ASSESSMENT OF PERSONALITY

Lewis R. Aiken
Pepperdine University

Allyn and Bacon
Boston   London   Sydney   Toronto

Series Editor: John-Paul Lenney
Series Editorial Assistant: Susan S. Brody
Production Administrator: Annette Joseph
Production Coordinator: Susan Freese
Editorial-Production Service: Kailyard Associates
Cover Administrator: Linda K. Dickinson
Cover Designer: Christy Rosso

We acknowledge the following for permission to reprint:

p. 91   From Petzelt, J. T., & Craddick, R. (1978). Present meaning of assessment in psychology.
         Professional Psychology: Research and Practice, 9, 587–591. Reprinted with permission.

p. 103   From Directions for scoring the High School Personality Questionnaire. Copyright © 1960,
         1969, Institute for Personality and Ability Testing, Inc. Reproduced by permission.

p. 134   From Bernard, H. W., & Huckins, W.C. (1978). *Dynamics of Personal Adjustment* (3rd ed.).
         Boston: Holbrook Press, pp. 420–421. Reprinted by permission of publisher.

p. 208   Reproduced by permission from the Jenkins Activity Survey. Copyright © 1979, 1969, 1966,
         1965 by The Psychological Corporation. All rights reserved.

continued on page 536

Library of Congress Cataloging-in-Publication Data

Aiken, Lewis R., 1931-
   Assessment of personality.

   Bibliography: p.
   1. Personality assessment.   I. Title.
BF698.4.A36   1988   155.2'8   88-7538
ISBN 0-205-11769-4

Printed in the United States of America

10 9 8 7 6 5 4 3 2 1   93 92 91 90 89 88

Contents

Part V Other Measures and Issues 389

Preface

This book is a survey of concepts, methodologies, psychometric procedures, and instruments concerned with the assessment of personality. The emphasis is on assessment methods and instruments, but since theories, research, and issues concerning human personality have influenced assessment, these matters are not neglected.

The term *personality assessment* refers to procedures designed to assess a person's characteristic modes of thinking and acting. Such assessment is not limited to the classification and measurement of types, traits, and temperaments but includes measures of interests, attitudes, values, perceptual styles, and other internal dynamics and behaviors characterizing the uniqueness of an individual.

Assessment of Personality is divided into five parts, consisting of two to four chapters each. The four chapters in Part I provide an overview of the foundations of personality assessment, including the history of personality assessment, theories of personality, and psychometric methods. The construction and administration of assessment instruments, as well as the interpretation and reporting of findings, are also described in Part I.

Two chapters in Part II are concerned with basic principles of behavioral observations, interviewing, ratings, and attitude measurement. Personality inventories, including rational-theoretical, factor-analyzed, and criterion-keyed inventories, are considered in detail in Part III. In addition, inventories for measuring interests and values, which are characteristics of personality, are also surveyed in Part III. The three chapters in Part IV are devoted to projective methods such as association, completion, and drawing techniques, as well as inkblot and apperception tests.

Physiological, perceptual, and cognitive measures of personality are discussed in the first chapter in Part V. The last chapter considers the major issues in personality assessment and future prospects for the field. Particular attention is given in this chapter, as elsewhere in the text, to the use of computers in designing, administering, and scoring assessment instruments, as well as in analyzing and reporting results. Advances in the methodology and theoretical foundations of personality assessment are also considered in Chapter 14.

Each of the fourteen chapters in the book ends with a summary, a set of exercises, and a list of suggested readings for further study of the topic. Numerous illustrations and examples are given to provide students with a background for selecting and using a variety of personality assessment devices and an understanding of their assets and limitations. Students are instructed to scrutinize the psychometric qualities (reliability, validity, standardization, etc.) of the various instruments carefully and to become thoroughly familiar with the administration, scoring, and interpretation procedures. The necessity for making multiple observations and measurements, depending on the goals of the psychological assessments, and integrating findings from different sources, is stressed as well. Procedures for reporting assessment results to appropriate persons and subsequent follow-up and retesting are also discussed.

Assessment of Personality is designed primarily for use in a one-semester course on personality assessment at the upper undergraduate or beginning graduate level. It is also appropriate to combine the text with lectures or readings on personality theories and research or with material on intellectual assessment (e.g., Aiken, 1987), and to include it in courses on personality or in a comprehensive course on psychological testing and assessment.

In addition to being a textbook, *Assessment of Personality* is a useful source book providing coverage of a wide range of instruments and procedures; lists of tests and distributors; a comprehensive glossary; and complete indexes of authors, subjects, and tests. As such, it will serve as a valuable reference for professional psychologists and researchers in the behavioral sciences. Nevertheless, the book has been written principally as an integrated, survey text, economical in style but comprehensive in content, rather than as a reference work.

Both the coverage and format of the book have been improved by the constructive reviews of James R. Council, Sampo V. Paunonen, and Harrison W. Voigt, in addition to the expert copyediting of Rebecca Davison of Kailyard Associates. I am extremely grateful to these individuals and to my students, whose reactions to my lectures on personality assessment helped make this book a better volume than it might otherwise have been.

L. R. A.

PART I

Foundations of
Personality Assessment

CHAPTER 1

History and Theories

No two people are exactly alike; everyone is unique. Even identical twins, who originate in the same fertilized egg and hence share the same heredity differ in significant ways. This is true whether they are reared in the same or different environments. On the other hand, everyone is similar to everyone else in certain respects. Despite differences in heredity, experiences, and culture, we share certain physical and mental qualities that distinguish us as human beings. Thus, people are both unique and similar; we possess a complex set of physical, mental, and behavioral characteristics that identify us as human and endow us with individual personalities.

The term *personality* is derived from the Greek *persona*, or mask, associated with a role played by an actor in a play. The dictionary defines personality in several ways. One definition emphasizes the public, social stimulus, or behavioral (both *General* verbal and nonverbal) characteristics of a person that are visible to and hence make an impression on other people. Another definition stresses a person's private, central, inner core. Included within this private core are the motives, attitudes, inter- *Fad* ests, beliefs, fantasies, cognitive styles, and other mental processes of an individual. Some definitions of personality emphasize its person quality, personal existence, or identity features. An extreme example is the view that personality is a mysterious charisma possessed only by Hollywood stars and other celebrities. Other meanings of personality are associated with specific disciplines or professions. Among these are selfhood, the ideal of perfection, and supreme value (philosophy); the individual members of the Trinity (theology); and a person having legal status (law) (Hunt, 1982).

A more global, or *holistic*, definition of personality views it as an organized composite of qualities or characteristics—the sum total of the physical, mental, emotional, and social qualities of a person. This is the way the term is employed in this book, and as such, it is essentially synonymous with the psychology of the individual (Murray, 1938). More specifically, we shall use the term personality to refer to a unique composite of inborn and acquired mental abilities, attitudes, temperaments, and other individual differences in thoughts, feelings, and actions. This collection of cognitive and affective characteristics, as it exists in a particular human being, is associated with a fairly consistent pattern of behavior.

The use of such a broad definition implies that the measurement, or more precisely *assessment*, of personality encompasses a wide range of variables. Among these variables are not only affective characteristics, such as emotion, temperament, character, and stylistic traits, but also cognitive variables, such as achievement, intelligence, and specific aptitudes, as well as various psychomotor abilities or physical skills and mannerisms. To assess these variables means to appraise or estimate their level of magnitude by methods such as observations, interviews, rating scales, checklists, inventories, projective techniques, and psychological tests.

This book focuses on the assessment of affective characteristics, which encompass the traditional, albeit somewhat limited, conception of personality variables. Reference is also made to cognitive and psychomotor variables, but they are not discussed at length. For a more complete description of the measurement of cognitive and psychomotor abilities the student should consult the *Assessment of Intellectual Functioning* (Aiken, 1987), *Psychological Testing and Assessment* (6th ed.) (Aiken, 1988), or similar volumes on psychological testing in general and the assessment of human abilities in particular.

Historical Foundations

The history of personality assessment goes back to a time when people first noticed individual differences in ways of behaving and thinking. Although there are no written records of the earliest behavioral observations, the *Epic of Gilgamesh* (c. 2000 B.C.) and the Bible contain citations indicating an awareness of personality differences. For example, in Judges 7:3, God says to Gideon: "Now therefore go to, proclaim in the ears of the people, saying. Whosoever is fearful and afraid, let him return and depart early from mount Gilead. And there returned of the people twenty and two thousand; and there remained ten thousand." Because the number remaining was still too large to constitute an effective fighting force, God further directed Gideon to bring the people down to the water (Judges 7:4–7).

> So he brought down the people unto the water: and the Lord said unto Gideon, Every one that lappeth of the water with his tongue, as a dog lappeth, him shalt thou set by himself; likewise every one that boweth down upon his knees to drink. And the number of them that lapped, putting their hand to their mouth, were three hundred men: but all the rest of the people bowed down upon their knees to drink water.
>
> And the Lord said unto Gideon, By the three hundred men that lapped will I save you, and deliver the Midianites into thine hand: and let all the other people go every man unto his place.

God presumably surmised that the men who lapped like dogs while drinking were more alert or wary and hence would prove to be more effective soldiers.

Although this biblical story is one of the earliest recorded instances of the use of a situational test of personality for the purpose of personnel selection, it was not the first personnel selection procedure to be employed. As early as 2200 B.C., the Chinese had begun using oral examinations to select government workers and determine periodically if civil servants remained fit to perform their duties. Both what was said by the examinee and how it was said were important in determining a pass or fail.

Ancient Greece and Rome

Attempts to analyze and assess human personality can also be seen in the writings of the ancient Greeks and Romans. The Greek physician Hippocrates (460–377 B.C.) proposed four humors in the human body—blood, yellow bile, black bile, and phlegm. (He also devised the first formal system of classifying mental disorders, a forerunner of the system proposed by Emil Kraeplin some 2,300 years later.) The major categories in Hippocrates' classification system were mania (overexcitability), melancholia (depression), and phrenitis (brain fever).

Around 200 A.D., Galen, a Roman physician who subscribed to Hipprocates' humoral theory, concluded from his observations that there were four types of temperament corresponding to an overabundance of each of the four humors. These four temperament types were sanguine, melancholic, choleric, and phlegmatic. An individual with a *sanguine* temperament purportedly had an excess of blood and was active, vigorous, and confident. An individual with a *melancholic* temperament was generally gloomy or sad and said to have a predominance of black bile. A person with a *choleric* temperament presumably had an excess of yellow bile and was easily angered, quick to act, and prone to violence. And a habitually unemotional or lethargic individual, referred to as a *phlegmatic* personality, had an overabundance of phlegm in the body.

The ancient Greeks were greatly interested in human characteristics and wrote extensively on the subject. Famous philosophers such as Plato (c. 428–347 B.C.) and Aristotle (384–322 B.C.), for example, had much to say on the subject of individual differences. Plato's distinction between rational and irrational human behavior and his analyses of conflict (as opposed to harmony) and repression undoubtedly influenced nineteenth-century psychoanalytic theorizing. The doctrine of the soul, which was initiated by the Pythagoreans, was also developed by Plato and Aristotle. To Plato the soul had three functions—nutritive, sensitive, and rational. Aristotle viewed the soul as a spirit moving in the body, a "perfect unity toward which bodily functions are directed."

Of particular interest to personality assessment are the 30 descriptions or sketches provided by Theophrastus (372–287 B.C.) who succeeded Aristotle as head of the Athenian Lyceum. These sketches, like the Hippocrates-Galen humoral theory, were based on overgeneralized observations of human behavior. Examples of the character types described by Theophrastus were the Flatterer, the Garrulous Man, the Liar, the Penurious Man, the Surly Man, and the Tasteless Man. Excerpts from two of these sketches, describing the dominant characteristics and typical style of action of a certain type of individual, are given in Report 1–1. Theophrastus presented no scientific evidence for the existence of such character types, although the sketches do make interesting reading.

The Middle Ages and the Renaissance

A number of other events, both ancient and modern, that have contributed to the interpretation and assessment of personality are listed in Table 1–1. As this chronology suggests, little genuine progress in the scientific analysis of personality was made until fairly recent times. Descriptive characterizations having a semblance of truth were provided by such writers as Cervantes in *Don Quixote* and Shakespeare in his plays. These works have supplied such descriptive terms as quixotic, Falstaffian, and Shylock to the English language. The characterizations of Cervantes, Shakespeare, and other writers, are, however, like those of Theophrastus, usually stereotypes or overgeneralizations. The scientific exploration and measurement of human personality did not begin in earnest until the late nineteenth century.

Until the Renaissance, the study of individuality and personality was held back by the same social and religious forces that hampered progress in art and science. The Middle Ages, which lasted approximately from the fall of the Roman Empire (late fifth century A.D.) until the fourteenth century, was, for most people, a time of unquestioning faith and a struggle to survive and do one's duty. Theologians such as Augustine emphasized introspective reflection; materialism and science were considered enemies of the Church. Due to a combination of social and economic forces, the Catholic Church began weakening during the fifteenth century. As a consequence, supernatural views and a preoccupation with death, demons, and the hereafter gave way to more temporal, earthly concerns.

The Renaissance, fourteenth to seventeenth century A.D., and the subsequent period of Enlightenment in the eighteenth century saw a return to the ancient Hellenistic view of the value of the individual. According to this ideal, people are capable of doing something to influence their circumstances in this life. Freed from

Sample Descriptions of the Characters of Theophrastus

The Garrulous Man

The Garrulous man is one that will sit down close beside somebody he does not know, and begin talk with a eulogy of his own life, and then relate a dream he had the night before, and after that tell dish by dish what he had for supper. As he warms up to his work he will remark that we are by no means the men we were, and the price of wheat has gone down, and there's a ship of strangers in town. . . . Next he will surmise that the crops would be all the better for some more rain, and tell him what he is going to grow on his farm next year, adding that it is difficult to make both ends meet . . . and "I vomited yesterday" and "What day is it today?" . . . And if you let him go on he will never stop (Edmonds, 1929, pp. 48–49).

The Penurious Man

A Penurious man is one who goes to a debtor to ask for his half-obol interest before the end of the month. At a dinner where expenses are shared, he counts the number of cups each person drinks, and he makes a smaller libation to Artemis than anyone. If someone has made a good bargain on his account and presents him with the bill he says it is too much. When his servant breaks a pot or a plate, he deducts the value from his food. If his wife drops a copper, he moves furnitures, beds, chests and hunts in the curtains. If he has something to sell he puts such a price on it that the buyer has no profit. He forbids his wife to lend anything—neither salt nor lampwick nor cinnamon nor marjoram nor meal nor garlands nor cakes for sacrifices. . . . To sum up, the coffers of the penurious men are moldy and the keys rust; they wear cloaks where hardly reach the thigh; a very little oil-bottle supplies them for anointing; they have hair cut short and do not put on their shoes until midday; and when they take their cloak to the fuller they urge him to use plenty of earth so that it will not be spotted so soon (quoted by Allport, 1937, p. 57).

the constraints of intolerance and censorship, they can use their abilities to understand the world and themselves, thereby improving their condition and that of their fellow humans.

Traditional church doctrine had held that people were basically evil, born in sin with only a hope and not a guarantee of a better life after death. In contrast, many philosophers during the Enlightenment and the succeeding Age of Romanticism maintained that human beings are either good or neither good nor bad by nature. The French philosopher Jean Jacques Rousseau, in his doctrine of the noble savage, maintained that people are born in a state of goodness and that naturalness is virtuous. This point of view came to influence a number of modern humanistic

Table 1–1	Noteworthy Events in the History of Personality Assessment

400 B.C.—Hippocrates relates personality characteristics to body types.

4th century B.C.—Theophrastus describes 30 personality or character types.

2nd century A.D.—Galen relates Hippocrates theory of body humors to temperament.

1800—Franz Gall and Johann Spurzheim establish the pseudoscience of phrenology, relating bumps on the skull to personality.

1884—Francis Galton describes methods for the measurement of character, including word associations and behavior sampling techniques.

1892—Emil Kraeplin uses word association technique in clinical contexts.

1896—Kraeplin's classification of mental disorders developed.

1900—*The Interpretation of Dreams* by Sigmund Freud is published.

1905—Carl Jung uses word association tests to detect and analyze mental complexes. First practical intelligence test, the Binet-Simon Scale by Alfred Binet and Theophilé Simon published.

1906—Heymans and Wiersma develop list of symptoms indicative of psychopathology.

1910—Kent-Rosanoff word lists published.

1919—Robert Woodworth's Personal Data Sheet, the first standardized personality inventory, based on the Heymans-Wiersma symptoms list, used in U.S. military selection. Pressey X-O Test published.

1920—Hermann Rorschach's Inkblot Test published.

1920s—Kurt Lewin and others begin experimental study of personality.

1925—Ernst Kretschmer describes his observations on the relationships of body build to personality and mental disorder.

1926—Florence Goodenough's Draw-a-Man Test published.

1927—First edition of Strong Vocational Interest Blank for Men published.

1928—Hartshore and May studies of character reported.

1934—Kuder Preference Record-Vocational published.

1930s—Levy and Beck popularize Rorschach Inkblot Test in United States.

1935—Thematic Apperception Test (TAT) developed by Murray and Morgan. Humm-Wadsworth Temperament Scale published. Louis Thurstone develops centroid method of factor analysis.

1937—Books on personality by Gordon Allport and Ross Stagner published.

1938—Henry Murray's *Explorations in Personality*, describing theoretical foundations of the Thematic Apperception Test, published. Bender Visual-Motor Gestalt Test for assessing personality and brain damage published.

1939—Lawrence Frank uses the term *projective techniques* to describe the Rorschach Inkblot Test and other unstructured methods of assessing personality.

1940—J. P. Guilford applies factor analysis to the construction of a personality inventory.

1941–45—Situational tests developed by U.S. Office of Strategic Services.

1942—Sheldon and Stevens report their research on the relationships of body build to temperament.

1943—Minnesota Multiphasic Personality Inventory by S. R. Hathaway and J. C. McKinley published.

(Continued)

1949—R. B. Cattell's Sixteen Personality Factor Questionnaire published.
1953—Q-sort technique devised by William Stephenson.
1954—Paul Meehl's *Clinical Versus Statistical Prediction* published.
1968—Walter Mischel's *Personality and Assessment* published. Kuder Occupational Interest Survey published.
1972—Holland's Self-Directed Search, a measure of interests and personality, published.
1975–1980—Growth of behavioral assessment techniques.
1985—*Standards for Educational and Psychological Testing* and ninth edition of *The Mental Measurements Yearbook* published.
1986—*Guidelines for Computer-Based Tests and Interpretations* published. Revised editions of MMPI and CPI published.

psychologists who saw the human struggle as one of attempting to realize the good or growth potential within oneself. On the other hand, the view that people are born in neither a state of goodness nor evil, that they are blank tablets or *tabula rasa* at birth, was favored by John Locke, Voltaire, and certain other philosophers. The writings of these empiricists influenced the conceptions of trait-factor and behavioristic psychologists during the twentieth century.

Pseudoscience and Personality Assessment

People have a natural curiosity about what motivates them and how they will turn out. Before the modern era, they often relied on oracles, soothsayers, and other fortune tellers to diagnose their character and foretell their future. Pseudosciences such as astrology, palmistry, phrenology, physiognomy, graphology, most of which have ancient origins, are still believed by many people.

Astrology   Among the oldest of these pseudosciences is *astrology*, which is based on the notion that the relative positions of the moon and planets in relation to the sun affect the fortunes of individuals. Each of the twelve signs of the *zodiac*, or constellations of these heavenly bodies, is supposedly associated with certain aspects of character, temperament, and aptitude. Given the exact time and place of a person's birth, an astrologer can prepare an individualized chart, or *horoscope*, of the planetary positions associated with that person. From this information, astrologers claim to be able to predict the person's future and advise him or her on decisions and possible actions.

Palmistry   Similar in some respects to astrology, and equally as old, is *palmistry*, or chiromancy. Palmists claim to be able to analyze a person's character and predict his or her destiny by analyzing the features of the hand. Special attention is given to the seven mounts (Jupiter, Saturn, Apollo or the Sun, Mercury, Mars, the Moon, and Venus) located at the bases of the thumb and fingers and the sides of the hand. The following descriptions are examples of characteristics said to be associated with the development of five of the mounts: development of Jupiter signifies ambition, concern for honor, interest in religion; overdevelopment reveals pride and superstition; high development of Mars indicates bravery and a martial character, and low development suggests cowardice; Saturn is related to luck and wisdom; Apollo (the Sun) to intelligence, and Venus to love. In addition to the seven mounts, palmists study the relative length and depth of the head, heart, life, and fortune lines of the hand: a short or broken life line points to an early death or serious illness; the head line is associated with intelligence, the heart line with affection, and the line of fortune predicts success and failure.

Phrenology   Related to palmistry, but with the focus on the head instead of the hand, is *phrenology*. Probably few people today believe in phrenology, but it was viewed more seriously by Thomas Jefferson, Edgar Allan Poe, and many other prominent individuals during the eighteenth and nineteenth centuries. As developed by Franz Gall (1758–1828) and his student Johann Spurzheim (1776–1832), phrenology is a pseudoscience. Abstract mental qualities such as acquisitiveness, agreeableness, amativeness, artistic talent, courage, greed, philoprogenitiveness, and pride are associated with the development of some thirty-seven so-called organs of the brain. Phrenologists believed that an overdevelopment of one or more of these brain organs results in a protuberance (bump) on the skull over the corresponding area (see Figure 1–1). If so, then personality or character could be interpreted by fingering the skull to analyze the configuration of bumps. By the end of the nineteenth century, the research of Pierre Flourens and other neurophysiologists had disproved the notion that specific brain areas are associated with the complex functions described by Gall and Spurzheim.

Physiognomy   Another pseudoscience that attempted to determine temperament and character from external bodily features, especially the face, is *physiognomy*. Remnants of physiognomy exist in contemporary personality assessment, for example, in the requirement that a personal photograph be submitted with an employment application and in the Szondi Test. The Szondi Test consists of six sets of photographs, with eight pictures per set, of mental patients having different psychiatric diagnoses (catatonia, depression, hysteria, mania, etc.). In taking the test, examinees select the two pictures they like most and the two they like least in each set. The basic assumption underlying the test is that the facial features of the mental patients depicted in the twelve selected and twelve rejected photographs have special meaning for the examinee, whose needs and personality are similar to those of the patients in the photographs they like most and dissimilar to those of the patients they like least.

Physiognomy should not be confused with the analysis of meanings or messages communicated by facial expressions such as smiling and crying (e.g., Ekman & Friesen, 1984). Physiognomy is concerned with determining personal characteristics from the form or features of the body, especially the face. The analysis of facial

Phrenological chart of brain functions   **Figure 1-1**

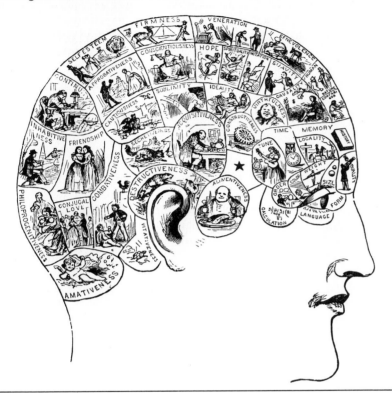

Courtesy of Bettman Archive.

expressions, however, is a more scientifically accepted and valid effort to determine the meanings and origins of nonverbal behavior.

Graphology   For hundreds of years, and by studying hundreds of books written on the subject, people have tried, without notable success, to assess individual personality by analyzing handwriting samples. Some graphologists attempt to interpret handwriting intuitively on the basis of overall impressions, whereas others are more analytic in stressing certain signs or clues such as the way the writer dots *i*'s or slants letters. To be fair, *graphology* is not at quite the same level of quackery as astrology or phrenology, and it continues to have many proponents. For example, many business organizations make use of the services of graphologists in employee selection. Unfortunately, the claims of these proponents are more often than not just as wrong as those of the phrenologists.

It does make some sense that handwriting, which is a type of stylistic behavior, could reflect personality characteristics to some extent (see Report 1–2). Graphologists are, however, not noted for the validity of their analyses, and even attempts to analyze handwriting by means of computers have not revealed graphology to be a valid method of personality assessment (Rothenberg, 1985). Furthermore, handwriting is affected by alcohol and other drugs, as well as by aging, disease, and factors other than personality (Kelly, 1987). After reviewing the scientific literature on graphology, Ben-Shakhar and his co-authors (1986) concluded that "graphological predictions would seem to play a role akin to that played by placebos in medicine: not completely ineffective, but for reasons other than those that make the real thing effective."

The Late Nineteenth and Twentieth Centuries

After the French Revolution of 1789, a more humane attitude toward the mentally ill developed through the influence of Philippe Pinel (1745–1826), who "struck the chains from the limbs of the insane" and instituted much needed reforms in mental hospitals throughout France. The emphasis of early nineteenth-century psychiatry was on an *organic* basis of mental illness, which was a marked improvement over the older belief that the mentally ill are possessed of devils that must be driven out by beating or burning the body or some other form of *exorcism*. But many later nineteenth-century and twentieth-century psychiatrists focused on *functional* causes of mental illness, such as faulty habits acquired by experience. As a consequence, psychological forms of treatment—hypnosis, reeducation, and psychotherapy—rather than medicine or surgery, were recommended in many mental illness cases. The French psychiatrists Jean-Martin Charcot (1825–1893) and Pierre Janet (1859–1947) were pioneers in the development of the concept of functional causes of mental illness and the use of hypnosis for treating certain mental disorders. In addition to treating these disorders, methods of diagnosing them—including various observational and testing techniques—were devised by French psychiatrists and psychologists.

By the end of the nineteenth century, psychology had been formally christened a science, and the scientific study of human behavior and mental life was well underway. Despite the disinterest of experimental psychology's founding father, Wilhelm Wundt (1832–1920) in the study of motivation, emotion, intelligence, thought, personality, and other individual-difference variables, certain psychologists began conducting research on individual differences in cognitive and affective characteristics.

In 1884, Francis Galton, whose primary research interest was the assessment of intellectual abilities, proposed to measure emotions by recording changes in heartbeat and pulse rate and to assess good temper, optimism, and other so-called

---

Israelis See Handwriting as True Personality Test

JERUSALEM—A young Israeli computer technician and his wife went apartment-hunting recently in a West Bank Jewish settlement near here and were surprised to learn that before being accepted as residents, they would have to submit samples of their handwriting for analysis.

"If you didn't pass the graphology test, then you couldn't be accepted at the settlement," said the technician, who asked not to be identified by name. "It kind of turned us off a little. It seemed like reading tea leaves."

The young couple did not take the test; they chose to live elsewhere. But every year, tens of thousands of other Israelis find their handwriting being analyzed in routine psychological and personality-screening procedures involved in getting a job, finding a place to live, even choosing a mate. Some volunteer; others are analyzed without their knowledge.

Throughout the world, handwriting analysis is an accepted criminal investigation tool. But its value as a mirror of personality is much more controversial. And in the United States, graphologists concede, their craft is often viewed as more fitting for a carnival sideshow than as serious psychological testing.

Most institutions in Israel are publicly ambivalent about it, even as they use it extensively to complement—in some cases, to substitute for—more conventional psychological tests.

In addition to many settlements on the West Bank, most Israeli kibbutzim and moshavim—collective and cooperative farms—use handwriting analysis to screen applicants. Officials say the unusually close relationships and interdependence characteristic of these communities put a premium on ideological and personal compatibility.

Graphology experts here say that up to 60% of Israeli companies use handwriting analysis to help identify unsuitable or untrustworthy job applicants. "Position Available" advertisements routinely request handwritten resumes.

A spokesman for Bank Leumi, Israel's largest financial institution, seemed slightly embarassed but confirmed that all potential employees must take a graphology test.

*   *   *

Graphology emerged in continental Europe in the 19th Century, and the fact that it is so much more popular here than in much of the English-speaking world may be because so many of Israel's founding fathers came from Central or Eastern Europe.

Handwriting experts say they can detect certain personality traits by the way a

(Continued)

person forms his letters and by the amount of pressure he uses. There are 19th-Century French books on the subject, and a daily newspaper in Leipzig, East Germany, started a graphological column in 1863.

The *International Herald Tribune* reported last year that the majority of French companies use handwriting analysis in recruiting executives. The paper said graphology is used extensively by companies in West Germany, Switzerland, Belgium, Italy, and Spain.

---

character traits. Among the methods described by Galton for measuring these variables was the behavior sampling technique of observing people in contrived social situations.

Galton was also the first psychological scientist to suggest the use of the *word association technique* for assessing personality. In this technique, a series of words is spoken to the examinee, who is directed to respond with the first word that comes to mind. The psychiatrist Emil Kraeplin, (1856–1926) who became famous for his method of classifying mental disorders into organic versus functional and psychoneurotic verses psychotic categories, also developed a word association technique in 1892. Several years later in 1905, the psychoanalyst Carl Jung used word association tests to detect and analyze mental complexes.

The extensive observations and descriptions of mental disorders provided by Emil Kraeplin, Richard von Krafft-Ebing, and other psychiatrists during the late nineteenth and early twentieth centuries also provided a framework for the later development of personality assessment instruments such as the Rorschach Inkblot Test and the Minnesota Multiphasic Personality Inventory (MMPI).

Alfred Binet (1857–1911), another psychologist whose primary claim to fame came from the measurement of intelligence, was also interested in the assessment of personality. Prior to his work in co-authoring the Binet-Simon Intelligence Scale in 1905, Binet had devised methods for studying the personality characteristics of eminent persons. One technique used by Binet involved responding to inkblots and telling stories about pictures (fantasy life); another was the collection and analysis of writing samples. In one study, Binet asked seven graphologists to analyze handwriting samples obtained from 37 highly successful men and 37 less successful men. In contrast to more recent research findings, Binet concluded that the diagnostic conclusions drawn by the graphologists were fairly accurate (Rothenberg, 1985).

Of particular significance in the history of personality assessment during the early twentieth century was the development and use in military selection during World War I of the first personality inventory—the Woodworth Personal Data Sheet. This paper-and-pencil, single-score inventory, which was a kind of standardized psychiatric interview, was designed to screen U.S. Army recruits for emotional disorders.

Other noteworthy events in personality assessment were the publication of Hermann Rorschach's Inkblot Test in 1920, the publication of Murray and Morgan's Thematic Apperception Test (TAT) in 1935, and the publication of Hathaway and McKinley's Minnesota Multiphasic Personality Inventory (MMPI) in 1943. All three of these instruments, which remain popular even to this day (Table 1–2), are discussed at length in later chapters. Also related to personality assessment is the extensive work conducted during the late 1920s and succeeding years on the measurement of interests, attitudes, and values (see Chapter 9). Experimental research by Kurt Lewin and his co-workers on conflict, frustration, and aspiration level also showed how personality could be studied and assessed scientifically.

A great number and variety of single-score and multiscore personality assessment instruments were developed during the twenties and thirties. Some of these instruments were designed to determine the presence of psychopathology, whereas others emphasized the analysis of personal adjustment, values, and other affective traits in normal individuals. During the forties and fifties, the growth of clinical, educational, industrial, and other fields of applied psychology, coupled with the development of more sophisticated procedures for constructing, scoring, and interpreting psychometric instruments, stimulated an even greater output of measures of human abilities and personality. Some of the most popular inventories, projectives, rating scales, and checklists for the assessment of personality that have resulted from these efforts are listed in Table 1–2. These personality tests are referred to with the greatest frequency in *The Ninth Mental Measurements Yearbook* (Mitchell, 1985), a standard, highly respected source of reviews of psychological tests and instruments.

A significant contemporary trend in psychological testing and assessment is the increasing use of high-speed digital computers in scoring, interpreting, and even administering psychological assessment instruments. The use of computers in connection with personality assessment, which began in the 1960s, has broadened and facilitated the applications of these instruments.

Despite, or perhaps because of, their extensive applications, the validity and implications of using personality assessment instruments have not gone unquestioned or uncriticized. Criticism can, of course, be healthy if it is not unwarranted or petty. Personality assessment, like any applied scientific enterprise, should be open to examination and evaluation. Consequently, a large portion of Chapter 14 of this book is devoted to criticisms and controversies in this field. Among the matters that have received the greatest attention, and are dealt with extensively in Chapter 14, are the relative importance of individual traits versus situational variables in determining behavior, the cross-situational and temporal consistency of personality measurements, the roles of heredity and environment in determining scores in these instruments, and the ethical considerations in their use.

Table 1–2	Personality Tests Having the Largest Numbers of References in *The Ninth Mental Measurements Yearbook*	

Test	Number of References	Rank
Minnesota Multiphasic Personality Inventory	339	1
State-Trait Anxiety Inventory	158	4
Bem Sex-Role Inventory	121	5
Eysenck Personality Inventory	91	8
Rorschach Inkblot Test	79	9.5
Present State Examination	71	11.5
16 Personality Factor Questionnaire	67	13.5
SCL-90-R	61	16.5
California Psychological Inventory	61	16.5
Tennessee Self-Concept Scale	60	18
Profile of Mood States	58	19
Thematic Apperception Test	51	20
Multiple Affect Adjective Check List	47	24
Personality Research Form	42	25.5
Jenkins Activity Survey	41	28.5
Group Embedded Figures Test	41	28.5
The Adjective Check List	39	31.5
Piers-Harris Children's Self-Concept Scale (The Way I Feel about Myself)	38	33
Eysenck Personality Questionnaire	32	36.5
Coopersmith Self-Esteem Inventories	32	36.5
Revised Behavior Problem Checklist	31	38.5
Personal Orientation Inventory	24	47
Fear Survey Schedule	23	49
The Draw-a-Person Test	23	49
Embedded Figures Test	23	49

More personality tests (350 out of 1,409, or 24.8% of the total) were reviewed in *The Ninth Mental Measurements Yearbook* than any other kind of test.

Theories of Personality

Theories of personality are conceptions of human behavior and experience that employ a set of psychological constructs (or concepts) in attempting to explain, predict, and control the actions of people. As personality theories, they are particularly concerned with individual differences and uniqueness in both socially acceptable and socially unacceptable behavior, but they also attempt to account for similarities among the actions and thought processes of people.

Although it is possible to adopt a fairly atheoretical, empirical approach in assessing personality, even psychologists such as B. F. Skinner who hold no great love for theories make some assumptions or have some preconceptions concerning the nature and expected outcomes of their research on behavior. At the other extreme from the radical empiricists, who would avoid psychological theories, are the extreme rationalists who attempt to develop intricate, all-encompassing explanatory models of human motives and actions. Unfortunately, such grandiose theories are frequently based on a minimum of actual observations of the objects of their efforts. Somewhere in the middle is the personality psychologist who uses theories in an *eclectic* way, selecting, it is hoped, the most useful aspects of different theories, to assist in interpreting the results of observations and other assessments.

At the very least it should be recognized that some frame of reference, some conceptual guidelines, can be helpful in the assessment and explanation of personality. Most people would not deny this. Almost everyone has some theory as to why people behave in the ways that they do. Like the descriptions of Theophrastus and Shakespeare, these theories of human nature and behavior typically consist of stereotypes or other overgeneralizations. Nevertheless, they do provide rough guidelines as to what can be expected of people and how we should act toward them. It is obviously important to have some explanation as to why people do the things they do and expectations of what they may do next. Our comfort and sometimes our very survival depend on the ability to understand and predict the behavior of our fellow humans and adjust to their idiosyncrasies and actions.

Psychologists realize that every individual is different from other individuals in many respects, and that human behavior is very complex and sometimes inconsistent. Consequently, the professional personality theorist is usually cautious in accepting the truth and explanatory power of common-sense theories. The individuality and intraindividual complexity of human behavior and mental life are so impressive to certain psychologists that they have abandoned efforts to discover general principles or laws to explain the seeming vagaries of human nature. Thus, they have dismissed the *nomothetic approach*—a search for general laws of behavior and personality—as unrealistic and inadequate to the task of understanding the individual. Rather, they advocate an *idiographic approach* of viewing each person as a lawful, integrated system worthy of analysis in his or her own right (Allport, 1937).

One of the major issues with which personality theorists have wrestled is the explanation of motivation—what drives people to behave in certain ways and to what extent this behavior is based on nature rather than nurture. Certain personality theorists appear to be more concerned with the structure than the dynamics of personality, but almost all recognize that accounting for human motivation—what makes people do the things they do—is an important part of the task of theory construction. Another concern is how social and nonsocial experiences shape personality both during childhood and later. Finally, theorists ask how the different characteristics or facets of personality are integrated or organized to produce unique patterns of perceiving, thinking, and acting. Not all personality theorists have

Table 1–3	Personality Assessment Methods Associated with Specific Theorists

Theorist	Assessment Methods
Alfred Adler	Analysis of birth order, early recollections, dream analysis, social interest (Crandall, 1975)
Gordon Allport	Idiographic content analyses of letters and diaries, Dominance-Submission Test, Study of Values
Arnold Buss and Robert Plomin	EASI Temperament Survey, EAS Temperament Survey for Adults
Raymond Cattell	Factor analysis (L-data, Q-data, T-data), psychological tests (16 Personality Factor Questionnaire and other questionnaire tests)
Erik Erikson	Psychohistorical analysis
Sigmund Freud	Free association, dream analysis, analysis of transference, analysis of resistance
Carl Jung	Word associations, method of amplification, symptom analysis, dream analysis, painting therapy
George Kelly	Role Construct Repertory Test
Abraham Maslow	Personality Orientation Inventory: A Measure of Self Actualization
David McClelland	Projective measures of need for achievement and need for power
Henry Murray	Thematic Apperception Test, situational (OSS) tests; concept of *needs* also used in Edwards Personal Preference Schedule and Adjective Check List.
Carl Rogers	Q-Sort (Stephenson, 1953), Experience Inventory (Coan, 1972), Experiencing Scale (Gendlin & Tomlinson, 1967; Klein et al., 1969)
Julian Rotter	I-E Scale, Interpersonal Trust Scale
William Sheldon	Somatotyping and temperament-typing
B. F. Skinner	Direct observations of behavior, self-report procedures, physiological measures of behavior
Herman Witkin	Body Adjustment Test, Rod and Frame Test, Embedded Figures Test

attempted to answer these questions, or even the same questions, in the same ways. There are many differences among theories of personality, differences that often seem to reflect the theorist's own personality as much as the actual nature of human behavior and mental life.

One important difference among personality theories is the relative emphasis placed on heredity and environment as molders of behavior. Another difference is the extent to which internal, personal characteristics of the individual rather than external, situational variables are the major determinants of human action. As these and other points of dispute among personality theorists indicate, there is no comprehensive theory of personality that is supported by all psychologists. On the contrary, theories and research findings in the field of personality and its assessment are constantly developing and changing. Be that as it may, it is important for students of personality assessment to be aware of the various theories of personality and the strengths and weaknesses of those theories. Despite their shortcomings, theories of personality can serve as guides to the measurement and understanding of personality. Certainly one must have some *apperceptive mass*, some ideational framework concerning personality and behavior, in order to interpret individual assessment findings. For this purpose, the theories constructed and tested by professional psychologists are probably more useful than the common-sense theories of the layperson.

The five groups of theories discussed here—typologies, trait-factor theories, psychoanalytic (or psychodynamic) theories, phenomenological (humanistic) theories, and social learning theories—have not been equally influential in the development of personality assessment instruments and procedures. However, theorists of all persuasions have developed and/or stimulated the development of various assessment techniques. Sometimes these have been very basic techniques, such as careful observations, and at other times quite complex procedures, such as projective tests. Table 1–3 lists the most prominent personality theorists and the assessment methods with which they are associated.

Type Theories

As we have seen in the discussion of Theophrastus's characters, one of the oldest approaches to personality is found in the theory of fixed categories or types of people. The Hippocrates-Galen humoral theory is such a *type theory*. Although this theory is now only of historical interest, there is some overlap even today (see Figure 1–3). The body-type theories of Kretschmer, Lombroso, and Sheldon are based somewhat more securely on observational data.

The notion that physique is related to personality is very old. For example, in Shakespeare's *Julius Caesar* (Act I, Scene II) Caesar observes:

> Let me have men about me that are fat,
> Sleek-headed men, and such as sleep a-nights.
> Yond Cassius has a lean and hungry look;

He thinks too much; such men are dangerous.

. . . .
Would he were fatter! . . . He reads much;
He is a great observer, and he looks
Quite through the deeds of men: He loves no plays,
As dost thou Antony; he hears no music;
Seldom he smiles; and smiles in such a sort
As if he mock'd himself, and scorn'd his spirit
That could be mov'd to smile at anything.
Such as he be never at heart's ease
While they behold a greater than themselves;
And therefore are they very dangerous.

Three centuries later, Ernst Kretschmer (1925), after making extensive measurements of the physiques of mental patients and others, concluded that both a thin, lanky, angular body build (asthenic physique) and a muscular body build (athletic physique) are associated with withdrawing tendencies (schizoid temperament). On the other hand, a rotund, stocky body build (pyknic physique) was found to be associated with emotional instability (cycloid temperament). Kretschmer maintained that the cycloid and schizoid temperament types are transitional stages, the cycloid leading to manic-depressive psychosis and the schizoid to schizophrenia.

Another body typologist, the criminologist Cesare Lombroso (1836–1909), believed that the physical characteristics of criminals are different from those of other people. Viewing criminals as being at a lower stage of biological development, Lombroso noted that they had large jaws, receding foreheads, and other primitive physical traits. The presence of these atavistic traits was interpreted by Lombroso as demonstrating that criminals were born to be criminals. The fact that many criminals did not possess the characteristics listed by Lombroso made his theory less credible.

William Sheldon and S. S. Stevens (1940, 1942) also proposed a typology theory. The Sheldon *somatotype* system classifies human physiques into three components according to their degree of *endomorphy* (fatness), *mesomorphy* (muscularity), and *ectomorphy* (thinness) on a scale of 1 to 7 (see Figure 1–2). Thus, an extreme endomorph would be a 7–1–1, an extreme mesomorph a 1–7–1, and an extreme ectomorph a 1–1–7. The degree of each component was judged by measurements taken from photographs of the person at various angles.

An excess of any one of the three somatotype components in the Sheldon-Stevens system was found to be related to the temperament types of *viscerotonia*, *somatotonia*, and *cerebrotonia*. An individual's score on each of the temperament dimensions, also rated on a 7-point scale, was determined by his or her ratings, obtained from questionnaires and observations, on 20 trait dimensions. Viscerotonics are characterized as jolly, sociable, and loving of comfort and eating; somatotonics are assertive, dominating, noisy, callous, have a youthful orientation, and love physical adventure and exercise. Cerebrotonics are restrained, fast in reacting, introversive,

---

Sheldon's somatotypes **Figure 1–2**

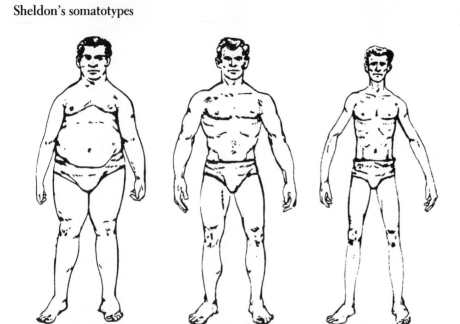

| Extreme | Extreme | Extreme |
| Endomorphy | Mesomorphy | Ectomorphy |

From *Elements of Psychology* (second edition) by David Krech, Richard Crutchfield, and Norman Livson. Copyright © 1969 by Alfred A. Knopf, Inc. Reprinted by permission of publisher.

hypersensitive to pain, have difficulty sleeping, and are oriented toward later periods of life. Moderate to high correlations have been found between ratings on endomorphy and viscerotonia, mesomorphy and somatotonia, and ectomorphy and cerebrotonia.

Body-type theories are interesting, but because of the many exceptions to the hypothesized relationships between body build and personality, their scientific status is not very high. In addition, different interpretations have been given to the correlations between physique and personality. Contemporary psychologists also object to typologies because they place people in categories and assign labels to them. Not only does labeling overemphasize internal causation of behavior, but it also acts as a self-fulfilling prophecy in which people tend to become what they are labeled as being. Thus, a person labeled as an introvert may be left alone by would-be friends, causing him or her to become even more socially isolated. Similarly, an extrovert may become more outgoing or sociable because other people expect the person to behave in an extroversive manner.

Trait Theories

Personality *trait*, or the predisposition to respond in a particular way to persons, objects, or situations, is narrower than *type*. One of the first and most prominent trait theorists was Gordon Allport (1897–1967). In 1936, Allport and Odbert began by listing the 17,953 words in the English language that refer to characteristics of personality and reducing them to a smaller list of trait names (Allport & Odbert, 1936). A *trait* was defined as a "neuropsychic structure having the capacity to render many stimuli functionally equivalent, and to initiate and guide equivalent (meaningfully consistent) forms of adaptive and expressive behavior" (Allport, 1961, p. 347). Allport visualized human personality as consisting of the dynamic organization of those traits that determine a person's unique adjustment to the environment. In order of their pervasiveness across different situations, there are *cardinal traits* (e.g., Machiavellianism, narcissism), *central traits* (e.g., sociableness, affectionateness), and *secondary traits* (e.g., food preferences or musical preferences). In terms of the extent to which they are general or shared among different people, Allport differentiated among *common traits* (e.g., aggression), *individual traits*, and *personal dispositions*. Although common traits and individual traits can be measured by standardized assessment instruments, personal dispositions are determined only by a careful study of a person.

Another trait theorist, R. B. Cattell (1905–) adopted a holistic position in which personality encompasses both affective and cognitive variables. Cattell classified personality traits in four ways: common versus unique, surface versus source, constitutional versus environmental-mold, and dynamic versus ability versus temperament. Like Allport, Cattell saw common traits as characterizing all people, and *unique traits*, which are Allport's individual traits, as peculiar to the individual. Regarding the surface source distinction, *surface traits* are easily observed in a person's behavior, but *source traits* can be discovered only by the mathematical processes of factor analysis, which are discussed in Chapter 2. Trait theorists such as Cattell, Eysenck, and Guilford have applied factor analysis to discover the underlying sources of consistency in behavior. Cattell's trait-factory theory also includes *constitutional traits* that depend on heredity and *environmental mold traits* that are derived from the environment. Finally, *dynamic traits* motivate the person toward a goal, *ability traits* determine the ability to achieve the goal, and *temperament traits* pertain to the emotional aspects of goal-directed activity. Cattell's trait-factor theory, which is much more elaborate than the brief description provided here, has served as a framework in constructing several personality inventories (see Chapter 7).

Many others psychologists, such as Hans Eysenck and J. P. Guilford, have theorized and conducted research on personality traits and instruments to measure them. Factor-analytic methods have been applied in much of this research, yielding a variety of personality dimensions. The two basic dimensions in Eysenck's system, which he believes have a biological basis, are introverted-extroverted and stable-

A two-dimensional classification of personality

Figure 1–3

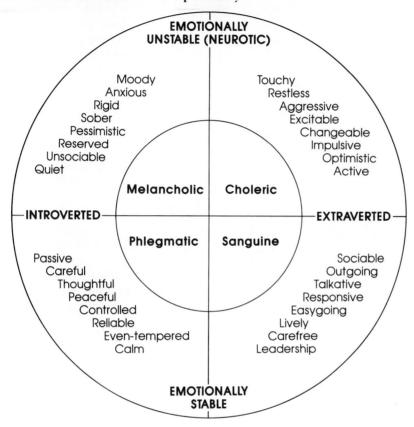

From *Personality and Individual Differences* by H. J. Eysenck and M. W. Eysenck, Plenum Publishing, 1958. Reprinted by permission of the publisher.

unstable. The positions of the 32 traits on the circle in Figure 1–3 indicate the direction and amount of the two basic dimensions comprising each trait. Individuals closer to the extroverted end of the horizontal scale are interested primarily in people or things outside themselves. In contrast, the focus of those closer to the introverted end of the scale is primarily on themselves and their private, inner lives. Also note the location of Galen's four temperament types on the circle. A melancholic individual is an unstable introvert; a choleric individual, an unstable extrovert; a phlegmatic person, a stable introvert; a sanguine person, a stable extrovert.

Psychoanalytic Theory

Sigmund Freud (1856–1939) viewed human personality as a kind of battleground where three combatants—id, ego, and superego—struggle for supremacy. The *id*, a reservoir of instinctive drives of sex and aggression housed in the unconscious part of the mind, acts according to the pleasure principle. It runs into conflict with the *superego* (the conscience), which acts according to the moral principle. Although the id is innate, the superego develops as the child internalizes the prohibitions and sanctions that parents place on his or her behavior. Meanwhile, the *ego*, acting according to the reality principle, serves as a mediator between the relentless struggle between the id and superego for control. The id says, "Now!", the superego says "Never!", and the ego says "Later" to an individual's basic desires. Although id impulses and the conflict of id with superego and ego are usually in the unconscious mind, they are expressed in thoughts and behavior in various disguised forms. The expression of unconscious drives and conflicts can occur in dreams ("the royal road to the unconscious"), under hypnosis, by having patients say whatever comes into their minds (free association), or by using a variety of other methods such as projective tests.

Freud also believed that human personality develops through a series of *psychosexual stages*. During each stage, a different region of the body (erogenous zone) is the center of sexual stimulation and gratification, and at that stage conflicts pertaining to the particular body region are predominant. The *oral stage* occurs from birth to one and a half years, during which time pleasure is derived primarily from stimulation of the mouth and lips, as in sucking, biting, and swallowing. During the *anal stage*, from about age one and a half to three years, interest and conflict center on the retention and expulsion of feces. Negativism, manifested by defiance of parental orders, and frequently associated with toilet-training, is most pronounced during the anal stage. Next in order is the *phallic stage*, from three to six years, during which the body region of greatest interest is the genital area. It is during the phallic stage—when rubbing, touching, exhibiting oneself, and looking are emphasized—that the Oedipus complex develops. The *Oedipus complex*, consisting of a composite of sexual feelings toward the mother and dislike of the father in three- to six-year-old boys, was viewed by Freud as a universal phenomenon. The comparable situation in girls—disliking the mother and loving the father—is referred to as the *Electra complex*.

Freud maintained that if a young boy is to progress from the phallic stage to the latency period of relative sexual inactivity during middle childhood, the Oedipus complex must either be resolved or repressed. In most instances it is resolved by the boy's learning to identify with, that is, trying to act like, his father. At the onset of puberty, the child who has successfully passed through the previous psychosexual stages enters the *genital stage*. Interest in the opposite sex then becomes predominant, ultimately culminating in heterosexual mating.

Freud's theory of personality was based almost entirely on uncontrolled clinical observations of approximately one hundred patients, and many parts of the theory have not been confirmed by subsequent research. Certain assumptions of the theory, for example, the universality of the Oedipus complex and the notion of a latency period, have been shown to be incorrect. But Freud and his followers did render an important service in pointing out the existence of infantile and childhood sexuality and its significance in personality development. Acknowledgement, however, of this contribution does not imply acceptance of the idea that all children invariably pass through the sequence of psychosexual stages outlined above or that adult personality structure is critically dependent on childhood sexual conflict.

Among the disciples and followers of Freud who took issue with or expanded his views were Carl Jung (1875–1961), Alfred Adler (1870–1937), Karen Horney (1885–1952), Erik Fromm (1900–1980), and Erik Erikson (1902–). In his *analytic psychology*, Jung differentiated between the *personal unconscious*, which was essentially the same as Freud's *unconscious*, and the *collective unconscious*. Jung's collective unconscious is a part of the mind that is shared with all humanity, a storehouse of archaic molds (*archetypes*) and propensities inherited from the individual's past. The collective unconscious contains both frightening memories and ancestral wisdom; it is the source of human creativity. Jung also distinguished between various personality types or dimensions—introversion versus extroversion, sensing versus intuition, thinking versus feeling, and judging versus perception. These form the theoretical basis of a personality inventory known as the Myers–Briggs Type Indicator (see Chapter 7).

Adler's *individual psychology* minimizes the effects of frustrated impulses and biological factors on the personality and stresses social factors instead. Adler is best known for his emphasis on feelings of inferiority (the "inferiority complex") as determiners of personality adjustment. These feelings, consisting of a sense of incompleteness or imperfection in one's life, result from frustration of the drive to mastery (the "will to power").

In comparison with Freud, modern psychoanalysts place more emphasis on social learning and culture than on biological instincts as determinants of personality. These neoanalysts, or *ego psychologists*, while admitting their intellectual debt to the founding father, have deviated substantially from Freud in their emphasis on the ego, the importance of social factors, and their stress on cross-cultural studies for understanding human personality and the development of personality theory. One of the most famous of the neoanalysts is Erik Erikson, whose psychohistorical analyses of Martin Luther and Mahatma Gandhi (Erikson, 1958, 1969) in particular, stimulated research on personality assessment through an analysis of the writings of and about famous people. Psychohistories have benefitted from both cross-cultural and interdisciplinary research efforts.

Phenomenological Theories

Stemming from a philosophical tradition that emphasizes the analysis of immediate, personal, subjective experience, *phenomenological* (humanistic or self) *theorists* maintain that trait theorists and others who attempt to analyze personality into a set of components do an injustice to the integrated, dynamic organization of personality. Consequently, phenomenological theorists have been quite critical of psychoanalytic, trait-factor, and behavioral theories of personality. In contrast to traditional psychoanalysis, which emphasizes the fundamental importance of sexual and aggressive impulses, the unconscious, and psychosexual stages in development, phenomenologists stress perceptions, meanings, feelings, and the self. Phenomenologists see a person as responding to the world in terms of his or her unique, private perceptions of it. These perceptions are determined by individual experiences and the meanings placed on those experiences in an effort to fully realize one's potentialities. That part of the environment that is perceived and has meaning for a person is known as the *phenomenal field*, a portion of which (the *self*) is related to the individual in a personal way. Finally, the evaluations—good or bad—that the individual places on the self are referred to as the *self-concept*.

According to Abraham Maslow, Carl Rogers, and other phenomenological theorists, the individual strives to attain a state of *self-actualization*—a congruence or harmony between his or her real self and ideal self. The basic direction of an individual's existence is toward self-actualization and pleasant relations with other people, but that effort can be inhibited in various ways. Rogers points out that most people are not open to or willing to accept the full range of their experiences. In the process of growing up, they learn that they are objects of *conditional positive regard*: parents and other significant people accept the child's behavior only if it conforms to expected standards (*conditions of worth*). Consequently, the child, who eventually becomes an adult, learns to recognize and accept only a part of his or her experiences. The result is an individual who cannot become totally functioning unless she or he receives *unconditional positive regard* from others—a state in which the person is accepted regardless of what he or she is or does.

Clinical practitioners of the phenomenological persuasion have tended to eschew more objective psychological tests and procedures in favor of case studies and open or unstructured interviews to study and assess human personality. Certainly Rogers himself has not been a great believer in the use of personality assessment instruments, and the influence of phenomenology on the construction of personality assessment instruments has not been nearly as great as that of psychoanalytic and trait-factor theories. Nevertheless, designers of instruments for assessing feelings and attitudes toward the self usually follow a phenomenological theory of personality. Illustrative of instruments in this category are *Q sorts* (Stephenson, 1953) and inventories such as the Tennessee Self-Concept Scale (TSCS) and the Piers-Harris Children's Self-Concept Scale (both available from Western Psychological Services), and the Coopersmith Self-Esteem Inventories (available from Consulting Psychologists Press). The one hundred self-descriptive items on the TSCS are written at a sixth-grade level; the 80 items on the Piers-Harris scale at a third-grade level. The TSCS is designed for individuals 12 years old and older, and the Piers-Harris for children in grades 3 through 12. There are two Coopersmith inventories, a school form for children aged 8 to 15 years, and an adult form for individuals aged 16 years and over. All of the self-concept instruments described above can be administered in 10 to 20 minutes.

Murray's Personology

A number of personality assessment instruments have been developed in the context of investigations of personality and behavior disorders. These efforts, although not totally devoid of theoretical foundations, have not been restricted to one particular theoretical position. Examples of this approach are many: the research of the Harvard personologists, which resulted in the Thematic Apperception Test and other instruments; research conducted at the Institute for Personality Assessment and Research in Berkeley, California, which produced the Omnibus Personality Inventory; and the applications of behavior modification, which have resulted in a variety of rating scales and questionnaires. Behavior modification, which is discussed in some detail in Chapter 5, is an outgrowth of the research of B. F. Skinner and other behaviorists. Research on personology was initiated and guided by Henry Murray during the 1930s through the 1950s.

As described in Murray's book *Explorations in Personality* (1938), *personology* was never a unique, fully developed theory of personality in the same sense as Freud's psychoanalytic theory. Murray's theoretical position was more holistic, incorporating ideas from psychoanalysis, trait theory, and other psychological systems. Like Allport, Murray believed that the field of personality is best served by intensive study of the single case, and the 20 "needs" enunciated by Murray are reminiscent of Allport's "traits." A basic principle of Murray's theorizing is that human beings are driven to reduce tensions generated by forces that are internal (*needs*) and external (*press*) to the person. Thus, behavior is a function of both needs and press, which are defined as follows (Murray, 1938):

> A need is a construct . . . which stands for a force (the physico-chemical nature of which is unknown) in the brain region, a force which organizes perception, apperception, intellection, conation, and action in such a way as to transform in a certain direction an existing unsatisfying situation.
>
> The press of an object is what it can *do to the subject* or *for the subject*—the power that it has to affect the well-being of the subject in one way or another. The cathexis of an object . . . is what it can *make the subject do.* (p. 121)

Murray labeled the actual, objective press from the environment *alpha press*, whereas the perceived press is *beta press*.

Analysis of Thematic Apperception Test stories in terms of needs and press, which is discussed in Chapter 12, was an important application of Murray's concepts in the area of personality assessment. Murray's list of physiogenic and psychogenic needs has also been used in the scoring of more objective instruments such as the Edwards Personal Preference Schedule and the Adjective Check List.

Two other concepts, or *hypothetical constructs*, in Murray's theory are thema and vector-value. A *thema*, of which behavior is a function, results from a combination of a particular need and a particular press. The concept of *vector-value*, or simply vector, was added by Murray in 1951 to emphasize the fact that needs, rather than existing alone, operate to serve some value or intent. To a large extent, the notion of *vector*, as a force that serves some value, came to replace that of *need* in Murray's thinking. Examples of such vectors, or behavioral tendencies, are avoidance, expression, reception, and rejection.

Social Learning Theory

Many other theoretical conceptualizations have influenced the development of personality assessment instruments. Among these are the behavioral concepts discussed in Chapter 5, George Kelly's (1955) theory of personal constructs (see Chapter 6), and the cognitive-behavioral approaches of social learning theorists such as Julian Rotter, Albert Bandura, and Walter Mischel. Only Rotter's and Bandura's conceptions will be discussed here, but Mischel's ideas are given extensive attention in Chapter 14.

Rotter's Theory   The first *social learning theory* per se was that of Julian Rotter (1954), who attempted to integrate the traditional behavioristic position on the role of reinforcement in learning with the cognitive conceptualizations of field theorists such as Kurt Lewin. Rotter was not the first to note that much human behavior is learned in a social context, but he made a more conscious effort than his forerunners to develop a systematic theory of how this takes place. The theory begins by differentiating between *reinforcement* (motivation) and *expectancy* (cognition): reinforcements result in movement toward or away from a goal, whereas cognitions are internal states such as expectancy and reinforcement value. The term expectancy refers to a subjective probability held by a person that a specific behavior performed in a certain situation will lead to reinforcement. Two *generalized expectancies* that have been measured and investigated by Rotter and others are internal-external locus of control (see Chapter 13) and interpersonal trust. *Locus of control* refers to the typical direction from which people perceive themselves as being controlled (internal, or from within oneself, verses external, or by other people). *Interpersonal trust* is concerned with the extent to which the individual believes that others tell the truth.

Reinforcement is important for performance, but not all reinforcements are equally valued by the individual: even when the probabilities of occurrence of different reinforcements are equal, certain objects or actions will have greater *reinforcement value* than others. Both reinforcement value and expectancies are affected by the psychological relevance or meaning of the situation to the individual, which must be understood in order to predict the individual's behavior in that situation.

Bandura's Observational Learning Theory   More important for its development of techniques for modifying maladaptive behavior than for the design of personality assessment instruments is Bandura's *social learning theory*. Conceptualizing psychological functioning as the reciprocal interaction of behavior, person variables (cognitions and other internal states), and environmental variables, Bandura emphasizes the fact that the individual is not a passive push-button apparatus who only acts when acted upon. People both influence and are influenced by the social environment, in which learning takes place by observation, imitation, and modeling. Unlike more traditional behaviorists such as Clark Hull and B. F. Skinner, Bandura (1977) maintains that much learning takes place without reinforcement—in the absence of rewards and punishments—but that reinforcement determines when the learned behavior will occur. Particularly important in learning is the process of *modeling* the behavior of others, the effectiveness of which depends on such factors as the personal characteristics of the model and the learner's motivational level. Aggression, fears, sex-typed behaviors and many other emotional and stylistic reactions are, according to Bandura, learned by observation and modeling.

Bandura also emphasizes the fact that learning and behavior are mediated by perceptions and cognitions: people form internal, symbolic representations of their environments, and it is these representations that mediate changes in behavior. By visualizing the consequences of certain actions, the individual learns to regulate his or her behavior.

Empirical Approaches to Personality Assessment

Rather than being designed in accordance with a specific theory of personality, many personality assessment instruments have been constructed on a purely empirical basis. For example, the items on the various scales of the Minnesota Multiphasic Personality Inventory (MMPI) were selected on the basis of their ability to distinguish between two contrasting groups of people (normals and selected psychiatric patient groups). No specific theory of personality was implied or involved in this empirical procedure; the MMPI items were simply validated against the specific criterion of psychiatric diagnoses of various samples of mental patients (see Chapter 8).

Summary

The study of personality is concerned with the unique patterns of psychological characteristics possessed by individuals. A holistic definition deals with both the affective and cognitive, behavioral and mental variables that differentiate among people. Various methods—observations, interviews, rating scales, inventories, projective techniques, tests—are used to assess the structure and function of personality, how it develops and what factors are responsible for its development.

The assessment of personality is as old as humanity, the earliest methods being observation and situational testing. Descriptions of types of character or temperament are found in the writings of the ancient Greeks, Romans, and other nationalities. Such generalized descriptions also appear in famous works of literature written during medieval, Renaissance, and modern times. One of the most widely cited typologies in ancient times was the four humors of Hippocrates and the corresponding temperaments—sanguine, melancholic, choleric, and phlegmatic.

Among the pseudosciences that have been concerned with the analysis of human personality, character, and destiny are astrology, palmistry, phrenology, physiognomy, and graphology. With the possible exception of graphology, none of these is now considered by psychologists to have any legitimacy.

The scientific assessment of personality began during the late nineteenth century in the research of Francis Galton, Alfred Binet, and other psychologists and psychiatrists. The first projective test was the word association test, introduced by Galton and adapted by Emil Kraeplin, Carl Jung, and others. The first personality inventory, a list of questions pertaining to psychopathological symptoms, was constructed by Robert Woodworth and his collaborators during World War I. This inventory, the Woodworth Personal Data Sheet, was designed initially to identify soldiers who might break down under the stresses of war.

The Rorschach Inkblot Test, the most widely used projective technique, was devised by Hermann Rorschach in the early 1920s. The second most popular projective technique, the Thematic Apperception Test, was constructed by Henry Murray and his collaborators in the 1930s. The most widely used personality inventory, the Minnesota Multiphasic Personality Inventory (MMPI), constructed by Hathaway and McKinley, was first published in the early 1940s.

To some extent one or more theories of personality stimulated or guided the construction, scoring, and interpretation of many personality assessment instruments. Psychoanalytic theories and various trait-factor theories have exerted the greatest influence on personality assessment, but a number of instruments also owe their development to phenomenological (self) and social learning (behavioral) theories. Different theories place different emphases on the structure and dynamic aspects of personality, and on the relative importance of biological and environmental determinants.

As examples of personality theories that have stimulated various assessment methods, the chapter considered the body-type theory of Sheldon and Stevens, the trait (or trait-factor) theories of Allport, Cattell, and Eysenck, the psychoanalytic theories of Freud, Jung, and Adler, and the self theory of Rogers. Three other theoretical, or descriptive, approaches to personality were described briefly: Murray's conception of needs and press and the social learning theories of Rotter and Bandura. Other theoretical conceptualizations, such as Kelley's theory of personal constructs and Mischel's social learning theory, are considered in Chapters 6 and 14.

In contrast to assessment devices that stem from a specific theory of personality, instruments such as the MMPI were designed on an empirical basis by their ability to differentiate among specific groups of people. Nevertheless, even these empirically devised instruments were developed on the basis of certain assumptions concerning what constructs the instrument should measure and what kinds of items it should contain. Thus, the invention of techniques of assessing personality does not occur in a vacuum but is based on certain assumptions concerning the nature of personality and its development in a particular sociocultural context.

Exercises

1. Identify each of the following terms:

ability traits	idiographic approach
alpha press	individual psychology
anal stage	individual traits
analytic psychology	interpersonal trust
apperceptive mass	locus of control
archetypes	melancholic
assessment	mesomorphy
astrology	modeling
beta press	need
cerebrotonia	nomothetic approach
choleric	Oedipus complex
collective unconscious	oral stage
common traits	organic
conditional positive regard	palmistry
conditions of worth	persona
constitutional traits	personal dispositions
dynamic traits	personal unconscious
ectomorphy	personality
ego	personology
ego psychologists	phallic stage
Electra complex	phenomenal field
endormorphy	phenomenological theorists
environmental mold traits	phlegmatic
exorcism	phrenology
expectancy	physiognomy
extrovert	press
functional	psychoanalytic theory
genital stage	psychosexual stage
graphology	Q sort
holistic	reinforcement
horoscope	reinforcement value
hypothetical constructs	sanguine
id	self-actualization

self-concept	trait theory
social learning theory	type theory
somatotonia	unconditional positive regard
somatotype	unconscious
source trait	unique traits
superego	vector-value
surface trait	viscerotonia
tabula rasa	word association test
temperament traits	zodiac
thema	

2. The relationships between body build and personality noted by Kretschmer, Sheldon and Stevens, and others do not *prove* that physique causes temperament, or vice versa. Correlation does not imply causation; it only implies prediction. In what way does body build influence personality development? In what way does personality influence physical development? Might not the relationship between personality and physical characteristics be dynamic, reciprocal, and interactive? Explain.

3. Both classical and modern literature are replete with descriptive examples of the presumed relationships of personality characteristics to facial form and movement (kinesics). List as many illustrations as you can find from the writings of William Shakespeare, Charles Dickens, and other famous writers of such presumed relationships. These writers also created many stereotypic characters, such as Falstaff, Othello, Uriah Heep, and Mr. Micawber, whose names have become synonymous with particular personality characteristics or syndromes. List as many stereotypes of this kind as you can think of.

4. Anonymously collect handwriting samples, other than signatures, from members of the class and attempt to match the students with their handwriting. What information or techniques did you use in making these matches, and how successful were you? Were you at least able to differentiate between the handwriting of males and females? A colleague of mine and I (Aiken & Zweigenhaft, 1978) found that, in a sample of men and women in Iran, not only were the signatures of women smaller than those of men, but people of higher social class had larger signatures than people of lower social class. Does this make sense? Would you expect similar results in more democratic countries such as the United States? Why or why not?

5. Of what does an effective theory of personality, or any psychological theory for that matter, consist? What does it attempt to do, and what are the criteria of its effectiveness?

6. Make a case for physiognomy and graphology as legitimate areas of research and application in personality assessment.

Suggested Readings

Allport, G. (1937). *Personality: A psychological interpretation*. New York: Holt.

Ben-Shakhar, G., Bar-Hillel, M., Bilu, Y., Ben-Abba, E., & Flug, A. (1986). Can graphology predict occupational success? Two empirical studies and some methodological ruminations. *Journal of Applied Psychology, 71*, 645–653.

Erikson, E. (1969). *Gandhi's truth*. New York: Norton.

Goldstein, G., & Hersen, M. (1984). Historical perspectives. In G. Goldstein & M. Hersen (Eds.), *Handbook of psychological assessment*. New York: Pergamon.

Hall, C. S., & Lindzey, G. (1985). *Introduction to theories of personality*. New York: Wiley.

Hergenhahn, B. K. (1984). *An introduction to theories of personality* (2nd ed.). Englewood Cliffs, NJ: Prentice-Hall.

Jung, C. G. (1923). *Psychological types*. London: Routledge & Kegan Paul.

Mischel, W. (1986). *Introduction to personality* (4th ed.). New York: Holt, Rinehart & Winston.

Murray, H. (1938). *Explorations in personality*. New York: Oxford University Press.

Richman, J. (Ed.). (1957). *A general selection from the works of Sigmund Freud*. Garden City, NY: Doubleday.

Schultz, D. (1986). *Theories of personality*. Monterey, CA: Brooks/Cole.

CHAPTER 2

Psychometrics I: Statistical Methods and Test Construction

$\mathbf{I}$n the assessment of personality, various procedures are used to collect data—observations, checklists, rating scales, personality inventories, projective techniques, and tests. The value of the resulting data depends on the effectiveness with which the various data-collection instruments are constructed and/or selected. This chapter and the next one consider some of the more technical features of instrument construction and selection, providing the reader with an introduction to the concepts and methods of psychological measurement.[1]

Measurement and Statistics

Measurement, the assignment of numbers to events, is one of the foundations of science. Almost any effort to describe and classify natural phenomena involves measurement of a sort, albeit sometimes a rather crude level of measurement. Measurements in psychology and the other social sciences are admittedly not as precise as those in natural sciences such as physics, but they can be useful in summarizing data on human behavior and drawing inferences from those data. The quantification of observations provides a more objective basis for making intra- and inter-individual comparisons, which is critical to an understanding of differences both within and between individuals.

Scales of Measurement

The lowest level of measurement, in which numbers are arbitrarily assigned designations of objects or events, is known as measurement on a *nominal scale*. An example of nominal measurement are the numbers on athletic uniforms, which typically reveal nothing about the player's skill or position on the team. Illustrative of personal/social variables measured on a nominal scale are sex (male vs. female) and ethnicity (black, white, etc.).

At a somewhat higher level is measurement on an *ordinal scale*, in which the numbers represent the rank orders or orders of merit of some object, person, or situation. Sequence (place) of finishing in a contest of some kind is an example of measurement on an ordinal scale. In personality assessment, scales used to rate behavior and personal characteristics represent measurement at an ordinal level.

Although many social science variables are measured on ordinal scales, this type of measurement is rather limited. For example, if John finishes second, Sue finishes fourth, and Joe finishes sixth in a contest, one cannot say that, although 4 − 2 = 6 − 4, the difference in whatever characteristic is being assessed is the same for John and Sue as it is for Sue and Joe. This is because, on an ordinal scale, equal numerical differences do not necessarily correspond to equal differences in whatever characteristic is being measured.

To make statements such as "the difference between a score of 2 and a score of 4 equals the difference between a score of 4 and a score of 6" requires that measurements be on an interval or ratio scale. A common example of an *interval scale* is the Celsius scale of temperature. On such a scale, if the temperature is 10° Celsius on Monday, 15° Celsius on Wednesday, and 20° Celsius on Friday, then it is correct to say that the difference in temperature (i.e., warmth) on Monday and Wednesday is equal to the difference in temperature on Wednesday and Friday. On the other hand, it requires measurement on a *ratio scale*, on which the number "0" is not an arbitrary zero (as on an interval scale), but rather an absolute zero, to say that it is twice as hot on Friday as on Monday. Since the "0" on the Celsius scale is an arbitrary zero, another type of instrument—a Kelvin thermometer, on which "0" represents a true zero—the absence of molecular motion, is needed to measure temperature on a ratio scale. Thus, it is correct to say that 20° Kelvin is twice as hot as 10° Kelvin (both are quite cold!).

Although the measurement of personality variables is usually on an ordinal scale, or somewhere between an ordinal and interval scale, we frequently employ interval-scale statistics in personality assessment. Thus, we may choose to summarize our data with interval-scale statistics such as the arithmetic mean, standard deviation, or standard scores rather than ordinal-scale statistics such as the median, semi-interquartile range, and percentile ranks. Usually, no great harm is done by this practice, as long as it is realized that all measurements of personality are fairly crude indicators and predictors. As we shall see, however, under certain circumstances it is more appropriate to employ statistics that assume a lower scale of measurement than interval or ratio.

Frequency Distributions and Percentiles

A number of questions need to be answered in order to describe psychological measurements obtained from a group of people: How many people made a given score? What is the average score? What is the spread or variability of the scores? How is one set of measurements related to another set of measurements? When the number of scores is sizable, answers to these and other statistical questions may be obtained more efficiently by grouping the measurements in the form of a *frequency distribution*. To illustrate the construction of a frequency distribution, consider the 90 numbers in Table 2–1. These numbers are the composite scores obtained from the personality ratings assigned by 90 college students to their professor in a political science class. For each of the following characteristics, the students were instructed at midterm to indicate, on a five-point scale (1 = lowest amount through 5 = highest amount), the extent to which the professor was

1. considerate
2. courteous
3. creative
4. friendly
5. interesting
6. knowledgeable
7. motivating
8. organized
9. patient
10. prepared
11. punctual

Thus, the possible sum of ratings on the eleven items ranged from 11 to 55.

It would be possible to group the scores in Table 2–1 into intervals having any desirable numerical width say of 5, yielding the intervals 10 to 14, 15 to 19, 20 to 24, and so on. To do so, however, would distort the data somewhat and is unnecessary when the number of different scores is not unduly large. Consequently, as shown in Table 2–2, we have constructed a frequency distribution having an interval width of 1. The actual (real) limits of an interval range from .5 below the lowest score to .5 above the highest score falling within the interval. Since the

Table 2–1		Raw Scores on Instructor Personality Rating Scale				
26	28	40	37	35	33	33
37	29	42	38	35	38	39
39	28	29	28	39	40	36
45	33	37	29	35	36	31
52	34	24	41	41	33	40
33	39	42	37	34	51	48
54	49	38	55	42	47	46
53	31	38	40	27	35	47
39	40	42	42	37	42	43
41	39	44	31	36	34	36
40	39	31	36	28	41	40
32	36	28	39	50	43	34
34	37	35	50	41	42	

interval width in Table 2–2 is 1, highest and lowest scores are identical, so the real limits range from 23.5 to 24.5 for the first interval, 24.5 to 25.5 for the second interval, etc.

In addition to listing the frequency of each score or score interval, Table 2–2 gives the cumulative percentage, or *percentile rank*, associated with that score. The percentile rank of a given score is the percentage of people obtaining that score or a lower score. For example, 15 people $(1 + 0 + 1 + 1 + 5 + 3 + 0 + 4)$ gave the teacher a score of 31 or below, so the upper real limit of score of 31, namely 31.5, corresponds to a percentile rank of $100(15/90) = 16.67$. Another way of saying the same thing is that 31.5 is the 16.67th (approximately 17th) *percentile*. Likewise, since 76 people gave the teacher a score of 43 (actually 43.5) or below, the percentile rank of the score of 43.5, is $100(76/90) = 84.44$. Alternatively, we can say that 43.5 is the 84.44th percentile.

Averages

One of the first statistics to be computed from a set of scores is an *average* or *measure of central tendency*. The three averages most often encountered are the mode, median, and arithmetic mean. The *mode*, or most frequently occurring score, is the easiest to compute. For example, the mode of the data in Table 2–2 is 39 because more students (8) gave a score of 39 than any other score.

The *median*, or 50th percentile, is the score below which 50 percent of the scores fall. It can be seen that 47.78 percent of the scores in Table 2–2 fall below a score of 37.5 and 52.22 percent of the scores fall below a score of 38.5. Consequently, the median is computed by interpolating within the interval 37.5 to 38.5,

	Frequency Distribution of Composite Rating Scores in Table 2–1		Table 2–2

Score Interval Midpoint	Frequency on Interval	Cumulative Percentage (Percentile Rank of Upper Limit)
24	1	1.11
25	0	1.11
26	1	2.22
27	1	3.33
28	5	8.89
29	3	12.22
30	0	12.22
31	4	16.67
32	1	17.78
33	5	23.33
34	5	28.89
35	5	34.44
36	6	41.11
37	6	47.78
38	4	52.22
39	8	61.11
40	7	68.89
41	5	74.44
42	7	82.22
43	2	84.44
44	1	85.56
45	1	86.67
46	1	87.78
47	2	90.00
48	1	91.11
49	1	92.22
50	2	94.44
51	1	95.56
52	1	96.67
53	1	97.78
54	1	98.89
55	1	100.00

of which 38 is the midpoint. This is easily accomplished by substracting 47.78 from 50, dividing the remainder by the difference between 52.22 and 47.78, and adding the result to 37.5: $(50 - 47.78)/(52.22 - 47.78) + 37.5 = 2.22/4.44 + 37.5 = 38.00$. Formulas for computing the median, in addition to other percentiles and percentile ranks, from a frequency distribution are given in textbooks on elementary statistics and introductory psychological testing (Aiken, 1988; McCall, 1986; Pagano, 1986).

The mode is the least popular and usually least representative measure of central tendency. More popular is the median, which is an appropriate measure of central tendency whenever measurements are made on an ordinal scale or the distribution of scores is markedly skewed (asymmetrical). Despite the fact that it can be greatly affected by extremely high or low scores, the most popular of all measures of central tendency is the *arithmetic mean*. The arithmetic mean ($\overline{X}$) is computed as the sum of the scores divided by the number of scores, $\overline{X} = \Sigma X/n$, where the Greek letter capital sigma Σ means "the sum of" and n is the total number of scores. Adding all the scores (sum of ratings) in Table 2–1 yields 3,428, so the arithmetic mean is 3,428/90 = 38.09.

Measures of Variability

It is usually important to know not only the average of a group of scores but also how much the scores vary from each other or from the average score. One such measure of variability is the range, computed as the highest minus the lowest score. The *range* of the scores in Table 2–2 is $55 - 24 = 31$. Unfortunately, this simply computed statistic is greatly affected by extreme scores and consequently tends to be unstable. Another, more stable kind of range is known as the semi-interquartile range. The *semi-interquartile range* (Q) is defined as half the difference between the 75th percentile and the 25th percentile. The 75th percentile of the scores in Table 2–2, computed by interpolating within the score interval 41.5 to 42.5 is $(75 - 74.44)/(82.22 - 74.44) + 41.5 = 41.57$. Similarly, the 25th percentile is computed as $(25 - 23.33)/(28.89 - 23.33) + 33.5 = 33.80$. Therefore $Q = (41.57 - 33.80)/2 = 3.89$.

The semi-interquartile range is an appropriate measure of variability to use when the median is the measure of central tendency. A third measure of variability, the *standard deviation,* is more suitable when the arithmetic mean is the reported measure of central tendency. The standard deviation (s) of a set of scores is computed as

$$s = \sqrt{[\Sigma X^2 - (\Sigma X)^2/n]/(n - 1)}.$$

To find ΣX^2, the sum of squares, each score (X) is squared and the squares are added; to find $(\Sigma X)^2$, the square of the sum, the values of X are added and then the sum is squared. For the data in Table 2–1, $\Sigma X = 3,428$ and $\Sigma X^2 = 134,482$. Therefore,

$$s = \sqrt{(134,482 - 3428^2/90)/89} = 6.63.$$

The square of the standard deviation is known as the *variance* (s^2), which is 43.97 for this problem.

Standard (z) Scores

Because the measurements obtained from different psychological variables may not be expressed in the same numerical units, it is convenient to have a uniform scale of measurement to which scores on different variables may be converted. Then an individual's performance on one variable can be directly compared with his or her standing on another variable. Various score transformations utilizing the arithmetic mean and standard deviation can be made. One popular transformation is the standard *z score*, where $z = (X - \overline{X})/s$. Just as the gram and centimeter are used as standard units of measurement of weight and length in the metric system, the z score is used as a standard unit in psychological measurement. The z score corresponding to a given raw score (X) indicates the number of standard deviation units that X is above (+) or below (−) the mean of all scores in the group.

To illustrate the computation of z scores, which themselves have a mean of 0 and a standard deviation of 1, the z score corresponding to a raw score of 45 from the data in Table 2–2 is $z = (45 - 38.09)/6.63 = 1.04$; the z score corresponding to a raw score of 35 is $(35 - 38.09)/6.63 = -.47$. Incidentally, the arithmetic mean of the z scores corresponding to a set of data is 0 and the standard deviation of z scores is 1.

Correlation and Regression

A correlation coefficient is an index number, usually ranging from −1.00 to +1.00, that indicates the degree and direction of the relationship between two variables. The closer the correlation is to +1.00 or −1.00, the greater the relationship between the two variables and the more accurately either variable can be predicted from the other. When the correlation is positive, low scores on one variable tend to go with low scores on the other variable, and high scores with high scores. When the correlation is negative, low scores on one variable go with high scores on the other variable.

There are many types of correlation coefficients, but we shall restrict our attention to two that are used frequently in the construction of personality assessment instruments and research involving those instruments—the *product-moment coefficient* and the *point-biserial coefficient*. It should be noted that both of these coefficients are based on the assumption of a linear (straight line) relationship between the two variables. If the relationship is nonlinear (or curvilinear), as is the relationship between certain variables—say performance efficiency and level of motivation—then the product-moment and point-biserial coefficients will give a distorted picture of the true relationship between the variables. However, even if they are not precisely linear, the relationships between many psychological variables are sufficiently close to linear to justify the use of these coefficients.

Product-Moment Coefficient Consider the 90 pairs of scores in the X and Y columns of Table 2–3, where X is a composite student rating of the personality of an

Table 2–3	Composite Ratings of Instructor (X) and Course (Y) by Student				
Student	X	Y	X²	Y²	XY
1	26	6	676	36	156
2	28	10	784	100	280
3	40	28	1600	784	1120
4	37	14	1369	196	518
5	35	14	1225	196	490
6	33	12	1089	144	396
7	33	21	1089	441	693
8	37	20	1369	400	740
9	29	18	841	324	522
10	42	21	1764	441	882
11	38	22	1444	484	836
12	35	19	1225	361	665
13	38	18	1444	324	684
14	39	23	1521	529	897
15	39	21	1521	441	819
16	28	19	784	361	532
17	29	12	841	144	348
18	28	9	784	81	252
19	39	15	1521	225	585
20	40	22	1600	484	880
21	36	22	1296	484	792
22	45	25	2025	625	1125
23	33	15	1089	225	495
24	37	15	1369	225	555
25	29	18	841	324	522
26	35	11	1225	121	385
27	36	16	1296	256	576
28	31	16	961	256	496
29	52	30	2704	900	1560
30	34	18	1156	324	612
31	24	11	576	121	264
32	41	21	1681	441	861
33	41	21	1681	441	861
34	33	10	1089	100	330
35	40	16	1600	256	640
36	33	16	1089	256	528
37	39	21	1521	441	819
38	42	19	1764	361	798
39	37	15	1369	225	555
40	34	13	1156	169	442
41	51	23	2601	529	1173
42	48	24	2304	576	1152
43	54	21	2916	441	1134

(Continued)

Student	X	Y	X²	Y²	XY
44	49	20	2401	400	980
45	38	20	1444	400	760
46	55	22	3025	484	1210
47	42	19	1764	361	798
48	47	19	2209	361	893
49	46	22	2116	484	1012
50	53	24	2809	576	1272
51	31	19	961	361	589
52	38	6	1444	36	228
53	40	19	1600	361	760
54	27	12	729	144	324
55	35	15	1225	225	525
56	47	20	2209	400	940
57	39	23	1521	529	897
58	40	17	1600	289	680
59	42	13	1764	169	546
60	42	20	1764	400	840
61	37	18	1369	324	666
62	42	20	1764	400	840
63	43	18	1849	324	774
64	41	19	1681	361	779
65	39	16	1521	256	624
66	44	24	1936	576	1056
67	31	15	961	225	465
68	36	15	1296	225	540
69	34	21	1156	441	714
70	36	18	1296	324	648
71	40	20	1600	400	800
72	39	23	1521	529	897
73	31	23	961	529	713
74	36	10	1296	100	360
75	28	20	784	400	560
76	41	18	1681	324	738
77	40	17	1600	289	680
78	32	19	1024	361	608
79	36	18	1296	324	648
80	28	14	784	196	392
81	39	13	1521	169	507
82	50	7	2500	49	350
83	43	8	1849	64	344
84	34	19	1156	361	646
85	34	14	1156	196	476
86	37	22	1369	484	814
87	35	23	1225	529	805
88	50	21	2500	441	1050
89	41	17	1681	289	697
90	42	30	1764	900	1260
Sums	3428	1611	134482	30963	62675

instructor given at midterm and *Y* is an end-of-term evaluation of a course taught by that instructor. The eleven items on the composite personality rating were listed earlier in the chapter. The six items included in the course evaluation score consist of five-point-scale ratings of the extent to which the course was considered:

1. helpful
2. informative
3. interesting
4. motivating
5. stimulating
6. valuable

The formula for determining the product-moment correlation coefficient between the *X* and *Y* variables is:

$$r = \frac{n\Sigma XY - (\Sigma X)(\Sigma Y)}{\sqrt{[n\Sigma X^2 - (\Sigma X)^2][n\Sigma Y^2 - (\Sigma Y)^2]}}$$

Note that the six values needed in the formula are n (the number of *X*, *Y* pairs of scores), the sum of the *X* scores (ΣX), the sum of the *Y* scores (ΣY), the sum of the squares of the *X* scores (ΣX^2), the sum of the squares of the *Y* scores (ΣY^2), and the sum of the cross-products of the *X* and *Y* scores (ΣXY). Substituting the appropriate numbers (see last row of Table 2–3) in the formula for *r* yields

$$r = \frac{90(62,675) - (3,428)(1,611)}{\sqrt{[90(134,482) - (3,428)^2][90(30,963) - (1,611)^2]}} = .4555.$$

Thus, there is a moderate, but significant, positive correlation between composite ratings of instructor personality at midterm and end-of-term evaluative ratings of the course. This indicates a tendency for students who rate the instructor's personality high at midterm to rate the course high at the end, and for students who assign low ratings to the instructor's personality at midterm to give low ratings to the course at the end.

Simple Linear Regression   Although correlation does not imply causation, it does imply prediction: the larger the value of r, in either a positive or negative direction, the more accurate the prediction of Y from X (or X from Y). The prediction of Y from X is facilitated by substituting the appropriate values of *b*, X, and a in the equation

$$Y_{pred} = bX + a,$$

where

$$b = [N\Sigma XY - (\Sigma X)(\Sigma Y)]/[N\Sigma X^2 - (\Sigma X)^2],$$

and

$$a = \overline{Y} - b\overline{X}.$$

For the data in Table 2–1:

$N = 90,$
$\Sigma XY = 62,675,$
$\Sigma X = 3,428,$
$\Sigma Y = 1,611,$
$\Sigma X^2 = 134,482,$
$\Sigma Y^2 = 30,963,$
$\overline{X} = 38.0889$
and
$\overline{Y} = 17.90.$

Consequently, $b = [90(62,675) - 3,428(1,611)]/[90(134,482) - (3,428)^2] = .3357$ and $a = 17.90 - .3357(38.0889) = 5.1136$. Entering any value of X, say X = 50, into the resulting *regression equation*, $Y_{pred} = .3357X + 5.1136$, yields a predicted Y value for a person with that X score, viz.: $Y_{pred} = .3357(50) + 5.1136 = 21.8986$, or approximately 22. This is only a predicted value, not necessarily an obtained Y value; a person who makes an X score of 50 may obtain a quite different Y score than 22. What the predicted Y score of 22 represents is the approximate mean Y score of all individuals whose X score is 50. Therefore, some individuals whose X score is 50 will have obtained Y scores below 22 and some will have obtained Y scores above 22.

Coefficient of Determination   Remembering that correlation implies prediction, a useful index of the accuracy of prediction can be derived by squaring the correlation coefficient. The resulting statistic (r^2), referred to as the *coefficient of determination*, is the proportion of variance in the predicted (or criterion) variable that can be accounted for or explained by variability in the predictor variable. For the above example, $r^2 = (.4555)^2 = .2075$, so approximately 21% of the variance in end-of-term ratings of the course can be accounted for by variability in midterm ratings of the instructor's personality. This leaves $100 - 21 = 79\%$ of the variability in end-of-term course ratings unaccounted for—a substantial percentage.

Multiple Linear Regression   As noted above, only 21% of the variance in the criterion variable (Y) was accounted for by variation in the predictor variable (X). One possible way of improving the predictability of Y from X is to include more independent variables in the regression equation. Thus, if we include two more independent variables in the equation, our prediction equation, now referred to as a *multiple regression equation*, becomes $Y_{pred} = b_1 X_1 + b_2 X_2 + b_3 X_3 + a$. Determination of the numerical values of the b's and a is somewhat complex and usually done on a computer.

There is no guarantee that including scores on other independent variables in the regression equation will improve the accuracy of prediction, but this is more likely to occur when the independent (X) variables have low correlations with each other and high correlations with the dependent (Y) variable. It is also important to recognize that a multiple regression approach assumes that each independent variable is linearly related to all the other variables in the equation and that scores on the dependent variable have a normal (bell-shaped) distribution.

Point-Biserial Coefficient   Equivalent to the product-moment coefficient when one of the variables is continuous and the other variable dichotomous is the point-biserial coefficient. The dichotomous (X) variable consists of two discrete groups of people, numerically designated 0 and 1. A formula for computing the point-biserial coefficient is

$$r_{pb} = \frac{(\bar{Y}_1 - \bar{Y})}{s} \sqrt{\frac{n_1 n}{(n - n_1)(n - 1)}},$$

where n = the total number of examinees, n_1 = the number of examinees in the group designated 1, $\bar{Y}_1$ = the Y mean of group 1, $\bar{Y}$ = the Y mean of both groups combined, and s = the Y standard deviation of both groups combined. The point-biserial coefficient is useful in a number of contexts, in particular for determining the extent to which the individual items on a test are related to total test scores—calculations that take place in the item analysis of a test. To illustrate the use of this formula, let sex (female = 0, male = 1) be the dichotomous variable to be correlated with the 90 composite personality ratings in Table 2–4. Then

$$r = \frac{(36.4722 - 38.0889)}{6.631} \sqrt{\frac{36(90)}{54(89)}} = -.2002.$$

The direction and magnitude of this coefficient indicates a very low negative relationship between sex and ratings of instructor personality; males viewed the instructor less positively than females, but not significantly so.

Factor Analysis

Table 2–5 is a matrix of correlations among the ratings given by the 90 students to the 11 instructor personality items described earlier in the chapter. If the matrix is divided into two triangular portions by drawing a line from the upper left to the

					Composite Instructor Ratings by Sex					Table 2–4

Composite Instructor Ratings by Sex

Females (n = 54)

26	40	35	33	33	37	38	38	39	28
29	28	39	36	45	29	35	36	31	34
40	33	37	51	54	49	38	55	42	47
46	53	38	35	47	39	42	42	43	39
34	36	40	36	41	40	50	43	34	34
35	50	41	42						

Males (n = 36)

28	37	29	42	35	39	40	33	37	52
24	41	41	33	39	42	34	48	31	40
27	40	37	42	41	44	31	36	39	31
28	32	36	28	39	37				

lower right corner, it can be seen that it is a symmetric matrix in which the first row contains the same values as the first column, the second row the same elements as the second column, and so on. Also notice that the numbers on the principal diagonal (upper left to lower right) are all 1.00s, the presumed correlation of each item with itself.[2]

The computation of the correlation coefficients given in this matrix is the first step in a *factor analysis*, a mathematical procedure for reducing the number of variables (items or tests) to a smaller number of dimensions, or *factors*, by taking into account the overlap (correlations) among the various measures. In psychological testing, the task of a factor analysis is to find a few salient factors that account for the major part of the variance in a group of scores on different tests or other psychometric measures. Thus, the factors extracted by a factor analysis should account for a large percentage of the overlap among the variances of the items or tests represented in the correlation matrix.

In this case, there are 11 items, or variables, so the object of the factor analysis is to find that matrix of *factor loadings*, or correlations between factors and items, that most effectively accounts for the correlations among the items. There are many approaches to factor analysis, but all involve two stages: factoring the matrix of correlations to produce an initial, or unrotated, factor matrix, and then *rotating* the factor matrix to provide the simplest possible configuration of factor loadings. The purpose of the factoring stage is to determine the number of factors required to account for the relationships among the various tests and provide initial estimates of the numerical loadings of each test on each factor. The purpose of factor rotation is to make the factors more interpretable by producing a configuration in which only a

Table 2–5

Matrix of Correlations Among 11 Instructor Personality Items

Item	1	2	3	4	5	6	7	8	9	10	11
1	1.000	.727	.424	.573	.343	.294	.458	.200	.425	.091	.078
2	.727	1.000	.304	.620	.287	.258	.363	.075	.459	.115	.127
3	.424	.304	1.000	.470	.510	.080	.691	.206	.304	.129	.112
4	.573	.620	.470	1.000	.336	.195	.390	.061	.528	.026	.022
5	.343	.287	.510	.336	1.000	.171	.638	.374	.203	.243	.244
6	.294	.258	.080	.195	.171	1.000	.108	.227	.159	.490	.430
7	.458	.363	.691	.390	.638	.108	1.000	.218	.314	.108	.065
8	.200	.075	.206	.061	.374	.227	.218	1.000	.085	.524	.421
9	.425	.459	.304	.528	.203	.159	.314	.085	1.000	.114	.187
10	.091	.115	.129	.026	.243	.490	.108	.524	.114	1.000	.611
11	.078	.127	.112	.022	.244	.430	.065	.421	.187	.611	1.000

few tests have high loadings and the majority of tests have low loadings on any given factor. One of the most common factoring procedures is the *principal axis* method, and a popular rotation procedure is *varimax rotation*. These are the procedures that we shall use in this instance.

The correlation matrix in Table 2–5 was factored by the principal axis procedure by using subprogram FACTOR of the computer package of statistical programs known as SPSS/PC+ (Norusis, 1985). The resulting unrotated factor matrix is shown in Table 2–6. Observe that the computer program yielded a three-factor solution, the three factors are designated A, B, and C. The decimal numbers listed under each factor column are the correlations, or *loadings*, of the 11 items on that factor. Thus, Item 1 has a loading of .754 on Factor A, −.271 on Factor B, and .250 on Factor C. The sum of the squared loadings for each item is the item's *communality*, or proportion of the variance of that item accounted for by the three common factors. For example, the communality of item 1 is $(.754)^2 + (−.271)^2 + (.250)^2 = .704$. This means that 70.4% of the variance of the item 1 scores is accounted for by these three factors.

It is also of interest to determine the proportion of total test (or item in this case) variance specific to a given test. To determine this *specificity* of a test (or item), we use the equation specificity = reliability − communality. Although the topic of reliability is not discussed until the next chapter, let it suffice for now to say that *reliability* refers to the extent to which test scores are free from errors of measurement. A *reliability coefficient* is an index number ranging from .00 (complete unreliability) to 1.00 (perfect reliability). Like communality and reliability, specificity ranges from .00 to 1.00; the larger a test's specificity, the more specific whatever that test measures is to that test itself. The larger a test's communality, the more common whatever that test measures is to the other tests in the group of tests being factor analyzed.

	Factor Loadings			
Item	*Factor* A	*Factor* B	*Factor* C	Communality
1	.754	−.271	.250	.704
2	.708	−.281	.415	.752
3	.689	−.206	−.440	.710
4	.702	−.392	.240	.704
5	.674	.063	−.500	.708
6	.442	.477	.402	.584
7	.714	−.216	−.485	.791
8	.434	.573	−.257	.582
9	.594	−.201	.330	.502
10	.408	.769	.063	.762
11	.388	.718	.122	.681

Unrotated Factor Matrix of Rated Instructor Personality Items   **Table 2–6**

The rotated factor matrix is shown in Table 2–7. The communality of each item is the same as in the unrotated factor matrix, but the rotated factors are much easier to interpret than those in Table 2–6. Varimax rotation is an orthogonal rotation procedure, in that the factor axes remain at right angles to each other. In contrast, the factor axes in *oblique rotation* make acute or obtuse angles with each other. Orthogonal factors are usually easier to interpret than oblique factors since the factors are uncorrelated, or independent.

In interpreting the rotated factor matrix, we pay particular attention to the items that have loadings of .50 or more on a given factor. It can be seen in Table 2–7 that four items—item 1 (considerate), item 2 (courteous), item 4 (friendly), and item 9 (patient) have high loadings on Factor A′. Consequently, an appropriate name for this factor might be "considerateness" or "interpersonal sensitivity." Four items also have high loadings on Factor B′: item 6 (knowledgeable), item 8 (organized), item 10 (prepared), and item 11 (punctual). Hence an appropriate name for this factor might be "preparedness." Lastly, three items have high loadings on Factor C′: item 3 (creative), item 5 (interesting), and item 7 (motivating). An appropriate name for Factor A′ might be "stimulating" or "motivating." These three factors make psychological sense in terms of the kind of personality students expect of a good teacher—one who shows consideration, is prepared for class, and has a style that interests and motivates learners.

There is much more to factor analysis that has been indicated here; entire books have been written on the topic (for example, Harman, 1976). As these books reveal, factor analysis is a complex topic that involves higher-order mathematics such as matrix algebra and the analytic geometry of space. The topic is also a

Table 2–7   **Rotated Factor Matrix of Rated Instructor Personality Items**

| | Factor Loadings | | | |
Item	Factor A'	Factor B'	Factor C'	Communality
1	.783	.090	.288	.704
2	.853	.089	.131	.752
3	.303	.015	.786	.710
4	.790	−.041	.280	.704
5	.148	.243	.792	.708
6	.353	.669	−.113	.584
7	.298	.009	.838	.791
8	−.082	.649	.392	.582
9	.691	.102	.120	.502
10	.011	.867	.100	.762
11	.052	.822	.048	.681

controversial one: not only is there disagreement concerning the most appropriate procedures of factoring and rotation, but the interpretation of factors and their psychological bases have been the source of dispute for many years. At the very least, however, factor analysis provides the psychometrician with one more tool for understanding the relationships among psychological variables and events. It has proven to be particularly useful in the design of psychological assessment instruments and in research concerned with the validity of those instruments.

Construction and Item Analysis of Assessment Instruments

The design and construction of personality assessment instruments has involved a variety of approaches, some based on theoretical or common-sense conceptions of the nature of personality and others on empirical or criterion-related approaches. Almost all of these efforts have employed some sort of statistical procedures to determine or demonstrate the validity of the instruments.

The construction of projective techniques such as the Rorschach Inkblot Test and the Thematic Apperception Test has typically relied on some theory or theoretical conceptions of personality structure and dynamics, although common sense and a kind of hit-or-miss empiricism have also played a role in their development. Details of how the best-known projectives were designed are discussed in chapters 10 through 12. Likewise, the design of personality and interest inventories is discussed in chapters 7 through 9. However, because the construction of personality inventories and rating scales has adhered more closely than projectives to statistical and psychometric methods, strategies for constructing the former instruments will be considered briefly at this point.

Strategies for Constructing Inventories and Rating Scales

Burisch (1984) describes three major strategies for constructing personality inventories and rating scales—the deductive, inductive, and external. The *deductive*, or content-based, strategy (also referred to as the rational, intuitive, or theoretical approach), entails quite a bit of sophisticated language about personality; a few theoretical conceptions concerning the structure and function of personality can also prove helpful. Using this knowledge base as a starting point, the person constructing the scale writes or designs a series of items that he or she hopes will assess the psychological constructs under consideration. This was the approach followed in preparing the 11-item instructor personality scale described earlier in the chapter.

The second strategy, the *inductive* one, involves the use of factor analysis or other correlation-based procedures. Although designers of personality inventories and rating scales usually have some initial ideas about what they desire to measure, the major feature of the inductive approach is to let the data speak for themselves. In other words, a large collection of items is first administered to a appropriate sample of examinees. Then a statistical and/or rational analysis of the responses determines the number of variabless being measured by the item aggregate and which items contribute to the assessment of which variables. This approach to inventory construction has also been labeled as internal, internal consistency, or itemetric.

The third strategy, labeled the *external, empirical*, or *criterion group* approach, has been characterized as the most accurate and generally useful. Various statistical procedures, including simple correlational methods, chi square, multiple regression analysis, and factor analysis, have been used in selecting items in the empirical methods of test construction. In the empirical strategy, as exemplified in the construction of the Minnesota Multiphasic Personality Inventory (MMPI) and the Strong Vocational Interest Blank, items are selected or retained according to their ability to differentiate between two (or more) criterion groups of examinees. Thus, in designing the MMPI, an item was placed on the schizophrenic scale if the responses given to the item by a group of known schizophrenics were significantly different from those given by a group of normal people. On the Strong Vocational Interest Blank for Men, an item became part of the "Banker" scale if a criterion group of bankers responded to the item in a significantly different way from a criterion group of men in general.

It is not always clear which of the three approaches to personality scale development is best. Burisch (1984) maintains that scales developed by the deductive approach have the advantages of being more economical to construct and communicating information more directly to the personality assessor. He admits, however, that deductively developed scales can be more easily faked and may not be as appropriate as empirical scales when it is advantageous to the examinee to dissemble. In any case, a combination of the three strategies has been employed in the construction of many personality inventories and rating scales. Even in the development of the simple 11-item instructor personality inventory discussed previously, two approaches—the deductive and inductive—were used.

Item Analysis and Item Response Theory

The process of constructing a personality test or inventory does not end with the first administration of the instrument to a sample group of people. Whatever strategy was employed in initial construction—deductive, inductive, external, or more likely some combination of these—the test author will almost always desire to conduct a *post hoc* analysis to determine whether all items constituting the test are functioning properly. That is, are they measuring what the test designer wants them to measure? Of course, careful construction of items, critical reading by other experts on test design, and preliminary tryouts with small groups of examinees can minimize the number of poor items revealed by an empirical item analysis. But try as they may, test designers never anticipate all the problems that can occur when the test is actually administered to a large, representative group of individuals. Consequently, an empirical item analysis usually reveals that many items are behaving in a different way than they are supposed to.

Traditional Procedures   Various statistical procedures are applied in a thorough item analysis of a test designed to measure a specified psychological charateristic, in particular measures of item difficulty (What percentage of the group gave the keyed answer to the item?) and item discrimination (To what extent do items discriminate between scores on the test as a whole or on some external variable?). If the test or section of the test was meant to measure a single characteristic or trait, then the scores on the items comprising the test or section should have high correlations with each other. An alternative procedure is to determine the correlation between the scores on each item and scores on the section or test as a whole. Items having low correlations with other items, or with total test (or section) scores, should then be revised or discarded. In addition to correlating items with each other or total scores, in order to possess external validity the item should be significantly correlated with other variables that presumably measure the same characteristic.

Other statistical methods, such as constructing frequency distributions of the various responses to the item and conducting factor analyses of the item scores, can reveal weaknesses (and strengths) of the test. But the analysis process is a neverending one; published and unpublished tests are still being item analyzed years after they first appeared. There are good reasons for the repetition: the results of an item analysis often vary markedly with the specific group that is tested in addition to when and under what conditions they are tested. For example, certain items may be answered differently by males than by females, by one ethnic group than by another, or by one socioeconomic group than by another. In constructing a standardized test of personality or ability, it has become common practice to examine each item and its associated statistics for indications of group discrimination or bias. The fact that test items are answered differently by one group than by another group, however, does not necessarily mean that the items are biased against one of the groups. An item is biased, in a technical sense, only when it measures something different—a different characteristic or trait—in one group than in another. If item scores reflect true differences in whatever ability or trait the item was designed to measure, the item is not biased in this sense.

Item Response Curves and Theory   A somewhat more complex item-analysis method with items having (0, 1) scoring begins with the construction of an item response curve for each item. In constructing an *item-response curve*, the proportion of examinees who answer the item in a specific way (on an ability test those who answer correctly) is plotted against scores on an internal criterion (e.g., total test scores) or performance on an external criterion (e.g., academic or occupational adjustment measures). Once the response curve is drawn for a particular item, a difficulty level and a discriminative index can be computed for that item. The *difficulty level* (*b*) is the criterion score (usually a standardized z score) at which 50 percent of the examinees answer the item in the specified manner, and the *discriminative index* (*a*) is the slope of the item-response curve at that point. However, an item-response curve goes further than a simple item analysis in providing a detailed picture of the functional relationships between the percentage of people answering the item in a specified way and scores on the internal or external criterion measure.

In *item-response theory* (IRT), item-response curves are constructed by plotting the proportion of people answering the item in a specified manner against estimates of the true standing of those individuals on the latent trait or characteristic of interest. These estimates are derived from a specific mathematical function known as a logistic equation (see Hulin, Drasgow & Parsons, 1983). Referred to as *latent-trait theory, item-characteristic curve theory* (ICC), or the *Rasch model*, the precise mathematical equations involved in this approach vary with the assumptions and estimation procedures prescribed by the approach. Basically, these item-analysis methods relate examinees' performances on test items to their estimated standings on a hypothetical latent psychological trait or continuum. Because a thorough understanding of how item-analysis models operate requires a fairly sophisticated background in mathematics, the technical details will not be described here. However, item-response theories provide not only a novel approach to item analysis but also procedures for constructing tests having certain specified characteristics.

Item-response approaches, which have been used quite successfully in the development, administration, and evaluation of ability tests, have not been applied extensively to personality assessment. There are differences between the measurement of ability and personality that make the application of IRT techniques to personality assessment more complex than in the case of ability testing (see Butcher, Keller, & Bacon, 1985). It can be argued that the item difficulty, discrimination, and guessing indexes, which are important parameters in item-response models, have their counterparts in personality testing, but there are other problems (lack of unidimensionality of whatever the test is measuring, greater ambiguity of the items, etc.) that make the application of IRT models to personality assessment more difficult. This is not to say that IRT procedures will not find a place in personality assessment, but only that there are significant problems to overcome and that alternative approaches may be more successful.

Sources and Standards for Personality Assessment Instruments

There are many facets to test interpertation and evaluation, and we have just scratched the surface of this important topic. Before continuing with the more technical details of the process, however, we shall pause briefly to consider the question of where one can find information about specific personality tests, or psychological tests in general. The sources provide both descriptive and evaluative, verbal and quantitative, information about a wide variety of affective and cognitive measuring instruments.

The number of personality assessment instruments, both published and unpublished, is truly overwhelming. *Tests in Print III* (Mitchell, 1983), a standard source of psychological and educational test descriptions, contains 576 separate personality test entries, the largest number in any category. Similarly, 350, or 24.8%, of the tests reviewed in *The Ninth Mental Measurements Yearbook* (Mitchell, 1985) are personality tests. If one adds to these published instruments an estimate of the number of inventories, checklists, rating forms, attitude scales, and other unpublished affective instruments listed in *Dissertation Abstracts*, the several volumes of the *Directory of Unpublished Experimental Mental Measures* (Goldman & Busch, 1978, 1982; Goldman & Osborne, 1985; Goldman & Saunders, 1974), and other sources, the total is undoubtedly well over a thousand. Not all of these instruments, by any means, fulfill the requirements for a good test listed in the *Standards for Educational and Psychological Testing* (American Educational Research Association et al., 1985). Nevertheless, they are or have been used to measure behavioral and mental characteristics in the affective domain.

As indicated by the more than 50 publishers and distributors of personality assessment instruments whose addresses are listed in the Appendix B, the development and marketing of personality tests has become a big business. Although not as many personality tests are sold as standardized achievement tests and other tests of ability (intelligence, special aptitudes, etc.), personality assessment is still a lucrative enterprise with customers in private practice, clinics, educational institutions, business and industry, and government.

Two of the major sources of information on tests and other assessment instruments are *Tests in Print III,* which provides a fairly exhaustive descriptive listing without evaluating the instruments and *The Mental Measurements Yearbooks,* which contain detailed reviews of a sizable number (1,409 in the ninth edition) of tests. Report 2–1 illustrates the type of information included in a review of a personality tests, in this case the Jenkins Activity Survey. In general, such a review should contain

- A detailed description of test content (title, author, publisher, date and place of publication, forms available, type of test, cost, sections of the test, kinds of items and how selected, theory or conceptual basis of the test, mental operations or characteristics the test is supposed to measure).

- Administration and scoring information (instructions, time limits, whole or part scoring, clarity of directions for administration and scoring).

- Description of norms (size and composition of test standardization group and how selected, kinds of norms reported, overall adequacy of standardization).

- Reliability data (kinds of reliability information reported in manual, nature and sizes of samples on which the reliability information was obtained and whether adequate).

- Validity data (kinds of validity information available and whether it is satisfactory in terms of the stated purposes of the test).

Other sources of information on personality assessment instruments include various journals (see Appendix A), textbooks concerned with the topic, and abstract and index series (e.g., *Psychological Abstracts, Child Development Abstracts, Dissertation Abstracts, Education Index*). A number of source books, directories, handbooks, annotated bibliographies, and collections of critical reviews of psychological assessment instruments have also been published during the past 15 years or so. Noteworthy among these are *Tests* (Sweetland & Keyser, 1983–1986) and *Test Critiques* (Keyser & Sweetland, 1984–1986). References for these volumes are listed at the end of this chapter under "Sources of Information on Personality Tests." Finally, the test catalogs provided free of charge by publishers and distributors whose addresses are given in Appendix B can serve to familiarize the student and professional to the names and purposes of various personality assessment instruments and the individuals or groups for whom they are suitable.

As will be discussed in Chapter 4, test distributors should require those who order their test materials to demonstrate some competency in psychological testing. All too often, psychological assessment materials are made available to individuals who are unknowledgeable or untrained in their use. In any event, when deciding what tests to order, the potential user should not be misled by the *jingle fallacy* (tests having similar names necessarily measure the same characteristics) or the *jangle fallacy* (tests having different names measure different characteristics). A specimen set of a particular instrument, which typically includes a copy of the test, answer sheet, and perhaps a scoring key, can be ordered by professional psychologists and counselors to help them determine whether the instrument is applicable to the individuals and for the purpose which the potential purchaser has in mind.

The test manual, containing a description of how the test was constructed, directions for administration and scoring, and perhaps norms, is usually not included in a specimen set and must be ordered separately. For some instruments, administration and scoring is covered in one manual and the statistical details of norms, reliability, and validity in a separate technical manual. However, even a technical manual does not necessarily give up-to-date data on the validity of the test; much of that information may have to be sought in reports of research investigations published in professional journals subsequent to publication of the manual.

Report 2–1	**Review of Jenkins Activity Survey**

Review of Jenkins Activity Survey by JAMES A. BLUMENTHAL, Assistant Professor of Medical Psychology, Department of Psychiatry, Duke University Medical Center, Durham, NC:

The Type A behavior pattern is a behavioral syndrome that has been demonstrated to be associated with increased risk for the development of coronary heart disease (CHD). Individuals displaying this pattern are characterized by extremes of competitiveness, striving for achievement and personal recognition, aggressiveness, haste, impatience, explosiveness and loudness in speech, and feelings of being under the pressure of time and challenge of responsibility. Type A individuals need not manifest all aspects of this profile to be classified as possessing it. However, Type A individuals display a predominance of these features, while individuals manifesting the converse, Type B behavior are identified by the relative absence of these characteristics.

Initially, the Type A behavior pattern was assessed by a standard behavioral interview which has become known as the Structured Interview (SI). Behavior pattern classification was based upon subjective clinical judgments by trained raters. In a large-scale prospective, epidemiologic study known as the Western Collaborative Group Study (WCGS), individuals classified as Type A by the interview method were observed to have roughly twice the incidence of CHD compared to their Type B counterparts.

The Jenkins Activity Survey (JAS) was developed in an attempt to duplicate the clinical assessment of the Type A behavior pattern by employing an objective psychometric procedure. The JAS is a self-administered, multiple-choice questionnaire that yields a composite Type A scale score and three factor analytically-derived subscales: Speed and impatience, Job involvement, and Hard-driving and competi-

(Continued)

tive. It was initially developed from an item pool based upon the structured interview and questions from clinical experience that discriminated interview-determined Type A from Type B individuals.

The manual presents a brief historical overview of the concept of "coronary-prone" behavior and various approaches to the measurement of Type A. It describes the development of the JAS beginning with the experimental 64-item questionnaire designed in 1964 to the present 1979 version. The current Form C consists of 52 of the items included in its predecessor, Form B. Some minor modifications in the format of the JAS were made to facilitate administration and scoring of the instrument. However, the item composition and scoring algorithms for each scale are identical to the third (1969) edition and the subsequent (1972) Form B revision. Consequently, all reliability, validity, and clinical data based on the 1969 edition, Form B, and the present Form C are considered together.

The normative data (T scores, Centiles) published in the manual are based on the 1969 JAS scores of the WCGS participants. The sample consisted of 2,588 employed middle class males ages 48 through 65 years at the time of testing. The Type A scale for the 1969 edition was derived from discriminant function procedures using as criterion groups those subjects who had scored strongly Type A and B on the previous editions of the test. Similarly, three factor scales were also derived from discriminant function procedures. The JAS was standardized to have mean of 0.0 and standard deviation of 10.0 for all four scales. Positive scores indicate Type A behavior, while negative scores denote Type B behavior. In addition to data from the WCGS population, means from other populations (usually white, middle class males) are also included in the manual.

The Type A scale consists of 21 items, while Speed and impatience (Factor S), Job involvement (Factor J) and Hard-driving and competitive (Factor H) contain 21, 24, and 20 items respectively. There are a number of items that overlap between different scales, and are assigned different scale weightings. The manual characterizes the correlations between the Type A scale and Factor S (.67), H (.58), and J (.42) to be rather modest, and the authors claim that the three factor scores make independent contributions to the assessment of Type A tendencies.

Reliability estimates for the JAS Type A scale appear to be adequate. For example, estimates of item reliabilities derived from squared multiple correlation coefficients range from .27 to .75, with the corresponding internal consistency reliability coefficient for the Type A scale reported to be .85. Test-retest reliability estimates generally range between .60 and .70 for retest intervals of from six months to four years. However, most of the correlations are based upon significant modifications in the items in the 1965 and 1969 versions of the JAS. The authors claim that the consistently high correlations between scores derived in the 1965 and 1969 editions indicate the relative equivalence of the several editions of the JAS. Alternate forms of the JAS are not currently available, however.

Several kinds of validational evidence are presented. Concurrent validity has

(Continued)

been established by comparing JAS scores to Type A ratings based upon the structured interview. Despite a statistically significant association between the two measures, as many as 30% of respondents are classified differently by the JAS and interview, and correlations between the JAS and interview in younger populations (e.g., college students) are less than .50. Recently, a comparison of the JAS and the interview method revealed that sources of common variance appear to be in measures of self-reported pressured drive and hostility and verbal competitiveness. The source of unique variance in the interview is the subject's speech style, while the source of unique variance in the JAS is self-reported time pressure. Evidence for the predictive validity of the JAS comes primarily from the prospective findings of the WCGS. Analysis of JAS Type A scores of 2,750 healthy men showed the Type A scale to distinguish the 120 future clinical cases of CHD from those men who subsequently remained healthy. Men scoring in the top third of the distribution (> +5.0) incurred 1.7 times the incidence of CHD over a four-year interval compared to those scoring in the lowest third (< −5.0). Numerous studies have also found patients with CHD to score higher on the JAS Type A scale than patients without CHD. However, compared to the interview, the power of the JAS Type A scale to predict CHD in the WCGS is clearly weaker than the interview, and none of the three subscales relate to any clinical manifestations of CHD. Other studies have shown the JAS to be related to increased rates of reinfarction and more extensive coronary atherosclerosis. It should be noted, however, that these results have not always been confirmed by other research groups, and more research is needed to document the relationship of the JAS to other clinical endpoints.

The JAS has been used concurrently with a number of standard psychological inventories, including the California Psychological Inventory (CPI), State-Trait Anxiety Inventory (STAI), Gough Adjective Checklist (ACL), Thurstone Temperament Schedule (TTS), Guilford-Zimmerman Temperament Survey (GZTS), and Strong Vocational Interest Blank (SVIB). Only the General Activity scale of the GZTS, the Active Scale of the TTS, and the Occupational level scales of the SVIB correlated with the JAS Type A scale .40 or greater. In several correlational studies, the JAS has also been shown to have negligible associations with measures of psychopathology, emotional distress, or psychiatric diagnoses.

The JAS has several major shortcomings. The norms cannot be considered representative of any population of broad general interest. The standardization sample did not include women, young or elderly, or persons with low socioeconomic status. While experimental versions of the JAS have been developed for individuals who are female, unemployed, elderly (Form N) and in college (Form T), these editions lack sufficient reliability and validity information and are not available for general use. Revisions of the norms on the basis of a more representative sample would be worthwhile. Local norms or norms for specific populations (patients in rural settings, minorities, individuals with low socioeconomic status,

(Continued)

patients in cardiac rehabilitation programs or family clinic settings, etc.) may be more suitable.

Many users may be disappointed by the susceptibility of the JAS to test-taking attitude. Measures of response set such as defensiveness or social desirability are not included, and the items are readily transparent. The hand-scoring system is also difficult because of the complex weighting system employed. Consequently, hand scoring is tedious and time consuming and is not recommended.

Reliability data is limited but adequate. However, the validity data is too tentative at the present time. While the JAS items include an adequate sampling of the Type A behavior pattern, other potential coronary-prone behaviors such as feelings of helplessness, anger, depression, job dissatisfaction, and lack of social support are not included. Consequently, the terms "Type A" and "coronary prone" cannot be considered equivalent. In addition, since Type A is currently viewed as a behavioral predisposition elicited by appropriate environmental demands, assessment of relevant situational influences is lacking and would appear warranted.

Agreement between the JAS and structured interview is less than acceptable, especially for certain groups such as women, people who are retired, unemployed, or in school. Indeed, the authors acknowledge that the JAS misclassifies too many subjects to allow its use in clinical settings. In addition, evidence that the JAS can accurately predict new cases of CHD is lacking. While the JAS has been shown to be associated with increased prevalence of CHD in population studies in the U.S. (and recently Europe), an individual score offers little prognostic value in a clinical setting, even when combined with traditional risk factors. Moreover, while determination of hypertension, hyperlipidemia, or diabetes is important for subsequent treatment, determination of Type A scores does not aid in modification of the behavior pattern.

While the authors offer several clinical vignettes, the JAS scores do not permit any precise descriptive or diagnostic information about personality functioning. Indeed, a major limitation of the JAS is a lack of information about how scores translate into overt behaviors for a given individual. Subcomponents of the Type A behavior pattern such as hostility or anger, hastened behavioral tempo, and feelings of time pressure may best be evaluated by employing other instruments.

The limitations of the Type A construct should also be noted. While an extended critique is beyond the scope of the present discussion, Type A is not considered a typology in the traditional sense, although a certain underlying consistency of behavior is implied. More work is needed to clarify the conceptual basis for understanding Type A behavior. Since it has been estimated that 50–70% of the general population may be classified as Type A, and the incidence of CHD is extremely low (roughly 3% in the middle aged U.S. population), the predictive value of the instrument is obviously limited.

In summary, the JAS is still in an experimental phase, and norms, reliabilities,
(Continued)

and validities are tentative. The primary positive features of the JAS are its easy to read booklet and test instructions, its relative brevity (it requires approximately 15 minutes to complete), its objective scoring system, and a well-documented record of its use in a variety of clinical and research settings. On the other hand, the test has several undesirable features including a complex scoring system, lack of safeguards against test-taking attitude, and limited practical utility. The JAS represents a valuable contribution to the advancement of research in the area of coronary heart disease, and is currently the most widely used instrument to assess Type A behavior. However, use of the JAS should be limited to experimental or clinical research. Clinical judgment remains the method of choice for assessment of the Type A behavior pattern, and for selecting appropriate individuals at risk for developing CHD.

From *The Ninth Mental Measurements Yearbook* edited by J. V. Mitchell, 1985, pp. 743–745, Buros Institute of Mental Measurements of The University of Nebraska-Lincoln. Reprinted by permission of the author and publisher.

Summary

Measurement, the quantification of variables, is a fundamental characteristic of science. As in all scientific enterprises, the assessment of personality involves classification and measurement of variables. The scale or level of such measurement varies with the mathematical operations that are meaningful with the scores obtained from the tests or other assessment procedures. Measurement of personality characteristics is usually at a somewhat lower level than an interval or ratio scale. On an interval scale, equal numerical intervals imply equal differences in the characteristic being assessed, and on a ratio scale equal numerical ratios imply equal ratios in the assessed characteristic. Typically, scores on personality assessment instruments represent measurement at an ordinal (rank order) scale or somewhere between an ordinal and an interval scale.

The analysis of personality assessment data usually involves the use of statistics, including the construction of frequency distributions and the computations of percentiles and percentile ranks, measures of central tendency (arithmetic mean, median, mode), variability (range, semi-interquartile range, standard deviation), standard scores (e.g., z scores and T scores), and measures of correlation (product-moment coefficient, point-biserial coefficient). Product-moment correlations between variables may be used in linear regression equations for predicting scores on a dependent (criterion) variable, and in a factor analysis to obtain a clearer picture of the basic dimensions underlying a set of intercorrelated variables.

A factor analysis of the scores obtained by a large sample of persons on a group of tests or items involves extracting the factors, rotating the factor axes, and interpreting the rotated factors. Factors are interpreted by inspecting the loadings of the various tests on the factor axes. Computation of the communality (common factor variance) and specificity (specific factor variance) can also aid in the interpretive process.

Three strategies for constructing ratings scales and personality inventories are deductive (content- or theory-based), inductive (internal consistency or factor-analytic), and external (empirical or criterion-group). Each strategy has advantages, the deductive approach being perhaps the most straightforward and economical and the external approach the most predictive of behavior.

The purpose of an item analysis of a test is to determine the extent to which the items comprising the test are functioning as they are supposed to: Are they of the appropriate difficulty level, and do they discriminate between high and low scores on the internal or external criterion? Traditional item analysis procedures involving the use of proportions and correlations to compute difficulty and discrimination indexes have been supplemented or replaced in recent years by more complex item response models involving the determination of item difficulty and discriminative parameters from item characteristic curves.

The various sources of information on personality assessment instruments include test publishers' catalogs and specimen sets of tests, articles in professional journals, descriptions in *Tests in Print III*, reviews in *The Mental Measurements Yearbooks*, as well as descriptions and critiques in the books listed below.

Exercises

1. Define each of the following terms in a sentence or two:

arithmetic mean	item-response theory
average	jangle fallacy
coefficient of determination	jingle fallacy
communality	latent trait theory
criterion group strategy	loadings
deductive strategy	measure of central tendency
difficulty level (of item)	measurement
discriminative index (of item)	median
empirical strategy	mode
external strategy	multiple regression equation
factor analysis	nominal scale
factor loadings	oblique rotation
factors	ordinal scale
frequency distribution	orthogonal rotation
inductive strategy	percentile
interval scale	percentile rank
item analysis	point-biserial coefficient
item characteristic curve	principal axis
item-response curve	product-moment coefficient

psychometrics	scales of measurement
range	semi-interquartile range
Rasch model	specificity
ratio scale	standard deviation
regression equation	variance
reliability	varimax rotation
reliability coefficient	z score
rotating (factor rotation)	

2.   The following scores were obtained by 30 students on a personality inventory. Find the arithmetic mean, variance, and standard deviation of the scores, and then convert each raw score to a z score.

65	72	79	49	45	70	53	32	53	56
67	70	74	66	45	33	73	54	42	76
51	56	74	66	23	46	48	36	57	29

3.   Construct a frequency distribution for the 30 scores in Exercise 2, using an interval width of 1. Find the mode, median, range, and semi-interquartile range of these scores from the frequency distribution. Is the frequency distribution of these scores fairly symmetrical, or is it skewed positively (more low scores than high scores) or negatively (more high scores than low scores)? Construct a second frequency distribution for these scores, with an interval width of 5. In what way does this wider grouping change the shape of the frequency distribution?

4. Compute the product-moment correlation coefficient between the following scores on an Achievement Orientation scale of a personality inventory (X) administered to a group of 30 college freshmen and the grade-point averages (Y) the students had attained at the end of their freshman year.

X	65	53	74	42	23	72	32	66	76	46
Y	3.2	1.5	2.9	1.8	1.5	3.5	1.3	2.5	3.5	1.8
X	79	53	45	51	48	49	56	33	56	36
Y	3.7	1.7	1.7	2.2	2.2	2.1	2.0	1.4	2.4	1.9
X	45	67	73	74	57	70	70	54	66	29
Y	1.8	2.3	2.0	3.5	2.4	2.8	2.6	1.6	3.0	2.1

What can you say about the relationship of Achievement Orientation scores to grade-point average at the end of freshman year? Is it positive or negative, high or low? Next determine the linear regression equation for predicting grade-point average (Y) from Achievement Orientation scores. Then find the predicted grade-point average for a student whose Achievement Orientation score is 40 and for a student whose Achievement Orientation score is 70.

5.   The following is an SPSS/PC+ computer program for a factor analysis of the correlation matrix in Table 2–5. If possible, run this program on a microcomputer that has SPSS/PC+ software, print out the results and interpret them.

```
DATA LIST MATRIX FREE
/ITEM01 TO ITEM11.
N 90.
BEGIN DATA.
1.000
 .727   1.000
 .424    .304   1.000
 .573    .620    .470   1.000
 .343    .287    .510    .336   1.000
 .294    .258    .080    .195    .171   1.000
 .458    .363    .691    .390    .638    .108   1.000
 .200    .075    .206    .061    .374    .227    .218   1.000
 .425    .459    .304    .528    .203    .159    .314    .085   1.000
 .091    .115    .129    .026    .243    .490    .108    .524    .114   1.000
 .078    .127    .112    .022    .244    .430    .065    .421    .187    .611   1.000
END DATA.
FACTOR READ=COR TRIANGLE
/VARIABLES=ITEM01 TO ITEM11
/PRINT=ALL
/FORMAT = SORT
ROTATION = VARIMAX
/ROTATION = OBLIMIN.
FINISH.
```

Did you obtain the same results as those listed in Tables 2–6 and 2–7? Do the two different types of factor rotation-orthogonal (VARIMAX) and oblique (OBLIMIN) yield different results? Ask your instructor or someone else who is knowledgeable about factor analysis to help you interpret your results.

6.   Most college and university libraries have copies of *The Ninth Mental Measurements Yearbook* (Mitchell, 1985), *Tests in Print III* (Mitchell, 1983), *Tests* (2nd ed.) (Sweetland & Keyser, 1986), and *Test Critiques* (Keyser & Sweetland, 1984–1986). Examine these volumes, paying particular attention to sections concerned with various kinds of personality assessment instruments (checklists, rating scales, personality inventories, projective techniques, etc.). Describe the various kinds of information contained in these volumes, especially as it relates to personality assessment.

Sources of Information on Personality Tests

Andrulis, R. S. (Ed.). (1977). *Adult assessment: A sourcebook of tests and measures of human behavior.* Springfield, IL: Thomas.

Beere, C. A. (1979). *Women and women's issues: A handbook of tests and measures.* San Francisco: Jossey-Bass.

Buros, O. K. (Ed.). (1970). *Personality tests and reviews.* Highland Park, NJ: Gryphon.

Buros, O. K. (Ed.). (1974). *Personality tests and reviews II.* Highland Park, NJ: Gryphon.

Chun, K. T., Cobb, S., & French, J. R. P., Jr. (1976). *Measures for psychological assessment.* Ann Arbor, MI: Institute for Social Research, University of Michigan.

Comrey, A. L., Backer, T. E., & Glaser, E. M. (1973). *A source book for mental health measures.* Los Angeles: Human Interaction Research Institute.

Educational Testing Service. (April, 1985). *Annotated bibliography of tests: Personality adjustment.* Princeton, NJ: Author.

Goldman, B. A., & Busch, J. C. (Eds.). (1978, 1982). *Directory of unpublished mental measures* (Vols. 2 & 3). New York: Human Sciences.

Goldman, B. A., & Osborne, W. L. (Eds.). (1985). *Directory of unpublished experimental mental measures* (Vol. 4). New York: Human Sciences.

Goldman, B. A., & Saunders, J. L. (Eds.). (1974). *Directory of unpublished experimental mental measures* (Vol. 1). New York: Human Sciences.

Goldstein, G., & Hersen, M. (Eds.). (1984). *Handbook of psychological assessment.* Elmsford, NY: Pergamon.

Groth-Marnat, G. (1984). *Handbook of psychological assessment.* New York: Van Nostrand Reinhold.

Johnson, O. G., & Bommarito, J. W. (1971). *Tests and measurements in child development: Handbook I.* San Francisco: Jossey-Bass.

Johnson, O. G. (1976). *Tests and measurements in child development: Handbook II.* San Francisco: Jossey-Bass.

Keyser, D. J., & Sweetland, R. C. (Eds.). (1984–1986). *Test critiques* (Vols. I–V). Kansas City, MO: Test Corporation of America.

Krug, S. E. (Ed.). (1984). *Psychware: A reference guide to computer-based products for behavioral assessment in psychology, education and business.* Kansas City, MO: Test Corporation of America.

Lake, D. G., Miles, M. B., & Earle, R. B. (1973). *Measuring human behavior: Tools for the assessment of social functioning.* New York: Teachers College Press.

Levy, P., & Goldstein, H. (1984). *Tests in education: A book of critical reviews.* New York: Academic.

Lyerly, S. B. (Ed.). (1978). *Handbook of psychiatric rating scales* (2nd ed.). Rockville, MD: National Institute of Mental Health.

Mitchell, J. V., Jr. (Ed.). (1983). *Tests in print III.* Lincoln, NE: Buros Institute of Mental Measurements of the University of Nebraska-Lincoln.

Mitchell, J. V., Jr. (Ed.). (1985). *The ninth mental measurements yearbook* (Vols. 1–2). Lincoln, NE: Buros Institute of Mental Measurements of the University of Nebraska-Lincoln.

Robinson, J. P., Athanasiou, R., & Head, K. B. (1974). *Measures of occupational attitudes and occupational characteristics.* Ann Arbor, MI: Institute for Social Research, University of Michigan.

Robinson, J. P., Rush, J. G., & Head, K. B. (1973). *Measures of political attitudes.* Ann Arbor, MI: Institute for Social Research, University of Michigan.

Robinson, J. P., & Shaver, P. R. (1973). *Measures of social attitudes* (Rev. ed.). Ann Arbor, MI: Institute for Social Research, University of Michigan.

Shaw, M. W., & Wright, J. M. (1967). *Scales for the measurement of attitudes.* New York: McGraw-Hill.

Sweetland, R. C., & Keyser, D. J. (Eds.). (1983). *Tests.* Kansas City, MO: Test Corporation of America.

Sweetland, R. C., & Keyser, D. J. (Eds.). (1986). *Tests* (2nd ed.). Kansas City, MO: Test Corporation of America.

Weaver, S. S. (Ed.). (1984). *Testing children.* Kansas City, MO: Test Corporation of America.

Endnotes

[1]This discussion of statistical methods employed in psychological assessment is quite brief, and the reader in encouraged to consult chapters 2, 4, and 5 of *Psychological Testing and Assessment* (Aiken, 1988), as well as other books on psychometrics and statistics (e.g., Nunnally, 1978; McClave & Dietrich, 1985) for a more complete description of statistics and measurement.

[2]For more details on factor analysis, see chapters 13 through 15 of Cliff (1987) or other books on multivariate analysis and psychometric theory and methods (e.g., Nunnally, 1978).

CHAPTER 3

Psychometrics II: Standardization, Reliability, and Validity

Item analysis is an important step in designing and evaluating a psychological test or other assessment instrument, but it is not the final step. Before a test can be used with some confidence that it is an accurate measure of the psychological construct it is supposed to measure, information concerning the reliability and validity of the test must be obtained. Furthermore, it is useful for purposes of score interpretation to have available data on the performance of a large group of people who are representative of those with whom the instrument will ultimately be used.[1] To accomplish this purpose, the test, inventory, rating scale, or other psychometric device must be standardized.

Standardization

Any standardized test has standard directions for administration and scoring that should be adhered to closely, leaving little room for personal interpretation or bias.

However, having standard directions for administration and scoring is necessary but not sufficient for a test to be considered standardized. In addition, the *standardization* of any personality test or other assessment instrument requires administering the instrument to a large sample of individuals (the *standardization sample*) selected as representative of the *target population* of persons for whom the instrument is intended. Of course the large size of a standardization sample, or *norm group*, does not guarantee that it is representative of the target population. To be representative of the population, the sample must be carefully selected.

The manner in which a standardization sample is selected from the target population varies from simple random sampling to more complex sampling strategies such as stratified random sampling and cluster sampling. In *simple random sampling*, every person in the target population has an equal chance of being chosen. However, randomness does not imply representativeness. Consequently, a more appropriate way to standardize a test is to begin by categorizing, or "stratifying," the target population on a series of demographic variables (sex, age, socioeconomic status, geographical region, etc.) presumed to be related to scores on the test. Then the number of individuals selected at random from each category or stratum produced in this way is made proportional to the total number of persons in the target population who fall in that stratum. Using this method, which is referred to as *stratified random sampling*, the likelihood of selecting an atypical, or biased, sample is minimized. Then the obtained norms will provide a sounder basis for interpreting scores on the test than norms obtained by simple random sampling.

More economical than stratified random sampling and more likely than simple random sampling to provide a representative sample of the target population is cluster sampling. *Cluster sampling* consists of dividing a designated geographical area or composite population into blocks or clusters. Then a specified percentage of the clusters is selected at random, and within each cluster a certain number of subunits (schools, houses, etc.) are randomly chosen. The final step is to question (i.e., test) all individuals within each subunit, or at least a random sample of those having designated characteristics.

Administering all items on a test to a stratified random sample or a cluster sample of individuals is tedious and time-consuming, so less costly strategies for determining test norms have been proposed. One such strategy is to sample test items as well as individuals. In *item sampling* different randomly selected examinees answer different sets of items. One group of examinees answers one set of items, and other groups answer other sets. The process is an efficient one, in that it enables the administration of more items to a large sample of people in a fixed period of time. The results can then be combined to conduct item analyses and determine norms for representative samples of examinees on a wide range of test content. Research employing such item-sampling procedures has shown that the resulting norms are quite similar to those obtained by the traditional but more laborious process of administering the entire test to a large representative sample of individuals (e.g., Owens & Stufflebeam, 1969).

Norms

Norms, which serve as a frame of reference for interpreting scores on tests or other psychological assessment instruments, are transformations of raw scores on a test obtained by the standardization group. In the case of achievement tests, norms are often expresssed as *age equivalents* or *grade equivalents*, determined by the average score made on the test by a certain age or grade group. In the case of personality assessment, norms are almost always expressed in terms of percentile ranks or standard scores by age, sex, or other demographic variables.

To serve effectively as a means of interpreting test scores, norms must be appropriate to the group or individual being evaluated. For example, a particular ninth-grader's test score may be higher than that of 80% of seventh graders and higher than that of 40% of college freshmen in the standardization sample. Although it may be of some interest to compare a ninth-grader's score with the scores of seventh graders and college freshmen, of primary concern is the ninth-grader's standing in his or her own grade group. In any case, whenever an examinee's raw score on the test is converted by referring to a table of norms, it is important to indicate the characteristics of the particular group (age, sex, ethnic group, educational and socioeconomic status, geographical region, etc.) on which the norms are based. Also important is the time or date when the norms were obtained. Spring norms are different from fall norms, and norms obtained during times of rapid social change may be different from those obtained during more stable periods. Regardless of the type of test—achievement, intelligence, specific aptitude, personality, interest, attitude—the norms can become outdated. Therefore, almost every test should be restandardized periodically.

Percentile Norms

Procedures for determining percentile ranks and standard scores were discussed in Chapter 2. When computed from a frequency distribution, both kinds of norms are based on the midpoints of the score intervals. Determination of the percentile (rank) norm of a given interval midpoint, say the midpoint score of 40 in Table 2–2, consists of computing the percentage of scores falling below that midpoint. The process begins by determining the cumulative frequency (cf) up to the interval containing that midpoint, adding to cf one-half the frequency ($.5f$) on the interval, dividing the resulting sum by the total number of scores (n) and multiplying the resulting quotient by 100, i.e., $100(cf + .5f)/n$. For the frequency distribution in Table 2–2 the percentile rank of a raw score of 40 is $100[55 + .5(7)]/90 = 65$, so a score of 40 is the 65th percentile.

Because they are easy to compute and understand, percentile norms are quite common in published tests. Tables of percentile norms within grades, ages, sex, occupations, and other groups are reported for many cognitive and affective instruments. Unfortunately, the unit of measurement is not equal on all parts of the percentile-rank scale. Percentile ranks are ordinal-level rather than interval-level measures, and consequently do not have the same meaning on all sections of the scale. The size of the percentile-rank unit becomes progressively smaller toward the center of the scale.

The tendency of percentile ranks to bunch up in the middle of the scale and spread out at the extremes causes difficulty in the interpretation of changes and differences in percentile norms. For example, the difference between percentile ranks of 5 and 10 (or 90 and 95) is greater, in terms of whatever psychological construct is being measured, than the difference between percentile ranks of 45 and 50 (or 50 and 55). On the percentile-rank scale 10 to 5 is greater than 50 to 45 because the unit of measurement for the first difference is larger than the unit of measurement for the second difference. With practice, however, it is not difficult to interpret percentile norms. One must simply remember to give greater weight to percentile rank differences at the extremes than to those toward the center of the scale.

Standard Score Norms

In contrast to percentile ranks, standard scores represent measurements on an interval scale. *Standard score norms* are converted scores having any desired mean and standard deviation. Many different types of standard scores—z scores, T scores, stanine scores, sten scores—are used in scoring and interpreting personality tests. Basically, all of these standard scores are transformations of z scores, which you will recall from Chapter 2 are computed by the formula $z = (X - \overline{X})/s$, where X is the raw score, $\overline{X}$ the arithmetic mean of the raw scores, and s the standard deviation of the raw scores.

Many z scores are negative numbers, which are somewhat troublesome to use, so a further transformation of z scores to *T scores* is often made. T scores, which are computed as $T = 10z + 50$, rounded to the nearest whole number, have a mean of 50 and standard deviation of 10. For example, the T scores corresponding to z scores of -1.00 and $+1.00$ are $10(-1.00) + 50 = 40$ and $10(1.00) + 50 = 60$. When computing T scores from a frequency distribution instead of raw scores, the T score corresponding to a given interval midpoint is somewhat more easily computed as $T = 10(\text{Midpoint} - \overline{X})/s + 50$. Computing T score norms in this way does not change the shape of the frequency distribution. If the frequency distribution of raw scores was skewed, the frequency distribution of T scores will be skewed in the same way—either positively or negatively; only the mean and standard deviation of the distribution are changed.

The percentile and T score norms corresponding to the frequency distribution of composite instructor-personality ratings in Table 2–2 are given in Table 3–1. Note that the average percentile norm, which is an ordinal-scale number, is 50, as is the average T score, an interval-scale number. Therefore, a score of 40, which is equivalent to a percentile norm of 65 and a T score norm of 53, is above average on either scale.

Percentile and T Score Norms for the Distribution of Raw Scores in Table 2-2		Table 3–1
Raw Score	Percentile Norm	T Score Norm
24	1	29
25	1	30
26	2	32
27	3	33
28	6	35
29	11	36
30	12	38
31	14	39
32	17	41
33	21	42
34	26	44
35	32	45
36	38	47
37	44	48
38	50	50
39	57	51
40	65	53
41	72	54
42	78	56
43	83	57
44	85	59
45	86	60
46	87	62
47	89	63
48	91	65
49	92	66
50	93	68
51	95	69
52	96	71
53	97	72
54	98	74
55	99	76

Normalized Standard Scores

The z and T score norms referred to above are simple linear transformations of raw scores. The distribution of converted scores has a different mean and standard deviation from the raw score distribution, but the shapes of the two distributions are the same. If the raw score distribution is symmetrical, the converted score distribution will also be symmetrical; if one is skewed, the other will also be skewed.

In order to make the scores on different tests more directly comparable, there is a transformation procedure that not only affects the mean and standard deviation but also changes the shape of the frequency distribution of raw scores to that of a normal distribution. The conversion of a group of raw scores to these *normalized standard scores* begins with the computation of the percentile ranks of the raw scores. Then, from a table of areas under the normal curve (see Appendix B of Aiken, 1988 or any elementary statistics book), the z score corresponding to each percentile rank is found. These normalized z scores may then be transformed to a distribution of scores having any desired mean and standard deviation. One popular scale is the *stanine* ("standard nine") *scale*, scores on which range from 1 to 9. The stanine scale has a mean of 5 and a standard deviation of 2, so stanines are computed from normalized z scores as Stanine = $2z + 5$. Another scale, used with the 16 Personality Factor Questionnaire and certain other inventories, is the *sten* ("standard ten") *scale*, the scores on which range from 1 to 10 and have a mean of 5.5.

Parallel and Equated Tests

In many situations involving applications and research with psychological tests, more than one form of a test is needed. Parallel forms of a test are equivalent in the sense that they contain the same kinds of items of equal difficulty and are highly correlated. Therefore, the scores that examinees make on one form of the test are very similar to their scores on another form at the same age or grade level as the first form. Parallel tests are, understandably, rather expensive and time consuming to create, a procedure that traditionally has entailed constructing two tests having the same number and kinds of items and yielding the same means and standard deviations when standardized on the same group of people. The resulting parallel forms are then equated, or rather made comparable, by converting the scores on one form to the same units as those on the other form. This may be done, for example, by the *equipercentile method* of changing the scores on each form to percentile ranks. Then a table of equivalent scores on the two forms is prepared by equating the score at the *p*th percentile on the first form to the score at the *p*th percentile on the second form.

Tests may also be equated, or made comparable, by anchoring the tests to a common test or pool of items, as is done every year with the Scholastic Aptitude Test (SAT). By using a set of common anchor items on each new form that are the same as a subset of items used on at least one earlier form of the test, scores on the new form of the SAT administered each year are equated to at least one previous form—going all the way back to the form administered to the initial standardization sample in 1941.

Item-response theory (IRT) was discussed briefly in the last chapter in connection with item analysis. The IRT approach, which prescribes methods of calibrating a set of test items on an operationally defined latent trait—usually standard scores on the horizontal axis of an item-characteristic curve—has also been applied to the task of equating tests. The procedure is economical in that item sampling, in which randomly selected subsets of items are administered to different randomly selected groups of people, is employed. But whatever the method of attempting to equate tests may be—equipercentile, item-response, linear or nonlinear score transformations—tests that either measure different psychological characteristics or have different reliabilities cannot be strictly equated. In almost every case, about the best that can be done is to make the two tests or other psychometric instruments comparable (American Educational Research Association et al., 1985).

Reliability

No assessment device can be of value unless it measures something consistently, or *reliably*. Consequently, one of the first things that should be determined about a newly developed assessment instrument is whether or not it is sufficiently reliable to measure what it was designed to measure. If, in the absence of any permanent change in a person (due to growth, learning, disease, personal trauma, etc.), a person's score on a given test varies widely from time to time or situation to situation, then the test is probably unreliable and cannot be used to explain or make predictions about the person's behavior. Note that *reliability* does not have the same meaning as *stability*; in determining the reliability of a measuring instrument, it is assumed that the instrument is measuring a relatively stable characteristic. Unlike instability, unreliability is a result of measurement errors produced by temporary internal (e.g., low motivation, temporary indisposition) or external (e.g., a distracting or uncomfortable testing environment) conditions.

Classical Reliability Theory

In *classical reliability theory*, it is assumed that a person's observed score on a test is composed of a true score plus some unsystematic error of measurement. A *true score* is defined as the average of the scores that would be obtained if a person took the test an infinite number of times. It should be emphasized that the true score can never be measured exactly but must be estimated from the person's observed score on the test. It is also assumed in classical test theory that the variance of observed scores (s_{obs}^2) for a group of examinees is equal to the variance of their true scores (s_{tru}^2) plus the variance of the unsystematic errors of measurement (s_{err}^2):

$$s_{obs}^2 = s_{tru}^2 + s_{err}^2. \tag{3.1}$$

Then test reliability is defined as the ratio of true variance to observed variance, or the proportion of observed variance that is accounted for by true variance:

$$r_{11} = \frac{s_{tru}^2}{s_{obs}^2.}$$ (3.2)

The proportion of observed variance accounted for by error variance, or unaccounted for by true variance, can be determined from formulas 3.1 and 3.2 to be:

$$\frac{s_{err}^2}{s_{obs}^2} = 1 - r_{11}.$$ (3.3)

The reliability of a test is expressed as a positive decimal number ranging from .00 to 1.00, $r_{11} = 1.00$ indicating perfect reliability and $r_{11} = .00$ the absence of reliability. Since the variance of true scores cannot be computed directly, reliability is usually estimated by analyzing the effects of variations in administration conditions and test content on examinees' scores. As noted previously, reliability is not affected by systematic changes in scores that affect all examinees similarly, but only by unsystematic changes that have different effects on different examinees. Such unsystematic factors influence the error variance of the test, and hence the test's reliability. Each of the several methods of estimating reliability—test-retest, parallel-forms, internal consistency—takes into account somewhat different conditions that may produce these unsystematic changes in test scores and consequently affect the magnitude of the error variance and hence reliability.

Test-Retest Coefficient

To determine whether an instrument is reliable from one time to another a *test-retest coefficient* may be computed. This consists of finding the correlation between the scores made by a group of people on one administration of the instrument with their scores on a second administration. The test-retest procedure takes into account errors of measurement produced by differences in conditions associated with the two occasions on which the test is administered. But because the same test is administered on both occasions, errors due to different samples of test items are not reflected in a test-retest coefficient. Furthermore, differences between conditions of administration are likely to be greater after a long rather than a short time interval, so the magnitude of the reliability coefficient will tend to be larger when the interval between initial test and retest is short (a few days or weeks) rather than long (months or years).

Parallel-Forms Coefficient

When the time interval between initial test and retest is short, on being retested examinees will usually remember many of the responses that they gave when they first took the test. This will undoubtedly affect their responses on the second administration, a fact that in itself would not change the test's reliability if all examinees remembered equal numbers of responses. But some examinees usually recall more responses than other examinees, reducing the correlation between test and retest. Consequently, what seems to be needed is a parallel form of the test, one consisting of similar but not the same items. Then a *parallel-forms* coefficient can be computed as an index of reliability.

The parallel forms idea is reasonable in principle: by administering a parallel form after a suitable interval following administration of the original form, a reliability coefficient reflecting errors of measurement due to different items and different times of administration can be computed. To control for the confounding effect of form with time of administration, Form A should be administered first to half the group and Form B to the other half; then on the second administration the first group takes Form B and the second group takes Form A.

Internal-Consistency Coefficients

Although parallel forms are available for a number of tests, particularly tests of ability (achievement, intelligence, special aptitudes), a parallel form is expensive and often quite difficult to construct. Therefore, a less direct method of taking into account the effects of different samples of test items on reliability was devised—the method of *internal consistency*. Errors of measurement caused by different conditions or times of administration are, however, not reflected by an internal-consistency coefficient. Consequently, internal-consistency coefficients are not truly equivalent to either test-retest or parallel-forms coefficients.

Split-Half Method   It is often convenient to view a single test as consisting of two parts (parallel forms), each of which measures the same thing. Thus, a test can be administered and separate scores assigned to every examinee on two arbitrarily selected halves of the test. For example, an examinee may be given one score on the odd-numbered items and a second score on the even-numbered items. Then the correlation (r_{oe}) between the two sets of scores is a parallel-forms reliability coefficient for a test half as long as the original test. Assuming that the two halves are equivalent, having equal means and equal variances, then the reliability of the test as a whole can be estimated by the *Spearman-Brown prophecy formula*:

$$r_{11} = \frac{2r_{oe}}{1 + r_{oe}} . \tag{3.4}$$

To illustrate the use of this formula, assume that the correlation between total scores on the odd numbered items and total scores on the even numbered items of a test is .80. Then the estimated reliability of the entire test is

$$r_{11} = 2(.80)/(1 + .80) = .89.$$

Kuder-Richardson Method Obviously there are many different ways of dividing a test into two halves. Since each way may yield a somewhat different value of r_{11}, it is not clear which halving strategy results in the best reliability estimate. The *Kuder-Richardson Method* solves this problem by taking the average of the reliability coefficients obtained from all possible half-splits as the overall reliability estimate. But even with a test of, say, 20 items, we shall need the help of a computer to compute and average the resulting 92,378 split-half coefficients.

Under certain circumstances the mean of all split-half coefficients can be estimated by one of the following formulas:

$$r_{11} = \frac{k}{k-1}\left[1 - \frac{\sum\limits_{i=1}^{k} p_i(1 - p_i)}{s^2}\right], \tag{3.5}$$

$$r_{11} = \frac{k}{k-1}\left[1 - \frac{\overline{X}(k - \overline{X})}{ks^2}\right], \tag{3.6}$$

In these formulas, k is the number of items on the test, $\overline{X}$ the mean of total test scores, s^2 the variance of total test scores (computed with n instead of $n-1$ in the denominator), and p_i the proportion of examinees giving the keyed response to item i. Formulas 3.5 and 3.6 are known as Kuder-Richardson (K-R) formulas 20 and 21, respectively. Unlike formula 3.5, formula 3.6 is based on the assumption that all items are of equal difficulty; it also yields a more conservative estimate of reliability and is easier to use than formula 3.5.

To illustrate the application of formula 3.6, assume that a test containing 75 items has a mean of 50 and a variance of 100. Then by formula 3.6

$$r_{11} = \frac{75}{74}\left[1 - \frac{50(75\text{-}50)}{75(100)}\right] = .84.$$

Coefficient Alpha Formulas 3.5 and 3.6 are specific cases of the more general coefficient alpha (Cronbach, 1951). *Coefficient alpha* may be defined as

$$\alpha = \frac{k}{k-1}\left[1 - \sum_{i=1}^{k} \frac{s_i^2}{s_t^2}\right], \tag{3.7}$$

where s_i^2 is the variance of scores on item i and s_t^2 is the variance of total test scores. Although the Kuder-Richardson formulas are applicable only when test items are scored 0 or 1, coefficient alpha is a general formula for estimating the reliability of a test consisting of items on which two or more scoring weights are assigned to answers.

All internal-consistency procedures (split-half, Kuder-Richardson, coefficient alpha) overestimate the reliability of speeded tests, that is, tests that most examinees do not finish in time. Consequently, internal-consistency procedures must be modified to provide reasonable estimates of reliability when a test is speeded. One recommendation is to administer two halves of the test at different but equal times. Then the scores on the two separately timed halves are correlated and the resulting correlation coefficient corrected by the Spearman-Brown prophecy formula. Test-retest and parallel-forms procedures may also be used to estimate the reliability of a speeded test.

Computer programs for calculating split-half, Kuder-Richardson, and alpha reliability coefficients are readily accessible. For example, coefficient alpha determined on the 11-instructor personality items rated by 90 students was found by SPSS–X subprogram RELIABILITY to be .824. This is a modest reliability coefficient, but not unusual for personality rating scales.

The reliability coefficients of affective instruments such as personality and interest inventories are typically lower than those of cognitive tests (achievement, intelligence, and special aptitudes). See Table 3–2. However, the reliabilities of personality inventories and other affective measures are sometimes quite high, and even cognitive tests may have low reliabilities.

Interscorer Reliability

In scoring projective tests and other types of instruments involving subjective scorer judgment, it is important to know the extent to which different scorers agree with each other in scoring the responses of different examinees and items. The most common approach to determining this *interscorer or interrater reliability* is to have two individuals score the responses of a sizable number of examinees and compute the correlation between the scores assigned by the two scorers, yielding an interrater or interscorer reliability coefficient. Procedures for computing these indexes are found in many statistics or psychometrics textbooks (e.g., Nunnally, 1978). Another approach is to have many people score the test responses of one examinee, or, better still, have many people score the responses of a number of examinees. This last approach yields an *intraclass coefficient* or *coefficient of concordance*, a generalized interscorer or interrater reliability coefficient. Procedures for computing these indexes are also found in many statistics or psychometrics texts (e.g., Nunnally, 1978). The author (Aiken, 1985) has also provided special procedures for computing test-retest and internal-consistency reliability coefficients from rating-scale data and for conducting statistical tests of significance on the coefficients.

Interpreting Reliability Coefficients

Because the square of the reliability coefficient is the proportion of variance in observed scores, accounting for variance in true scores on the test, r_{11}^2 is actually a better index of the reliability of measurement than r_{11}. Thus, even when the reliability of a test is .90, only 81% of the observed variance is true score variance and 19%

Table 3–2

Reliability Coefficients Obtained with
Various Psychological Assessment Instruments

	Reliabilities		
Type of Instrument	*Low*	*Medium*	*High*
Achievement Test Batteries	.66	.92	.98
Scholastic Ability Tests	.56	.90	.97
Aptitude Test Batteries	.26	.88	.96
Objective Personality Tests	.46	.85	.97
Interest Inventories	.42	.84	.93
Attitude Scales	.47	.79	.98

G. C. Helmstadter, *Principles of Psychological Measurement,* © 1964, p. 85. Reprinted by permission of Prentice-Hall, Inc. Englewood Cliffs, NJ.

is error variance. And a reliability coefficient as low as .70, which is not an uncommon figure in personality assessment, means that more than half the variance of observed scores is due to errors of measurement.

How high must the reliability coefficient be for a test to be useful? The answer depends on what one plans to do with the test scores. If a test is used to determine whether the mean scores of two groups of people are significantly different, then a reliability coefficient as low as .65 may be satisfactory. But if the test is used to compare one person's score with that of another person, a coefficient of at least .85 should be obtained.

Variability and Reliability

As is the case with other measures of relationship, reliability tends to be greater when the variance of the variables of concern (test scores, item scores, ratings, etc.) is large than when it is small. Since test score variance is related to test length, one common method of increasing reliability is to add more items to the test. The general Spearman-Brown formula is an expression of the effect on reliability of lengthening a test by adding more items of the same type. This formula, a generalization of formula 3.4, is

$$r_{mm} = \frac{mr_{11}}{1 + (m-1)r_{11}}, \tag{3.8}$$

where m is the factor by which the test is lengthened, r_{11} the reliability of the original, unlengthened test, and r_{mm} the estimated reliability of the lengthened test. For example if a 20-item test having a reliability coefficient of .70 is made three times as long by adding 40 more items to the test, the estimated reliability of the new test will be $3(.70)/[1+ 2(.70)]= .875$. By solving formula 3.8 for m, one can also compute how many times longer a test of reliability r_{11} must be made in order to attain a desired reliability (r_{mm}).

In addition to being dependent on the number of items comprising the test, the variance and reliability of the test are affected by the heterogeneity of the group of people who take the test. The greater the range of individual differences among a group of people on a certain characteristic, the larger the variance of their scores on a measure of that characteristic. Consequently, the reliability coefficient of a test or other assessment measure will be higher in a more heterogeneous group, which has a larger test-score variance than in a more homogeneous group with a smaller test-score variance. The fact that the reliability of a test varies with the nature of the group tested is reflected in the practice of reporting separate reliability coefficients for different age, grade, sex, and socioeconomic groups.

Standard Error of Measurement

Less frequently reported in the context of personality assessment than in ability testing is a statistic known as the *standard error of measurement* (s_m). This statistic is an estimate of the standard deviation of the normal distribution of test scores an examinee would presumably obtain if he or she took the test an infinite number of times. The mean of this hypothetical frequency distribution is the examinee's true score on the test. The standard error of measurement is computed as

$$s_m = s\sqrt{1 - r_{11}} \, , \tag{3.9}$$

where s is the standard deviation of test scores and r_{11} the test-retest reliability coefficient.

To illustrate the computation and meaning of the standard error of measurement, assume that the standard deviation of a test is 6.63 and the test-retest reliability coefficient is .85; then $s_m = 6.63\sqrt{1-.85} = 2.57$. Therefore, if Joe's raw score on the test is 40 it can be concluded with 68% confidence that Joe is one of a group of people with an observed score of 40 whose true score on the test falls between $40 - 2.57 = 37.43$ and $40 + 2.57 = 42.57$. It can also be concluded with 95% confidence that Joe is one of a group of examinees with an observed score 40 whose true score on the test falls between $40 - 1.96(2.57) = 34.96$ and $40 + 1.96(2.57) = 45.04$.

As can be seen by inspecting formula 3.9, the standard error of measurement increases as reliability decreases. When $r_{11} = 1.00$, there is no error at all in estimating a person's true score from his or her observed score; when $r_{11} = .00$, the error of measurement is a maximum and equal to the standard deviation of observed scores. Of course, a test having a reliability coefficient close to .00 is useless because the correctness of any decisions made on the basis of the scores will be no better than chance.

Percentile Bands An examinee's score on certain tests is expressed not as a single number but rather as a score band, or *percentile band*, having a width of one standard error of measurement (or the percentile-rank equivalents of s_m) on either side of the examinee's observed test score. This practice is merely an acknowledgement of the fact that a test score is not a fixed, unvarying measure of a characteristic but only an approximation. The standard error of measurement is an estimate of the average error in that approximation.

When a person's scores on several tests are plotted in the form of a profile, it is useful to draw a band having a width of one or two standard errors of measurement around the score points. Then small differences between the scores of the same person on two different tests or the scores of two persons on the same test are less likely to be viewed as significant. In general, the difference between the scores of two people on the same test should not be interpreted as significant unless it is at least twice the standard error of measurement of the test. On the other hand, the difference between the scores of the same individual on two different tests should be greater than twice the standard error of measurement of *either* test before the difference can be interpreted as significant. This is so because the standard error of the difference between the scores on two tests is larger than the standard error of measurement of either test alone.

Reliability and Standard Error of Score Differences

The above rules of thumb for using the standard error of measurement to interpret score differences are useful, but they are not as revealing as two other statistics for diagnostic purposes. These statistics are the *reliability of score differences* and the *standard error of score differences*. As shown in the following formula, the reliability of differences between scores on two tests depends not only on the reliability of both tests but also on the correlation between the tests:

$$r_{dd} = \frac{r_{11} + r_{22} - 2r_{12}}{2(1 - r_{12})},$$
(3.10)

where r_{11} is the reliability of the first test, r_{22} the reliability of the second test, and r_{12} the correlation between the two tests. For example, if the reliability of test 1 is $r_{11} = .90$, the reliability of test 2 is $r_{22} = .80$, and the correlation between the two tests is $r_{12} = .70$, then the reliability of the difference between the scores on tests 1 and 2 is $[.90 + .80 - 2(.70)]/2(1 - .70) = .50$. In general, unless the two tests are uncorrelated, the reliability of the difference scores will always be less than the reliability of either test alone.

The second statistic, the standard error of score differences, can be used to establish confidence limits for the difference between an individual's true scores on two tests. Assuming that the standard deviations of the two tests are equal ($s_1 = s_2 =$

s), as they will be if scores on the two tests are converted to the same standard-score scale, a simple formula for the standard error of the difference scores is

$$s_{md} = s\sqrt{2 - r_{11} - r_{22}} \, . \tag{3.11}$$

As seen in this formula, the standard error of the difference scores varies inversely with the reliabilities of the two tests. The more reliable the tests, the smaller the standard error of the difference, and hence the greater the likelihood that the difference between the scores on two tests or part scores on a single test or test composite will be significant and interpretable. A conservative rule of thumb is that the difference between the scores of a person on two tests is significant if it equals two or more standard errors of the difference.

Generalizability Theory

Since the 1950s there has been growing dissatisfaction within the psychometric community with the classical test theory that developed during the first half of this century, and a number of alternative approaches have been devised. These approaches have been grounded more solidly in modern statistical theory and also influenced by advances in high-speed computing. One of these is *generalizability theory*, which considers a test score to be a single sample from a universe of possible scores. The reliability of that score is the precision with which it estimates a more generalized universe value of the score (the true score). In the computations of generalizability theory, the statistical procedures of analysis of variance are applied to determine the generalizability, or dependability, of test scores as a function of the following: changes in the person(s) taking the test, different samples of items comprising the test, the situations or conditions under which the test is administered, the methods or people involved in scoring the test. A *generalizability coefficient*, similar to a traditional reliability coefficient, may then be computed as the ratio of the expected variance of scores in the universe to the variance of scores in the sample. Finally, a *universe value* of the score, similar to the true score of classical reliability theory, can be estimated (Cronbach et al., 1972). Despite its greater statistical sophistication, however, generalizability theory has not replaced the classical theory of reliability and validity.

Validity

Reliability is a necessary but not a sufficient condition for validity; a measuring instrument can be reliable without being valid, but it cannot be valid without being reliable. The validity of a test can be no higher than the square root of its parallel-forms reliability. Furthermore, *validity*, the extent to which an instrument measures what it was designed to measure, is more specific to time and place than reliability. We say that a test is *valid* for such and such a purpose, not *generally valid*.

Obviously, validity is a more important characteristic of a test than reliability. A valid test is good for something, for assisting the psychologist in predicting and understanding behavior and mental functioning. To this end, there are three types of validity, or, more precisely, three ways of obtaining information on a test's validity: content validity, criterion-related validity, and construct validity.

Content Validity

Sometimes inaccurately referred to as *face validity*, *content validity* is concerned with whether the appearance or content of a measuring instrument supports the assertion that it is a measure of a certain psychological variable. Thus, one would expect a test of mechanical ability to contain mechanical problems and a test of reading achievement to contain reading passages. However, the matter is not quite so simple as merely looking at the test: the content must be examined closely by experts in the subject-matter of the test, while they systematically arrive at a decision concerning its content validity. Content validity is of greatest concern on tests of academic achievement and other cognitive skills, but it also has a place in evaluating personality assessment instruments. For example, a personality test designed to assess certain constructs of Jung's analytic theory should contain items related to the theory (e.g., the Myers-Briggs Type Indicator).

Criterion-Related Validity

The *criterion-related validity* of a test is determined by correlating test scores with measures on an external criterion of whatever the test is supposed to assess. Scores on the criterion may be obtained at the same time as the test is administered (*concurrent validity*) or at a later time (*predictive validity*). Concurrent validation is one of the approaches used in validating the MMPI: the ability of MMPI items to correctly classify mental patients was evaluated by determining the extent to which the inventory placed a sample of mental patients into the same diagnostic categories as they were placed by psychiatrists using other techniques. In addition to using the criterion of diagnosis or personality analyses obtained from interviews by psychiatrists or clinical psychologists, the concurrent validity of a test may be assessed by comparing the descriptions of examinees obtained from their test performance with descriptions of the same persons obtained from case histories and observations of behavior. Another frequently employed procedure in concurrent validation is the *method of contrasting groups:* two groups of people falling in different diagnostic, occupational, or other relevant categories are compared in terms of their test performance.

Among the criteria that have been used to determine the predictive validity of personality tests are changes in personality and behavior resulting from psychotherapy and other treatments, school or job performance, and other behavioral events (e.g., suicide attempts, violence). An illustration of predictive validity is the significant correlation (r = .455) between midterm ratings of instructor personality and end-of-term ratings of the course described in Chapter 2. The use of a linear regression equation for predicting scores on the criterion measure from scores on the predictor (test) variable is an integral part of the predictive validity process.

Standard Error of Estimate   A useful statistic to compute when the predictive validity of a test is of interest is the *standard error of estimate* (s_e). This statistic is computed as

$$s_e = s_Y\sqrt{1 - r^2}, \tag{3.12}$$

where s_y is the standard deviation of the criterion (Y) scores and r the correlation between predictor (X) and criterion (Y) scores. The standard error of estimate is used to establish a numerical interval within which it can be concluded, with a specified degree of confidence, that the obtained Y score of a person having a certain X score is likely to fall. Using as an example the instructor personality (X) and course evaluation (Y) scores given in Chapter 2, the standard error of estimate for predicting Y from X is

$$s_e = 4.88\sqrt{1 - .455^2} = 4.35.$$

Now assume that Maureen's X score is 40; substituting X = 40 in the regression equation $Y_{pred} = .3357X + 5.1136$, yields a predicted Y value of 18.54. Therefore, the chances are 68 out of 100 that Maureen is one of a group of people with the same X score (40) whose obtained Y scores fall between $18.54 - 4.35 = 14.19$ and $18.54 + 4.35 = 22.89$; similarly, the chances are 95 out of 100 that Maureen is one of a group of people with an X score of 40 whose obtained Y scores fall between $18.54 - 1.96(4.35) = 10.01$ and $18.54 + 1.96(4.35) = 27.07$. As suggested by this example, a person's actual Y score may be quite different from his or her predicted Y score. This is especially likely when the correlation between X and Y is modest. The smaller the correlation coefficient is, the larger is the standard error of estimate and hence the less accurate the prediction of Y from X.

Cross-Validation   Whenever a test's predictive validity is being determined for the first time, it is important to *cross-validate* (i.e., re-validate) the results on a second sample of individuals before they are reported. Reporting the validity coefficient and regression equation based on a single sample can be misleading, the reason being that chance factors can spuriously inflate the original validity coefficient. Consequently, the size of this coefficient may undergo considerable shrinkage when applied to a second sample of people. Cross-validation is also important with respect to concurrent validation. For example, using the method of contrasting groups one may find a set of scores or signs on a projective test that appear to differentiate between two psychiatric groups or between mentally disturbed and normal individuals. But the significance of these signs can easily disappear when the test is administered to a second sample.

Criterion Contamination   The validity of a test is limited not only by the reliabilities of the test and the criterion but also by the validity of the criterion itself as a measure of the particular variable of interest. Sometimes the criterion is made less valid, or is contaminated, by the particular method in which the criterion scores are determined. For example, a clinician who knows from other information that a group of examinees have already been diagnosed as psychotic may readily see psychotic signs in examinees' responses to a projective test. Then the method of contrasting groups in which the test scores of the psychotics are compared with those of normals will yield false evidence for the validity of the test. Such contamination of the criterion (psychotic vs. normal) can be controlled by *blind analysis*, that is, by making available to the clinician no information about the examinees other than their test scores before attempting a diagnosis. Many clinical psychologists maintain, however, that blind analysis is unnatural in that it is not the way in which tests are used in actual practice. Clinical diagnosticians typically have a great deal of additional information about a client or patient and attempt to find consistencies or congruences among the various test and nontest sources when making a diagnosis or treatment recommendation.

Base Rate   Another factor that can affect the magnitude of a criterion-related validity coefficient, and hence the identification or prediction of a certain kind of characteristic or behavior, is the base rate of that characteristic or behavior in the overall population. The *base rate* refers to the proportion of people in the general population who manifest the characteristic or behavior of interest. A test designed to predict a particular type of behavior is most effective when the base rate is 50% and least effective when it is very high or very low. Thus, characteristics or behaviors such as psychoticism, brain damage, or suicide, which have a low base rate in the general population, are much more difficult to assess, and hence diagnose, than those with higher base rates (e.g., neuroticism, sexual deviation, spouse or child abuse).

Incremental Validity   In deciding whether the use of a particular assessment instrument for predictive or diagnostic purposes justifies the cost, the concept of *incremental validity* should be taken into account: How much more accurate are predictions and/or diagnoses when the instrument is used than when it is not? Other methods of assessment (observation, interview, biographical inventory, etc.) may be less expensive and fulfill the purposes of assessment almost as well without administering the additional assessment instrument. *Multiple regression analysis*, a statistical procedure described briefly in Chapter 2, can be applied in answering the question of a test's incremental validity in a specific situation.

Construct Validity

Predictive validity is of greatest concern in situations involving occupational or educational selection and placement. Ability tests of various kinds, and sometimes personality and interest tests, are used for this purpose. Of greater concern with respect to personality tests, however, is construct validity (Cronbach & Meehl, 1955; Jackson, 1971). The *construct validity* of a psychological assessment instrument refers to the extent to which the instrument is a measure of a particular *construct*, or psychological concept, such as anxiety, achievement motivation, extraversion-introversion, or neuroticism. The construct validity of a test, which is the most general type of validity, is not determined in a single way or by one investigation. Rather it involves a network of investigations and procedures designed to discover whether an assessment instrument constructed to measure a certain personality variable is an effective measure of that variable.

Evidence for Construct Validity   Among the sources of evidence for the construct validity of a test are the following:

1. Experts' judgments that the content of the test pertains to the construct of interest.
2. An analysis of the internal consistency of the test.
3. Studies of the relationships, in both experimentally contrived and naturally occurring groups, of test scores to other variables on which the groups differ.
4. Correlations of the test with other tests and variables with which the test is expected to have a certain relationship, and factor analyses of these intercorrelations.
5. Questioning examinees or raters in detail about their responses to a test or rating scale in order to reveal the specific mental processes that occurred in deciding to make those responses.

As noted in the above list, various kinds of information, involving such procedures as a rational or statistical (e.g. factor analysis) analysis of the variables assessed by the instrument and studies of the ability of the instrument to predict behavior in situations in which the construct is known to be operative, contribute to the establishment of the construct validity of the instrument. Experimental demonstrations such as those used in the construct validation of the Taylor Manifest Anxiety Scale (TMAS) (Taylor, 1953) are particularly significant in establishing a test's construct validity. In this case it was predicted that, assuming anxiety is a drive, people with a high anxiety level would acquire a conditioned eyeblink in a light-airpuff-eyeblink classical conditioning situation more quickly than less anxious people. Furthermore, if the TMAS is a valid measure of the construct *anxiety*, then high TMAS scorers should be conditioned more readily in this situation than low TMAS scorers. The verification of this prediction contributed significantly to establishing the construct validity of the TMAS.

Convergent and Discriminant Validation   To possess construct validity, an assessment instrument should have high correlations with other measures of (or methods of measuring) the same construct (*convergent validity*) and low correlations with measures of different constructs (*discriminant validity*). Evidence pertaining to the convergent and discriminant validity of an instrument can be obtained most convincingly by comparing correlations between measures of (1) the same construct using the same method, (2) different constructs using the same method, (3) the same construct using different methods, and (4) different constructs using different methods. This *multitrait-multimethod approach* (Campbell & Fiske, 1959) provides evidence for the construct validity of the instrument when correlations between the same construct measured by the same and different methods are significantly higher than correlations between different constructs measured by the same or different methods. Unfortunately, the findings are not always as desired: sometimes correlations between different constructs measured by the same method are higher than correlations between the same construct measured by different methods. In this case, the method (paper-and-pencil inventory, projective technique, rating scale, interview, etc.) is more important in determining whatever is measured than the construct or trait supposedly being assessed.

Summary

A test or other assessment instrument that is *standardized* has standard directions for administration and scoring and a set of *norms* based on a representative sample of people for whom the test was designed. The various types of norms, which serve as a frame of reference for interpreting scores, obtained on personality assessment instruments are percentile norms, T scores, stanine (standard nine), and sten (standard ten) scores by sex, age, and other demographic variables. Stanine and sten scores are normalized standard scores that not only have different means and standard deviations from the corresponding raw scores but are also normally distributed regardless of the shape of the raw-score distribution.

The concept of the *reliability* of a test or other assessment instrument is concerned with the extent to which the scores are free from errors of measurement. Three procedures for obtaining information on an instrument's reliability are test-retest, parallel forms, and internal consistency. Three different types of internal consistency are split-half, Kuder-Richardson, and coefficient alpha. Inversely related to a test's reliability is its standard error of measurement, a numerical index of how accurately a person's obtained test score estimates his or her true score on the test. Interpreting differences between the scores of two people on the same test or one person on two different tests is facilitated by computing the reliability and standard error of the score differences.

A test can be reliable without being valid, but it cannot be valid without being reliable. *Validity* is the extent to which the test measures what it was designed to measure. Depending on the type of test (achievement, aptitude, personality), three types of validity are of interest: content validity, criterion-related validity (concurrent validity, predictive validity), and construct validity. The criterion-related validity of a test is determined by correlating test scores with criterion scores obtained at the same time (concurrent validity) or at some later time (predictive validity). A linear regression equation for predicting criterion scores from test scores and a measure of the error in this prediction (standard error of estimate) can also be computed. The most comprehensive type of validity, and the one of greatest concern on personality assessment instruments, is construct validity. Information on an instrument's construct validity is obtained by various procedures designed to determine the extent to which the instrument is a valid measure of a specified psychological construct or concept.

Exercises

1. Define each of the following terms in a sentence or two:

age equivalents	item sampling
base rate	item-response theory (IRT)
blind analysis	Kuder-Richardson method
classical reliability theory	multiple regression analysis
cluster sampling	multitrait-multimethod approach
coefficient alpha	norm group
coefficient of concordance	norm-referenced test
concurrent validity	normalized standard scores
construct validity	norms
content validity	parallel-forms coefficient
convergent validity	parallel test
criterion-referenced test	percentile bands
criterion-related validity	percentile norms
cross-validate	percentile ranks
discriminant validity	predictive validity
equated tests	reliability
equipercentile method	reliability of score differences
face validity	simple random sampling
generalizability coefficient	Spearman-Brown prophecy formula
generalizability theory	stability
grade equivalents	standard error of estimate
incremental validity	standard error of measurement
internal-consistency coefficient	standard error of score differences
interrater reliability	standard score norms
interscorer reliability	standardization
intraclass coefficient	standardization sample

stanine scale	test-retest coefficient
sten scale	true score
stratified random sampling	universe value
T scores	validity
target population	z scores

2. Find the percentile ranks, z score, and T score norms corresponding to the interval midpoints of the following frequency distribution of ratings of instructor (X) and course (Y), where $\overline{X} = 38.17$, $s_x = 6.68$, $\overline{Y} = 17.92$, $s_y = 4.90$.

Instructor Ratings		Course Ratings	
Interval	*Frequency*	*Interval*	*Frequency*
54–56	2	30–31	2
51–53	3	28–29	1
48–50	4	26–27	0
45–47	4	24–25	4
42–44	10	22–23	12
39–41	20	20–21	17
36–38	16	18–19	19
33–35	15	16–17	8
30–32	5	14–15	11
27–29	9	12–13	6
24–26	2	10–11	5
		8–9	2
		6–7	3

3. Calculate both Kuder-Richardson reliability coefficients on the following responses of ten examinees on a ten-item test, where 1 indicates the keyed response and 0 the nonkeyed response:

Item	Examinee									
	A	B	C	D	E	F	G	H	I	J
1	1	1	0	1	1	0	1	0	1	0
2	1	0	0	0	0	1	0	0	0	1
3	1	1	1	1	1	0	1	0	0	0
4	1	1	1	0	0	1	0	1	0	0
5	1	0	1	1	0	0	0	0	0	0
6	1	1	1	0	1	1	1	0	0	0
7	1	0	1	1	0	0	1	1	0	1
8	1	1	1	0	1	1	0	0	1	0
9	1	1	0	1	1	1	0	1	0	0
10	1	1	1	1	1	0	0	0	1	0
Total Scores	10	7	7	6	6	5	4	3	3	2

The mean ($\overline{X}$) of total scores is 5.30 and the variance (s^2) of total scores is 5.21.

4. Compute the standard error of measurement (s_m) of a test having a standard deviation of 10 and a parallel-forms reliability of .84. Then use the obtained value of s_m to find the 95% confidence interval for the true scores corresponding to obtained scores of 40, 50, and 60.

5. Derive formula 3.11 from formulas 3.9 and 3.10.

6. Plot a series of curves on a single graph illustrating how test reliability (r_{mm}) varies as a function of test length (m) and initial reliability (r_{11}). Use formula 3.8 and values of m equal to 2, 3, 4, and 5 and values of r_{11} equal to .60, .65, .70, .75, .80, .85, and .90. The horizontal axis of your graph should be r_{11} and the vertical axis r_{mm}. Plot one curve for each value of m.

7. What is the standard error of estimate (s_e) when the standard deviation (s_y) of the criterion measure equals 10 and the correlation between test and criterion is .60? Within what two values are you 95% confident that the obtained Y score of a person whose predicted Y score is 30 will fall? A person whose obtained Y score is 70 will fall?

Suggested Readings

American Educational Research Association, American Psychological Association, & National Council on Measurement in Education (1985). *Standards for educational and psychological testing* (pp. 9–24). Washington, DC: American Psychological Association.

Baker, F. (1985). *The basics of item response theory.* Portsmouth, NH: Heinemann.

Cronbach, L. J., & Meehl, P. E. (1955). Construct validity in psychological tests. *Psychological Bulletin, 52,* 281–302.

Dudek, F. J. (1979). The continuing misinterpretation of the standard error of measurement. *Psychological Bulletin, 86,* 335–337.

Felner, R. D. (1987). Reliability of diagnoses. In R. J. Corsini (Ed.), *Concise encyclopedia of psychology* (pp. 970–971). New York: Wiley.

Livingstone, S. A. (1985). Reliability of test results. In T. Husen & T. N. Postlethwaite (Eds.), *International encyclopedia of education* (Vol. 7, pp. 4268–4275). New York: Wiley.

Sumner, R. (1985). Test norms. In T. Husen & T. N. Postlethwaite (Eds.), *International encyclopedia of education* (Vol. 9, pp. 5205–5209). New York: Wiley.

Zeller, R. A. (1985). Validity. In T. Husen & T. N. Postlethwaite (Eds.), *International encyclopedia of education* (Vol. 9, pp. 5413–5422). New York: Wiley.

Endnote

[1]The distinction between norm-referenced and criterion-referenced measurement, which has been applied to achievement testing, can also be made for personality tests. A *criterion-referenced test* can be defined as one in which, by a consensus of people knowledgeable in the construct(s) being assessed, certain responses or a specified number of responses of

a certain kind are considered indicative of satisfactory adjustment, mental disorder, a paranoid condition, or some other designated psychological construct. Thus, criterion-referenced personality assessment is similar in concept to a *rational* or *theory-based* definition of adjustment or abnormality. However, *norm-referenced test*, in which interpretations or diagnoses are made with reference to the frequency distribution of specified responses defining a construct, is similar to a statistical definition of adjustment or abnormality. Both approaches have been applied in personality assessment, with the criterion-referenced approach perhaps being favored by clinicians and psychiatrists and the norm-referenced approach by their more psychometrically-oriented colleagues.

CHAPTER 4

Administration and Reporting

The process of personality assessment does not begin with the construction or selection of a personality assessment instrument. It begins with a need to know something about personality in general or about a particular personality. It can be either practical, as in counseling, or theoretical, as in research. To become operational, the need must be expressed as a question or statement specifying what someone wants to know about another person or group of people: Why does Bobby have so much trouble getting along with other children? Is Joan so maladjusted that she requires psychological help or perhaps even institutionalization? Does Frank have organic brain damage, or is his problem psychological? What personality variables are related to performance on this job?

Questions such as these, and consequently the need for personality assessment, are not limited to a specific situation. Personality assessments are made in a variety of settings (Petzelt & Craddick, 1978, p. 590):[1]

- In mental health settings as an aid in diagnosis, treatment, and residential placement
- In educational settings as an aid in formulating proper remediation measures

- In legal settings as an aid in court evaluations, such as sanity hearings, as well as assisting the judicial branch in planning rehabilitation measures
- In medical settings as an aid in hospital consultation to various clinics in evaluating the psychological aspects of illness
- In psychotherapeutic settings as an aid in planning and evaluating psychotherapy and chemotherapy, and in offering referring therapists better initial understanding of the client's dynamics and important focal issues
- As a research and teaching tool in the study of human personality, particularly with special populations, for example, prisoners and juvenile delinquents
- In various evaluations required by law, such as cases involving federal compensation

Once the needs of assessment have been specified, the goals can be set and decisions made about what kinds of data are required to attain those goals. The general goals of psychological assessment are to provide an accurate description of personality and behavior and to make predictions concerning future behavior. However, the goals in particular cases and/or settings are usually more specific: to determine the presence or absence of certain characteristics or conditions. The available assessment procedures or instruments employed in these settings are not limited to standardized tests and scales; observations, interviews of the client and others, application blanks or biographical data forms, homemade rating scales, autobiographies, diaries, and other nonstandardized information may also prove useful.

To a great extent, both the goals of personality assessment and the procedures selected to reach those goals vary with the particular assessment theory or model that is followed—psychodynamic, psychometric, or behavioristic. Although clinical assessors of all theoretical persuasions may play a role in deciding what questions require answers and what assessment techniques should be employed, assessors who follow a *psychodynamic* or *psychodiagnostic* model place more emphasis on the judgment of the assessor in collecting, organizing, and summarizing assessment data, as well as making diagnoses and prognoses on the basis of the findings. Interviews and projective techniques are most often used by psychodynamic assessors to provide an in-depth, multifaceted picture of personality dynamics.

In contrast, assessors who follow a *psychometric* model maintain that psychological assessment is valid only when it is objective and that subjective interpretations of personality inventories, rating scales, and other assessment data should be minimized. According to the psychometric model, examinees' scores on the traits or factors measured by objectively scored instruments should be interpreted by comparing them with the scores (norms) obtained from representative samples of individuals. Psychometric assessors are also more likely to advocate a statistical or cookbook approach to combining assessment data and making predictions and classifications.

Assessors who follow a *behavioristic* model emphasize the determination of what people do and where, when, and under what circumstances they do it (Schuldberg & Korchin, 1985). The goal of behavioristic assessment is to discover the antecedent and consequent events that elicit or control certain undesirable behaviors, as a prerequisite to designing a behavior modification program to change those behaviors. Traditionally, behavioristic assessors have collected data by means of objective observations of people in naturalistic, contrived, and role-playing situations, in addition to using checklists and rating scales to record and evaluate the objectively observed behavior. However, today's behavioristic assessors, especially those of the *cognitive-behavioral* mold, also use less objective approaches such as interviews to determine not only what examinees do but also what thoughts, feelings, aspirations, and other internal states they are experiencing.

Whatever theoretical background or assessment model an assessor may follow, the process of personality assessment begins with an expressed need, after which the goals of assessment should be stated and the instruments or procedures that will provide information relevant to the attainment of those goals are selected or constructed. Although several instruments and procedures are typically used in collecting personality data, a shotgun approach of administering every available device in the hope that it might provide some significant information and minimize the need for subjective judgment is not advisable. In conducting a comprehensive psychological assessment several procedures and instruments may be required to gain a clear, valid understanding of the client. However, it is inadvisable to overwhelm the client with assessment materials; care should be taken at the outset to select procedures or instruments that can be administered in a reasonable period of time, that consider the examinee's age and condition, and that provide useful information. After deciding what approaches and materials are appropriate, the standardized or nonstandardized data are collected, combined, and reflected upon to arrive at interpretations, diagnoses, predictions, and recommendations.

Instrument Selection and Administration

Observations and interviews, which are considered in detail in Chapter 5, are the most popular psychological assessment procedures. Even in making observations and conducting interviews, however, one must be aware of the sociocultural background of the person and be prepared to communicate in language that he or she understands. In a fairly thorough examination of a person, observations, usually uncontrolled, are made throughout the assessment period. Interviewing, which itself is a kind of observation of the interviewee and others who have information about the case, may occur before or after the formal testing period, depending on the circumstances and the individual who is being assessed.

Selection of the specific personality assessment instruments to be administered depends on the purposes of the assessment, as well as the age, ability, and temperament of the examinee and the skill, time, and theoretical frame of reference of the examiner. For example, personality inventories and scales require less training and time to administer than projective techniques. Preliminary observational and interview data are often helpful, not only in providing assessment data in their own right but also in suggesting what additional procedures or instruments may be appropriate for a given examinee. In any event, as illustrated by the citations in *Tests in Print III* (Mitchell, 1983) and *The Ninth Mental Measurements Yearbook* (Mitchell, 1985), the number of personality assessment instruments from which to choose is extensive. The most popular of these instruments, at least as indicated by the number of times they are cited in the psychological research literature, are listed in Table 1–2.

The results of a survey of the members of the Society for Personality Assessment (Piotrowski, 1985) also shed some light on what personality assessment instruments are viewed most favorably by professional psychologists. The two projective tests that over 90% of the respondents felt professional practitioners should be competent in using are the Rorschach and the Thematic Apperception Test. Approximately 50% of the respondents felt that practioners should also be competent in the Sentence Completion and Draw-A-Person tests, and approximately 25% felt they should be competent in the House-Tree-Person Test, the Bender-Gestalt Test, and the Children's Apperception Test. Concerning personality inventories with which professional practitioners should be competent, 87% of the respondents in Piotrowski's (1985) survey listed the Minnesota Multiphasic Personality Inventory. Somewhat more than 25% listed the California Psychological Inventory and the 16 Personality Factor Questionnaire, and approximately 10% listed the Edwards Personal Preference Schedule, the Millon Clinical Multiaxial Inventory, and the Personality Research Form.

Several additional recommendations concerning the collection of personality assessment data, which have been adapted from Sundberg (1977), can be made:

1. First survey the examinee's overall life situation and problems, and then obtain more details in areas of particular relevance to the assessment.
2. Be sensitive to the sociocultural and ethnic background of the examinee, as well as his or her age and sex, if relevant.
3. Use more objective, as opposed to subjective, techniques and data whenever possible. (This recommendation is somewhat controversial, because instruments such as the Rorschach Inkblot Test are more subjective but strongly preferred by examiners who subscribe to a psychodynamic orientation.)
4. Obtain the *right kind* of information, not just *more* information, pertaining to the specific situation and purposes of the assessment.

Test Administration

The procedure for collecting test data and other personality information depends on the type of information desired (oral, written, behavioral, etc.) and the examinee to whom it pertains (child or adult, normal or disabled, etc.). Methods of collecting observational and interview data, and procedures for administering specific objective and projective instruments are discussed in later chapters. In this section, we shall focus on general procedures of test administration. These recommendations apply particularly to standardized test administration, both affective and cognitive, but they also have implications for other methods of collecting personality assessment data. Because test administration procedures vary with the nature of the test and the examinee, the amount and type of training needed by the examiner also depend on these factors. Formal licensing or certification by an appropriate state agency, or at least supervision by a certified practitioner, is required to administer most individual pscyhological tests. Such a requirement helps ensure that the examiner has sufficient knowledge and skill in test administration and is essential in third-party insurance claims for psychological services.

Ethical Principles and Assessment Standards

Because personality assessment skills cannot be attained without considerable training, in most states a psychological examiner is required to be licensed or certified as a clinical psychologist, a counseling psychologist, or a school psychologist in order to conduct formal assessments of personality. Improper practices, which represent a violation of the ethical code of the American Psychological Association, can lead to revocation of a license or certificate. The meaning of this code is expressed succinctly in the first paragraph of its preamble (American Psychological Association, 1981):

> Psychologists respect the dignity and worth of the individual and strive for the preservation and protection of fundamental human rights. They are committed to increasing knowledge of human behavior and of people's understanding of themselves and others and the utilization of such knowledge for the promotion of human welfare. While pursuing these objectives, they make every effort to protect the welfare of those who seek their services and of the research participants that may be the object of study. They use their skills only for purposes consistent with these values and do not knowingly permit their misuse by others. While demanding for themselves freedom of inquiry and communication, psychologists accept the responsibility this freedom requires: competence, objectivity in the application of skills, and concern for the best interests of clients, colleagues, students, research participants, and society. (p. 633)

Realizing that the development, distribution, and use of personality tests and other psychological assessment instruments requires carefully formulated standards and clear ethical controls, a joint committee of the American Educational Research Association, the American Psychological Association, and the National Council on Measurement in Education, formulated and published a set of *Standards for Educational and Psychological Testing* (American Educational Research Association et al., 1985). The core of this pamphlet is the list of 180 standards for constructing, evaluating, administering, scoring, and interpreting psychological assessment instruments. Separate chapters describe standards for the application of tests in various contexts and with different groups. Any practicing psychologist (clinical, counseling, school, personnel/industrial) should be thoroughly familiar with these standards and adhere to them as closely as possible.[2]

Several of the *Standards for Educational and Psychological Testing* are relevant to test administration (American Educational Research Association et al., 1985):

> *Standard 6.6.* Responsibility for test use should be assumed by or delegated only to those individuals who have the training and experience necessary to handle this responsibility in a professional and technically adequate manner. Any special qualifications for test administration or interpretation noted in the manual should be met.

> *Standard 6.10.* In educational, clinical, and counseling applications, test administrators and users should not attempt to evaluate test takers whose special characteristics—ages, handicapping conditions, or linguistic, generational, or cultural backgrounds—are outside the range of their academic training or supervised experience. A test user faced with a request to evaluate a test taker whose special characteristics are not within his or her range of professional experience should seek consultation regarding test selection, necessary modifications of testing procedures, and score interpretation from a professional who has had relevant experience.

> *Standard 15.1.* In typical applications, test administrators should follow carefully the standardized procedures for administration and scoring specified by the test publisher. Specifications regarding instructions to test takers, time limits, the form of item presentation or response, and test materials or equipment should be strictly observed. Exceptions should be made only on the basis of carefully considered professional judgment, primarily in clinical applications.

> *Standard 15.2.* The testing environment should be one of reasonable comfort and with minimal distractions. Testing materials should be readable and understandable. In computerized testing, items displayed on a screen should be legible and free from glare, and the terminal should be properly positioned. (pp. 42, 43, 83)

Directions for Administration

As the above standards imply, psychological examiners should be thoroughly familiar with the tests they administer and the kinds of individuals for whom the tests are appropriate. On both individual and group tests, directions concerning the method of presenting the test materials, the phrasing of test questions, and the time limits (if any) for responding must be followed carefully. Differences in the way in which verbal instructions are phrased may affect test performance, even when those differences are subtle (Klopfer & Taulbee, 1976). The directions should be read slowly and clearly, informing the examinees how to indicate their responses but not what responses to make. As illustrated in Figure 4–1, written instructions to be read by

---

Directions for High School Personality Questionnaire

Figure 4–1

Jr.-Sr.

HSPQ

FORM A

1968-69 Edition

WHAT TO DO: Before you open this booklet, write your name, age, and sex in the correct areas on the answer sheet.

Inside this booklet are some questions that ask about your likes, dislikes, and interests.

Read each question, select the answer that is correct for *you*, and mark the correct space on the answer sheet. For some questions, it may be hard to choose one answer over the other. With these questions, decide which answer is *mostly true for you* and mark that answer on the answer sheet.

If you can't decide between the "a" or "c" answers, then select the "b" answer. *But use this as little as possible.*

The examples below are like the questions inside this booklet.

EXAMPLES:

1. I like to watch team games.
   a. yes (often), **b. sometimes,** **c. no (never).**

2. People say I'm impatient.
   a. true, **b. uncertain,** **c. false.**

3. I prefer friends who are:
   a. quiet, **b. in between,** **c. lively.**

4. Adult is to child as cat is to:
   a. kitten, **b. dog,** **c. baby.**

There are some questions that do have a right answer, like the last example. The right answer to this question is kitten, but there are few such reasoning questions.

In answering the questions, keep these five things in mind.

1. For each question, choose the one answer that is *true for you*.

2. Don't spend too much time thinking over each question. Give the first natural answer as it comes to you.

3. Answer every question, starting with number 1 and continuing until you've answered all the questions.

4. You should mark the *a* or *c* answer *most* of the time. Use the *b* answer *only* when you feel you have to.

5. If you change your mind after answering a question, *erase* the first answer completely.

You may ask for help if you have questions at any time.

DO NOT TURN PAGE UNTIL TOLD TO DO SO

---

examinees are usually printed on the front cover of a personality inventory or scale. These instructions tell examinees how and where the questions or items are to be answered. (See Figure 4–2 for a sample answer sheet.)

Repeating or rephrasing a question may be permitted on individual tests, but going beyond the directions printed in the manual is strictly against the rules. Departures from standard directions, even when they clarify the task, result in a different task being presented to examinees than the test designers had in mind. Consequently, if the directions deviate from those given to the group on whom the test was standardized (the *norm group*), the scores may not have the same meaning as those of the norm group. The result will be the loss of a useful frame of reference for interpreting examinees' scores.

There are, of course, occasions on which modifications of standard procedure will result in better information than strict adherence to the standard conditions of administration. Examples of such modifications are using a different sense or response modality (auditory rather than visual, oral rather than written), translating the test items to a different language, or increasing the time limits. Again, however, the examiner must bear in mind that when such modifications in testing procedure are employed, the resulting data cannot be interpreted with reference to test norms obtained under standard conditions.

Not only must the directions for administration be understood and adhered to, but other information in the test manual (reliability, validity, norms, etc.) and the content of the test itself should be familiar to the examiner. To attain familiarity with test content, it is recommended that the examiner take the test, as well as score and interpret the results, before attempting to administer it to anyone else.

Physical and Psychological Environments

As with psychological assessment instruments in general, personality tests should be administered under good physical conditions, including appropriate seating, lighting, ventilation, temperature, and noise level. A room familiar to the examinees and free from distractions is preferred. Individual testing should be conducted in a private room with only the examiner and examinee present, or, if absolutely necessary, one additional person such as a parent or guardian.

In addition to the physical environment, it is important to consider the psychological environment when conducting a psychological examination. Except in rare instances, such as stress interviewing, the examiner should not purposely attempt to make examinees more uneasy than they already are. In the past, there has been much discussion of the importance of *rapport*—a cordial, accepting relationship between examiner and examinee—in encouraging the latter to respond honestly on personality tests and up to his or her potential on ability tests. But the examiner will not appear the same to all examinees, and rapport may be difficult to establish or maintain in some cases. Even examiners who adhere closely to the directions for

Figure 4–2 Hand-scoreable answer sheet for High School Personality Questionnaire.

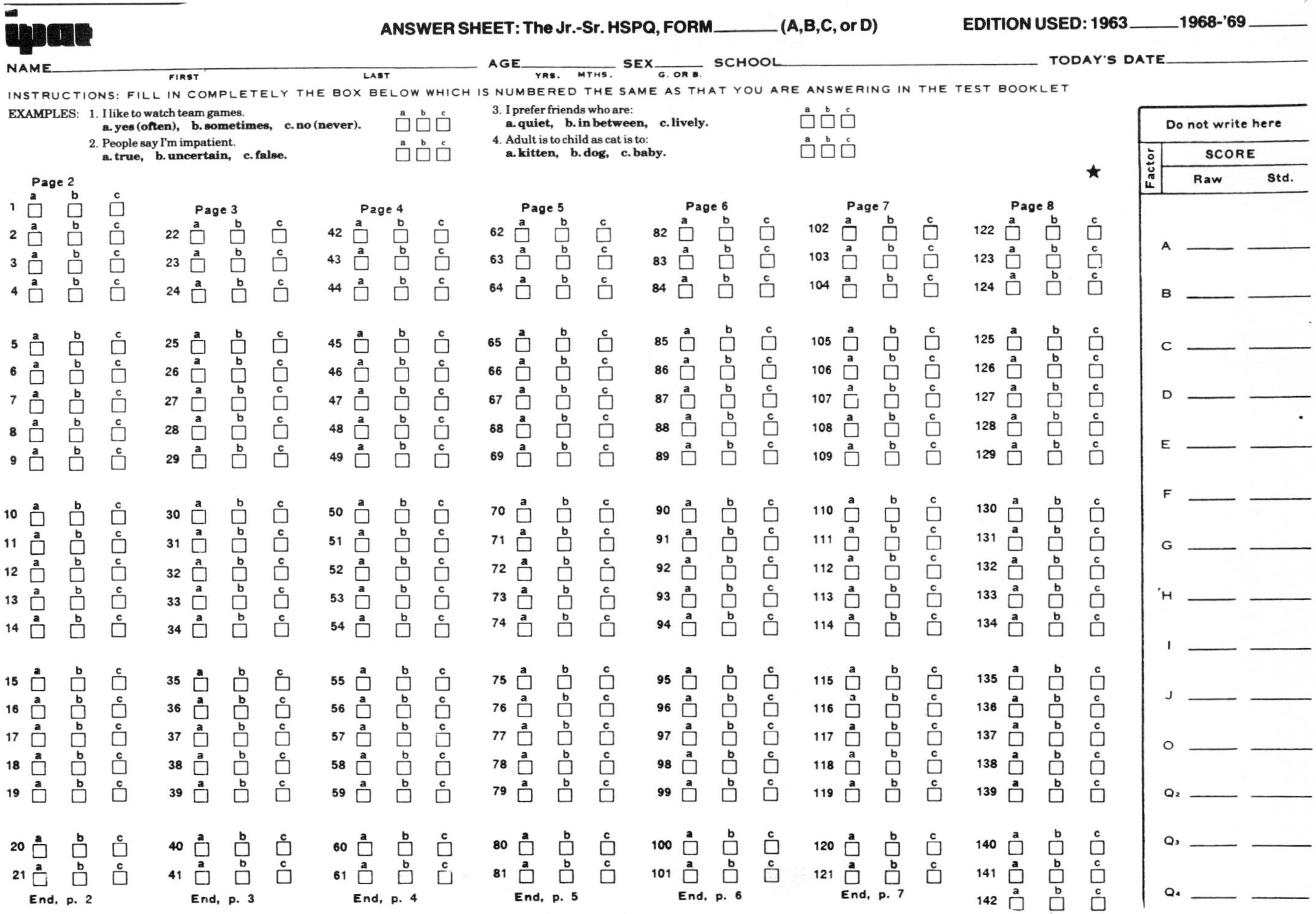

ANSWER SHEET: The Jr.-Sr. HSPQ, FORM ______ (A,B,C, or D) EDITION USED: 1963 ______ 1968-'69 ______

NAME ______ FIRST ______ LAST ______ AGE ______ YRS. MTHS. SEX ______ G. OR B. SCHOOL ______ TODAY'S DATE ______

INSTRUCTIONS: FILL IN COMPLETELY THE BOX BELOW WHICH IS NUMBERED THE SAME AS THAT YOU ARE ANSWERING IN THE TEST BOOKLET

EXAMPLES:
1. I like to watch team games. **a. yes (often), b. sometimes, c. no (never).** a ☐ b ☐ c ☐
2. People say I'm impatient. **a. true, b. uncertain, c. false.** a ☐ b ☐ c ☐
3. I prefer friends who are: **a. quiet, b. in between, c. lively.** a ☐ b ☐ c ☐
4. Adult is to child as cat is to: **a. kitten, b. dog, c. baby.** a ☐ b ☐ c ☐

★

Page 2	Page 3	Page 4	Page 5	Page 6	Page 7	Page 8
1 a ☐ b ☐ c ☐						
2 a ☐ b ☐ c ☐	22 a ☐ b ☐ c ☐	42 a ☐ b ☐ c ☐	62 a ☐ b ☐ c ☐	82 a ☐ b ☐ c ☐	102 a ☐ b ☐ c ☐	122 a ☐ b ☐ c ☐
3 a ☐ b ☐ c ☐	23 a ☐ b ☐ c ☐	43 a ☐ b ☐ c ☐	63 a ☐ b ☐ c ☐	83 a ☐ b ☐ c ☐	103 a ☐ b ☐ c ☐	123 a ☐ b ☐ c ☐
4 a ☐ b ☐ c ☐	24 a ☐ b ☐ c ☐	44 a ☐ b ☐ c ☐	64 a ☐ b ☐ c ☐	84 a ☐ b ☐ c ☐	104 a ☐ b ☐ c ☐	124 a ☐ b ☐ c ☐
5 a ☐ b ☐ c ☐	25 a ☐ b ☐ c ☐	45 a ☐ b ☐ c ☐	65 a ☐ b ☐ c ☐	85 a ☐ b ☐ c ☐	105 a ☐ b ☐ c ☐	125 a ☐ b ☐ c ☐
6 a ☐ b ☐ c ☐	26 a ☐ b ☐ c ☐	46 a ☐ b ☐ c ☐	66 a ☐ b ☐ c ☐	86 a ☐ b ☐ c ☐	106 a ☐ b ☐ c ☐	126 a ☐ b ☐ c ☐
7 a ☐ b ☐ c ☐	27 a ☐ b ☐ c ☐	47 a ☐ b ☐ c ☐	67 a ☐ b ☐ c ☐	87 a ☐ b ☐ c ☐	107 a ☐ b ☐ c ☐	127 a ☐ b ☐ c ☐
8 a ☐ b ☐ c ☐	28 a ☐ b ☐ c ☐	48 a ☐ b ☐ c ☐	68 a ☐ b ☐ c ☐	88 a ☐ b ☐ c ☐	108 a ☐ b ☐ c ☐	128 a ☐ b ☐ c ☐
9 a ☐ b ☐ c ☐	29 a ☐ b ☐ c ☐	49 a ☐ b ☐ c ☐	69 a ☐ b ☐ c ☐	89 a ☐ b ☐ c ☐	109 a ☐ b ☐ c ☐	129 a ☐ b ☐ c ☐
10 a ☐ b ☐ c ☐	30 a ☐ b ☐ c ☐	50 a ☐ b ☐ c ☐	70 a ☐ b ☐ c ☐	90 a ☐ b ☐ c ☐	110 a ☐ b ☐ c ☐	130 a ☐ b ☐ c ☐
11 a ☐ b ☐ c ☐	31 a ☐ b ☐ c ☐	51 a ☐ b ☐ c ☐	71 a ☐ b ☐ c ☐	91 a ☐ b ☐ c ☐	111 a ☐ b ☐ c ☐	131 a ☐ b ☐ c ☐
12 a ☐ b ☐ c ☐	32 a ☐ b ☐ c ☐	52 a ☐ b ☐ c ☐	72 a ☐ b ☐ c ☐	92 a ☐ b ☐ c ☐	112 a ☐ b ☐ c ☐	132 a ☐ b ☐ c ☐
13 a ☐ b ☐ c ☐	33 a ☐ b ☐ c ☐	53 a ☐ b ☐ c ☐	73 a ☐ b ☐ c ☐	93 a ☐ b ☐ c ☐	113 a ☐ b ☐ c ☐	133 a ☐ b ☐ c ☐
14 a ☐ b ☐ c ☐	34 a ☐ b ☐ c ☐	54 a ☐ b ☐ c ☐	74 a ☐ b ☐ c ☐	94 a ☐ b ☐ c ☐	114 a ☐ b ☐ c ☐	134 a ☐ b ☐ c ☐
15 a ☐ b ☐ c ☐	35 a ☐ b ☐ c ☐	55 a ☐ b ☐ c ☐	75 a ☐ b ☐ c ☐	95 a ☐ b ☐ c ☐	115 a ☐ b ☐ c ☐	135 a ☐ b ☐ c ☐
16 a ☐ b ☐ c ☐	36 a ☐ b ☐ c ☐	56 a ☐ b ☐ c ☐	76 a ☐ b ☐ c ☐	96 a ☐ b ☐ c ☐	116 a ☐ b ☐ c ☐	136 a ☐ b ☐ c ☐
17 a ☐ b ☐ c ☐	37 a ☐ b ☐ c ☐	57 a ☐ b ☐ c ☐	77 a ☐ b ☐ c ☐	97 a ☐ b ☐ c ☐	117 a ☐ b ☐ c ☐	137 a ☐ b ☐ c ☐
18 a ☐ b ☐ c ☐	38 a ☐ b ☐ c ☐	58 a ☐ b ☐ c ☐	78 a ☐ b ☐ c ☐	98 a ☐ b ☐ c ☐	118 a ☐ b ☐ c ☐	138 a ☐ b ☐ c ☐
19 a ☐ b ☐ c ☐	39 a ☐ b ☐ c ☐	59 a ☐ b ☐ c ☐	79 a ☐ b ☐ c ☐	99 a ☐ b ☐ c ☐	119 a ☐ b ☐ c ☐	139 a ☐ b ☐ c ☐
20 a ☐ b ☐ c ☐	40 a ☐ b ☐ c ☐	60 a ☐ b ☐ c ☐	80 a ☐ b ☐ c ☐	100 a ☐ b ☐ c ☐	120 a ☐ b ☐ c ☐	140 a ☐ b ☐ c ☐
21 a ☐ b ☐ c ☐	41 a ☐ b ☐ c ☐	61 a ☐ b ☐ c ☐	81 a ☐ b ☐ c ☐	101 a ☐ b ☐ c ☐	121 a ☐ b ☐ c ☐	141 a ☐ b ☐ c ☐
End, p. 2	End, p. 3	End, p. 4	End, p. 5	End, p. 6	End, p. 7	142 a ☐ b ☐ c ☐

Do not write here

Factor	SCORE Raw	SCORE Std.
A	______	______
B	______	______
C	______	______
D	______	______
E	______	______
F	______	______
G	______	______
H	______	______
I	______	______
J	______	______
O	______	______
Q_2	______	______
Q_3	______	______
Q_4	______	______

administering a test may, through differences in appearance and manner, vary in the amount of encouragement or threat they communicate.

Although the effect of the examiner's behavior on the examinee's emotional and motivational level will vary from person to person, it is recommended that the examiner be neither encouraging nor discouraging, maintaining a somewhat bland and noncommittal facial expression and tone of voice during the examination (Rosenthal, 1966). Neither approval nor disapproval of particular responses should be shown, lest it act as reward or punishment for what is the examinee's typical behavior or inform him or her of the correctness or incorrectness of a given response. Be that as it may, the examiner must be alert to the feelings of examinees and respond to their questions without being critical or condescending in voice or manner. The purpose of the examination and how the results will be used should be explained in a manner appropriate to the examinee's level of ability and need to know.

Examiners are, of course, not robots or creatures encased in stone, and the examination process may create disturbed or mixed feelings in examiners as well as examinees. For example, what intelligence-tester could resist being moved by the tears of a little girl who realizes that if she doesn't do well she will be placed in "the dummy class" and other children will make fun of her? Or who could fail to sympathize with an ex-mental patient who admits that he still hears voices but has learned to deny them and give the right answers on personality tests and in interviews so he will not be returned to the mental hospital?

Clearly there are circumstances in which examiners need to be especially active and encouraging. A testing situation creates a certain amount of tension in almost anyone, and occasionally examinees may become quite anxious. In addition, testing very young or very old, mentally disturbed, physically handicapped, or culturally disadvantaged people presents special problems of administration. In such cases, examiners must not only be thoroughly skilled in administering the test materials, but also quite sensitive, patient, and alert for emergencies. Examiners are seldom prepared to handle every emergency situation that can occur (e.g., an epileptic seizure or violent outburst), but experience in a variety of testing situations is crucial in developing the skills required to cope with such problems. When testing the very young, the elderly, and the handicapped, it may be necessary to use shorter testing periods and be prepared to take a longer total amount of time. Awareness of fatigue, anxiety, and the presence of sensory-motor deficits is also important.

Deviations from Standard Procedure

Some flexibility is usually permitted in administering nonstandardized instruments and even certain standardized tests. But, as Standard 15.1 of the *Standards for Educational and Psychological Testing* (American Educational Research Association et al., 1985, p. 83) makes clear, ". . . only on the basis of carefully considered professional judgment, primarily in clinical applications." And Standard 15.4 recommends, "In school situations not involving admissions and in clinical and counseling applications, any modification of standard test administration procedures or scoring should be described in the testing reports with appropriate cautions regarding the possible effects of such modifications on validity" (pp. 83–84). In any event, the manual of administration for the test should make clear to what extent deviations from standard procedure are permissible and what effects they may have on score interpretation.

After the Test

After the testing process has been completed, the examiner should make certain that examinees are taken care of, perhaps by offering reassurance, a small reward or privilege in the case of a young child, and returning examinees to the appropriate places. In individual clinical testing, it is usually important to interview a parent or other person who accompanies an examinee, perhaps both before and after the test. After the test, some information on what will be done with the test results and how they are to be used can be provided to the examinee and/or the accompanying party. The examiner will promise to report the results and interpretations to the appropriate person(s) or agency and to recommend what further action might be taken.

Following administration of a test to a group of people, the examiner collects the answer sheets, test booklets, pencils, scratch paper, and other materials. The test booklets and answer sheets are counted, and all other collected materials checked to make certain that none are missing. Only then are the examinees dismissed and the tests prepared for scoring.

Administration by Computer

Programming a computer to administer a personality inventory, rating scale, or checklist, or to conduct a structured interview, is fairly straightforward. In the case of individual tests and unstructured interviews, however, the process is more complex, and not completely satisfactory.

As indicated previously, Standard 15.2 of the *Standards for Educational and Psychological Testing* (American Educational Research Association et al., 1985, p. 83) includes the statement that "In computerized testing, items displayed on a screen should be legible and free from glare, and the terminal should be properly positioned." However, the Standards are incomplete in their recommendations concerning the application of computers in testing. For this reason, a set of *Guidelines for Computer-Based Tests and Interpretations* was developed to assist professionals in applying computer-based assessments competently and in the best interest of their clients and to guide test developers in establishing and maintaining the quality of new products (American Psychological Association, 1986). Among the eight guidelines pertaining to test administration by computer are recommendations that

The environment in which the testing terminal is located should be quiet, comfortable, and free from distraction;

Test items presented on the display screen should be legible and free from noticeable glare;

Equipment should be checked routinely and should be maintained in proper working condition;

Test performance should be monitored, and assistance to the test taker should be provided, as is needed and appropriate;

Test takers should be trained on proper use of the computer equipment;

Reasonable accommodations must be made for individuals who may be at an unfair disadvantage in a computer testing situation. (pp. 11–12)

Test Scoring

Objective tests of personality can be scored either by hand, using special scoring keys (stencil, strip, etc.), or by machine. Special machines for scoring objective tests have been in use for over a half century, and the increased availability of high-speed computers has made test scoring much more rapid and flexible. Computerized scoring is not limited to group-administered, multiple-choice tests; programs have also been devised for administering, scoring, and interpreting individual tests.

Numerous test scoring services are now in business, and Standard 15.5 of the *Standards for Educational and Psychological Testing* requires that these services document the procedures that they follow to ensure accurate scoring and to monitor and report (on request) their scoring-error rates. Other recommendations concerning test scoring are made in Chapter 15 of the Standards, but they apply primarily to ability testing rather than personality assessment.

Despite the growing importance of computerized test scoring, the majority of personality inventories, projectives, and other instruments continue to be scored by hand. Some of the responses to projective techniques and other individual tests can be scored during the examination, but final scoring should wait until the examinee has been dismissed. Scoring during the test should obviously be done as unobtrusively as possible, and at no time should the scores be revealed to the examinee.

The ethical problems of having personality tests scored by clerks who are not trained in psychology and do not always preserve confidentiality should also be mentioned. There is no easy solution to the problem, especially when scoring hundreds or thousands of personality inventories or rating scales. At the very least, however, test-scoring clerks should be made aware of the great necessity for accuracy in scoring, for keeping test records securely under lock and key, and not revealing the scores to anyone without authorized permission.

In most cases, directions for scoring specific personality assessment instruments are described in the chapters of this book in which those instruments are discussed. However, it may be instructive to consider the procedure for scoring one objective instrument at this time. The scoring of personality inventories such as the High School Personality Questionnaire (HSPQ) is entirely objective and, as seen in the following instructions, can be done by a clerk (Cattell, Cattell & Johns, 1984):

1. Check that each question has one, and only one, answer.

2. Place this key over the left-hand side of the answer sheet. Adjust it to position by means of the two "check stars."

3. There are seven "raw scores" to be obtained with each key, one given by each of the seven horizontal "layers" or strips across the key. The answers seen through the holes count either 2 or 1, as indicated by the number adjacent to the hole.

4. The Factor A score is obtained by adding the weights for the answers visible in the Factor A horizontal strip. Record the sum on the answer sheet in the Raw Score column beside the A.

5. Repeat this process for the other factor strips.

Because errors in scoring can result in a quite different picture of an individual's personality, it is important to double check the handscoring of paper-and-pencil inventories and other personality assessment devices. On the HSPQ, for example, errors in counting the differentially weighted answer marks occur very easily.

After the raw scores on a personality inventory have been obtained, they can be converted to percentile norms or standard scores and a profile constructed from these converted scores before beginning the process of interpreting the results (see figure in Report 4–1. The sten (standard ten) scores to which the raw scores have been converted range from 1 to 10 in the profile in Report 4–1; sten scores have a mean of 5.5 and a standard deviation of 2.0. The following designations of sten scores are used: Low = 1 to 3, Average = 4 to 7, High = 8 to 10.

In converting raw scores to standared scores or other norms, it is crucial that the set of norms appropriate for the examinee's age, sex, and other relevant characteristics be used. Certain students in my psychological assessment course have understandably been greatly concerned when the results of a personality inventory that they took, scored, and then transformed the raw scores to norms, revealed them to be quite extreme on certain traits. After I rescored the inventory and reconverted the raw scores to norms, the students were usually relieved to discover that they were much less abnormal than they had concluded from the initial results.

Unfortunately, not all personality assessment instruments can be scored as objectively as the High School Personality Questionnaire. For example, the procedures for scoring projective techniques such as the Rorschach and the Thematic Apperception Test are quite subjective and impressionistic. Considering the fact

Report 4–1

High School Personality Questionnaire

This report is intended to be used in conjunction with professional judgment. The statements it contains should be viewed as hypotheses to be validated against other sources of data. All information in this report should be treated confidentially and responsibly.

February 4, 1987

NAME–Bob Sample
ID NUMBER–123456789

AGE–13
SEX–M

HSPQ PROFILE

SCORE			LOW MEANING	1	2	3	4	5	6	7	8	9	10	HIGH MEANING	%
F	R	S													
A	11	6	Cool, Reserved											Warm	60
B	6	5	Concrete Thinking											Abstract Thinking	40
C	8	5	Easily Upset											Calm, Stable	40
D	8	4	Unexcitable											Excitable	23
E	10	5	Submissive, Unassertive											Dominant, Assertive	40
F	13	7	Sober, Serious											Enthusiastic, Cheerful	77
G	6	3	Disregards Rules											Conforming	11
H	8	4	Shy, Timid											Bold, Adventurous	23
I	7	6	Tough-Minded											Sensitive	60
J	5	3	Zestful, Participating											Guarded, Withdrawn	11
O	12	7	Self-Assured											Self-Blaming, Insecure	77
Q2	5	3	Group-Oriented											Self-Sufficient	11
Q3	11	6	Undisciplined											Self-Disciplined	60
Q4	11	6	Relaxed											Tense, Driven	60

"F" designates the factor scale, "R" designates the Raw score for each factor and "S" designates the Sten score for each factor.

Name: Bob Sample   -2-   February 4, 1987

PRIMARY PERSONALITY CHARACTERISTICS OF SPECIAL INTEREST

Regard for rules and respect for fine moral obligations is not high.

At school and elsewhere, he is a solid member of a group, zestfully playing his part and sharing the experiences of his group. This characteristic is high.

He has some lack of self-sufficiency and prefers to be a joiner and depend on going along with the group.

BROAD INFLUENCE PATTERNS

This person is neither extraverted nor introverted but is approximately average with a score of 6.4.

This individual's anxiety score of 6.4 is average.

His propensity toward alert and decisive responses, reflected in a score of 6.1, may be considered average.

The tendency of this individual toward independent and self-directed behavior is expressed by a score of 2.6, which can be thought of as low.

The degree of social responsibility and control he has achieved is reflected in a score of 4.1 that may be considered below average.

A score of 6.9 indicates that his accident proneness is above average.

The following projections about this individual's promise in the areas of academic achievement, leadership, creativity and vocational success are made relative to his educational opportunities, his aptitudes, and the appropriate peer setting.

His general capacity to work creatively, to transcend custom, and to generate new ideas, indicated by a score of 4.6, is average.

A score of 5.0 on leadership potential suggests that the probability of his effectively accepting a role of authority and direction in any group situation is average.

Estimating this individual's score of 2.7 from known relationships between personality and scholastic performance indicates that his level of achievement in main school subjects will be low.

The capacity of this individual to adjust to the demands of a skilled occupation and to grow into a job is expressed in a score of 3.6 that may be regarded as below average.

A score of 4.6 suggests that his ability to perform dependably in a job or task which is repetitive or tedious is average.

ITEM SUMMARY

Item responses have not been provided.

This report was processed using male norms for Form A.

that the scoring directions or guidelines for many items on personality tests and even individual tests of intelligence are not always clear, it is not surprising that a wide range of scores may be assigned to the same test responses. One might expect that this would be more likely to occur in the case of individuals who have less experience in using a particular instrument, but even experienced examiners and scorers are not immune to inaccurate and biased scoring.

Personality assessments are, of course, rarely conducted blindly, in the sense that the scorer knows nothing about the examinee other than the latter's test responses, chronological age, and the date on which the test was administered. More commonly, the scorer has enough additional information to form a distinct affective impression or attitude about the examinee. Knowing the sex, ethnic group membership, socioeconomic status, occupation, and other information about the examinee may make different impressions on different scorers. Unfortunately, these impressions, which may be positive or negative and lead to different kinds of expectations or degrees of bias, can affect the scoring of the test.

Interpreting Assessment Findings

A substantial amount of training is needed to interpret the results of a personality assessment or evaluation. Not only must the examiner consider the subscores and overall scores and their corresponding norm equivalents on the standardized instrument(s), but this information must be combined with the results of behavioral observations, interviews, and other nonstandardized test and nontest data. Consequently, the examiner should not only be proficient in administering the required psychological instruments but also an alert observer and a sensitive interviewer.

Case Study

A complete case study involves more than a psychological examination, interview, and observational data. A case study may be conducted in a clinical (*clinical case study*) or educational context to determine the cause(s) of a specific problem of behavioral or mental functioning. Details of the individual's background and characteristics are obtained both from the individual him- or herself and other people who play an important role in the person's life; follow-up data are also collected over a period of time. The following information may be attained:

- family (who is in home, home attitudes)
- culture (cultural group, cultural deviation and conflict)
- medical examinations and history (medical examination, physical development, physical conditions especially related to adjustment, sex development)
- developmental history (prenatal period and birth, early developmental signs, intellectual development, speech development, emotional development, social development)

- educational history (school progress, educational achievement, school adjustment, educational aspirations and plans)
- economic history in the case of older children and adults (occupation, occupational history, vocational plans and ambitions)
- legal history (delinquencies, arrests)
- and the person's life (daily routines, interests, hobbies, recreations, fantasy life, sex, social adjustments)

After the assessment data have been collected and integrated, a summary of the examinee's strengths and weaknesses is prepared and recommendations for clinical, educational, or vocational interventions may be made.

When a case study is conducted to determine the cause(s) of a specific psychological problem, hypotheses or conclusions as to the cause may be formulated and specific recommendations made concerning treatment—psychotherapy, drugs or other medical treatment, special education, etc. A follow-up assessment to evaluate the effectiveness of the prescribed treatment program should also be conducted after an appropriate time interval.

Despite its yield of potentially useful information for forming an overall picture as well as an in-depth understanding of the individual, a clinical case study has some notable weaknesses. These include the retrospective nature of the data (memory is seldom completely accurate), the fact that the person conducting the study is frequently biased in selecting and evaluating certain kinds of data or measurements, and the extent to which the findings are generalizable across situations or circumstances encountered by the individual. Employing a variety of assessments in a systematic sample of situations and being aware of the likelihood of bias in selection and evaluation can help reduce, although not eliminate, misinterpretations and overgeneralizations.

Psychodiagnosis and DSM-III

Psychodiagnosis is the process of examining a person from a psychological viewpoint to determine the nature and extent of a mental or behavioral disorder. In the traditional *medical model* of mental disorders, the psychodiagnostician (psychologist or psychiatrist) observes, interviews, and tests the patient to determine the presence or absence of certain psychological (and physical) symptoms. The psychodiagnostician then compares the patient's symptoms with standard descriptions of abnormal behavior to determine in which category of disorders the patient best fits. The end result of the process is the assignment of a psychiatric classification or label to the patient. In addition to diagnosing the disorder, a *prognosis*, or prediction of its likely outcome—if treated or untreated—is made.

The most popular system of psychodiagnosis, although by no means the only one, is that described in the *Diagnostic and Statistical Manual* of the American

Psychiatric Association. In the first two editions of the *Diagnostic and Statistical Manual*, which were published in 1952 and 1968, the categories of mental disorders used by Sigmund Freud, Emil Kraeplin, and other psychiatric classifiers were combined. The third edition of the manual (DSM-III), which grouped 200 specific disorders and conditions into 15 major categories, represented a radical departure from its predecessors. A revision of DSM-III (DSM-III-R), published in 1987, incorporated further changes in diagnostic criteria. Like DSM-III, the DSM-III-R system is multiaxial in that there are five separate axes or dimensions on which a person may be classified. Explicit criteria and decision-branching sequences for reaching a diagnosis are provided, the various disorders being grouped according to very specific behavioral symptoms without specifying their origins or methods of treatment. Among the changes introduced in DSM-III-R are a new classification and criteria for sleep disorders, an expanded section on substance abuse, a reorganization of Axes I and II, and a refinement of Axis IV to be more clinically useful.

In a multiaxial evaluation employing the DSM-III-R system, each case is assessed on five axes referring to different kinds of information about the patient. Axis I consists of the Clinical Syndromes and V Codes (Conditions Not Attributable to a Mental Disorder That Are a Focus of Attention or Treatment), and Axis II of Developmental Disorders and Personality Disorders. The major headings of these two axes are listed in Figure 4–3. In addition to labeling and numbering each disorder with a five-digit code on Axis I and Axis II, the severity of the disorder may be specified as mild, moderate, severe, or in partial or complete remission. Axis III of DSM-III-R provides a classification of Physical Disorders and Conditions, Axis IV a classification of Severity of Psychosocial Stressors, and Axis V a Global Assessment of Functioning (GAF) on a numerical scale.

As with its previous editions, DSM-III-R permits making multiple diagnoses on Axes I and II to describe a patient's condition. Such diagnoses may become quite complex, as indicated by the following example (American Psychiatric Association, 1987):

Axis I: 296.23   Major Depression, Single Episode, Severe without Psychotic Features
            303.90   Alcohol Dependence
Axis II: 301.60   Dependent Personality Disorder (Provisional, rule out Borderline Personality Disorder)
Axis III: Alcoholic cirrhosis of liver
Axis IV: Psychosocial stressors: anticipated retirement and change in residence, with loss of contact with friends
Axis V: Current GAF: 44
          Highest GAF past year: 55

Although DSM-III and DSM-III-R would, by providing more precise criteria for psychodiagnosis, appear to possess greater reliability than previous psychodiag-

Figure 4–3   A sample of the DSM-III-R classification system

DSM-III-R Classification: Axes I and II

DISORDERS USUALLY FIRST EVIDENT IN INFANCY, CHILDHOOD, OR ADOLESCENCE

Developmental Disorders
(These are coded on Axis II)
Mental Retardation
Pervasive Developmental
Disorders
Specific Developmental Disorders
Other Developmental Disorders

Disruptive Behavior Disorders
Anxiety Disorders of Childhood or
Adolescence
Eating Disorders
Gender Identity Disorders
Tic Disorders
Elimination Disorders
Speech Disorders Not Elsewhere
Classified
Other Disorders of Infancy, Childhood, or Adolescence

Organic Mental Disorders
Dementias Arising in the Senium
and Presenium
Psychoactive Substance-Induced
Organic Mental Disorders
Organic Mental Disorders associated with Axis II physical disorders or conditions, or whose
etiology is unknown

Psychoactive Substance Use Disorders

Schizophrenia

Delusional (Paranoid) Disorder

**Psychotic Disorders Not Elsewhere
Classified**

Mood Disorders
Bipolar Disorders
Depressive Disorders

**Anxiety Disorders (or Anxiety and
Phobic Neuroses)**

Somatoform Disorders

**Dissociative Disorders (or Hysterical
Neuroses, Dissociative Type)**

Sexual Disorders
Paraphilias
Sexual Dysfunctions
Other Sexual Disorders

Sleep Disorders
Dyssomnias
Parasomnias

Factitious Disorders

Impulse Control Disorders Not Elsewhere Classified

Adjustment Disorder

**Psychological Factors Affecting
Physical Condition**

Personality Disorders (These
are coded on Axis II)
Cluster A (Paranoid, Schizoid, etc.)
Cluster B (Antisocial, Histrionic, Narcissistic, etc.)
Cluster C (Avoidant, Dependent, Obsessive compulsive, etc.)

Reproduced by permission of the American Psychiatric Association from *Diagnostic and Statistical Manual of Mental Disorders* (Third Edition-Revised), 1987.

nostic systems, questions concerning the validity of the DSM system have been raised. Some authorities have argued that the criteria are too rigid to apply to all patients (Finn, 1982). Others question the appropriateness and possible dangers of any kind of psychiatric labeling.

Diagnostic labels such as schizophrenia and depression are not always assigned consistently. In addition to varying with the theoretical orientation and personal biases of the examiner, and the socioeconomic status and ethnicity of examinees, diagnoses vary from institution to institution (e.g., mental hospitals), community to community, and country to country (Cooper et al., 1972).

Variations in diagnoses of the same disorder are a product of the preoccupations or concerns of the diagnostician. In general, clinical psychologists and psychiatrists have tended to be more concerned with detecting signs of abnormality than indicators of health or coping abilities. But, depending on the perceived repercussions or payoffs for making a patient appear more or less disordered, the diagnostician may either exaggerate or downplay the severity of symptoms. For example, if a government agency or private insurance company pays for treatment and/or awards other compensation to patients diagnosed as psychotic or brain damaged but not for certain other diagnosed conditions, the result may be a greater number of diagnoses of psychosis and brain damage. On the other hand, as is true in some states, if a person loses many of his or her legal rights when diagnosed as psychotic, the diagnostitican may be reluctant to assign this label.

In defense of psychodiagnostic classification, advocates of the system point out that by reducing long-winded explanations diagnostic terms can improve communication among mental health professionals. Furthermore, classification can assist in making diagnostic predictions and conducting research on abnormal behavior (Meehl, 1962, Spitzer, 1976).

Some additional statements with respect to exercising caution in diagnostic labeling should be made. In using a diagnostic system such as DSM-III-R, great care must be taken in selecting the appropriate terms or categories to be included in a psychological report. Labels such as "psychotic," "neurotic," "psychopathic," and the like too often act as self-fulfilling prophecies in which the examinee becomes—at least in the eyes of others—what he or she is labeled as being (see Rosenhan, 1973). When using DSM-III-R, or any other diagnostic system, it is wise to follow the recommendation of Standard 16.6 of the *Standards for Educational and Psychological Testing:* "When score reporting includes assigning individuals to categories, the categories chosen should be based on carefully selected criteria. The least stigmatizing labels, consistent with accurate reporting, should always be assigned" (p. 86).

Clinical versus Statistical Prediction

The conventional or traditional procedure of combining assessment data and making interpretations and behavioral predictions is for the assessor to rely on his or her clinical experience concerning personality. This *impressionistic approach*, however, is viewed by many psychometricians as too subjective and biased to provide a valid picture of personality. Consequently, they have opted for the statistical or actuarial approach of applying empirically derived statistical formulas in making diagnoses and predictions.

The question of the relative merits of these procedures—using one's head (*clinical judgment*) versus using a formula (*statistical prediction*) has been debated for many years. This debate, which has filled many pages in psychological journals and books (e.g., Meehl, 1954, 1965; Holt, 1970; Sines, 1970), is discussed in detail in Chapter 14, but a few relevant comments are appropriate here. To Paul Meehl, a proponent of the statistical approach: ". . . there are occasions when you should use your head instead of the formula. . . . But which occasions they are is not, emphatically *not*, clear. What *is* clear from the available clinical data is that these occasions are much rarer than most clinicians suppose." (Meehl, 1973, p. 235)

Taking a somewhat more middle-of-the-road position, Korchin and Schuldberg (1981) cite evidence that clinicians are superior to standardized assessment instruments in collecting information on personality and behavior but statistical procedures are more accurate than clinical impressions in combining or integrating the data in predicting behavior. Arkes (1985) also points out that the clinician is needed to decide what information to look for in the first place.

Factors Detracting from Clinical Judgments

Why are clinical judgments apparently so poor, even when compared with simple linear regression equations? Among the factors cited by Arkes (1985) as detracting from clinical judgments are (1) preconceived notions, (2) failure to give adequate consideration to base rates, (3) hindsight bias, (4) serious overconfidence in one's own judgments.

Preconceived notions detract from clinical judgment in several ways. Memory tends to be distorted by becoming more consistent with preconceived hypotheses. Current information gets distorted toward (even tentative) hypotheses. And, finally, judgment is warped. One such preconceived notion is the *illusory correlation problem* of basing a clinical judgment on the number of times a symptom and a disorder have occurred together and overlooking the proportion of the time they have not occurred together. Illusory correlation occurs when clinicians tend to notice or recall whatever fits their expectations and to ignore or forget whatever is contrary to their expectations (Anastasi, 1988).

Arkes's (1985) second factor that can detract from clinical judgment, the *base rate*, refers to the proportion of people in a population who possess a specific characteristic or condition. If the base rate is low, then it is much more difficult to identify or diagnose the condition, by whatever assessment methods are available. Illustrative of conditions having low base rates, and hence difficult to predict, are suicide and homicide. On the other hand, neurotic behavior has a much higher base rate and is consequently easier to predict.

The third factor cited by Arkes (1985) as affecting clinical judgment, *hindsight bias* (Fischhoff, 1975), pertains to the belief, after an event has already occurred, that one could have predicted the event if asked to do so beforehand. There is, for example, the all-too-human tendency to view an acquaintance who has committed an antisocial or bizarre act as always having been strange or uncontrollable. Clearly, hindsight bias may prevent a clinician from learning as much from the occurrence of an event as he or she should.

A fourth factor impairing clinical judgment is the tendency of those who judge least accurately to be most confident in their judgments (Arkes, 1985). For example, merely formulating a rule such as "psychotics are often pale" is sufficient to convince some clinicians that the rule is valid. *Overconfidence* in one's own judgments can lead a person to believe that assistance, correction, or remediation from others is unnecessary, thereby solidifying the overconfidence and its false consequences (Lichtenstein, Fischhoff & Phillips, 1982).

Arkes (1985) cites two reasons why these four impediments to accurate judgment are so pervasive. The first reason is that many shortcuts or heuristics used by people in everyday decision-making actually work fairly well. One shortcut that is misleading is to assume that events that are remembered more easily have occurred more frequently. Thus a single dramatic occurrence of a certain disorder can create the illusion that it has occurred more often. A second reason for the pervasiveness of inaccurate clinical judgment is the fact that people apparently have limited awareness of the bases on which they make judgments. Obviously, improving judgments is difficult when one is unable to remember what factors initially influenced those judgments.

Reporting Assessment Data

A psychological assessment is often prompted by a referral from an agency or person, and as such there is usually an accompanying referral question or questions: Is this person psychotic? Is he or she brain damaged? What are the chances that the person will be able to succeed in a certain educational, vocational, or therapeutic program? In such instances the primary goal of the report is to answer the referral question. Whether or not there is a formal, specific referral question, the overall goals of a personality assessment include: diagnosis of mental, behavioral, or organic disorders; determination of the predominant adaptive and maladaptive psychological traits or characteristics of a person; educational or vocational selection, placement and remediation; research on personality structure and dynamics. Whatever the purposes and goals of the examination may be, some form of written report of the findings is usually required.

The content and style of a psychological test report vary with its purposes, the readers for whom it is intended, and the background and orientation of the writer. However, the outline given in Figure 4–4 is representative. Undoubtedly the most

Figure 4–4   Suggested Format for report of psychological examination

Name of Examinee: _____ Sex: _____
Birthdate: _____ Age: _____ Education: _____
Referred by: _____
Place of Examination: _____ Date of Exam: _____
Examined by: _____ Date of Report: _____
Tests Administered: _____

Reason for Referral. State briefly why the examinee was referred for psychological testing. What was the purpose of the referral, and what person or facility made it?

Observations and Interview Findings. Briefly describe the appearance and behavior of the examinee during the examination. Give the examinee's own story, as well as that of other observers if available. Describe the examinee's physical and psychological history and characteristics, educational and employment situation. In the case of children in particular, information on the home and family (social status, characteristics of parents, siblings, etc.) is also important to obtain. Serious sensory or psychomotor handicaps, as well as the presence of emotional disorder should also be noted.

Results and Interpretations. Give a detailed description of the results of the tests or other instruments administered and how they should be interpreted. If the examiner is interpreting the results according to a particular theory of personality, make certain that the reader understands the language and assumptions of the theory. Be as specific and individualized as possible in interpreting the results. Describe the examinee's characteristics, his or her approach to the tasks, level of motivation and emotionality, and any other factors that might have affected the results.

Conclusions and Recommendations. Briefly describe the conclusions (descriptive, dynamic, diagnostic) stemming from the observational, interview, and standardized or unstandardized test data. What recommendations are warranted by the results? Include appropriate interpretative cautions, but don't hedge or deal in generalities. Additional psychological assessment (be specific), neurological or other medical examinations, counseling or psychotherapy, special class placement and training, vocational rehabilitation and institutionalization are among the recommendations that might be made. If a handicap or disability exists, is it remediable?

Name and Signature of Examiner

_____

important part of Figure 4–4 is the "Conclusions and Recommendations" section since this is the end result of describing, evaluating, and diagnosing the individual. If the conclusions and recommendations are not thoughtful and sound, the entire process of psychological evaluation and the time of many people will have been wasted. Report 4–2, which was prepared by a college student for a class project, is an example of such a report. The reader should study this report and note where it fails to meet the requirements discussed in this section.

In preparing the report, the writer must keep clearly in mind the questions that need to be answered about the mental functioning and behavior of the examinee, including dynamics, development, and probable outcomes (prognosis). The examinee's characteristics and their interrelationships should be described as fully and specifically as possible, avoiding vague generalizations, stereotypes, and banalities (Kleinmuntz, 1982). For example, the following personality description could be true of almost anyone but gives the misleading impression that it is an individualized analysis (Forer, 1949):

> You have a strong need for other people to like you and for them to admire you. You have a tendency to be critical of yourself. You have a great deal of unused capacity which you have not turned to your advantage. While you have some personality weaknesses, you are generally able to compensate for them. Your sexual adjustment has presented some problems for you. Disciplined and controlled on the outside, you tend to be worrisome and insecure inside. At times you have serious doubts as to whether you have made the right decision or done the right thing. You prefer a certain amount of change and variety and become dissatisfied when hemmed in by restrictions and limitations. You pride yourself as being an independent thinker and do not accept others' opinions without satisfactory proof. You have found it unwise to be too frank in revealing yourself to others. At times you are extroverted, affable, sociable, while at other times you are introverted, wary, reserved. Some of your aspirations tend to be pretty unrealistic. (p. 120)

Thirty-seven students in a class of fifty whom I questioned rated it as a good or excellent description of their personalities. These students were victims of the *Barnum effect* or *Aunt Fanny error* (because the report applies to anyone—even one's "Aunt Fanny") of accepting as correct a personality description phrased in generalities, truisms, and other statements that sound specific to a given person but could actually be true of almost anyone.[3]

A report of psychological findings should be written in a clear, comprehensive style that can be understood by the person(s) for whom it is intended. Therefore the report writer should ascertain in advance who the audience for the report is; it may even be necessary to prepare different reports of the same findings for different audiences. Unfortunately, many psychological reports are too abstract, ambiguous, overgeneralized, awkward in wording, and go beyond the data. It should be remembered that a report is of little value if it is not understood or not read by people who can use the information to help make decisions pertaining to the examinee's future and well-being.

Report 4–2

Psychological Assessment Report

Name of Examinee: David C. Lake   Sex: Male
Birthdate: April 14, 1965   Age: 21 years, 11 months
Address: 211 Oaks Avenue, Lawrence, CA   Education: College senior
Examined by: Dorothy R. Brown   Date: March 19, 1987
Tests Administered: Jackson Personality Inventory,
                      Rotter Incomplete Sentences Blank

Observations and Interview Findings

David Lake, a somewhat overweight (200 pounds), blonde-haired young man of average height (5'10") and a senior psychology major at Johnson College, volunteered to take the personality tests because of an expressed curiosity about the tests and an interest in "what makes me tick." The tests were administered as an assignment in Psychology 429 (Psychological Assessment) at Johnson College during the Spring of 1987. An interview was conducted prior to administering the tests.

David stated that his health was good, but he regrets that he is not more skilled in athletics. Except for the weight problem, he is a neat, fairly attractive young man who has been married for two years. He admits having been involved in the "drug culture" at the last college he attended and to having some marital difficulties. His primary concern at the present time appears to be his occupational future, namely being able to find a job after college graduation.

David stated that both he and his wife are very religious. His father is a church minister, and David views his childhood as having been warm and loving. He reportedly maintains close ties with his parents. David and his wife attended another church-related college before he enrolled at Johnson College, but he stated that he is happier and making higher grades at Johnson. His wife is currently working as a cashier for the college, but she is both anxious to finish college and to start a family.

David feels that he is "rather hard on myself" for not living up to his potential, but he appears generally optimistic in his outlook and looks forward to a bright future. He stated that he would like to work as a counselor in a church-related context after graduating from college.

Test Results and Interpretations

David worked dililgently on the personality test materials, sighing deeply on occasion but persisting in the tasks without interruption. The interview and testing lasted approximately two hours, and it was apparent toward the end of the session that David was getting somewhat tired. He did not complain, however, and was quite interested in obtaining the results.

(Continued)

The standard T score equivalents (male norms) of David's raw scores on the Jackson Personality Inventory scales are as follows:

Anxiety	53	Responsibility	40
Breadth of Interest	39	Risk Taking	57
Complexity	64	Self-esteem	55
Conformity	56	Social Adroitness	63
Energy Level	49	Social Participation	38
Innovation	49	Tolerance	49
Interpersonal Affect	56	Value Orthodoxy	51
Organization	43	Infrequency	44

All of these scores are within the normal range (30–70), but the pattern of high and low scores indicates a conforming, socially-adroit individual who is, however, not very socially participative. On the whole he is a conventional individual with some insecurities, a fairly narrow range of interests, and moderately high self-esteem. He has some problems of organization and responsibility, and he prefers deep, more complex explanations and interpretations of things.

David's responses to the Rotter Incomplete Sentences Blank confirm his statements during the interview that he is not applying himself fully, gives up too quickly, and is missing something in life. Fears of not being accepted are also apparent in his responses to the Rotter: he stated that during childhood he often felt like an outsider. David is obviously rather severe on himself, perhaps because of parental pressures toward perfectionism. He expresses a lack of self-confidence and a need to achieve his potential more fully. In general, he has feelings of aloneness and of being an outsider. Although optimistic in his expectations for the future, he is self-critical and has rather strong feelings of failure.

Conclusions and Recommendations

The results of the personal interview, the Jackson Personality Inventory, and the Rotter Incomplete Sentences Blank yield a picture of a sensitive, self-critical young man of average to above-average abilities who is not living up to his own expectations and perhaps not those of his parents. He has high moral and personal standards but has violated those standards on occasion and feels that he may do so again. Although fairly content in his marriage, there are some problems. Financial security (finding a job) is obviously a pressing problem, and success in work may well ease some of the tension and insecurity that he obviously feels. Clearly David needs to develop some closer friendships and learn to relax a bit more. He might well benefit from some personal counseling, a field that he is interested in entering.

Dorothy R. Brown, Senior Psychology Major
Johnson College

The aim of psychological report writing is efficient communication of the results of the tests and other assessment instruments, as well as the observational and interview findings. Thoughtful writers always keep their potential readers in mind, attempting to bridge the gap between the minds of the writer and the readers in the most straightforward manner. Consequently, wordiness, alliterations, poetic expressions, mixed metaphors, and other circumlocutions or distractions are inappropriate. Colloquialisms, clichés, and vulgar expressions are also bad form, as are scientificisms and similar jargon. A basic rule of professional communication is that if there is more than one way to say something, one should choose the simplest way. This does not mean that only a terse, telegraphic style of writing is acceptable. It is possible to write economically but interestingly, avoiding abrupt transitions and choppy wording.

Every well-structured paragraph in an integrated report contains a topic sentence and one or more additional statements elaborating on the theme. As in the case of each paragraph, the report as a whole is well integrated, the writing flowing or "gliding" from paragraph to paragraph in an organized, goal-oriented manner. The writer knows where he or she is going and communicates this to the reader. Jumping from topic to topic—within or between paragraphs—is avoided, as are misspellings, grammatical errors, and other irregular, nonstandard constructions.

Computerized Reports

Growing in popularity during recent years are computer-prepared psychological test reports. The first computer test-interpretation programs were developed at the Mayo Clinic, the Hartford Institute of Living, and the University of Alabama during the early 1960s (Swenson & Pearson, 1964; Rome et al., 1962; Glueck & Reznikoff, 1965). These programs were designed to score, profile, and interpret responses to the Minnesota Multiphasic Personality Inventory (MMPI). Subsequently, more complex programs for the automated interpretation of the MMPI and other measures of personality and cognitive abilities became available.

Today a variety of companies provide computer test scoring and interpretation services and market microcomputer software for interpreting personality tests such as the MMPI, the California Psychological Inventory, the 16 Personality Factor Questionnaire, and the Millon Clinical Multiaxial Inventory. A representative, but by no means exhaustive, list of companies that score and interpret personality tests and/or sell packages of computer software for performing these functions is given in Appendix C. A sample report generated by a computer program designed to interpret the High School Personality Questionnaire (HSPQ) is given in Report 4–1. The system that prepared this report converts raw scores on the HSPQ to sten scores and generates a written interpretation of the scores.

Computer-generated test interpretations, such as Report 4–1, are usually not as individualized as those produced impressionistically by a clinical or counseling psychologist. Many computer programs are designed to take the age, sex, and other demographics of the examinee into account, but no program considers all the examinee's personal attributes (American Psychological Association, 1986). Consequently, psychological examiners may wish to supplement computer-generated test reports with additional interpretive statements. However, as the *Guidelines for Computer-Based Tests and Interpretations* (American Psychological Association, 1986) make clear, this should not be done routinely but only for good and compelling reasons. The important ethical issues pertaining to computer-based testing and interpretation, a topic addressed at length in Chapter 14, is only beginning to be dealt with and can be expected to grow as a matter of concern in the future.

Informed Consent and Confidentiality

There has been a great deal of concern in recent years about improper disclosure of test data, especially data identified by the names of examinees. The expanding use of computers and associated data banks has increased the need for vigilance in ensuring that test scores maintained in electronic files in particular are adequately protected against improper disclosure. As indicated by Standard 16.3 of the *Standards for Educational and Psychological Testing,* unless otherwise required by law, informed consent of the test taker or his or her legal representative is needed to release test results by name of the examinee to any other person or institution.

Not only do examinees have the legal right of access to the findings in their own test reports, but they can arrange for transmittal of their test scores to educational, clinical, or counseling agencies for any appropriate use (Standard 16.4). At the same time, every effort must be exerted to maintain confidentiality of test scores and other personal information. The Family Educational Rights and Privacy Act of 1974 specifies, for example, that test results and other student records maintained by educational institutions receiving federal funds can be made available in a personally identifiable way to other people only with the written consent of the student or his or her parents. However, this act does permit parents and school personnel with a "legitimate educational interest" to review student records, as does Public Law 94–142 in the case of handicapped children.

Consultations and Conferences

A written report is only one way in which the results of a psychometric evaluation are communicated to those who have a legitimate right to know. Clinical-case conferences or consultations in mental health contexts, and parent-teacher or parent-counselor conferences in school settings, may occur both before and after a psychological evaluation. When conducting a post-testing conference with a person who is unsophisticated in psychological testing, such as a typical parent, the counselor should describe, in language appropriate to the listener, the test results and whatever conclusions can reasonably be drawn from them. In general, qualitative rather than quantitative descriptions and interpretations should be employed. The purpose and nature of the tests, why these particular tests were selected, and the limitations of the tests and results should also be discussed. Descriptive statements rather than labels and score ranges that take into account the standard error of measurement rather than specific scores should be used.

When reporting and explaining test results to examinees and/or their parents, facilities for counseling people who become emotionally upset during the consultation session should also be available. In any event, the consultation will involve the discussion of options and decisions—for treatment, remediation, rehabilitation, or other intervention—and information on referral sources will be provided. Following the consultation, the examiner will send a copy of the examination report to the referral source and other responsible individuals. The examiner should also retain a copy of the report and any notes from observations and interviews (see Standard 15.9 of *Standards for Educational and Psychological Testing*).

Summary

Personality assessment begins with a need to know something about personality in general or a certain personality in particular. Information obtained from personality assessments is useful in a variety of settings: clinical, educational, legal, medical, and employment. Following specification of the need(s), the assessment goals are established and decisions made concerning the kinds of data required to attain those goals.

The goals of personality assessment vary to some extent with the model—psychodynamic (psychodiagnostic), psychometric, or behavioristic—espoused by the assessor. Those who follow a psychodynamic model are more likely to favor projective techniques and other in-depth procedures; those of the psychometric persuasion make greater use of personality inventories and other measures of personality traits; behavioristic-oriented assessors place more emphasis on objectively observed and measured behavior.

In addition to observations and interviews, popular assessment procedures include projective tests (Rorschach, Thematic Apperception Test, Sentence Completion and Draw-A-Person tests, House-Tree-Person Test, Bender-Gestalt Test, Children's Apperception Test) and personality inventories such as the Minnesota Multiphasic Personality Inventory, the California Psychological Inventory and the 16 Personality Factor Questionnaire.

The ethical code of the American Psychological Association and the *Standards for Educational and Psychological Testing* serve as guides for constructing, evaluating, administering, and interpreting psychological assessment instruments. As indicating in the Standards, except in highly unusual circumstances examiners should follow the directions for administration, scoring, and interpretation printed in the manual accompanying a standardized test. Care must be taken not only in reading the test directions and presenting the test materials properly, but in arranging the testing environment—both physical and psychological—for the comfort and convenience of examinees.

It is a simple matter to administer an objective personality inventory or rating scale by computer, but interviewing and administering projective techniques are more difficult. Although test scoring is now done routinely with computerized scoring systems, handscoring of answer sheets is still commonplace. The scoring of projective techniques and other nonobjective instruments is a subjective process that can be greatly influenced by examiner biases and perceptions of demographic and other characteristics of examinees.

Interpreting the results of personality assessment is also a fairly subjective process, involving the integration of observational, interview, biographical, test, and other data sources to form a coherent picture of the examinee's personality dynamics and his or her areas of strength and weakness. The most extensive assessments entail a thorough case study of the individual, frequently for psychodiagnostic and other clinical purposes.

Psychodiagnosis consists of an analysis of psychological and physical symptoms to classify and label an individual as belonging in a particular psychiatric category. In the United States, the most widely used classification system for mental disorders is the one described in the revision of the third edition of the *Diagnostic and Statistical Manual* (DSM-III-R) of the American Psychiatric Association. Although DSM-III-R is probably an improvement over its predecessors, certain psychologists and psychiatrists emphasize the shortcomings and dangers of any sort of psychopathological labeling and the subjectivity of the process.

Numerous studies have shown that statistical (actuarial) prediction of behavior is superior to clinical (impressionistic) prediction. It is recognized that clinicians are needed to make judgments in collecting data on personality, but clinical judgments can be notoriously inaccurate when subject to preconceived notions, failure to give adequate consideration to base rates, the hindsight bias, and serious overconfidence in one's own judgments.

In preparing a report of personality assessment findings, the writer should avoid vague generalizations, stereotypes, and banalities. The report should address itself to the questions that need to be answered concerning the mental functioning and behavior of the examinee. It should also be as brief as possible, communicating efficiently but comprehensively and following the rules of syntax and good composition style. Growing in popularity, but still somewhat controversial, are computer-generated reports that attempt to integrate test and demographic data into a series of descriptive and diagnostic statements about an individual.

Whether psychological assessment findings are communicated in writing or orally, there are laws and legal sanctions governing the disclosure of this information. Psychological test data should be kept confidential and, with some exceptions, shared with other people only after the written consent of the examinee or his or her legal guardians or counsel has been obtained. This information may be communicated in a consultative conference, expressed in language that the conferees can understand and with the welfare of the examinee foremost in mind.

Exercises

1. Define each of the following terms in a sentence or two:

Aunt Fanny error	informed consent
Barnum effect	medical model
base rate	norm group
behavioristic model	overconfidence
clinical case study	preconceived notions
clinical judgment	prognosis
clinical prediction	psychodiagnosis
cognitive-behavioral	psychodiagnostic model
computer-prepared test	psychodynamic model
interpretation	psychometric model
confidentiality	rapport
hindsight bias	statistical prediction
impressionistic approach	

2. At the beginning of the chapter, seven settings in which personality assessments are made were described. Consider any three of these settings, and obtain as much information as you can on personality assessment instruments that are used to help make decisions about people in these settings and how the instruments are applied.

3. What are the differences between the psychodynamic, psychometric, and behavioristic models of assessing personality? What assessment instruments or procedures are emphasized by each of the three models, and what are their goals of application?

4. Why is it necessary to have an explicit code of ethics for the practice of psychology, considering the fact that psychologists are professional people who have the welfare of the public uppermost in mind and also scientists who eschew the exploitation of others in their search for the truth? In framing your answer, refer to the following publications of the American Psychological Association: *Ethical Principles of the American Psychological Association* (1981), *Standards for Educational and Psychological Testing* (1985), *Guidelines for Computer-Based Tests and Interpretations* (1986), *General Guidelines for Providers of Psychological Services* (1987).

5. Ask a clinical psychologist, psychiatrist, or medical librarian to let you examine a copy of the *Diagnostic and Statistical Manual of Mental Disorders* (Third Edition-Revised), and write a brief description of this system for classifying

mental disorders. In addition, summarize the descriptions given in DSM-III-R of the following disorders: anxiety disorders, delusional disorders, dissociation disorders, mood disorders, schizophrenia, somatoform disorders.

6. To what extent have your own judgments of people been affected by the four factors listed by Arkes (1985): (1) preconceived notions that you had about the person(s); (2) failure to give adequate consideration to base rates, that is, how common the perceived characteristics are in the general population; (3) the hindsight bias, or believing, in retrospect, that you could have predicted that a person would behave in such a manner; (4) overconfidence in the accuracy of your own judgments? In addition, how influential do you believe these factors are in selecting employees or students, in jury decisions, in the persistence of social prejudice, and in other nonclinical situations? Provide examples from your own observations and experiences.

7. Show the personality description on page 113 to several of your friends. How many agreed that it was a fairly accurate description of their personalities?

8. Most departments of psychology and education keep on file specimen sets of standardized rating scales, checklists, personality inventories, or other personality assessment instruments, including the instrument itself and associated descriptive and interpretive materials (administration manual, norms, etc.). Select an available personality assessment instrument, and prepare a review of it by following an outline such as the one given below. Whenever possible, fill in the outline with information obtained from reading the manual and examining the instrument itself. Do not consult a review of the test in the *Mental Measurements Yearbooks, Test Critiques,* or other sources before completing your own review.

Content. List the title, author(s), publisher, date and place of publication, forms available, type of assessment instrument, and cost. Give a brief description of the sections of the instrument, the kinds of items or materials of which it is composed, and the personality or behavioral characteristics it is supposed to measure. Describe how the instrument was constructed and whether the construction procedure and/or theory on which it is based are clearly described in the manual.

Administration and Scoring. Describe any special instructions, whether the assessment instrument is timed, and if so the time limits. Give details concerning scoring—as a whole, by sections or parts, and so on. Indicate whether the directions for administration and scoring are clear.

Norms. Describe the group(s) (composition, size, etc.) on which the instrument was standardized and how the samples were selected (systematic, stratified random, etc.). What kinds of norms are reported in the administration and scoring manual or in technical supplements? Does the standardization appear to have been adequate for the recommended uses of the instrument?

Reliability. Describe the kinds of reliability information reported in the manual (internal consistency, parallel forms, test-retest, etc.). Are the nature and sizes of the samples on which reliability information is reported adequate with respect to the stated uses of the instrument?

Validity. Summarize the available information on the validity (content, predictive, concurrent, construct) of the instrument reported in the manual. Is the validity information satisfactory in terms of the stated purposes of the instrument?

Summary Comments. Give a summary statement of the design and content of the assessment instrument, and comment briefly on its adequacy as a measure of whatever it was designed to measure. Does the manual include satisfactory descriptions of the design, content, norms, reliability, and validity of the instrument? What further information and/or data are needed to improve the instrument and its uses?

Suggested Readings

Aiken, L. R. (1980). Problems in testing the elderly. *Educational Gerontology, 5*, 119–124.

American Educational Research Association, American Psychological Association, & National Council on Measurement in Education (1985). *Standards for educational and psychological testing* (Chaps. 6, 7, 9, & 15). Washington, DC: Author.

Arkes, H. R. (1985). Clinical judgment. In R. J. Corsini (Ed.), *Encyclopedia of psychology* (Vol. 1, pp. 223–224). New York: Wiley.

Finn, S. E. (1982). Base rates, utilities, and DSM-III: Shortcomings of fixed-rule systems of psychodiagnosis. *Journal of Abnormal Psychology, 9*, 294–302.

Groth-Marnat, G. (1984). The psychological report. In *Handbook of psychological assessment* (pp. 346–407). New York: Van Nostrand Reinhold.

Hollis, J. W., & Donna, P. A. (1979). *Psychological report writings: Theory and practice.* Muncie, IN: Accelerated Development.

Kellerman, H., & Burry, A. (1981). *Handbook of psychodiagnostic testing* (Chaps. 14–15). Orlando, FL: Grune & Stratton.

Korchin, S. J., & Schuldberg, D. (1981). The future of clinical assessment. *American Psychologist, 36*, 1147–1158.

Matarazzo, J. D. (1986). Computerized clinical psychological test interpretations: Unvalidated plus all mean and no sigma. *American Psychologist, 41*, 14–24.

Matarazzo, J. D., & Pankratz, L. D. (1985). Diagnoses. In R. J. Corsini (Ed.), *Encyclopedia of psychology* (Vol. 1, pp. 369–372). New York: Wiley.

Moreland, K. L. (1985). Validation of computer-based test interpretations: Problems and proposals. *Journal of Consulting and Clinical Psychology, 53*, 816–825.

Endnotes

[1]In many of these settings, psychological assessments are conducted both before and after some treatment or other intervention is imposed in order to determine its effectiveness.

Assessments may also be conducted periodically (i.e., repeatedly) to monitor changes in a person as a result of natural or externally applied conditions.

[2]Psychological assessment specialists are also expected to be familiar with the *General Guidelines for Providers of Psychological Services* (American Psychological Association, 1987), "a set of aspirational statements for psychologists which encourage continual improvement in the quality of practice and service." (p. 2)

[3]Despite the fact that ability tests such as the Scholastic Aptitude Test and various intelligence tests are usually more psychometrically sound (more reliable, valid, etc.), the results of one survey of college students revealed that they believed that personality tests they had taken provided a more accurate portrayal of their personalities than intelligence tests gave of their mental abilities (Aiken & Romen, 1984).

PART II

Observing, Interviewing, and Rating

CHAPTER 5

Observations and Interviews

Observations and interviews, whether formal or informal, are the two oldest methods of assessment. Long before the invention of writing, people made judgments and evaluations of others by observing their behavior and talking with them. For example, oral examinations, during which both the examinee's statements and behavior were recorded, were used to evaluate governmental employees in ancient China and to test students in the Middle Ages at institutions such as Oxford University and the University of Bologna. Not until the nineteenth century did uniform testing with written essay examinations become the primary mode of evaluating academic achievement. And despite the progress made in mental measurement during the last century, observing and interviewing have retained their popularity in educational, employment, and clinical situations.

The methods of observation and interviewing are, of course, similar in that both procedures involve observing nonverbal and verbal behavior and drawing conclusions from the findings. The difference is that in interviewing the interviewer interacts with the person being observed (the interviewee), focusing primarily on the verbal responses made by the interviewee to a series of questions. By their very nature, interviews are typically more obtrusive than noninteractive observations since interviewees are keenly aware of being observed. The potential price to pay for the obtrusiveness of interviews is that interviewees may behave less naturally or be more inclined to role-play than if they did not know they were being observed. On the other hand, interviewing offers a greater opportunity than observation to obtain details on a person's thoughts, aspirations, attitudes, and other internal states, as well as information about the person's past behavior. Finally, there are advantages and disadvantages in the fact that both observations and interviews may impose less structure on the process of obtaining information and hence greater subjectivity in recording and interpreting responses than more standardized paper-and-pencil techniques.

Observations

Certainly the most widely employed and probably the most generally understood and accepted method of personality assessment is some form of observation. When using the method of observation, which is basic to all science, the observer simply takes note of events and perhaps makes a written record of what is observed. Whether aware of it or not, everyone engages in casual or informal observation of other people and events. Some perceptive individuals are better than others in observing and describing other people and in drawing conclusions and making predictions from these observations. The following quotation from the short story "Four Meetings" by Henry James illustrates how keenly a writer can observe people and provide detailed, graphic descriptions of his or her observations. "I saw her but four times, though I remember them vividly. She made an impression on me. Close upon thirty, by every presumption, she was made almost like a little girl and had the complexion of a child. She was artistic, I suspected. Her eyes were perhaps too round and too inveterately surprised, but her lips had a mild decision, and her teeth, when she showed them, were charming." Painstaking observation is also a tool or characteristic of individuals whose profession necessitates an in-depth understanding of other people, whether for the purpose of helping or manipulating them.

Uncontrolled and Controlled Observations

Although more systematic in their observations than the average layperson, psychological researchers and psychodiagnosticians also obtain much of their information about other people from the *uncontrolled observation* of behavior informally with no attempt to restrict it to a contrived situation or set of circumstances. Observing the activities of children on a playground and the behavior of people in a waiting line are illustrations of uncontrolled, naturalistic observation.

Observations can be uncontrolled and yet systematic and objective. For example, teachers can be trained to make objective observations of the behavior of schoolchildren and accurate records, *anecdotal records*, of whatever behavior seems significant. Realizing that when Johnny pulls Mary's hair it is not invariably an act of aggression, a well-trained teacher-observer indicates in the anecdotal record precisely what was observed and differentiates between the observation and the interpretation placed on it.

An illustration of uncontrolled observation in the world of work is the *critical incidents technique* (Flanagan, 1954). Supervisors and others who are familiar with a particular job are asked to identify specific behaviors that are critical to job performance or that distinguish between good and poor workers. These behaviors, or "incidents," are critical because they have either highly positive or highly negative consequences. Examples are "secures machinery and tidies up place of work when finished" and "follows up customers' requests promptly." Identification of a large number of such incidents supplies valuable information on the nature of the job and the requirements for effective performance.

In contrast to uncontrolled observation, *controlled observation* consists of observations made in prearranged, or contrived, situations, with the purpose of determining how people behave in those situations. For example, a developmental psychologist may arrange or structure a situation beforehand to determine if a child will cheat or behave honestly under a certain set of conditions. Or a psychological researcher may use a one-way mirror to observe the interaction between an adult and a child in a certain prearranged situation. The use of the one-way mirror, through which the researcher can see the interaction of the adult and child but they cannot see the researcher eliminates the reactive effects of the observer's presence on the behavior of the performers. People often find it difficult to behave naturally when they know they are being observed. They tend to behave as if they were on stage, engaging in role-playing to some extent. This reaction has been referred to as the *guinea pig effect*, the person perceiving herself or himself as a guinea pig in an experiment (Selltiz, Jahoda, Deutsch & Cook, 1959).

Participant Observation

Although people who are aware of being observed may tend, at least initially, to behave atypically, sometimes it is advantageous to have the observer interact with the individual who is being observed. In such *participant observation*, the observer becomes a part of the observational situation and can make observations at first hand and experience what it is like to be in the situation oneself. Participant observation has been used extensively by cultural anthropologists, so much so that at one time it was quipped that a typical aborigine family consisted of a mother, a father, two children, and a cultural anthropologist! Realizing that they must take into account the likelihood that the observer's own behavior will affect the responses of other people in the situation, proponents of participant observation maintain that active involvement in a real-life situation can provide insights unobtainable by other methods.

Clearly, both clinical interviewing and psychotherapy involve participant observation, in that the interviewer or therapist is not merely an impassive, inactive recorder of the interviewee's or patient's behavior but is dynamically involved in influencing the behavior of the interviewee/patient. Much of what is known about the dynamics of personality and mental disorder is the result of observations made by people in clinical settings. Obviously, this *clinical method* is not completely objective: not only does the therapist-observer affect the patient's behavior, but the patient also affects the reactions of the therapist. Consequently, the accuracy of clinical observations and the interpretations placed on them should be carefully checked by other observers and procedures. For example, to what extent does the following description provide a valid, specific picture of the child's behavior during the examination rather than reflecting the observer's own personality and preconceptions?

> Michael is an attractive child with long, straight brown hair and freckles. He seemed a bit anxious during the examination, squirming around in his chair, but not excessively. He tended to give up easily on more difficult tasks, and also showed other indications of a low frustration tolerance (sighing deeply, reluctant to attempt certain tasks). However, he was fairly cooperative during the examination and seemed mildly interested in the tasks; he showed signs of fatigue toward the end of the examination period. In general, he was attentive and energetic, answering questions briefly, but was not especially talkative. He did not smile during the entire time, and responded in a laconic, occasionally uncertain manner.

Notice that even the description by Henry James quoted previously contains as many elements of interpretation as objective observation, and it is not entirely clear where one ends and the other begins.

Situational Testing and Leaderless Group Discussion

A classic research study that used a controlled observation procedure known as *situational testing* was the Character Education Inquiry of Hartshorne and May (1928). In this series of investigations, children were surreptitiously given an opportunity to demonstrate their honesty, altruism, and other character traits. For example, to test the children's honesty, the investigators placed them in a situation where they could copy test answers, seemingly without being detected. Among the findings of the study were that older children, less intelligent children, children of lower socioeconomic status, and more emotionally unstable children tended to be less honest in all of the situations. Perhaps the most important outcome of the investigations was that honesty and other traits of character varied as much with the situation as with the individual. In other words, a child's honesty, altruism, and other character traits were typically highly dependent on the situation in which the child was observed.

Situational testing for military uses was introduced by the Germans and subsequently adapted by the British and American armed forces during World War II. A series of simulated situational tests administered by the U.S. Office of Strategic Services (OSS) was designed to select espionage agents, and, as in the Hartshorne and May (1928) studies, entailed deceiving the candidates. For example, in the "wall problem," a group of men was assigned the task of crossing a "canyon." Unknown to the real candidate, the men assigned to assist him were knowledgeable about the experiment. One of the *plants* acted obstructively by making unrealistic suggestions and insulting or worrisome remarks; another plant pretended not to understand the task and passively resisted directions from the candidate. The real candidate, not knowing that those assigned to help him were accomplices of the examiners, was observed during his efforts to complete the task in the face of these frustrating circumstances.

One interesting variation of situational testing is the *leaderless group discussion* (LGD) test, which has been used, for example, in the *assessment center approach* to select executive personnel. In this technique, a small group of examinees (typically 12 or fewer) is asked to discuss an assigned topic—say a specific administrative, political, or social problem—for a period of time (30 minutes to one hour). The performances of individual members of the group are rated by observers and the other examinees. It has been found that reliable ratings in the LGD situation are usually made in terms of three dimensions: ascendance, task facilitation, and sociability (Couch & Carter, 1953).

Despite their real-life quality, it has proven difficult to determine the effectiveness of situational testing procedures for selection purposes. Even in the OSS assessment program, examinees frequently realized that the test situations were contrived. For this and other reasons, the reliabilities and predictive validities of situational tests are usually rather low in comparison with their expense. For example, in another assessment context—the selection of clinical psychology students—situational testing proved to be of questionable validity (Kelly & Fiske, 1951).

Self-Observation and Content Analysis

Self-observation, which most people typically do to some extent, is an appealing data-collection method in both research and clinical contexts. The appeal of the method lies in both its economy and the fact that it is the only way to get at private mental events such as thoughts and feelings. A problem with self-observations is that they are likely to be even more biased than observations made by others; people are seldom entirely objective in describing their own thoughts and behavior (Wolff & Merrens, 1974). However, as with observations made by others, people can be trained to make more objective, systematic observations of themselves (Thoreson & Mahoney, 1974). Thus, they can learn to distinguish what they are actually feeling, thinking, or doing from what they should or would like to feel, think, or do.

By keeping a continuous written record of one's thoughts, feelings, and actions, a wealth of self-observational data can be accumulated. Unfortunately, it is not always clear what to do with such an abundance of data—how it should be analyzed and interpreted? As seen in the *content analysis* of diaries, autobiographies, letters, drawings, and other personal documents, important insights into personality and behavior can be gained from interpreting self-observational data (Allport, 1965). But the complexity and laboriousness of content analysis have kept this interpretative approach from being applied routinely in clinical or other applied contexts.

A detailed content analysis involves specifying the objectives of the analysis, locating pertinent data, collecting contextual evidence, developing a detailed sampling plan, and devising appropriate data coding procedures (Borg & Gall, 1983). Computer programs have been written to facilitate the process of content analysis, the most widely used one being the General Inquirer (Stone et al., 1962). These programs process the material by systematically identifying instances of words (nouns, verbs, adjectives, etc.) and phrases (e.g., statements expressing negative, positive, or neutral feelings) specified by the investigator. The program determines their frequency of occurrence, prints and graphs the frequencies, conducts statistical analyses of the data, and classifies the words and phrases to determine the extent to which they fit a particular classificatory model.

Improving the Accuracy of Observations

One of the chronic problems of observational methods is that of objectivity. Consequently, a number of special procedures have been recommended for improving the objectivity and accuracy of observations. Because time frequently plays tricks on memory, it is better to record observed events immediately rather than retrospectively. Immediate recording can be facilitated by the use of a standard observation form or schedule, such as those described by Simon and Boyer (1974). Video and/or audio recordings are also helpful when they are not obtrusive. A more recent technique, computer-assisted observation, can assist not only in recording and transcribing observational events, but, with the proper equipment, transfer the observed data from coding sheets into computer storage, clean up the data, analyze it, and interpret the results. An example of an observation-recording device that can be used in conjunction with a computer is the Behavioral Event Recording Package (BERP), a multichannel event-recording and data-storage device designed to record and time ten independent observational events (Borg & Gall, 1983).

In addition to forms and machines for recording observations, methodological procedures such as subject sampling, time sampling, and incident (event) sampling have proven useful in increasing the objectivity and efficiency of observations. Before beginning a clinical or research investigation involving observational procedures, the investigator must make a number of decisions, foremost among them are what, how, when, and where the observations are to be made, and who is to be observed. With respect to the last question, that of subject sampling, it is obviously impractical to observe everyone who might possess the characteristics in which one is interested. Consequently, a representative sample of the pool of potential subjects must be selected. However, even a relatively small sample of subjects cannot be observed all the time. Continuous observation of the behavior of a single person yields a voluminous amount of data, not all of which is significant or pertinent to the clinical or research questions. For this reason, it is usually wise to focus on a limited number of specific, predetermined incidents or *target behaviors*. Then a manageable but representative number of those behaviors is observed. For example, a certain target behavior may consist of incidents of aggression. Then the frequency and duration of objectively defined occurrences of aggression may be recorded. In addition to this *incident sampling* procedure, the efficiency of observation may also be improved by *time sampling*, or interval recording, that is, making a series of observations lasting only a few minutes each over a period of a day or so.

Training Observers

Special procedures and devices such as those listed above are helpful in improving the accuracy of observations, but perhaps even more critical is the training of human observers to be as perceptive and objective as possible. People typically filter their observations through their own personal biases and needs. Consequently, untrained observers usually have a great deal of difficulty making accurate observations and separating observation from interpretation or fact from opinion.

The training of observers begins by describing the form or schedule on which the observations are to be made, going over the objective definition of each target behavior and how its occurrence and duration are to be recorded. Common errors made in recording behaviors and the importance of not letting one's own biases, expectancies, personality, attitudes, or desires interfere with what is observed are emphasized. Observers must be aware of the effects of their own biases, backgrounds, and behaviors on what is being observed, and the tendency to confuse fact with interpretation.

Because previous knowledge about the individuals being observed may lead observers to assume or expect that the former should behave in a certain manner, observers must be given only that information that they absolutely need about the individuals they are observing. In addition, to minimize the bias in observations created by a desire to provide the researcher or supervisor with supporting data, observers should be given minimal information concerning the purposes of the research project and no details on the specific hypotheses or expected outcomes. When the observer is visible to the person(s) being observed, the former should be cautioned to remain as unobtrusive and unreactive as possible, staying in the background and recording what is seen and heard without any undue display or emotion, approval or disapproval. Observer-trainees should also be given an opportunity to practice or role-play their observational activities and have their performance critiqued before going into the field or laboratory to make *bona fide* observations. Finally, in the interest of greater reliability, two or more observers are better than one, and defining the behaviors to be observed as specifically as possible is better than using general descriptive observational categories.

Nonverbal Behavior

Most people realize that interpersonal communication is not entirely verbal, but they are usually unaware of the extent to which movements of the hands, feet, eyes, and mouth, as well as body posture and tone of voice are interpreted as messages. Sigmund Freud (1905) was cognizant of these nonverbal cues: "He that has eyes to see and ears to hear may convince himself that no mortal can keep a secret. If his lips are silent, he chatters with his fingertips; betrayal oozes out of him at every pore" (p. 94).

During the past 25 years or so, a great deal of research interest has been shown in *nonverbal behavior*. According to the findings of one investigation (Mehrabian & Weiner, 1967), 65 to 90% of the meaning of interpersonal communications comes from nonverbal cues. Studies of both expert (Dittmann, 1962) and nonexpert (Ekman, 1965a, 1965b) evaluators of behavior reveal that interpretations of nonverbal messages are often quite reliable. For example, the following body movements have been found to be reliably associated with the corresponding emotions (Mahl, 1968; Ekman & Friesen, 1968):

> Moderate scratching and rubbing of the nose—depression
> Playing with one's wedding ring—feelings of marital conflict
> Movements of the hands—feelings about the self
> Movements of the feet—anger, annoyance, and irritation

Kinesics   Certain kinds of nonverbal cues are more important than others in message transmissions. Particularly significant are *kinesics*, which are movement of small (*microkinesics*) or large (*macrokinesics*) body parts. Also of interest are the kinesic cues obtained from eye contact and gaze. Among the findings on this topic are (Bernard & Huckins, 1978, pp. 420–421):

1. Eye contact may be used by dependent individuals to communicate positive attitudes to, and to elicit positive attitudes from, others. Eye contact almost can establish an obligation to interact.

2. Individuals who are looked at most tend to be perceived and tend to perceive themselves as possessing group power and status.

3. Dominant people speak more and look less. Long gazers, however, tend to be seen as more dominant than senders of short glances.

4. Extroverts look more frequently. Their percentage of gaze is greater and their glances are longer.

5. People tend to maximize eye contact with communicants of moderately high social status. They respond to high status with a moderate amount of looking, and they spend the shortest time of all with those of low social status.

6. Eye contact may increase or decrease with psychological distance. That is, when people are too close, they look less. When they are farther away (i.e., from three to ten feet), they look more.

7. Amount of gaze varies with degree of topic intimacy. The more intimate the topic, the less gaze.

8. When persons communicate to deceive others, they usually look less.

9. Glances are used for synchronizing conversation. If the speaker does not look at the listener when about to conclude an utterance, the latter lacks permission to speak. When the listener looks away, the speaker is notified that he or she has talked long enough and that the listener is getting ready for his or her turn. (pp. 420–421)

Proximics   Another class of nonverbals is *proximics*, which refers to the distance zone between communicators (personal space or territoriality). Hall (1969) grouped communication distances into four categories: intimate distance (0 to 18 inches), personal distance (18 inches to 4 feet), social distance (4 to 12 feet), and public distance (12 feet and over). When two people are situated at an *intimate distance*, they can touch or make other physical contact easily. Verbalization is relatively unimportant at this distance because messages can be sent and received by all the senses. *Personal distance* is approximately the same as personal space, the kind of invisible territorial bubble that an individual carries around from place to place. The extremes of this distance are too great for discussing personal topics and becoming mutually involved. People spend most of their time and are usually most comfortable at a *social distance* of 4 to 12 feet. It is easy to keep from becoming personally involved and to get away at this distance. Of course, social distance varies with culture, social relationships, sex, age, and other factors. Personal involvement does not occur at all at the *public distance* of 12 feet or more. The topics discussed are usually formal or impersonal at this distance, being limited to what can be seen and heard.

Paralinguistics   A third class of nonverbal message transmitters is *paralinguistics*, which includes tone of voice, rate of speaking, and other nonverbal aspects of speech. Five categories of paralinguistic cues and the emotions reportedly communicated by cue dimension are as follows (Scherer, 1974):

Amplitude variation (moderate to extreme)—pleasantness, activity, happiness, fear

Pitch variation (moderate to extreme)—anger, boredom, disgust, fear, pleasantness, activity, happiness, surprise

Pitch contour (down to up)—pleasantness, boredom, sadness, potency, anger, fear, surprise

Pitch level (low to high)—pleasantness, boredom, sadness, activity, potency, anger, fear, surprise

Tempo (slow to fast)—boredom, disgust, sadness, pleasantness, activity, potency, anger, fear, happiness, surprise

The relationship of culture and proximics—the fact that people in certain cultures stand closer when conversing than people in other cultures—was referred to earlier. Culture also affects mode of dress, eating habits, postures, and a wealth of other nonverbal behaviors that convey specific messages to those who are familiar with the cultures. These habits or behaviors are collectively referred to as *culturics*. Western visitors to non-Western countries might save themselves considerable grief and embarrassment by becoming familiar not only with the culturics of the country but also with the kinesic, proximic, and paralinguistic communications characteristics of the culture. For example, joining the forefinger and thumb is interpreted differently in the United States ("okay"), Japan ("okane" or money), and Mexico ("You're a dirty name!").

Interpretive Accuracy   Although most people probably succeed more often than not in interpreting nonverbal messages in their own culture correctly, mistakes do occur. The poker-faced gambler and the glad-handed sales representative or politician are renowned for their ability to deceive others with nonverbal behavior. I once interviewed a mental patient who refused to speak to me at first. After sitting quietly for a time, during which neither of us spoke (I was determined to remain silent until he responded to my previous question.), he unexpectedly asked: "Why do you want to kick me out of here?" Somewhat surprised, I looked at my crossed legs and observed that my right foot was moving back and forth. Although the patient interpreted this foot movement as my desire to get rid of him, on reflection I realized that it was I who wanted to leave and the foot movement was an implicit walking out of the room on my part! In any event, such nonverbal messages are often a better reflection of the truth than a person's verbalizations. It is considered easier to lie or distort one's true feelings by word of mouth than by body movements.

The PONS   Nonverbal behaviors and characteristics (*nonverbals*) are interpreted more accurately when the observer has some knowledge of the specific situation or context in which the behavior occurs. In addition, some people are better than others at interpreting nonverbals, although the ability does not appear to be related to intelligence. Research findings do indicate, however, that sensitivity to nonverbal messages is associated with personality. Rosenthal et al. (1979) devised a test, the Profile of Nonverbal Sensitivity (PONS), consisting of a 45-minute film in which viewers are presented with a series of scenes such as facial expressions or spoken phrases heard as tones or sounds but not as words. After each scene is presented, the viewer selects one of two appropriate descriptive labels. The authors of the PONS report that men and women who score high on the test tend to have fewer friends but warmer, more honest, and more satisfying sexual relationships than those who score low.

Reasoning that sensitivity to nonverbal messages is an important ability for diplomats to possess, David McClelland used the PONS in an applicant screening program for the U.S. Information Agency (USIA). Short taped segments from the test were played to USIA job applicants, who were then asked to indicate what emotion was being expressed. It was discovered that applicants who scored high on the PONS were considered significantly more competent by their colleagues than those who scored low (Rosenthal et al., 1979, pp. 304–306).

Another contribution to the assessment of nonverbal behavior is the Facial Action Coding System (FACS) by P. Ekman and W. V. Friesen (Consulting Psychologists Press, 1978). Designed as a method for objectively describing and measuring facial expressions, the FACS consists of material (photographs, films, etc.) for training observers in scoring dozens of facial Action Units. Also useful in training observers to judge emotion from facial expressions are the Pictures of Facial Affect by W. V. Friesen and P. Ekman (Consulting Psychologists Press, 1975), consisting of 110 black-and-white pictures expressing fear, anger, happiness, sadness, surprise, or disgust (plus a neutral expression).

Observations for Behavior Modification

Behavior modification is a technical term for a set of psychotherapeutic procedures, based on learning theory and research, designed to change inappropriate behavior to more personally and/or socially accepted behavior. Inappropriate behaviors may consist of excesses, deficits, or other inadequacies of action that are correctable through behavioral techniques such as systematic desensitization, counterconditioning, and extinction. To assess the effectiveness of any of these techniques in modifying the behavior in question, a *baseline* (operant) level of the frequency and/or intensity of the behavior is determined before the technique is applied. The baseline results may then be compared with the incidence or strength of the behavior after the technique has been applied to determine whether there has been any improvement.

Among the maladaptive behaviors that have received special attention by behavior modifiers are specific fears (or phobias), smoking, overeating, alcoholism, drug addiction, underassertiveness, bedwetting, chronic tension and pain, and sexual inadequacies of various kinds. Whatever the *target behaviors* or responses may be, they should be defined precisely and occur with sufficient frequency to be recordable and modifiable. Although target behaviors have typically been rather narrowly defined, behavior therapists of a more cognitive inclination have also tackled less specific problems such as negative self-concept and identity crisis. Furthermore, the target behaviors consist not only of nonverbal movements but also of verbal reports of thoughts and feelings.

In contrast to the dynamic approaches of psychoanalysis, trait-factor theories, and to some extent phenomenology, behavior therapists have attempted to under-stand behavior by studying the antecedents, including both its social learning history and current environment, and the results or consequences of that behavior. A basic tenet of behavior modification, adopted from operant learning theory, is that behav-ior is controlled by its consequences. Therefore, to design a program for correcting problem behavior one must identify the reinforcing consequences that sustain the behavior, in addition to the conditions that precede and trigger it. Following this approach, the process of behavior modification is preceded by a *functional analysis* of the problem behavior(s), consisting of an A-B-C sequence in which A stands for the *antecedent conditions*, B the problem behavior, and C the *consequences* of that behavior; B is modified by controlling for A and changing C. The antecedents and consequences of the target behavior may be either overt, objectively observable conditions or covert mental events reported by the person whose behavior is to be modified.

A variety of procedures are used in analyzing or assessing the antecedents and consequences of behavior. Among these procedures, which vary with the specific therapeutic methods and goals, are observations, interviews, checklists, rating scales, and questionnaires completed by the patient or a person acquainted with him or her. On occasion behavior modifiers have even used projective techniques, employing the responses as samples of behavior (see Maloney & Ward, 1976).

The observational procedures used in a behavior analysis involve taking note of the frequency and duration of the target behaviors and the particular contingen-cies (antecedents and consequences) of their occurrence. Depending on the context and the age of the patient, behavioral observations can be made and recorded by teachers, parents, nurses, nursing assistants, or any person acquainted with the patient. For example, diagnoses of psychopathology can be facilitated by observa-tions made by nurses and psychiatric aids of the behavior of patients on the ward. Rating scales such as the Nurses' Observation Scale for Inpatient Evaluation (NOSIE-30) (Honigfeld & Klett, 1965) and the Ward Behavior Inventory (Burdock et al., 1968) are useful devices for assessing patients' aggressive, communicative, and cooperative behaviors as well as other behaviors and appearance.

Perhaps the easiest and most economical way of determining how frequently and under what circumstances a particular target behavior occurs is self-observation. As noted earlier in the chapter, although self-observation is not always reliable, people can be trained to make accurate and valid observations of their own behavior (Kendall & Norton-Ford, 1982). In self-observation, for purposes of behavioral analysis and modification, the person is instructed to carry with him or her at all times materials such as index cards, a notepad, a wrist counter, and a timer to keep a record of occurrences of the target behavior and the time, place, and circumstances under which it occurs. This self-observational procedure, referred to as *self-monitoring*, can be fairly reliable when the patient is carefully trained. Interestingly enough, the very process of self-monitoring—observing and tabulating occurrences of specific behaviors in which one engages—can affect the occurrence of those behaviors, sometimes in a therapeutic way (Ciminero, Nelson & Lipinski, 1977). For example, a heavy smoker may find himself smoking less when he has to keep track of how often and how long he smokes. Other assessment procedures and instruments used in analyzing behavior for purposes of behavior modification are discussed in the next section and the next chapter.

Interviews

Interviewing is one of the oldest and most widely used methods of personality assessment. Not only does it yield much of the same kind of behavioral information as observation, but information on what a person says as well as what he or she does is obtained. The interviewee's nonverbal behavior, including body postures and poise, gestures, eye movements, and the quality and pattern of speech, are important and should be noted. The major emphasis in interviewing is, however, on the content of verbal statements made by the interviewee. For this reason, the interview may be defined as a "face-to-face verbal interchange in which one person, the interviewer, attempts to elicit information or expressions of opinion or belief from another person or persons" (Maccoby & Maccoby, 1954, p. 449). The information obtained in interviews consists of details of the interviewee's background or life-history, in addition to data on feelings, attitudes, perceptions, and expectations that are not usually observable.

Successful interviewing is not an easy task; it requires skill and sensitivity and may be quite time consuming and laborious. It is as much an art as a science, and some individuals are more effective than others in putting interviewees at ease or establishing rapport. The approach of the interviewer varies with the purpose and context of the interview, but, as in any interpersonal situation, the personality and actions of both participants influence the outcomes. Thus, an interview is not a one-way, master-slave situation in which the interviewer remains unaffected; in almost every case it is a dynamic, two-way interchange in which the participants mutually influence each other. Not only do the actions of the interviewer affect the behavior of the interviewee, but the latter's own responses can shape the behavior of the former.

The interview can be an end in itself, but it may also function as a way to get acquainted or warm up, a lead-in to other assessment procedures. Most clinical and counseling psychologists like the face-to-face closeness of the interview because it enables them to get a feel for the patient or client and his or her problems and coping abilities. They, together with personnel psychologists, employment counselors, and other interviewers, usually justify the time and expense of the interview by their belief that private information of the sort obtained in this way is not available by any other means. Finally, patients, counselees, and applicants usually express feelings of being more involved when interviewed than when they are merely asked to fill out paper-and-pencil questionnaires or applications and are not given an opportunity to communicate their problems, needs, opinions, and circumstances in person.

Interviewing Techniques and Structure

A personal interview can take place anywhere, but it is usually better to conduct it in a quiet room that is free from distractions. Both the interviewer and interviewee should be comfortably seated facing each other. Because interviewing is a complex interpersonal skill that is to some extent a function of the interviewer's personality, effective interviewing is not easily taught. Attention to the following recommendations, however, can improve one's interviewing skills.

Professional interviewers are usually friendly but neutral, interested but not prying in reacting to the interviewee; they are warm and open, and they nonjudgmentally accept the interviewee for what he or she is without showing approval or disapproval. They do not begin with leading questions of the "How often do you beat your wife?" type, or ask questions that imply a certain answer, "You still do that, don't you?" By properly timing the questions and varying their content with the situation, effective interviewers are able to develop a conversation that flows from topic to topic. But they are also comfortable with silences, allowing the interviewee sufficient time to answer a question completely, and listening to the answer without interrupting. In addition, they pay attention not only to what the interviewee says but also the manner in which it is said. Realizing that the interviewer's behavior (activity level, amount and speed of talking, etc.) tends to be imitated by the interviewee, interviewers are patient and comfortable and do not hurry the inteviewee. Skilled interviewers also check their understandings, impressions, and perceptions of the interviewee's statements by asking for clarification or repetition. They may rephrase the interviewee's answers to clarify them, making certain that they do not misunderstand, or ask direct questions to fill in the gaps. They are, however, not voyeurs who unremittingly probe or relish the discussion of certain topics and consciously or unconsciously reinforce the interviewee's statements pertaining to those matters.

Although the effective interviewing behaviors described above are generally applicable, specific techniques vary with the theoretical orientation (behavioral, client-centered, psychoanalytic, etc.) of the interviewer, as well as the goals and stage of the interview. Most interviewers outside of clinical contexts, as well as many clinicians, are fairly eclectic in their orientation, following no particular theory of personality but applying relevant concepts from a variety of theories.

Structured versus Unstructured Interviews The degree to which an interview is structured should depend primarily on the goals of the interview, but it is also important to consider the interviewee and interviewer. Some interviewees respond more readily to a relatively unstructured, open-ended approach; others supply more relevant information when the interview follows an *interviewing guide* and is quite consistent in the questions posed. In addition, certain interviewers feel more comfortable and accomplish more using the highly structured procedure of asking a series of questions similar to those found on an application blank or personal history form. Less experienced interviewers typically find it easier to handle a *structured* *interview*, the results of which can be reliably quantified for purposes of analysis. They tend to feel more comfortable with a standard set of questions of the sort prepared by Spitzer et al. (1964). On the other hand, many experienced interviewers prefer greater flexibility in the content and timing of interview questions, in other words, less structure. Perhaps the most unstructured interview of all begins with a question such as "Will you tell me about yourself?"

It requires more skill and time to conduct an *unstructured interview*, but the interviewer can follow up interesting leads or concentrate on details that seem significant. To accomplish this, the interviewer encourages the interviewee to feel free to discuss his or her problems, interests, behaviors, or whatever else appears relevant to the goals of the interview. Those goals also affect the amount of structure used in an interview. When answers to a large number of specific questions are needed, as in employment selection situations, then a fairly structured interview is appropriate. When the goal is to obtain an in-depth picture of the individual's personality, or to define the nature of certain problems and their causes, a more unstructured interview is called for. Whether highly structured or relatively open-ended, the sequence of questions in an interview should usually proceed from the general to the specific and from less personal to more personal topics.

Most professional interviewers are able to vary their approach with the personality of the interviewee and the objectives of the interview. They begin by asking a series of nonthreatening, open-ended questions to establish rapport and get the conversation going, and then become more specific in their questioning as the interview proceeds.

Interview Topics and Questions The specific questions asked depend on the purposes of the interview, but it is helpful to plan for an interview by outlining the topics to be covered if not the specific questions to be asked. A general topical outline for an interview designed for a comprehensive assessment of personality is given in in the list below. A complete life-history interview, whether conducted in a clinical, social service, employment, or research situation, requires obtaining the kinds of information listed below. Not all of these topics need be covered in a specific situation; the interviewer can concentrate on those areas that are considered most important. In any event, the specific interview questions, framed in language with which the interviewee is familiar and comfortable, can be developed from the following outline.

General Outline for Assessment Interview

1. *Identifying Data*: name, age, sex, education, ethnic group, nationality, address, date of birth, marital status, date of interview, and so forth.
2. *Purpose of Interview*: employment, psychiatric intake, psychodiagnostic, problem solving or troubleshooting, performance evaluation, termination or exit.

3. *Physical Appearance:* clothing, grooming, physical description (attractiveness, unusual features, etc.), obvious or apparent physical disorders or disabilities.
4. *Behavior:* attitudes and emotions (cooperative, outgoing or reserved, friendly or hostile, defensive, etc.); motoric behavior (active versus passive, posture, gait, carriage); level of intellectual functioning (bright, average, retarded—estimated from vocabulary, immediate and long-term memory, judgment, abstract thinking); signs of mental disorder (distorted thought processes—bizarre constructions, thought blocking, etc.; distorted perceptions—delusions, hallucinations, disorientation in time or space, etc.; inappropriate or extreme emotional reactions—depression, mania; unusual mannerisms, postures, or facial expressions).
5. *Family:* parents, siblings, other family members; sociocultural group; attitude(s) toward family members.
6. *Medical History:* present health, health history, physical problems.
7. *Developmental History:* Physical, intellectual, language, emotional, and social development; irregularities or problems of development.
8. *Education and Training:* schools attended, performance level, adjustment to school, plans for further education and training.
9. *Employment:* nature and number of jobs or positions held, military service (rank and duties), job performance level(s), job problems.
10. *Legal Problems:* arrests and convictions, nature of misdemeanors or felonies.
11. *Sexual and Marital History:* sexual activities and problems, marriages, marital problems, separations and divorce(s), children.
12. *Interests and Attitudes:* hobbies, recreational activities, social activities and attitude(s) toward others, level of self-acceptance and satisfaction, aspirations or goals.
13. *Current Problems:* details of current problems and plans for solving them.

Clinical Interviews

Interviews are used in various contexts and for a wide range of purposes. In research contexts, they are used for polling, surveys, and to obtain in-depth information on personality and behavior to test some hypothesis or theoretical proposition. In employment situations, interviews are used for selection and screening, evaluation or appraisal, troubleshooting, and termination. In clinical contexts, intake interviews of patients and their relatives are essential in collecting case histories for making medical and/or psychological diagnoses (diagnostic interviews). In addition, there are therapeutic interviews that are a part of the psychological treatment process and exit interviews designed to determine whether an institutionalized individual is ready to be released.

In clinical interviews conducted for intake purposes at a social agency or mental hospital, in diagnostic interviews to determine the causes and correlate of an individual's problems, and in therapeutic interviews (counseling, psychotherapy), it is recommended that, among other things, the interviewer

1. assures the interviewee of confidentiality of the interview;
2. conveys a feeling of interest and warmth (rapport);
3. tries to put the interviewee at ease;
4. tries to "get in touch" with how the interviewee feels (empathy);
5. is courteous, patient, and accepting;
6. encourages the interviewee to express his or her thoughts and feelings freely;
7. adjusts the questions to the cultural and educational background of the interviewee;
8. avoids psychiatric or psychological jargon;
9. avoids leading questions;
10. shares personal information and experiences with the interviewee (self-disclosure) if appropriate and timed accurately;
11. uses humor sparingly, and only if appropriate and not insulting;
12. listens without overreacting emotionally;
13. attends not only to what is said but also to how it is said;
14. and takes notes or makes a recording as inconspicuously as possible.

Of course, many of these recommendations are not restricted to clinical interviews.

When conducted properly, a diagnostic or therapeutic interview can provide a great deal of information about the interviewee: the nature, duration, and severity of his or her problems, how the problems are manifested (inwardly or outwardly), what past influences are related to present difficulties, the interviewee's resources and limitations for coping with the problems, the kinds of psychological assistance the interviewee has had in the past, and what kinds of assistance are expected and might be of help now.

In many instances, structured diagnostic interviewing can be made less difficult, as well as more objective and efficient, by using a standard form such as the Psychiatric Diagnostic Interview (PDI) by E. Othmer, E. C. Penick, and B. J. Powell (Western Psychological Services, 1981). Based on the clinical criteria of DSM-III (see Chapter 4), the PDI can be administered by a psychologist, a psychiatrist, or a trained and supervised technician, to a normal person in 15 to 30 minutes or to an individual having two or more psychiatric syndromes in about one hour. From the interviewee's yes or no responses to a series of questions pertaining to basic psychiatric syndromes, the PDI reveals whether the interviewee has, or has ever had, any of 15 major psychiatric disorders or one of three combination syndromes. Another widely used clinical interview questionnaire is the Present State Examination by J. K. Wing, J. E. Cooper, and N. Sartorius (Cambridge University Press,

1967–1974). This form requires rating psychiatric symptoms reported by the patient as having occurred during the preceding months. The ratings are scored by computer on 38 psychiatric syndromes.

Mental Status Interview   A special type of diagnostic interview known as a *mental status interview* is used in both clinical and legal contexts to determine the mental competence of an individual for legal and psychiatric purposes. A mental status interview is designed to obtain in-depth information about the interviewee's emotional state (affect and mood), intellectual and perceptual functioning (attention, concentration, memory, intelligence, judgment), style and content of thought processes and speech, level of insight into his or her mental status and personality problems, psychomotor activity, as well as the patient's general appearance, attitude, and insight into his or her condition. The categories covered and examples from a report on an interview of the mental status of a particular patient are given in Table 5–1.

Illustrative interview and observational schedules or questionnaires employed in mental status examinations are listed in Appendix D. Related instruments include the Brief Psychiatric Rating Scale (Overall & Klett, 1972), Missouri Automated Mental Status Examination Checklist (Hedlund, Sletton, Evenson, Altman & Cho, 1977), Missouri Automated Psychiatric History (Eaton, Sletton, Kitchen & Smith, 1971), and Mini-Mental Status Examination (Folstein, Folstein & McHugh, 1975). Examples of instruments with a more symptom-specific orientation are The Dementia Scale (Blessed, Tomlinson & Roth, 1968) and the Hamilton Depression Scale (Hamilton, 1960). The instruments described in Appendix D are basically highly structured interviews requiring little clinical experience as long as the interviewer has been adequately trained in how to complete the particular schedule. For example, the Schedule for Affective Disorders and Schizophrenia (SADS) consists of a series of questions concerning the interviewee's background, psychological disturbances, and specific occurrences of abnormal behavior. Not all of the questions need be asked; a branching procedure enables the interviewer to skip certain questions depending on the interviewee's answers to other questions. In any event, after completing the schedule, the interviewer makes a diagnostic decision depending on the specific answers given.

Computer Interviewing   Structured psychodiagnostic interviewing can be automated by storing a set of questions and instructions in a computer. The computer presents a series of questions concerning the past history, present illness, and mental functioning on a screen; the examinee responds by typing an answer, which is recorded by the computer. Although more difficult to program than a structured interview, computer-controlled, semi-structured interviews have been devised so that, after asking a question and receiving the interviewee's response, the computer decides what question to ask next. Technically this is called *conditionally branching* (Kleinmuntz & McLean, 1968; Kleinmuntz, 1982, pp. 199–207). Representa-

	Table 5–1

**Categories and Examples from
Report of a Mental Status Interview**

Category	Example of Report
General appearance, attitude, and behavior	He is friendly and cooperative. Has made no complaints about ward restrictions. He smiles in a somewhat exaggerated and grotesque manner.
Discourse	He answers in a deep loud voice, speaking in a slow, precise, and somewhat condescending manner. His responses are relevant but vague.
Mood and affective fluctuations	His facial expressions, although not totally inappropriate, are poorly correlated with subject of discourse or events in his environment.
Sensorium and intellect	The patient's orientation to place, person, and time is normal. His remote and recent memory also are normal. Two brief intelligence measures indicate about average intelligence.
Mental content and specific preoccupations	He readily discusses what he calls his "nervous trouble." He complains of "bad thoughts" and a "conspiracy." He reports hearing voices saying, "Hello, Bill, you're a dirty dog."
Insight	The patient readily accepts the idea that he should be in the hospital. He feels that hospitalization will help him get rid of these "bad" thoughts. He is not in the least defensive about admitting to auditory and visual hallucinations or to the idea that everyone on earth is his enemy.

Based on Kleinmuntz, 1982, 1985. Reprinted by permission of Robert Krieger Publishing Company.

tive of the available computer software packages for psychological interviewing and report preparation are the Psychological/Psychiatric Status Interview and the Psychological/Social History Report (both available from Slosson Educational Publications, Inc.), the Diagnostic Interview for Children and Adolescents (available from Multi-Health Systems, Inc.), and the Giannetti On-Line Psychosocial History (GOLPH) (available from National Computer Systems). The first of these packages is designed for an initial psychological or psychiatric interview, and the second for a structured, psychological, intake interview. The third and fourth packages conduct diagnostic interviews structured according to DSM-III (see Chapter 4).

Among the advantages of *computer interviews* are savings in professional time, broader coverage of topics, greater flexibility than rigid questionnaires, and greater reliability than person-to-person interviews. In general, a high degree of agreement has been obtained between the information provided by computer interviews and that elicited from standard psychiatric interviews and questionnaires (Lucas et al., 1977). Furthermore, being interviewed by a computer is not objectionable to most people. On the other hand, it is somewhat expensive and has certain other disadvantages, including the need to abbreviate or bypass the system in crisis cases, limited utility with children and adults of low mental ability, and insufficient flexibility for use with the wide range of problems and symptoms found in psychiatric patients (Haynes, 1984). Other potential disadvantages of computer interviews include the fact that they have difficulty with anything other than structured, verbal information and that they are unable to tailor the wording of questions (Erdman, Klein & Greist, 1985).

Behavioral Interviews   A *behavioral interview* is a type of clinical interviewing that focuses on obtaining information to plan a behavior modification program. As discussed earlier in the chapter, this entails describing, in objective behavioral terms, the problem behaviors of the interviewee as well as their antecedent conditions and reinforcing consequences. To conduct such an interview successfully, the interviewee must be encouraged (and taught if necessary) to respond in specific behavioral terms rather than in the more customary language of motives or traits. After obtaining the necessary information to develop a behavior modification program, the program must then be explained to the client and he or she motivated to follow it.

Stress Interviewing   The usual role of cordiality toward the interviewee is suspended in a *stress interview*. The goal of stress interviewing, which is used in clinical, selection, and interrogation contexts, may be to determine the interviewee's ability to cope or solve a specific problem under conditions of emotional stress. Stress interviewing may also be appropriate when time is short or when the interviewee is very repetitive, emotionally unresponsive, or quite defensive. An attempt is made to produce a valid emotional response—to get beneath the superficial social mask (*persona*) of the interviewee—by asking probing, challenging questions in a kind of police interrogation atmosphere. A great deal of professional expertise is obviously required in order to make a stress interview appear realistic and not let it get out of control.

Methode Clinique and Morality Research   The clinical method of interviewing in which the interviewer asks probing questions to test the limits or obtain in-depth information about a person has been employed extensively in research by Sigmund Freud, Jean Piaget, and many other famous psychologists. In fact, most of Freud's theoretical conceptions concerning the nature of human personality were obtained by interviewing only about a hundred patients. The use of clinical interviewing in research, referred to as the *methode clinique*, requires considerable skill.

An example of a research instrument involving the use of the methode clinique is Lawrence Kohlberg's Moral Judgment Scale. Kohlberg (1969, 1974) maintains that the development of personal morality progresses through three ascending levels, consisting of two stages each. At the lowest level (*premoral level*), moral judgments are guided either by punishment and obedience or by a kind of naive pleasure-pain philosophy. At an intermediate level (*morality of conventional rule conformity*), morality depends either on the approval of other people (good boy/good girl morality) or on adherence to the precepts of authority. In the first stage of the last level (*morality of self-accepted moral principles*), morality is viewed in terms of acceptance of a contract or democratically determined agreement. In the second stage of the last level, the individual has developed an internal set of principles and a conscience that directs his or her judgment and behavior.

The Moral Judgment Scale is administered by presenting to the examinee nine hypothetical moral dilemmas and obtaining judgments and reasons for the judgment pertaining to each dilemma. Scoring entails making rather subjective evaluations of the examinee's responses in terms of Kholberg's levels/stages.

Personnel Interviews

Almost all production and service organizations use interviews, not only for employee selection, classification, and placement purposes, but also for counseling, troubleshooting, termination (exit interview), and research. Because the interviewing process is expensive and time consuming, it is reasonable to wonder if it is the most efficient procedure for obtaining data on job applicants. Much of the information from a structured interview, which is the preferred approach in most employment settings, can be obtained from an application blank or questionnaire. But job applicants are often more willing to reveal matters of significance in the personal atmosphere of an interview than in writing. In any event, a personnel interview is the final step in the employee selection process for all but the lowest-level jobs in the great majority of organizational settings.

Employment interviewers usually have available a variety of other information about an applicant, including that supplied by the completed application form, letters of recommendation, test scores, and the like. The interviewer's task is to integrate data available from all these sources and from the personal interview to make a recommendation or job decision about the applicant.

An employment interviewer must be cautious in asking questions concerning private matters, not only because they can place the interviewee under an emotional strain but also because it may be illegal to ask them. Interpretive guidelines issued by the Equal Employment Opportunity Commission indicate that it is permissible to ask the following questions in an employment interview ("Interview Questions," 1980, p. 8):

How many years experience do you have?

(To a housewife) Why do you want to return to work?

What are your career goals?

Who have been your prior employers?

Why did you leave your last job?

Are you a veteran? Did the military provide you with job-related experience?

If you have no phone, where can we reach you?

What languages do you speak fluently?

Can you do extensive traveling?

Who recommended you to us?

What did you like or dislike about your previous jobs?

What is your educational background? What schools did you attend?

What are your strong points? Weaknesses?

Do you have any objection if we check with your former employer for references?

On the other hand, it is considered illegal to ask the following questions:

What is your age?

What is your date of birth?

Do you have children? If so, how old are they?

What is your race?

What church do you attend?

Are you married, divorced, separated, widowed, or single?

Have you ever been arrested?

What kind of military discharge do you have?

What clubs or organizations do you belong to?

Do you rent or own your own home?

What does your wife (husband) do?

Who lives in your household?

Have your wages ever been attached or garnisheed?

What was your maiden name (female applicants)?

Reliability and Validity of Interviews

The interview is an important psychological tool, but it shares with observational methods problems of reliability and validity. Reliability demands consistency, but interviewers vary in their appearance, approach, and style, and, consequently, the impressions they make on interviewees. These differing impressions of the same interviewer result in differences in behavior: with one interviewer a person may be friendly and outgoing, whereas with another he or she may be hostile and remote. In addition, the interviewer's perceptions of the interviewee can be distorted by his or her own experiences and personality (Raines & Rohrer, 1960).

The reliability of an interview is usually determined by comparing the ratings given to the interviewee's responses by two or more interviewers. The resulting *interrater reliability coefficient* varies with the specificity of the questions asked and the behaviors rated, and is higher for structured and semistructured than for unstructured interviews (Schwab & Heneman, 1969; Bradley & Caldwell, 1977; Disbrow, Doerr & Caulfield, 1977). But even in the case of fairly specific, objective questions asked in a structured format, the reliability coefficients are moderate, usually ranging no higher than .80.

Because the interviewer is the assessment instrument in an interview, many of the reliability problems of interviews are associated with the characteristics and behavior of the interviewer. The interviewer is almost always in charge in an interviewing situation, the personality and biases of the interviewer usually being more important than those of the interviewee in determining what kinds of information are obtained. The socio-emotional tone of the interview is determined more by the interviewer's actions than by those of the interviewee: the interviewer usually talks more, and the length of the interviewee's answers is directly related to the length of the interviewer's questions. In addition to being too dominant, the interviewer may fail to obtain complete, accurate information by asking the wrong questions, by not encouraging or not allowing enough time for complete answers, and by not recording the responses correctly.

Other shortcomings of interviewers are the tendency to give more weight to first impressions and to be affected more by unfavorable than by favorable information about an interviewee. Errors that affect ratings (see Chapter 6) also occur in interviewers' judgments. An example is the *halo effect* of making judgments, both favorable and unfavorable, on the basis of a general impression or a single prominent characteristic of the interviewee. This effect occurs when a person who is actually superior (or inferior) on only one or two characteristics is given an overall superior (or inferior) evaluation. In addition, the *contrast error* of judging an average interviewee as being inferior if the preceding interviewee was superior or as superior if the preceding interviewee was inferior, can occur.

Because an interviewer's impressions are influenced by the neatness, posture, and other nonverbal behaviors of the interviewee, as well as the latter's verbal answers, prospective interviewees would do well to prepare themselves, both mentally and physically for interviews. In the case of employment interviews, interviewees should have some knowledge of the organization and its philosophy. They should be prepared to give a synopsis of their background and aspirations, but refrain from controversial comments and engaging in bad habits such as smoking or nailbiting during the interview.

A consistent finding of research pertaining to the validity of an interview as an employment selection or clinical diagnostic method is that it is overrated (Arvey, 1979; Reilly & Chao, 1982). Interviews can be made more valid, but they must be carefully planned or structured and the interviewers extensively trained. Interview findings are also more valid when the interviewer focuses on specific (job or clinical) information and when answers are evaluated question by question, preferably by at least two evaluators, rather than as a whole. To facilitate this process, the entire interview should be recorded on audiotape or videotape for later playback and evaluation. In this way the task of interpreting an interviewee's responses can be separated more effectively from the actual interviewing process.

Application Blanks and Biographical Inventories

Interviewing is the most common procedure for obtaining biographical or life-history data. Demographic and experiential information about an individual is also available in personal documents and various data bases. However, much of this information can be obtained more efficiently from *application blanks* and *biographical inventories*.

Employment Application Blanks

Although information provided by completed application blanks and other life-history forms is useful in clinical, educational, and other contexts, the most systematic use of biographical data obtained in this manner has taken place in employment situations. A sizable portion of the data is highly factual and verifiable from other sources (applicant's name, birthdate, marital status, number of dependents, employment history), but a substantial amount is derived from the applicant's self-observations and impressions (e.g. past experiences, interests, attitudes, aspirations).

A completed application blank is both a formal request for employment and a brief description of the applicant's fitness for a job. It provides a personnel department with an efficient, inexpensive way of determining whether an applicant meets the minimum requirements for a job. Following a series of questions to identify the applicant (name, address, employment desired, etc.), detailed background information (education, physical handicaps, military record, previous employment, and experience) is requested. If the completed application is not filed away and forgotten, it can also serve as as informational guide for any subsequent interviews of the applicant. Furthermore, the demographic and descriptive information obtained from a completed application blank can be numerically weighted to predict quality of work, absenteeism, turnover, and other job performance criteria.

Biographical Inventories

More formal biographical inventories, or biodata forms, which are comprised of a variety of items pertaining to the life history of the applicant (family relationships, friendships, extracurricular activities, interests, etc.), have been designed and used by a number of production and service organizations, both public and private. A great deal of research on these longer forms of the weighted application blank has been conducted during the past two or three decades (see Owens, 1976). Catalogs of life-history items, from which personnel administrators or recruiters may construct their own biographical inventories, have even been prepared (Glennon, Albright, & Owens, 1966).

Not only have biographical inventories proved to possess substantial content validity; they are also effective predictors of performance in a variety of job contexts ranging from unskilled work to high-level executive responsibilities. As noted previously in the discussion of interviews, however, legal problems are associated with requests for certain kinds of information (e.g., age, sex, ethnicity, religion, marital status, number of children) on application blanks and biographical inventories. In a sense this is unfortunate because many of these items are good predictors of on-the-job performance. Furthermore, although the information provided by application blanks and biographical inventories has fairly high validity, applicants may object to certain items (personal finances, family background, and other intimate details) as being too personal or otherwise offensive (Rosenbaum, 1973). Consequently, one would expect answers to these kinds of items to be of questionable validity.

References and Recommendations

A section of a typical application blank is usually provided for the names, addresses, and telephone numbers of former employers or other associates of the applicant who can be contacted for additional details and recommendations. Information from an applicant's listed references, whether obtained by letters, telephone calls, interviews, or questionnaires, can be useful despite some obvious limitations. *Letters of recommendation* have perhaps the greatest limitations in that they often provide an incorrect picture of the applicant. Because former employers or other reference sources are frequently reluctant to make negative comments about a person in writing, one telephone call is sometimes worth a dozen letters of recommendation. In fact, laudatory letters of recommendation are so much the rule that personnel administrators and other selection officials often become overly sensitized to anything less than very positive written statements about an applicant. There is also a tendency to interpret short letters as indicative of disapproval of the applicant and longer letters as more complimentary.

Summary

Observations of behavior and personal interviews are the oldest, if not the most precise, methods of personality assessment. Observations may be formal or informal, controlled or uncontrolled, depending on their purpose and the situation in which they take place. Uncontrolled, or naturalistic, observation—a group of children on a playground, a crowd at a sports event, or people on the street going about their business—are situations where the individuals being observed are unaware of the observer. This is the most common and least expensive form of observation. However, it is usually not as objective or scientifically useful as controlled observation of individual behavior or interactions between people in a prearranged, contrived situation.

Special types of observational procedures include participant observation, in which the observer is a participant in the situation which he or she observes; situational testing, in which a person or persons are given a task to solve in a seemingly realistic but prearranged situation under frustrating circumstances; and self-observation, in which the individual makes a detailed record of his or her own behavior. Self-observations obtained from diaries and other personal documents are sometimes interpreted by content analysis procedures.

The objectivity and efficiency of observations can be improved by methodological procedures such as subject, time, and incident sampling; electronic recording and analysis; and careful training of observers. Observers are trained to attend to both the nonverbal behaviors (kinesics, proximics, paralinguistics, culturics) and other activities of those persons who are being observed. Some success in selecting observers who are most perceptive of nonverbal behavior has been attained in using tests such as the Profile of Nonverbal Sensitivity (PONS).

Although the procedures used in collecting observational data for behavior modification purposes are not radically different from procedures for obtaining observations for other purposes, the behavioral model emphasizes careful self-observations of the target behavior (*B*), the antecedent conditions (*A*), and the consequences (*C*) of the behavior. The observer records the occurrence and duration of the target behavior to establish an operant level or baseline and changes in the rate and duration of the behavior after the behavior modification program is instituted. A common approach in behavior modification is to have the patient record his or her own target behaviors, a procedure referred to as self-monitoring.

An interview is a face-to-face verbal interchange in which one person attempts to elicit information or expressions of opinion or belief from another person. The obtained information usually concerns the background or life-history of the interviewee, in addition to the feelings, perceptions, and attitudes of the interviewee. Although anyone who likes to converse with others can conduct an interview of sorts, certain individuals, usually those who have been trained extensively, are more effective interviewers than others.

A professional interviewer begins by establishing rapport with the interviewee and then, depending on whether the interview is structured, semistructured, or unstructured, asks both general and specific questions to derive a psychological portrait of the interviewee. Variations from a standard format are the rule in unstructured interviewing, in which the interviewer feels free to follow up interesting leads by asking additional questions. The interviewer must be cautious about asking certain questions, not only because they may embarrass the interviewee but because they may be illegal in personnel selection contexts.

Structured interviews, in which a sequence of objective, preplanned questions is asked, are simpler to conduct and usually more reliable than unstructured interviews. However, they lack the flexibility of less structured interviews, which are more likely to reveal in-depth information about the interviewee. The particular approach of the interviewer varies with the context and purpose of the interview. In personnel or employment contexts (selection interview, placement interview, performance-appraisal interview), more emphasis is placed on whether the interviewee can perform, can learn to perform, or is effectively performing a certain job. In clinical contexts, the emphasis is more on determining the nature and causes of a person's (patient's, client's) psychological problems and whether the person is competent.

Special types of clinical interviews include the mental status interview, conducted for psychiatric and legal purposes to determine the mental competence of an interviewee; the computer interview, which entails programming a computer to ask a series of questions in a structured or semistructured format; the behavioral interview, designed to obtain information for planning a program of behavior modification; and the stress interview, to break down an individual's defenses by treating him or her in a hostile manner and asking stress-provoking questions in a cross-examination atmosphere.

The reliability of an interview is usually determined by correlating two or more interviewers' judgments or ratings of the same person. The resulting interrater reliability coefficients are typically quite modest. The reliabilities are higher for structured than for unstructured interviews and higher with trained than untrained interviewers. The training of interviewers emphasizes efforts to minimize the effects of the biases, expectations, and personality of the interviewer on the responses of the interviewee and making an objective recording of the interview.

Much of the objective data about a person's life-history or background can be obtained more efficiently from an application blank or biographical inventory than from an interview. Information from the first two sources is also useful for the interviewer to have on hand to guide his or her questioning of the interviewee in an attempt to verify the data and obtain supplementary or in-depth information. Additional information about applicants in personnel contexts can be made available from letters of recommendation and telephone calls to former employers or other individuals who are acquainted with the applicant. Letters and telephone calls to relatives, physicians, and others who have come in contact with a patient are also helpful in making diagnoses and prescribing treatments in clinical contexts.

Exercises

1. Define each of the following terms in a sentence or two:

anecdotal records	assessment center approach
antecedent conditions	baseline
application blanks	behavior modification

behavioral interview
biographical inventories
clinical method
computer interviews
conditional branching
consequences
content analysis
contrast error
controlled observation
critical incidents technique
culturics
functional analysis
guinea pig effect
halo effect
incident sampling
interrater reliability coefficient
interviewing guide
intimate distance
kinesics
leaderless group discussion test
letters of recommendation
macrokinesics
microkinesics
mental status interview
methode clinique

morality of conventional rule
 conformity
morality of self-accepted moral
 principles
nonverbal behavior
nonverbals
paralinguistics
participant observation
persona
personal distance
plants
premoral level
proximics
public distance
self-monitoring
self-observation
situational testing
social distance
stress interview
structured interview
target behaviors
time sampling
uncontrolled observation
unstructured interview

2.   Select a person in one of your classes as a subject for observation—preferably someone whom you do not know and toward whom you have neutral feelings. Observe the person over a period of three or four class meetings, inconspicuously recording what he or she does and says. Try to be as objective as possible, looking for consistent, typical behaviors, as well as noting responses that occur infrequently. At the end of the observation period, write a two to three page characterization of the person. Without having access to any other information about this person (what other students say about the person, how well he or she does in college, etc.), how would you describe this person's personality and characteristic behavior? Finally, check your observations against those of other people who know or have observed this person. After this experience of close observation using a time sampling technique, how do you feel about objective observation as a method of assessing personality? Is it valid and useful?

3.   Ask six people, one at a time, to make facial expressions indicative of each of the following emotions: anger, disgust, fear, happiness, sadness, surprise. Make notes on the facial expressions differentiating the various emotions. Did your actors find the task difficult? Was there appreciable consistency from person to person in

the expressions characterizing a particular emotion? Were certain emotions easier to express and more consistently expressed than others?

4. Referring to the outline on pages 141–142 and other interviewing guidelines available to you, conduct a structured personal interview of someone whom you do not know well. Write up the results as a formal report, giving identifying information, a summary of the interview findings, and recommendations pertaining to the interviewee.

5. Consult the editions of *Tests in Print*, various editions of *The Mental Measurements Yearbook*, *Tests*, and *Test Critiques* for descriptions and reviews of the observational and interview instruments listed in Appendix D, as well as the following instruments referred to in this chapter: Profile of Nonverbal Sensitivity (PONS), Nurses' Observation Scale for Inpatient Behavior, Ward Behavior Inventory, Psychiatric Diagnostic Interview, Brief Psychiatric Rating Scale, Missouri Automated Mental Status Checklist, Missouri Automated Psychiatric History, Mini-Mental Status Examination, Dementia Scale, Hamilton Depression Scale, Psychological/Psychiatric Status Interview, Psychological/Social History Report, Diagnostic Interview for Children and Adolescents, Giannetti On-Line Psychosocial History, Moral Judgment Scale. What conclusions can you draw concerning the design and use of these instruments?

6. Conduct a simulated employment interview with an acquaintance. A fairly structured interview is most appropriate if you are a beginning interviewer. A list of questions to be asked during the interview should be prepared beforehand. However, you should feel free to deviate from the interview schedule if you later think of questions that are more pertinent to the applicant's job performance. Make certain that all questions you ask are job-related and legally acceptable.

Suggested Readings

Argyle, M. (1975). *Bodily communication*. New York: International Universities Press.

Ciminero, A. R., Calhoun, K. S., & Adams, H. E. (1986). *Handbook of behavioral assessment* (2nd ed.). New York: Wiley.

Cone, J. D., & Foster, S. L. (1982). Direct observation in clinical psychology. In P. C. Kendall & J. N. Butcher (Eds.), *Handbook of research methods in clinical psychology* (Chap. 10). New York: Wiley.

Cormier, W. H., & Cormier, L. S. (1979). *Interviewing strategies for helpers: A guide to assessment, treatment, and evaluation*. Monterey, CA: Brooks/Cole.

Erdman, H. P., Klein, M. H., & Greist, J. H. (1985). Direct patient computer interviewing. *Journal of Consulting and Clinical Psychology, 53*, 760–773.

Greenspan, S. I. (1981). *The clinical interview of the child: Theory and practice*. New York: McGraw-Hill.

Hersen, M., & Bellack, A. S. (Eds.) (1982). *Behavioral assessment: A practical handbook* (2nd ed.). New York: Pergamon.

Hersen, M., & Turner, S. M. (1985). *Diagnostic interviewing*. New York: Plenum.

Lifton, R. J., & Olson, E. (1974). *Explorations in psychohistory*. New York: Simon & Schuster.

Siassi, I. (1984). Psychiatric interviews and mental status examinations. In G. Goldstein & M. Hersen (Eds.), *Handbook of psychological assessment* (pp. 259–275). New York: Pergamon.

CHAPTER 6

Rating Scales and Attitude Measurement

Information obtained from controlled and uncontrolled observations or structured and unstructured interviews may be recorded and analyzed in a variety of ways. Because of the large quantity of data yielded by a lengthy observational session or a comprehensive interview, the findings must be summarized and interpreted in a form suitable for a report to the referring individual or organization. Those who will read the report are busy people and not necessarily patient with tedious, rambling descriptions of insignificant or irrelevant behavior, so the report should still contain enough information to give a clear picture of the observational or interview results and what they appear to indicate.

Simplifying and summarizing the findings of a lengthy observational session or a comprehensive, in-depth interview can be facilitated by the use of a properly constructed checklist or rating scale. A checklist consists of a list of descriptive terms, phrases, or statements pertaining to actions and thoughts that the checker endorses (checks, underlines, or in some other way indicates acceptance of). The person to whom the checklist items pertain may be the checker himself (herself) or someone else about whom the checker has sufficient information to make the required judgments.

Unlike the items on a checklist, which necessitate only a dichotomous decision, a rating scale requires a response on a multicategory or continuous (straight line) scale. Different categories, or different points on the continuum, of a rating scale are checked for different frequencies or intensities of a particular behavior or characteristic being rated.

Although checklists and rating scales have been in use since the last century, a renewed interest in constructing standardized instruments of these kinds and conducting both theoretical and applied research on them has been kindled during the past quarter century or so. One reason for this interest is the growing recognition that the effectiveness of mental health, educational, and other social intervention programs cannot be taken for granted but must be periodically evaluated. The need to determine whether these programs, which are frequently supported by governmental or private grants, produce the appropriate behavioral, cognitive, and affective changes in the recipients of their services has led to a search for more carefully designed and standardized evaluation instruments. In many instances, in particular those programs calling for repeated, periodic evaluations, multiple forms of the same instrument are required. Consequently, checklists and rating scales, which are among the simplest types of psychometric instruments to construct, have been produced in increasing numbers.

Checklists

A *checklist* is a relatively simple, highly cost-effective, and fairly reliable method of describing or evaluating a person. More easily constructed than rating scales or personality inventories (see Chapters 7 and 8), and sometimes just as valid, checklists can be administered as self-report or observer-report instruments. In completing a checklist, the respondent is instructed to mark the words or phrases in a list that apply to the individual being evaluated (oneself or another person). When a number of judges or checkers evaluate a person on the same items of a checklist, then that person's score on each item can be set equal to the number of judges who checked it.

An example of a checklist that can be used repeatedly, in this case to note the presence of behaviors indicative of anxiety, is shown in Figure 6–1. Used in connection with desensitization, a behavior modification procedure, the observed behaviors can be checked over several time periods to obtain more reliable measures or to detect changes due to treatment or other circumstances.

Critical Incidents

In employment situations, checklists for appraising job performance and attitudes have been constructed from a set of critical incidents pertaining to job behavior. In the *critical incidents technique* (Flanagan, 1954), supervisors and others who are familiar with a particular job are asked to identify specific behaviors that are critical

Behavioral checklist for performance anxiety   **Figure 6–1**

Behavior Observed	Time Period							
	1	2	3	4	5	6	7	8
1. Paces								
2. Sways								
3. Shuffles feet								
4. Knees tremble								
5. Extraneous arm and hand movement (swings, scratches, toys, etc.)								
6. Arms rigid								
7. Hands restrained (in pockets, behind back, clasped)								
8. Hand tremors								
9. No eye contact								
10. Face muscles tense (drawn, tics, grimaces)								
11. Face "deadpan"								
12. Face pale								
13. Face flushed (blushes)								
14. Moistens lips								
15. Swallows								
16. Clears throat								
17. Breathes heavily								
18. Perspires (face, hands, armpits)								
19. Voice quivers								
20. Speech blocks or stammers								

to job performance or which distinguish between good and poor workers. These behaviors, or incidents, are critical because they have either highly positive or highly negative consequences. Examples are "secures machinery and tidies up place of work when finished" and "follows up customers' requests promptly." Identification of a large number of such incidents supplies valuable information on the nature of the job and the requirements for effective performance.

Standardized Checklists

Special-purpose checklists for use in specific situations or for certain purposes can be prepared in clinical, educational, and industrial-organizational contexts. The problem with such home-grown instruments is that they are rarely adequately validated or standardized, reliability data is meager, and consequently one is uncertain whether the checklist is serving its intended purpose.

Several dozen checklists, a selection of which are described in Appendix E, have been designed and standardized for identifying various characteristics of behavior and personality. Certain checklists are concerned specifically with *adaptive behavior*, or the degree of independent functioning and maintenance as well as the ability to meet cultural demands for personal and social responsibility; an example is the Normative Adaptive Behavior Checklist. Other checklists, such as the Children's Problems Checklist and the Mooney Problem Check Lists focus on problem behaviors.

Mooney Problem Check Lists Among the oldest instruments in the checklist category are the Mooney Problem Check Lists (MPCL) by R. L. Mooney and L. V. Gordon (The Psychological Corporation, 1950). Each of the four levels of the MPCL—junior high school (grades 7–9), high school (grades 9–12), college (grades 13–16), and adult—consists of a list of 210 to 330 statements of problems in areas such as health and physical development, home and family, boy and girl relations, morals and religion, courtship and marriage, economic security, school or occupation, social and recreational, and so forth. The specific areas depend on the level. The problem statements were constructed from a list of problems obtained from two sources—clinical case histories and personal problems identified by several thousand individuals. Problems in seven areas are evaluated at the junior high level, in eleven areas at the high school and college levels, and in nine areas at the adult level. Examinees are directed to underline problems that are of some concern to them, circle the numbers of the problems of most concern, and then write a summary of their problems.

The MPCL can be scored for the number of problems in each area. Summary counts and distributions of problems checked are sometimes prepared for local use, but no norms have been published. Responses are interpreted either impressionistically or by comparing them with locally obtained norms. With respect to other psychometric characteristics, the 1950 manual reports test-retest reliability coefficients of .90 or higher for ranks (order of importance) of the problem areas for each examinee. The case for the validity of the MPCL, as with problem checklists in general, is usually made on the basis of content.

Although the majority of checklists measure a variety of personality and behavioral characteristics and are more general in their purpose, others are designed for a specific purpose or to assess a specific characteristic or symptom. Illustrative of omnibus checklists that yield a number of scores are the Adjective Check List (ACL), the Louisville Checklist, and the Multiple Affective Adjective Check List; in contrast, the Sexual Activities Checklist (Bentler, 1968) and the Depression Adjective Check List focuses on one type of psychological problem or area. Finally, the Marital Evaluation Checklist, the Mental Status Checklist–Adults, and the School Behavior Checklist are examples of instruments designed for a specific purpose or group of people. This was also true originally of the Jesness Behavior Check List, which was constructed in a juvenile corrections context but extended in its use to nondelinquent adolescents.

Adjective Check List (ACL)   In contrast to the non-normative approach of the Mooney Problem Check Lists, the Adjective Check List (ACL) by H. G. Gough and A. B. Heilbrun (Consulting Psychologists Press, 1965, 1980) consists of 300 adjectives, arranged alphabetically from absent-minded to zany. Examinees take 15 to 20 minutes to mark those adjectives that they consider to be self-descriptive. Responses may then be scored on the 37 scales described in the 1983 manual: 4 modus operandi scales, 15 need scales, 9 topical scales, 5 transactional analysis scales, and 4 origence-intellectence scales. Scores on the first four, or modus operandi scales (total number of adjectives checked, number of favorable adjectives checked, number of unfavorable adjectives checked, communality) pertain to the manner in which a respondent has dealt with the checklist. The need scales (5–19) are based on Edwards's (1954) descriptions of 15 needs in Murray's (1938) needs-press theory of personality. Each of the topical scales (20–28) assesses a different topic or component of interpersonal behavior (e.g., counseling readiness, personal adjustment, creative personality, masculine attributes). The transactional analysis scales (29–33) are described as measures of the five ego functions of Berne's (1966) transactional analysis. The origence-intellectence scales (34–37) are described as measures of Welsh's origence-intellectence (i.e., creativity and intelligence) dimensions of personality.

For purposes of interpretation and counseling, raw scores on the ACL scales are converted to standard T scores. As an illustration, the 37 T scores and the associated profile of the case described in Report 6–1 are given in Table 6–1. The T scores are interpreted with reference to the appropriate norms listed in the manual. In addition to normative data on 5,238 males and 4,144 females, the manual provides profiles and associated interpretations for six sample cases. The 1983 ACL manual lists test-retest coefficients for the separate scales ranging from .34 for the high-origence–low-intellectence scale to .77 for the aggression scale, with a median of .65. The manual also describes many uses of the ACL and research investigations that have employed it.

Reviews of the ACL (Teeter, 1985; Zarske, 1985) are fairly positive, concluding that the instrument is well developed and has had its greatest usefulness in self-concept studies. The internal consistency reliabilities of most of the 37 scales are reasonably high, but data on the test-retest reliabilities of the scales are limited. Furthermore, the scales are significantly intercorrelated and should therefore not be interpreted as independent factors. The ACL has been used principally with normal people, and its validity in psychodiagnosis and treatment planning has not been determined.

Table 6–1	Scales and Sample T Scores on the Adjective Check List	

Scale Name and Designation	Standard Scores for Case in Report 6–1
Modus Operandi	
1 Total number of adjectives checked (No. Ckd)	37
2 Number of favorable adjectives checked (Fav)	62
3 Number of unfavorable adjectives checked (Unfav)	59
4 Communality (Com)	68
Need Scales	
5 Achievement (Ach)	57
6 Dominance (Dom)	50
7 Endurance (End)	53
8 Order (Ord)	57
9 Intraception (Int)	57
10 Nurturance (Nur)	44
11 Affiliation (Aff)	53
12 Heterosexuality (Het)	46
13 Exhibition (Exh)	44
14 Autonomy (Aut)	49
15 Aggression (Agg)	58
16 Change (Cha)	58
17 Succorance (Suc)	41
18 Abasement (Aba)	56
19 Deference (Def)	49
Topical Scales	
20 Counseling Readiness (Crs)	55
21 Self-control (S-Cn)	48
22 Self-confidence (S-Cfd)	59
23 Personal Adjustment (P-Adj)	53
24 Ideal Self (Iss)	64
25 Creative Personality (Cps)	63
26 Military Leadership (Mls)	52
27 Masculine Attributes (Mas)	54
28 Feminine Attributes (Fem)	69
Transactional Analysis	
29 Critical Parent (CP)	62
30 Nurturing Parent (NP)	48
31 Adult (A)	56
32 Free Child (FC)	46
33 Adapted Child (AC)	41
Origence-intellectence	
34 High Origence, Low Intellectence (A-1)	47
35 High Origence, High Intellectence (A-2)	64
36 Low Origence, Low Intellectence (A-3)	44
37 Low Origence, High Intellectence (A-4)	63

Adapted from *The Adjective Check List Manual* by Harrison G. Gough, Ph.D. and Alfred B. Heilbrun, Jr., Ph.D. Copyright 1983. Published by Consulting Psychologists Press Inc.

| Case Description Accompanying Adjective Check List Scores in Table 6–1 | **Report 6–1** |

Case 4 was a 19-year-old undergraduate student majoring in biology. She maintained an A grade average and planned to go to graduate school. She was brought up in a close-knit, large family, and had warm feelings about her parents and her childhood. Before college, she had always lived in small towns or semirural areas. Coming to an urban college required quite an adjustment, but she liked the excitement and stimulation of city life. She retained her religious beliefs and regularly attended church. She viewed herself as a political and economic conservative. Standard scores (mean of 50 and standard deviation of 10) from ratings by 18 staff observers were 64 for Energy Level, 54 for Femininity, 61 for Intellectual Competence, 57 for Need: Achievement, 58 for Originality, 46 for Sense of Responsibility, and 58 for Personal Soundness. She was rated as unusually effective in leaderless group discussion, but only average in charades. Her life-history interviewer described her in the following way:

> She is an intelligent, vivacious, attractive young woman, enthusiastic about her life at the University. Although she views herself as introverted, her behavior is more extraverted; she was talkative, outgoing, candid, and not hesitant to assume a leadership role. Her parents were strict, expected the children to assume responsibilities, and placed a high value on academic achievement. She described her mother as a demanding, extremely shy woman who participated in social activities from a sense of duty. She said her father was somewhat intimidating, but affectionate; she feels closer to him now than she did when she was growing up. Being at school—away from home and the relative isolation of that environment—is very exciting.

Scores on her ACL profile are in agreement with the case-history data and staff evaluations. Moderate elevations occur on the scales for Achievement, Self-confidence, and Personality Adjustment, and scores of 60 or greater on the scales for Ideal Self, Creative Personality, and A-2 (high origence, high intellectence). The ACL profile also revealed scores of 60 or greater on the scales for Favorable, Communality, Femininity, Critical Parent, and A-4 (low origence, high intellectence). Although the staff rating of 54 on Femininity was above average for the sample of 80 students included in this project, it is not as high as the score of 69 on her self-descriptive ACL. Because she had scores greater than 50 on *both* Masculinity and Femininity, she is in the androgynous cell in the interaction diagram between the two scales. Contemporary research (Spence and Helmreich, 1978) suggests that psychologically androgynous women are more likely to do well in intellectual and professional pursuits than women in the other three categories defined in the fourfold table. The profile also revealed elevated scores on *both* Favorable and Unfavorable, which suggests she is more complex, internally differentiated, and less repressive than her peers.

Depression Adjective Check List and Multiple Affect Adjective Check List-Revised   Designed with a sharper clinical focus than the ACL are the Depression Adjective Check Lists (DACL) and the Multiple Affect Adjective Check List-Revised (MAACL-R). The purpose of the DACL by B. Lubin (EdITS, 1967–1981) is to provide for the repeated measurement of transient depressive mood, feeling, or emotion in adolescents (grades 9–16) and adults. The DACL consists of seven forms or lists: lists A, B, C, and D consist of 32 adjectives each, and lists E, F, and G of 34 adjectives each. The examinee checks the adjectives that are descriptive of how he or she feels at that time. The percentile norms for the DACL are based on a national probability sample of 621 adolescents and 3,011 adults. Internal-consistency reliability coefficients of the seven lists are high (.81–.90), but test-retest reliabilities over a one-week interval are low (.19–.24). The DACL was used in the National Survey of Depression, in addition to other clinical, epidemiological, and experimental investigations. In a critique of the instrument, Petzel (1985) concluded that the DACL is useful in research and group categorization, but that evidence for its use in individual diagnosis is weak.

The MAACL-R by M. Zuckerman and B. Lubin (EdITS, 1981) consists of 132 adjectives describing feelings; examinees check those adjectives that indicate how they generally feel (on the trait form) or how they feel today or at present (on the state form). Standard T scores on both the trait and state forms of the MAACL-R are obtained on five basic scales: Anxiety (A), Depression (D), Hostility (H), Positive Affect (PA), and Sensation Seeking (SS). Two summary standard scores—Dysphoria (Dys = A + D + H) and Positive Affect and Sensation Seeking (PASS = PA + SS) are also computed. Norms for the trait form of the MAACL-R are based on a representative, nationwide sample of 1,491 individuals aged 18 years and over; norms for the state form are based on a (nonrepresentative) sample of 538 students at a midwestern college. With the exception of the Sensation Seeking scale, the internal-consistency reliability coefficients for the scales on both the trait and state forms of the MAACL-R are adequate. The test-retest reliabilities are satisfactory for the trait scales but, as expected, low for the state scales. The results of validity studies on various populations, including normal adolescents and adults, counseling clients, and patients from clinics and state hospitals, are reported in the MAACL-R manual (Zuckerman & Lubin, 1985). Scores on the MAACL-R correlate in the expected direction with other measures of personality (e.g., MMPI, PONS, peer ratings, self-ratings, psychiatric diagnoses).

Reviewing the MAACL-R, Templer (1985) concluded that it is definitely superior to its predecessor, the MAACL, and listed a number of advantages of the instrument: brevity and ease of administration, provision of both state and trait measures, assessment of five affect dimensions, sensitivity to changes over time, good reliability, relative independence of response sets, commendable construct validity, and a wide range of research applications with both normal and abnormal populations, especially in assessing temporal changes.

Rating Scales

Since their introduction by Francis Galton during the latter part of the nineteenth century, rating scales have become popular assessment devices in mental health, business/industrial, and educational contexts. Rating scales are fairly easy to construct and versatile in their applications. Ratings may be made by the person being rated (ratee), in which case they are referred to as self-ratings, or by another person (rater) who has knowledge of the ratee's behavior, capabilities, and other characteristics.

A rating scale requires that judgments concerning the behavior or personality of another person be made on an ordered scale containing enough categories or points (usually 5 to 7) to provide sufficient response variability to differentiate among ratees. Consequently, the numbers obtained when scoring rating scales represent measurement on at least an ordinal scale (see Chapter 2).

Rating scales are generally considered superior to checklists but less precise than personality inventories and more superficial than projective techniques. Their superiority to checklists is particularly apparent when the number of raters or judges is small. However, when the number of raters is large, a well-constructed checklist may discriminate just as accurately as a rating scale.

Types of Rating Scales

A rating scale may be unipolar or bipolar. On a *unipolar scale*, a single term or phrase referring to a behavior or trait is used; the rater indicates the extent to which the ratee possesses that behavior or trait. For example, degree of dominance may be rated on a scale of 1 to 7, where 1 is the lowest amount and 7 the greatest amount of dominance. This unipolar scale can be converted to a *bipolar scale* by using two adjectives—submissive and dominant to designate the two extreme categories; the middle category represents equal amounts of dominance and submission.

Rating scales may be classified in ways other than unipolar or bipolar. For example, there are numerical rating scales, semantic-differential scales, graphic rating scales, standard rating scales, behaviorally anchored scales, and forced-choice scales.

Numerical Rating Scale   On a *numerical rating scale*, the ratee is assigned one of several numbers corresponding to particular descriptions of the characteristic to be rated, such as "sociability" or "intelligence." All that is required is that the ratings be made on a series of ordered categories, different categories being assigned different numerical values. For example, in rating an individual on "sociability," five categories, ranging from very unsociable (1) to very sociable (5), may be used.

Semantic-differential Scale   A special example of a numerical rating scale is a *semantic-differential scale*, a technique originally employed in research concerned with the connotative meanings that concepts such as "father," "mother," "sickness," "sin," "hatred," and "love" have for different people (Osgood, Suci & Tannenbaum, 1957). The procedure begins by having a person rate a series of concepts on several seven-point, bipolar adjective scales. For example, the concept of "mother" might be rated on the following three seven-point scales:

Bad	____	____	____	____	____	____	____	Good
Weak	____	____	____	____	____	____	____	Strong
Slow	____	____	____	____	____	____	____	Fast

In actual practice, ten or more such bipolar scales are used on a semantic-differential instrument.

After the rater has rated all concepts of interest on the various scales, the responses to each concept are scored on several semantic dimensions and compared with the rater's responses to the remaining concepts. The principal connotative meaning (semantic) dimensions that have been determined by factor analyses of ratings given to a series of concepts on many different adjectival scales by different raters are "evaluation," "potency," and "activity." A *semantic space* may be constructed by plotting the rater's scores on the rated concepts on these three dimensions. Concepts falling close to each other in the semantic space presumably have similar connotative meanings for the rater.

Graphic Rating Scale   Another popular type of rating scale is a *graphic rating scale*, containing graphic descriptions of the end points and perhaps various intermediate points on a scale continuum. An illustration is:

What are the student's chances of succeeding in college course work?

Will fail most subjects	Will do poorly in some subjects, average in others	Will be an average student	Will do above average in some subjects, average in others	Will do above average in all subjects

The rater makes a mark on a series of lines such as this containing descriptive terms or phrases pertaining to a certain behavior or characteristic. The verbal description at the left end of the line usually represents the lowest amount or frequency of occurrence, and the description at the right end the highest amount of frequency of occurrence.

Standard Rating Scale   On a *standard rating scale*, the rater supplies, or is supplied with, a set of standards against which ratees are to be compared. An example of a standard rating scale is the *man-to-man scale* for rating individuals on a specified trait such as "cooperativeness." Raters begin by thinking of five people falling at different points along a hypothetical continuum of cooperativeness. Then they compare each person to be rated with these five individuals and indicate which one the ratee is most like with respect to cooperativeness.

Behaviorally Anchored Scales   Developed by Smith and Kendall (1963) and based on Flanagan's (1954) critical incidents technique, *behaviorally anchored scales* represent attempts to make the terminology of rating scales more descriptive of actual behavior and hence more objective. Understandably, terms such as "anxiety," "self-confidence," "aggressiveness," and other nouns or adjectives used in traditional trait-oriented rating scales may be interpreted differently by different raters. This is particularly true when raters receive little or no training in how they should interpret such terms in rating themselves or others. A tongue-in-check illustration of a behaviorally anchored scale for rating five employee performance factors is given in Figure 6–2.

Constructing a behaviorally anchored rating scale involves convening a group of individuals who possess expert knowledge of a particular job or other situation and having them, through discussion and painstaking deliberation, attempt to reach a consensus on a series of behaviorally descriptive, critical incidents from which an objective, highly reliable rating scale can be constructed. Behavioral descriptions that survive repeated reevaluation by the group, or other groups, may then be prepared as a series of items to be rated. One might expect that the emphasis on objectively observable behavior and the concentrated group effort, which are features of behaviorally anchored scales, would make these scales psychometrically superior to other rating scales. In addition, the fact that the technique requires group involvement and consensus in constructing the scale, and hence a greater likelihood of group acceptance, would seem to be an advantage. However, a review of the research literature on the topic concluded that behaviorally anchored scales are not necessarily an improvement over graphic rating scales (Schwab, Heneman & De Cotiis, 1975).

Forced-Choice Rating Scale   On the simplest type of *forced-choice rating scale*, the rater is given two descriptive words, phrases, or statements that are closely matched in desirability. The rater is told to indicate which one best applies to the ratee. When the rating scale contains three or more descriptions, raters are told to indicate which is most applicable and which least applicable to the ratee. In the case of a scale containing four descriptions, say an item consisting of two equally desirable and two equally undersirable descriptions, the rater is instructed to mark the statement that is most applicable and the one that is least applicable to the ratee. Only one desirable and one undesirable statement discriminate between high and low ratees on the criterion—whatever it may be (job performance, behavioral adjustment, etc.), but the raters presumably do not know which of the four statements these are. A hypothetical example of a four-statement, forced-choice item that might be used to evaluate supervisors or other leaders is

Assumes responsibility easily.

Doesn't know how or when to delegate.

Has many constructive suggestions to offer.

Doesn't listen to others' suggestions.

Note that the first and third statements are positive and the second and fourth statements are negative. But which is most positive and which least negative? Presumably, only the scale designer knows.

Errors in Rating

Like the U.S. Army, which reportedly switched back from the forced-choice to the man-to-man rating scale for evaluating officers, raters sometimes find the forced-choice procedure difficult and distasteful. Cumbersome as it may be to select one of four descriptions that is most characteristic and one that is least characteristic of a person, forced-choice ratings do have the advantage of controlling for certain errors in ratings, such as the *constant error*, the *halo effect*, the *contrast error*, and the *proximity error*. Not all raters are equally susceptible to these errors, since, as with any other evaluation method that relies on observations, the background and personality of the rater affects his or her perception, judgment, and style of responding. However, one type of error to which all raters are susceptible is the *ambiguity error* caused by poor descriptions of the various locations on the scales and by scales consisting of items about which the rater has insufficient information (Kleinmuntz, 1982). Other types of errors made in rating are described below.

Constant Errors   These errors occur when the assigned ratings are higher (*leniency* or *generosity error*), lower (*severity error*), or more often in the average category (*central tendency error*) than they should be. Transforming ratings to standard scores or other convenient units can assist in coping with such constant errors, but making raters aware of the various kinds of errors that can occur in rating is probably more effective.

Halo Effect   The halo effect is the tendency of raters to respond to the general impression made by the ratee or to overgeneralize by assigning favorable ratings on all traits merely because the individual is outstanding on one or two. There is also such a thing as a negative halo effect, in which one bad apple, or rather one bad characteristic, spoils the ratings on all characteristics. Related to the halo effect is the *logical error* of giving a person similar ratings on characteristics that the rater believes to be logically associated.

Contrast Error   This term has been used in at least two different senses. In one sense it refers to the tendency to assign a higher rating than justified if an immediately preceding person received a very low rating, or to assign a lower rating than

Figure 6–2   "Tongue-in-cheek" behaviorally anchored rating scale for employee appraisal

Guide to Employee Performance Appraisal

Performance Degrees

Performance Factors	Far Exceeds Job Requirements	Exceeds Job Requirements	Meets Job Requirements	Needs Some Improvement	Does Not Meet Minimum Requirements
Quality	Leaps tall buildings with a single bound.	Must take running start to leap over tall buildings.	Can only leap over a short building or medium with no spires.	Crashes into buildings when attempting to jump over them.	Cannot recognize buildings at all, much less jump.
Timeliness	Is faster than a speeding bullet.	Is as fast as a speeding bullet.	Not quite as fast as a speeding bullet.	Would you believe a slow bullet?	Wounds self with bullets when attempting to shoot gun.
Initiative	Is stronger than a locomotive.	Is stronger than a bull elephant.	Is stronger than a bull.	Shoots the bull.	Smells like a bull.
Adaptability	Walks on water consistently.	Walks on water in emergencies.	Washes with water.	Drinks water.	Passes water in emergencies.
Communication	Talks with God.	Talks with the angels.	Talks to himself.	Argues with himself.	Loses those arguments.

Adapted from *The Industrial-Organizational Psychologist*, 1980, 17(4), p. 22, and used with permission.

justified if the preceding person received a very high rating. In a second sense, the contrast error refers to the tendency of a rater to compare or contrast the ratee with himself or herself (i.e., the rater) in assigning ratings on certain behaviors or traits.

Proximity Error   The actual location of a particular rating item on the printed page may affect the ratings assigned to it. In the proximity error, the rater tends to assign similar ratings to a person on items that are closer together on the printed page. Likewise, if a person is consistently rated high, low, or average on the majority of a set of items located close together on the printed page, other items that are situated near these items may also be rated in the same way—a kind of spread of response or response set.

Improving Ratings

It is not easy to make reliable and valid ratings of people under any circumstances and particularly when the behaviors or personality characteristics are poorly defined or highly subjective. In addition, the meanings of the scale units may be unclear and hence interpreted differently by different raters.

Personal biases can obviously affect ratings: if you like someone you will probably give him or her higher ratings, and if you dislike the person you will tend to give him or her lower ratings than someone whom you neither like nor dislike. Furthermore, raters frequently are insufficiently familiar with the person being rated to make accurate ratings, or they may be familiar with the person's behavior in certain situations but not in others. Training in how to make ratings more objective—by being aware of the various kinds of errors that can occur, by becoming more familiar with the person and characteristics being rated by the instrument, and by omitting items that the rater feels unqualified to judge, can improve the accuracy of ratings. In addition to training, selection of raters is important. Some individuals are simply not interested, clearly too biased, or unwilling to invest the time required to become an objective rater; such individuals should not be used as raters if they cannot be motivated and trained to be conscientious and objective.

Another way of improving ratings is to balance out the biases of individual raters by combining the responses of several raters. In addition, careful attention to the design of rating scale items can result in greater reliability and validity. Both the behaviors or traits being rated and the scale points should be designated in precise behavioral terms that will be interpreted in the same way by different raters. Matters of format, such as arranging the items on the rating sheets so they can be easily completed and scored, making certain that bipolar scales are not all in the same direction, that items are not too close together (one per page is preferable but probably impossible), and that the rating form is not unnecessarily long, are also important in providing accurate, meaningful results.

Reliability and Validity of Rating Scales

Because of the many errors involved in ratings, the reliabilities and validities of various rating scales are frequently marginal. However, reliabilities may be improved by careful training of raters, reaching the .80s and even .90s. Among the most reliable ratings obtained in various groups (college students, industrial supervisors, military personnel, etc.) are those given by the ratee's peers (Kane & Lawler, 1980; Reynolds, 1966).

As in the case of interviews, interrater or interjudge reliability, computed as a coefficient of correlation or concordance among the ratings assigned by several raters or judges, is a common method of expressing the reliability of a rating scale. However, test-retest, parallel forms, and internal-consistency reliability coefficients may also be determined. With respect to validity, all the different types of validity—content, criterion-related (predictive, concurrent), and construct validity are of interest in evaluating an instrument consisting of a series of rating scales.

Commercially Available Rating Scales

Although the great majority of rating scales are nonstandardized, special purpose instruments designed for a particular research investigation, many standardized scales for rating behavior and personality traits in children and adults are commercially available. Researchers in the fields of child development, special education, and behavior disorders in particular, have constructed dozens of rating instruments for assessing behavioral changes resulting from specific educational, therapeutic, and other intervention procedures. A handbook describing many psychiatric rating scales is available from the National Institute of Mental Health (Lyerly, 1978). A number of unpublished rating scales and checklists, listed in *Tests in Microfiche*, can also be ordered from Educational Testing Service.

A dozen commercially available rating scales are described in Appendix F. Note that some of these instruments are oriented more toward behavioral assessments, others have a trait-factor orientation, and still others were developed in a dynamic, psychiatric context. Also useful in clinical settings are the Behavioral Rating Instrument for Autistic and Other Atypical Children (Stoelting Company, 1977), the Inpatient Multidimensional Psychiatric Scale (Lorr et al., 1966), and the Wittenborn Psychiatric Rating Scale (Wittenborn, 1964). Furthermore, many standardized interview and observation instruments involve ratings of behavior and personality and hence consist in part of rating scales (see Appendix D).

Q Sorts

A special type of rating scale, the *Q sort*, introduced by William Stephenson (1953), has been used extensively in research in clinical and social psychology. The Q sort technique requires that the respondent, who may be the person being described or someone else (e.g., an acquaintance or expert observer), sort a set of 100 descriptive statements of personality into a series of nine categories (piles) varying from "most descriptive" to "least descriptive" of the person. Each card in a Q sort deck contains a statement such as (Block, 1961)

Has a wide range of interests.

Is productive; gets things done.

Is self-dramatizing; is histrionic.

Is overreactive to minor frustrations; is irritable.

Seeks reassurance from others.

Appears to have a high degree of intellectual capacity.

Is basically anxious.

In sorting the statement-bearing cards in a Q sort deck, the respondent is directed to make his or her choices so that a certain number of cards fall in each category and the resulting frequency distribution of statements across categories will have a predetermined shape, usually normal. To approximate a normal distribution for a Q sort of 100 statements, Block (1961) recommends instructing sorters to place the following numbers of statements into categories 1 through 9: 5, 8, 12, 16, 18, 16, 12, 8, 5. The response to each statement on a Q sort instrument is assigned an integer ranging from 1 to 9, depending on the category assigned to the statement by the respondent. The results obtained from different sorters can then be correlated by using the product-moment correlation formula and factor analysis or cluster analysis procedures (see Chapter 2).

Q sort statements may be written specifically for a particular applied or research use, but standard sets of statements are also available. Commercially distributed sets include the California Q-Sort Deck by J. Block and adapted by D. Bem and the California Child Q-Sort Set by J. Block and J. Block, both of which are published by Consulting Psychologists Press (1978, 1980 respectively) and consist of 100 cards containing descriptive statements of personality.

Certain investigations of changes in self-concept resulting from psychotherapy or other experiences have required research subjects to make before-and-after Q sorts of a series of statements to describe their feelings and attitudes. In several investigations (e.g., Rogers & Dymond, 1954), each subject was asked to make separate Q sorts according to his or her perceived "real self" and "ideal self." According to phenomenological (self) theory, in effective counseling and psychotherapy the differences between the "real" and "ideal" self-sorts should be smaller after therapy than before.

Selecting People

Instead of sorting statement-bearing cards, one can sort or select people according to certain criteria. Illustrative of this approach is the *sociometric* or peer nomination technique, the *guess-who technique*, and the Role Construct Repertory Test.

Sociometric Technique   Using this technique the respondent is asked to select two subsets of people from a larger group: those with whom he or she would like to engage in a certain activity and those with whom he or she would dislike or prefer not to engage in the activity. Alternatively, only acceptances (choices) may be requested. For example, the individuals in a school class, place of work, military unit, or any other organization may be asked to select individuals with whom they whould like to study, work, serve, or engage in any other activity. The resulting acceptances (and rejections) of each person can then be listed and analyzed, revealing which group members need assistance or attention and whether the physical arrangement of the group members is satisfactory in terms of efficiency and morale.

The sociometric process can be facilitated by depicting the results as a *sociogram* such as the one in Figure 6–3. Each circle or triangle in this sociogram represents a fifth grader who was asked, "Which three children in this class would you like to invite to a party?" Choices are indicated by arrows from the chooser to the chosen, mutual choices by bisected lines. *Stars*, such as Barbara and Joe, are people who are chosen most often; *isolates*, such as Emily and Lucy, are chosen by no one; *mutual admiration societies* or *cliques*, such as Fremont, Elton, and Joe, consist of groups of people who choose each other.

Guess-Who Technique   Another example of selecting people, based on a guessing game for children, is known as the guess-who technique. Children in a classroom, or any other group of acquaintances, are given a list of behavior descriptions such as "Someone who always seems rather sad, worried, or unhappy" and "Someone who is very friendly, who is nice to everybody," and asked to write down the names of persons whom they think fit the description (Cunningham et al., 1951). As in the case of the sociometric technique, the results can help to identify children who have problems and need help.

Role Construct Repertory Test   A final example of a assessment procedure in which people are selected (and compared) is the Role Construct Repertory Test (Rep) (Kelly, 1955). According to George Kelly's theory of personal constructs people are scientists, albeit not necessarily good ones. Like scientists, they conceptualize or categorize their experiences in what appears to them to be a logical way. But many people, particularly those who are considered neurotic, perceive or construe the world incorrectly and develop faulty systems of constructs. Consequently, Kelly believes that to help the neurotic individual the psychotherapist must begin by identifying the system of constructs used by the former in interpreting those people who are important to her or him.

Figure 6–3   Sociogram of a fifth-grade class

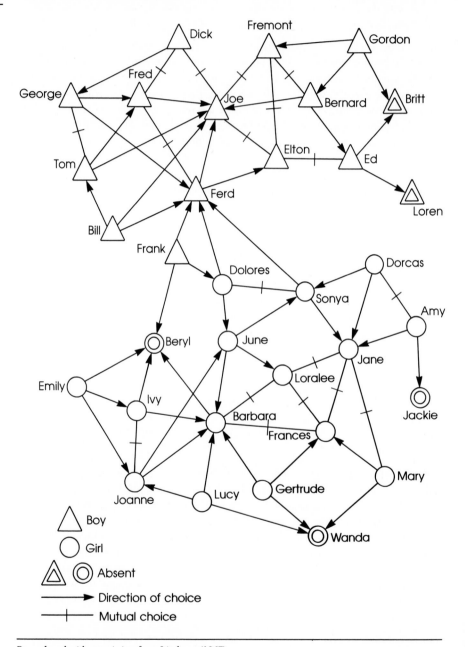

One procedure that Kelly devised for identifying a person's system of constructs is the Role Construct Repertory (Rep) Test. The first step in administering the Rep Test is to have the examinee list the names of the 22 people in his or her life who fill each of the following roles:

1. yourself
2. your mother
3. your father
4. brother nearest to you in age (or person most like a brother)
5. sister nearest to you in age (or person most like a sister)
6. your spouse (or closest friend of opposite sex)
7. friend of opposite sex after person in 6
8. closest friend of same sex as you
9. person once a close friend but no longer
10. religious leader with whom you could discuss feelings about religion
11. your medical doctor
12. neighbor you know best
13. person you know who dislikes you
14. person for whom you feel sorry and would like to help
15. person with whom you feel uncomfortable
16. recent acquaintance you would like to know better
17. most influential teacher when you were in your teens
18. teacher you disagreed with most
19. employer or supervisor under whom you worked while experiencing stress
20. most successful person you know
21. happiest person you know
22. most ethical person you know

After designating the 22 people, the examinee is instructed to compare them in groups of three corresponding to the three circles on each row of Figure 6–4. Thus, the first comparison is among persons 20, 21, and 22, and the second comparison among persons 17, 18, and 19. Then on the appropriate row under the column headed "Construct," the examinee writes a word or phrase, for example "motivated," describing how two of the three people are alike; under "Contrast" the examinee writes a word or phrase, for example, "lazy," describing how the third person is different from the other two. Next the examinee writes an X in the circles corresponding to the two people on that row who are alike. For the remaining 19 people on the row, the appropriate box is checked if the "Construct" part applies to them and left blank if it does not apply. This process is continued for the remaining 21 constructs, or as many or few constructs as the examinee wishes to list. Six construct-contrast examples are included in Figure 6–4.

The examinee's performance on the Rep Test is analyzed by noting how many constructs are used and what they are, what aspects of people are emphasized in the

Figure 6–4   Typical form used for the Role Construct Repertory Test

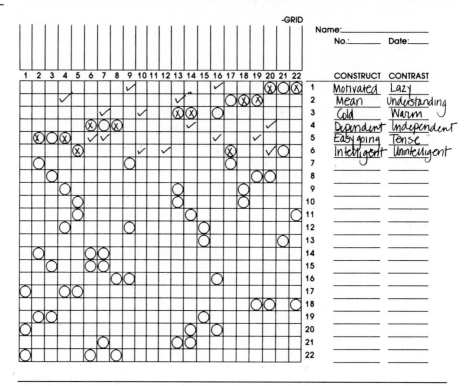

Adapted and reproduced with permission from Kelly (1955).

constructs (physical, social, etc.), and which people are most like or different from the examinee. Interpreting the test results is a laborious, subjective process because the Rep Test is as much a projective test as a rating scale. In the absence of an objective scoring system it should not be surprising that, although the grid responses appear fairly reliable, the Rep Test has not been widely used for either clinical or research purposes, and its validity is largely unknown.

Attitude Measurement

An *attitude* is a learned predisposition to respond positively or negatively to a certain object, situation, institution, or person. As such it consists of cognitive (knowledge or intellect), affective (emotion and motivation), and performance (behavior or action) components. Although the concept of attitude is not distinct from interest, opinion, belief, or value, there are differences in the manner in which these terms are employed. An *interest* is a feeling or preference concerning one's own activities. Unlike attitude, which implies approval or disapproval (a moral judgment), being interested in something simply means that the person spends time thinking about or reacting to it, regardless of whether those thoughts and reactions are positive or negative. An *opinion* is a specific reaction to certain occurrences or situations, whereas an attitude is more general in its effects on a person's responses toward a broad class of events or people. Furthermore, people are aware of their opinions, but they may not be fully conscious of their attitudes. Opinions are similar to *beliefs*, in that both are judgments or acceptances of certain propositions as facts. But the factual support for an opinion is usually weaker than that for a belief. Finally, the term *value* refers to the importance, utility, or worth attached to particular activities and objectives, usually as ends but potentially as both means and ends.

Attitudes, interests, opinions, beliefs, and values can all be viewed as personality characteristics or motivators of behavior, and items designed to assess each of them are often found on personality assessment instruments. Cattell (1965a) views attitudes, which he defines as "readinesses to act," as at a lower level than other personality variables. Attitudes, which are the starting point in Cattell's dynamic lattice model of personality, are subservient to *sentiments*. Sentiments, in turn, are subservient to *ergs*—biologically based needs or drives that are satisfied by means of attitudes and sentiments. For example, a liking for plays and films (attitude level) may stem from an involvement with photography (sentiment level), which in turn may satisfy various needs (sex, gregariousness, curiosity) at the ergic level.

Despite some interest on the part of clinical psychologists and personality theorists such as Cattell, the measurement of attitudes has been of greater concern to social and industrial/organizational psychologists than to clinical psychologists. The reason for discussing the topic in this book is that attitude measurement is a part of personality assessment and attitude scales are similar in design and structure to rating scales and checklists.

Methods of Measuring Attitudes

Different methods can be used to obtain information on a person's attitude, including direct observation of how the person behaves in relation to certain things. That is, what does the person actually do or say in situations in which the attitude object or event is present? Willingness to do a favor, sign a petition, or make a donation to some cause are examples of behavioral measures of attitudes.

Direct observation of behavior is informative, particularly with certain individuals (e.g., young children) or when other methods are considered obtrusive. However, obtaining a representative sample of behavior, across time and situations, is very time consuming and expensive. In addition, behavioral measures of attitudes often yield different results from other methods. Among these methods are projective techniques and attitude questionnaires or scales.

Showing a set of ambiguous pictures to people and instructing them to make up a story about each picture is a *projective technique*. Because the pictures can be interpreted in different ways, the stories told by the respondents should reveal something about their attitudes toward the characters, scenes, or situations in the pictures.

The most popular method of measuring attitudes is to administer an attitude scale. An *attitude scale*, consisting of a set of positive and negative statements concerning a subject of interest (a group of people, an institution, a concept, etc.), can be constructed in a number of different ways. One of the first attitude scales was the Bogardus Social Distance Scale (Bogardus, 1925), on which respondents were asked to indicate their degree of acceptance of various racial and religious groups by ranking them. The Borgardus scale proved useful in research on regional differences and other variables associated with racial prejudice, but it permitted attitude measurement on only an ordinal scale and was somewhat crude by present-day standards. More precise measures of attitudes were subsequently made possible by the work of Louis Thurstone, Rensis Likert, Louis Guttman, and other psychometricians.

Thurstone Scales

During the late 1920s, Louis Thurstone and his colleagues began attempting to put attitude measurement on the level of interval measurement by using the methods of *pair comparisons* and *equal-appearing intervals*. The first step in constructing an attitude scale by either method is to collect a large number of statements expressing a wide range of positive and negative attitudes toward a given topic. The next step in the method of pair comparisons is for a group of experts to compare every statement with every other statement and make a judgment about which statement in each pair expresses a more positive attitude. Because the pair comparisons procedure proved to be cumbersome and time consuming, the method of equal-appearing intervals has been more popular.

The first step in the method of equal-appearing intervals is to have several dozen expert judges sort the 200 or so attitude statements into eleven categories, varying from least favorable (category 1) to most favorable (category 11) attitude toward the object. The judges are instructed to think of the 11 categories as lying at equal intervals along a continuum. After all judges have completed the sorting process for all statements, a frequency distribution for each statement is constructed by counting the number of judges who placed the statement in each of the 11 categories. Next the median (scale value) and semi-interquartile range (ambiguity index) is computed from the frequency distribution for each statement. The final attitude scale consists of 20 or so statements selected in such a way that the 20 scale values are approximately equidistant in numerical value, the range of scale values is as wide as possible, and the ambiguity indexes are low. A portion of one of the many attitude scales constructed by

L. L. Thurstone and his colleagues by this method is shown in Figure 6–5. Note that the scale values of the statements shown, which are concerned with attitudes toward capital punishment, range from .1 (highly negative toward) to 11.0 (highly positive toward). An examinee's score on such a scale is the median of the scale values of the statements with which she or he indicates agreement.

Thurstone and his co-workers constructed some 30 attitude scales by the method of equal-appearing intervals, which was generalized by Remmers (1960) in his *master attitude scales*. Nine commercially available Master Attitude Scales by H. H. Remmers (Purdue Research Foundation) measure attitudes toward: any school subject, any vocation, any institution, any defined group, any proposed social action, any practice, any homemaking activity, individual and group morale, and the high school. Like the Thurstone scales in general, the reliabilities of the Master Attitude Scales are mostly in the .80s.

Despite the fairly high reliabilities of instruments constructed by this procedure, the method of equal-appearing intervals has been criticized on a number of points: (1) the great amount of work required in constructing an attitude scale, (2) the lack of uniqueness in a respondent's score, and (3) the effects of the judges' own attitudes toward the scale values of statements (Selltiz, Wrightsman, & Cook, 1976). Considering the availability of new timesaving techniques, the first criticism is not so serious. The second criticism refers to the fact that the same score, which is simply the median scale value of the statements checked, may be obtained by checking different statements. The third criticism refers to the fact that not everyone is capable of playing the role of a neutral judge. Bruvold (1975) concluded, however, that careful instruction of the judges reduces the judgmental bias to a level that does not seriously distort the equal-interval properties of these scales. A final criticism, which is not limited to Thurstone-type attitude scales, is that these scales represent measurement at only an ordinal, not an interval level (Petrie, 1969). Although the actual level of measurement of equal-appearing interval scales probably lies somewhere between the ordinal and interval levels, the matter is debatable.

Likert Scales

Like the method of equal-appearing intervals, R. Likert's (1932) *method of summated* ratings begins with the collection of a large number of statements expressing a variety of positive and negative attitudes toward a specified object or event. Next a group of 100 to 200 people, not necessarily expert judges as required by the method of equal-appearing intervals, indicate on a four- to seven-point scale the extent to which they agree or disagree with each statement. In the typical case of a five-point scale, positively stated items are scored 0 for strongly disagree, 1 for disagree, 2 for undecided, 3 for agree, and 4 for strongly agree; negatively stated items are scored 4 for strongly disagree, 3 for disagree, 2 for undecided, 1 for agree, and 0 for strongly agree. A respondent's total score on the initial attitude item set is computed as the sum of scores for the individual items. After obtaining the total

Figure 6–5 **Twelve of the twenty-four items on a scale of attitudes toward capital punishment***

This is a study of attitude toward capital punishment. Below you will find a number of statements expressing different attitudes toward capital punishment.

√Put a checkmark if you agree with the statement.
X Put a cross if you disagree with the statement.

Try to indicate either agreement or disagreement for each statement. If you simply cannot decide about a statement you may mark it with a question mark.
This is not an examination. There are no right or wrong answers to these statements. This is simply a study of people's attitudes toward capital punishment. Please indicate your own convictions by a checkmark when you agree and by a cross when you disagree.

Scale Value	Item Number	
(0.1)	12	I do not believe in capital punishment under any circumstances.
(0.9)	16	Execution of criminals is a disgrace to civilized society.
(2.0)	21	The state cannot teach the sacredness of human life by destroying it.
(2.7)	8	Capital punishment has never been effective in preventing crime.
(3.4)	9	I don't believe in capital punishment but I'm not sure it isn't necessary.
(3.9)	11	I think the return of the whipping post would be more effective than capital punishment.
(5.8)	18	I do not believe in capital punishment but it is not practically advisable to abolish it.
(6.2)	6	Capital punishment is wrong but is necessary in our imperfect civilization.
(7.9)	23	Capital punishment is justified only for premeditated murder.
(9.4)	20	Capital punishment gives the criminal what he deserves.
(9.6)	17	Capital punishment is just and necessary.
(11.0)	7	Every criminal should be executed.

*The items are arranged in order of scale values, and the scale values are listed, neither of which is the case on the actual scale.

Used by permission from Peterson & Thurstone (1933).

scores of all respondents on the initial item set, a statistical procedure (t-test or item discrimination index) is applied to each item. Then equal numbers of positively and negatively stated items (usually 10 of each) that significantly differentiate between respondents whose total scores fall in the upper 27% from those whose total scores fall in the lower 27% are selected. Ten items from an attitude scale constructed by this method are shown in Figure 6–6. A person's total score on this scale is the sum of the numerical weights (0, 1, 2, 3, or 4) of the responses which he or she checks.

Ten of the twenty items on a scale of attitudes toward socialized medicine* | **Figure 6–6**

Please indicate your reaction to the following statements, using these alternatives:

Strongly Agree = SA
Agree = A
Undecided = U
Disagree = D
Strongly Disagree = SD

*1. The quality of medical care under the system of private practice is superior to that under a system of compulsory health insurance.

2. A compulsory health program will produce a healthier and more productive population.

*3. Under a compulsory health program there would be less incentive for young persons to become doctors.

4. A compulsory health program is necessary because it brings the greatest good to the greatest number of people.

*5. Treatment under a compulsory health program would be mechanical and superficial.

6. A compulsory health program would be a realization of one of the true aims of a democracy.

*7. Compulsory medical care would upset the traditional relationship between the family doctor and the patient.

*8. I feel that I would get better care from a doctor whom I am paying than from a doctor who is being paid by the government.

9. Despite many practical objections, I feel that compulsory health insurance is a real need of the American people.

10. A compulsory health program could be administered quite efficiently if the doctors would cooperate.

---

*The asterisked items are scored 0,1,2,3,4 for SA, A, U, D, and SD; the remaining items are scored in the opposite direction.

From I. Mahler (1953). "Attitudes toward Socialized Medicine." *Journal of Social Psychology*, 38, pp. 273–282. Reprinted with permission of the Helen Dwight Reid Educational Foundation. Published by Heldref Publications, 4000 Albermarle St., N.W., Washington, D.C. 20016. Copyright © 1953.

Not all published attitude scales referred to as Likert-type scales have been constructed by item-analysis procedures (Triandis, 1971). In many cases a set of declarative statements, each with five agree-disagree response categories, is simply put together as an instrument without any specific theoretical construct in mind or without following the Likert attitude-scaling procedure. Consequently, one cannot be certain that a questionnaire that looks like a Likert scale was actually constructed by the Likert scaling procedure.

Despite misuses of Likert's method of summated ratings, it has several advantages over Thurstone's method of equal-appearing intervals (Selltiz, Wrightsman & Cook, 1976). Because it does not require expert, unbiased judges, constructing a Likert scale is easier than constructing a Thurstone scale. Also unlike Thurstone scales, Likert scales permit the use of items that are not clearly related to the attitude being assessed as long as they are significantly correlated with total scores. Finally, a Likert scale is likely to have a higher reliability coefficient than a Thurstone scale consisting of the same number of items. Like Thurstone scales, however, Likert scales have been criticized for the fact that different patterns of responses can yield the same score, and that at best the scores represent ordinal measurement.

Guttman Scales

The Thurstone and Likert attitude-scaling procedures have been widely used, but a third procedure—Louis Guttman's *scalogram analysis*, has been employed less frequently. The purpose of scalogram analysis (Guttman, 1944) is to determine whether the responses to the items chosen to measure a given attitude fall on a single dimension. When the items constitute a true, unidimensional Guttman scale, the respondent who endorses a particular item also endorses every item having a lower scale value. This condition is more likely to be realized with cognitive than with attitude statements and other affective items.

As in the Bogardus (1925) approach to attitude-scale construction, scalogram analysis aims to produce a cumulative, ordinal scale. Guttman realized the difficulty of creating such a true scale with attitudinal items, but he felt that it could be approximated. The extent to which a true scale is obtained is indicated by the *reproducibility coefficient*, computed as the proportion of actual responses that fall into the perfect pattern of a true Guttman scale. That is, what proportion of the respondents who endorse a particular item endorse all items below it on the scale? An acceptable value of the reproducibility coefficient is .90 (see Edwards, 1957a).

Other Attitude Measurement Procedures

A number of other procedures have been devised or applied to the process of attitude-scale construction, including the semantic-differential technique, Q technique, and facet analysis. The first two of these were discussed earlier in the chapter, and the last will be touched on very briefly. *Facet analysis* is a complex, multidimensional procedure for item construction and analysis that can be applied to any attitude object or situation (Castro & Jordan, 1977). The procedure has been used to construct attitude-behavior scales pertaining to a number of psychosocial conditions and situations, including mental retardation (Jordan, 1971) and racial-ethnic interaction (Hamersma, Paige & Jordan, 1973).

It has become increasingly clear during the past decade or so that attitude measurement is multidimensional rather than unidimensional, requiring more complex assessment procedures than those of Thurstone and Likert. For example, factor analysis (see Chapter 2) is now commonly used in constructing attitude instruments (Steiner & Barnhart, 1972; Wiechmann & Wiechmann, 1973). The trend away from unidimensional scales is also seen in the increasing use of complex statistical procedures such as multidimensional scaling (van der Kamp, 1973), latent structure analysis (Lazarsfeld, 1957), latent-partition analysis (Hartke, 1979), and the repertory-grid technique (Duckworth & Entwhistle, 1974).

Sources and Psychometric Characteristics of Attitude Scales

A volume compiled by Shaw and Wright (1967) describes 176 attitude scales of various types, covering attitudes toward a variety of issues, concepts, groups, and institutions. In addition, a series of books published by the Institute for Social Research at the University of Michigan describes many different scales for assessing social attitudes (Robinson & Shaver, 1973), political attitudes (Robinson, Rush & Head, 1973), and occupational attitudes (Robinson, Athanasiou & Head, 1974). Several dozen attitude measures, covering a wide range of areas, are also listed in *Tests in Microfiche* and can be ordered from Educational Testing Service.

Many publishers and distributors of psychological assessment instruments (see Appendix B for names and addresses) market attitude questionnaires and scales. For example, the Master Attitude Scales are available from the Purdue University Bookstore; the Survey of School Attitudes and the Survey of Study Habits and Attitudes are available from The Psychological Corporation; the Employee Attitude Inventory is available from London House.

As with attitude questionnaires in general, the reliabilities of the standardized instruments listed above are lower than those of standardized tests of cognitive abilities. However, the test-retest and internal-consistency coefficients of Thurstone- and Likert-type scales often reach into the .80s and .90s. With respect to validity, scores on attitude scales appear to make a small, but significant contribution to the prediction of performance in academic and certain other organizational settings. But attitude measures have not generally correlated very highly with actual behavior, and research reviews have concluded that they are not very accurate predictors of specific behavior (see Gardner, 1975). It has been argued, however, that specific behavior can be predicted from measures of attitude toward the specific behavior, especially when the attitude statements are expressed in behavioral terms (Ajzen & Fishbein, 1977).

Summary

Checklists and rating scales serve many different purposes, among which are summarizing and objectifying the results of observations and interviews. Checklists are similar to rating scales in that they require a decision concerning the presence or absence of a particular behavior or characteristic. But unlike rating scales, which require responses to be made on a multicategory continuum, checklists demand only a Yes-No or other dichotomous decision. Both checklists and rating scales are useful in assessing whether individuals possess certain behaviors or traits and if changes have occurred in these variables. Such changes frequently result from the application of a particular treatment, educational program, or other intervention process; checklists and rating scales can be used to evaluate the effectiveness of such interventions.

A checklist can usually be constructed quite simply, but it is more behaviorally oriented, and hence more objective, when the items deal with critical incidents—specific behaviors that are necessary for effective performance or some other criterion. Commerically available checklists of problems, such as the Mooney Problem Check Lists, and adjectives, such as the Adjective Check List and the Depression Adjective Check Lists, have been used extensively for both diagnostic and research purposes in educational, clinical, and industrial-organizational contexts. Although checklists are not usually considered to measure as precisely as rating scales, summing the responses checked by a large number of persons in assessing other persons can produce fairly stable scores.

The effective use of rating scales requires that judgments (ratings) concerning behaviors, personality traits, or other characteristics of individuals (ratees) be made by objective, unbiased raters. Depending on the nature of the concept rated, and thus the origin of the scale, a rating scale may be unipolar or bipolar. Depending on whether the various scale positions are numbers, verbal descriptions, or more behavioral descriptions, a rating scale may be numerical, graphic, or behaviorally anchored. A semantic differential is a special form of a numerical scale used to assess the connotative meanings of specified concepts to the rater. Another type of rating scale is the standard rating scale, such as the man-to-man scale, on which ratees are compared against a set of standards.

Different kinds of errors that occur in making ratings include the ambiguity error, constant errors (leniency, severity, and central tendency errors), contrast error, logical error, proximity error, and halo effect. The forced-choice rating procedure, on which the rater is required to choose between two equally desirable descriptions and perhaps between two equally undesirable descriptions as well, controls for some of these errors, but it is cumbersome to use and disliked by many raters. Ratings may be transformed to standard scores as a statistical control for constant errors, but perhaps the most effective procedure for reducing the effects of all types of errors in rating is to train the raters carefully and make them aware of the various kinds of errors.

Although standardized rating scales tend to be more reliable than unstandardized scales, ratings are not typically as reliable as scores on personality inventories or cognitive tests. However, when a rating scale is carefully constructed to be as objective as possible and the raters are carefully trained, reliability coefficients in the .80s or even in the .90s can be attained. Averaging the ratings of several raters also improves the reliability coefficient of a rating scale.

Q sorts are modified rating scales in which the respondent sorts a set of a hundred or so cards containing personality descriptions into nine piles to form a normal distribution of statements across piles. The Q sort procedure has been used in studies concerned with the effectiveness of psychological counseling and in other research and applied contexts.

Personality assessment approaches similar to checklists and ratings are the sociometric technique, guess-who technique, and Role Construct Repertory (Rep) Test. All three procedures involve selecting and comparing people according to various criteria or dimensions. The results of applying the sociometric and guess-who techniques can be used to identify individuals in a group who have personal and social problems. The Rep Test is a complex procedure based on George Kelly's theory of personal constructs.

Attitudes are learned predispositions to respond positively or negatively to some object, situation, or person. As such, attitudes are personality characteristics, although at a more superficial level than temperaments, values, and other traits. Attitudes can be assessed in a number of ways, the most popular being an attitude scale. The procedures for scaling attitudes devised by Thurstone (method of equal-appearing intervals), Likert (method of summated ratings), and Guttman (scalogram analysis), particularly the first two, have been commonly employed. Other attitude-scaling procedures include the semantic-differential technique, Q sorts, and facet analysis. Multivariate techniques such as factor analysis, multidimensional scaling, latent-structure analysis, latent-partition analysis, and the repertory grid technique have also been applied to the scaling of attitudes.

Judging by the variety of attitude instruments that have been devised, an individual can have an attitude toward almost anything—any school subject, any vocation, any defined group, any institution, any proposed social action, any practice. The great majority of the hundreds of attitude scales and questionnaires listed in various reference sources are unstandardized instruments designed for a particular research investigation or application. However, a number of standardized instruments for assessing attitudes, especially toward school and school subjects, work and work supervisors, are available from publishers of psychological and educational tests.

Exercises

1.   Define each of the following terms in a sentence or two.

adaptive behavior   ambiguity error
adjective checklist   attitude

attitude scale	master attitude scale
behaviorally anchored scales	mutual admiration societies
belief	numerical rating scale
bipolar scale	opinion
central tendency error	pair comparisons
checklist	projective technique
cliques	proximity error
constant error	Q sort
contrast error	rating scale
critical incidents technique	reproducibility coefficient
equal-appearing intervals	scalogram analysis
ergs	semantic-differential scale
facet analysis	semantic space
forced-choice rating scale	sentiments
generosity error	severity error
graphic rating scale	sociogram
guess-who technique	sociometric technique
halo effect	standard rating scale
interest	stars
isolates	summated ratings
leniency error	unipolar scale
logical error	value
man-to-man scale	

2. Make a copy of the Behavioral Checklist for Performance Anxiety (Figure 6–1) and use it to record your observations of a person over eight time periods of ten minutes each. Put a check mark after the behavior in the appropriate time period column if the behavior occurs during that time. Make multiple check marks if the same behavior is observed more than once during the time period. How consistent was each of the behaviors across the eight time periods, and how many times did each behavior occur? Would you characterize the person whom you observed as an "anxious person"? Do you believe that all of the 20 behaviors listed in Figure 6–1 are indicative of "anxiety"? Why or why not?

3. Consulting a dictionary or thesaurus, select a sample of 50 adjectives referring to traits or characteristics of personality. Try to choose a mixture of positive and not-so-positive terms that are not synonyms or antonyms. Make multiple copies of the alphabetized list of terms, with a short blank line after each adjective, and administer the list to a sample of students. Ask the students to check each adjective that they believe to be generally descriptive of themselves. Summarize the results, comparing them with what you already know about the individuals from other reports and observations.

4. To construct an attitude scale by Thurstone's method of equal-appearing intervals, suppose that each of 50 judges sorts 200 attitude statements into 11 piles.

The number of judges who place statements X, Y, and Z into each category are given in the three frequency distributions listed below. Compute the scale value (median) and ambiguity index (semi-interquartile range) of each statement by methods described in Chapter 2. Use the pile number (1, 2, . . . , 11) plus .5 as the upper exact limit of the interval.

Pile Number	Statement X	Statement Y	Statement Z
1	3		
2	4		
3	6	8	
4	8	10	
5	13	12	6
6	10	9	9
7	6	8	10
8		3	18
9			7
10			
11			

5. Administer the Thurstone attitude scale in Figure 6–5, (Attitudes Toward Capital Punishment, and the Likert attitude scale in Figure 6–6, (Attitudes Toward Socialized Medicine), to several people. The statements in Figure 6–5 will have to be retyped in order according to their item number, omitting the scale values, before administering this scale. The person's total score on the scale of attitudes toward capital punishment is determined by adding the scale values of the statements checked by the person and dividing this sum by the total number of statements (12). The score on the scale of attitudes toward socialized medicine is determined in the following manner by adding the points corresponding to the response (SA, A, U, D, SD) indicated for each item: on items 2, 4, 6, 9, and 10; $SA = 4$; $A = 3$; $U = 2$; $D = 1$; and $SD = 0$; on items 1, 3, 5, 7, and 8; $SA = 0$; $A = 1$; $U = 2$; $D = 3$; and $SD = 4$. Question your examinees about the causes of their attitudes toward capital punishment and socialized medicine, and summarize the results. Do you perceive any relationship between their attitudes and their personalities?

6. Ask each member of a small college class or other regularly meeting group of people who know each other fairly well to write, on a slip of paper, the names of three people in the group with whom he or she would most like to engage in a certain activity (e.g., study for the next test). Assign a numerical or letter code to each person in the group, and construct a sociogram of the results similar to the one in Figure 6–3. Interpret your sociogram in terms of the social dynamics of the group, taking note of the stars, isolates, cliques, and mutual admiration societies.

7. In what sense are attitudes indicators of personality? Give examples from your own experience or from fiction (short stories, novels, plays, films, etc.) and

history illustrating how a person's attitudes can reveal significant facts about his or her personality.

Suggested Readings

Aiken, L. R. (1980). Attitude measurement and research. In D. A. Payne (Ed.), *Recent developments in affective measurement* (pp. 1–24). San Francisco: Jossey-Bass.

Aiken, L. R. (1985). Rating scales. In R. J. Corsini (Ed.), *Encyclopedia of psychology* (Vol. 3, pp. 206–207). New York: Wiley.

Davis, D., & Ostrom, T. M. (1985). Attitude measurement. In R. J. Corsini (Ed.), *Encyclopedia of psychology* (Vol. 1, pp. 97–99). New York: Wiley.

Dickinson, T. L., & Zellinger, P. M. (1980). A comparison of the behaviorally anchored rating and mixed standard scale formats. *Journal of Applied Psychology, 65,* 147–154.

Kelman, H. C. (1974). Attitudes are alive and well and gainfully employed in the sphere of action. *American Psychologist, 19,* 310–324.

Saal, F. E., Downey, R. G., & Lahey, M. A. (1980). Rating the ratings: Assessing the psychometric quality of rating data. *Psychological Bulletin, 88,* 413–428.

Teeter, P. A. (1985). Review of the Adjective Check List. In J. V. Mitchell, Jr. (Ed.), *The ninth mental measurements yearbook* (Vol. I, pp. 50–52). Lincoln, NE: University of Nebraska Press.

PART III

Personality Inventories

CHAPTER 7

Rational-Theoretical and Factor-Analyzed Inventories

$\mathbf{A}$ *personality inventory* consists, as does a personality rating scale or checklist, of items concerning personal characteristics, thoughts, feelings, and behavior. Personality inventories, however, typically measure a broader range of variables and are usually more carefully constructed and standardized than rating scales and checklists. These inventories are frequently designed to yield scores on several personality variables, but many single-score or single-purpose inventories are also available. They have been used, with mixed success, for a variety of purposes, including research on personality, psychiatric diagnosis, personality counseling, educational and vocational counseling, occupational selection and placement, and premarital, marital, and family counseling.

In the history of personality assessment, the initial focus was on the development of instruments to serve a very practical purpose—that of identifying and diagnosing maladjusted or mentally disordered individuals. Even today, as seen in the popularity of tests used in clinical and counseling situations to detect mental illness, behavioral disorders, and delinquency, and to predict various kinds of personally and socially destructive behaviors, the emphasis in personality assessment continues to be on the pathological. Nevertheless, personality inventories designed for so-called normal individuals and that focus on more positive features and coping behaviors are used extensively—primarily in research, but also in guidance, self-exploration, personal development, and applicant selection. The use of these inventories is not limited to mental hospitals and mental health clinics; they are also administered in schools, colleges, business-industrial contexts, and other organizational situations.

Despite decades of criticism of personality assessment devices, an increase in research and development in personality assessment during the 1970s and 1980s has given rise to many new instruments. A number of these are special-purpose instruments designed for a particular research program concerned with, say, depression, suicide, cardiovascular disease, or criminal behavior. Others are general-purpose instruments designed with greater psychometric sophistication than their predecessors to measure a host of personality variables. Table 7–1 indicates which personality inventories are the most popular. It lists the 13 personality inventories referred to the greatest number of times in *The Ninth Mental Measurements Yearbook* (Mitchell, 1985). Note that the Minnesota Multiphasic Personality Inventory (MMPI) is by far the most frequently cited inventory.

Psychometric Characteristics

The assessment instruments discussed in this chapter and the next have been called *objective* measures, in the sense that they consist of true-false or multiple choice items that can be scored objectively. Respondents are required to select a response from a dichotomy (true-false, yes-no, agree-disagree, etc.) or from a list of three or more alternatives (e.g., completely false, mostly false, partly false and partly true, mostly true, completely true; strongly disagree, disagree, neutral, agree, strongly agree). A trained psychologist or other mental health professional is not needed to score a personality inventory; it can be done by a clerk. Another advantage of personality inventories is that a large number of items, covering a wide range of topics, can be answered in a relatively short period of time to provide a comprehensive description of various features of an examinee's personality.

Scale Construction Strategies

Strategies for constructing personality inventories, rating scales, and checklists were described briefly in Chapter 2. Although the terms differ somewhat depending upon who is doing the describing, most authorities agree that there are basically three approaches to the development of a personality inventory.

Rational-Theoretical Strategy   The first strategy has been referred to in a variety of ways: content-based, deductive, rational, intuitive, judgmental, logical-content,

	Table 7–1

Reference Frequencies and Ranks for the 13 Personality Inventories in a Group of 50 Tests in *The Ninth Mental Measurements Yearbook* Generating the Largest Number of References

Personality Inventory	Number of References	Rank
Minnesota Multiphasic Personality Inventory	339	1
State-Trait Anxiety Inventory	158	4
Eysenck Personality Inventory	91	8
16 Personality Factor Questionnaire	67	13.5
SCL-90-R	61	16.5
California Psychological Inventory	61	16.5
Tennessee Self-Concept Scale	60	18
Profile of Mood States	58	19
Personality Research Form	42	25.5
Jenkins Activity Survey	41	28.5
Piers-Harris Children's Self-Concept Scale	38	33
Eysenck Personality Questionnaire	32	36.5
Coopersmith Self-Esteem Inventories	32	36.5

Adapted from *The Ninth Mental Measurements Yearbook* by permission of the Buros Institute of Mental Measurements. Copyright 1985 by the Buros Institute of Mental Measurements of the University of Nebraska–Lincoln.

face-value, common-sense, or theoretical. We will use Lanyon and Goodstein's (1982) term *rational-theoretical strategy*, which emphasizes its origins in both reasoning and theory.

Obviously, a test designer must start somewhere. In the rational-theoretical strategy, he or she starts with a conception of personality derived from a variety of sources—common sense, professional judgment, research findings, and perhaps one or more theories of personality. Illustrative of this approach are the personality inventories and rating scales derived from the work of the trait theorists Gordon Allport and Henry Murray. Murray's needs-press theory of personality, in particular, stimulated the development of a number of instruments, including the Adjective Check List, the Edwards Personality Preference Schedule, and the Personality Research Form. Other theories of personality that have played a role in the development of assessment instruments are psychoanalytic theory (Freud, Jung), the theory of personal constructs (Kelly), internal-external locus of control theory (Rotter), and various theories of concepts such as anxiety, depression, and repression-sensitization. The Myers-Briggs Type Indicator, based on concepts from Carl Jung's analytic theory, is a good example of a *theory-based inventory*.

Factor-Analytic Strategy   A second strategy of personality test construction has been referred to as the inductive, internal consistency, clustering, itemetric, or factor-analytic. In this approach, which we shall call the *factor-analytic strategy*, the emphasis is on developing a set of internally consistent scales consisting of a collection or pool of highly intercorrelated items. In order to measure different personality variables, the correlations among scores on the various scales must be low. The development of such scales, in which the items within scales are highly intercorrelated but the scales themselves have low correlations with each other, relies on the methods of factor analysis. Illustrative of personality inventories constructed by this factor-analytic strategy are the Guilford-Zimmerman Temperament Survey, the 16 Personality Factor Questionnaire, and the Eysenck Personality Inventory.

Criterion-Keyed Strategy   The third strategy for developing personality assessment instruments is variously referred to as the external, empirical, group-contrast, criterion group, criterion-validated, or criterion-keyed strategy. We shall use the last term, *criterion-keyed strategy*, to emphasize the fact that item selection and instrument validation by this strategy consist of determining the extent to which the items and scores on specific scales differentiate between specified criterion groups. Depending on the purpose of the inventory, the two criterion groups may be dichotomies such as physicians versus men in general, psychiatric patients versus normals, delinquents versus nondelinquents, or high-anxious versus low-anxious people. The criterion-keyed strategy, which was used initially in selecting items for the Strong Vocational Interest Blank for Men, was subsequently applied in the development of the Minnesota Multiphasic Personality Inventory, the California Psychological Inventory, the Jesness Inventory, and certain other psychometric instruments.

Each of the above strategies has its advantages and disadvantages. For example, inventories developed using a rational-theoretical approach have greater face validity and can be constructed more easily than criterion-keyed inventories, but they are more easily faked than the latter (Burisch, 1984). In terms of their effectiveness in predicting external criteria, Goldberg (1972) found that scales produced by the three methods were equally effective. Criterion-keyed inventories did possess certain advantages over rational-theoretical and factor-analyzed inventories, but these advantages were not impressive.

The three strategies for developing personality tests are not mutually exclusive, and those who construct tests frequently try to capitalize on the merits of all three approaches by employing a combination of them in forming a personality inventory. The development of a scale to measure a specific personality variable or construct begins with a careful definition of the construct based on reasoning and theory, followed by preparation of a large pool of items designed to measure the construct. Items may consist of terms, phrases, statements, or questions. The item pool is then administered to a sample of subjects (a pilot group) representative of the target population. The responses of the pilot group are analyzed to identify items that require editing or discarding. Items answered (or not answered) in a particular direction by an excessive number of respondents and items having low correlations with total scores on the scale are particularly suspect. The statistical analysis typically involves internal consistency checks and perhaps factor analysis. Next the revised items are administered to a new sample of people, and these results are analyzed to determine their psychometric properties (reliability, validity, norms, etc.). Of particular interest is the ability of the scale to differentiate between criterion groups, that is, a group of people known from independent evidence to possess a high degree of the variable or construct and a group known to possess a low amount of it. This process may continue, of course, including additional research on the reliability and validity of the scale and any other scales comprising the inventory.

Faking and Response Sets

It was assumed by early developers of personality inventories that respondents were aware of their own characteristics and would answer the test questions honestly and accurately, interpreting the words and phrases of the items in the same way as other people. Unfortunately, these assumptions have not always been justified, and response validity has continued to be a serious problem in the case of personality inventories. Not only may people be unwilling to tell the truth about themselves, as they know it; they may not even know what the truth is and unintentionally give incorrect answers.

Depth-psychologists and other critics of self-report questionnaires have long alleged that these instruments tap only surface or conscious aspects of personality and can therefore by easily falsified. According to these critics, projective tests are more valid than personality inventories because they get at deeper layers of personality and are less subject to faking. These criticisms are not without merit: research findings demonstrate that people can distort their responses to personality inventories when directed to do so (e.g., Noll, 1951; Wesman, 1952). However, outright lying or faking on self-report measures of personality administered in counseling and job placement situations is probably not as common as one might be led to believe (see Schwab & Packard, 1973). In any event, faking is usually more of a problem on personality inventories than it is on ability tests and can contribute to the lower reliabilities of the former. Other factors, such as situational specificity and changeability of responses over time, which are more characteristic of measures of personality than ability, also affect the reliabilities of the former instruments.

Outright malingering (faking bad) and faking good are not the only response tendencies that affect the validity of personality test scores; acquiescence, social desirability, overcautiousness, extremeness, oppositionalism, and other *response sets* or response styles also contribute to a distorted picture of personality. All of these response sets are tendencies to respond to an item in a particular way, regardless of its content. *Acquiescence* (yea-saying), which causes particular problems on true-false items, refers to the tendency to agree (answer *true*) rather than disagree (answer *false*) when in doubt. The *social desirability* response set is the tendency to respond in a more socially acceptable manner, giving the answer that the examinee believes will create a more favorable impression.

Designed specifically to measure the social desirability response set are the Edwards Social Desirability (SD) Scale (Edwards, 1957b) and the Crowne-Marlowe Social Desirability Scale (Crowne & Marlowe, 1964). The former instrument consists of 39 true-false items on which a group of people (judges) showed perfect agreement when directed to answer in a socially desirable direction. Scores on the Edwards SD scale have been shown to correlate positively with personality scales that measure socially desirable traits (agreeableness, cooperativeness, responsibility, objectivity, etc.) and negatively with personality scales measuring socially undesirable traits (anxiety, hostility, insecurity, neuroticism, etc.) (Edwards, 1970). These findings prompted a debate within psychology as to whether measures of personality merely assess the ability to detect responses that are socially acceptable or unacceptable.

The controversy concerning whether personality inventories and scales measure something other than the ability to perceive what is socially desirable has not been completely resolved. It has, however, led to greater awareness of the effects of perceived socially desirable behavior on responses to personality test items and a need to control for this response set. Efforts to control for the social desirability response set have taken various forms, among which are developing separate social desirability scales on multiscore inventories and designing inventories in such a way that either the item format controls for social desirability or the items are neutral in terms of their social desirability (Block, 1965).

The response sets of acquiescence and social desirability have been of particular concern because the items on so many personality inventories are of the true-false variety and therefore seemingly more susceptible to these response sets. The meanings of the other response sets referred to above should be fairly obvious: *overcautiousness* means being excessively careful in answering, *extremeness* means tending to give more extreme responses than even mentally disordered people would give, and *oppositionalism* is the tendency to answer the opposite of what one believes to be true. Research has also been conducted on these three variables but not nearly as extensively as research on acquiescence and social desirability.

It may have occurred to the reader that response sets themselves may be characteristics of personality. For example, some people just can't seem to say no (acquiescence), and some are preoccupied with presenting themselves in the most favorable light (social desirability). A case can be made for viewing response sets as personality characteristics, but in general they have been seen as a source of difficulty in getting examinees to respond to the content rather than the form of an item and revealing their true personality. Edwards (1957b) has argued that the social desirability response set in particular is so strong in responding to true-false items such as those on the MMPI that it interferes significantly with a correct understanding and psychodiagnosis of the examinee.

Checks and Controls for Truthfulness in Responding

Various methods have been devised to determine whether examinees have responded truthfully to the items on a personality inventory:

1.   Count the number of items omitted by the examinee. If this number is quite different from the average number of omissions in the norm group, the examinee has probably responded incorrectly.

2.   Count the number of items that the normative sample rarely answered in the same way as the examinee. If this number is quite large, doubt may be cast on the validity of the examinee's responses. An example are *infrequency scales* on various inventories that consist of a set of items that relatively few people in the normative sample endorsed.

3.   Compute the examinee's scores on special scales developed to detect faking or response sets. If these scores are significantly larger than expected, the validity of the examinee's responses should be questioned. An example are *social desirability scales* that consist of items that are varied in content but designed to detect responding in a socially desirable direction.

The third item above, the special validity scales, is devised by administering the inventory with special directions: to fake good, to fake bad, to answer in the socially desirable direction, to answer like a mentally ill person, and so on. The item responses of examinees who were given the special directions are then compared with the responses of examinees given the standard directions, and the significance of the differences are determined. Items showing significant response differences are then formed into a special validity scale, which is cross-validated and standardized. The obtained norms on the special scale can then be used to detect faking or the given response set.

A number of procedures used in designing self-report questionnaires have also been used to control for response sets. An important control for the acquiescence response set on true-false questionnaires is to make the number of items keyed *true* approximately the same as the number keyed *false*. To control for the social desirability response set, some inventories are designed with a forced-choice item format, in which two or more phrases or statements designed to be equal in social desirability comprise each item; examinees select one as being more characteristic or descriptive of themselves. In addition, judges can rate the social desirability of items as they are constructed; items with an extremely high social desirability rating can then be eliminated.

It would be wrong to leave the reader with the impression that all responses to personality inventories bear the taint of response sets and that it is impossible to count on these inventories to reveal anything of significance about an individual's personality. Although the possibility of response sets should never be overlooked, the great majority of people probably tell the truth as they see it on a personality inventory as long as it is not against their self-interest to do so. Researchers in personality assessment (e.g., Block, 1965; Wiggins, 1973) recognize that, in constructing and using self-report inventories, one needs to be aware of the possibility of faking and response sets. Nevertheless, the content of a personality inventory is still an important factor in determining the validity and significance of the obtained responses.

Norms, Reliability, and Validity

Unlike many checklists and rating scales, norms have been obtained for most personality inventories. Unfortunately, the norms are frequently based on small and perhaps unrepresentative samples and must therefore be interpreted with caution. A special problem exists with respect to the norms on forced-choice inventories in that they are *ipsative*: examinees' scores on the various scales comprising the inventory are related to or affect each other. Consequently, one cannot interpret a score on a given ipsative scale in any absolute sense, but only with respect to scores on other ipsative scales. This lack of independence of scores on the various scales causes difficulty in comparing a person's scores with those of other people.

The reliability coefficients of personality inventories, as with all affective measuring instruments, are almost always smaller than those of ability tests. This is understandable when one considers that responses to personality test questions are more variable across time and situations than ability test questions. This does not necessarily mean that personality traits are less stable—although they may well be—but rather that personality test items are less concrete or objective and hence the manner in which they are answered is more susceptible than ability test questions to transitory differences in attitude or mood.

For the most part, personality inventories are also quite limited in their validities. One factor related to validity is the tendency of the user of a personality inventory to believe that inventory scales having similar names necessarily measure the same variable (the jingle fallacy) or that scales having different names measure different variables (the jangle fallacy). Thus, the anxiety scales on two different inventories may have a lower correlation with each other than the anxiety scale on one inventory and the depression scale on the other. Furthermore, even when similarly named scales on two different inventories are highly correlated one must consider the possibility of a common response set. As noted above, response sets and faking prevent personality inventories from having greater validities for diagnostic and predictive purposes.

Early Inventories

Although more recently published personality inventories are far from perfect, they are psychometrically more sophisticated than early inventories such as the Personal Data Sheet, the A-S Reaction Study, and the Adjustment Inventory. Early inventories were rather crude according to today's standards, but in their time they were employed extensively in research, counseling, and selection.

Single-Score Inventories

The Personal Data Sheet, constructed in 1918 by R. S. Woodworth to identify U.S. Army recruits who were most likely to break down in combat, was the first personality inventory of any significance. Some years before, Heymans and Wiersma (1906) had constructed a list of symptoms indicative of psychopathology, a list that was revised by Hoch and Amsden (1913) and Wells (1914). However, the Personal Data Sheet was the first personality inventory to be administered on a mass basis. Designed to detect emotional disorders, this paper-and-pencil inventory consisted of 116 yes-no questions reduced from an original group of 200 questions concerning physical symptoms, abnormal fears and worries, social and environmental adjustment, unhappiness, obsessions, compulsions, tics, nightmares, fantasies, and other feelings and behaviors. The questions, similar to those asked in psychiatric screening interviews, were based on common neurotic symptoms, as well as feelings and behaviors described and observed in soldiers who had not been able to adjust to the stresses of military life. These neurotic symptoms were included as items only if they occurred at least twice as frequently in a group of individuals already diagnosed by psychiatrists as neurotics as in normals. Some illustrative items from the Personal Data Sheet are (Hollingworth, 1920)

> Do you feel sad and low-spirited most of the time?
> Are you often frightened in the middle of the night?
> Do you think you have hurt yourself by going too much with women?
> Have you ever lost your memory for a time?
> Do you usually feel well and strong?
> Do you ever walk in your sleep?
> Do you ever feel an awful pressure in or about your head?
> Are you troubled with the idea that people are watching you on the street?
> Do you make friends easily?
> Are you troubled by shyness?
> Did you have a happy childhood?
> Are you ever bothered by a feeling that things are not real? (pp. 120–126)

The Personal Data Sheet was a single-score instrument, a person's score being the total number of items answered in the direction judged to be characteristic of maladjustment or neurosis. Only items answered in the keyed direction by less than 25% of a sample of normal individuals were included in the final form of the inventory (Woodworth, 1920). It was completed too late during the war to be used in the selection of military personnel, but in its final form, known as the Woodworth Psychoneurotic Inventory, it served as a basis for the development of other paper-and-pencil inventories.

Other pioneering personality inventories of the single-score type were the X-O Test (Pressey & Pressey, 1919) and the A-S Reaction Study (G.W. and F.A. Allport, Houghton-Mifflin, 1928). On the X-O Test, examinees were directed to cross out (X) each of 600 words that they considered unpleasant, described activities they considered to be wrong (e.g., smoking, spitting in public), or referred to things that they worried about or made them anxious (e.g., money, pain). The A-S Reaction Study, a multiple choice inventory used in a number of social-psychological investigations, was designed to measure a person's disposition to be ascendant (A) or submissive (S) in everyday social relationships.

Multiscore Inventories

The first *multiscore inventory* to become commercially available was the Bernreuter Personality Inventory (1931). The Bernreuter consisted of 125 items to be answered *yes, no, or ?* in 25 minutes or so by high school students, college students, and adults; the inventory was administered to individuals as young as age 13. Different numerical weights were assigned to items to yield scores on six variables: Neurotic Tendency, Self-Sufficiency, Introversion-Extroversion, Dominance-Submission, Sociability, and Confidence. Despite the fact that its 1938 norms are outdated by almost a half-century, the Bernreuter is still commercially available through the Stoelting Company.

Another multiscore personality inventory published in the 1930s but still in use as recently as the 1970s (Lubin, Wallis & Paine, 1971) is the Adjustment Inventory by H. M. Bell (Consulting Psychologists Press, 1934, 1963). Like the Personal Data Sheet, the A-S Reaction Study and the Bernreuter Personality Inventory, the Adjustment Inventory was developed by rational or content-validated procedures. However, the six scales (Home, Health, Submissiveness, Emotionality, Hostility, Masculinity) on the inventory were refined by internal-consistency procedures and validated against various external criteria. Separate forms were provided for students (grades 9–16) and adults.

Contemporary Rational-Theoretical Inventories

Items on the first personality inventories were all derived by reasoning and logical judgment about the nature of personality and maladjustment. Many of the questions, such as those on the Personal Data Sheet, were of the same kind that a clinical psychologist or psychiatrist might ask in trying to develop a symptom picture and arrive at a psychodiagnosis. Similar psychiatrically oriented inventories, which provide several scores rather than a single maladjustment index, are popular today. An example is the SCL-90-R (L. R. Derogatis, 1975–1979; available from the author). This 90-item, self-report symptom inventory is designed to reflect the psychological symptom patterns of psychiatric and medical patients on nine primary dimensions (somatization, obsessive-compulsive, interpersonal sensitivity, depression, anxiety, hostility, phobic anxiety, paranoid ideation, psychoticism) plus three distress indices (global severity index, positive symptom distress index, positive symptom total). Unfortunately, a reviewer of the SCL-90-R concluded that "There is no evidence that it can be used clinically either for psychiatric screening, or for purposes of psychiatric diagnosis" (Payne, 1985 p. 1329).

Although the major purpose of early multiscore inventories such as the Bernreuter Personality Inventory and the Adjustment Inventory was also to identify personality adjustment difficulties, the focus was more on milder problems than on severe psychological disorders. The items on subsequent *rational-theoretical* or *content-validated inventories*, like those on the early inventories, were selected because they seemed to those who developed the tests to measure significant characteristics or constructs. Although this *a priori* approach is, as indicated previously, flawed, it continued to be used in constructing such multiscore instruments as the California Test of Personality and the Omnibus Personality Inventory.

Rational or Content-Validated Inventories

Many multiscore personality inventories were constructed during the 1940s and 1950s, a number of which were widely used for a time and then declined in popularity. Revisions and new editions kept some of these inventories from going out of print, one of which was the Taylor-Johnson Temperament Analysis.

Taylor-Johnson Temperament Analysis (T-JTA) Developed by R. J. Johnson and R. M. Taylor (Psychological Publications, Inc., 1941–1984), the T-JTA is applicable to adolescents and adults and may be answered by oneself or by one person on another in criss-cross fashion. The latest normative data, published in 1985, are used to interpret scores on nine bipolar traits: nervous-composed, depressive-lighthearted, social-quiet, responsive-inhibited, sympathetic-indifferent, subjective-objective, dominant-submissive, hostile-tolerant, self-disciplined-impulsive, plus test-taking attitude. Still widely used, particularly in premarital, marital, and family counseling, the T-JTA has received high marks from reviewers for its design and scoring and its use in youth work and relationship counseling (Stahman, 1978; Small, 1984). It is somewhat unique in that it is available in five languages and has a special edition for the blind.

Two other multiscore inventories published originally in the 1940s and 1950s are the California Test of Personality, which was widely administered in American schools, and the Omnibus Personality Inventory for college students.

California Test of Personality   Unlike many personality inventories, which have been designed for only one or two age levels, usually adolescence and adulthood, the California Test of Personality by L. P. Thorpe et al. (CTB/McGraw-Hill, 1942, 1953) has five levels: Primary (kindergarten–grade 3), Elementary (grades 4–8), Intermediate (grades 7–10), Secondary (grade 9–college), and Adult. The test at each level consists of 180 yes-no questions divided into two sections having six parts of 15 items each. The six parts in the first section are scored for Self-Reliance, Sense of Personal Worth, Sense of Personal Freedom, Feeling of Belonging, Freedom from Withdrawing Tendencies, and Freedom from Nervous Symptoms, with an overall section score on Personal Adjustment. The six parts in the second section are scored for Social Standards, Social Skills, Freedom from Anti-Social Tendencies, Family Relations, School Relations, and Community Relations, with an overall score on Social Adjustment. Combining the scores on Personal Adjustment and Social Adjustment yields a Total Adjustment Score. All 15 scores can be plotted as a profile of standard scores.

Like many other yes-no inventories, the California Test of Personality is easy to fake, but it has been quite popular over the years. Reliability studies of all levels of the test have yielded Kuder-Richardson and equivalent-forms coefficients ranging from the low .50s to the high .90s for the 15 scores, with most of the coefficients being in the .80s. Reliabilities of the two section scores and the total score are, as expected, higher than those of the 12 part scores. Furthermore, many of the part scores have substantial correlations with each other, making the interpretation of part-score differences risky. Numerous studies pertaining to the validity of the test have been conducted, but there are no controls or special scales for response sets.

Omnibus Personality Inventory   Another multiscore inventory devised by a rational or content-validated strategy, the Omnibus Personality Inventory by P. Heist et al. (The Psychological Corporation, 1959, 1968), is a 385 true-false item questionnaire developed in connection with a personality research project at the Institute for Personality Assessment and Research of the University of California. Construction of this inventory was based on general psychological knowledge and the results of personality research rather than any specific theory. It was designed for older adolescents and adults, and standardized on 3,540 male and 3,743 female college freshmen in 37 different institutions. The inventory is scored on the 14 scales listed in Table 7–2; an Intellectual Disposition Category is also determined by combining scores on six of the regular scales. Raw scores are converted to T scores, having a mean of 50 and a standard deviation of 10, and plotted in the form of a profile. Sample standard scores for one examinee are given in the last column of Table 7–2. This 17-year-old college freshman male was described as possessing intellectual interests, a high potential for scholarship, a willingness to work with a variety of people, and a highly integrated personality.

Scales and Sample Scores on the Omnibus Personality Inventory	**Table 7–2**

Scale and Description	Standard Scores of Sample Examinee
Thinking Introversion (TI): Liking for reflective thought, ideas and abstractions, and academic activities.	67
Theoretical Orientation (TO): Preference for dealing with theoretical matters and problems and for using scientific methods.	65
Estheticism (Es): Interest in, and sensitivity of response to, painting, sculpture, music, literature, and drama.	67
Complexity (Co): Tolerance or liking for flexibility in viewing and organizing phenomena with emphasis on the novel and experimental, as constrasted with a rigid or simplistic view.	73
Autonomy (Au): Drive for personal independence, intellectual and political liberalism, and tolerance; freedom from judgmental or authoritarian thinking.	66
Religious Orientation (RO): Extent of involvement, commitment, and belief in conventional religious doctrines and practices.	57
Social Extroversion (SE): Interest in seeking and enjoying social activities as contrasted with a tendency to withdraw from social contacts and responsibilities.	64
Impulse Expression (IE): Readiness to express impulses (including feelings of sensuality, rebellion, and aggression), and to seek gratification either in thought or in overt action.	66
Personal Integration (PI): Attitudes and behaviors that characterize the socially adjusted or integrated person as contrasted with the socially alienated or disturbed person.	56
Anxiety Level (AL): Freedom from symptoms of anxiety related to social maladjustment and poor self-concept.	49
Altruism (Am): Affiliation, trusting, and ethical concern for the feelings and welfare of others as opposed to a distant impersonal view.	61
Practical Outlook (PO): Interest in the practical and utilitarian applications of ideas and things: tendency to set a high value upon material possessions and concrete accomplishments.	35
Masculinity-Femininity (MF): Interests and attitudes common to members of one's sex.	52
Response Bias (RB): An indicator of test-taking attitude, reflecting the tendency to try to make a good or a bad impression.	58

Kuder-Richardson reliabilities of the Omnibus Personality Inventory scales, based on a sample of 7,283 college freshmen, are reported as ranging from .67 for the Response Bias scale to .89 for the Personal Integration scale. Several case studies of individuals who took the inventory are presented in the manual to illustrate its use. Tables of correlations of the scales with scores on other personality inventories and tests of ability, along with other evidence pertaining to validity, are also given.

Single-Construct Inventories

A number of personality measures focus on a single construct, such as depression, sex-role identity, anxiety, and self-concept, or a specific disorder, but provide two or more separate scores for that construct. Various measures of single constructs are considered throughout the book, but here we shall limit our descriptions to two—anxiety and self-concept.

State-Trait Anxiety Inventory (STAI)   Perhaps the most popular of all single-construct measures of personality, the STAI by C. D. Spielberger (Consulting Psychologists Press, 1968–1983), is a self-evaluation anxiety inventory consisting of two forms of 20 statements (e.g., "I feel calm," or "I am jittery") each, an A-State and an A-Trait. On the A-State questionnaire, examinees are instructed to indicate how they feel at the moment on a four-point scale (*not at all, somewhat, moderately so, very much so*). On the A-Trait form, examinees indicate how they generally feel by responding to each statement (e.g., "I am inclined to take things hard" or "I am a steady person") on another four-point scale (*almost never, sometimes, often, almost always*). The manual for Form Y, the most recent version of the STAI, includes extensive normative and validity data and discussions of research uses. Also available is a Children's State-Trait Anxiety Inventory by C. D. Spielberger et al. (Consulting Psychologists Press, 1968–1970), labeled the How-I-Feel Questionnaire and designed to measure state and trait anxiety in upper-elementary and junior high children.[1]

In a review of the State-Trait Anxiety Inventory, Chaplin (1984) concluded that the inventory provides a better measure of state-anxiety than of trait-anxiety. Walker and Kaufman's (1984) review of the State-Trait Anxiety Scale for Children is mainly positive but the reviewers do point to a reading level problem when the scale is administered to younger children.

Beck Depression Inventory   The Beck Depression Inventory (BDI) by A. T. Beck (The Psychological Corporation, 1961), is a widely used instrument for identifying and assessing the intensity of depression as well as distinguishing depression from anxiety. It contains 21 items in the following categories that purportedly reflect the affect, attitudes, and behavior stated in the language of clinically depressed patients:

1. Sadness
2. Pessimism/Discouragement

3. Sense of Failure
4. Dissatisfaction
5. Guilt
6. Expectation of Punishment
7. Self-Dislike
8. Self-Accusation
9. Suicidal Ideation
10. Crying
11. Irritability
12. Social Withdrawal
13. Indecisiveness
14. Body Image Distortion
15. Work Retardation
16. Insomina
17. Fatigability
18. Anorexia
19. Weight Loss
20. Somatic Preoccupation
21. Loss of Libido

The BDI items are expressions of three highly related symptoms of negative attitudes, performance impairment, and somatic disturbances comprising the general syndrome of depression. Designed for ages 13 to 80 and taking only five to ten minutes to complete, each of the 21 items is rated on a scale of 0 to 3. Norms based on various samples are expressed in terms of score ranges for various levels of depression.

Although there is no manual for the BDI, internal-consistency reliabilities in the .80s and .90s have been reported in the literature (Beck, 1970). The case for the validity of the BDI is made primarily on the basis of its content, but correlations in the .60s and .70s have been obtained with psychiatrists' ratings and other measures of depression. Despite its deceptive simplicity, the BDI has been used effectively in clinical and research settings to identify and diagnose depression—especially with individuals who are motivated to reveal their true emotional state (Stehouwer, 1985).

Measures of Self-Concept   An individual's perception and evaluation of him- or herself—the self-concept—is a significant factor in mental health and an important construct in phenomenological theories such as that of Carl Rogers. Various *self-concept scales* have been published, the most popular being the Tennessee Self-Concept Scale, the Piers-Harris Children's Self-Concept Scale, and the Coopersmith Self-Esteem Inventories.

Tennessee Self-Concept Scale (TSCS)   The TSCS by W. H. Fitts (Western Psychological Services, 1964–1984) is a widely used measure of self-concept, consisting of

100 self-descriptive statements to be answered on a scale ranging from 1 (completely false) to 5 (completely true). Written at a sixth-grade reading level, the TSCS can be administered in 10 to 20 minutes to persons aged 12 years or older. The Counseling Form is scored on 14 variables, including self-criticism, nine self-esteem scores (identity, self-satisfaction, behavior, physical self, moral-ethical self, personal self, family self, social self, and total), three variability-of-responses scores (variation across the first three self-esteem scores, variation across the last five self-esteem scores, and total), and a distribution score. The Clinical and Research Form yields the above 14 scores plus 15 other scores.

In a critique of the TSCS, Walsh (1984) concluded it is the most ambitiously and comprehensively conceived scale of self-concept in existence today, having been constructed in an orderly and reasonable manner, and having satisfactory normative data. On the negative side, the method by which the items were selected imposes certain constraints on the TSCS. The reliability data are considered to be inappropriate and inadequate, and the results of validity studies on the TSCS are mixed. Walsh (1984) concludes that the TSCS should not be used in counseling an individual concerning the nature and dynamics of his or her problems, but rather for initiating discussions about self-concept.

Piers-Harris Self-Concept Scale   Also known as The Way I Feel about Myself, the Piers-Harris Children's Self-Concept Scale by E. V. Piers and D. B. Harris (Western Psychological Associates, 1969, 1984) consists of 80 yes-no statements written at a third-grade level. The scale is used with children in grades 4 through 12. Percentile and stanine scores, based on a standardization group of 1,183 Pennsylvania schoolchildren in grades 3 through 11, are obtained on a total Self-Concept scale and six subscales (Behavior, Intellectual and School Status, Physical Appearance and Attributes, Anxiety, Popularity, Happiness and Satisfaction).

The Piers-Harris is a direct measure of self-concept that is easy to administer and score. The six subscales have high internal-consistency reliabilities, and low to high test-retest reliabilities. Among the limitations of the scale are limited standardization and only moderate correlations with other measures of self-concept. The scores are also substantially influenced by response sets, fake good, and fake bad (Cosden, 1984).

Coopersmith Self-Esteem Inventories (CSEI)   Created by S. Coopersmith (Consulting Psychologists Press, 1981), the CSEI has three forms: School Form and School Short Form for ages 8 through 15 and Adult Form for ages 16 and above. It consists of 25 to 50 dichotomous items (*Like Me, Unlike Me*). These inventories can be scored for General Self, Social Self-Peers, Home-Parents, School-Academic, Total Self, and Lie Scale.

The CSEI is a widely used inventory. The School Form is particularly popular. The manual, which is based on Coopersmith's (1981) book, *The Antecedents of Self-Esteem*, goes beyond the usual test manual in providing specific suggestions to counselors and teachers on how to improve students' self-esteem. However, the reliability, validity, and standardization data, both as reported in the manual and in other publications, are inadequate (Adair, 1984). Furthermore, no exact criteria for evaluating self-esteem, which is categorized as low, medium, and high, are given.

Health-Related Inventories

It is common knowledge that psychological factors play an important role in both the genesis and progression of physical disorders. In fact, a specific field of medicine known as psychosomatic medicine is concerned with the diagnosis and treatment of stress- connected disorders such as gastrointestinal, neuromuscular, and cardiovascular problems of various kinds. Although the influence of stress, attitudes, and other psychological factors on physical illness has been appreciated thoughout this century, certain physical disorders, such as coronary heart disease and anorexia nervosa, have become topics of intensive interdisciplinary research efforts during the past decade or so. The development of special psychological assessment instruments for pinpointing the relationships of personality factors to the particular physical disorder has assisted research in this field. Examples of personality inventories of this type are the Jenkins Activity Survey and the Eating Disorders Inventory.

Jenkins Activity Survey (JAS)   Psychological examinations of patients who manifest symptoms of coronary heart disease have revealed a pattern of behavior, known as *Type A behavior*, characterized as aggressive, ambitious, extremely competitive, preoccupied with achievement, impatient, restless, and associated with feelings of being under pressure and challenged. Contrasting with the Type A pattern is the Type B behavior pattern. People who are Type B do not show a proneness to coronary disorder. They are characterized as more relaxed, easy-going, and patient; they speak and act more slowly and evenly (Jenkins, Zyzanski & Rosenman, 1979). Compared with Type Bs, Type A individuals manifest a significantly higher incidence of heart attacks, even when differences in age, serum cholesterol level, smoking frequency, and blood pressure are taken into account. The American Heart Association recognizes the Type A behavior pattern as a significant psychosocial factor in heart and blood vessel diseases, but not as important a risk factor as smoking, high blood pressure, or high blood cholesterol (Schulte, 1985).

Each of the A and B types can be divided further into two subtypes (A1 and A2, B3 and B4), depending on the degree to which Type A or Type B characteristics are manifested. A1 people show most Type A characteristics to an intense degree, whereas Type A behavior is entirely absent in B4 people. The behaviors of A2 and B3 people are intermediate between the A1 and B4 extremes. These four behavior patterns can be assessed by either a clinical interview or a personality inventory, the Jenkins Activity Survey (JAS), which was developed by C. D. Jenkins, S. J. Zyzanski, and R. H. Rosenman (The Psychological Corporation, 1965–1979).

The JAS, which takes about 20 minutes to complete, is a 52-item, self-report questionnaire for adults aged 25 to 65 years. It is scored on Type A, as well as three factorially independent scales: Speed and Impatience, Job Involvement, and Hard Driving and Competitive. Illustrative items from each of the three scales are as follows:

1. When you listen to someone talking, and this person takes too long to come to the point, do you feel like hurrying him along?

2. How often do you bring your work home with you at night or study materials related to your job?

3. Nowadays, do you consider yourself to be:
   a. Definitely hard-driving and competitive?
   b. Probably hard-driving and competitive?
   c. Probably more relaxed and easy-going?
   d. Definitely more relaxed and easy-going?

The JAS was standardized on 2,588 middle- to upper-level managers between the ages of 48 and 65 in ten large California corporations. Results obtained from structured interviews and through retrospective and predictive studies of coronary heart disease occurrence are cited as support for the validity of the JAS.

Despite its wide usage and a number of positive features, the JAS was viewed by Blumenthal (1985) as still in the experimental phase. The reliabilities, validities, and norms of this instrument are tentative, the scoring system is complex, and controls for test-taking attitude are lacking. Blumenthal (1985) concludes that use of the JAS should be limited to research, and that clinical judgment is a more accurate method of selecting individuals who are prone to coronary heart disease.

In any event, the psychological dynamics of heart disease remain unclear. According to certain researchers (e.g., Ragland & Brand, 1988), it is not necessarily a high achievement drive per se but rather frustration resulting from a discrepancy between ambition and achievement that promotes cardiovascular illness. Research findings (see Shulte, 1985) also point to hostility, characterized by a lack of trust in other people or fear that others are out to get the person, as an important psychological variable in the blockage of coronary arteries.

The results of a long-term followup of patients who took part in a 1960s study that helped to advance Type A theory call into question the original findings. The followup study found that people with Type A personalities are no more likely to die suddenly of heart attacks that Type Bs (Ragland & Brand, 1988). Of 257 men who suffered heart attacks between the time they took part in the original (1960s) study and 1983, twenty-six died within 24 hours after suffering the attack. But there was no significant difference in the death rates of those identified as Type As and the Type Bs. Furthermore, among the 231 men who survived at least 24 hours after an attack the death rate for the Type As was only 58% of that of the Type Bs. Such a finding might lead one to conclude that, rather than increasing the risk of death after a heart attack, a Type A personality may actually serve to decrease the risk or protect the victim against death.

Eating Disorders Inventory (EDI)   The EDI by D. M. Garner and M. P. Olmstead (PAR, 1984) consists of 64 self-report statements concerning behaviors, feelings, and thoughts about eating, in addition to self-perceptions, and attitudes. The statements, were selected from a pool of 146 statements written by experienced clinicians to assess a broad range of psychological and behavioral traits common to anorexia nervosa and bulimia. Of the 11 psychological constructs that the authors of the EDI originally planned to measure, only eight met the established reliability and validity criteria. The minimum acceptable reliability coefficient (alpha) for each scale was set at .80 for the anorexia nervosa samples; the minimum item-total correlation, set at .40, was met by almost all accepted items.

The eight scales on which the EDI is scored include Drive for Thinness, Bulimia, Body Dissatisfaction, Ineffectiveness, Perfectionism, Interpersonal Distrust, Interoceptive Awareness, and Maturity Fears. However, the significant positive correlations among the majority of the eight scales show that they do not represent independent dimensions. The percentile norms for the EDI are based on 215 female primary anorexia nervosa patients, 770 female university students, 981 female high school students, and 223 male college students. The majority of the correlations of the EDI scales with scores on several personality inventories and clinicians' ratings are modest but significant. Sample cases and a few research studies employing the EDI are also described in the manual. From these data, it can be tentatively concluded that the EDI has promise as a clinical screening tool, an outcome measure, and an adjunct to clinical judgments of patients with *eating disorders*.

Millon Behavioral Health Inventory (MBHI)   Unlike the Jenkins Activity Survey and the Eating Disorders Inventory, which focus on specific disorders, the purpose of the MBHI by T. Millon et al. (National Computer Systems, 1982) is more general in its relationship to health and thus in assisting clinicians (physicians, nurses, psychologists) in formulating a comprehensive treatment plan for physically ill and behavioral-medicine adult medical patients. The MBHI consists of 150 true-false, problem-descriptive statements that can be answered in 20 minutes or so by adults. The inventory is scored on 20 scales grouped into four broad categories: eight Basic Coping Styles (likely style of dealing with health care personnel and medical regimens), six Psychogenic Attitudes (problematic psychosocial attitudes and stressors), six Psychosomatic Correlates (similarity to patients with psychosomatic complications), and Prognostic Indexes (possible treatment difficulties). A computer-generated interpretive report for the MBHI is prepared by National Computer Systems based on norms obtained from 1,194 physically ill adults (clinical group) and 452 men and women from various settings (nonclinical group). The report indicates how the patient will probably relate to health care personnel, what psychosocial attitudes and stressors are likely to cause problems, and the patient's similiarity to people with psychosomatic complications or those who respond poorly to medical treatment. The test-retest and internal-consistency reliabilities (KR-20) of the MBHI are comparable to those of other multivariable inventories (median correlation equals .80), and a variety of psychometric and empirical research data pertaining to the construct validity of the MBHI are described in the manual (Millon, 1982a).

In a review of the MBHI, Allen (1985) maintains that the manual does not adequately describe the test construction, standardization, and interpretation procedures. The reviewer points out that the reliabilities of the 20 MBHI clinical scales are moderate in a nonpatient sample and unknown among patients; the scales also have rather high correlations with each other, making profile analysis difficult. Finally, Allen (1985) feels that the evidence for the validity of the computer narrative interpretations of the MBHI scores is insufficient.

Theory-Based Inventories

Construction of the personality inventories described previously in this chapter was not guided by a specific theory of personality, although informal theories or constructs played a role in the development of some of them. For example, theories pertaining to the self undoubtedly had some effect on the construction of the Tennessee Self-Concept Scale and the Coopersmith Self-Esteem Inventories.

Two theories that have been particularly influential in the design of personality inventories are Henry Murray's needs-press theory and Carl Jung's analytic theory. Among the instruments that have employed concepts from Murray's theory are the Adjective Check List, the Edwards Personal Preference Schedule, the Personality Research Form, and the Thematic Apperception Test. Two inventories that are based on Jung's typology are the Myers-Briggs Type Indicator and The Singer-Loomis Inventory of Personality.

Edwards Personal Preference Schedule (EPPS)   The EPPS by A. L. Edwards (The Psychological Corporation, 1953–1959), which consists of 225 pairs of statements pertaining to individual likes and feelings, is one of the most widely researched of all personality inventories. Each forced-choice statement pair pits two psychological needs against each other; the examinee is instructed to indicate which statement is more descriptive or characteristic of him- or herself. In an effort to control for the social desirability response set, the two statements comprising each item were selected to be approximately equal in social desirability. An example of such a statement pair is

A. I like to do things by myself.
B. I like to help others do things.

The 15 needs on which the EPPS is scored are achievement, deference, order, exhibition, autonomy, affiliation, intraception, succorance, dominance, abasement, nurturance, change, endurance, heterosexuality, and aggression; consistency and profile stability scores are also obtained. Percentile and T score norms for each scale are based on over 1,500 students in 29 colleges and approximately 9,000 adults in 48 states; separate norms for high school students are also available. Split-half reliabilities of the scores range from .60 to .87 and test-retest reliabilities from .74 to .88.

As is the case with all forced-choice inventories, scores on the EPPS are *ipsative* rather than *normative* and must be interpreted accordingly. By endorsing statements pertaining to certain needs, the respondent *ipso facto* rejects statements pertaining to other needs. Thus, a person's score on one need is relative to his or her scores on the other needs. Consequently, scores on the various need scales are not statistically independent, a circumstance that creates problems of score interpretation.

Although the forced-choice format of the EPPS controls to some extent for the social desirability reponse set (see Feldman & Corah, 1960 and Wiggins, 1966), many examinees find the format awkward and difficult. In addition, the validity of the EPPS scales as measures of psychological needs is questionable. For example, the scores do not correlate very highly with other measures of similar variables.

Edwards reportedly designed the EPPS as an exercise in personality test construction rather than as a serious competitor with other inventories. It has stimulated a great deal of research, but remains, after 30 years, an interesting research and instructional tool rather than a diagnostic device applicable to clinical situations (see Drummond, 1984).

Myers-Briggs Type Indicator (MBTI) The MBTI by I. B. Myers (Consulting Psychologists Press and The Psychological Corporation, 1943–1977) is a research inventory composed of 166 (Form F) or 126 (Form G) two-choice items concerning preferences of inclinations in feelings and behavior. Following Carl Jung's theory of personality types, it can be scored on four bipolar scales: Introversion-Extraversion, Sensing-Intuition, Thinking-Feeling (only on Form F), and Judging-Perceptive. Combinations of scores on these four two-part categories, which are described below the drawing in Figure 7–1, result in 16 possible personality types. Thus, as shown in the profile in Figure 7–1, an ENFP type is a person whose predominant modes are Extraversion, Intuition, Feeling, and Perceptive. On the other hand, an ISTJ type is a person whose predominant modes are Introversion, Sensing, Thinking, and Judging. Unfortunately, no measures of test-taking attitude are provided, a shortcoming that could lead to errors of diagnosis and screening (Willis, 1984).

Percentile norms for the four indicator scores, based on small samples of high school and college students, are given in the MBTI manual (Myers & McCaulley, 1985). Split-half reliabilities of the four scores are reported as being in the .70s and .80s, and a number of small-scale validity studies are also described. Although the conceptualization of personality in terms of types is not viewed with favor by most American psychologists, an impressive array of materials on the Myers-Briggs Type Indicator has been published by Consulting Psychologists Press. Included in these materials are books, computer software, and the Myers-Briggs Type Development Indicator (Research Edition). These materials should be studied extensively by the

Figure 7–1   Report form for Myers-Briggs Type Indicator

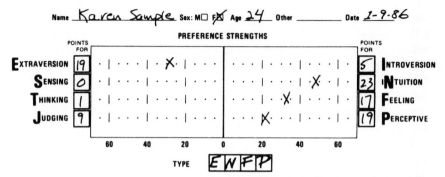

Indicator questions deal with the way you like to use your perception and judgment, that is, the way you like to look at things and the way you like to go about deciding things. The answers given reflect four separate preferences called EI, SN, TF and JP. The profile above shows your score on each preference. The four letters of your "type" tell how you came out on all four preferences. What each preference means is shown below.

E An E for extraversion probably means you relate more easily to the outer world of people and things than to the inner world of ideas.

I An I for introversion probably means you relate more easily to the inner world of ideas than to the outer world of people and things.

S An S for sensing probably means you would rather work with known facts than look for possibilities and relationships.

N An N for intuition probably means you would rather look for possibilities and relationships than work with known facts.

T A T for thinking probably means you base your judgments more on impersonal analysis and logic than on personal values.

F An F for feeling probably means you base your judgments more on personal values than on impersonal analysis and logic.

J A J for the judging attitude probably means you like a planned, decided, orderly way of life better than a flexible, spontaneous way.

P A P for the perceptive attitude probably means you like a flexible, spontaneous way of life better than a planned, decided, orderly way.

Each combination of preferences tends to be characterized by its own set of interests, values and skills. On the back of this page are very brief descriptions of each type. Find the one matching your four letters and see whether or not it fits you. If it doesn't, try to find one that does. Whatever your preferences, of course, you may still use some behaviors characteristic of contrasting preferences, but not with equal liking or skill. This tendency may be greater if preference strength on a scale is low (under 15). For a more complete discussion of the types and their vocational and personal implications, see *Introduction to Type* by Isabel Briggs Myers, or consult your counselor.

user as a background for obtaining the necessary skills to administer and interpret the MBTI.

Factor-Analyzed Inventories

The common goal of researchers who apply factor-analytic techniques to the analysis of personality has been to isolate a relatively small number of personality factors or traits that would account for variations in scores on different inventories and then construct a measure of each factor. The first published application of factor analysis to the study of personality was made by Webb (1915). Webb had large groups of males in schools and colleges make ratings on 40 or more qualities that they considered to have "a general and fundamental bearing on the total personality."

Treatment of the data by an early form of factor analysis led Webb to conclude that "consistency of action resulting from deliberate volition, or will" is the most basic characteristic of personality.

J. P. Guilford, whose research and development work began in the late 1930s and early 1940s (Guilford, 1940; Guilford & Martin, 1943), deserves credit for being the first person to construct a personality inventory by using factor-analytic techniques. The construction of his initial inventories—the Guilford-Martin Inventory of Factors, Guilford-Martin Personnel Inventory, and Inventory of Factors STDCR, which were influenced by Jung's introversion-extroversion types, involved correlating a large number of existing personality tests with each other. Guilford's tests were carefully reviewed by Louis and Thelma Thurstone, who then constructed their own personality inventory—the Thurstone Temperament Schedule (1949–1953). This 140-item inventory was scored on seven traits (Active, Vigorous, Impulsive, Dominant, Stable, Sociable, Reflective), but the reliabilities of these trait measures were not very high.

Current Factor-Scored Inventories

Guilford-Zimmerman Temperament Survey   Following Thurstone and Thurstone's analysis of Guilford's data, the latter reanalyzed his own earlier findings and published a ten-factor condensation of his three earlier inventories. Known as the Guilford-Zimmerman Temperament Survey (GZTS) (Guilford & Zimmerman, 1956) by J. P. Guilford and W. S. Zimmerman (Sheridan Psychological Services, 1949–1978), this inventory was designed for high school through adult levels and scored on ten 30-item trait scales: General Activity, Restraint, Ascendance, Sociability, Emotional Stability, Objectivity, Friendliness, Thoughtfulness, Personal Relations, and Masculinity. Three verification keys for detecting false and careless responses are also provided. Percentile and standard score norms for the ten scales, which have moderate reliabilities, are based mainly on samples of college students. Although still in print, the GZTS has never been as popular as the more clinically oriented Minnesota Multiphasic Personality Inventory.

Cattell's Questionnaires   Perhaps the most comprehensive series of inventories for assessing personality in individuals six years and older was designed by R. B. Cattell (Institute for Personality and Ability Testing, 1949–1986). Cattell began his personality research with a list of 17,953 personality-descriptive adjectives, which Allport and Odbert (1936) had gleaned from the dictionary. By combining terms having similar meanings, the list was first reduced to 4,504 real traits, then to 171 trait names; subsequent factor analyses of scores on these trait dimensions produced 31 surface traits and 12 source traits of personality. Cattell devised a number of measures of these traits and four others isolated in his later work, but his major instrument is the 16 Personality Factor Questionnaire (16 PF). Two parallel forms of the 16 PF at each of three vocabulary proficiency levels (educationally disadvantaged through newspaper-literate adults), in addition to a tape-recorded form for the educationally disadvantaged, were published.

The personality variables measured by the 16 PF are listed in Report 7–1. In addition to 16 primary traits of personality, the 16 PF can be scored for three validity or test-taking attitude scales—Motivational Distortion (MD) or faking good, Faking Bad, and Random response as well as a number of combined scores or patterns (see Report 7–1). Standard score norms (sten scores) for the 16 PF scales, based on large, representative samples of high school students, college students, and adults, are given in a special supplement supplied with the manual. Separate norms are given for males, females, and males and females combined in three groups (high school seniors, college students, adults). These sten scores, which range in value from 1 to 10, have a mean of 5.5 and a standard deviation of 2. Sten scores of 4 and below are considered low, and scores of 7 and above high.

Scores on the 16 PF may be interpreted by the *profile-matching technique* of comparing the examinee's scores with those of selected groups, for example, delinquents or neurotics. A second interpretive technique, known as *criterion estimation*, involves the use of statistical equations in which each score is multiplied by a specified numerical weight to predict selected behaviors or classifications. A somewhat less complex interpretative procedure begins with an examination of the examinee's scores on the three validity scales to determine whether the scores are sufficiently valid to warrant interpretation. If so, then scores on the second-order factors (Introversion vs. Extraversion, Low Anxiety vs. High Anxiety, Tender-minded Emotionality vs. Tough Poise, Subduedness vs. Independence) are examined, followed by an examination of the 16 primary factors (Karson & O'Dell, 1976). The following example shows how a clinical psychologist interpreted a specific pattern of sten scores on the 16 PF, using no information other than the person's age (23) and sex (female):

Factor	A	B	C	E	F	G	H	I	L	M	N	O	Q_1	Q_2	Q_3	Q_4	MD
Score	3	8	6	10	8	4	4	7	5	10	9	8	7	8	1	6	4

This is an extremely dominant and aggressive young lady who shows a severe inability to bind anxiety (Q_3 = 1). Her relatively high F of 8 indicates marked immaturity coupled with relatively low group conformity (G = 4) and high superego introjection (O = 8). Her average ego strength (C = 6) suggests that she has some good capacity for improved personal adjustment. This, and her good intelligence (B = 8), both indicate that she may be able to respond to psychotherapy. Her extremely high dominance (E = 10) and relatively high Q_1 of 7 suggest that she would be a difficult person to live with in view of her critical, castrating tendencies. She is seen as a highly sophisticated person who apparently needs to learn to get more gratification from people rather than from things. Her extraordinarily high tendency toward fantasy activity (M = 10) suggests that too much of her potential energy is perhaps wasted on impractical day-dreams rather than put to constructive use. It is hoped that her employment does not require careful attention to details and attending to the task at hand, since she is not cut out for this type of work. Her 16 PF profile suggests that she is a sporadic individual with a variable level of ego functioning who is unable consistently to apply her energies to the task at hand. She might well be able to use some psychotherapy.

A serious shortcoming of the 16 PF is its low to moderate reliabilities. The split-half reliabilities of the 16 PF factors are as low as .54, and the equivalence coefficients (correlations between primary factor scales on different test forms) are also low. Test-retest coefficients over short time intervals (dependability coefficients) are in the .70s and .80s, which are lower than the reliabilities of many other personality inventories. Evidence for the validity of the 16 PF is found in the results of numerous research investigations, many of them cross-cultural in nature (see Gynther & Gynther, 1976). A case for the construct validity of the questionnaire is made on the basis of multiple correlations between scores on items loading significantly on a factor and scores on the factor itself (direct construct validity) or multiple correlations between scores on the primary factors and scores on other factors (indirect construct validity).

An attractive feature of the 16 PF is the computer report of scores, including a score profile, personal counseling observations, intervention considerations, primary personality characteristics of significance, broad influence patterns, and vocational observations (see Report 7–1). Unfortunately, the 16 PF norms, in addition to the reliability and validity information, are rather dated. Be that as it may, the 16 PF is widely used in counseling and research, enterprises for which it would doubtless be even more valuable if it were restandardized (Wholeben, 1985).

Three inventories designed by Cattell as downward extensions of the 16 PF are the High School Personality Questionnaire for ages 12 through 18 (see Report 4–1 and Figures 4–1 and 4–2), the Children's Personality Questionnaire (for ages 8 through 12), and the Early School Personality Questionnaire (for ages 6 through 8). Like their parent instrument, the 16 PF, these questionnaires have some problems with reliability but are generally well constructed and have proven useful in educational and research contexts. In addition, Cattell designed several single-score instruments (e.g., Anxiety Scale Questionnaire, Neuroticism Scale Questionnaire, Depression Scale) as measures of more general factors of personality. By factor analyzing 16 PF items related to psychological disorders, 12 new factors were obtained, and a new inventory, the Clinical Analysis Questionnaire, was then constructed to assess scores on these 12 factors in clinical populations.

Eysenck Personality Questionnaire (EPQ)   This revision by H. J. and B. J. Eysenck (EdITS, 1975–1976) of the Eysenck Personality Inventory (1963–1969) and the Junior Eysenck Personality Inventory (1963–1970) represents a more parsimonious conception of personality than the inventories of Guilford and Cattell.

Report 7–1 Sample Report

16 P F C L I N I C A L R E P O R T

by

Samuel Karson, Ph.D.

Name: Mr. Sample
Date: January 26, 1987
Sex: Male
Age: 25

This confidential report is designed for use by appropriately qualified professionals. The presentation of information is compact and the language of the Report is technical. It was not intended to be used for patient feedback.

The report is intended to be used in conjunction with professional judgment. The statements it contains should be viewed as hypotheses to be validated against other sources of data. All information in this report should be treated confidentially and responsibly.

For additional information about the Report and its contents, please refer to the "Manual for the Karson Clinical Report", available through IPAT.

Name: Mr. Sample   -2-   January 26, 1987

TEST-TAKING ATTITUDE

Faking good attempts are slightly higher than normal. There is little or no evidence of a response set to look bad or to fake anxiety symptoms deliberately. Indications are that he read the items carefully and clearly understood what was required. The random index is within normal limits.

PERSONALITY CAPSULE DESCRIPTION

A strong need for dominance and marked evidence of assertiveness are clear in his personality makeup. He is not a particularly sophisticated or shrewd person, but instead he tends to be direct and forthright in his interpersonal relationships. This suggests a lack of experience in social situations. His obsessive-compulsive defense mechanisms are not currently operating satisfactorily. This suggests that he has not satisfactorily resolved his own identity problems. A history of conflicting family relationships is suggested that has probably succeeded in interfering with his ability to empathize with other people, and which makes him tend to move away from them. His capacity for abstract verbal skills appears to be high. He is a cool, tough-minded, realistic person who is not apt to lose control of himself in emergencies. He may resort to fantasy activity or daydreaming at a time when he ought to be responding to the exigencies of the stimulus situation confronting him. Consequently, attending to routine details is probably not his strong suit.

He is basically a shy, timid, restrained person who finds it difficult to handle threats of any kind successfully. He is seen as someone who tends to be suspicious of other people's motives and who displaces and projects his angry feelings. Superego introjection is somewhat below average, but not seriously so. He probably has little problem with depression originating in conflict with his superego. He tends to be an accepting person who is respectful of traditions and of the "establishment." He does not adopt a critical and radical approach to authority. Much dependency gratification is required from the people he encounters in his life and in his job in particular. His free-floating anxiety is above average and suggests higher than average feelings of tension and frustration.

(Continued)

Name: Mr. Sample

PRIMARY PERSONALITY TRAITS

	Low 1 2 3	Average 4 5 6 7	High 8 9 10		
A	Warmth	3
B	Intelligence	8
C	Ego Strength	5
E	Dominance	9
F	Impulsivity	6
G	Group Conformity	6
H	Boldness	4
I	Tender-Mindedness	3
L	Suspiciousness	7
M	Imagination	8
N	Shrewdness	2
O	Guilt Proneness	4
Q1	Rebelliousness	4
Q2	Self-Sufficiency	4
Q3	Compulsivity	2
Q4	Free-Floating Anxiety	7

CLINICAL SIGNS AND SYNDROMES

ANX	Anxiety	6.4
NEU	Neuroticism	4.2
PSY	Psychoticism	7.3
SOC	Sociopathy	6.9

INTERPERSONAL PATTERNS

EX	Extraversion	5.0
LD	Leadership	5.0
IN	Independence	7.3

Name: Mr. Sample

COGNITIVE FACTORS

CORT	Tough Poise	6.9
CR	Creativity	6.7
AC	Academic Achievement	6.9

NEED PATTERNS

ABA	Abasement	4.5
ACH	Achievement	8.2
AFF	Affiliation	2.6
AGG	Aggression	7.5
AUT	Autonomy	6.8
CHG	Change	6.2
DEF	Deference	2.4
DOM	Dominance	5.1
END	Endurance	4.3
EXH	Exhibition	6.9
HET	Heterosexuality	6.1
INT	Intraception	5.2
NUR	Nurturance	2.3
ORD	Order	3.3
SUC	Succorance	5.2

RAW SCORES

A: 6	B: 10	C: 18	E: 20	F: 14	G: 15	H: 10	I: 5
L: 9	M: 18	N: 4	O: 5	Q1: 6	Q2: 7	Q3: 8	Q4: 12

Faking Good: 8 Faking Bad: 0 Random: 3

The sten scores used to generate the report were corrected for distortion.

The personality profile pattern code is 2223.

This report was processed using male adult (GP) norms for Form A.

ITEM SUMMARY

Item responses have not been provided.

Eysenck's earlier inventories (the Maudsley Personality Inventory and the Eysenck Personality Inventory) were scored for two basic dimensions of personality—Neuroticism (N) and Extroversion (versus Introversion) (E)—which had emerged from his factor-analytic research. A measure of a third dimension, Psychoticism (P), and a Lie Scale (L) were added in designing the EPQ. The EPQ has a wide age range (7 through adulthood) and takes only 10 to 15 minutes to complete.

Test-retest reliabilities for the N, E, P, and L scales of the EPQ range from .78 to .89 over a one-month interval; internal-consistency coefficients are in the .70s and .80s. Norms on the two forms (A and B), based on American college students and adults, are appropriate for individuals aged 16 years and above. Norms on the Junior EPQ were obtained from samples of 7- to 15-year-old children.

The EPQ and its predecessors have been used extensively in personality research but less frequently in clinical and other applied contexts. Eysenck (1965, 1981) has used scores on the introversion-extroversion and neuroticism factors in particular to predict how individuals will react in experimental situations and has related personality patterns to body type, for example, introverts are taller and leaner than extroverts, (also see Chapter 13).

Profile of Mood States   Requiring even less testing time (3–5 minutes) than the Eysenck Personality Questionnaire is the Profile of Mood States (POMS) by W. J. Eichman and T. E. Weckowicz, (EdITS, 1971). Designed for ages 18 through adult, the POMS consists of 65 adjectives describing feeling and mood. For each adjective, examinees are instructed to fill in the circle corresponding to the term or phrase that best describes how they have been feeling during the past week including today. Possible responses on the five-point scale are *Not at all, A little, Moderately, Quite a bit, Extremely*. In the sense that it aspires to measure short-term or transitory conditions, the POMS is similar to the State Scale of the State-Trait Anxiety Inventory, the Multiple Affect Adjective Check List (see Chapter 6), and other instruments, for example, the Sickness Impact Profile by Bergner and Gilson (1981).

The POMS is scored on six factors derived from repeated factor analyses: Tension-Anxiety (*T*), Depression-Dejection (*D*), Anger-Hostility (*A*), Vigor-Activity (*V*), Fatigue-Inertia (*F*), Confusion-Bewilderment (*C*). Scores on the six factors may also be summed to yield a Total Mood Disturbance (TMD) score. Internal-consistency reliability coefficients (K-R 20) for the six factors range from .84 to .95, and test-retest coefficients from .43 to .52. As expected with transitory moods, the test-retest coefficients are quite low. A variety of studies pertaining to the validity of the POMS are described in the manual, including short term psychotherapy studies, controlled outpatient drug trials, and studies of emotion-inducing conditions. Normative data are based on several hundred psychiatric outpatients and college students, but they are probably not representative.

Peterson and Headen (1984) gave the POMS a fairly positive review. It is seen as a relatively valid measure of momentary mood states, particularly in psychiatric outpatients and for use in research on the effects of medical or psychological interventions. There are problems concerning the appropriateness of the norms and the factor structure of the POMS, but it is convenient and easy to use.

Comrey Personality Scales Another widely used multifactor inventory, the Comrey Personality Scales (CPS) by A. L. Comrey (EdITS, 1970) was designed to provide a profile description of the normal socially functioning individual. The CPS consists of 180 items to be answered on seven-point scales ranging from *Always* to *Never* or from *Definitely* to *Definitely Not*. It can be completed in 35 to 50 minutes by respondents of high school age or above and is scored on eight personality factors: Trust versus Defensiveness *(T)*, Orderliness versus Lack of Compulsion *(O)*, Social Conformity versus Rebelliousness *(C)*, Activity versus Lack of Energy *(A)*, Emotional Stability versus Neuroticism *(S)*, Extraversion versus Introversion *(E)*, Masculinity versus Femininity *(M)*, and Empathy versus Egocentrism *(P)*. Scores are also provided on an eight-item Validity Check *(V)*, designed to detect random or inappropriate responding, and a twelve-item measure of Response Bias *(R)*, defined as the tendency to answer items in a socially desirable manner. T score norms for college males and females, split-half reliability coefficients for the various scales in the .80s and .90s, and data pertaining to the validity of the CPS are reported in the manual. Significant relationships among CPS scales and criteria of success in a variety of occupational situations have been obtained, and evidence for the construct validity of the inventory is found in the results of studies pointing to considerable cross-cultural stability of the eight scales.

Despite Comrey's efforts to develop an effective factor-analyzed inventory for relatively normal personalities, the CPS has been criticized on a number of important points (Merenda, 1985). The manual is obviously out-of-date. A restandardization to produce norms that are more representative of the general population is needed. The factor structure of the CPS, which, like the norms, is based on restricted student samples, also needs improving. Another shortcoming is the lack of reported test-retest or parallel forms (only one form is published) reliability coefficients; only internal-consistency (split-half) reliabilities are given. The case for the criterion-related validity of this inventory is based mainly on concurrent correlations between CPS scales and on similar scales on other personality inventories. Merenda (1985) finds the results of construct validity studies on the CPS disappointing and concludes that it fails to meet acceptable standards for psychological tests.

Perspective on Factor Analysis in Personality Assessment

Many other personality inventories have been constructed using factor-analytic methodologies, some of which are described in the next section. However, most specialists in this field do not believe that factor analysis, regardless of its mathematical sophistication, reveals true dimensions of personality in any substantive sense. Rather, by revealing internal consistencies and differences among test items and scales, it helps clarify the relationships among personality constructs or variables.

The criterion-related validities of personality inventories constructed by factor analysis tend to be either low or unknown. Consequently, these inventories are generally less helpful in making behavioral predictions and decisions (diagnostic, intervention, training, etc.) in clinical and other applied psychological contexts than content-validated and criterion-keyed inventories. Nevertheless, applications of factor analysis to inventory construction and even more basic research on the nature of human personality remain appealing to certain psychologists. There is fairly good agreement that a large number of personality inventories measure at least the two factors defined by Eysenck, extroversion-introversion and neuroticism (emotionality). In addition, there is substantial support for a five-factor model of personality, defined as extroversion or surgency, agreeableness, conscientiousness, emotional stability, and culture by Goldberg (1980) and as neuroticism, extroversion, openness, agreeableness, and conscientiousness by Costa and McCrae (1986). Costa and McCrae (1986) define these five factors as follows: *neuroticism*—worrying versus calm, insecure versus secure, self-pitying versus self-satisfied; *extroversion*—sociable versus retiring, fun-loving versus sober, affectionate versus reserved; *openness*—imaginative versus down to earth, preference for variety versus preference for routine, independent versus conforming; *agreeableness*—soft-hearted versus ruthless, trusting versus suspicious, helpful versus uncooperative; *conscientiousness*—well-organized versus disorganized, careful versus careless, self-disciplined versus weak willed. The five factors appear to be highly consistent across different groups of people and situations.

Combining Strategies in Inventory Construction

Recent efforts to construct personality inventories have taken place in an atmosphere of renewed interest in research on personality and a greater appreciation of its complexities. Rather than relying on a single strategy, however, the development of certain inventories has involved a combination of approaches. Representative of personality inventories employing a mixture of rational-theoretical and factor-analytic strategies are the instruments designed by D. N. Jackson and the NEO Personality Inventory.

Jackson's Inventories

Representative of a new level of sophistication in the construction of personality inventories are the instruments designed by D. N. Jackson (Research Psychologists Press). Jackson's overall approach begins with detailed descriptions of the characteristics to be measured. Then a large pool of items is prepared and administered to a sizable, representative sample of examinees. Using the trait descriptions prepared at the outset, judges' ratings of the examinees on these traits are also obtained. In analyzing the data, the item responses of separate samples of examinees are subjected to different items analyses. A statistical, computer-based procedure is employed to ensure that the correlations among the items constituting a given scale are high but that the correlations among different scales are low. Realization of this goal results in the reliabilities of subtest score differences being high, thereby facilitating effective differentiation among scores on different subtests.

Personality Research Form (PRF)   The PRF (1965–1974) is a true-false personality inventory designed for grade 6 through adulthood. It takes 45 to 75 minutes to administer, depending on the form. There are five forms: Form E consists of 352 items, parallel Forms AA and BB of 440 items each, and parallel Forms A and B of 300 items each. Based on Henry Murray's trait theory of personality, each of the 15 scales of Forms A and B and the 22 scales of Forms AA, BB, and E consists of 20 items. Many of these scales bear the same names as those listed in the description of the Edwards Personal Preference Schedule (see above). In addition to the content scales, all forms are scored on an Infrequency scale consisting of rarely marked items; Forms AA, BB, and E are also scored on a Social Desirability scale.

The PRF was standardized on 1,000 men and 1,000 women in 30 colleges. Internal-consistency and test-retest reliability coefficients for the 14 content scales common to all five forms cluster around .80, but the reliabilities of the six additional content scales on Forms AA, BB, and E fall into the .50s. Validity coefficients obtained by correlating the content scales with behavior ratings and scores on a specially devised trait rating form are in the .50s. Evidence for convergent and discriminant validity is also reported in the PRF manual.

One might assume from the psychometric sophistication with which the PRF was constructed that it would escape much criticism. However, as seen in Tinsley's (1985) review this is not the case. Tinsley faults the PRF for the impoverished conceptualization of personality underlying its development, for its inadequate reliabilities, for its lack of adequate norms, and for difficulties in interpreting the scores because of insufficient information in the manual as to what the scores mean. In addition, little validity information concerning the relationships between PRF scores and real-life criteria is provided. Finally, even the removal of variation due to the social desirability response set from PRF scores is viewed by Tinsley as a mistake that probably leads to a loss of information. He recommends that the PRF not be used in practical or applied settings, and concludes that the Omnibus Personality Inventory, the California Psychological Inventory, and the Jackson Personality Inventory are more appropriate for research purposes.

Jackson Personality Inventory (JPI)   Like the PRF, the JPI (1976), which consists of 320 true-false items, was designed for adolescents and adults and takes about an hour to complete. But the JPI has a more social or interpersonal orientation than the PRF, providing a method of predicting behavior in a variety of practical settings (business, industrial, educational, recreational) as well as clinical and counseling situations. The construction methodology for the JPI was even more sophisticated than that for the PRI: two separate item analyses of a large item pool administered to two separate samples of people were conducted to maximize content variance in relation to social desirability variance, to maximize item variance, and to minimize the overlap among scales.

The JPI is scored on 15 substantive, or content, scales (Anxiety, Breadth of Interest, Complexity, Conformity, Energy Level, Innovation, Interpersonal Affect, Organization, Responsibility, Risk Taking, Self-Esteem, Social Adroitness, Social Participation, Tolerance, Value Orthodoxy), plus an Infrequency scale. Norms on samples of 2,000 males and 2,000 females from 43 North American colleges and universities, in addition to separate high school norms, are available. Internal-consistency reliability coefficients for the separate scales range from .75 to .95, averaging around .90. With respect to the validity of the JPI, the correlations of scores on the 15 scales with ratings of the same traits are moderate (.38 with peer ratings, .56 with self ratings, .70 with relevant adjective checklist variables). The manual reports correlations with various other criteria (occupational preference, attitude toward marijuana use, etc.). As with the Personality Research Form, the Jackson Personality Inventory has good potential. But neither inventory has experienced wide-spread use, and so that potential has yet to be realized.

In a review of the JPI, Dyer (1985) states that it is an impressive instrument and scored on positive personality dimensions relevant to the way in which we think about people rather than in negative, deviant terms. However, he criticizes the JPI manual as being too brief and perhaps too cryptic for educational users. In addition, evidence for the reliability and criterion-related validity for clinical use is not given in the manual. Dyer concludes that the JPI should be used primarily in research contexts, particularly research on personality correlates of occupational criteria and specific teacher-learning situations or styles.

NEO Personality Inventory

An even more recent personality inventory constructed by a combination of rational and factor-analytic methods is the NEO Personality Inventory (NEO-PI) by P. T. Costa, Jr. and R. R. McCrae (PAR, 1985). Designed for adults (ages 20–90), the NEO-PI consists of 181 items for self-reports (Form S) or observer ratings (Form R) on a five-point scale (Strongly Disagree, Disagree, Neutral, Agree, Strongly Agree). The inventory is scored on five personality domains—Neuroticism *(N)*, Extroversion *(E)*, Openness to Experience *(O)*, Agreeableness *(A)*, Conscientiousness *(C)*. The N, E, and O domains can also be scored on six different facet scales: Anxiety, Hostility, Depression, Self-Consciousness, Impulsiveness, and Vulnerability facets for domain N; Warmth, Gregariousness, Assertiveness, Activity, Excitement-Seeking, and Positive Emotions facets for domain *E*; Fantasy, Aesthetics, Feelings, Actions, Ideas, and Values facets for domain *O*.

Internal-consistency reliabilities for both forms of the NEO-PI range from .85 to .93 for the domain scales and from .60 to .86 for the facet scales. Test-retest reliabilities (six months) range from .86 to .91 for the domain scales and from .66 to .92 for the facet scales. Evidence for the validity of the NEO-PI is still somewhat scanty, but correlations with other personality inventories, expert ratings, and sentence completion tests are reported in the manual.

Summary

Personality inventories were originally designed to identify and diagnose maladjustment and psychiatric disorders, but they were expanded to include the assessment of a wide range of normal and abnormal characteristics. These inventories are objective, in the sense that they can be scored reliably by individuals having no special psychological training. They can also tap a variety of personality variables in a fairly short time period.

Three strategies that have been applied to the construction of personality inventories are the rational-theoretical strategy, the factor-analytic strategy, and the criterion-keyed strategy. Inventories devised by the first two strategies are described in this chapter, and those designed by the third strategy are examined in Chapter 8. No single strategy is uniformly superior to the others; each has its advantages and disadvantages, and a combination is usually best.

The problem of truthfulness in responding to items on personality inventories, including faking good, faking bad, and response sets such as acquiescence and social desirability, has been dealt with in a number of ways. Counting the number of items omitted by the examinee, counting the number of items that the examinee answers differently from the normative sample, and the use of special validity scales are three methods for detecting faking (good or bad) and response sets on personality inventories. The use of special response formats, such as the forced-choice technique, can assist in controlling for response sets.

Norms on personality inventories are typically not as representative of the target population as are those on tests of achievement and intelligence. Special problems also occur in interpreting the results of ipsative scales, in which the responses to items on one scale affect responses to items on other scales. Furthermore, the reliabilities of personality inventories tend to be lower than those of ability tests. Personality inventories are also limited in their ability to diagnose and predict behavior, and many inventories should be restricted in their uses to research purposes.

The first personality inventory to be administered on a mass basis was the Woodworth Personal Data Sheet, for identifying soldiers likely to break down in combat. Other early single-score inventories included the X-O Test and the A-S Reaction Study. Two of the first multiscore personality inventories were the Bernreuter Personality Inventory and the Bell Adjustment Inventory. Among the most popular rational or content-validated, multiscore inventories first published in the 1940s and 1950s are the California Test of Personality and the Omnibus Personality Inventory. Widely administered, special-purpose inventories such as the State-

Trait Anxiety Inventory and various measures of self-concept made their initial appearances during the 1960s.

The Jenkins Activity Survey was designed to detect a pattern of behavior (Type A) associated with coronary heart disease. Other health-related instruments are the Eating Disorders Inventory for identifying anorexia nervosa, bulimia, and related eating problems having a psychological basis, and the Millon Behavioral Health Inventory for assisting in formulating a comprehensive treatment plan for adult medical patients.

Two personality theories or systems that have greatly influenced the development of personality inventories are Henry Murray's need-press theory and Carl Jung's analytic theory. Instruments designed to measure the psychological needs postulated by Murray include the Edwards Personal Preference Schedule, the Personality Research Form, the Jackson Personality Inventory, and the Adjective Check List (Chapter 6). The Myers-Briggs Type Indicator and the Singer-Loomis Inventory of Personality are examples of instruments designed to assess an individual's standing on the various Jungian types.

The use of factor analysis in the development of personality inventories stems from the pioneering work of J. P. Guilford during the early 1940s. Prominent instruments in this category include the Guilford-Zimmerman Temperament Survey, the 16 Personality Factor Questionnaire (R. B. Cattell), and the Eysenck Personality Questionnaire (H. G. Eysenck). Also noteworthy are the Profile of Mood States and the Comrey Personality Scales. Factor analysis cannot be said to reveal the true structure of personality, although it does assist in the understanding of personality structure and what is being measured by various inventories and tests.

Perhaps the best examples, from a psychometric viewpoint, of personality inventories constructed by combining rational-theoretical and factor-analytic strategies are the Personality Research Form and the Jackson Personality Inventory. Another inventory in this category is the NEO Personality Inventory.

Exercises

1. Define each of the following terms in a sentence or two:

acquiescence	overcautiousness
content-validated inventory	personality inventory
criterion estimation	profile-matching technique
criterion-keyed strategy	rational-theoretical strategy
eating disorders	response set
extremeness	self-concept scale
factor-analytic strategy	social desirability
infrequency scale	social desirability scale
ipsative	theory based inventory
multiscore inventory	Type A behavior
oppositionalism	Type B behavior

2. With respect to the issue of dissimulation or faking on personality inventories, write five true-false items that you think would be answered "true" more often by fakers than by nonfakers. Then write five items that you believe would be answered "false" more often than "true" by fakers than by nonfakers.

3. Construct an inventory consisting of ten true-false statements that you consider to be effective measures of the social desirability response set. Phrase the statements in such as way that for five of them the keyed response is true and for the other five the keyed response is false.

4. Construct a ten item self-concept inventory, using a true-false item format. On half the statements the keyed answer should be "true," and on the other half the keyed answer should be "false." Administer your self-concept inventory to several students, computing total scores (0–10) as the number of responses given in the keyed direction. Did you find generally low or generally high scores? How variable were the scores? What evidence can you offer in support of your ten-item inventory as a valid measure of self-concept?

5. Consult *The Ninth Mental Measurements Yearbook* (Mitchell, 1985) and preceding volumes as well as *Test Critiques* (Keyser & Sweetland, 1984–1986) for reviews of any three personality inventories discussed in this chapter. Are the reviews generally positive or negative? What are the most common sources of criticism of the inventories?

6. Take the following personality inventory devised by Willerman (1975); then make multiple copies and administer it to several other people.

Directions: For each statement, circle the number that indicates how true the statement is of you.

	How true is this of you?				
		Hardly				A Lot
1.	I make friends easily.	1	2	3	4	5
2.	I tend to be shy.	1	2	3	4	5
3.	I like to be with others.	1	2	3	4	5
4.	I like to be independent of people.	1	2	3	4	5
5.	I usually prefer to do things alone.	1	2	3	4	5
6.	I am always on the go.	1	2	3	4	5
7.	I like to be off and running as soon as I wake up in the morning.	1	2	3	4	5
8.	I like to keep busy all of the time.	1	2	3	4	5
9.	I am very energetic.	1	2	3	4	5
10.	I prefer quiet, inactive pastimes to more active ones.	1	2	3	4	5
11.	I tend to cry easily.	1	2	3	4	5

(Continued)

12.	I am easily frightened.	1	2	3	4	5
13.	I tend to be somewhat emotional.	1	2	3	4	5
14.	I get upset easily.	1	2	3	4	5
15.	I tend to be easily irritated.	1	2	3	4	5

From *Individual and Group Differences* by L. Willerman, New York: Harper's College Press, 1975. Reprinted with permission.

Scoring: For all items except numbers 2, 4, 5, and 10 the score is simply the number circled; for items 2, 4, 5, and 10, reverse the numbers before scoring (1 = 5, 2 = 4, 3 = 3, 4 = 2, 5 = 1). Add the scores on items 1 through 5 to yield an index of Sociability, the scores on items 6 through 10 to yield an index of Activity Level, and the scores on items 11 through 15 to yield an Emotionality index. Interpret your scores and those of other people to whom you administer the inventory with respect to the following average ranges within which 68% of samples of female and male students at the University of Texas at Austin scored on the three scales:

Index	Average Range for Females	Average Range for Males
Sociability	15–20	13–19
Activity Level	13–20	13–19
Emotionality	11–18	9–16

Scores outside these ranges can be interpreted as high or low on the particular characteristic. Why is it important for you to be cautious in your interpretations of scores on this inventory?

Suggested Readings

Allport, G. W., & Odbert, H. S. (1936). Trait-names, a psycholexical study. *Psychological Monographs, 47*(1).

Allport, F. H., & Allport, G. W. (1921). Personality traits: Their classification and measurement. *Journal of Abnormal and Social Psychology, 16,* 6–40.

Burisch, M. (1986). Methods of personality inventory development—a comparative analysis. In A. Angleitner & J. S. Wiggins (Eds.), *Personality assessment via questionnaires* (pp. 109–123). New York: Springer.

Coopersmith, S. (1981). *The antecedents of self-esteem.* Palo Alto, CA: Consulting Psychologists Press.

Goldberg, L. R. (1981). Language and individual differences: The search for universals in personality lexicons. In L. Wheeler (Ed.), *Personality and school psychology review* (Vol. 2, pp. 141–165). Beverly Hills, CA: Sage.

Gynther, M. D., & Green, S. B. (1982). Methodological problems with self-report inventories. In P. C. Kendall & J. N. Butcher (Eds.), *Handbook of research methods in clinical psychology* (pp. 355–386). New York: Wiley.

Hamann, D. L. (1985). The assessment of trait-state anxiety and musical performance. In C.

D. Spielberger & J. N. Butcher (Eds.) *Advances in personality assessment* (Vol. 5, pp. 133–155). Hillsdale, NJ: L Erlbaum.

Rorer, L. G. (1983). Personality structure and assessment. In M. R. Rosenzweig & L. W. Porter (Eds.), *Annual Review of Psychology* (Vol. 34, pp. 431–463). Palo Alto, CA: Annual Reviews, Inc.

Endnote

[1]A similar distinction between the state and trait aspects of an emotion has been made with respect to anger. The State-Trait Anger Expression Inventory (STAXI) (C. D. Spielberger, Psychological Assessment Resources, 1987), which was designed to assess the state-trait anger distinction, consists of 44 items yielding three measures: State-Anger, Trait-Anger, and Anger Expression. The Anger-Expression Scale (AX), which is similar in conception if not construction to Rosenzweig's Picture-Frustration Study (see Chapter 10) and consistent with physiological research on anger (see Chapter 13), is scored on Anger-in (suppressed anger) and Anger-out (anger expressed toward other people and the environment). Additional information on types of trait anger, anger control, and the direction of expressed anger is provided by various subscales of STAXI.

CHAPTER 8

Criterion-Keyed
Inventories

$\mathbf{R}$ather than relying on rational-theoretical or factor-analytic strategies in determining what items to include on an affective inventory, certain psychologists decided quite early to adopt the empirical strategy of letting the items speak for themselves. One of the first psychologists to use this approach was E. K. Strong. Each item on the Strong Vocational Interest Blank for Men was keyed (scored) on a particular occupational scale only if the item significantly differentiated between men in that occupation and men in general. In this *criterion-keyed* or group-contrast approach to inventory construction items are given a numerical scoring weight (keyed) for a particular group variable if they discriminate between members of that group (the contrast group) and a control group. When constructing a vocational interest inventory, the contrast groups may be salespeople, physicians, engineers, or members of other occupational groups. In developing a personality inventory, the contrast group may consist of anxious people, depressed people, delinquents, schizophrenics, or whatever diagnostic group the inventory is designed to identify.

Although atheoretical, the empirical or criterion-keyed approach to inventory construction is not totally *irrational*: reason, based on common sense and psychological experience, is involved in the original selection or construction of items on which to compare the contrast and control groups. Nevertheless, the items on a criterion-keyed inventory are typically rather heterogeneous and may not seem as face-valid as the items on inventories constructed by rational-theoretical or factor-analytic strategies. One of the items keyed for the Banker scale of the original Strong Vocational Interest Blank for Men, for example, was "I like men with gold teeth." Items such as this, which are a source of perplexity when they appear on personality inventories, have been the subject of quips by social satirists and others critical of personality assessment. Consider, for example, the following 14-item, true-false personality inventory devised by the humorist Art Buchwald ("I was an Imaginary Playmate," 1965):

> When I was young, I used to tease vegetables.
>
> Sometimes I am unable to prevent clean thoughts from entering my mind.
>
> I am not unwilling to work for a jackass.
>
> I would enjoy the work of a chicken flicker.
>
> I think beavers work too hard.
>
> It is important to wash your hands before washing your hands.
>
> It is hard for me to say the right thing when I find myself in a room full of mice.
>
> I use shoe polish to excess.
>
> The sight of blood no longer excites me.
>
> It makes me furious to see an innocent man escape the chair.
>
> As a child, I used to wet the ceiling.
>
> I am aroused by persons of the opposite sexes.
>
> I believe I smell as good as most people.
>
> When I was a child, I was an imaginary playmate. (p. 990)

It is doubtful that many, if any, of these "rationally-constructed" items would distinguish between two psychologically different groups, but they may effectively discriminate between less deceptive persons and those who delight in making fun of psychology!

Minnesota Multiphasic Personality Inventory

Although by far the most famous, the Minnesota Multiphasic Personality Inventory (MMPI) (available from National Computer Systems) was not the first criterion-keyed inventory of personality. An early instrument of this kind was the A-S Reaction Study by G. W. and F. H. Allport (1929–1938); items on this inventory were retained only if they differentiated between groups of individuals rated as ascendent or submissive by their peers. In addition, experience with earlier inventories such as the Humm-Wadsworth Temperament Scale (1935), by psychologist S. R. Hathaway and psychiatrist J. C. McKinley, served as a background for the development in 1940 of the MMPI. The original purpose of the MMPI was, like that of the Personal Data Sheet constructed by Woodworth two decades before, to distinguish between psychologically normal and psychologically abnormal people. The inventory has been used extensively for diagnostic and research purposes in clinics and mental hosptials, where examinees' scores on the several scales are analyzed for evidence of psychological problems and disorders.

Constructing the MMPI

Hathaway and McKinley began by assembling hundreds of statements concerning psychological symptoms from a variety of sources (e.g., psychological reports and textbooks). After eliminating ambiguous and similar statements, 504 items remained. These statements were then administered to groups of psychiatric patients who had been previously diagnosed as hypochrondriacal, depressed, hysterical, psychopathic, paranoid, psychasthenic, schizophrenic, or hypomanic, and their responses compared with those of approximately 700 persons having no history of psychiatric problems. Items that significantly differentiated between a particular diagnostic group and presumably normal people were included on the scale for that disorder. Comparisons were also made between the responses of each diagnostic group and the responses of all other diagnostic groups combined. The resulting eight diagnostic scales were then cross-validated by comparing the scores of new groups of patients having each diagnosis with the scores of a new normal group and patients in all other diagnostic groups combined.

Later, the original pool of 504 items was expanded to 566 by including a *Masculinity-Femininity scale* that was originally designed to identify homosexuals but succeeded only in differentiating between males and females. In addition, a scale for measuring Social Introversion (*Si*) was developed by Drake (1946) that contrasted the responses of college women involved in extracurricular activities with those who were less involved. This brought to 14 the number of scales on the standard MMPI: four validity scales, nine clinical scales, and the *Si* scale.

Description of the MMPI

Designed for persons 16 years and older with a minimum of a sixth-grade education, the statement items on the MMPI are to be answered *true or mostly true* (T) or *false or not usually true* (F). Statements that do not apply to the examinee or that the examinee does not know about can be left blank, but respondents are encouraged to answer all items. The statements are concerned with attitudes towards education, marriage, family, and occupation; as well as emotions; motor disturbances; psychosomatic symptoms; sexual, political, and religious values; obsessive-compulsive and phobic behaviors; delusional and hallucinatory experiences; sadomasochistic thoughts and behaviors; and other thoughts; feelings; and behaviors indicative of psychological problems or disorders. Examples are

I am happy most of the time.

I enjoy social gatherings just to be with people.

I have never had a fainting spell.

I believe I am a condemned person.

There are 566 statements in all, 16 of which are repeated. Only 399 items are actually scored for the basic scales, each of which consists of 15 to 78 items. Because many items appear on more than one scale, the scales are not independent and certain scales have substantial correlations with each other.

The MMPI is available in a variety of forms (group booklet, cards, hardcover booklet [Form R], tape recording, etc.) and in several languages. It is usually administered in booklet form, the card form being used only when the examinee is quite disturbed or has a low educational or intellectual level. Several short forms containing fewer than the standard number of items are also available, examples being Kincannon's (1968) 71-item Mini-Mult; Dean's (1972) 86-item Midi-Mult; Overall and Gomez-Mont's (1974) MMPI-168; and Faschingbauer's (1974) FAM.

MMPI Scales

The validity scales, the nine original clinical scales, the *Si* (Social Introversion) scale, and their correlates are described in Table 8–1. Many special scales have been developed from the MMPI item pool during the course of hundreds of research investigations over the past half century. However, the majority of these special scales, which were designed to measure such variables as accident proneness, alcoholism, anxiety, caudality (frontal vs. nonfrontal cortical damage), control, dependency, dominance, ego strength, low back pain, originality, prejudice, repression, social responsibility, and social status, are used infrequently. Among the most commonly used are the A (Anxiety) scale, R (Repression) scale, *Es* (Ego Strength) scale, and *Mac* (MacAndrew Alcoholism) scale. By isolating clusters of items having high intercorrelations, Wiggins (1966) also developed a set of 13 content scales having high internal consistencies. These scales (Social Maladjustment, Depression, Feminine Interests, Poor Morale, Religious Fundamentalism, Authority Conflict, Psychoticism, Organic Symptoms, Family Problems, Manifest Hostility, Phobias, Hypomania, Poor Health) were found to have some validity for college undergraduates, psychiatric inpatients, and patients at a military medical facility (Wiggins, Goldberg & Appelbaum, 1971; Jarnecke & Chambers, 1977; Lachar & Alexander, 1978).

Descriptions of MMPI Scales, Illustrative Items, and Correlates	Table 8–1

Validity (or Test-taking Attitude) Scales:

? (Cannot Say) Number of items left unanswered. Suggests uncooperativeness or defensiveness if over 30 items are left unanswered.

L (Lie) Fifteen items of overly good self-report, such as, "I smile at everyone I meet." (True) Measures the tendency to claim an excessive amount of virtue. High scores reflect a tendency to present an overly favorable self-image.

F (Frequency or Infrequency) Sixty-four items answered in the scored direction by 10 percent or less of normals, such as, "There is an international plot against me." (True) Measures the tendency to endorse rare or unusual attributes. High scores may suggest faking, confusion, disorganization, or severe disturbance.

K (Correction) Thirty items reflecting defensiveness in admitting to problems, such as, "I feel bad when others criticize me." (False) Measures an individual's unwillingness to disclose personal information. High scores reflect defensiveness or the individual's unrealistic view of himself or herself.

Clinical Scales:

1 or Hs (Hypochondriasis) Thirty-three items derived from patients showing abnormal concern with bodily functions, such as, "I have chest pains several times a week." (True) Measures the neurotic tendency to develop or claim somatic problems. High scorers have many vague physical complaints. They are described as unhappy, complaining, demanding, hostile, and attention-seeking.

2 or (D) (Depression) Sixty items derived from patients showing extreme pessimism, feelings of hopelessness, and slowing of thought and action, such as, "I usually feel that life is interesting and worthwhile." (False) Low mood, low self-esteem, and feelings of inadequacy are reflected in high scores on this scale. High scores are described as shy, moody, pessimistic, despondent, over-controlled, guilt-ridden, and depressed.

3 or Hy (Conversion Hysteria) Sixty items from neurotic patients using physical or mental symptoms as a way of unconsciously avoiding difficult conflicts and responsibilities, such as, "My heart frequently pounds so hard I can feel it." (True) High scorers rely on repression and denial to manage conflict. They tend to develop physical symptoms under stress. They are described as naive, gullible, outgoing, visible, demanding, manipulative, and noninsightful.

4 or Pd (Psychopathic Deviate) Fifty items from patients who show a repeated and flagrant disregard for social customs, an emotional shallowness, and an inability to learn from punishing experiences, such as, "My activities and interests are often criticized by others." (True) Scale 4 measures anti-social behavior such as impulsivity, poor social judgment, disregard for rules and authority, hostility, and aggressiveness. High scorers are found to be extraverted, likeable, exhibitionistic, controlling and manipulative in social situations, immature, and to have difficulties in interpersonal relationships.

5 or Mf (Masculinity-Femininity) Sixty items from patients showing homoeroticism and items differentiating between men and women, such as, "I like to arrange flowers."

(Continued)

(True, scored for femininity.) This scale measures sex role attitudes and behavior. High scoring males are viewed as being passive, sensitive, effeminate, and as having broad interests; conflicts over heterosexual behavior are often found. High scoring females are viewed as masculine, aggressive, adventurous, and as having narrow interests.

6   or Pa (Paranoia) Forty items from patients showing abnormal suspiciousness and delusions of grandeur or persecution, such as, "There are evil people trying to influence my mind." (True) This scale reflects characteristics such as suspiciousness, aloofness, shrewdness, and guardedness that are found among paranoid individuals. High scorers tend to be hostile, argumentative, angry, resentful, and to externalize blame.

7   or Pt (Psychasthenia) Forty-eight items based on neurotic patients showing obsessions, compulsions, abnormal fears, and guilt and indecisiveness, such as, "I save nearly everything I buy, even after I have no use for it." (True) This scale measures anxiety, obsessive-compulsive behavior, and general maladjustment. Individuals who score high on this scale are seen as tense, worried, preoccupied, and phobic. They tend to intellectualize and ruminate about problems.

8   or Sc (Schizophrenia) Seventy-eight items from patients showing bizarre or unusual thoughts or behavior, who are often withdrawn and experiencing delusions and hallucinations, such as, "Things around me do not seem real," (True) and, "It makes me uncomfortable to have people close to me." (True) High scorers on this scale have unconventional, schizoid, and alienated life styles. They are withdrawn, moody, feel confused, and have unusual ideas. Very high scores reflect bizarre mentation, personality disorganization, delusions, and hallucinations.

9   or Ma (Hypomania) Forty-six items from patients characterized by emotional excitement, overactivity, and flight of ideas, such as, "At times I feel very 'high' or very 'low' for no apparent reason." (True) High scores reflect energetic, sociable, impulsive, overly optimistic characteristics. These individuals tend to be irritable, moody, impatient, and grandiose. Some evidence of mood disturbance and flight of ideas may be present in very high scoring individuals.

0   or Si (Social Introversion) Seventy items from persons showing shyness, little interest in people, and insecurity, such as, "I have the time of my life at parties." (False) High scores on this scale suggest social introversion. Characteristics of overcontrol, shyness, lethargy, tension, guilt proneness, and withdrawal are present for high scorers. Low scoring individuals are viewed as extraverted. They are outgoing, undercontrolled, visible, socially forward, aggressive, and impulsive.

After Sundberg (1977) and Butcher & Keller (1984). Adapted and reproduced by permission of the publishers. The Minnesota Multiphasic Personality Inventory, Copyright © 1943, renewed 1970 by the University of Minnesota.

Examining Scores on the Validity Scales

Before attempting to interpret scores on the clinical or special scales of the MMPI, attention should be directed to scores on the four validity scales—the *? (Cannot Say) scale,* the *L (Lie) scale,* the *F (Frequency or Infrequency) scale,* and the *K (Correction) scale.* A score on the *?* scale consists of the number of items that the examinee leaves blank. A high "?" score can be interpreted as "defensiveness" or "uncertainty," and, if too high, may invalidate scales on which many items are unanswered. Although there is no set maximum *?* score that invalidates an MMPI profile, if 10% or more of the items are omitted there is serious doubt as to the validity of the profile as a whole. For this reason, examinees are encouraged to respond to every statement even when in doubt.

The *L* (raw lie), or *fake good score*, is the number of items out of 15 in a special set of statements that the examinee answered in such a way as to be placed in a more favorable light. For example, examinees who answer true to many statements of the sort that they "always tell the truth, never get mad, read every editorial in the newspaper every day, and have as good manners at home as when out in company" tend to obtain high *L* scores. An *L* score of 10 or more, which is at least two standard deviations above the mean, certainly suggests that the profile is invalid.

The *F*, or *fake bad score* ("F" originally stood for "feeblemindedness"), is a measure of randomness in responding or highly deviant responding. Examples of the 64 items on the *F* scale that are rarely endorsed by the general population are "Everything tastes the same" and "I see things, animals, or people around me that others do not see." A high *F* score of, say, 16 or more, suggests that the examinee is trying to appear very emotionally disturbed, has not read the items carefully, or does not understand them. Graham (1977) found that people who see themselves as being in need of psychological help may answer as many as 25 of the items in the *F* score direction. Failure to comply with the directions, for whatever reasons, and faking are also associated with high *F* scale scores.

The *K* score is a measure of overcriticalness or overgenerousness in evaluating oneself; high *K* scores indicate defensiveness in responding and are related to the social desirability response set. Examples of the 30 items on the *K* scale are "At times I feel like swearing" and "At times I feel like smashing things." High *K* scorers tend to deny personal inadequacies and deficiencies in self-control, whereas low scorers are willing to say socially undesirable things about themselves. The authors of the MMPI maintained that subtracting a portion of *K* from certain clinical scales improves the discriminatory power of these scales. Consequently, fractions of the *K* score may also be applied as correction factors to the raw scores on clinical scales 1, 4, 7, 8, and 9. However, the value of these corrections has been questioned, and they are not always made. The *F* and *K* scores can also be used in combination, as an *F* minus *K* index, to discern the tendency to fake good or fake bad. When *F−K* is more positive than +11, the examinee is probably trying to fake bad; when *F−K* is more negative than −11, he or she is probably trying to fake good.

Interpreting Scores on the MMPI Clinical Scales

Although a generally high profile on the nine clinical scales of the MMPI suggests serious psychological problems, a T score of 70 or above on a given clinical scale is not necessarily indicative of the disorder with which the scale is labeled. For this and other reasons, the nine clinical scales are now usually referred to by numerical rather than diagnostic category designations. In addition, a psychiatric diagnosis or personality analysis is not made on the basis of a single score but from a consideration of score combinations.

Paired Scores   One popular approach to MMPI interpretation, proposed some years ago by Paul Meehl (1951), is *paired scores*, two scales having T scores of 70 or above. To illustrate, Table 8–2 provides descriptions and possible diagnoses associated with 20 two-point code types. Pairs of scales having T scores of 70 or above are given in the left column and the associated personality characteristics and diagnoses in the right column. Because it is not clear what they mean, extremely low scores usually play little role in the interpretation of an MMPI profile.

Coded Scores   A more recent approach bases the interpretation and psychiatric diagnosis on the pattern displayed by the entire group of scores on the clinical scales. First the given score profile is coded according to one of several systems, after which it is interpreted. In addition to placing the examinee into one or more diagnostic categories, behaviors typically associated with various high scores are also described.

Several coding systems for analyzing MMPI score profiles have been devised, those of Hathaway and Welsh being the most popular (Marks, Seeman, & Haller 1974; Duckworth & Anderson, 1986). The coding process begins by arranging the numerical designations of the nine clinical scales and the Social Introversion scale (scale 0), from left to right, in descending order of T scores. Performing this ranking process on the profile in Figure 8–1 yields 1362749850. In Welsh's profile coding system, a * (asterisk) designates T scores of 90 or greater, a " (quotation mark) T scores of 80 to 89, ' (apostrophe) for T scores of 70 to 79, a - (hyphen) after the last scale having a T score of 60 or above, and a / (solidus) after the last scale having a T score of 50 or above. The number designations of scales having T scores within one point of each other are underlined, and scores on the L, F, and K scales are placed after the profile code. Applying this system, the complete Welsh code for the profile in Figure 8–1 is 13'6-27 498/50:   KL/F?:. Associated with coding systems for the MMPI scales are cookbooks for interpreting profiles (Hathaway & Meehl, 1951; Marks, Seeman & Haller, 1974). However, actuarial interpretation of MMPI profiles by reference to such cookbooks eventually yielded to the more mechanized computer interpretations.

Profile Interpretation   The process of interpreting an MMPI profile usually begins by inspecting scores on the validity scales. Assuming that the validity scale scores are satisfactory, attention is then given to scales with T scores of 70 or above. Scale 2 is considered to be a measure of depression and scale 7 a measure of anxiety, tension, or alertness to unknown danger. Because depression and anxiety are the most common symptoms of mental disorder, psychiatric patients generally have a high score on scale 2 or 7 or both. As noted in Table 8–2, high scores on both scales 2 and 7 point to a combination of anxiety and depression. Other patterns of high scores indicate other symptoms. High scores on scales 4 and 9 suggest impulsive-

	Descriptions of Some MMPI Two-Point Code Types	**Table 8–2**

Code Types	Descriptions
1–2,2–1	Depressed, worried, pessimistic, somatic overconcern; frequent diagnosis is hypochondriasis.
1–3,3–1	Immature, egocentric, demanding; hysterical characteristics; diagnosis of hysterical conversion reaction when scale 2 ten points or more lower.
1–8,8–1	Confused, disoriented, difficulty concentrating, limited ability to deal with stress, feelings of alienation, difficulty controlling feelings of hostility; possible diagnosis of schizophrenia when accompanied by elevated *F* scale score.
1–9,9–1	Tense, anxious, great emotional turmoil, expect high level of achievement from themselves but unclear goals, basically passive-dependent; possible brain damage, when diagnosis not made on basis of MMPI alone; possible diagnosis of passive-aggressive personality if scales 4 and 6 elevated; hypochondriasis and manic state also common diagnoses.
2–3,3–2	Lacking in energy, apathetic, listless, depressed and anxious, feelings of hopelessness and inadequacy; both men and women immature and dependent, but men more ambitious, industrious, and competitive and women more apathetic, weak, and depressed; common diagnosis is dysthymic disorder.
2–4,4–2	Difficulty controlling impulses, immature, dependent, egocentric, vacillates between self-pity and blaming others for difficulties, difficulty in social relations, resentment of authority figures; possible diagnoses are antisocial or passive-aggressive personality, or adjustment disorder with depressed mood.
2–6,6–2	Extreme sensitivity to real or imagined criticism; usually openly hostile, aggressive, and resentful toward others (chip on shoulder); diagnosis of paranoid schizophrenia likely when scales 7, 8, and possibly 9 also high; well-defined paranoid system also suggested when scales 2, 6, and *F* moderately elevated; other diagnoses are dysthymic disorder and passive-aggressive personality (when scale 4 elevated).
2–7,7–2	Most common code in psychiatric populations, characterized by depression, agitation, pessimism, and nervousness, as well as somatic complaints, preoccupation with personal deficiencies, and guilt; usual diagnosis is depressive and/or anxiety disorder.
2–8,8–2	Depressed, anxious, agitated, hostile, and aggressive impulses with potential for self-destructive behaviors; periods of confusion, thought retardation, and difficulty concentrating; usually diagnosed as major depressive disorder, schizophrenia, or schizoaffective disorder.
2–9,9–2	Anxious, depressed, high energy level, extremely narcissistic and preoccupied with self-worth; may indicate identity crisis in young person or reaction to physical disability or involutional depression in older person; can also indicate certain types of brain injury or cyclothymic disorder.

(Continued)

3–4,4–3	Immature, self-centered, seemingly conforming on the outside but with a high level of anger which is difficult to express; usual diagnosis is passive-aggressive personality.
3–8,8–3	Disoriented, difficulty concentrating, lapses of memory, may regress and develop delusional thinking, feelings of unreality and emotional inappropriateness; frequent diagnosis is schizophrenia, but hysterical disorder also possible.
4–5,5–4	Nonconforming and defiant, aggressive and antisocial, emotionally passive, sexual identity concerns and possible homosexual impulses in men; women with this code type are usually rebelling against feminine role.
4–6,6–4	Hostile, brooding, distrustful, irritable, self-centered, usually unable to form close relationships; men often psychotic (especially paranoid schizophrenia) or prepsychotic; women may be psychotic or prepsychotic but more likely passive-aggressive personalities.
4–7,7–4	Cyclical patterns of impulsive acting out followed by periods of guilt and remorse, with guilt out of proportion to actual behavior, frequent somatic complaints and insensitivity to feelings of others; chronic pattern usually diagnosed as antisocial personality or anxiety disorder.
4–8,8–4	Strange, eccentric, suspicious, hostile, irritable, may have ideas or reference, unpredictable, changeable, nonconforming; associated with violent crime in the case of men; usual diagnosis is schizoid personality, paranoid personality, or paranoid schizoprenia.
4–9,9–4	Impulsive, sensation-seeking, irresponsible, untrustworthy, shallow, pleasure-oriented, manipulative, superficial, immoral, narcissistic, hedonistic, free from anxiety and guilt, poor judgment, unconventional; associated with delinquency in adolescents; usual diagnosis in adults is antisocial personality, but may indicate manic or schizophrenic state when score on scale 8 also high.
6–8,8–6	Hostile, withdrawing, apathetic, suspicious, uncooperative, poor judgment, difficulty concentrating, bizarre thought content, delusions of persecution and/or grandeur, hallucinations; usual diagnoses are paranoid schizophrenia (especially if scale 4 high), paranoid state, or schizoid personality.
7–8,8–7	Passive, agitated, lacking in self-confidence, difficulty sustaining mature heterosexual relationships; feelings of inadequacy, guilt, insecurity, inferiority, confusion, worry, and fear; risk of suicide; diagnosis of schizophrenia or alienated personality disorder; when scale 2 score also high, possibility of dysthymic or obsessive-compulsive disorder.
8–9,9–8	Highly energetic, emotionally labile, tense, disorganized, possible delusions of grandeur, goals and expectations unrealistic, interpersonal relationships immature; usually fearful, distrustful, irritable, and distractible; delusions and hallucinations likely; modal diagnosis is schizophrenia, but schizoaffective, manic, or drug-induced psychosis also possible.

Adapted from Groth-Marnat (1984, pp. 291–308) and Newmark (1985, pp. 37–49).

ness, low frustration tolerance, rebelliousness, and hostile aggression; high scores on scales 6 and 8 point to withdrawal, apathy, and paranoid delusions.

Special terms have come to be associated with certain patterns of high scores. Scales 1, 2, and 3 are referred to as the *neurotic triad* because high scores on all three of these scales are so frequently associated with psychoneurotic problems. When the T scores on these three scales are all above 70 but the score on scale 2 is lower than those on scales 1 and 3, the profile is referred to as a *conversion* V and suggests a diagnosis of conversion hysteria. At the other end of the profile, scales 6, 7, 8, and 9 are referred to as the *psychotic tetrad* because high scores on these four scales are so often associated with psychotic disorders. When the T scores on these four scales are all above 70 but scales 7 and 9 are lower than scales 6 and 8, the profile is referred to as a *paranoid valley* and suggests a diagnosis of paranoid schizophrenia.

Computer-Based Interpretation

A number of interpretive computer programs based on prerecorded rules for the configural or *pattern analysis* of MMPI scores and available for mainframe and microcomputers have been developed (see pp. 717–720 of *The Ninth Mental Measurements Yearbook*, Mitchell, 1985, for reviews). For example, Report 8–1 is a computer-generated interpretation of the MMPI responses of the individual whose scale score profile is given in Figure 8–1. Despite the seeming expertness and plausibility of many computer-based interpretations, one must be cautious about overmechanizing the process of test interpretation. Computers, as well as people, make mistakes, and one should remember that the instructions (programs) followed by the computers were written by fallible human beings. Furthermore, the ready availability of computer interpretations of the MMPI may encourage their use by inadequately trained individuals.

Reliability, Norms, and Group Differences

The test-retest reliability coefficients of the MMPI scales reported in the manual are based on data obtained many years ago from relatively small samples of normal people and psychiatric patients. The coefficients are not atypical for instruments of this kind, ranging from .50 to .90 over relatively short time periods (days and weeks). After an interval of a year or more, however, the test-retest coefficients drop to a median of .30 to .40. The substantial drop in test-retest reliabilities over long periods is, of course, not unexpected. The extent of psychological disturbance registered on the MMPI fluctuates over time as the examinee receives psychological treatment, experiences personal crises or a decrease or increase in stress, and when coping skills become more or less effective. As might be expected, the internal-consistency coefficients are higher than the test-retest correlations: median r of approximately .70 and as high as .90 for certain scales.

Figure 8–1   Profile of scores on the Minnesota Multiphasic Personality Inventory

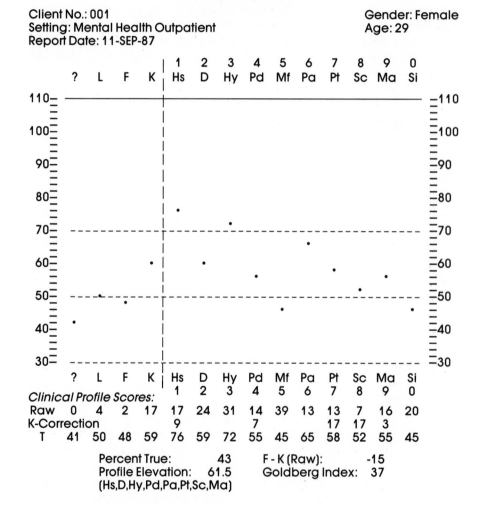

THE MINNESOTA REPORT
for the Minnesota Multiphasic Personality Inventory : Adult System
by James N. Butcher, Ph.D.
CLINICAL PROFILE

Client No.: 001   Gender: Female
Setting: Mental Health Outpatient   Age: 29
Report Date: 11-SEP-87

	?	L	F	K	Hs 1	D 2	Hy 3	Pd 4	Mf 5	Pa 6	Pt 7	Sc 8	Ma 9	Si 0
Clinical Profile Scores:					1	2	3	4	5	6	7	8	9	0
Raw	0	4	2	17	17	24	31	14	39	13	13	7	16	20
K-Correction					9			7			17	17	3	
T	41	50	48	59	76	59	72	55	45	65	58	52	55	45

Percent True: 43   F - K (Raw):   -15
Profile Elevation: 61.5   Goldberg Index: 37
(Hs,D,Hy,Pd,Pa,Pt,Sc,Ma)

Welsh Code: 13'6-27 498/50: KL/F?:

THE MINNESOTA REPORT™	**Report 8–1**

for the Minnesota Multiphasic Personality Inventory™: Adult System

by James N. Butcher, Ph.D.

Client No.: 001	Gender: Female
Setting: Mental Health Outpatient	Age: 29
Report Date: 11-SEP-87	
PAS Code Number: 00139430 764 0005	

PROFILE VALIDITY

This client's approach to the MMPI was open and cooperative. The resulting MMPI profile is valid and probably a good indication of her present level of personality functioning. This suggests that she is able to follow instructions and to respond appropriately to the task, and may be viewed as a positive indication of her involvement with the evaluation.

SYMPTOMATIC PATTERN

Her MMPI profile presents a rather mixed pattern of symptoms in which somatic reactivity under stress is a primary difficulty. Because of somatic symptoms, the client presents a picture of physical problems and a reduced level of psychological functioning. Her physical problems may be vague, may have appeared suddenly after a period of stress, and may not be traceable to actual organic changes. She may be manifesting fatigue, vague pain, weakness, or unexplained periods of dizziness.

She may view herself as highly virtuous and show a "Pollyanish" attitude toward life. She may not appear greatly anxious or depressed over her symptoms and may show "La belle indifference." Apparently sociable and rather exhibitionistic, she seems to manage conflict by excessive denial and repression.

In addition, the following description is suggested by the content of this client's responses. She may have a great need for affection and may seek attention from others. She tends to avoid confrontation and ignores problems so as not to alienate other people, and may view people in a naively trusting way.

NOTE: This MMPI interpretation can serve as a useful source of hypotheses about clients. This report is based on objectively derived scale indexes and scale interpretations that have been developed in diverse groups of patients. The personality descriptions, inferences, and recommendations contained herein need to be verified by other sources of clinical information since individual clients may not fully match the prototype. The information in this report should most appropriately be used by a trained, qualified test interpreter. The information contained in this report should be considered confidential.

(Continued)

INTERPERSONAL RELATIONS

She tends to be somewhat passive-dependent and demanding in interpersonal relationships. She may attempt to control others by developing physical symptoms.

She has an average interest in being with others and is not socially isolated or withdrawn. She appears to meet and talk with other people with relative ease and is not overly anxious when in social gatherings.

BEHAVIORAL STABILITY

The personality pattern characterized by this profile is long-standing and quite stable. The client is likely to have a hysteroid adjustment to life, but under stress may experience periods of exacerbated symptom development. Some individuals with this profile develop patterns of "invalidism" in which they become incapacitated and dependent upon others.

DIAGNOSTIC CONSIDERATIONS

Individuals with this profile typically show a neurotic pattern of adjustment and would probably receive a clinical diagnosis of Conversion Disorder or Somatization Disorder. They might also receive an Axis II diagnosis of Dependent Personality.

There is some possibility that she is having difficulties of an addictive nature. She may be abusing or over-using addicting subtances. Further evaluation of alcohol or drug usage is recommended.

TREATMENT CONSIDERATIONS

The client will probably be resistant to psychological treatment since she has little psychological insight and seeks medical explanations for her disorder. She is probably defensive and reluctant to engage in self-exploration. In addition, she seems to experience little anxiety over her situation, and may have little motivation to change her behavior. Some individuals with this profile respond to placebos or mild suggestion, or to stress-innoculation training if it is not too threatening. They will probably require long-term commitment to therapy before their personality will change substantially. However, individuals with this profile often terminate treatment early.

The criterion groups on which the original clinical scales were based were rather small and not necessarily representative of psychiatric populations in general. And because the correlations among the clinical scales are appreciable in some instances, the reliabilities of differences among scores on the clinical scales—and hence the accuracy of differential diagnosis among psychiatric groups—are somewhat low. The significant correlations among the clinical scales indicate that the number of factors measured by the MMPI is less than the number of scales. According to Dahlstrom, Welsh, and Dahlstrom (1975), perhaps as few as two factors ("general psychological adjustment" and "control over one's feelings and actions") account for a large percentage of the variability in MMPI scores.

Separate norms for men and women were derived in the original standardization of the MMPI in the early 1940s. Despite the provision of separate sex norms, research indicates that standardized interpretations of MMPI scale scores are more accurate for men than for women (Kelley & King, 1979). Also with respect to the sex variable, the M-F (Masculinity-Femininity) scale, which was constructed from items answered differently by males than by females, is more a measure of sex differences in interests than in sex role or sexual identity. Consequently, men who score low on the M-F scale are not necessarily more feminine in their sexual identity (or more likely to be homosexual as was originally thought), and women who score high on the M-F scale are not necessarily more masculine in their sexual identity (see Bem, 1975).

In scoring the MMPI no distinction is made among different age or ethnic groups, although age and ethnic differences in scores have been reported. Hathaway and McKinley, authors of the MMPI, were undoubtedly unaware of the fact that comparisons of the MMPI profiles of samples of blacks and whites would reveal several pronounced differences, suggesting greater psychopathology in the former group. In particular, blacks tend to score higher than whites on scales 8 and 9, the differences being related to education, place of residence, and degree of separation from white culture. Gynther (1972) argues that black-white differences in MMPI profiles should not be interpreted as meaning that blacks are more maladjusted than whites. Rather, he concludes that blacks have different attitudes, interests, and expectations than whites (the most striking attitude being distrust of white society) and that these factors affect the responses of blacks to items on the MMPI.

Considering their datedness and the methodologically crude way in which they were collected, it is surprising that the original MMPI norms are as good as they are (Colligan, Osborne & Swenson, 1982). Be that as it may, the need for new norms has been recognized for some years. Psychiatric classification has changed markedly during the past half century. In addition, more people now describe themselves as depressed and more appear to have antisocial tendencies. In any event the long-awaited restandardization of the MMPI, which took place in the early 1980s and was heralded by the publication of new norms in 1987, was quite welcome.

Restandardizing the MMPI

In addition to providing new, up-to-date norms, restandardization of the MMPI by the University of Minnesota Press was undertaken to broaden the item pool by (1) including content not represented in the original version, (2) revising and rewording the language of some of the existing items that were dated, awkward, or sexist, and

(3) providing separate forms of the inventory for adults and adolescents. All 550 of the original MMPI items were retained in the Adult and Adolescent revised versions, although 14% of the original items were changed because of dated language or awkwardness in wording. Words more characteristic of the 1940s (e.g., streetcar, sleeping powder, and drop the handkerchief) were omitted, and other modifications to update statements (e.g., *I like to take a bath.* became *I like to take a bath or shower.*) were made. As with the items of the original forms, the revised MMPI items were written at a sixth-grade level.

The original 550 items, along with the rewritten ones, are included in the new form, but the 16 repeated items in the old form have been deleted. The adult version also contains 154 new experimental items designed to assess certain areas of psychopathology not well represented in the original version of the MMPI (e.g., eating disorders, Type A personality, drug abuse). The Adolescent Version contains 104 new items concerned specifically with adolescent problems. In addition, the tendency for normal adolescents in a temporary state of turmoil to score like adult psychopaths on the old edition has been corrected. Despite the various changes in content, the MMPI can still be scored on the original clinical scales.

The samples of normal adolescents and adults tested in restandardizing the MMPI consisted of 15,000 Americans and Canadians from eight states and Toronto, selected at random from telephone books and replies to magazine advertisements. An effort was made to test people who were representative of the general population in terms of rural-urban and geographic residence, as well as demographic characteristics such as age, sex, education, and ethnicity. The original clinical scales have been evaluated on several new clinical populations, and studies on psychiatric samples (e.g., inpatient alcoholics and outpatient medical samples) conducted.

Problems and Prospects

The MMPI has been referred to by one writer as a "psychometric nightmare" (Rodgers, 1972) and by another as ". . . matchless as the objective instrument for the assessment of psychopathology" (King, 1978, p. 938). In the light of such seemingly divergent statements, one might well conclude that this is another example of beauty lying in the eye of the beholder. But strange as it may seem, both characterizations are probably correct. The MMPI certainly has a host of problems: the true-false keying of items on many scales (e.g., L, K, 7, 8, 9) is lopsided, that is, many more items are keyed "true" than "false" or vice versa; different scales contain many of the same items (as many as six items overlap between scales); the fact that extreme groups were used in constructing the scales makes the use of the MMPI with less extreme groups questionable; the use of groups of normal people in the criterion-keying procedure by which the scales were developed does not seem appropriate for scales used to differentiate among psychiatric groups. Faced with these and other psychometric difficulties, it may seem miraculous that the MMPI has not been replaced by one of several contenders (e.g., Jackson Personality Inventory, Millon Clinical Multiaxial Inventory). Yet the MMPI remains the objective personality inventory of choice by over 90% of clinical psychologists. It is difficult to know whether the popularity of the MMPI is a cause or an effect of the 7,000 or more research investigations that have been conducted with this inventory and the fact that it has been translated into dozens of languages. Since it appears unlikely that the MMPI will be replaced during the remainder of this century, it is hoped that the new norms, the computer interpretations, and the hundreds of new investigations with this instrument will result in improvements in the validity and manner in which the MMPI is used.

California Psychological Inventory

Like the Stanford-Binet in intelligence testing, the MMPI has been a kind of parent instrument for a number of other personality inventories. One of these offspring was the Minnesota Counseling Inventory (MCI), which was based on the MMPI and the older Minnesota Personality Scale. In contrast to the MMPI, which has a psychiatric orientation, the MCI was designed as a measure of adjustment in boys and girls in grades 9 through 12. The MCI, which is now out of print, has been replaced to a large extent by the California Psychological Inventory.

The most carefully researched of the several MMPI-like inventories that have been devised for normal people is the California Psychological Inventory (CPI), which is available from Consulting Psychologists Press (1956–1987). In constructing the original version of the CPI, 178 of its 480 true-false statements were taken from the MMPI; the remaining CPI items were specially prepared. The items are written at a fourth-grade level and have been administered to individuals as young as 12 years and as old as 75. However, the CPI is most suitable for high school, college age, and young adults. Unlike the MMPI categories, which emphasize maladjustment and psychiatric disorders, the CPI scoring categories stress more positive, normal aspects of personality. The author of the CPI, Harrison Gough, intended it to be a measure of interpersonal behavioral attributes common to all cultures and societies—what he referred to as *folk constructs*.

The original CPI is scored for the 18 scales listed in Table 8–3, plus six additional scores (Empathy, Independence, Management Interests, Work Orientation, Leadership, Social Maturity), which are included when the inventory is scored by the publisher. The scales in each of the first three classes have intuitive or logical connections with each other: the Class I scales are concerned with feelings of interpersonal adequacy, the Class II scales with acceptance or rejection of social norms and values, and the Class III scales with intellectual and academic variables. The three scales in Class IV are not related in any significant way.

Table 8–3	Scales on California Psychological Inventory

Class I. Measures of Poise, Ascendancy, Self-Assurance, and Interpersonal Adequacy

1. Do (Dominance) To assess factors of leadership ability, dominance, persistence, and social initiative.

2. Cs (Capacity for status) To serve as an index of an individual's capacity for status (not his actual or achieved status). The scale attempts to measure the personal qualities and attributes that underlie and lead to status.

3. Sy (Sociability) To identify persons of outgoing, sociable, participative temperament.

4. Sp (Social presence) To assess factors such as poise, spontaneity, and self-confidence in personal and social interaction.

5. Sa (Self-acceptance) To assess factors such as sense of personal worth, self-acceptance, and capacity for independent thinking and action.

6. Wb (Sense of Well-being) To identify persons who minimize their worries and complaints, and who are relatively free from self-doubt and disillusionment.

Class II. Measures of Socialization, Maturity, Responsibility, and Intrapersonal Structuring of Values

7. Re (Responsibility) To identify persons of conscientious, responsible, and dependable disposition and temperament.

8. So (Socialization) To indicate the degree of social maturity, integrity, and rectitude that the individual has attained.

9. Sc (Self-control) To assess the degree and adequacy of self-regulation and self-control and freedom from impulsivity and self-centeredness.

10. To (Tolerance) To identify persons with permissive, accepting, and nonjudgmental social beliefs and attitudes.

11. Gi (Good impression) To identify persons capable of creating a favorable impression and who are concerned about how others react to them.

12. Cm (Communality) To indicate the degree to which an individual's reactions and responses correspond to the modal ("common") pattern established for the inventory.

Class III. Measures of Achievement Potential and Intellectual Efficiency

13. Ac (Achievement via conformance) To identify those factors of interest and motivation that facilitate achievement in any setting where conformance is a positive behavior.

14. Ai (Achievement via independence) To identify those factors of interest and motivation that facilitate achievement in any setting where autonomy and independence are positive behaviors.

(Continued)

15. Ie (Intellectual efficiency) To indicate the degree of personal and intellectual efficiency that the individual has attained.

Class IV.   Measures of Intellectual and Interest Modes

16. Py (Psychological-mindedness) To measure the degree to which the individual is interested in, and responsive to, the inner needs, motives, and experiences of others.

17. Fx (Flexibility) To indicate the degree of flexibility and adaptability of a person's thinking and social behavior.

18. Fe (Femininity) To assess the masculinity or femininity of interests. (High scores indicate more feminine interests, low scores more masculine.)

From H. G. Gough, (1975). *Manual for the California Psychological Inventory* (pp. 10–11). Palo Alto, CA: Consulting Psychologists Press, Inc. Reprinted by permission.

Fifteen of the 18 CPI scales listed in Table 8–3 are personality scales, and three are validity or response bias scales. Eleven of the personality scales were constructed empirically by using contrasting (criterion) groups identified by a behavioral index or judges' ratings. For example, items were included on the Dominance scale if they differentiated among persons rated high in dominance and persons rated low in dominance by their peers. Four of the scales (Social Presence, Self-Acceptance, Self-Control, Flexibility) were developed by a combination of rational selection of items and internal-consistency analysis.

Validity Scales

Three of the CPI scales—Sense of Well-Being (Wb), Good Impression (Gi), and Communality (Cm)—are validity scales. Two of the validity scales were constructed from items that tended to be responded to in a certain way by normal people who were asked to fake bad (Wb) or fake good (Gi), whereas the Cm scale consists of a group of items that 95% or more of the examinees answered in a particular manner. Examinees with very high Wb scores (originally called Dissimulation) are probably denying or minimizing their problems; those with very low Wb scores are probably exaggerating their problems or trying to appear more maladjusted than they actually are. Similarly, high scores on the Gi scale, a measure of the social desirability response set, indicate a tendency to minimize problems and deny pathological symptoms. Finally, low scores on the 28-item Cm scale indicate that examinees are responding to the items randomly or otherwise incorrectly.

Administration and Scoring

The CPI can be administered to high school or college students, either individually or in a group. There is no time limit, but 45 minutes to one hour is usually required to answer the 480 items. A 240-item shorter version of the CPI (Burger, 1975) takes somewhat less time but is not as reliable. Items on both versions are answered true or false by making an X in the appropriate space on the separate answer sheet.

Handscoring the CPI involves placing each of 16 plastic templates over the answer sheet and counting the X's that show through. The raw score on each scale is then converted to a T score by use of a profile sheet. Machine scoring, which involves mailing the answer sheets to Consulting Psychologists Press or National Computer Systems, is obviously more efficient when testing a large group of people.

Interpreting the CPI

Interpretation of scores on the 18 CPI scales typically begins by inspecting the T scores on the three validity scales (*Wb*, *Gi*, and *Cm*). If these scores are extremely high (70 or greater) or extremely low (30 or less), the profile is probably invalid and should not be interpreted further. Otherwise, interpretation proceeds by noting the overall profile elevation and the pattern of low and high scores. Effective social and intellectual functioning is indicated by T scores above the mean (50), but, of course, scores may not be uniformly high or low on all scales. For example, scores in one class of scales may be mostly high while those in another are mostly low. After examining the elevation of the profile as a whole and of the scales in each of the four classes, high and low scores on specific scales and the variability of the profile are noted. The descriptions given in the manual of high and low scorers on each scale can assist in the interpretation process. McAllister's (1986) *A Practical Guide to CPI Interpretation* is recommended for more details on the four-step interpretative process that focuses on the total profile, the individual CPI scales, various score configurations, and two dozen regression equations to predict performance in various areas. A number of case examples are also presented in this guide. As with other personality inventories, computer scoring and interpretation of the CPI has become more popular than handscoring in recent years.

Norms, Reliability, and Validity

The CPI was more extensively standardized than any other criterion-keyed inventory and, with the exception of the MMPI, is the most thoroughly researched. The standard score norms from the original standardization are based on the responses of 6,000 males and 7,000 females of varying ages and socioeconomic status. Persons of various ages, socioeconomic levels, and geographical locations were included in the standardization sample, and separate norms were obtained for males and females. Means and standard deviations for 19 samples (psychiatric patients, prison inmates, juvenile delinquents, different occupational group members, etc.) are also provided in the 1975 manual.

Reported test-retest reliability coefficients for the various CPI scales range from .38 to .77 (average $r = .66$) for normal high school students and adults over a period of one year; short-term (1–4 weeks) test-retest coefficients are higher (average $r = .77$). Split-half coefficients for males and females range from .63 to .86 (average $r = .78$), indicating greater internal consistency for the CPI than the MMPI scales. As in the case of the MMPI, a number of items appear on more than one scale. The fact that the correlations among CPI scales are rather high (many scales correlate .50 or greater) and the reliabilities fairly modest creates problems of intraindividual differentiation among scores. The situation is better with respect to group differentiation: research results have demonstrated, for example, the validity of the inventory for identifying delinquents and predicting school dropouts.

As with its parent, the MMPI, an extensive volume of research pertaining to the validity of the CPI has been conducted. With respect to its construct validity, factor analyses reveal that five factors are represented by the 18 scales: I. Positive Adjustment, II. Social Poise, Extroversion, or Interpersonal Effectiveness, III. Independent Thought and Action, IV. Test Taking Attitude, V. Masculinity-Femininity. Megaree (1972) summarized the evidence for the concurrent and predictive validity of the CPI. Scores on the CPI scales tend to be significantly correlated with measures of emotional adjustment, but the majority of the coefficients are low. Determining multiple regression equations for combining scores on several scales can improve the usefulness of the CPI as a predictor of various behavioral criteria (delinquency, dropouts, grades, marital adjustment, parole violations, smoking cessation, drug abuse, choice of contraception, leadership, time estimation, etc.). These findings are consistent with Gough's initial recommendation that scores on the various scales be entered in appropriate multiple regression equations to predict whatever socially acceptable or unacceptable behavior is of concern. In addition to the multiple regression approach, research employing discriminant analysis and correlates of different types of profiles would be useful. Despite its shortcomings, the CPI remains a popular test: the results of a survey conducted by Piotrowski and Keller (1983) of graduate programs in clinical psychology revealed that among five objective personality tests with which the respondents thought Ph.D. candidates should be familiar, the CPI was second only to the MMPI.

Revision of the CPI

A revision of the CPI published in 1986 consists of 462 items retained or reworded from the original 480-item inventory. Two new scales—Empathy and Independence—were also added to the original 18 listed in Table 8–3. The scales of the new CPI are classified into three groups. The first group, the folk concept measures, consists of the 18 original scales and the two new ones. The second group of measures consists of the special purpose scales, indices, and regression equations developed by Gough and others (social maturity, Type A living style, etc.). The third group represents a theoretical model containing three major themes in the CPI— interpersonal orientation, normative perspective, and realization. Vectors 1, 2, and 3 (v.1, v.2, v.3) assess these three themes. The interpersonal orientation (internality vs.

externality) theme, which is inherent in the Capacity for Status, Dominance, Self-Acceptance, Sociability, and Social Presence scales, is measured by the new 34-item *structural scale* v.1. The normative perspective (norm-favoring vs. norm-doubting) theme, involving intrapersonal values of the sort assessed by the Responsibility, Socialization, and Self-Control scales, is measured by the new 36-item structural scale v.2. The realization (or competence) theme, involving the Achievement via Conformance, Achievement via Independence, Intellectual Efficiency, Sense of Well-Being, and Tolerance scales, is measured by the new 58-item scale v.3. Scores on the three themes are independent of each other, but are significantly correlated with the folk concept scales.

Scores on v.1 and v.2 were classified, separately for 1000 males and 1000 females, to create the four-fold typology depicted in Figure 8–2. These four types represent four ways of living or lifestyles. Note the descriptions of the alpha, beta, gamma, and delta personality types given at each of the v.3 levels of the figure. Although the exact description varies slightly with the level of v.3, in general *alphas* are characterized as "externally oriented and norm-favoring," *betas* as "internally oriented and norm-favoring," *gammas* as "externally oriented and norm-questioning," and *deltas* as "internally oriented and norm-questioning."

The third theme, v.3, measures the degree to which the potentials associated with each of the four types have been realized. There are seven levels of competence or effectiveness within v.3; Figure 8–2 shows cross-sections at levels 1, 4, and 7. Level 1 is described as "poor integration and little or no realization of the positive potential of the type" and Level 7 as "superior integration and realization of the positive potential of the type" (the "type" being alpha, beta, gamma, or delta). Levels between 1 and 7 are assigned descriptions intermediate between these two extremes. Thus, various scores on the v.1, v.2, and v.3 themes can be combined to produce a total of 4 types x 7 levels = 28 different personality configurations.

Millon Clinical Multiaxial Inventory

The description of the original and revised versions of the CPI should make clear that it is not merely an extension of the MMPI to normal adolescents and adults—a sane person's MMPI so to speak. Instruments such as the California Psychological Inventory have extended and supplemented the MMPI rather than replaced it. Nevertheless, it is widely recognized that the MMPI is faulty in a number of respects and new inventories have emerged that aspire to succeed it. One of the candidates for succession is the Millon Clinical Multiaxial Inventory (MCMI) (see Widiger et al., 1986).

The MCMI-I and its successor, the MCMI-II by T. Millon (National Computer Systems, 1987), are both composed of 175 brief, self-descriptive statements to be answered "true" or "false." Written at an eighth-grade level, these inventories were designed for clinical patients aged 17 years and older. In revising the MCMI-I

Personality Model of the California Psychological Inventory, Revised Edition **Figure 8–2**

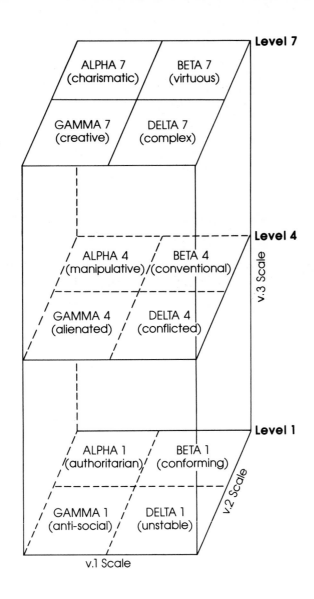

to produce the MCMI-II, 45 of the items were reworded or replaced and the number of clinical scales was increased to 25. The inclusion of items on the various scales entailed a combination of theoretical, internal-consistency, and criterion-keyed approaches. The first step was to write and select items to fit the constructs of Millon's theory. Next the frequency distributions of the items and the correlations between item and total scale scores were examined. Then the ability of the items to discriminate between individuals in a particular diagnostic category and an undifferentiated sample of psychiatric patients was examined. Finally, the items were cross-validated on new samples of patients.

The designations of the MCMI-I scales follow the personality theory described in Theodore Millon's *Modern Psychopathology* (1969) text, a theory which also played an important role in the development of the third edition of the *Diagnostic and Statistical Manual of Mental Disorders* (American Psychiatric Association, 1980). Similarly, the MCMI-II was designed to coordinate with the categories of personality disorders and clinical syndromes incorporated in the revised version of DSM-III (DSM-III-R).

The 25 diagnostic scales of the MCMI-II, which were designed to assess both relatively enduring *trait* features of personality as well as more transient *state* features of acute clinical syndromes, are grouped into five categories. These five categories and the 25 diagnostic scales grouped under them are listed in the extreme left and right columns, respectively, of Figure 8–3. The woman on whom the profile in this figure is based was characterized as an anxious, dependent individual, preoccupied with her health, with poor emotional control and high self-destructive potential.

Administration and Scoring

Administration of the MCMI-II follows a procedure similar to that for other personality inventories but takes less time (25–30 minutes) than the longer MMPI and CPI inventories. The MCMI-II can be scored with a set of hand-scoring templates and a supplement to the manual, but it is usually machine scored by National Computer Systems. Raw scores on the various scales are weighted and converted to *base rate scores*, which take into account the incidence of a particular characteristic or disorder in the general population. By determining the incidence of a particular personality disorder or trait in a specified population, raw scores can be transformed in such a way that the ratio of the number of correct classifications (valid positives) to the number of incorrect classifications (false positives) is minimized. The MCMI-II is scored and interpreted by National Computer Systems on the 25 diagnostic scales; the scores are listed and a score profile such as the one in Figure 8–3 and a narrative interpretation are provided. The narrative portion of the report makes a statement concerning the validity of the responses, gives interpretations for both Axis I (Clinical Syndromes) and Axis II (Personality Patterns), and lists statements involving noteworthy responses made by the examinee, parallel DSM-III-R multiaxial diagnoses, and therapeutic implications. Score profiles and interpretive guidelines for various DSM-III-R diagnostic groups are provided in the *Manual for the MCMI-II* (Millon, 1987).

Profile of scores on the Millon Clinical Multiaxial Inventory-II

Figure 8–3

MILLON CLINICAL MULTIAXIAL INVENTORY-II
FOR PROFESSIONAL USE ONLY

ID NUMBER = 168252   VALID REPORT
PERSONALITY CODE = 3 8B ** - * 2 1 8A + - " 4 7 6B 6A 5   // - ** - * //
SYNDROME CODE = S ** - * // - ** - * //
DEMOGRAPHIC = 00001056/ON/F/40/W/F/H10/C/MA/SC/30900/04/08/30160/ 920 0033

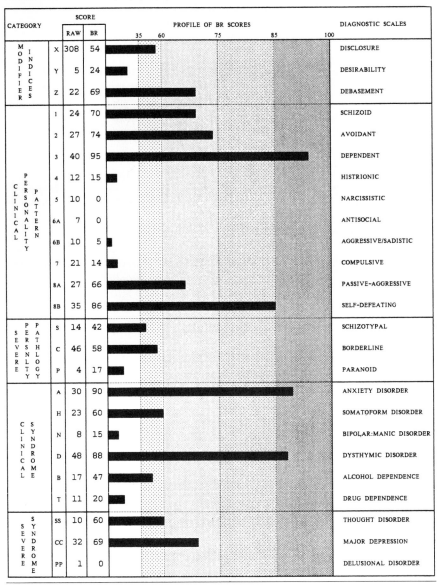

CATEGORY			SCORE RAW	SCORE BR	PROFILE OF BR SCORES	DIAGNOSTIC SCALES
MODIFIER INDICES		X	308	54		DISCLOSURE
		Y	5	24		DESIRABILITY
		Z	22	69		DEBASEMENT
CLINICAL PERSONALITY PATTERN		1	24	70		SCHIZOID
		2	27	74		AVOIDANT
		3	40	95		DEPENDENT
		4	12	15		HISTRIONIC
		5	10	0		NARCISSISTIC
		6A	7	0		ANTISOCIAL
		6B	10	5		AGGRESSIVE/SADISTIC
		7	21	14		COMPULSIVE
		8A	27	66		PASSIVE-AGGRESSIVE
		8B	35	86		SELF-DEFEATING
SEVERE PERSONALITY PATHOLOGY		S	14	42		SCHIZOTYPAL
		C	46	58		BORDERLINE
		P	4	17		PARANOID
CLINICAL SYNDROME		A	30	90		ANXIETY DISORDER
		H	23	60		SOMATOFORM DISORDER
		N	8	15		BIPOLAR:MANIC DISORDER
		D	48	88		DYSTHYMIC DISORDER
		B	17	47		ALCOHOL DEPENDENCE
		T	11	20		DRUG DEPENDENCE
SEVERE SYNDROME		SS	10	60		THOUGHT DISORDER
		CC	32	69		MAJOR DEPRESSION
		PP	1	0		DELUSIONAL DISORDER

Norms, Reliability, and Validity

Norms for the MCMI-I are based on 1,591 men and women inpatients and outpatients in several hospitals, clinics, and private practice situations in the United States and Great Britain. The manual for the MCMI-II (Millon, 1987) describes standardization data from various samples. The data on which the base rate norms are computed were obtained from 1,292 patients in more than 70 clinical settings. The average reliabilities of both the MCMI-I and MCMI-II scales are quite good for a personality inventory. The average test-retest reliabilities for the MCMI-II, which are based on patients in treatment, range from the low .50s to the low .90s over a period of 3 to 5 weeks; internal-consistency coefficients are mostly in the .80s. The MCMI-II scales have generally low correlations with each other, a distinct improvement over the MCMI-I that permits more effective differential diagnosis.

Evaluation

Reviewers (e.g., Hess, 1985; Widiger, 1985b; Widiger et al., 1986) have generally given fairly positive evaluations to the theoretical foundation, construction methodology, and research agenda of MCMI-I. As on the MMPI and the CPI, there is some item overlap among the MCMI-I and the MCMI-II scales. The scale overlap, which is worse for the MCMI-I than the MCMI-II, decreases the reliability of differences among scale scores and hence increases the difficulty of interpreting profiles of scores on the inventory. And because the base rates for a particular syndrome are not necessarily the same in a particular local situation as those assumed by Millon, MCMI-I scores are probably not as accurate as they would be if computed from local base rates. Finally, the expressed relationship of the MCMI-I to the DSM-III axes has not been satisfactorily demonstrated. But despite its shortcomings, reviewers concur that the MCMI-I has potential and has not received the attention and use that it deserves from clinicians. Perhaps this situation will be improved with MCMI-II, which appears to be psychometrically superior to MCMI-I.

Criterion-Keyed Inventories for Children and Adolescents

Instruments such as the Missouri Children's Picture Series (MCPS) by J. O. Sines and others (Psychological Assessment and Services, 1963–1971) and the Personality Inventory for Children are related to the MMPI but different from it in many respects. Although not widely used, the MCPS is an interesting inventory in that it attempts to assess children's personalities by utilizing a series of line-drawn pictures on cards of what a sample of children had indicated they liked or did not like to do. By sorting the 238 cards into two piles a child who takes the test indicates whether or not whatever is pictured looks like fun. Responses are then scored on eight variables (conformity, masculinity-femininity, maturity, aggression, inhibition, activity level, sleep disturbance, somatization). Information on the psychometric properties of the MCPS is insufficient to recommend its usage in clinical situations, but it is an interesting inventory with good potential for research on personality development and disorders in children.

Personality Inventory for Children

More popular than the MCPS and more directly related to the MMPI is the Personality Inventory for Children (PIC) by R. D. Wert and others (Western Psychological Services, 1977). Unlike the MMPI, however, the PIC is an inventory of observed behavior rather than self-report: the child's personality profile is determined from a parent's (usually the mother's) or other caretaker's responses to 600 true-false items concerning the child's behavior. Consequently, the resulting personality profile may reflect the attitudes and perceptions of the adult observer as much as the child's behavior.

PIC Scales The 16 primary scales on which the PIC is scored consist of three validity scales (Lie, Frequency or Deviant Responding, and Defensiveness), 12 clinical scales (Achievement, Intellectual Screening, Development, Somatic Concern, Depression, Family Relations, Delinquency, Withdrawal, Anxiety, Psychosis, Hyperactivity, Social Skills), and a screening scale (Adjustment) to identify children needing psychological evaluation. Scores on four factor scales and 17 experimental scales may also be determined. The Frequency scale consists of a set of items rarely answered in a particular direction, and the Defensiveness scale contains items designed to assess the observer's defensiveness about the child's behavior. The clinical scales were designed to identify certain emotional and interpersonal problems, in addition to assessing the child's cognitive development, academic achievement, and the psychological climate of the family. Two of the validity scales and five of the clinical scales were constructed by the criterion-keying procedure of selecting items according to observers' judgments of the relevance of the item to children's actual behavior; one validity scale and seven clinical scales were constructed by a content-validated or internal-consistency procedure or both.

Standardization, Reliability, and Validity The PIC was standardized during 1958 and 1962 on 2,390 normal boys and girls aged 5½ through 16½ years (approximately 100 boys and 100 girls at each year interval) and 200 normal boys and girls aged 3 through 5 years. The test-retest reliabilities vary widely (from the mid-.30s to the .90s), depending on the scale, the nature of the group tested, and the test-retest interval. Internal-consistency reliabilities are reported as ranging from the low .60s to the high .80s. A number of studies concerned with the validity of the PIC have been conducted. For example, an investigation of 3,431 inpatients and outpatients in a Michigan child guidance facility (Lachar & Gdowski, 1979) provided empirical cutoff scores on each scale for use in diagnosing disorders such as mental retardation, cerebral dysfunction, childhood psychosis, and delinquency, and 37 diagnostically descriptive paragraphs to serve as interpretive hypotheses. Lachar and Gdowski's (1979) *Actuarial Assessment of Child and Adolescent Personality: An Interpretive Guide for the Personality Inventory for Children Profile* provides additional information on the psychometric characteristics and use of the PIC.

Evaluation   Reviews of the PIC have been mixed in their evaluations. Achenbach (1981) faulted the PIC scales for being constructed from old personality theories. Reynolds (1985) concluded that there were serious psychometric deficiencies in the standardization, norming, and reliability of the inventory. Reviews by Dreger (1982), Rothermel and Lovell (1985) and Tuma (1985) are more positive. Tuma (1985) characterizes the PIC as "probably as sophisticated and psychometrically sound an instrument currently available for assessing children" (p. 1159). However, even Tuma decried the lack of a straightforward, integrated, user-oriented manual that might increase the clinical usefulness and decrease confusion and misuse of the PIC.

Millon Adolescent Personality Inventory

Similar to the MCMI-I in the coordination of its scoring with DSM-III is the 150-item Millon Adolescent Personality Inventory (MAPI) by T. Millon, C. J. Green, and R. B. Meager (National Computer Systems 1982). Item selection and scale development for the MAPI, which was designed for individuals aged 13 through 18 years, involved a three-stage process: theoretical-substantive, internal-structural, and external-criterion. After passing each of the three stages, the items were cross-validated on additional samples.

Scales, Scoring, and Interpretation   Also similar to the MCMI-I is the fact that the eight Personality Styles scales (Introversive, Inhibited, Cooperative, Sociable, Confident, Forceful, Respectful, Sensitive) of the MAPI are based on Millon's theory of personality (Millon, 1969, 1981). In addition, the MAPI is scored on eight Expressed Concerns scales (Self-Concept, Personal Esteem, Body Comfort, Sexual Acceptance, Peer Security, Social Tolerance, Family Rapport, Academic Confidence), four Behavioral Correlates scales (Impulse Control, Societal Conformity, Scholastic Achievement, Attendance Consistency), as well as reliability and validity indexes for identifying poor test-taking attitudes and confused or random responding. The MAPI is scored and interpreted by National Computer Systems, yielding a score profile and narrative report of personality patterns, expressed concerns, behavioral correlates, noteworthy responses, and therapeutic implications. Eight descriptive case illustrations are also presented in the manual (Millon, 1982b).

Reliability and Validity   Test-retest reliabilities of the 20 MAPI clinical scales range from .53 to .82 over five months and .45 to .75 over one year; internal-consistency coefficients range from .67 to .84. The manual also presents the results of a principal components, varimax-rotation factor analysis of the 20 scales from which four factors were extracted. Correlations with the CPI, 16 PF, and the EPPS are also listed in the manual.

Evaluation Like those of the PIC, reviews of the MAPI have been mixed. On the positive side, Brown (1985) refers to the MAPI as an excellent addition to the list of personality assessment instruments available for adolescents and lauds its use of modern statistical procedures in standardization and its well-written manual. Widiger (1985a) concludes that the MAPI is potentially useful for describing adolescent personality. However, both reviewers feel that the personality theory underlying the instrument is weak and the interpretation of MAPI scores complex and tentative: the language of the computer-generated report is said to be too adult and too pathologically-oriented for young teenagers. Widiger (1985a) maintains that the MAPI scales have little empirical foundation and that the cutoff points for the scales were chosen on the basis of unspecified base rates and that the percentages of correct decisions were not cross-validated. Both reviewers feel that the inventory needs additional empirical support before being relied on extensively in the personality assessment of adolescents.

Summary

Six inventories developed, in whole or in part, through criterion-keying procedures are discussed in this chapter: the Minnesota Multiphasic Personality Inventory (MMPI), the California Psychological Inventory (CPI), the Millon Clinical Multiaxial Inventory (MCMI-I and II), the Missouri Children's Picture Series (MCPS), the Personality Inventory for Children (PIC), and the Millon Adolescent Personality Inventory (MAPI). The MMPI, the PIC, and the MCMI-I and II were designed primarily for diagnosing mental disorders, the CPI for assessing the personality characteristics of normal people, and the MCPS and MAPI for assessing normal adolescents as well as those with personality problems.

The most widely used of these six inventories, and of all objective measures of personality for that matter, is the MMPI. The MMPI is also the oldest of the six inventories, having been constructed during the early 1940s at the University of Minnesota. The 566 true-false items on the MMPI were selected and placed on one or more clinical scales by comparing the responses of particular diagnostic groups with the responses of a sample of normal people. The inventory is scored for 14 standard scales (4 validity scales, 9 clinical scales, and Social Introversion), and may also be scored for numerous additional scales that have been developed.

Interpretation of scores on the MMPI proceeds in several different ways. Inspecting scores on the validity scales to determine if the profile is valid is usually followed by an analysis of pairs and patterns of high scores on the clinical scales (T scores above 70). National Computer Systems and certain other companies offer computer scoring and interpretation services for the MMPI; a narrative report of scores and item responses is provided to assist in diagnosis and treatment.

The MMPI has numerous psychometric problems, but it remains popular with clinicians. It was restandardized in 1986 and will undoubtedly continue to be the leader in the field of objective measures of personality for some years to come.

Second only to the MMPI in popularity among practicing psychologists is the California Psychological Inventory (CPI). This 480-item true-false inventory was constructed from a combination of items borrowed from the MMPI and new items to provide an empirically keyed inventory for the assessment of personality in normal high school and college students and adults. The CPI is scored on 18 scales divided into four categories. Scores on three of the scales (*Wb, Gi, Cm*) serve as a check on the validity of the inventory; they also contribute to the analysis of scores on all 18 scales. Multiple-regression equations for predicting group membership or diagnosis are provided in McAllister's (1986) excellent interpretive manual.

Like the MMPI, the CPI can be scored by hand or machine, but computer scoring and the associated interpretive narrative reports are becoming more popular. In interpreting a valid CPI profile, attention is first given to the overall profile elevation, then to categories containing consistently high or low scores, and finally to scores on the individual scales. The initial standardization of the CPI was more representative than that of the MMPI, and the scales of the former inventory tend to be more homogeneous than those of the latter. A recent revision of the CPI consisting of 462 items employs even more sophisticated scoring and interpretation procedures than its parent instrument.

It can be argued that the most sophisticated and carefully constructed of the personality inventories discussed in this chapter is the Millon Clinical Multiaxial Inventory (MCMI-I and II). Based on Theodore Millon's theory of psychopathology, which contributed to the design of DSM-III, this true-false inventory was designed for clinical patients aged 17 years and older. Included among the 25 diagnostic scales on which the MCMI-II is scored are three modifier indices, ten clinical personality pattern scales, three severe personality pathology scales, six clinical syndrome scales, and three severe syndrome scales. Inclusion of items on particular scales was based on a combination of rational, empirical, and cross-validation procedures.

The scoring of the MCMI-II is unique, in that it takes into account the base rate of a particular psychopathological disorder or personality type. The test-retest and internal-consistency reliabilities of the various scales are as high as those of most personality inventories, and the validity of the inventory is attested to by correlational evidence presented in the manual (Millon, 1987). Despite its developmental sophistication and brevity, however, the MCMI-II will not likely replace the MMPI in the hearts and minds of clinical psychologists.

Perhaps the most popular criterion-keyed personality inventory for children is the Personality Inventory for Children (PIC). This 600 true-false item behavioral inventory, for individuals aged 6 through 16 years, is somewhat unique among instruments of this kind in that it is completed by a parent or other observer acquainted with the examinee's behavior. In addition to three validity scales (Lie, Frequency, and Defensiveness), the PIC is scored for 12 clinical scales and a screening scale; scores on 17 other experimental and four factor scales may also be determined.

The PIC norms are rather old (25 or more years), and the reliabilities vary widely from scale to scale. However, a substantial amount of research concerned with the validity of this inventory has been conducted, and it is probably as well constructed and useful as any available personality assessment instrument for children.

The Millon Adolescent Personality Inventory (MAPI), a 150-item true-false inventory of adolescent personality, has received mixed reviews from critics. The three-stage strategy by which it was designed is similar to that of the MCMI. But the MAPI has a weak theoretical foundation, and the results of administering the inventory are sometimes difficult to interpret. Both the MAPI and MCMI-I and II are scored and interpreted by National Computer Systems on the basis of scores (base rate scores) that take into account the incidence of a particular disorder or personality type in the population. The MAPI is scored for eight Personality Styles, eight Expressed Concerns, four Behavioral Correlates, and two reliability and validity indexes. The reliability coefficients of the MAPI are satisfactory for an instrument of this kind, but evidence for its validity is inadequate.

Exercises

1. Define each of the following terms in a sentence or two:

alphas	gammas
base rate score	K (correction) scale
betas	L (lie) scale
? (cannot say) scale	Masculinity-Femininity scale
clinical scales	neurotic triad
coded scores	paired scores
communality scale	paranoid valley
conversion V	pattern analysis
criterion-keyed inventory	psychotic tetrad
deltas	question scale
diagnostic scale	structural scale
F (frequency or infrequency) scale	syndrome
fake bad score	validity index
fake good score	vectors
folk constructs	

2. The following is a list of personality inventories discussed in Chapters 7 and 8. Describe the characteristics and uses of as many of these inventories as you

can. Which ones are appropriate for children? For adults? Which ones are used in clinical settings in the diagnosis of psychopathology?

Beck Depression Inventory
California Psychological Inventory
California Test of Personality
Comrey Personality Scales
Coopersmith Self-Esteem Inventories
Early School Personality Questionnaire
Eating Disorders Inventory
Edwards Personal Preference Schedule
Guilford-Zimmerman Temperament Survey
High School Personality Questionnaire
Jackson Personality Inventory
Jenkins Activity Survey
Millon Adolescent Personality Inventory
Millon Behavioral Health Inventory
Millon Clinical Multiaxial Inventory
Minnesota Multiphasic Personality Inventory
Missouri Children's Picture Series
Myers-Briggs Type Indicator
NEO Personality Inventory
Omnibus Personality Inventory
Personality Research Form
Personality Inventory for Children
Piers-Harris Self-Concept Scale
Profile of Mood States
SCL-90-R
16 Personality Factor Questionnaire
State-Trait Anxiety Inventory
Taylor-Johnson Temperament Analysis
Tennessee Self-Concept Scale

3. Read reviews of any two of the following personality inventories in the *Ninth Mental Measurements Yearbook* (Mitchell, 1985, and previous editions by Buros) or *Test Critiques* (Keyser & Sweetland, 1984–1986). Summarize the good and bad features of the two inventories according to the reviewers.

California Psychological Inventory (CPI)

Millon Adolescent Personality Inventory (MAPI)

Millon Clinical Multiaxial Inventory (MCMI-I and II)

Minnesota Multiphasic Personality Inventory (MMPI)

Missouri Children's Picture Series (MCPS)

Personality Inventory for Children (PIC)

4. Compare the criterion-keyed approach, discussed in Chapter 8, with the rational-theoretical and factor-analytic approaches, discussed in Chapter 7, to personality inventory construction. In your opinion, which approach is best and why?

5. Arrange to take the California Psychological Inventory or the 16 Personality Factor Questionnaire, and have your scores interpreted by your instructor or another qualified person. Are your scores consistent with your own subjective assessment of your personality? After taking it, what criticisms of the personality inventory do you have?

6. Following the procedure outlined in exercise 8 of Chapter 4, prepare a critical review of any of the personality inventories listed in exercise 2 (above).

Suggested Readings

Butcher, J. N., & Keller, L. S. (1984). Objective personality assessment. In G. Goldstein & M. Hersen (Eds.), *Handbook of psychological assessment* (pp. 307–331). New York: Pergamon.

Butcher, J. N., & Finn, S. (1983). Objective personality assessment in clinical settings. In M. Hersen, A. Kazdir, & A. S. Bellak (Eds.), *The clinical pyschology handbook* (pp. 329–344). New York: Pergamon.

Dyer, F. J. (1985). Millon Adolescent Personality Inventory. In D. J. Keyser & R. C. Sweetland (Eds.), *Test critiques* (Vol. IV, pp. 425–433). Kansas City, MO: Test Corporation of America.

Graham, J.R. (1987). *The MMPI: A practical guide* (2nd ed.). New York: Oxford University Press.

Groth-Marnat, G. (1985). *Handbook of psychological assessment* (Chap. 7 & 8). New York: Van Nostrand Reinhold.

Hess, A. K. (1985). Review of Millon Clinical Multiaxial Inventory. In J. V. Mitchell, Jr. (Ed.), *The ninth mental measurements yearbook* (Vol. II, pp. 984–986). Lincoln, NE: University of Nebraska Press.

Moreland, K. L., & Dahlstrom, W. G. (1983). A survey of MMPI teaching in APA-approved clinical psychology programs. *Journal of Personality Assessment, 147,* 115–119.

Newmark, C. S. (1985). The MMPI. In C. S. Newmark (Ed.), *Major psychological assessment instruments* (pp. 11–63). Newton, MA: Allyn & Bacon.

Widiger, T. A. (1985). Review of Millon Clinical Multiaxial Inventory. In J. V. Mitchell, Jr. (Ed.), *The ninth mental measurements yearbook* (Vol. II, pp. 986–988). Lincoln, NE: University of Nebraska Press.

CHAPTER 9

Assessment of Interests and Values

Interests and values are associated but not identical concepts; they are also related to attitudes, beliefs, opinions, sentiments, and personal orientations. An *interest* is a feeling or preference concerning activities, ideas, and objects, whereas a *value* is concerned with the importance or worth attached to particular activities, ideas, and objects. Unlike personality inventories, which were originally designed to detect and diagnose maladjustment or mental disorder, measures of interests developed primarily within the context of vocational psychology. In this context they have made important practical contributions to vocational counseling and selection. Measures of values, on the other hand, stemmed mainly from research on social psychology, and only secondarily have they contributed to vocational psychology.

Interests and values are related not only to each other but to attitudes, beliefs, opinions, sentiments, personal orientations, and many other psychological variables. Similar to *attitudes*, which are discussed at length in Chapter 6, are *beliefs* and *opinions*. Both beliefs and opinions are judgments or acceptances of propositions as facts, but the factual supports for opinions are substantially weaker than those for beliefs. In terms of the extent to which their formation is based on factual information, attitudes are in lowest place, opinions next, and beliefs at the top. However, opinions and beliefs are less pervasive or generalized and less resistant to change than attitudes. This chapter will focus on the measurement of interests and values since that is where most of the research and theorizing has been concentrated.

Interests and Personality

Super (1970) conceptualizes interests and values as they relate to needs:

> Traits, values, and interests derive from needs. The need . . . leads to action, and action leads to modes of behavior or traits that seek objectives formulated in generic terms (values) or in specific terms (interests). Traits are ways (styles) of acting to meet a need in a given situation. Values are objectives that one seeks to attain a need. Interests are the specific activities and objects through which values can be attained and needs met. (pp. 189–190)

Super views *needs* as more characteristic than values, and values as more general than interests. Needs, values, and interests can all be satisfied by various types of activities, but the relationship to goal-oriented activities is closer for interests than for values and closer for values than for needs. Both values (the objectives or goals of behavior) and interests (the activities in which values are pursued or sought) are more closely related than needs to the actual decisions or choices made by the individual.

Super's description of the relationships among interests, values, and needs underscores the fact that what are called interests (vocational, educational, recreational, social, etc.) and values are actually personality variables; they induce people to act in certain ways and consequently function as dynamisms or motivators of behavior. Thus, certain activities and goals are selected by a person because they are seen as having the potential for satisfying his or her needs. However, not only do specific personality characteristics result in behavior that shapes or determines a person's environment, but the environment also affects personality. People with similar personality characteristics tend to select similar occupations, and exposure to a particular occupation for a prolonged period of time tends to change an individual in such a way that his or her personality becomes more like the personalities of other people in that occupation (Osipow, 1983).

H. D. Carter (1940) introduced the idea that interests are dynamic characteristics that form a part of the individual's self-concept and direct his or her choice of career. Later Bordin (1943), Forer (1948), and other psychologists elaborated on this idea. Forer appears to have been the first person to construct a personality inventory composed of items concerned with interests and activities; he also demonstrated how an interest inventory (Kuder Preference Record) could be used to differentiate between medical and psychiatric groups ranging from asthmatics to schizophrenics. Darley and Hagenah (1955) and Super (1972) emphasized the fact that interests become differentiated in the process of personality development, and that consequently interest inventories are actually measures of personality. Two other influential figures who have theorized and conducted research on the relationships of interests to personality are Anne Roe and John L. Holland.

Psychoanalytic and Developmental Theories

Rather than viewing interests simply as acquired characteristics produced by fortuitous experiences, many psychologists consider them as expressions of deep-seated individual needs and personality traits (Darley & Hagenah, 1955). Since Freud, psychoanalysts have maintained that personality traits influence selection of a particular vocation. Freud and other psychoanalysts emphasized the roles of sublimation (the channeling of frustrated sexual or aggressive drives into a substitute activity) and identification in the formation of interests. With respect to sublimation, a person with strong sadistic impulses might become interested in being a surgeon and a person whose sexual impulses were frustrated might write romantic poetry or enter an occupation concerned with decoration or use of the body (modeling, acting, sports, etc.). Although evidence for the operation of sublimation in determining interests and vocational choice is not clear-cut, data pertaining to the role of identification with parents and significant other people in one's life is more substantial. Consistent with the concept of identification are Nachmann's (1960) findings of differences in the acceptance of aggressive impulses, the emphasis on fairness and obedience to authority, and the relative dominance of the mother and father in families of lawyers, dentists, and social workers. The influence of parents is also underscored by Steimel and Suziedelis's (1963) finding that college students who were influenced more by their fathers were more likely to major in the exact sciences and students influenced more by their mothers tended toward the liberal arts. Additional research on the role of identification with parents in determining vocational interests is reported by Stewart (1959), Crites (1960), and Heilbrun (1969).

Needs and Other Personality Traits   Related but not restricted to a psychoanalytic conception of interests is research linking vocational and educational interests to specific needs and other personality characteristics. For example, significant correlations have been found between scores on interest inventories and personality inventories (Utz & Korben, 1976). Introversion is more common among people with scientific interests, aggressiveness is related to an interest in selling, and the incidence of psychoneurosis is greater among individuals with strong literary and aesthetic interests (Darley & Hagenah, 1955; Osipow, 1983; Super & Bohn, 1970). Other researchers (Sternberg, 1955; Siegelman & Peck, 1960) have delineated specific patterns of personality characteristics associated with choice of college major or career. Siegelman and Peck described chemists as curious, imaginative, intellectual, creative, relating to objects, and emotionally involved in their work; ministers are described as nurturant, personally insecure, and more likely to feel vocationally inadequate; military officers are characterized as valuing security and variety in associations and living quarters, dedicated to country, accepting of responsibility and authority, and concerned with loyalty and honesty.

Super's Developmental Theory   Recognizing the importance of identification and role-play in the development of interests but stressing the changes in self-concept and interests with growth, Super (1957) described a two-stage process in an individual's search for identity through the achievement of vocational maturity. The search begins in the *exploratory stage*, which is composed of a tentative substage, a transition substage, and finally an uncommitted trial substage. The second or *establishment stage* is composed of a committed trial substage and an advancement substage. Progress through these stages involves five developmental tasks occurring during specific chronological age periods: crystallization of a vocational preference (ages 14–18), specification of a vocational preference (ages 18–21), implementation of the preference (ages 21–24), stabilization of the preference (ages 25–35), and consolidation of status and advancement (late-30s to mid-40s).

Ginzberg's Developmental Theory   Another stage theory of vocational decision making is Ginzberg, Ginsburg, Axelrad, and Herma's (1951) conception of three major periods in the process of vocational choice: fantasy, tentative, and realistic. During the *fantasy period*, children's occupational preferences are arbitrary and unrealistic. During the four substages of the *tentative period* (interest, capacity, value, and transition), which begins at about age 11 and ends by about age 18, children begin considering possible vocations by asking themselves what they most like to do and are interested in. As they progress through the four substages of the tentative period, children begin to realize that not only do certain vocations require more ability than others but that some vocations are more intrinsically or extrinsically valued than others. The final, or *realistic*, period begins with an exploratory stage and progresses through a crystallization stage occurring between the ages of 19 and 21. During this stage the successes and failures experienced during the exploratory stage lead to a clear vocational pattern, and finally to a specification stage in which a position or professional speciality is selected.

According to Ginzberg et al. (1951), the adequacy of an adolescent's vocational choice process depends on the extent to which he or she is able to test reality, develop a suitable time perspective, defer gratification, accept and implement compromises in vocational plans, and identify suitable vocational role models at the appropriate time. Ginzberg et al. (1951) maintain that these factors and other intrinsic characteristics are important in determining whether the individual learns to delay gratification and becomes primarily work-oriented or is unable to delay gratification and becomes primarily pleasure-oriented. Another personality variable that influences vocational choice is whether the person is an active problem solver who attacks problems and attempts to solve them or a passive problem solver who merely waits for events to happen to him or her (Osipow, 1983).

Roe's Person-Environment Theory of Career Choice

Based to some extent on psychoanalytic theory and Maslow's (1954) hierarchy of needs theory, as well as the results of her own research, is A. Roe's three-dimensional conception of career choice (Roe & Siegelman, 1964) (see Figure 9–1). The findings of her initial research on the personalities of physical, biological, and social scientists led Roe to conclude that these scientists could be distinguished by the degree of their interest in people versus their interest in things. A strong interest in people leads an individual to enter more person-oriented vocational environments, which include general cultural, arts, entertainment, services, and business contact occupations. A strong interest in things, on the other hand, leads to more nonperson-oriented vocations (e.g., scientific, outdoor, technological, and organizational activities). Roe theorizes that these differences in orientation result from childhood experiences, in particular the rewards and punishments delivered for various activities and the psychological climate of the home (warm or accepting vs. cold or avoiding). A warm family environment is said to result in a greater interest in people and a cold environment in a greater interest in things.

As diagrammed in Figure 9–1, Roe and Klos (1969) subsequently modified the theory to that of a three-dimensional conical model. The left-to-right line of this figure depicts the dimension of Orientation to Personal Relations versus Orientation to Natural Phenomena, while the near-to-far line depicts the dimension of Orientation to Resource Utilization versus Orientation to Purposeful Communication. The third or vertical dimension, Low Level versus High Level, refers to the skill level (professional, skilled, unskilled) required by the occupation; lower-level (unskilled) occupations are closer to the pointed end of the cone and higher-level (professional) occupations closer to the broader end. The fact that the cross-sectional circles are larger near the top than near the bottom of the cone is consistent with Roe's belief that variability on the first two (horizontal) dimensions is greater among professional occupations than among the lower-skilled occupations located further toward the tip of the cone.

The specifics of Roe's three-dimensional model have not been well-supported by research (Osipow, 1983). For example, a variety of orientations are possible within a single career: both scientists and artists may work with both people and things in various contexts. Furthermore, differences among the interests of people in low-level occupations may be as great as those in high-level occupations. Osipow (1983) concludes that even the assertion that people are either person- or nonperson-oriented in their interests and that this orientation influences vocational choice cannot be stated unequivocally. However, Roe's model has been applied to the construction of several vocational interest inventories, including Ramak (Meir & Barak, 1974), the California Occupational Preference System Interest Inventory, the Hall Occupational

Figure 9–1   Roe's three-dimensional conical model of career choice

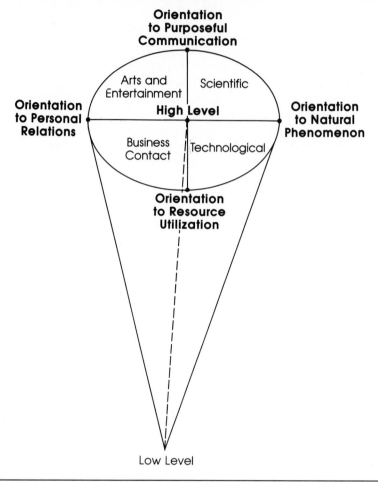

Orientation Inventory, and the Vocational Interest Inventory. On the Ramak, which is Hebrew for "a list of occupations," respondents indicate their preferences for 72 different occupational environments arranged by field and level according to Roe's classification scheme. The Ramak is scored on eight fields and three levels within each field. A companion instrument is based on occupational course titles.

COPS Interest Inventory   This inventory by R. R. Knapp and L. Knapp (EdITS, 1966–1982) is designed for seventh grade through college and takes 30 to 40 minutes to complete. The items are in Likert-type format (L = like very much, l = like moderately, d = dislike moderately, D = dislike very much). Based on factor analyses of items reflecting Roe's (1956) classification of occupations into clusters and levels within each cluster, the COPS Interest Inventory is scored on eight major cluster scales (Arts, Service, Science, Business, Technology, Outdoor, Clerical, Communication). The first five scales have two levels—Professional and Skilled; the Technology scale also has a third level—Consumer Economics. The clusters are keyed both to curriculum choices and to detailed job information sources such as the *Dictionary of Occupational Titles* (U. S. Dept. of Labor, 1982) and the *Occupational Outlook Handbook* (U.S. Dept. of Labor, 1986–1987).

Three additional forms of the COPS are the professional level COPS-P, which is designed for senior high school and college students as well as adult professionals; an intermediate level COPS II, designed for elementary through high school students; and the COPS-R for sixth grade through high school. The COPS-R is written in simplified language and uses a single norms profile. All of the COPS inventories may be used, in conjunction with measures of abilities (CAPS) and work values (COPES), for purposes of career counseling.

The COPS has, over the years, received mixed reviews, but a recent review by Bauerfeind (1986) is generally positive. Although there are admittedly weaknesses in regard to the norms and predictive validities for the COPS and some problems in understanding the manual (Knapp & Knapp, 1984), Bauerfeind concludes that the items are well written and highly relevant to real-life job activities and that the answer sheets are convenient to use and easily scored. Students seem to enjoy taking the COPS, and it should serve as an effective stimulus for career exploration.

Hall Occupational Orientation Inventory (HOOI)   The HOOI by L. G. Hall and R. B. Tarrier (Scholastic Testing Service, 1968–1976) focuses on 22 job and personality characteristics. It is based on a personality-need theory inspired by Abraham Maslow and adapted by A. Roe to the area of occupational choice. The HOOI is appropriate for individuals from grade three through adulthood and takes 30 to 40 minutes to complete. Three levels are available: Intermediate HOOI for grades 3 to 7, Young Adult/College HOOI for high school and college students and professionals, and an Adult Basic HOOI for reading handicapped adults.

Because scores on the HOOI scales were designed to be interpreted idiographically rather than nomothetically, no normative data are given: scores are described in somewhat normative fashion, however, as high, average, or low. Rather than being a measurement device in the true sense of the word, the HOOI appears to have been designed primarily for instructional purposes. Examinees administer, score, and interpret the inventory by themselves, as an aid to career exploration; in this way it can serve as a career development and counseling resource but not a true test or interest inventory (see Lee, 1984).

Vocational Interest Inventory (VII)   The VII by P. W. Lunneborg (Western Psychological Services, 1981) consists of 112 forced-choice items, and is designed for grade 3 through adulthood and takes 30 to 40 minutes to complete. It focuses on eight occupational areas delineated by Roe: Service, Business Contact, Organization, Technical, Outdoor, Science, General Cultural, and Arts and Entertainment. These interest areas overlap with those of the COPS Interest Inventory.

An effort was made in constructing the VII to balance sex differences in items and combined sex norms are used in score interpretation. Despite these efforts, sex differences in scores remain, particularly on scales 6 (Science) and 8 (Arts and Entertainment). Furthermore, the sample on which the norms are based (University of Washington-bound high school students) is limited, and no evidence for the predictive validity of the VII for occupational entry is given in the manual (see Hansen, 1985).

Holland's Vocational Personalities-Work Environments Theory

Even more influential than Roe's theoretical model is J. L. Holland's theory of vocational personalities and work environments. Holland (1985) maintains that the complementary match between the personality type of an individual and the psychological environment in which the individual finds him- or herself determines the individual's behavior in that environment. If people receive sufficient reinforcements and satisfactions in their environment, they will tend to remain in it; otherwise they will either change their environment or change themselves. Personality type, of course, is influenced by past and present physical and sociocultural environment as well as an individual's hereditary makeup.

According to Holland's hexagonal model (see Figure 9–2), there are six types of vocational personalities and six work environments: Realistic (R), Investigative (I), Artistic (A), Social (S), Enterprising (E), and Conventional (C). A *realistic type* of person likes to manipulate tools, machines, and other objects, and to be outdoors and work with plants and animals, but dislikes educational and therapeutic activities. He or she tends to possess athletic, mechanical, and technical competencies but is deficient in social and educational skills. Consequently, such a person, who is characterized as practical, conforming, and natural, is likely to avoid situations requiring verbal and interpersonal skills and to seek jobs such as automobile mechanic, farmer, or electrician.

The *investigative type* of individual prefers activities that demand a great deal of thinking and understanding, for example, scientific enterprises. He or she likes to observe, learn, investigate, analyze, evaluate, and solve problems, but tends to avoid situations requiring interpersonal and persuasive skills. This scholarly individual is characterized as rational, cautious, curious, independent, introversive, and more likely to be found in fields such as chemistry, physics, biology, geology, and other sciences.

The *artistic type* of person is described as imaginative, introspective, complicated, emotional, expressive, impulsive, noncomforming, and disorderly. He or she tends to prefer unstructured situations in which creativity or imagination can be

---

Holland's hexagonal model of interests   **Figure 9–2**

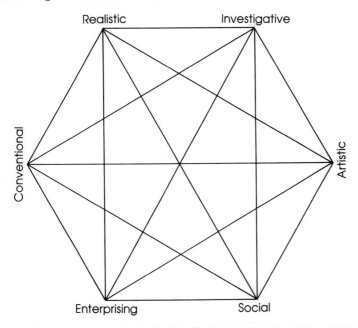

From *Differential Psychology* by H. L. Minton and F. W. Schneider. Copyright © 1980 by Wadsworth, Inc. Reprinted by permission of the publisher, Brooks/Cole Publishing Company, Monterey, California.

expressed. Consequently, jobs such as actor, musician, or writer are likely to appeal to people in this category.

The *social type*, who is verbally and interpersonally skilled, likes to work with people—developing, enlightening, informing, training, curing, and helping or supporting them in various ways. Individuals in this category tend to be humanistic, empathic, and to have teaching abilities; the mechanical and scientific abilities of these persons are minimal. Such individuals are viewed as cooperative, friendly, helpful, persuasive, tactful, and understanding, and are likely to be found in clinical or counseling psychology, speech therapy, and teaching.

The *enterprising type*, described as aggressive, ambitious, energetic, domineering, pleasure seeking, self-confident, and sociable, tends to have high verbal and leadership abilities. Such a person likes to influence and persuade others, and to lead or manage organizations for economic gain. Jobs such as manager, business executive, or salesperson are preferred by these individuals.

The *conventional type* is described as conscientious, efficient, inflexible, obedient, orderly, persistent, practical, and self-controlled. He or she tends to have good arithmetic and clerical ability, and is consequently adept at filing, record keeping, and data processing. These skills are congruent with his or her emphasis on business and economic achievement, leading to jobs such as banker, bookkeeper, or tax expert.

Corresponding to the six personality types are six model environments— realistic, investigative, artistic, social, enterprising, and conventional, each of which is sought by persons with corresponding skills, abilities, attitudes, values, and personality traits. Behavior in a particular environment is, according to Holland, determined by the interaction between the individual's personality and the type of environment. People tend to seek environments that are congruent with their personalities and tend to be happier, more satisfied, and more productive in such environments than in environments that are incongruent with their personalities. However, both the personality types and the environmental types are idealizations; a given individual or environment is typically a composite of more than one ideal type.

As depicted by their proximity in the model in Figure 9–2, according to Holland some of the $6(5)/2 = 15$ pairs of personality types are more closely related to each other, and hence more consistent. *Consistency* refers to the degree to which personality types or environmental types (models) are related to each other, the consistency of a person's interest pattern being indicated by the extent to which he or she scores high on interest types that are close to each other on the hexagonal model. Figure 9–2 shows, for example, that the investigative and conventional types are closer, and hence more consistent, with the realistic type, whereas the artistic and enterprising types are more consistent with the social type.

Other important concepts in Holland's theory are differentiation, identity, congruence, and calculus. A person who has only one or two high scores has a greater degree of *differentiation* than a person with several high scores. Holland maintains that high consistency and differentiation of personality types are characteristic of people who cope effectively with their vocational problems. A second concept, *identity*, may be either personal or environmental. In the case of *personal identity* the individual has a clear and stable picture of his or her goals, interests, and talents, a condition associated with having a small number of vocational goals in a few major categories. *Environmental identity* is concerned with whether the goals, tasks, and rewards of the environment are stable over time. A third concept, *congruence*, refers to the fact that different personality types function best in different environments, environments that provide opportunities and rewards that are congruent with a person's abilities and preferences. Finally, the concept of *calculus* refers to the fact that personality types or environments are orderable according to a hexagonal model (see Figure 9–2) in which the distances between types or environments are consistent with the theoretical relationships between them.

An impressive amount of research, much of which is longitudinal in design, has been conducted with respect to Holland's theory. Although Osipow (1983) maintains that the theory is limited in its ability to explain the process of personality development and its role in vocational selection, he concludes that "with respect to the research testing it, the record of Holland's theory is extremely good. The research program has been broad, varied, and comprehensive." (p. 112) Much of this research has employed the two instruments described below.

Self-Directed Search, 1985 Revision (SDS)   The SDS by J. L. Holland (Psychological Assessment Resources, 1985) consists of a 16-page assessment booklet that assists the user in making a thoughtful evaluation of his or her own interests and abilities, and a 16-page Occupations Finder for actively exploring the entire range of possible occupations. There are six scores, *RIASEC scores*: Realistic (*R*), Investigative (*I*), Artistic (*A*), Social (*S*), Enterprising (*E*), and Conventional (*C*). The norms are incorporated in a three-letter occupational code, and the Occupations Finder contains over 1,100 occupational titles keyed to the three-letter code.

In a review of the SDS, Dolliver (1985) points out that it "has become a prototype of a self-administered, self-scoring, and self-interpretive vocational interest measure." (p. 1347) Some concern is expressed about the accuracy with which high school students are able to identify their three-letter occupational code, and supervision is recommended. Students who have taken the SDS should also consult a vocational counselor. Another area of concern is the gender-relatedness of the SDS: females tend to score higher on the *A* and *S* scales and males on the *R*, *I*, and *E* scales. However, Dolliver (1985) agrees with Holland's assertion that these differences are related to gender differences in the world of work and hence do not represent a sex bias.

Vocational Preference Inventory, 1985 Revision (VPI)   The VPI by J. L. Holland (Psychological Assessment Resources, 1985) is a supplement to the Self-Directed Search and other interest inventories. It is based on Holland's theory that occupations can be described in terms of personality characteristics. Examinees indicate whether they like or dislike each of 160 or more different occupations, the responses being scored on 11 scales: Realistic, Investigative, Artistic, Scientific, Enterprising, Conventional, Self-Control, Status, Masculinity-Femininity, Infrequency, and Acquiescence. The first six (RIASEC) scores can be used with the SDS Occupations Finder for purposes of career exploration and vocational guidance. Different patterns of high scores on these six types result in the examinee's being assigned to different vocational categories. For example, a person who scores high on the *C*, *E*, and *S* scales falls in the same category as advertising agents and sales representatives.

In a review of the previous (seventh) edition of the VPI, Rounds (1985) concludes that this inventory cannot be recommended because of "unsubstantiated clinical and personality interpretations that might easily mislead the unwary user" (p. 1684) and its failure to provide adequate reliability, validity, and normative data. The situation has improved somewhat with the current (1985) edition and the new manual, but the psychometric characteristics of the VPI still leave something to be desired.

Personality Inventories as Measures of Interests

Personality inventories of the sort described in chapters 7 and 8 typically contain a number of questions concerning interests and attitudes, as well as other aspects of personality. Consequently, scores on many of these inventories may be used in vocational counseling and guidance. An example is the 16 Personality Factor Questionnaire, which can be scored and interpreted by computer at the Institute for Personality and Ability Testing in terms of occupational variables corresponding to Holland's themes. An examinee's profile of scores on these variables (venturous-influential, nurturing-altruistic, creative-self-expressive, procedural-systematic, analytic-scientific, mechanical-operative) can then be compared with the profiles of 52 occupations to determine the similarity of the examinee's interests to those of people in each occupation. Another personality inventory, scored on six occupational scales (Service Orientation, Reliability Stress Tolerance, Clerical Potential, Sales Potential, Managerial Potential), as well as six other personality dimensions (Intellectance, Adjustment, Prudence, Ambition, Sociability, Likeability) is the Hogan Personality Inventory by R. Hogan (National Computer Systems, 1985).

Perhaps the most favorably reviewed of the inventories in this category is the Self-Description Inventory (SDI) by C. B. Johansson (National Computer Systems, 1975–1983). Designed for grades nine and over, the SDI yields scores on 11 personal description scales (Caution vs. Adventurous, Nonscientific vs. Analytical, Tense vs. Relaxed, Insecure vs. Confident, Conventional vs. Imaginative, Impatient vs. Patient, Unconcerned vs. Altruistic, Reserved vs. Outgoing, Soft-spoken vs. Forceful, Lackadaisical vs. Industrious, Unorganized vs. Orderly) and six vocationally oriented scales based on Holland's themes (Realistic, Investigative, Artistic, Social, Enterprising, Conventional). Scores on several administrative indices (total responses; percentages of items answered *Yes, Sometimes,* and *No;* response check) provide a check on validity biases. The SDI must be scored by computer, which also provides a narrative interpretation of results.

The SDI was standardized on samples of males and females between the ages of 15 and 55, and its reliability and validity appear fairly satisfactory. Test-retest reliabilities for the personality scales range from .70 to .94 and for the vocationally oriented scales from .76 to .91. Moderate correlations with various other personality inventories are reported in the manual, but additional validity data confirm the ability of the SDI scores to differentiate among people in varying occupational groups who are experienced and satisfied with their work.

Criterion- and Content-Validated Interest Inventories

Unlike instruments based on the theories of Roe and Holland, the majority of interest inventories have not been constructed according to a specific theoretical framework. Inventories such as the Strong Vocational Interest Blank eventually incorporated certain theoretical concepts such as Holland's thematic categories into their interpretive structure, but the items comprising these inventories were originally selected only if they were significantly related to a specified external or internal criterion or on the basis of common and psychological sense.

The work of James Miner marks the beginning of systematic efforts to develop criterion- and content-validated measures of interests. The interest questionnaire constructed by Miner in 1915 prompted an historic seminar on interest measurement held at Carnegie Institute of Technology in 1915. One result of that seminar was E. K. Strong, Jr.'s research on interest measurement and the development and refinement of the Strong Vocational Interest Blank for Men, the first standardized interest inventory. Other noteworthy events in the history of interest measurement were the publication by G. F. Kuder in 1939 of the Kuder Preference Record and the research on objective interest measures conducted by U.S. Army Air Corps psychologists during World War II. Many interest inventories have been published since World War II, but modifications of the inventories developed originally by Strong and Kuder continue to be the most popular.

The Strong Inventories

As a result of research conducted during the 1920s, Strong discovered consistent, significant differences in people's reports of what they like and dislike. Deciding to construct an inventory to assess these individual differences in interests, he administered a variety of items concerning preferences for specific occupations, school subjects, amusements, activities, and types of people, in addition to a scale for rating their own abilities and characteristics, to groups of men employed in specific occupations. By comparing the responses of these occupational groups to those of men in general, Strong was able to develop a series of occupational scales consisting of items that significant numbers of men in specific occupations answered differently from men in general. Several dozen of these occupational scales for men were devised, and a separate women's blank that could be scored on over two dozen occupational scales was constructed a few years later.

For various reasons, including the desire to comply with Title IX of the Civil Rights Act of 1964 and to meet allegations of sexism, in 1974 the men's and women's blanks of the SVIB were combined into a single instrument—the Strong-Campbell Interest Inventory (SCII). An attempt was made to remove sex bias in the content of the items and the occupational labels and create a more unisex inventory. Sex bias was reduced but not entirely eliminated in constructing the SCII.

Format of the SVIB-SCII   The latest edition of the Strong-Campbell Interest Inventory, the SVIB-SCII by E. K. Strong Jr., J. Hansen, and D. P. Campbell (Consulting Psychologists Press), was published in 1985. The SVIB-SCII consists of 325 items grouped into the following seven parts:

I.   *Occupations*   Each of 131 occupational titles is responded to with like (L), indifferent (I), or dislike (D).
II.   *School Subjects*   Each of 36 school subjects is responded to with like (L), indifferent (I), or dislike (D).
III.   *Activities*   Each of 51 general occupational activities is responded to with like (L), indifferent (I), or dislike (D).
IV.   *Amusements*   Each of 39 amusements or hobbies is responded to with like (L), indifferent (I), or dislike (D).
V.   *Types of People*   Each of 24 types of people is responded to with like (L), indifferent (I), or dislike (D).
VI.   *Preference between Two Activities*   For each of 30 pairs of activities, preference between the activity on the left (L) and the activity on the right (R), or no preference (–), is indicated.
VII.   *Your Characteristics*   Each of 14 characteristics is responded to with Yes, ?, or No, depending on whether or not they are self-descriptive.

Although the items, format, and administration procedure are essentially unchanged from the previous edition, the profile has been expanded to include 106 occupations represented by 207 occupational scales.

SVIB-SCII Scales   The SVIB–SCII is scored on five groups of measures: administrative indexes, general occupational themes, basic interest scales, occupational scales, and special scales. Before attempting to interpret a person's scores on the last four groups of measures, scores on the ten administrative indices, particularly the total responses (TR) and infrequent responses (IR), should be checked. The TR and IR indexes are recorded at the top left of the upper half of the SVIB-SCII profile form (see Figure 9–3). If the TR index is less than about 305, the examiner should inspect the answer sheet to ascertain the problem. The IR index, which is based on infrequently selected response choices, is used to determine whether the answer sheet was marked correctly; a negative *IR* index should lead one to question the validity of the SVIB-SCII profile. The remaining eight administrative indexes are the response percentages given at the bottom right of the lower half of the profile form (see Figure 9–4). If the Like (*LP*), Indifferent (*IP*), or Dislike (*DP*) percentages are outside the 20 to 55 range, there is an unusual circumstance of some sort that should be investigated before interpreting the profile (Hansen & Campbell, 1985).

As shown in Figures 9–3 and 9–4, the SVIB-SCII profile form is divided into six thematic sections based on Holland's (1973) vocational personalities system: Realistic, Investigative, Artistic, Social, Enterprising, and Conventional. The examinee's standard T score on each occupational theme is indicated below the label of the theme. The norm group for scoring the general occupational themes consisted of 300 men and 300 women, referred to as the "general reference sample," considered to represent the interests of people in general.

The 23 basic interest scales, one to five of which are listed under each of the six occupational themes, were constructed by grouping items having high in-

SVIB-SCII Profile Form, upper half (Page 1)

Figure 9–3

STRONG-CAMPBELL INTEREST INVENTORY OF THE
STRONG VOCATIONAL INTEREST BLANK

PROFILE REPORT FOR:
JAMES JON C
ID: 562432008
AGE: 20   SEX: M

DATE TESTED: 01/13/88
DATE SCORED: 1/ 15/ 88

SPECIAL SCALES: ACADEMIC COMFORT 42
INTROVERSION-EXTROVERSION 32

TOTAL RESPONSES: 324 INFREQUENT RESPONSES: 6

OCCUPATIONAL SCALES

Occupational Scale	F	M
REALISTIC		
Marine Corps enlisted personnel (CRS)		17
Navy enlisted personnel	25	7
Army officer	42	24
Navy officer	32	23
Air Force officer	32	21
Air Force enlisted personnel (CI)		9
Police officer	40	30
Bus driver	22	33
Horticultural worker	14	13
Farmer	25	19
Vocational agriculture teacher	14	11
Forester	8	12
Veterinarian (IR)		9
Athletic trainer (SR)	8	
Emergency medical technician	9	9
Radiologic technologist	9	3
Carpenter	9	6
Electrician	12	9
Architect (ARI)	19	
Engineer	14	1
INVESTIGATIVE		
Computer programmer	12	5
Systems analyst	15	11
Medical technologist	0	5
R & D manager	12	9
Geologist	6	6
Biologist (I)	-6	
Chemist	1	-2
Physicist	-12	-11
Veterinarian (RI)	0	
Science teacher	0	6
Physical therapist	8	13
Respiratory therapist	12	6
Medical technician	7	0
Pharmacist	10	32
Dietitian (CSE)	24	
Nurse, RN (SI)		16
Chiropractor	28	20
Optometrist	14	8
Dentist	6	8
Physician	5	11
Biologist (IR)		14
Mathematician	-1	-3
Geographer	21	21
College professor	20	30
Psychologist	23	33
Sociologist	19	27
ARTISTIC		
Medical illustrator	4	7
Art teacher	-3	31
Artist, fine	28	24
Artist, commercial	18	36
Interior decorator	49	47
Architect (RIA)		
Photographer	32	37
Musician	13	34
Chef (EA)	12	
Beautician (E)		45
Flight attendant	46	46
Advertising executive	59	55
Broadcaster	60	57
Public relations director	59	61
Lawyer	52	59
Public administrator	58	53
Reporter	58	41
Librarian	34	36
English teacher	45	47
Foreign language teacher (SA)		37

STANDARD SCORES: VERY DISSIMILAR, DISSIMILAR, MODERATELY DISSIMILAR, MID-RANGE, MODERATELY SIMILAR, SIMILAR, VERY SIMILAR — 15 25 30 40 45 55

REALISTIC

GENERAL OCCUPATIONAL THEME - R
Very Low 36

BASIC INTEREST SCALES (STANDARD SCORE)
AGRICULTURE Mod Low 43
NATURE Low 37
ADVENTURE Very High 67
MILITARY ACTIVITIES Average 47
MECHANICAL ACTIVITIES Very Low 36

INVESTIGATIVE

GENERAL OCCUPATIONAL THEME - I
Mod Low 42

BASIC INTEREST SCALES (STANDARD SCORE)
SCIENCE Very Low 35
MATHEMATICS Low 36
MEDICAL SCIENCE Mod. Low 43
MEDICAL SERVICE Mod. Low 41

ARTISTIC

GENERAL OCCUPATIONAL THEME - A
Mod High 55

BASIC INTEREST SCALES (STANDARD SCORE)
MUSIC/DRAMATICS Mod. High 53
ART Average 48
WRITING Mod High 59

CONSULTING PSYCHOLOGISTS PRESS
577 COLLEGE AVENUE
PALO ALTO, CA 94306

83 82 1 N

(Continued)

Figure 9–4

SVIB-SCII Profile Form, lower half (Page 2)

STRONG CAMPBELL INTEREST INVENTORY OF THE
STRONG VOCATIONAL INTEREST BLANK

PROFILE REPORT FOR: JAMES JON C
ID: 562432008
AGE: 20   **SEX:** M

DATE TESTED: 01/13/88
DATE SCORED: 1/ 15/ 88

OCCUPATIONAL SCALES

	STANDARD SCORES		VERY DISSIMILAR	DISSIMILAR	MODERATELY DISSIMILAR	MID-RANGE	MODERATELY SIMILAR	SIMILAR	VERY SIMILAR
	F	M							

SOCIAL

GENERAL OCCUPATIONAL THEME - S   Mod. High 55

BASIC INTEREST SCALES (STANDARD SCORE)
- TEACHING   Mod. Low 42
- SOCIAL SERVICE   Average 47
- ATHLETICS   Mod. High 60
- DOMESTIC ARTS   Average 46
- RELIGIOUS ACTIVITIES   High 62

Scale	F	M
Foreign language teacher	16	(AS)
Minister	30	45
Social worker	43	53
Guidance counselor	47	48
Social science teacher	44	51
Elementary teacher	19	12
Special education teacher	28	24
Occupational therapist	5	26
Speech pathologist	39	29
Nurse, RN	22	(ISR)
Dental hygienist	16	N/A
Nurse, LPN	12	19
Athletic trainer	(RIS)	18
Physical education teacher	11	14
Recreation leader	47	57
YWCA/YMCA director	46	53
School administrator	49	49
Home economics teacher	18	N/A

ENTERPRISING

GENERAL OCCUPATIONAL THEME - E   Mod. High 61

BASIC INTEREST SCALES (STANDARD SCORE)
- PUBLIC SPEAKING   Very High 66
- LAW/POLITICS   High 62
- MERCHANDISING   Mod. High 59
- SALES   High 66
- BUSINESS MANAGEMENT   Mod. High 60

Scale	F	M
Personnel director	60	59
Elected public official	52	54
Life insurance agent	54	50
Chamber of Commerce executive	49	57
Store manager	51	56
Agribusiness manager	N/A	24
Purchasing agent	51	54
Restaurant manager	46	47
Chef	(AR)	32
Travel agent	46	62
Funeral director	39	41
Nursing home administrator	(CSE)	48
Optician	25	16
Realtor	53	56
Beautician	20	(AEI)
Florist	34	39
Buyer	39	57
Marketing executive	47	55
Investments manager	46	47

CONVENTIONAL

GENERAL OCCUPATIONAL THEME - C   Average 45

BASIC INTEREST SCALES (STANDARD SCORE)
- OFFICE PRACTICES   Average 45

Scale	F	M
Accountant	21	33
Banker	40	57
IRS agent	32	45
Credit manager	30	40
Business education teacher	21	32
Food service manager	(CS)	32
Dietitian	(ISR)	31
Nursing home administrator	37	(ESC)
Executive housekeeper	30	42
Food service manager	28	(CES)
Dental assistant	17	N/A
Secretary	35	N/A
Air Force enlisted personnel	17	(R)
Marine Corps enlisted personnel	24	(RC)
Army enlisted personnel	30	17
Mathematics teacher	8	5

ADMINISTRATIVE INDEXES (RESPONSE %)

OCCUPATIONS	41 L%	6 I%	52 D%
SCHOOL SUBJECTS	50 L%	0 I%	50 D%
ACTIVITIES	63 L%	4 I%	33 D%
LEISURE ACTIVITIES	62 L%	5 I%	33 D%
TYPES OF PEOPLE	46 L%	8 I%	46 D%
PREFERENCES	43 L%	10 =%	47 R%
CHARACTERISTICS	64 V%	0 ?%	36 N%
ALL PARTS	50 %	5 %	45 %

Reproduced by special permission of the distributor, Consulting Psychologists Press, Inc., Palo Alto, CA, for the publisher, Stanford University Press, from the Strong-Campbell Interest Inventory of the Strong Vocational Interest Blank by Jo-Ida Hansen and David Campbell. Copyright 1985 by the Board of Trustees of the Leland Stanford Junior University.

tercorrelations. Scores on these basic interest scales represent the strength and consistency of special areas of interest (agriculture, science, music-dramatics, teaching, public speaking, office practices, etc.) Raw scores on the basic interest scales are transformed to a standard score scale and designated as very low, low, moderately low, average, moderately high, high, or very high, separate scales and scores being provided for men and women.

Listed on the right sides of Figures 9–3 and 9–4 are the names of 207 scales, representing 106 different occupations, and the examinee's standard score on each scale. Each of these occupational scales was constructed by comparing the SVIB-SCII item repsonses of men or women employed in a particular occupation with the responses of a reference group of men or women in general. All but five of the scales were matched with opposite-sex scales and standardized separately by sex. A person's raw score on a given occupational scale is determined by adding the numerical weights assigned to his or her responses on the scale, the weight assigned to a response depending on the direction in which the item discriminates between men or women employed in that occupation and men or women in general. After all weights assigned to a person's responses to the items on a particular scale are summed, the obtained raw score is converted to a standard (T) score. A verbal description (*very dissimilar, dissimilar, moderately dissimilar, mid-range, moderately similar, similar, very similar*) is also used to indicate the degree of similarity between the examinee's score and that of the occupational standardization group (see Figures 9–3 and 9–4).

Two empirically derived scales on the SVIB-SCII were developed for special purposes (see top left of Figure 9–3). These special scales are Academic Comfort (AC) and Introversion-Extroversion (IE). The AC scale was constructed by comparing the responses of high school and college students attaining high marks in school with the responses of those attaining low marks. Scores on the scale are related to the tendency to persist or stay in school. The IE scale was constructed by comparing the SVIB responses of individuals classified as introverts with those classified as extroverts on the basis of their scores on the MMPI.

Scoring the SVIB-SCII   The SVIB-SCII can be scored only by computer, the item weights and scoring procedure being a trade secret. Completed inventories must be sent to Consulting Psychologists Press for computerized scoring, profiling, and interpretation. The results of computer scoring and interpretation are printed as a Strong Interpretive Report. This report, which provides a narrative explanation of the examinee's score pattern, focuses on the three highest General Occupational Themes and related Basic Interest and Occupational Scales; both vocational and avocational pursuits are suggested.

Reliability   Median test-retest reliabilities of the SVIB-SCII over two-week, thirty-day, and three-year periods are listed in the manual as .91, .86, and .81 for the General Occupational Themes, .91, .88, and .82 for the Basic Interest Scales, and .92, .89, and .87 for the Occupational Scales, respectively. The median internal-consistency coefficients are also satisfactory, being in the low .90s. The long term reliabilities of the SVIB, on which the SVIB-SCII is based, are given as .75 over 20 years and .55 over 35 years (Strong, 1955). These figures indicate that interests, as measured by the Strong inventories, are sufficiently stable to use in the vocational counseling of older adolescents and adults.

Validity   Until his death in 1962, E. K. Strong, Jr. continued his research on the validity of the SVIB; this work was continued by David P. Campbell and Jo-Ida C. Hansen at the University of Minnesota. In Strong's (1955) follow-up study of the occupations and interests of 663 men who initially took the SVIB when they were in college, scores on the inventory, administered eighteen years earlier, were highly successful in predicting occupational satisfaction. The results of this study and others have demonstrated that interest inventories can be used to predict occupational satisfaction, as well as persistence in an occupation, but they cannot forecast how successful a person will be in that occupation. Similarly, in academic settings interest inventories can predict ratings of satisfaction with one's major or field of study but not course grades (French, 1961).

Kuder Interest Inventories

In contrast to the varied-item format of the SVIB-SCII, G. F. Kuder employed a forced-choice format in constructing all of his interest inventories. To construct his first inventory, the Kuder Vocational Preference Record, Kuder administered a list of statements concerned with activities to college students and determined from their responses which items clustered together. As a result, ten scales of items having low correlations across scales but high correlations within scales were constructed. Then triads of items, each member of a triad belonging to a different interest scale, were formed and administered in forced-choice format. In this way an examinee's interests in different areas were pitted against each other.

Forced-Choice Item Format   Each item on the Kuder inventories consists of three statements of activities (see Figure 9–5); the examinee is directed to blacken the circles marked M or L to indicate which of the three activities he or she *most* prefers and which activity he or she *least* prefers. The responses given to the first item triad indicate that the examinee would most like to visit a museum and least like to visit an art gallery. Of the activities listed in the second item triad, the examinee would most like to collect coins and least like to collect stones.

Ipsative Measurement   The forced-choice item format selected by Kuder has both advantages and disadvantages. Although it tends to minimize certain response sets (acquiescence, social desirability, etc.), examinees sometimes find it awkward. Another problem with the forced-choice format is the ipsative nature of the responses, in that by accepting or rejecting an activity falling on one scale the respondent does not select or reject an activity falling on another scale. Consequently, respondents'

Two examples of Forced-Choice Item format

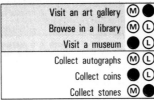

Figure 9–5

From the *Kuder General Interest Survey*, Form E, Answer Sheet, by G. Frederic Kuder. © 1985, 1976, 1963, G. Frederic Kuder. Reprinted by permission of the publisher, Science Research Associates, Inc.

scores on a particular scale are affected by their responses to items on other scales and it is impossible to obtain uniformly high or uniformly low scores across all scales. A typical score pattern on a forced-choice inventory consists of high scores on one or more scales, low scores on one or more scales, and average scores on the remaining scales.

GIS and OIS   Brief descriptions of three Kuder inventories currently available (Science Research Associates) are given in the list below. The two most recently published inventories, the Kuder General Interest Survey (GIS, 1976) and the Kuder Occupational Interest Survey (OIS, 1976), are improvements and downward extensions of earlier Kuder inventories. The GIS, which was designed for grades 6–12, yields scores on a person's interests in ten general interest areas. In scoring the OIS, which was designed for grades 10 through adult, the examinee's responses are compared with those of people satisfied with their occupational choices and with those of college students majoring in particular fields of study.

Kuder Form C: Vocational Preference Record

Use. For counseling and placement of high school students and adults.

Format. One hundred sixty-eight triads of statements describing activities, one activity in each triad to be marked "Most Liked" and one "Least Liked."

Range and Time Limit. High school. No time limit; takes 30–40 minutes.

Forms and Scoring. CP—hand scored; CM—machine-scored.

Scales. Ten interest scales: outdoor, mechanical, scientific, computational, persuasive, artistic, literary, musical, social service, and clerical. One verification (V) score, based on items having extreme response splits.

Standardization Data (Norms). Percentile ranks for men and women; score profile in ten interest areas may be plotted on percentile rank scale. Stanines for men and women in forty-one occupational families. Manual groups occupations according to major interest area or pair of interest areas.

Reliability. Kuder-Richardson reliabilities of the ten scales are in the .70s and .80s.

Validity. Several studies of the relationships between Kuder Form C and job satisfaction support its validity.

Kuder Form E: General Interest Survey

Use. Developed as a downward extension and revision of Kuder Form C; useful in vocational counseling of junior and senior high school students to help them make sound choices in school and think about education and careers.

Format. One hundred sixty-eight triads of statements describing various activities, one activity in each triad to be marked "Most Preferred" and one "Least Preferred."

Range and Time Limit. Grades 6–12. No time limit; takes 30–40 minutes.

Forms and Scoring. Hand scored (pin-punch) and machine scored versions; individual interest scores given on both male and female profiles indicating level of interest in each job family group as compared with either males or females in the grade group.

Scales. Ten interest scales: outdoor, mechanical, scientific, computational, persuasive, artistic, literary, musical, social service, clerical; one verification (V) score.

Standardization Data (Norms). In compliance with Title IX regulations, separate percentile norms based on stratified sample of U.S. boys and girls in grades 6–8 and 9–12.

Reliability. Test-retest reliabilities after six weeks, by sex and grade level (6–8 and 9–12), in .70s and .80s.

Validity. No long-term evidence of validity available; transparency program designed to help students interpret their Kuder Form E scores.

Kuder Form DD: Occupational Interest Survey

Use. For selection, placement, and counseling in employment centers, personnel agencies, and industrial retraining programs.

Format. One hundred triads of statements describing various activities, one activity in each triad to be marked "Most Preferred" and one "Least Preferred."

Range and Time Limit. Grade 11—adult. No time limit; usually takes 30–40 minutes.

Scales. Results divided into four sections: Dependability (extent to which results can be relied upon); Vocational Interest Estimates (how examinee's attraction to ten different interest areas—Artistic, Clerical, Computational, Literary, Mechanical, Musical, Outdoor, Persuasive, Scientific, Social

Service—compares with those of groups of males and females in general); Occupational Scales (how examinee's interest pattern compares with those of people in approximately 100 occupations for men and women combined); College Major Scales (how examinee's interest pattern compares with those of students in approximately forty college majors).

Scores on Vocational Interest Estimates are expressed as percentiles; scores on Occupations and College Majors are lambda coefficients describing the strength of the relationship between the responses of the inventory taker and those of people in the specified occupational or college major group.

GIS Norms and Report Form   Separate percentile norms for four groups (males and females in grades 6–8, males and females in grades 9–12) were obtained in 1987. The availability of separate sex norms permits examinees to compare their GIS scores with those of both boys and girls. Figure 9–6 is a semi-narrative report of the percentile scores obtained by one examinee who took the GIS. The report format provides a rank-order listing of percentiles in the ten interest areas, as well as the three areas in Holland's six-part classification scheme in which the examinee ranks highest (1) with respect to other males and (2) with respect to other females. Although the provision of separate sex norms helps to control for sex bias resulting from combined norms, sex differences in interests can be seen in the fact that, on the average, boys score higher on the mechanical, computational, scientific, and persuasive scales while girls score higher on the artistic, literary, musical, social service, and clerical scales of the GIS.

OIS Scores   The OIS is scored in a different manner from other Kuder inventories. A person's score on any of the OIS occupational or college major scales is a modified biserial correlation coefficient (*lambda coefficient*) between his or her responses to the items and the proportion of individuals in the specified occupational group or college major who endorsed each item. The higher the lambda coefficient, the more closely the person's score resembles the interest pattern of the corresponding occupational group or major. Figure 9-7 illustrates that the report of scores on the OIS lists the lambda coefficients for occupational and college major scales by sex of norm group. In interpreting a person's lambda coefficients, the highest coefficients are emphasized; the associated occupations or majors are those in which the examinee has the greatest interests. However, occupations or majors falling within .06 units of the highest coefficients should also be considered.

Reliability and Validity of the GIS and OIS   The short-term test-retest reliability coefficients of the GIS and OIS scales are in the .80s and .90s, and the scores are fairly stable over a decade or more (Zytowski, 1976). In general, the evidence indicates that the content validity of both the GIS and OIS is adequate. With respect to the predictive validity of the OIS, Zytowski (1976) found that over half the individuals tested with the OIS 12 to 19 years earlier had entered occupations on which they had scored within .07 to .12 points of their highest lambda coefficients.

Figure 9–6 Sample interest profile on Kuder General Interest Survey-Form E

```
 S R A ®      KUDER GENERAL INTEREST SURVEY
              Form E Narrative Report
Name     THOMPSON ALEX               Numeric Grid   343434343434343
Sex      M                           Process Number 0001 00011
Level    GRADES 9 - 12               Norm Group     GRADES 9 - 12

Recently you took the KUDER GENERAL INTEREST SURVEY, FORM E. You were  Ⓐ
asked to indicate which of three activities you most preferred and which
you least preferred. Your V score of 006 indicates that you marked your
answers carefully and sincerely. This means that you can have confidence
in the accuracy of your results.

Your results show how your interest in ten vocational areas compares to
that of other students.  The numbers in the charts below indicate the
proportion of students whose interest in these ten areas is less than   Ⓑ
yours. Your scores are ranked from highest to lowest and grouped into
HIGH, AVERAGE, and LOW interests. The charts below show which of the
vocational areas fall within each of these groups. The vocational areas
in which your interests are highest extend into the HIGH areas of the
chart; those in which your interests are about the same as other
students extend only into the AVERAGE area; and those that are lowest
extend only into the LOW area.
Ⓓ
Compared to other males:                Compared to females:
    Ⓕ
   Low....Avg..High....                    Low....Avg..High....
Ⓒ       Ⓔ
Persuasive 96-------:----:-------    Persuasive 98-------:----:-------
Literary   96-------:----:-------    Scientific 93-------:----:----
Scientific 78-------:----:-         Literary   88-------:----:-------
Soc Serv   78-------:----:-         Computat'l 68-------:----:
Musical    66-------:----           Musical    54-------:----
Computat'l 60-------:----           Mechanical 36-------:----:-
Artistic   21-------                Soc Serv   33-------:-
Outdoor    18------                 Outdoor    24-------
Clerical   14------                 Artistic   18------
Mechanical 02-                      Clerical   07----

Because there are differences in the interests of males and females,    Ⓖ
results are provided separately by sex. Generally you will be interested
in the results for your own sex; however, if your interests are
nontraditional, you may learn something from seeing how you compare with
the other sex.

A number of reference books in which you may find occupational          Ⓗ
information are keyed to the following personality type codes: Realistic,
Investigative, Artistic, Social, Enterprising, and Conventional. Your
scores rank you highest on the following:

Compared to other males:                Compared to females:

     Enterprising                            Enterprising
     Investigative                           Investigative
     Social                                  Social

For more information on the vocational areas and scores discussed here,
read your Interpretive Leaflet. If you have any questions regarding
these results, please see your counselor or teacher.
                                     SCIENCE RESEARCH ASSOCIATES, INC.
  © 1987, 1963 G. Frederic Kuder     S R A  155 North Wacker Drive, Chicago, Illinois 60606
  Printed in U.S.A. All rights reserved
                                     An IBM Company        Code 27-3898
```

(Continued)

(A) V score (a measure of reliability that flags unusual or doubtful results) is reported and interpreted

(B) Explanation of test and its interpretation

(C) Score ranking by percentile (compared to norm group) on each scale

(D) Every student compared to both male and female norms

(E) Both graphic and numerical results shown

(F) High, average, and low interest graphically differentiated

(G) Every student is encouraged to look at results on both male and female norms

(H) Conversion to RAISEC codes

From the KUDER GENERAL INTEREST SURVEY, Form E, Interest Profile © 1977, 1963 by G. Frederic Kuder. Reprinted by permission of the publisher, Science Research Associates, Inc.

Other General Interest and Special Purpose Inventories

Although the Strong and Kuder inventories have been the most popular interest inventories, many other general interest surveys and special purpose instruments have been constructed since the 1920s and 1930s. The majority of these instruments have focused on vocational interests, but several have also been designed primarily to assess school-related interests. Many special-purpose inventories designed to measure the interests of children, the disadvantaged, and people who plan to enter nonprofessional occupations have also become available. Because of space limitations, the discussion will be limited to three of the most carefully-designed and validated of these inventories—the Ohio Vocational Interest Survey, the Jackson Vocational Interest Survey, and the Career Assessment Inventory.

Ohio Vocational Interest Survey, 2nd ed. (OVIS-II)   The OVIS-II (The Psychological Corporation, 1981), which is designed for students in grade 7 through college and adults, takes approximately 45 minutes to complete. Examinees respond on a five-point scale ranging from *like very much* to *dislike very much* to items consisting of 253 job activities representing the entire spectrum of occupations listed in the *Dictionary of Occupational Titles* (4th ed.) (DOT), published by the U.S. Department of Labor (1982). The DOT system, which classifies occupations as involving "data, people, and things," is used to group responses into interest clusters represented by 23 scales; each scale consists of 11 job activities.

Evidence for the validity of OVIS-II given in the manual is inadequate: no concurrent or predictive validity information of any kind is presented. In addition, no adult norms are given to support the proposed use of this inventory with mid-career-change adults. Despite its recognized shortcomings, Crites (1985) concludes that OVIS-II is a well constructed and conceptualized inventory of job activity preferences explicitly related to the occupational structure and should be useful with high school and college students in career planning and cognate educational choices.

Figure 9–7   Report of scores on Kuder Occupational Interest Survey

Kuder Occupational Interest Survey Report Form

Name   BYER ALEC J

Sex   MALE   Date   12/05/86

Numeric Grid No.   SRA No.   00110

1 **Dependability:** How much confidence can you place in your results? In scoring your responses several checks were made on your answer patterns to be sure that you understood the directions and that your results were complete and dependable. According to these:

YOUR RESULTS APPEAR
TO BE DEPENDABLE.

2 **Vocational Interest Estimates:** Vocational interests can be divided into different types and the level of your attraction to each type can be measured. You may feel that you know what interests you have already — what you may not know is how strong they are compared with other people's interests. This section shows the relative rank of your preferences for ten different kinds of vocational activities. Each is explained on the back of this report form. Your preferences in these activities, as compared with other people's interests, are as follows:

Compared with men		Compared with women	
HIGH		HIGH	
SOCIAL SERVICE	97	SOCIAL SERVICE	87
AVERAGE		MUSICAL	80
MUSICAL	75	AVERAGE	
COMPUTATIONAL	63	COMPUTATIONAL	71
PERSUASIVE	51	MECHANICAL	70
SCIENTIFIC	49	PERSUASIVE	62
MECHANICAL	27	SCIENTIFIC	58
OUTDOOR	25	OUTDOOR	27
LOW		LOW	
ARTISTIC	23	CLERICAL	12
CLERICAL	15	ARTISTIC	11
LITERARY	03	LITERARY	01

3 **Occupations:** The KOIS has been given to groups of persons who are experienced and satisfied in many different occupations. Their patterns of interests have been compared with yours and placed in order of their similarity with you. The following occupational groups have interest patterns *most* similar to yours:

Compared with men		Compared with women	
ELEM SCH TEACHER	.38	AUDIOL/SP PATHOL	.39
SOCIAL WORKER	.38	RELIGIOUS ED DIR	.37
AUDIOL/SP PATHOL	.35	SOCIAL WORKER	.37
MINISTER	.35	FILM/TV PROD/DIR	.35
COUNSELOR, HS	.35	INSURANCE AGENT	.35
NURSE	.34	COUNSELOR, HS	.35
PHARMACEUT SALES	.33	DEPT STORE–SALES	.35
PODIATRIST	.32	COL STU PERS WKR	.33
		NURSE	.33
THESE ARE NEXT		NUTRITIONIST	.33
MOST SIMILAR:		DIETITIAN	.33
		DENTIST	.33

MOST **SIMILAR, CONT.**   Compared with men

AUTO SALESPERSON	.30
FILM/TV PROD/DIR	.29
PHYS THERAPIST	.29
PERSONNEL MGR	.28
OPTOMETRIST	.27
LAWYER	.27
PSYCHOLOGIST	.26

THE REST ARE
LISTED IN ORDER
OF SIMILARITY:

PHYSICIAN	.23
SCIENCE TCHR, HS	.23
CLOTHIER, RETAIL	.23
TRAVEL AGENT	.23
INSURANCE AGENT	.22
PHARMACIST	.22
SCHOOL SUPT	.22
ACCT, CERT PUB	.21
MATH TCHR, HS	.21
REAL ESTATE AGT	.20
DENTIST	.20
FLORIST	.20
BUYER	.20
RADIO STATION MGR	.20
PHOTOGRAPHER	.19
X-RAY TECHNICIAN	.19
TRUCK DRIVER	.18
SUPERVSR, INDUST	.18
PLANT NURSRY WKR	.17
INTERIOR DECOR	.17
POLICE OFFICER	.17
STATISTICIAN	.17
POSTAL CLERK	.16
LIBRARIAN	.16
TV REPAIRER	.16
BANKER	.16
BRICKLAYER	.15
FARMER	.15
EXTENSION AGENT	.14
METEOROLOGIST	.14
VETERINARIAN	.14
BOOKSTORE MGR	.14
CHEMIST	.13
BOOKKEEPER	.13
COMPUTER PRGRM	.13
WELDER	.13
ENGINEER	.13
PLUMBING CONTRAC	.12
PAINTER, HOUSE	.12
MATHEMATICIAN	.12
ARCHITECT	.11
ELECTRICIAN	.11
CARPENTER	.11
MACHINIST	.11
AUTO MECHANIC	.10

From the Kuder Occupational Interest Survey, Form DD, KOIS Report Form © 1985; Science Research Associates, Inc. Reprinted by permission of the publisher.

Compared with women		Compared with men		Compared with women	
THESE ARE NEXT MOST SIMILAR:		REST, CONT.			
		BLDG CONTRACTOR	.09		
PHYSICIAN	.32	PLUMBER	.08		
DENTAL ASSISTANT	.32	PRINTER	.08		
PHYS THERAPIST	.32	FORESTER	.07		
BANKER	.31	JOURNALIST	.05		
PSYCHOLOGIST	.31				
BEAUTICIAN	.29				
ELEM SCH TEACHER	.29				
ACCT, CERT PUB	.29				
FLORIST	.29				
OCCUPA THERAPIST	.28				
EXTENSION AGENT	.28				
LAWYER	.28				
BANK CLERK	.27				
SECRETARY	.27				
BOOKKEEPER	.27				
X-RAY TECHNICIAN	.27				

4 College Majors: Just as for occupations, the KOIS has been given to many persons in different college majors. The following college major groups have interest patterns *most* similar to yours:

Compared with women		Compared with men		Compared with women	
THE REST ARE LISTED IN ORDER OF SIMILARITY:		SOCIOLOGY	.36	ELEMENTARY EDUC	.41
		ELEMENTARY EDUC	.33	HOME ECON EDUC	.40
		PHYSICAL EDUC	.30	SOCIOLOGY	.40
				MUSIC & MUSIC ED	.39
MATH TEACHER, HS	.25	THESE ARE NEXT MOST SIMILAR:		PHYSICAL EDUC	.39
OFFICE CLERK	.24			DRAMA	.39
VETERINARIAN	.24			FOREIGN LANGUAGE	.37
ARCHITECT	.24	PSYCHOLOGY	.29	NURSING	.37
JOURNALIST	.23	MUSIC & MUSIC ED	.29	PSYCHOLOGY	.36
SCIENCE TCHR, HS	.23	FOREIGN LANGUAGE	.28	HEALTH PROFESS	.36
ENGINEER	.23	POLITICAL SCI	.27		
COMPUTR PRGRAM	.22	PRERED/PHAR/DENT	.27	THESE ARE NEXT MOST SIMILAR:	
LIBRARIAN	.22	HISTORY	.26		
BOOKSTORE MGR	.21	ECONOMICS	.24		
INTERIOR DECOR	.18			POLITICAL SCI	.34
		THE REST ARE LISTED IN ORDER OF SIMILARITY:		HISTORY	.33
				BUSINESS EDUC	.33
				MATHEMATICS	.33
				ENGLISH	.30
		BIOLOGICAL SCI	.23	BIOLOGICAL SCI	.30
		BUSINESS ADMIN	.21		
		SERV ACAD CADET	.21	THE REST ARE	
		MATHEMATICS	.19	LISTED IN ORDER	
		AGRICULTURE	.17	OF SIMILARITY:	
		ENGLISH	.17		
		ENGINEERING	.16	ART & ART EDUC	.20
		PHYSICAL SCIENCE	.15		
		ANIMAL SCIENCE	.14		
		ART & ART EDUC	.12		
		ARCHITECTURE	.12		
		FORESTRY	.08		

Experimental Scales.

V-SCORE 49

M	.18	MBI	.26	N	.29	NBI	.26
S	.21	F	.24	D	.42	AO	.35

Jackson Vocational Interest Survey (JVIS)   The JVIS by D. N. Jackson (Research Psychologists Press, 1976–1977) is based on the results of an extensive research program consisting of 289 forced-choice pairs of statements descriptive of job-related activities. The statements comprising an item pair refer to two equally popular interests, and the examinee is directed to indicate a preference between them. Designed for high school age and beyond, the JVIS takes 45 to 60 minutes to complete. Initial scoring is on 34 basic interest scales representing 26 *work role* and eight *work style* dimensions. The definitions of the work role and work style dimensions were refined by referring to job descriptions in the DOT. Another approach to scoring the JVIS is through ten occupational themes (Expressive, Logical, Inquiring, Practical, Assertive, Socialized, Helping, Conventional, Enterprising, Communication). These themes are based both on Holland's six vocational personality themes and a factor analysis of responses to the JVIS. Scores on the ten themes are highly reliable (test-retest coefficients between .82 and .92), as are scores on the 34 basic interest scales (median r = .84). With respect to the validity of the JVIS, a large study conducted at Pennsylvania State University found that JVIS profiles did a better job of predicting choice of academic major than any previously reported combination of interest and aptitude measures.

Reviews of the JVIS have praised its careful construction and factorially pure scales, but some have noted that more evidence for its validity is required (Davidshofer, 1985; Thomas, 1985). In addition, the JVIS is a rather long inventory and hence takes more time to administer than certain other inventories with a similar format (e.g., the Kuder OIS).

Career Assessment Inventory (CAI)   Although certain scales on the SVIB-SCII, the Kuder OIS, and other general interest inventories pertain to interests in nonprofessional occupations, none of these inventories was designed specifically for that purpose. Since World War II, a number of inventories have focused on the nonprofessions and are somewhat simpler in content and vocabulary than the Strong and Kuder instruments. The CAI by C. B. Johannson (National Computer Systems, 1975–1982) has been more carefully designed, standardized, and researched than other instruments in this category.

The CAI is modeled after the Strong inventories; in fact, it has been called the working man's SVIB. Examinees respond on a five-point scale (*L*, like very much; *l*, like somewhat; *I*, indifferent; *d*, dislike somewhat; and *D*, dislike very much) to each of the 305 items covering activities, school subjects, and occupational titles. The inventory is written at a sixth-grade level and can be completed in 30 to 40 minutes (Johannson, 1984). Similar to the SVIB-SCII, the computer T score report of the CAI consists of four sections:

    I.   Administrative Indices (Total Responses; Response Consistency; Response Percentages on Activities, School Subjects, and Occupations)

   II. General Themes (Realistic, Investigative, Artistic, Social, Enterprising, Conventional)

The 25 Basic Interest Area Scales and the 111 Occupational Scales are grouped under Holland's six themes. Scores on four Special Scales (Fine Arts-Mechanical, Occupational Extraversion-Introversion, Educational Orientation, Variability of Interests), a computer-generated narrative report, and a counselor's summary are provided. The CAI is well designed from a psychometric viewpoint and has good reliability. On the negative side, McCabe (1985) notes the lack of predictive validity studies in the manual and the fact that the CAI is relatively expensive to score. Overall, however, he rates it as a very important test that fills a significant need and is well developed and engineered to be easily and appropriately used.

Using Interest Inventories in Counseling

Young men and women are often unrealistic about their academic and vocational plans. For example, many more high school students expect to graduate from college than actually do, and the career aspirations of college students are frequently inconsistent with their career possibilities (Flanagan, Tiedeman, & Willis, 1973). Career aims and decisions are affected not only by environmental factors such as the economic situation and the kinds of jobs that are available, but also by psychosocial variables such as one's sex, socioeconomic status, physical and mental abilities, interests, and a knowledge of what particular occupations entail. Consequently, academic and vocational counselors should be informed about what kinds of activities particular occupations involve and whether the abilities, interests, and resources of students or other counselees are appropriate for entering or preparing for those occupations.

Properly trained counselors are prepared to obtain personal data from counselees and supply them with information on various training programs and occupations. However, vocational counseling must be done with caution. Both jobs and people are multifaceted and dynamic: they possess many different characteristics and those characteristics may change with time. The job of psychologist, for example, involves different activities in different situations, and the nature of the job has changed over the years. Even in the same situational context and time frame, many jobs have enough diversity so that people with different abilities and interests can adjust and perform satisfactorily.

Despite the need for a flexible, realistic approach to vocational counseling in which advice and predictions are couched in terms of likelihoods, counselors must make some interpretation of scores on psychological tests and inventories. Furthermore, in interpreting the results of an interest inventory they should explain that *interest* is not equivalent to *ability*. It is not uncommon for a student to conclude from the results of an interest inventory that he or she has the abilities required to succeed in a certain occupation when actually all that has been revealed is that the student's interests are similar to those of people in that occupation. For this and other reasons, it is unwise to leave the task of interpreting a self-administered inventory to the examinee, especially a young examinee. In any case, scores on interest inventories should be employed in counseling in the light of other information about the counselee—test scores, accomplishments (grades, awards, extracurricular activities), work experiences, and interests. Also useful to experienced vocational counselors are books such as the *Dictionary of Occupational Titles* (U.S. Dept. of Labor, 1982), the *Occupational Outlook Handbook* (U.S. Dept. of Labor, 1986), and the *Guide for Occupational Exploration* (U.S. Government Printing Office, 1979), in addition to various career exploration and development materials obtainable from commercial testing companies (see Appendix B).

Values and Personal Orientations

As indicated at the beginning of the chapter, values are more general or abstract than interests: they are concerned with the usefulness, importance, or worth attached to particular activities or objects. Milton Rokeach (1973), who has conducted extensive international and cross-cultural research on the topic, defines a value as "an enduring belief that a specific mode of conduct or end-state of existence is personally or socially preferable to an opposite or converse mode of conduct or end-state of existence." (p. 5) This definition implies that values are of two kinds—those concerned with modes of conduct (*instrumental values*) and those concerned with end-states (*terminal values*). Although vocational psychologists have in large measure limited their attention to terminal values, Rokeach has defined several subcategories of both instrumental and terminal values and designed an instrument to measure them.

Rokeach's Value Survey

Milton Rokeach classified instrumental values as being of two kinds—*moral values* and *competence values*. The former category is concerned with interpersonal modes of conduct, which produce guilt feelings when violated. The latter category, competence values, has to do with intrapersonal, self-actualizing modes of conduct, the violation of which leads to feelings of inadequacy. Terminal values are also further subdivided into *personal values* and *social values*. Personal values, which include such end-states as peace of mind and salvation, are self-centered; social values, which include end-states such as equality and world peace, are society-centered.

Rokeach's Value Survey consists of a series of 18 instrumental and 18 terminal value terms or phrases for assessing the relative importance of these values to people (see Table 9–1). The respondent is directed to rank order the 18 items in each list according to their importance to him or her. No other instrument measures as many

Items on Rokeach's Value Survey		Table 9–1
Instrumental Values	Terminal Values	
Ambitious	A comfortable life	
Broadminded	An exciting life	
Capable	A sense of accomplishment	
Cheerful	A world at peace	
Clean	A world of beauty	
Courageous	Equality	
Forgiving	Family security	
Helpful	Freedom	
Honest	Happiness	
Imaginative	Inner harmony	
Independent	Mature love	
Intellectual	National security	
Logical	Pleasure	
Loving	Salvation	
Obedient	Self-respect	
Polite	Social recognition	
Responsible	True friendship	
Self-controlled	Wisdom	

Copyright by Milton Rokeach, 1967. Reproduced with permission of Halgren Tests, 873 Persimmon Ave., Sunnyvale, CA 94087.

values, a fact which, coupled with the speed of its administration and scoring and its inexpensiveness, may account for its popularity. The reliability of the Value Survey for comparing different groups, a purpose for which it has been employed in hundreds of investigations for more than two decades, is adequate. It has been found that people of different nationalities and in different walks of life rank the items on the Value Survey differently. For example, Rokeach (1973) reported that Israeli students, perhaps understandably, assigned highest rankings to "a world at peace" and "national security," whereas American students placed higher value on "a comfortable life" and "ambition."

Study of Values

Over the past several decades social and vocational psychologists have constructed many different instruments to measure values. Undoubtedly the most popular of these instruments has been the Study of Values by G.W. Allport et al. (Riverside Publishing Company, 1931–1970), a popularity attested to by its administration in numerous research investigations concerned with personality, perception, social psychology, and vocational guidance. Based on Eduard Spranger's (1928) classification of people into six value types, the Study of Values (SV) assesses the relative strength of an individual's values in six areas: theoretical, economic, aesthetic, social, political, and religious. Appropriate for high school students, college students and adults, the SV is untimed but takes approximately 20 minutes to complete. On the 30 items of Part I, respondents indicate a relative preference for two activities by dividing up three points among them, or by dividing the three points between affirmative and negative responses. On the 15 items of Part II, respondents rank four choices in order of preference. Scores on the six areas, which are ipsative in nature, are plotted as a profile showing the relative strength of the respondent's values. The manual lists mean scores on each of the six SV areas for a sample of over 8,000 college students of both sexes and various occupational groups; the most recent norms, based on a nationwide sample of 6,000 high school students, were obtained in 1968. Test-retest reliabilities of the separate area scales over an interval of two months are in the .80s.

The theoretical foundation, the ipsative nature of the scoring system, and the fair amount of education required to understand the SV items have all been criticized (Rabinowitz, 1984). In addition, some of the content seems too old-fashioned for the 1980s, and the norms are obviously dated. Despite these shortcomings, the Study of Values continues to be used for instructional and research purposes.

Vocational Values

Although there is no reason why Rokeach's Value Survey and the Study of Values could not be used in vocational counseling situations, these inventories were not designed specifically for that purpose. More closely related to work choices and satisfactions are instruments such as the Work Values Inventory, the Values Scale, and the Temperament and Values Inventory. Such *vocational values* vary from individual to individual and within the same individual from time to time. For example, Super (1973) found that people in upper-level occupations are more motivated by the need for self-actualization, an intrinsic goal, whereas extrinsic values are more likely to be subscribed to by people in lower-level occupations.

Work Values Inventory   This inventory, developed by D. E. Super (Riverside Publishing Company, 1968–1970), consists of 45 Likert-type items and was designed to assess 15 values considered to be significant in vocational success and satisfaction. Examples of these values, each measured by only three items, are achievement, supervisory relations, independence, aesthetics, and creativity. For each statement, respondents indicate, on a five-point scale, the degree of importance they attach to the value represented by the statement. Percentile norms by grade (7–12) for each of the 15 values are based on data collected in the spring of 1968 on a representative national sample of approximately 9,000 high school boys and girls. Test-retest reliability coefficients, obtained from retesting 99 tenth graders after two weeks, range from .74 to .88 for the 15 scales. Evidence for the content, concurrent, and construct values of the Work Values Inventory is described in the manual.

The Work Values Inventory has been praised for its excellent psychometric foundations and its continuing research uses (Bolton, 1985), but it has not gone uncriticized. The manual needs to be revised and brought up to date by incorporating the findings of research studies conducted since 1970, in particular occupational validity studies based on the current form of the inventory. In addition, reliability data based on college students and adults, not just tenth graders, and new normative data are required.

Values Scale   Developed by the Work Importance Study, an international consortium of vocational psychologists in America, Asia, and Europe and written by D. D. Neville and D. E. Super (Consulting Psychologists Press, 1986), this instrument possesses characteristics of both the Work Values Inventory and Rokeach's Value Survey. The purpose of the consortium and the Values Scale was to understand values that individuals seek or hope to find in various life roles and to assess the relative importance of the work role as a means of realizing one's values in the context of other life roles. The Values Scale, which takes 30 to 45 minutes to administer, consists of 106 items and is scored for 21 values (5 items per value): Ability Utilization, Achievement, Advancement, Aesthetics, Altruism, Authority, Autonomy, Creativity, Economic Rewards, Life Style, Personal Development, Physical Activity, Prestige, Risk, Social Interaction, Social Relations, Variety, Working Conditions, Cultural Identity, Physical Prowess, Economic Security. The reliabilities of all scales are adequate for individual assessment at the adult level; the reliabilities of ten scales are high enough for individual assessment at the college level, and the reliabilities of eight scales are adequate at the high school level. The means and standard deviations for three samples (high school, college, adult), as well as data on the construct value of the instrument, are given in the manual. Because of the newness of the instrument (1986), no predictive validity data are given. However, the Values Scale appears to have good potential for research on vocational counseling and selection, and particularly for cross-cultural or cross-national, comparative studies.

Temperament and Values Inventory   Similar in concept to the Self-Description Inventory discussed earlier in the chapter, the Temperament and Values Inventory (TVI) was constructed by C. B. Johannson and P. L. Webber (National Computer Systems, 1976–1977). It measures both more traditional personality or temperament variables and more work-related, value-interest dimensions. Designed to complement information obtained from ability tests and vocational interest inventories, this carefully constructed instrument consists of 230 items divided into two sections: 133 true-false items scored on seven Temperament Scales (Personal Characteristics) and 97 Likert-type items scored on seven Values Scales (Reward Values). The seven bipolar Temperament Scales are Routine-Flexible, Quiet-Active, Attentive-Distractible, Serious-Cheerful, Consistent-Changeable, Reserved-Social, and Reticent-Persuasive. The seven Values Scales are Social Recognition, Managerial/Sales Benefits, Leadership, Social Service, Task Specificity, Philosophical Curiosity, and Work Independence. The TVI is designed primarily for high school students and adults, takes approximately 30 minutes to complete, and is computer scored and interpreted. The scales were developed on an initial sample of 802 males and females and verified on a separate sample of 456 high school students. The standard T score scale norms are based on males and females in three age groups (15–19 years, 20–25 years, 26–55 years). Test-retest reliabilities, computed on small samples retested over 1 to 2 weeks, are fairly satisfactory, .79 to .93. Comparisons with other related inventories are made to support the construct validity of the TVI, and data on the ability of the inventory to differentiate between relatively small samples of individuals in a rather narrow range of occupations is reported to support the claim for concurrent validity.

The TVI has received fairly positive evaluations (e.g., Wheeler, 1985; Zuckerman, 1985), especially for its careful construction and well-designed manual. Among its psychometric shortcomings are a lack of long-term reliability data, a need for convergent and discriminant validity studies, and norms based on fairly small and nonrepresentative samples.

Personal Orientations

Similar to inventories of interests and values are measures of *personal orientations*, which cut across a wide range of personality variables and are similar in concept to the cognitive and perceptual styles discussed in Chapter 13. One example of a personal orientation is the masculinity versus femininity variable, included in many personality and interest inventories. Differences between the preferences and activities of males and females are so commonplace that it has been routine procedure to standardize psychological tests separately by sex. But, regardless of sex differences, sex discrimination may be found in all areas of human enterprise. For example, it has been alleged, with some justification, that the Strong Vocational Interest Blanks and other early interest inventories contributed to sex discrimination by directing young women into traditional women's occupations such as teaching, nursing, and clerical work (Diamond, 1979).

Bem Sex-Role Inventory Concern over sex discrimination and an interest in the nature and origin of sex differences in psychological characteristics has prompted the development of a number of measures of sex-role during the past decade or so. The most prominent of these is the Bem Sex-Role Inventory (BSRI) by S. L. Bem (Consulting Psychologists Press, 1978–1981). The short form of the Bem Sex-Role Inventory (Short BSRI), which was designed to classify individuals according to their sex-role orientation, consists of 60 words or phrases to be rated on a seven-point scale on which 1 means *never or almost never true* and 7 means *always or almost always true*. Twenty of the items refer to characteristics considered significantly more desirable in men than in women (e.g., acts as a leader, aggressive, ambitious), 20 items refer to characteristics considered significantly more desirable in women than in men (e.g., affectionate, cheerful, childlike), and 20 items are presumably sex-neutral (e.g., adaptable, conceited, conscientious). Scores on three scales—Masculinity (*M*), Femininity (*F*), and Androgyny (*A*)—are determined first. Next the examinee may be placed in one of the following four categories according to his or her scores on the *M*, *F*, and *A* scales: Masculine (above median on *M* and below median on *F*), Feminine (above median on *F* and below median on *M*), Androgynous (above median on both *M* and *F*), or Undifferentiated (below median on both *M* and *F*).

Payne (1985) concludes that the Short BSRI provides promising indices of stereotypically sex-linked descriptions, which have significant correlations with various indices of adjustment. The test-retest and internal-consistency reliabilities of the Short BSRI are generally satisfactory, but the validity data are meager. In addition, researchers are cautioned not to rely on the norms reported in the BSRI manual since they are based solely on samples of Stanford University undergraduates.

Similar in content and scoring, but not perfectly correlated with the BSRI, is the Personal Attributes Questionnaire (PAQ) (Spence & Helmreich, 1978). Like the BSRI, data obtained from the PAQ support a dualistic rather than a bipolar conception of masculinity and femininity in that the two constructs are viewed as different dimensions rather than simply opposite ends of the same continuum.

Other measures of personal orientations include inventories such as the Orientation Inventory (ORI) by B. M. Bass (Consulting Psychologists Press, 1962–1977) and the Personal Orientation Inventory. The ORI consists of 27 forced-choice interest and opinion items that are scored on three scales (Self-Orientation, Interactional-Orientation, and Task-Orientation) based on Bernard Bass's theory of interpersonal behavior in organizations (Bass & Berg, 1961).

Personal Orientation Inventory (POI) This widely used inventory by E. L. Shostrom (EdITS, 1962–1968) was designed to measure values and behaviors that are important in the development of the self-actualizing person. Such a person develops and uses all of his or her potential and is free of the inhibitions and emotional turmoil that characterize less self-actualized people. The POI consists of 150 forced-choice items appropriate for high school students, college students, and adults. The inventory is scored first for two major orientation ratios: Time Ratio (Time Incompetence/ Time Competence, which indicates whether time orientation is primarily in the present or past and/or the future); and Support Ratio (Other/Inner, which indicates whether a person's reactions are basically toward others or the self). Secondly, the POI is scored for the following ten scales: Self-Actualizing Value, Existentiality, Feeling Reactivity, Spontaneity, Self-Regard, Self-Acceptance, Nature of Man, Synergy, Acceptance of Aggression, Capacity for Intimate Contact. Percentile norms based on a sample of 2,607 western and midwestern college freshmen (1,514 males and 1,093 females), in addition to mean scores and profiles based on a smaller sample of adults, are given in the manual. Test-retest reliabilities of the individual scales, computed on a sample of 48 college students, are moderate (mostly in the .60s and .70s). Correlations with other personality scales and other evidence for the validity of the POI are also reported.

Summary

Interests and values are personality characteristics that have received the greatest attention by vocational and social psychologists. Theories relating interests to personality and behavior have been proposed by researchers of various persuasions and emphases—psychoanalytic, developmental, trait-factor, and social learning. Psychoanalysts have emphasized the roles of sublimation and identification (modeling) in the growth of vocational interests and career choice. Illustrative of developmental theories of vocational interests and maturation are the theories of E. Ginzberg and Donald Super. Ginzberg and his colleagues view vocational decision making as a three-stage process beginning with a fantasy period, progressing through a tentative period, and ending with a realistic period; the last two stages have four and two substages, respectively. Emphasizing developmental changes in self-concept and interests, the two-stage theory of Super and his co-workers conceptualizes this process as beginning with an exploratory stage consisting of three substages and ending with an establishment stage having two substages.

Two other theories that have greatly influenced both research and instrument construction concerned with vocational interests are Roe's person-environment theory and Holland's theory of vocational personalities and work environments. Roe's three-dimensional conical model of career choice consists of Orientation to Personal Relations versus Orientation to Natural Phenomena, Orientation to Resource Utilization versus Orientation to Purposeful Communication, and level of skill (professional, skilled, unskilled) involved in the occupation. Interest inventories based on Roe's theory include the COPS Interest Inventory, the Hall Occupational Orientation Inventory, and the Vocational Interest Inventory.

Perhaps most influential of all theories of interest and career choice is Holland's hexagonal model and the associated concepts. According to this model there are six types of vocational personalities—realistic, investigative, artistic, social, enterprising, and conventional; six kinds of vocational environments corresponding to the personality types are also described. The concepts of consistency (the degree to which personality types or environmental types are related to each other), differentiation (making high scores on only one or two dimensions), identity (personal or environmental), congruence (the fit between personality types and environments), and calculus (ordering of the personality types or environments according to a hexagonal model) are also used in the theory. The major career-planning instruments designed on the basis of Holland's theory are the Self-Directed Search and the Vocational Preference Inventory, but the development and scoring of a number of other interest inventories have also been influenced by the theory.

Not only are interest inventories considered to be measures of personality, but personality inventories can also be scored on interest categories and used in career planning. Among the personality inventories that have been employed in career counseling and decision making are the 16 Personality Factor Questionnaire, the Hogan Personality Inventory, and the Self-Description Inventory.

Historically, the most popular interest inventories, such as the Strong Vocational Interest Blanks and the various Kuder instruments, were designed not on the basis of a particular theory but either by criterion-keying or content-validated procedures. Over the years, the Strong and Kuder inventories have moved closer together in their use of a combination of criterion-keyed and content-validation. For examples, the occupational scales of the SVIB-SCII are criterion-keyed, but the basic interest scales are content-validated. Similarly the scales of the Kuder General Interest Survey are content-validated, whereas the occupational and college-major scales of the Kuder Occupational Interest Survey were developed by criterion-keyed procedures.

Although the SVIB-SCII, the General Interest Survey, and the Occupational Interest Survey are the most popular of all interest inventories, many other instruments of this kind are available. Three of the most carefully designed interest inventories are the Ohio Vocational Interest Survey, the Jackson Vocational Interest Survey, and the Career Assessment Inventory. Particularly noteworthy is the Career Assessment Inventory, which was designed by criterion-keyed procedures to assess interests in nonprofessional occupations. Special purpose instruments to measure the interests of children as well as disadvantaged and handicapped individuals are also available. As is the case with all vocational interest inventories, these instruments are useful in career counseling when applied in conjunction with information on the aptitudes, experiences, motivations, and other characteristics of counselees.

Values are generally conceived of as being on a higher, more abstract conceptual plane and less directly related to behavior than interests. Hence measures of values have been employed less frequently than interest inventories in vocational counseling and career decision-making. Rokeach differentiated between instrumental values and terminal values and devised a checklist, the Value Survey, to measure two kinds of instrumental values (moral and competence) and two kinds of terminal values (personal and social). However, the most time-honored measure of values is the Study of Values, an ipsative instrument that measures a person's values in six areas: theoretical, economic, aesthetic, social, political, and religious.

More frequently applied in vocational counseling than either the Value Survey or the Study of Values are the Work Values Inventory (WVI), the Values Scale (VS), and the Temperament and Values Inventory (TVI). The WVI and VS, which measure 15 and 21 values, respectively, are the products of research by Super and his colleagues on the values that people seek in various life roles and the work role in particular. The TVI, which is scored on seven bipolar temperament scales and seven values scales, is a carefully designed instrument developed and scored at National Computer Systems.

Personal orientations, such as self-actualization and sex-role identification, cut across a somewhat wider range of personality variables than either interests or values. The most energetic researcher in the area of sex-role identification is Sandra Bem, whose Bem Sex-Role Inventory has been used in numerous investigations to differentiate between the masculine, feminine, and androgynous roles. Research with the Bem Sex-Role Inventory, the Personal Attributes Questionnaire, and similar instruments has revealed that masculinity and femininity are two different psychological constructs and not simply polar opposites on a single dimension. Other multiscale measures of personal orientations include instruments such as The Orientation Inventory (ORI) and the Personal Orientation Inventory (POI). The most popular of these is the POI, which measures various aspects of self-actualization.

Exercises

1. Define each of the following terms in a sentence or two:

artistic type	instrumental values
attitudes	interest
basic interest scales	investigative type
beliefs	lambda coefficient
calculus	moral values
competence values	need
congruence	occupational scales
consistency	opinions
content-validated interest inventory	personal identity
conventional type	personal orientations
criterion-validated interest inventory	personal values
	realistic period
differentiation	realistic type
enterprising type	RIASEC scores
environmental identity	social type
establishment stage	social values
exploratory stage	tentative period
fantasy period	terminal values
forced-choice item format	value
general occupational themes	vocational values
identity	

2. Assign ranks of 1 (most important) through 18 (least important) to each of the 18 instrumental values in Table 9–1, and then repeat the process with the 18 terminal values listed in the table. The ranks may then be compared with the

median ranks for American men and women and the composite ranks for college men from four different countries given on pages 249 and 251 of *Differential Psychology* (1980) by Minton and Schneider. Finally, significant differences between the reader's ranks and those assigned by other people (your classmates or those given in Minton and Schneider) may be interpreted.

3.   Compare the SVIB-SCII with the Kuder OIS (Form DD) in terms of design, scoring, and interpretation.

4.   Defend the thesis that interests are characteristics of personality and consequently that interest inventories are measures of personality. Cite specific theories, research findings, and specific instruments in support of your position.

5.   Arrange to take the Allport-Vernon-Lindzey Study of Values, score your responses on the six scales, draw a profile of the scores, and interpret the scores or have them interpreted by your instructor.

6.   Administer the following Educational Values Inventory to five or ten people varying in background and nationality if possible, and score the responses. Construct and compare the profiles of scores of your examinees on the six educational values scales.

Educational Values Inventory

Part I Each of the items in this section refers to a possible goal or emphasis of higher education. Check the appropriate letter after each of the following statements to indicate how important you believe the corresponding goal should be. Use this key: U = Unimportant, S = Somewhat important, I = Important, V = Very important, E = Extremely important.

1.   Ability to lead or direct other people.   U   S   I   V   E
2.   Appreciation of the beautiful and harmonious things in
       life.   U   S   I   V   E
3.   Preparation for a vocation or profession of one's choice.   U   S   I   V   E
4.   Gaining insight into the meaning and purpose of life.   U   S   I   V   E
5.   Understanding of social problems and their possible
       solutions.   U   S   I   V   E
6.   Understanding of scientific theories and the laws of nature.   U   S   I   V   E
7.   Acquiring the ability to express oneself artistically.   U   S   I   V   E
8.   Understanding how to direct others in the accomplishment
       of some goal.   U   S   I   V   E
9.   Development of a personal philosophy of life.   U   S   I   V   E
10.   Learning how to succeed in a chosen occupation or field.   U   S   I   V   E
11.   Learning about scientific problems and their solutions.   U   S   I   V   E
12.   Understanding people of different social classes and
       cultures.   U   S   I   V   E

Part II Check the appropriate letter after each of the following items to indicate your estimate of how valuable the particular kinds of college courses are to students in general. Use this key: N = Not at all valuable, S = Somewhat valuable, V = Valuable, Q = Quite valuable, E = Extremely valuable.

13. Courses concerned with how to direct and organize
      people.   N   S   V   Q   E
14. Courses in one's chosen vocation or professional field.   N   S   V   Q   E
15. Courses dealing with philosophical and/or religious ideas.   N   S   V   Q   E
16. Courses concerned with understanding and helping
      people.   N   S   V   Q   E
17. Courses in science and mathematics.   N   S   V   Q   E
18. Courses in music, art, and literature.   N   S   V   Q   E

Part III Check the appropriate letter after each of the following items to indicate how much attention you feel should be given to each kind of college course in the education of most college students. Use this key: N = No attention at all, L = Little attention, M = Moderate degree of attention, A = Above average attention, E = Extensive amount of attention.

19. Courses concerned with how to understand and be of help
      to other people.   N   L   M   A   E
20. Courses in the vocational professional field of your
      choice.   N   L   M   A   E
21. Courses in art, literature, and music.   N   L   M   A   E
22. Courses in scientific and mathematical fields.   N   L   M   A   E
23. Courses concerned with philosophy and religion.   N   L   M   A   E
24. Courses concerned with organizing and directing people.   N   L   M   A   E

The responses to each item on the Educational Values Inventory are scored on a scale of 1 to 5 from left (U or N) to right (E), respectively. The sum of scored responses to items 2, 7, 18, and 21 is the Aesthetic Value score; items 1, 8, 13, and 24, the Leadership Value score; items 4, 9, 15, and 23 the Philosophical Value score; items 5, 12, 16, and 19 the Social Value score; items 6, 11, 17, and 22 the Scientific Value score; items 3, 10, 14, and 20 the Vocational Value score.

Suggested Readings

Darley, J. B., & Hagenah, T. (1955). *Vocational interest measurement*. Minneapolis: University of Minnesota Press.

Dawes, R. V. (1980). Measuring interests. In D. A. Payne (Ed.), *New directions for testing and measurement: No. 7. Recent developments in affective measurement* (pp. 77–92). San Francisco: Jossey-Bass.

Deaux, K. (1984). From individual differences to social categories: Analysis of a decade's research on gender. *American Psychologist, 39*, 105–116.

Holland, J. L. (1985). *Making vocational choices: A theory of vocational personalities and work environments* (2nd ed.). Englewood Cliffs, NJ: Prentice-Hall.

Osipow, S. H. (1983) (3rd ed.). *Theories of career development.* Englewood Cliffs, NJ: Prentice Hall.

Roe, A., & Siegelman, M. (1964). *The origin of interests.* Washington, DC: American Personnel and Guidance Association.

Super, D., & Bohn, M. J., Jr. (1970). *Occupational psychology.* Belmont, CA: Wadsworth.

Utz, P., & Korben, D. (1976). The construct validity of the occupational themes on the Strong-Campbell Interest Inventory. *Journal of Vocational Behavior, 9,* 31–42.

PART IV

Projective Techniques

CHAPTER 10

Associations, Completions, and Drawings

*P*rojective technique is a term introduced by Lawrence Frank (1939) for ambiguous stimuli on which respondents can project their inner needs and states. Frank (1948) defined a projective technique as "a method of studying the personality by confronting the subject with a situation to which he will respond according to what the situation means to him and how he feels when so responding." (p. 46) The essential feature of a projective technique was described as evoking from a person ". . . what is in various ways expressed in his private world and personality processes." (Frank, 1948, p. 42)

Concepts and Examples

Projective techniques are composed of relatively unstructured stimuli that examinees are asked to describe, tell a story about, complete, or respond to in some other manner. In contrast to the more structured personality inventories and rating scales, projective techniques are usually less obvious in their intent, have no right or wrong answers, and therefore are presumably less subject to faking and response sets. Because projectives are relatively unstructured in content and usually open-ended in terms of the responses required, it is assumed that whatever structure is imposed on the stimulus material represents a projection of the observer's own individual perceptions of the world. It is also maintained that the more unstructured the task, the more likely the responses are to reveal important facets of personality.

Because projectives attempt to reveal unconscious mental processes, interpretations of responses to these instruments have been greatly influenced by psychoanalytic theory. Consequently, it is not surprising that the period of greatest increase in the use of projectives was 1940 to 1960, when psychoanalysis had a pronounced effect on personality assessment, research, and theory.

In addition to being influenced by psychoanalysis and other psychodynamic theories, those who interpret projective test protocols usually try to form an overall impression of the patient's or examinee's personality by searching for consistencies and outstanding features in the pattern of responses. As a consequence, administering and scoring a typical projective test necessitates more extensive training and sensitivity than required for a self-report inventory. Psychologists who are well trained in projective techniques, however, often disagree in their interpretations.

Detractors and Supporters

Opponents of projective techniques view these instruments as little more than an opportunity for the imagination and intuition of the interpreter to have free play and even run riot (e.g., Eysenck, 1960). Even proponents of these instruments admit that projective techniques (1) are highly fakable in either a good or bad direction (Albert, Fox & Kahn, 1980; Exner, 1978); (2) are very susceptible to the conditions under which they are administered (phrasing of directions and questions, personality of examiner, degree of encouragement given to examinee, etc.) (Klopfer & Taulbee, 1976); (3) are scored and interpreted differently by examiners with different theoretical orientations and personality dynamics (Hamilton & Robertson, 1966); (4) have inadequate, unrepresentative norms or no norms at all (Anastasi, 1988); (5) are poorly validated and cross-validated (Kinslinger, 1966). But despite repeated criticisms and some decline in popularity during recent years, projectives continue to be used not only by clinical and developmental psychologists and psychiatrists but by anthropologists, market researchers, and other specialists in human behavior.

An early 1980s survey of psychologists in various clinical and counseling contexts found that the Rorschach technique, the Sentence Completion Test, the Thematic Apperception Test, the House-Tree-Person Technique, and the Draw-a-Person Test were the five projective tests among the top ten tests of all kinds in terms of frequency of usage (Lubin, Larsen, & Matarazzo, 1984). However, only one of these projective tests—the Rorschach—is listed among the top ten according to number of times cited in *The Ninth Mental Measurements Yearbook* (Mitchell,

1985). This suggests that, although projectives continue to be widely administered, research and publications concerned with the techniques have slowed down considerably during recent years. Consistent with the decline of research on projectives is the finding that a majority of clinical psychology faculty in universities express negative attitudes toward projectives and do not recommend that time devoted to teaching about them be increased (Piotrowski & Keller, 1984). Be that as it may, projective techniques continue to be popular, a phenomenon that Lubin, Larsen and Matarazzo (1984) attribute in part to recent refinements in scoring and interpretive systems such as that of Exner (1974).

According to their advocates, projectives can get at deeper layers of personality of which even the examinee may be unaware. But Frank's (1948) unfortunate analogy that projective techniques can provide a kind of X-ray of the mind should not be interpreted as meaning that projectives are an open sesame to the unconscious. Furthermore, the lack of structure in projectives is a double-edged sword in that it makes for scoring difficulties. Consequently, most projective techniques do not meet conventional standards of reliability and validity. The validity coefficients of these techniques, employing various criteria, are generally low; the low coefficients reflect situational factors as well as subjectivity in scoring and interpretation.

Influence of Psychoanalytic Theory

The use of projective techniques such as word associations, early recollections, inkblots, and picture stories goes back to the late nineteenth and early twentieth centuries. However, the period from the late 1930s through the 1950s may be characterized as the zenith of these assessment methods. In particular, the decade following World War II, which witnessed the rapid growth of clinical psychology, was a time of extensive development, use, and research on projective techniques. It was also during this period that personality inventories such as the MMPI became increasingly influential, and projectives acted to some extent as a counter to the reportedly more superficial personality analyses and psychodiagnoses provided by personality inventories and rating scales.

From the time of their first clinical application during the early 1900s, projectives have been associated with psychoanalytic theory and attendant efforts to reveal and analyze deeper, unconscious aspects of personality. The psychoanalytic concept of *projection* holds that individuals, both defensively and nondefensively, project their own motives, desires, problems, and conflicts onto external situations or stimuli. In theory, the same unconscious forces that are revealed in distorted, symbolic form in dreams, hypnotic or drug-induced states, slips of the tongue and pen, free verbal associations, and other external manifestations can also elude the mental censor and be expressed in responses to relatively amorphous, unstructured test situations. Unconscious forces lead the person to structure ambiguous material in ways that express the operation of these forces. Consequently, an understanding of the dynamics of individual personality should be obtainable by analyzing how the person perceives, organizes, relates to, or otherwise responds to projective test materials. These responses provide *signs* of underlying personality structure and functioning, revealing the nature of unconscious forces and conflicts.

In addition to being influenced by psychoanalysis and other psychodynamic theories of personality, psychologists who interpret projective test protocols usually try to form an overall impression of the examinee's personality by searching for consistencies and outstanding features in the pattern of responses. As a consequence, administering, scoring, and interpreting a typical projective test usually demands greater sensitivity and more clinical experience than that required by self-report inventories. But even psychologists who are well trained in the use of projectives frequently disagree in their interpretations of responses. Furthermore, research has shown that responses to projectives vary with the method of administration, the personality of the examiner, and the mood or attitude of the examinee. If such responses are highly unstable, the ability of projectives to reflect deeper, more abiding features of personality structure and dynamics should be questioned.

Classification

A well-known classification system (Lindzey, 1959) groups projectives, according to the response required, into five categories: *association* (to words or inkblots), *construction* (of stories, sequences, etc.), *completions* (of sentences or stories), *arrangement* or *selection* (of pictures or verbal options), and *expression* (through drawings, play, etc.). Examples of association techniques are word associations, early memories, and the Rorschach Inkblot Test. Construction techniques include such instruments as the Thematic Apperception Test, the House-Tree-Person Technique, and the Make-a-Picture-Story Test. Illustrative completion techniques are various sentence completion tests and the Rosenzweig Picture Frustration Study. Arrangement or selection techniques include the Szondi Test and the Kahn Test of Symbol Arrangement. Finally, handwriting analysis, painting, and psychodrama—the last two of which are also psychotherapeutic methods—are examples of expression techniques.

This chapter focuses on association and completion techniques, as well as construction techniques requiring drawings. However, because of its extensive clinical and research usage, discussion of the most popular of all association techniques—the Rorschach Inkblot Test—is postponed until Chapter 11. The second most popular projective technique—the Thematic Apperception Test—and related picture story tests are discussed in Chapter 12.

Association Techniques

Inkblots, pictures, words, and other stimuli designed to elicit a variety of associations were used by Binet, Dearborn, Sharp, Wundt, and other psychologists during the late nineteenth century to study imagination, memory, and other cognitive abilities. However, the systematic analysis of personality and the diagnosis of mental disorders by using such stimulus material was not undertaken until sometime later. Following the emphasis of nineteenth-century psychology on the structure and functioning of the mind, American and British psychologists of the time were more interested in individual differences in intelligence than personality. Furthermore, greater attention was devoted to pure, theoretical science than to applying scientific findings and techniques in clinical or other practical situations.

Early Recollections

Ruth Munroe (1955) describes Alfred Adler's use of *early recollections* as the first truly projective test to be used in a clinical context. In keeping with the psychoanalytic emphasis on the importance of early experiences in the formation of personality, the technique involves instructing the examinee to "Tell me your earliest memory," with the further condition that the memory should be a specific, concrete, single one. The requirement that the memory be specific rather than general is what differentiates an early recollection from a report. In any case, three to six distinct memories are usually obtained so that common themes may be determined (Armstrong, 1985).

The following two quotations from Corsini and Marsella (1983) are examples of earliest memories:

1. I remember being on a train seated between my parents and I was bored and restless. I was looking through the window and all I saw was telephone poles and I wanted to get away but I was hemmed in and so I began to inch my way down without my parents knowing and I finally got to the floor and began to look around and I noticed the legs of people and I remember the smell of the floor and the dust there. And I began to move forward being careful not to let anyone know I was there. And I came upon an oil can; it was brass and shiny. And I picked it up and began to squirt oil on the shoes of a man. Suddenly, the man cried out and he reached down and pulled me out. And the conductor came and picked me up while I was screaming and I was brought to my father who began to spank me.

2. I was about ten years of age and I wanted to build a wooden automobile using tires from any old baby carriage. And I announced this to everyone. But most kids who made one of these used two strings to steer the wagon, but I wanted a steering wheel. My father wanted to help me but I said I would do it alone. However, when I came to making the steering wheel, I couldn't figure out how to do it. So, I secretly got rid of the car, how much I had done and I reported to everyone that someone had stolen my car, and that was the end of it. However, I felt that my father had known what I had done. (pp. 605–607)

Interpreting an earliest memory is an impressionistic, subjective process, entailing good common sense and some conceptual or theoretical guides. Each early recollection given by the examinee is analyzed for its cognitive and behavioral patterns, and an effort is made to determine the broad themes unifying the early recollections and the frame of reference reflected in them. The characteristic outlook and attitude revealed by the behavior rather than the behavior itself is what is important. Manaster and Pergman (1974) devised a scoring manual for categorizing the content of early recollections into the seven categories of characteristics, themes, concern with detail, setting, activity level, source of control, and emotion. The two memories listed above were interpreted as follows (Corsini & Masella, 1983):

1. You are a wanderer, and you move not only from place to place but also from person to person, a kind of Don Juan. You are easily bored and always restless, and on the go, and you want excitement and will do things in a mischievous manner to get excitement. However, you know you won't succeed in getting away with your mischief and you expect to be caught and to be punished.

2. He is overambitious, trying to do better and bigger things than others, but he goes over his head and can't complete what he starts out doing; eventually he gives up but will not admit that he tried to do more than he could. (pp. 605–607)

Research on early recollections has provided some support for Adler's view that they reflect the examinee's frame of reference (Mosak, 1969). Other psychologists have successfully identified homosexuality and predicted occupational choice (Friedberg, 1975; Manaster & Perryman, 1974) from early recollections, but research has failed to show that psychodiagnoses can be made solely on the basis of information obtained from early recollections (Armstrong, 1985).

Word Associations

The method of *word associations* was introduced by Francis Galton (1879), later (1880) used in association experiments in Wundt's psychological laboratory, and applied in clinical situations by Emil Kraepelin (1892) and Carl Jung (1910). It was Jung who first used word associations to detect mental complexes and neurotic conflicts. His procedure was to read to a patient a list of 100 words representing common emotional problems (anger, fear, death, etc.). Signs of emotional disturbance revealed in the patient's associations to the words included abnormal response content, long response times, and emotional reactions. Of some interest is the fact that the pioneering work of Carl Jung on word association tests is related to the development of the lie detector (see Chapter 13).

In administering a word association test today, a list of words is read aloud, one at a time, to an examinee who has been instructed to respond to each word with the first word that comes to mind. The examiner begins by making a statement such as the following: "I am going to read a list of words, one at a time. After I read a word, please answer with the first word that comes into your mind." Individualized clinical application of the word association technique involves interspersing certain emotionally loaded words, or words of special significance to the examinee, among neutral words. Long response times or unusual associations may be symptomatic of emotional disturbance. The form or part of speech represented by the response may also be significant. For example, a general principle guiding the psychoanalytic interpretation of language is that nouns are more likely than verbs to be disguised expressions of needs and conflicts. This is so because, according to Freudian theory, it is easier to alter the object of a desire (a noun) than its direction (a verb).

Many clinical psychologists prefer to construct their own word lists, but standardized lists are available. An illustration is the Kent-Rosanoff Free Association Test by G. H. Kent and A. J. Rosanoff (Stoelting Co., 1910), a standard list of 100 nouns, adjectives, and verbs first published in 1910. Unlike Jung's word list, the words on the Kent-Rosanoff Test are neutral rather than emotionally loaded. Also unlike Jung, Kent and Rosanoff determined norms by administering the words to 1,000 normal people and obtaining their associations. Responses were classified as common or individual reactions. Individual reactions include categories such as juvenile responses, neologisms, repetitions, parts of speech, associations to a previous stimulus or response, and word complements. Twenty-five types of associative disturbances and six reproduction disturbances are included in the system. Appelbaum's (1960) addition to the scoring system of the Kent-Rosanoff includes repetitions, blockings, multi-words, self-references, perseverations, and repetitions of stimulus words; this system is used primarily with brain-damaged individuals.

Another standard word list was provided by Rapaport, Gill and Schafer (1946) (see Table 10–1) and used at the Menninger Clinic. Twenty of the 60 nouns in the list are traumatic (they have aggressive, excretory, or sexual connotations) and 40 are nontraumatic. A complex system of scoring responses focuses on the stimulus words that produce disturbances in the associative process and behavior of the examinee.

Word associations represent an economical and sometimes enlightening psychodiagnostic procedure. Infrequent or unusual responses to standard or specially prepared word lists are considered indicative of emotional disturbance, but this conclusion has not been found to be consistently valid. Furthermore, limiting the examinee's response to one word usually provides insufficient information for a useful content analysis. The response time pressure experienced by examinees also tends to result in mechanical, stimulus-bound responses. For these reasons, along with the decline of the psychoanalytic model that inspired their usage in the clinical situation, word associations are not as popular as they once were. In the main, they have been replaced by techniques such as sentence completions and apperception tests that elicit richer, more detailed associations.

Various modifications in the technique of word associations have been introduced over the years. Siipola, Walker, and Kolb (1955) required the examinee to delay responding until he or she found a response that was personally satisfying. According to the findings of Dunn, Bliss and Siipola (1958), associations obtained

Table 10–1	Revised Word List from Rapaport, Gill and Schafer	
1. rat	21. suicide	41. cut
2. lamp	22. mountain	42. movies
3. love	23. smoke	43. cockroach
4. book	24. house	44. bite
5. father	25. vagina	45. dog
6. paper	26. tobacco	46. dance
7. breast	27. mouth	47. gun
8. curtain	28. horse	48. water
9. trunk	29. masturbation	49. husband
10. drink	30. wife	50. mud
11. party	31. table	51. woman
12. spring	32. fight	52. fire
13. bowel movement	33. beef	53. suck
14. rug	34. stomach	54. money
15. boy friend	35. farm	55. mother
16. chair	36. man	56. hospital
17. screen	37. taxes	57. girl friend
18. penis	38. nipple	58. taxi
19. radiator	39. doctor	59. intercourse
20. frame	40. dirt	60. hunger

Rapaport, Gill, and Schafer, *Diagnostic Psychological Testing* Vol. 2. Chicago: Year Book Publishers, 1946, p. 84. Reproduced with permission of the publisher.

under this delayed condition are related to the degree of impulsivity and the values of the respondent.

Sutherland and Gill (1970) introduced an approach that combines word associations with sentence completions. A list of 100 stimulus words is prepared, and the examinee is directed to respond to each word with a complete sentence. A response to the stimulus word "garden," for example, might be "I hate working in a garden" or "Gardening is a good hobby." Sutherland and Gill claim that requiring complete sentences in responding makes possible a more thorough quantitative analysis of ego functioning in a variety of situations. They advocate scoring responses on six dimensions:

1. form of expression
2. syntactical use of the stimulus word
3. self and other references
4. mode of communication (generalizations and personal statements)
5. affective tone
6. affective reference in four key areas

Despite its plausibility, this combined technique has rarely been used for purposes of clinical diagnosis.

Completion Techniques

Completion techniques in which the examinee is told to complete an incomplete sentence, story, picture, or in other ways construct a whole from a part are more structured than the Rorschach and many other projective tests. Perhaps for this reason these techniques, although tending to yield more superficial responses, have greater reliability than less structured projectives. Despite the fact that they presumably tap more conscious or surface features of personality than inkblots, the three completion techniques discussed in this section—sentence completions, story completions, and the Rosenzweig Picture Frustration Study—still provide clues to the examinee's attitudes, conflicts, and problems. An examinee's responses to completion techniques standardized on representative samples can be interpreted by comparing them with normative data obtained from various groups of people, normal and pathological.

Sentence Completions

Asking a person to complete specially written incomplete sentences is a flexible, easily administered, and nonthreatening semiprojective method that can identify a broad range of psychological concerns in a short period of time. *Sentence completion* is appropriately labeled "semi-projective" because sentence stems are more structured, more apparent in their intention, and hence more fakable than the Rorschach, the Thematic Apperception Test, and most other projectives. As with other projectives, however, it is assumed that the completed sentences reflect the underlying attitudes, desires, and fears of the respondent.

Because their purpose is not disguised well and examinees can more easily censor their responses, Phares (1985) concluded that sentence completions often yield little information that is not obtainable from an intensive interview. However, many psychologists have been impressed with the utility of the technique, which Murstein (1965) considers "probably the most valid of all projective techniques." (p. 777) Concurring with this evaluation, Goldberg (1965) deemed sentence completions to be one of the most valid of all projectives for diagnostic and research purposes.

Historical Background   Sentence completions were used initially by Ebbinghaus (1897) as an intelligence test, and even more recently by Copple (1956) as a creative-response test of intelligence. Two of the first psychologists to use the technique for assessing personality were Payne (1928) and Tendler (1930). Sentence completions were employed in a variety of military situations during World War II, for example, in the psychological evaluation and selection of pilots, army officers, and OSS (Office of Strategic Service) candidates. They have also been used for personnel selection in business and industry. During the decade immediately following World War II standardized sentence completion instruments were developed by Rotter (1946), Rohde (1947), Sacks and Levy (1950), Forer (1950), and Holsopple and Miale (1954).

Sentence completion tests have been designed for individuals of all ages, ranging from early childhood through later life. Responses are usually written, but they may be given orally. The test may be administered either individually, in which case hesitations, emotional reactions, and other overt behaviors can be observed, or simultaneously to a group of people. The number of sentence fragments on a form ranges from about 20 to 100, sufficient space being provided after each fragment for the examinee to write his or her response.

Content and Scoring   A variety of sentence fragments relating to attitudes, emotions, and conflicts can be constructed, for example

My greatest fear is_____ _____.

I only wish my mother had _____.

The thing that bothers me most is _____.

Other examples of incomplete sentences are given in Figure 10–1, a form that I designed for use with children of school age. Typically, examinees are instructed to finish each item by making a complete statement expressing their true feelings. Stems are usually written in the first person, and there is no time limit. It has been maintained, however, that responses are less likely to be censored when the test is speeded up, and the stems are written in the third person (Hanfmann & Getzels, 1953).

Most clinicians evaluate and interpret the responses impressionistically and in the light of other information about the examinee. The accuracy of impressionistic evaluations and predictions made from sentence completions varies, of course, with the skill of the evaluator in making such subjective judgments. In addition to possessing high interpersonal sensitivity and clinical judgment, an effective evaluator understands the limitations of the sentence completion technique and takes into account information obtained from behavior observations, interviews, and other tests, as well as the situation in which the sentences are completed and his or her own theoretical biases.

In interpreting responses, affective tone (negative or positive), the examinee's role (active or passive), form of the response (specific or qualified, imperative or declarative), temporal orientation (past, present, future), degree of commitment (wholehearted vs. hedging), degree of definiteness from one response to another (definite vs. vague), and variation in verbalization from one response to another should be kept in mind (Rabin & Zlotogorski, 1981). Objective scoring systems that

---

A sentence completion test for children   **Figure 10–1**

Directions: Finish these sentences to show your real feelings.

1. I like _____.

2. The best time _____.

3. My mother _____.

4. I feel _____.

5. I can't _____.

6. Other children _____.

7. I need _____.

8. My father _____.

9. This school _____.

10. I want _____.

11. I don't like _____.

12. I am very _____.

13. My teacher _____.

14. I worry about _____.

15. I am sorry that _____.

---

can be followed by nonprofessionals have been provided for several published instruments in this category. For example, the Rohde Sentence Completions, one of the oldest blanks, is scored on 38 variables, including inner integrates, inner state, and general traits. In addition to content scoring, noncontent properties of responses may be evaluated. Among the noncontent properties scored in such a formal analysis are length of completion, use of personal pronouns, response time, verb/adjective ratio, range of words used, grammatical errors, and first word used (Benton, Windle & Erdice, 1957).

Sentence completions do not easily lend themselves to computer scoring, but computer programs for scoring limited or restricted responses are available. An example is the program for scoring the One-Word Sentence Completion Test (Veldman, Menaker & Peck, 1969). Interscorer and test-retest reliabilities of certain sentence completion tests are in the .80s and .90s, high enough for making diagnostic differentiations among individuals. However, relatively few sentence completion tests can meet accepted standards for test construction and standardization.

The majority of sentence completion tests are unpublished and unstandard-ized instruments designed for a specific purpose in a given situation. However, the instruments listed in Appendix G are representative of published sentence comple-tion tests. Two of these, the Rotter Incomplete Sentences Blank and the Bloom Sentence Completion Survey, will be discussed at some length.

The Rotter Incomplete Sentences Blank (ISB)   Consisting of three forms (high school, college, adult), each containing 40 sentence fragments written mostly in the first person, the ISB is one of the most carefully designed and standardized of sentence completion tests. The ISB by J. Rotter (pronounced "rotor") and J. E. Rafferty (The Psychological Corporation, 1950) is scored for conflict (C) or un-healthy responses (e.g., "I hate . . . almost everyone."); positive responses (P) (e.g., "The best . . . is yet to come."); and neutral responses (N) (e.g., "Most girls . . . are females." Weights for C responses are $C1 = 4$, $C2 = 5$, and $C3 = 6$, from lowest to highest degree of the conflict expressed. Weights for P responses are $P1 = 2$, $P2 = 1$, and $P3 = 0$, from least to most positive response. N responses receive no numerical weight. After scoring each response, an overall adjustment score is ob-tained by adding the weighted ratings in the conflict and positive categories. The overall adjustment score ranges from 0 to 240, higher scores being associated with greater maladjustment. The 1950 ISB manual (Rotter & Rafferty, 1950) provides a number of case examples to demonstrate scoring of the ISB.

Interscorer reliability of the ISB ranges from .88 to .96 (Lah & Rotter, 1981; Rotter & Rafferty, 1950), and the adjustment score correlates significantly with other measures of maladjustment (Goldberg, 1965). Research has shown that ISB scores can correctly classify examinees into adjusted and maladjusted categories and hence be used in screening for overall maladjustment (Rotter & Rafferty, 1950). Norms based on the original standardization group for the ISB (299 entering fresh-man at Ohio State University) are admittedly out of date (Lah & Rotter, 1981), and the test definitely warrants restandardization. Perhaps a Rotter-rooter could be found who would be willing to undertake it!

Bloom Sentence Completion Survey (BSCS)   Peterson's (1985) review of the BSCS begins with the question: "What has forty stems but only one Bloom and smells like a rose?" (p. 204) Peterson's question and the answer—the Bloom Sen-tence Completion Survey by W. Bloom (Stoelting Co. 1974–1975)—reveal some-thing of his generally favorable evaluation of this test. There is only one form but two levels (student and adults) on the BSCS, which is designed to assess attitudes toward important factors in everyday living. Eight scores can be determined on this individually administered test: age mates (student) or people (adults), physical self, family, psychological self, self-directedness, education (students) and work (adults), accomplishment, and irritants.

The forty stems on the BSCS are arranged in groups of eight items represent-ing each of the eight areas, repeated at equal intervals throughout the test; this format facilitates scoring the five items in each area. Item responses are scored +

(positive, favorable, or well disposed), − (negative, unfavorable, or ill-disposed), or 0 (concrete or objective description, a response that does not fit the dichotomy or a completely tangential one). Scores on each of the five items constituting an area are added to yield a total area score having an 11-point range (-5 to $+5$).

Evidence for the reliability of the BSCS is fairly scanty; interrater reliability coefficients are reported to be over .90 for technicians having a high school education. Validation data indicate that the BSCS had some ability to differentiate between individuals who were retained in the U.S. Air Force and those who were discharged for psychological reasons. Statistically significant negative correlations between BSCS scores and scores on the State-Trait Anxiety Inventory are also reported in the manual. Apparently less anxious people tend to make higher scores than more anxious people on the BSCS, which is one bit of evidence for the construct validity of the instrument.

Story Completions

As indicated above, sentence completions have been used in the personality assessment of all age groups. However, because of the limited ability of most children to express their feelings in writing, the technique may not be as revealing as other approaches. Techniques that involve the use of materials and activities that are more appropriate or characteristic of children usually yield richer, more meaningful responses. For example, observing how children play with dolls, puppets, and other constructions can provide useful insights into their thoughts and behavior.

Children are active creatures who enjoy playing, but they also like to listen to and tell stories. Consequently, presenting a child with the beginning of a story, that is, at least one complete sentence representing the start of a plot, and asking him or her to complete the story can be quite motivating to the child and informative to the examiner. Such story fragments, as with sentence fragments, may be tailor-made for the particular child and purposes of the assessment, but standard sets of incomplete stories are also available. Among these are the Madeline Thomas Stories and the Duss (Despert) Fables. Two of the 15 incomplete stories in the former series are (Zlotogorski & Wiggs, 1986):

> A boy (or girl) goes to school. During recess he (she) does not play with other children; he (she) stays by himself (herself) in a corner. Why?
>
> A boy fights with his brother. Mother comes. What is going to happen? (p. 196)

Two of the incomplete stories or fables from the Duss (Despert) series are as follows (Rabin & Zlotogorski, 1981):

> A boy (or girl) took a very nice walk in the woods alone with his mother (or her father, for the girl). They had lots of fun together. When he returned home the boy found that his father did not look as he usually did. Why? (Similarly, upon returning the girl finds that the mother does not look the same as usual.)

> A child comes home from school. Mother says to him (her), "Don't start your home-work right away—I have something to tell you." What is the mother going to say to the child? (p. 141)

The purpose of the first Madeline Thomas story is to give the child an opportunity to explain reasons for withdrawal from the group (fears, shame, guilt, etc.), whereas the second story involves sibling rivalry. Equally obvious is the Oedipal theme in the first Duss (Despert) fable; the last story is designed to reveal some of the fears and desires of the child.

Story completions are interpreted impressionistically and in the light of other diagnostic information. As with sentence completions, however, it is possible to classify and quantify the responses according to a predetermined conceptual or theoretical scheme. The examiner may also structure or direct the child's responses to the incomplete stories by presenting stories that encourage a particular class of responses, by providing the child with a sample completed story, and by asking specific questions pertaining to the story after the child has finished it.

Although story completions would seem to possess face validity, there is little psychometric evidence for the reliability and validity of the technique. According to certain critics of the technique, "face validity" should be modified to "faith validity" as far as story completions are concerned.

Rosenzweig Picture-Frustration Study

Another projective (or semi-projective) device that requires examinees to construct verbal responses to verbal stimuli is the Rosenzweig Picture-Frustration Study (P-F) by S. Rosenzweig (Psychological Assessment Resources, 1944–1981). Each of the three forms—Children (ages 4–13), Adolescent (ages 12–18), and Adult (ages 18 and over)—of this instrument consists of 24 comic-strip pictures in an 8-page standard size (8 ½ inch by 11 inch) booklet. Every picture contains two people, the person on the left being depicted as saying words that are frustrating to the person on the right or which describe the frustrating situation. The examiner reads the instructions with the examinee, the latter being instructed to indicate, by writing in the balloon above the frustrated person's head, the first verbal response that comes to mind as being made by this anonymous person (see Figure 10–2). In the case of younger examinees, the examiner writes the examinee's spoken response.

Psychoanalytic in its rationale, the P-F focuses on the characteristic manner in which the individual responds to ego- or super-ego blocking situations. Based on the assumption that the typical response to frustration is some sort of aggression, the P-F is scored according to the direction of aggression and the type of aggression expressed. Included under Direction of Aggression are: *extraggression* or E-A (out-wardly, or toward the environment); *intraggression* or I-A (inwardly, toward one-self); *imaggression* or M-A (avoidance or nonexpression of aggression). (The terms used for extraggression, intraggression, and imaggression in the older research litera-

---

Item from the Rosenzweig Picture-Frustration Study

Figure 10–2

---

ture on the Rosenzweig P-F are extrapunitive, intrapunitive, and impunitive.) Included under Type of Aggression are: obstacle-dominance or O-D (the frustrating object stands out); etho-defense or E-D (the examinee's ego predominates to defend itself); need-persistence or N-P (the goal is pursued despite the frustration). After the examinee has responded to all items, the examiner conducts a post-test interrogation or inquiry to assist in interpreting and classifying the responses, a task facilitated by an extensive list of scored examples included in the manual.

Scores on the six variables listed above are combined in a three by three matrix to yield nine factors, making a total of 15 scores. In addition to these 15 scores, a Group Conformity Rating (GCR) indicating how closely the examinee's responses correspond to those given most frequently by a norm group, and a trends score designed to reflect changes in responses to frustration in the first and second halves of the P-F may be determined. The fact that responses to the 24 pictures are assigned to specific categories results in ipsative scoring, in which high and low scores in the various categories balance out. Finally, Rosenzweig (1978) emphasizes that, in addition to quantitative scoring, responses to the P-F should be evaluated impressionistically.

The P-F is typically administered individually as part of a battery of psychological assessment instruments. With some loss of scoring accuracy, it can be administered simultaneously to a group of people. It is also possible to give it orally to handicapped individuals and young children by reading aloud the comments of the figure on the left and then recording the examinee's response.

Like sentence completion tests, the P-F is a semi-projective technique that can be scored quantitatively and more reliably than most projectives. Interscorer agreement in scoring the nine factors is reported to be approximately 85%. However, the test-retest reliabilities of the three forms are fairly modest (.50s and .60s for E-A, M-A, E-D, and N-P, and even lower for other variables). Norms on many special groups are reported in the manual. The most recent norms for the adolescent form (1978) are based on 813 junior and senior high school students in the Midwest, the great majority of whom were white and middle class. The P-F has been employed throughout the world for over 40 years in a large number of research investigations concerned with the nature of frustration and its correlates (Rosenzweig, 1978). Significant relationships have been found between P-F scores and age trends, cultural differences, hypnotizability, other personality tests, psychiatric reports, sex differences, and various physiological measures.

Projective Drawings

Instruments requiring oral or written responses to words and sentences represent only one of many tests falling in the category of projective techniques. Among the materials that have been employed on projective tests are clay, paints, building materials, and colored chips. Although it has not received wide acceptance among professional psychologists, handwriting analysis (graphology), which was discussed briefly in Chapter 1, also has its advocates (e.g., Holt, 1974) as a psychodiagnostic technique. Graphologists use either an analytic or a pattern approach to interpreting handwriting. In the analytic approach, characteristics of individual letters (e.g., angularity, curvature, slant, width) presumably indicate certain traits of personality and character. In the pattern approach, the writer's script is analyzed for consistent patterns composed of various elements.

More widely respected than handwriting analysis by clinical psychologists are *projective drawings* of people (alone or doing something together) and objects. Three examples of instruments in this category—the Draw-a-Person Test, the House-Tree-Person Technique, and the Bender Visual-Motor Gestalt Test—are described below.

Draw-a-Person Test

The first psychologist to use drawings in formal psychological assessment was Goodenough (1926). Goodenough's Draw-a-Man Test was designed primarily as a performance test of intelligence, but it became apparent that various features of the drawing (e.g., facial expression, size, boldness, and position of the drawing on the page) reflect other personality characteristics. Subsequently, Karen Machover

(1949, 1951) developed a Draw-a-Person Test (DAP) specifically to assess personality characteristics and functioning. On this test, the examinee is presented with a blank sheet of paper and instructed to "draw a person." Following completion of the figure, the examinee is usually directed to draw, on the other side or a separate sheet, a picture of a person of the opposite sex from that of the first figure. Finally, he or she is asked to tell a story about each person, including age, ambitions, educational level, fears, and other facts about the person.

The DAP is interpreted in terms of the placement of various features in the drawings (e.g., size, body details, position, clothing). Machover (1949) maintained that there is a tendency for examinees to project impulses that are acceptable to them onto the same-sex figure and impulses that are unacceptable onto the opposite-sex figure. The relative sizes of the male and female figures reportedly reveal clues concerning the sexual identification of the examinee. Other details of the drawings that are considered to be indicative of certain personality characteristics or psychopathological conditions are: large eyelashes are associated with hysteria, exaggerated eyes indicate suspiciousness; many clothing details suggest neurosis; large drawings suggest acting out impulses; dark, heavy shading suggests strong aggressive impulses; small drawings, few facial features, or a dejected facial expression point to depression; few body periphery details reveal suicidal tendencies; few physical features suggest psychosis or organic brain damage. Other features that are noted and interpreted include disproportionate body parts, missing parts, erasures, and symmetry or asymmetry.

To Machover, a disproportionately large or small head—the center of intellectual power, control of bodily impulses, and social balance—indicates functional difficulties in these areas. Machover made a number of sweeping generalizations about heads, such as "Disproportionately large heads will often be given by individuals suffering from organic brain disease." and "The sex given the proportionately larger head is the sex that is accorded more intellectual and social authority."

Although many of the interpretative signs and generalizations that Machover claimed were based on her clinical experience make psychoanalytic and even common sense, they have not held up under close scrutiny. Swensen (1957, 1968) criticized Machover's system of interpreting the DAP and urged caution in applying her hypotheses concerning the psychological meanings revealed by the drawings. Some evidence has been found for a positive relationship between the judged quality of drawings and overall psychological adjustment (Lewinsohn, 1965; Roback, 1968), but most of Machover's interpretative hypotheses have not been supported by research.

House-Tree-Person Technique

One variation on the DAP test is the Draw-a-Person Quality Scale (Wagner & Schubert, 1955). In this technique, the person drawn by the examinee is rated on an artistic scale ranging from zero to eight. A more popular variation is the House-

Tree-Person Technique (HTP) by J. N. Buck (Western Psychological Services, 1948–1980), which, along with the DAP and several other projectives, was listed among the top ten tests in terms of usage by clinical and counseling psychologists (Lubin, Larsen, & Matarazzo, 1984). In administering the HTP, the examinee is given a number 2 pencil and sheets of 7 inch by 8½ inch white paper, on which he or she makes freehand drawings of a house, a tree, and a person. The house drawing is made with the longer axis of the sheet placed horizontally; the tree and person drawings are made on separate sides with the longer axis of the sheet vertical. After the drawings are completed in pencil, they are taken away and the examinee is given crayons to make drawings of a house, a tree, and a person. Lastly, he or she is asked to answer some 20 questions about each drawing; the questions involve descriptions and interpretations of the drawings and their backgrounds.

The drawings may be scored quantitatively on a number of variables: drive (level and control), primary needs and assets, psychosexual concerns (satisfaction and conflicts), interpersonal relationships, and interenvironmental matters (reality level and extratensive-intratensive) (Siipola, 1985). However, the drawings are usually interpreted impressionistically and holistically.

In theory, the house represents the examinee's home, arousing associations or perceptions concerning his or her home-life and familial relationships. The tree is said to reflect the examinee's deeper, more *unconscious* feelings about him- or herself. The condition of the tree is related to the examinee's vivacity or attitude toward life: a dead tree points to emotional emptiness, a full-blown tree to liveliness, a weeping willow to weakness, and a spiky tree to aggressiveness. The person, representing the self and interpreted similarly as on the DAP test, is said to reflect a more conscious view of the examinee's self and his or her relationship with the environment.

The HTP has been used extensively in clinical practice as well as in many research investigations involving assorted groups, but it has not been standardized on a specific population. The reliability and validity of the HTP vary with the scoring criteria and the nature of the individuals tested. Swensen (1968) concluded that global ratings of the HTP are more reliable than ratings of the details of the drawings. In any case, the reliability coefficients are typically quite modest. Buck (1948) reported that the HTP was validated by comparing personality evaluations made from HTP responses with diagnoses by staff psychiatrists, intimate friends, and the Rorschach Inkblot Test. However, evidence for the reliability and validity of the HTP, like that of most projectives, is rather skimpy.

Bender Visual-Motor Gestalt Test

The Bender Visual-Motor Gestalt Test by L. Bender (The Psychological Corporation, 1938–1977) consists of nine geometric designs borrowed from Wertheimer (1923). The examinee is directed to copy the designs, which are presented individually on 4 inch by 6 inch white cards (see Figure 10–3); afterwards, he or she may

---

The Bender Visual-Motor Gestalt Test figures   **Figure 10–3**

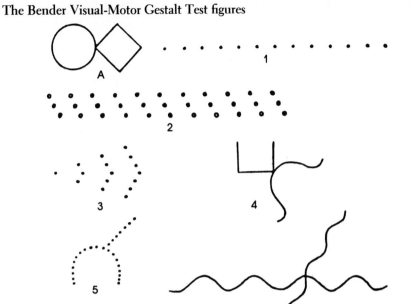

From the *Bender® Visual-Motor Gestalt Test* published by the American Orthopsychiatric Association, 1938.©

---

also be asked to reproduce the designs from memory. The Bender-Gestalt was introduced as a measure of visual-motor coordination, but its primary clinical application has been to detect central nervous system impairment (brain damage or organicity) in persons aged 4 years through adult. It can be completed in a few minutes or so, and is frequently administered as part of a battery of tests to assess perceptual/cognitive functioning and learning disabilities. Many clinicians administer a brief projective test such as the Bender-Gestalt or the HTP at the beginning of the testing period to establish rapport.

Evaluating the Drawings   Scoring of the Bender-Gestalt to detect neurological impairment focuses on the number and types of reproduction errors made. Children eight years or older and of normal intelligence usually make no more than two errors. Errors that suggest organic brain damage are: shape distortions; rotating the design; problems in integrating the design; disportionate, overlapping, or fragmented drawings; perseverations. A restandardization of the Bender-Gestalt, including norms for ages five through ten years, was published in 1975; these scores are highly correlated with intelligence quotients up to ages nine through ten (Koppitz, 1975). The drawings can also be evaluated as projective responses. For example, figure reversals suggest negativism (Hutt, 1969) and exact reproductions point to obsessive-compulsive personality traits (Tolor & Schulberg, 1963).

Hutt Adaptation of the Bender-Gestalt   A number of modifications of the Bender-Gestalt materials and procedure have been published, including the Bender Visual-Motor Gestalt Test for Children, the Watkins-Bender Test Scoring System (to detect learning disabilities), the Canter Background Interference Procedure for the Bender-Gestalt (the designs must be reproduced on a background of intersecting sinusoidal lines), and the Hutt Adaptation of the Bender-Gestalt Test (Hutt, 1977).

Responses in the Hutt Adaptation, which uses nine designs similar to those of the Bender-Gestalt but more uniform in size, can be evaluated by an objective approach, a projective approach, or a configurational analysis approach. In the objective approach, the designs are scored on a Psychopathology Scale and a Scale for Perceptual Adience-Abience. The Psychopathology Scale consists of 17 factors, almost all of which are weighted one to ten points. The norms on this scale are based on relatively small samples of normal and mentally disordered groups, and the test-retest reliability coefficients over two weeks are in the .80s. With respect to its validity, scores on the Psychopathology Scale differentiated significantly between normal people and psychotic people but not between brain-damaged and chronic schizophrenic individuals.

The Scale of Perceptual Adience-Abience was designed to assess the examinee's perceptual orientation or style—openness (approach) versus closedness (avoidance). There are 12 factors on this scale, which is significantly correlated ($r = .69$) with the Psychopathology Scale. Like those for the Psychopathology Scale, norms for the Scale of Perceptual Adience-Abience are based on limited samples. Some evidence for the construct validity of the latter scale is reported by Hutt (1970, 1977), but the validity data are actually rather meager.

In the projective approach to evaluating responses to the Hutt Adaptation, evidence is sought in the drawings for the individual's style of adaptation, cognition, affect, areas of conflict, defensive methods, and maturational characteristics. To provide the required data for the projective approach, the examinee begins by copying the designs, then redraws them to make them more pleasing to him or her, and finally indicates what the originally copied and redrawn designs look like or suggest.

A third approach to scoring the Hutt Adaptation—configurational analysis—consists of determining the presence or absence of specific signs characteristic of five clinical syndromes: brain damage, depression, mental retardation, psychoneuroses, schizophrenias. Cutting scores on various measures are used to differentiate among psychiatric groups. However, as with the projective approach, configurational analysis of responses is not sufficiently valid to make good diagnostic decisions. Although the objective approach to scoring the Hutt Adaptation warrants higher marks than the other two approaches, Sattler (1985) concludes in his review of this instrument that extreme caution should be exercised in using it as a projective technique.

Summary

In a 1982 survey of clinical and counseling psychologists, the Bender Visual-Motor Gestalt Test, Rorschach, Thematic Apperception Test, sentence completion tests (all kinds), House-Tree-Person Test, and Draw-a-Person Test, in that order, were among the top ten of all tests mentioned. These findings, which would probably not be much different today, point to the continuing popularity of projective techniques. Despite persistent criticisms of projectives, they have not been replaced by personality inventories, rating scales, or other more objective personality assessment techniques.

With the possible exception of completely unstructured interviews, projectives are the most unstructured of all personality assessment devices. Projectives have been categorized as association, completion, construction, arrangement or selection, and expression techniques. Examples of instruments in these categories are given in this chapter and in Chapters 11 and 12. Included in the present chapter are: association techniques such as early recollections and word associations; completion techniques such as sentence completions, story completions, and the Rosenzweig Picture-Frustration Study; projective drawings (expression techniques) such as the Draw-a-Person Test, the House-Tree-Person Technique, and the Bender Visual-Motor Gestalt Test.

Early recollections, a technique in which examinees attempt to recall their earliest memories and provide associations to those memories, are sometimes used in the personality assessment of children. The examinee is directed to recall three to six specific, concrete, single memories from which common themes are determined. Interpretation of the memories is impressionistic, but a system of categorizing responses has been devised by Manaster and Perryman (1974).

Clinicians have used word association, in which an examinee is directed to respond to each of a series of individually presented words with the first word that comes to mind, to detect conflicts, complexes, and other sources of emotional disturbance. Standard word lists such as the Kent-Rosanoff Free Association Test, responses to which are compared to norms and content analyzed, are available. Modifications of the word association technique, such as requiring that sentence responses be given to stimulus words (Sutherland & Gill, 1970), have been introduced. However, because of its poor yield of information, word association is not one of the most popular projective techniques.

More popular and reliable than word associations and many other projectives are sentence completions. In this technique, the examinee completes a series of sentence fragments in any way that he or she chooses. Although unstandardized incomplete sentence tests are frequently constructed by clinicians for a specific purpose, many published, standardized tests in this category are available. Two examples are described in this chapter: the Rotter Incomplete Sentences Blank (ISB) and the Bloom Sentence Completion Survey. Of these two, the Rotter ISB is more popular and time-honored. Although the norms are rather dated, the ISB is a highly reliable instrument that can be scored for conflict or unhealthy responses, positive responses, neutral responses, and an overall adjustment score.

Story completions are an infrequently used technique in which the examinee (typically a child) is given the beginning of a story and asked to complete it. Standard sets of incomplete stories include the Madeline Thomas Stories and the Duss (Despert) Fables. Responses are interpreted impressionistically and by referring to other diagnostic information concerning the child.

The Rosenzweig Picture-Frustration Study consists of 24 comic-strip pictures, each of which depicts an individual in a frustrating situation; the examinee indicates what the frustrated person's response to the situation is likely to be. The Rosenzweig P-F is scored according to the direction of aggression (extraggression, intraggression, imaggression) and type of aggression (obstacle-dominance, etho-defense, need-persistence) revealed by the examinee's responses. In addition to these six categories, separate scores on the three by three combinations of direction and type of aggression, a group conformity rating, and a trends score may be obtained. Like sentence completion tests, the Rosenzweig P-F is considered a semi-projective instrument.

The personalities of both children and adults are frequently revealed through expressive behavior, as in drawing a person or object. The most popular projective drawing tests are the Draw-a-Person Test and the House-Tree-Person Technique. On the Draw-a-Person Test, the examinee is asked to draw a person on a sheet of white paper and then draw on another sheet a person of the opposite sex from the first drawing. The drawings are analyzed impressionistically in terms of sex, body details, position, clothing, and other features. Following Machover, psychoanalytic-based interpretations are made in terms of various signs revealed by the drawings. With the House-Tree-Person Technique, the examinee makes pencil and crayon drawings of a house, a tree, and a person. In the impressionistic interpretation of the drawings, the house is said to arouse associations or perceptions concerning home life, the tree reflects the examinee's unconscious feelings about himself, and the person is interpreted as reflecting a more conscious view of the self.

The Hutt Adaptation of the Bender Visual-Motor Gestalt Test, in which the examinee copies a series of nine geometrical designs presented individually, is another projective technique of the drawing type. Responses to the Hutt may be evaluated objectively, projectively, or by configurational analysis. The objective approach, which yields scores on a Psychopathology Scale and a Scale of Perceptual Adience-Abience, is considered to be more reliable and valid than the projective and configurational analysis approaches to evaluating the Hutt drawings.

Exercises

1. Define each of the following terms and identify the tests:

arrangement (technique)
association (technique)
completion (technique)
construction (technique)
Draw-a-Person Test
early recollections
expression (technique)
extraggression
House-Tree-Person Technique
imaggression
intraggression

Picture-Frustration Study
projection
projective drawings
projective technique
selection
sentence completions
signs
story completions
Visual-Motor Gestalt Test
unconscious
word associations

2. Ask several of your friends or relatives to tell you two or three of their earliest memories, and see what reasonable interpretations you can make of the memories. In addition, it might be interesting to obtain such recollections from individuals who are fairly unknowledgeable about psychology and presumably less likely than psychology majors to interpret and perhaps censor or embellish their psychologically significant memories. Whether viewed from a common sense, psychodynamic, or other theoretical perspective, do the memories lend themselves to unambiguous interpretations? Do the interpretations make sense and are they consistent with what you know about the individual from other sources?

3. Construct an alphabetical list of 25 nouns pertaining to subjects of interest to people in your age group (college, grades, graduation, failure, sex, marriage, religion, mother, father, career, health, and so on), and administer it to a dozen acquaintances. Ask each person to respond to every word on the list as quickly as possible with the first word that comes to mind. Record the response time (in seconds) and the response to each word. Summarize the results in terms of the number of responses of a particular kind made to each stimulus word, average response times, and insights provided into the personalities of the respondents. You might also wish to construct a list of other parts of speech (verbs, adjectives, etc.) and see if the responses are more revealing than they are to nouns.

4. Construct ten incomplete sentences pertaining to matters of concern to college students. Type (double space) your ten sentence fragments on a sheet of paper and make multiple copies. Administer your sentence completion test to several college students, instructing each person to complete every sentence fragment with a word or phrase that has a personal meaning or refers to a matter of concern to her or him. Study the responses given to the sentence fragments, and try to analyze them in terms of what you already know or have observed about the personalities of the respondents. Write a report summarizing your findings.

5.   What are the principal advantages and limitations of projective techniques? What factors have led to the decline of their use in clinical diagnosis, and why do they remain fairly popular among clinical psychologists?

6.   Construct two incomplete stories that you believe will reveal something about the respondent's personality when he or she is asked to complete the stories. Try out your stories on several of your classmates or friends. Does the content of the complete stories suggest anything significant about the respondent's personality? Do you consider this technique of personality assessment to be reliable and valid? Why or why not?

Suggested Readings

Canter, A. (1985). The Bender-Gestalt Test. In C. S. Newmark (Ed.), *Major psychological assessment instruments* (Vol. I, pp. 217–248). Newton, MA: Allyn & Bacon.

Cummings, J. A. (1986). Projective drawings. In H. M. Knoff (Ed.), *The assessment of child and adolescent personality* (pp. 245–272). New York: Guilford.

Groth-Marnat, G. (1984). *Handbook of psychological assessment* (pp. 91–147). New York: Van Nostrand Reinhold.

Hammer, E. F. (1985). The House-Tree-Person Test. In C. S. Newmark (Ed.), *Major psychological assessment instruments* (Vol. I, pp. 135–164). Newton, MA: Allyn & Bacon.

Handler, L. (1985). The clinical use of the Draw-A-Person Test (DAP). In C. S. Newmark (Ed.), *Major psychological assessment instruments* (Vol. I, pp. 165–216). Newton, MA: Allyn & Bacon.

Hart, D. H. (1986). The sentence completion technique. In D. H. Hart (Ed.), *The assessment of child and adolescent personality* (pp. 245–272). New York: Guilford.

Krall, V. (1986). Projective play techniques. In A. I. Rabin (Ed.), *Projective techniques for children and adolescents* (pp. 264–278). New York: Springer.

Rabin, A. I. (1981). Projective methods: A historical introduction. In A. I. Rabin (Ed.), *Assessment with projective techniques: A concise introduction* (pp. 1–22). New York: Springer.

Rabin, A. I., & Zlotogorski, Z. (1981). Completion methods: Word association, sentence, and story completion. In A. I. Rabin (Ed.), *Assessment with projective techniques: A concise introduction* (pp. 121–150). New York: Springer.

Zlotogorski, Z., & Wiggs, E. (1986). Story- and sentence completion techniques. In A. I. Rabin (Ed.), *Projective techniques for children and adolescents* (pp. 195–211). New York: Springer.

CHAPTER 11

The Rorschach Technique

Little did Swiss psychiatrist Hermann Rorschach realize when he unexpectedly died in 1922 that the ten inkblots, which were to bear his name, would be at the pinnacle of the psychodiagnostic methods known as projective techniques. Few testing instruments provide broad band idiographic data yielding such dynamic formulations and personality descriptions as the Rorschach. In effect, the technique is a real-life sample of behavior that yields data from which description, explanation, and, it is hoped, prediction of a person's mental life and behavior can be made.

The question of whether the Rorschach is actually a projective technique, a problem-solving strategy, a perceptual-cognitive task, an apperceptive process, a structured interview, or an X-ray of the mind continues to be debated even today. Nevertheless, the basic hypothesis that lies at the heart of the interpretive foundation of the Rorschach is as true today as it was four decades ago (Frank, 1948):

This chapter was prepared by Chris Piotrowski

What is of major significance for understanding the individual personality is that the individual organizes experience as he warps, twists, distorts, and otherwise fits every situation, event, and person into the framework of his private world, giving them the affective significance which they must have for him in his private world. (p. 15)

Format and Foundations

The Rorschach consists of ten inkblots, almost all of which are bilaterally symmetrical on a white 5½ inch by 9½ inch card. Cards I, IV, V, VI, and VII, which are noncolored or achromatic, are printed in varying shades of black and gray. Cards II and III are printed in black and red, whereas the remaining cards, VIII, IX, and X, are multicolored and somewhat more elaborate than the others. These ten inkblots,

Figure 11–1   An inkblot figure similar to those on the Rorschach

which are reproduced from those originally published by Hermann Rorschach, have been standardized worldwide and are available from Hans Huber in Bern, Switzerland. An inkblot similar to those on the Rorschach test is illustrated in Figure 11–1.

Rationale and Administration Procedure

The theoretical rationale underlying the Rorschach is that an ambiguous, unstructured stimulus such as an inkblot presents an organizational, perceptual, or problem-solving task to an examinee who responds in the unique way he or she responds to any experience. A person's idiosyncratic motives, desires, needs, and ways of relating to the animate and inanimate world are presumably reflected in his or her approach in responding to each inkblot.

In administering the Rorschach, each card is presented individually, in order, and viewed at no greater than arm's length; the examinee is permitted to turn the card in viewing it. Administration of all ten inkblots usually takes 45 to 55 minutes, involving two phases and sometimes a third phase referred to as the *testing the limits phase*. During the first, or *free association phase*, the examiner, who is usually a psychologist, presents one card at a time to the examinee and records verbatim the latter's oral responses to it. The examiner also records the examinee's response time to each card and the position(s) of the card while the latter is holding it. Upon completion of the free association phase, the *inquiry phase* begins. In this phase the examiner determines how the examinee arrived at each response. Through nondirective questioning or probing, the examiner determines what characteristics of the inkblot provoked each response. The examinee's reported perceptions of the characteristics of the inkblots, for example, form, reference to color, shading, and animate or inanimate movement, are known as *determinants* and are critical features of formal Rorschach scoring and protocol interpretation.

Historical Background

Although people have long been fascinated by their own responses, as well as those of others, to ambiguous visual stimuli such as clouds, it was not until the early 1900s that inkblots were used in a systematic manner to investigate mental phenomena. Early investigators of the technique, for example, Alfred Binet, T. Rybakow, and Stella Sharp, used inkblots to test and research imagination, but their efforts were not concerned with personality assessment per se. In 1911 the Swiss psychiatrist Hermann Rorschach began working on what was to develop into the *psychodiagnostic method*. Rorschach and his mentor, Konrad Gehring, employed inkblots in their experiments with school children in Zurich. But it was not until 1917 that Rorschach began to synthesize his observations of normal adults and psychiatric patients into a clinical and theoretical framework, an endeavor which culminated in a monograph entitled *Psychodiagnostik* (Rorschach, 1921). Rorschach was quite interested in applying psychoanalytic concepts to his research, but his interpretation of responses to the inkblots focused on the *formal* aspects of percept formation rather than response content.

Unfortunately, Rorschach's efforts were interrupted by his untimely death shortly after the publication of *Psychodiagnostik*. However, a small group of followers continued his work in Switzerland. One of these individuals, Emil Oberholzer, taught the Rorschach method to David Levy and Samuel Beck, who were instrumental in bringing credibility to the technique in America. Many other psychologists and psychiatrists who emigrated from Europe to the United States during the 1930s stimulated acceptance and development of the Rorschach method. The major proponents of the technique were Samuel Beck, Marguerite Hertz, Bruno Klopfer, Zygmunt Piotrowski, and David Rapaport. All of these individuals developed their own formulations and methodology, and eventually five distinct Rorschach systems evolved.

Beck was the first student to fulfill a dissertation requirement by investigating the Rorschach, and several years later he developed the first American Rorschach scoring system. In 1937 Beck presented his novel approach to the Rorschach in his book, *Introduction to the Rorschach Method*. About this same time, Marguerite Hertz completed her dissertation on the Rorschach and developed a Rorschach system. Hertz's prolific scholarly publications presented a distinct Rorschach System that evolved during the 1940s.

Bruno Klopfer was introduced to the Rorschach in Zurich, having completed his Ph.D. some ten years earlier. Upon immigrating to the United States, Klopfer accepted an academic position at Columbia University where he conducted graduate seminars on the Rorschach. In 1937, he founded the periodical *Rorschach Research Exchange* to provide a research outlet and network of communication among the ever-increasing number of adherents to the Rorschach technique. This periodical was subsequently renamed the *Journal of Projective Techniques and Personality Assessment* and is currently known as the *Journal of Personality Assessment*. This official journal of the Society for Personality Assessment continues to publish research on projective techniques in general and the Rorschach in particular.

Zygmunt Piotrowski received a Ph.D. in 1927, having been trained in the European experimental tradition in Poland. Several years later, while involved in postdoctoral work at Columbia University, Piotrowski participated in Klopfer's seminars on the Rorschach and became interested in how neurologically impaired patients responded to the ambiguous nature of the inkblots. During the 1940s Piotrowski gradually shifted away from the Klopfer and Beck Systems and created his own scoring and interpretive approach. He emphasized the use of signs, single characteristics—either formal or content—which the examiner uses to draw certain clinical conclusions. Not until 1957, in his popular text *Perceptanalysis*, did Piotrowski expound on the intricacies of his scoring system. Some years later, he developed a computerized scoring method based on some 1,000 rules, which is referred to as the Piotrowski Automated Rorschach (PAR).

The fifth major Rorschach system was developed by David Rapaport during his many years at the Menninger Foundation in Topeka, Kansas. Since Rapaport had a keen interest in psychoanalytic theory and particularly psychopathological thinking, the rich clinical data derived from Rorschach responses provided a useful tool in his clinical and research endeavors. Together with some outstanding colleagues, Rapaport collaborated on a research project that involved the Rorschach, which was subsequently described in an influential book entitled *Diagnostic Psychological Testing* (Rapaport, Gill & Schafer, 1946). Rapaport's system, which deviated from the other four well-established Rorschach systems and espoused a psychoanalytic approach, drew many adherents at the time. Although Rapaport's approach did not have a dramatic impact, one of his colleagues, Roy Schafer, was quite influential in keeping the approach alive for many years to come.

As this brief history indicates, development of the Rorschach was not very consistent or uniform. By the mid-1950s five Rorschach systems were in use, and the evident debate among major innovators was rather poignant. At times, it appeared that the Rorschach itself was in the midst of a family feud. Nonetheless, the inkblot test survived the internal struggles of its proponents, as well as many criticisms and attacks from opponents. Why did the Rorschach flourish and command so much attention in academic and clinical circles?

For three decades following publication of *Psychodiagnostik* several trends were evident in American clinical psychology. The spirit of the times was predominantly psychoanalytic and, of course, the Rorschach lent itself to many Freudian and neoFreudian conceptualizations. Due to the inkblots' projective nature, many clinicians and researchers found in the Rorschach a measurement tool for the study of unconscious processes. Furthermore, the role of the clinician during this time was largely that of diagnostician, and psychologists were hard pressed to find sound diagnostic tests or instruments. There was dissatisfaction with objective (paper-and-pencil) tests in the evolving special area of clinical psychology. Finally, the inkblot method seemed intriguing and captured the attention of many creative thinkers. The Rorschach engendered much theoretical speculation, diagnostic acumen, and appeared to be a judicious means of assessing the human mind.

Despite these strong trends that seem to sway opinion in Rorschach's favor, the technique had a number of shortcomings. There was no standard system by which to evaluate interpretations and theoretical suppositions. In fact, all five Rorschach systems had idiosyncrasies of their own and were for all practical purposes five distinct methods. Moreover, the five systems were not based on any one systematic theory. The Rorschach survived for several decades in this precarious state until the mid-1970s and the energetic, creative work of John Exner.

Popularity of the Rorschach

Despite the Rorschach's precarious status in the clinical community, it has withstood the attacks of critics (some of which were justified) for over a half century. Nonetheless, the Rorschach has remained a popular and frequently used instrument in both academic and clinical settings. In a series of articles on test use, Lubin and his colleagues (1984, 1985, 1986) reported that the Rorschach was rated fourth in frequency of usage by psychodiagnosticians. Lubin, Larsen, and Matarazzo (1984) point out that "Recent refinements in scoring and interpretive systems might account for the persistence of popularity for some of the projective techniques. Several write-in comments suggested this possibility in the case of Exner's work with the Rorschach." (p. 452)

Several studies of testing practices have shed some light on the use of the Rorschach by professionals in various organizations. Piotrowski and Keller (1984) surveyed the membership of the Association for Advancement of Behavior Therapy (AABT) regarding their attitudes toward clinical assessment. As expected, AABT members were quite pessimistic about projective techniques; however, approximately one-third of those who responded indicated that professional practicitioners should be competent in the Rorschach. Recently, these same authors surveyed the members of the Society for Personality Assessment concerning their usage of psychodiagnostic tests; the Rorschach ranked second in usage among a variety of personality assessment instruments (Piotrowski, Sherry & Keller, 1985).

In a recent survey of the attitudes of academic clinical faculty toward projective techniques, 71% of the respondents indicated that it was *very important* or *somewhat important* for the Rorschach to be mastered by practicing clinicians; 65% of the respondents believed that course work in the technique should be required (Pruitt, Smith, Thelen & Lubin, 1985). In support of this trend, a report (Ritzler & Alter, 1986) on teaching of the Rorschach found that 88% of the programs placed major emphasis on the Rorschach in at least one assessment course; there were no differences between the ratings of highly experienced and moderately experienced instructors; instructors as a group rated the Rorschach highly as a clinical tool and teaching aid, but gave it generally low ratings as a research instrument; and the results clearly indicate that the Exner Comprehensive System is widely used as an instructional method.

What conclusions can be drawn from the foregoing discussion of the Rorschach's status in contemporary clinical psychology? First, despite the widely held opinion that projective techniques are empirically and practically moribund, the Rorschach has survived the barrage of attacks by critics for some 50 years (Piotrowski, 1984). In fact, a resurgence of interest in the Rorschach, particularly from clinicians outside academic settings, has occurred since the publication of Exner's *Comprehensive System* (Exner, 1978; Exner & Weiner, 1982; Exner, 1986).

With respect to its value in stimulating research, according to *Tests in Print III* (Mitchell, 1983) by the early 1980s the Rorschach had been the subject of approximately 6,000 research studies. Although the Rorschach has lost its dominance to the MMPI in recent years, both instruments continue to be popular in published research (Polyson, Peterson & Marshall, 1986).

In sum, the Rorschach technique has been dethroned from its previous high estate, but is still considered a worthwhile tool in the hands of highly trained psychodiagnostic clinicians (Weiner, 1983). In fact, since the introduction of Exner's work in the mid-1970s the Rorschach has gained renewed interest from adherents and respect from opponents of personality assessment.

Five Major Systems and Alternative Approaches

By 1957 there were five distinct Rorschach systems, as well as many varied approaches differing in their administrative, scoring, and interpretative features. This state of affairs led to much dissension among proponents of the major systems, and critics were quick to seize the opportunity to refer to the chaos and disunity as unscientific in merit. Surprisingly, the Beck, Klopfer, Hertz, Piotrowski, and Rapaport-Schafer systems survived side-by-side with little consensus among them, each system having a unique approach to the Rorschach inkblots. A brief description of the idiosyncrasies of each system is given below.

Beck's System

The approach of Samuel Beck, a dedicated follower of Hermann Rorschach, was highly empirical and experimental, but Beck welcomed evidence from clinically validated data. He emphasized standardized procedures and in many ways viewed his approach as a "continuing experiment in perception," with an emphasis on objectivity (Beck, 1944). At the same time, Beck was criticized for not providing enough information on the nature of the clinical population and procedures by which samples were selected.

Klopfer's System

Probably due to the influence of his European training, Bruno Klopfer's approach was largely based on phenomenology and as such contrasted with a behavioral-empiricistic perspective. His methodology involved little statistical analyses but emphasized the subjective, experiential view of the examiner. Klopfer's qualitative approach was obviously at odds with the scientific-empirical tradition evident in the United States. He developed a rather elaborate scoring system, but was criticized for his subjective, unsystematic guidelines.

Hertz's System

The system proposed by Marguerite Hertz closely followed the tenets originally prescribed by Rorschach and was consistent with the empirical-statistical emphasis prevalent in American psychology. Originally, Hertz sided with Beck's objective approach, but later developed her own method with a focus on standardization.

Rapaport-Schafer System

The popularity of this system is probably attributable to the fact that it is heavily slanted toward psychoanalytic theory. In addition, *Diagnostic Psychological Testing* (Rapaport, Gill & Schafer, 1946) and *Psychoanalytic Interpretation in Rorschach Testing* (Schafer, 1954) proved to be popular references and textbooks in psychodiagnostic training. However, the Rapaport-Schafer system, which because of its strong psychoanalytic emphasis and unacceptability to behavioral-empiricists, had few adherents and was never formalized into a true major system.

Piotrowski's System

Of the five major Rorschach systems, the final one was developed by Zygmunt Piotrowski. Piotrowski's system rests soundly on clinical observation and the application of a sign approach to diagnostic formulations. Much of his creative thinking and imagination are reflected in the book *Perceptanalysis* (Piotrowski, 1957). One of Piotrowski's many novel adaptations, far removed from Rorschach's original work, is concerned with the meaning and importance of the *movement response*. Although clinicians were attracted to some of Piotrowski's novel insights and unique approaches to the inkblots, his system has had few adherents and the approach is rarely used today.

Content Analysis

A rather novel alternative to scoring Rorschach responses is the focus on *content* rather than on formal percept analysis; that is, an emphasis on *what* is perceived as opposed to *where* and *how*. The focus on *content analysis* and its relationship to the psychological characteristics of the individual has been discussed by Aronow and Reznikoff (Aronow & Reznikoff, 1983; Reznikoff, Aronow & Rauchway, 1982). The approach is clinical in nature, in that interpretations are based on the attributed *meaning* of responses for an individual. Relationships between particular responses and their clinical significance are obviously difficult to substantiate, even within the context of an individual's own experiential life.

Clinicians and researchers have also developed numerous scoring methods based on developmental level, hostility, anxiety, and body image, in addition to signs or indicators of homosexuality, suicide ideation, neurotic tendencies, and schizophrenia (see Goldfried, Stricker & Weiner, 1971). For example, hostility responses may include animals fighting, a killed animal, an angry face, people arguing, a squashed bug, or a wolf devouring its prey. The content approach to Rorschach analysis is employed largely in conjunction with one of the major systems. However, many clinicians use the content approach as an adjunct to interviewing an individual when performing a clinical assessment of a person.

Holtzman Inkblot Technique

Although the Rorschach has had a few inkblot competitors (measures utilizing inkblots different from Rorschach's), most of them have received little attention in the literature and are of interest today only for their historical significance. The single instrument that has captured the attention of empirically conscious clinicians is the Holtzman Inkblot Technique (HIT), but recent surveys indicate that its current usage is not extensive. According to Holtzman (1981), the HIT was designed to overcome psychometric limitations in the Rorschach. Unlike the Rorschach, the HIT consists of two parallel forms (A and B) of 45 inkblots each. Designed for ages five years and over, the blots were selected on the basis of their high split-half reliabilities and the ability to differentiate between normal and pathological individuals. The blots, some of which are asymmetric, are more varied in color, form, and shading than those on the Rorschach, and only one response per card is permitted. A brief inquiry immediately follows each response. Group administration of the HIT by means of a projector and screen is also quite feasible.

Scoring of the HIT involves 22 quantitative variables (location, space, form appropriateness, color, shading, etc.) that were isolated by analyzing hundreds of test protocols obtained from eight groups, including children and adults, normal and psychiatric samples. The quality of response content is characterized as anxiety, hostility, barrier penetration, and pathognomic verbalization.

The HIT was originally standardized on 1,334 individuals ranging in age from five years to adult; raw scores on the 22 variables are converted to percentile ranks for interpretative purposes. Six factors appear to account for the common variance among the 22 variables; among these factors are perceptual maturity, perceptual sensitivity, psychopathology of thought, and perceptual differentiation.

The results of reliability and validity studies of the HIT are highly satisfactory. HIT scores are related to the developmental level of children and have been used in the differential diagnoses of psychiatric disorders. Although the HIT has experienced problems gaining acceptance from clinical practitioners, it represents a noteworthy effort to provide an inkblot technique having acceptable psychometric properties. A comprehensive appraisal of the HIT (Holtzman, 1981) and an annotated bibliography of the technique (Swartz, Reineher & Holtzman, 1983) are available to interested readers.

Exner's Comprehensive System

Quite early it became apparent that clinicians and academicians were using the Rorschach in unstandardized ways, and even those who espoused one of the major Rorschach systems personalized the administration, scoring, and interpretation of the test. A survey of academic instructors conducted during the 1960s found that inexperienced, unmotivated faculty were frequently teaching the Rorschach; in fact, few instructors had any clinical experience at all with the technique (Jackson & Wohl, 1966). Subsequent investigations in the academic setting found that junior faculty members, who were often inexperienced and uninterested in the Rorschach, were assigned to teach courses on projective techniques. With such poor role models, it is not surprising that exposure to the Rorschach was rather cursory and that instruction in the Rorschach systems was inadequate. Over several decades, this superficial indoctrination of students, coupled with the lack of cohesion among Rorschach's followers, led to gross misuse and improper adaptations of the technique. Exner and Exner (1972) found that the majority of clinicians were using idiosyncratic approaches in scoring the Rorschach and actually combining features of the major systems. It was obvious that someone with patience, fortitude, and intellectual prowess was needed to bring order out of the chaos.

In 1974, after many years of painstaking work, John Exner introduced the *Comprehensive System* to the Rorschach community. According to Exner, even into the 1960s none of the Rorschach systematizers was reconciled to synthesis or compromise. A project was undertaken to draw from each system those features that under careful scrutiny yielded valid and substantive data. Exner (1986) found many disparities among the systems, even with respect to such fundamental issues as seating arrangement and introductory instruction in the subject. Furthermore,

> differences in scoring led to many differences concerning interpretation. They differed significantly about which scores should be calculated in a quantitative summary of the record and what relationships between scores would be important to interpretation. They differed concerning the meaningfulness of many variables and which configurations of variables might be interpretively important. In spite of their substantial differences, several interpretive postulates appeared in each of the systems that were the same or similar. For the most part these were drawn from Rorschach's original work, but to the casual observer that common thread could easily convey the impression that the systems were much more similar than was actually the case. Major differences existed across the systems on issues about which Rorschach was not definitive or had offered no procedures or postulates. (p. 19)

Exner performed an extensive analysis of the Rorschach literature and selected 700 research reports that he considered methodologically sound. This collection served as a data bank from which various elements of each of the five systems could be carefully studied. The features that could be empirically validated, from all the systems, were subsequently integrated. In sum, the Comprehensive System represents a combination of the psychometrically credible aspects of all the major Rorschach systematizers.

Administrative Procedures in the Comprehensive System

The seating arrangement is usually side-by-side, and after a brief introduction concerning the purpose of the test the examiner hands Card I to the examinee and asks, "What might this be?" If the examinee offers only one response to Card I, the examiner might prompt him or her with "If you take your time and look some more, I think that you will find something else, too." No further prompting is encouraged and if questions arise, the examiner answers in a neutral and judicious manner. Responses to all ten inkblots are recorded verbatim during this association phase; the position in which the examinee holds the card is also noted. An inquiry phase is conducted after all ten inkblots have been responded to. The intent of the inquiry is to obtain sufficient information to score each response accurately, that is, what was perceived that formed the subject's response? Exner (1986) recommends that the examiner introduce the inquiry with

> O.K., we've done them all. Now we are going to go back through them. It won't take long. I want you to help me see what you saw. I'm going to read what you said, and then I want you to show me where on the blot you saw it and what there is there that makes it look like that, so that I can see it too. I'd like to see it just like you did, so help me now. Do you understand? (p. 72)

Information obtained from the inquiry should permit scoring and coding of all responses according to location (where on the blot was the percept seen?), determinant (what made it look or appear like that?), and content (what actually is it?). Responses are also noted on the location sheet, a one-page chart with miniature versions of all ten inkblots; the examinee's responses to each inkblot are simply outlined on this sheet.

Scoring in the Comprehensive System

The first scoring category is *location*, that is, the area or part of the blot used by the examinee or with which each response is associated. If the entire blot is involved, it is scored as a whole response and designated by the symbol W. Responses to major segments of the blot are scored D (common detail) or Dd (uncommon detail), depending on the frequency with which a normative group used the area in responding. If the white space area is used in the response its notation is WS, DS, DdS, depending on the area of the percept. Location responses are then scored for degree of organization or differentiation, such as v (vague response) denoting a diffuse impression of the percept without any attribution to structural features.

In the second scoring category, *determinants*, the examiner notes the features or characteristics of each inkblot that contributed to the response process. These features encompass three major classifications: form and movement, color, and shading. According to Exner (1986), the symbols and criteria selected for determinant scoring in the Comprehensive System involve 24 symbols representing nine categories. These symbols and the associated criteria are given in Table 11–1.

The form (F) response describes the perceived object, based on its shape or

Table 11–1	Symbols and Criteria for Determinant Coding	
Category	Symbol	Criteria
Form	F	*Form answers.* To be used separately for responses based exclusively on form features of the blot, or in combination with other determinant symbols (*except* **M & m**) when the form features have contributed to the formulation of the answer.
Movement	M	*Human movement response.* To be used for responses involving the kinesthetic activity of a human, or of an animal or fictional character in human-like activity.
	FM	*Animal movement response.* To be used for responses involving a kinesthetic activity of an animal. The movement perceived must be congruent to the species identified in the content. Animals reported in movement *not* common to their species should be coded as **M.**
	m	*Inanimate movement response.* To be used for responses involving the movement of inanimate, inorganic, or insensate objects.
Chromatic Color	C	*Pure color response.* To be used for answers based exclusively on the chromatic color features of the blot. *No* form is involved.
	CF	*Color-form response.* To be used for answers that are formulated primarily because of the chromatic color features of the blot. Form features *are* used, but are of secondary importance.
	FC	*Form-color response.* To be used for answers that are created mainly because of form features. Chromatic color is also used, but is of secondary importance.
	Cn	*Color naming response.* To be used when the colors of the blot or blot areas are identified by *name*, and with the intention of giving a response.
Achromatic Color	C′	*Pure achromatic color response.* To be used when the response is based exclusively on the gray, black, or white features of

(Continued)

Category	Symbol	Criteria
		the blot, when they are clearly used as color. *No* form is involved.
	C′F	*Achromatic color-form response.* To be used for responses that are formulated *mainly* because of the black, white, or gray features, clearly used as color. Form features are used, but are of secondary importance.
	FC′	*Form-achromatic color response.* To be used for answers that are based mainly on the form features. The achromatic features, clearly used as color, are also included, but are of secondary importance.
Shading-Texture	**T**	*Pure texture response.* To be used for answers in which the shading components of the blot are translated to represent a tactual phenomenon, with no consideration to the form features.
	TF	*Texture-form response.* To be used for responses in which the shading features of the blot are interpreted as tactual, and form is used secondarily, for purposes of elaboration and/or clarification.
	FT	*Form-texture response.* To be used for responses that are based *mainly* on the form features. Shading features of the blot are translated as tactual, but are of secondary importance.
Shading-Dimension	**V**	*Pure vista response.* To be used for answers in which the shading features are interpreted as depth or dimensionality. *No* form is involved.
	VF	*Vista-form response.* To be used for responses in which the shading features are interpreted as depth or dimensionality. Form features are included, but are of secondary importance.
	FV	*Form-vista response.* To be used for answers that are based mainly on the form features of the blot. Shading features are also interpreted to note depth and/or dimensionality, but are of secondary importance to the formulation of the answer.

(Continued)

Category	Symbol	Criteria
Shading-Diffuse	**Y**	*Pure shading response.* To be used for responses that are based exclusively on the light-dark features of the blot that are completely formless and do not involve reference to either texture or dimension.
	YF	*Shading-form response.* To be used for responses based primarily on the light-dark features of the blot. Form features are included, but are of secondary importance.
	FY	*Form-shading response.* To be used for responses that are based *mainly* on the form features of the blot. The light-dark features of the blot are included as elaboration and/or clarification and are secondary to the use of form.
Form Dimension	**FD**	*Form-based dimensional response.* To be used for answers in which the impression of depth, distance, or dimensionality is created by using the elements of size and/or shape of contours. *No* use of shading is involved in creating this impression.
Pairs & Reflections	**(2)**	*The pair response.* To be used for answers in which two identical objects are reported, based on the symmetry of the blot. The objects must be equivalent in all respects, but must *not* be identified as being reflected or as mirror images.
	rF	*Reflection-form response.* To be used for answers in which the blot or blot area is reported as a reflection or mirror image because of the symmetry of the blot. The object or content reported has no specific form requirement, as in clouds, landscape, shadows, etc.
	Fr	*Form-reflection response.* To be used for answers in which the blot or blot area is identified as reflected or a mirror image, based on the symmetry of the blot. The substance of the response is based on form features, and the object reported has a specific form demand.

From *The Rorschach: A Comprehenisve System* (2nd ed.), by J. E. Exner. Copyright 1986. Reproduced by permission of the author.

form features. For example on Card IV the subject may attribute seeing a "giant monster" to "there's the head with its arms and legs here, the center forms the body." Clearly, form characteristics have determined this percept. According to Exner, form features are the most frequently used determinant category and are included in about 95% of the total responses.

Some empirical evidence has supported the notion that the three types of movement responses (human, animal, inanimate) actually reflect different psychological processes. The symbol *M* denotes human activity, both active and passive movement, for example, "two Indians fighting" or "a girl sitting and thinking." Animal movement is denoted by *FM*, such as "a bat flying." However, if animals are involved in human-type activities such as "two elephants laughing," the percept should be scored *M*. The symbol *m* denotes nonhuman/animal motion; some common responses include rocks falling, explosions, and objects floating. All movement responses are also labeled as either *active* or *passive*, although there is disagreement on the precise criteria for various responses (see Exner, 1986, pp. 106–110).

Chromatic color responses (*C, CF, FC*) are indicated when the percept involves the spectrum of hues other than black, white, or gray. At times, these classifications are difficult and the examiner must determine whether the primary criterion for the percept is color-form, form-color, or color alone. The response "sun" followed by "it's all yellow and the rays are shining outward, plus there's some sunspots" would be coded *CF*. The primary emphasis is on color with some secondary form features. Obviously, the examiner is hard pressed at times to determine whether color is primary, secondary, or the sole characteristic of a percept; however, a thorough inquiry should facilitate the decision. *Achromatic color* determinants, initially discussed by Klopfer and Kelley (1942), are responses in which gray, black, and white parts of the inkblot are used as color and represented by *C', C'F,* or *F'C*. The response "a black bat" to Card V denotes the use of achromatic color as a secondary feature and is therefore scored *F'C*. The critical factor for both the chromatic and achromatic color responses is whether form is primary or secondary for clarification or elaboration of the percept or not at all.

The *texture* determinant represents tactual features such as furry, rough, grainy, and silky. A response of actually rubbing the color confirms either a pure texture (*T*), texture-form (*TF*), or form-texture (*FT*) response. Although a pure texture response is rare, a *TF* response is quite common, for example "some fur." In short, a *TF* response should indicate shaded features as texture with elaboration based on form characteristics. Conversely, *FT* response involves primary form requirements with reference to texture in a secondary manner. Many of the common animal skin responses to Card VI are coded *FT*.

The use of the light-dark features of the inkblots usually indicates a *shading* determinant. The shading response could include variations in hue or a diffusion of light-dark tones. *FY* refers to percepts that are based primarily on form with shading features used for elaboration, such as "a light from a lighthouse with some dark and light areas." Shading-form (*YF*), and pure shading (*Y*) responses occur infrequently.

Table 11–2	Symbols and Criteria for Coding Form Quality		
Symbol	**Definition**	**Criterion**	
+	Superior-elaborated	The unusually precise articulation of the use of form in a manner that tends to enrich the quality of the response without sacrificing the appropriateness of the form use. The + answer need not be original, but rather unique by the manner in which details are defined and by which the form is used and specified.	
o	Ordinary	The obvious, easily articulated use of form features to define an object reported frequently by others. The answer is commonplace and easy to see. There is no unusual enrichment of the answer by overelaboration of the form features.	
u	Unusual	A low-frequency response in which the basic contours involved are not significantly violated. These are uncommon answers that are seen quickly and easily by the observer.	
–	Minus	The distorted, arbitrary, unrealistic use of form in creating a response. The answer is imposed on the blot structure with total, or near total, disregard for the structure of the area being used in creating the response. Often arbitrary contours will be created where none exist.	

From *The Rorschach: A Comprehensive System* (2nd ed.), by J. E. Exner. Copyright 1986. Reproduced by permission of the author.

Shading determinants have been one of the most unsettled and controversial aspects of Rorschach testing, involving various methods of coding from all five major systems. Responses that use shading with a percept of depth or dimension are coded as vista-form (VF), form-vista (FV), or pure vista (V). These shading dimension responses usually attribute depth or contour to the percept.

Several determinants specific to the Comprehensive System have been incorporated into the scoring in recent years; they are referred to as form-dimension and pair and reflections responses (see Table 11–1). In addition, three other elements, blend, organizational activity, and form quality, have critical significance in the Rorschach record and should be evaluated carefully. A *blend* response occurs when more than one determinant is attributed to a percept. Exner (1986) states that approximately 20% of the responses in a given protocol are scored as blends and that each response to a percept must be scored separately. The response "rows of trees on both sides of a mountain" qualifies as a blend response. *Organizational activity* (Z) refers to responses that integrate two or more detail areas of a blot in a meaningful, organized fashion. Form must always be involved in the percept, for example, "two elephants dancing around a drum trying to push each other away." Z scores reveal the level of cognitive activity and possibly the individual's intellectual efficiency. Third, *form quality* is the level of perceptual accuracy or "goodness of fit" of each response in the protocol. In other words, does the examinee's use of form correspond well with the actual inkblot percept? Whereas most of the systems in the past used "good form/poor form," the Comprehensive System involves a four-category coding system that permits differentiation of form quality (see Table 11–2).

The third scoring category is the coding of the content of responses. Originally, Rorschach included only six distinct scoring categories for content, human, human detail, animal, animal detail, landscape, and inanimate objects. To permit finer discriminations of responses, Exner selected a list of 27 categories for the scoring of content. Table 11–3 summarizes the criteria for each of the content categories used in the Comprehensive System.

Popular responses are common percepts given quite frequently by normative samples. Exner reports that in a sample of 7,500 protocols, 13 popular responses were produced at least 2,500 times. The most up-to-date listing in the Comprehensive System includes 15 popular responses; the criteria for each of these responses are summarized in Table 11–4.

Some responses, because of their peculiar nature, require a *special score*. Currently, there are 12 special scores in the Comprehensive System, including five that deal with unusual verbalizations and typically signal the presence of a thought disorder. Some other scores, referred to as inappropriate combinations (*INCOM, FABCOM,* and *CONTAM*), reflect unrealistic relationships and syntheses between objects and activities. These inappropriate percepts indicate that the examinee's cognitive processes may be seriously affected. *Perseveration* occurs when redundant responses are given to the same percept or to a number of inkblot cards throughout the protocol. Again, these types of cognitive distortions usually indicate pathological preoccupations.

Structural Summary

The *structural summary* includes Rorschach elements such as location features, determinants, form quality, contents, and special scoring (see Figure 11–2), as well as various ratios, percentages, and derivations. Some of the critical quantitative formulas used for personality description and interpretation in a structural summary are discussed briefly below.

The various formulas indicate the comparisons and proportions between Rorschach elements. The *experience balance* (*erlebnistypus* or EB) is the relationship between all human movement (M) responses and the weighted sum of the chromatic color responses. EB reflects a preferential response style referred to as *introversive* and *extratensive*. Introversive designates a person who utilizes inner

Table 11–3		Symbols and Criteria Used in Scoring for Content
Category	Symbol	Criterion
Whole Human	H	Involving or implying the percept of a whole human form.
Whole Human (fictional or mythological)	(H)	Involving or implying the percept of a whole human form of a fictional or mythological basis, that is, gnomes, fairies, giants, witches, King Midas, Alice in Wonderland, monsters (human like), ghosts, dwarfs, devils, and angels.
Human Detail	Hd	Involving the percept of an incomplete human form, that is, a person but the head is missing, an arm, fingers, two big feet, and the lower part of a woman.
Human Detail (fictional or mythological)	(Hd)	Involving the percept of an incomplete human form of a fictional or mythological basis, that is, the hand of God, the head of the devil, the foot of a monster, the head of a witch, and the eyes of an angel.
Whole Animal	A	Involving or implying the percept of a whole animal form.
Whole Animal (fictional or mythological)	(A)	Involving or implying the percept of a whole animal form of a fictional or mythological basis, that is, unicorn, flying red horse, black beauty, Jonathan Livingston Seagull, and a magic frog.
Animal Detail	Ad	Involving the percept of an incomplete animal form, that is, the hoof of a horse, the claw of a lobster, the head of a fish, the head of a rabbit.
Animal Detail (fictional or mythological)	(Ad)	Involving the percept of an incomplete animal form of a fictional or mythological basis, that is, the wing of the bird of prey, Peter Rabbit's head, the head of Pooh Bear, the head of Bambi, and the wings of Pegasus.
Abstraction	Ab	Involving the percept which is clearly an abstract concept, that is, fear, depression, elation, and anger, abstract art, or any form of symbolism.
Alphabet	Al	Involving percepts of Arabic numerals, such as 2, 4, and 7, or the letters of the alphabet, such as A, M, and X.

(Continued)

Category	Symbol	Criteria
Anatomy	*An*	Involving the percept of anatomy (internal organs) of either human or animal content, that is, a heart, lungs, stomach, a bleached skull of a cow, a brain of a dog, and the insides of a person's stomach.
Art	*Art*	Involving percepts of paintings, plus other art objects, that is, a family crest, the seal of the president, and a sculpture of a bird.
Anthropology	*Ay*	Involving percepts which have a specific cultural relationship, that is, a totem pole, a helmet like those used by Romans, a Viking ship, or Lindberg's airplane.
Blood	*Bl*	Involving the percept of blood, either human or animal.
Botany	*Bt*	Involving the percept of any plant life, that is, flowers, trees, bushes, and seaweed.
Clothing	*Cg*	Involving the percept of any clothing ordinarily associated with the human, that is, hat, boots, jacket, trousers, and tie.
Clouds	*Cl*	Involving the percept of clouds. Variations of this category, such as fog, mist, and so on, should be scored as *Na*.
Explosion	*Ex*	Involving percepts of an actual explosion, occurring most commonly to Card IX, as an atomic explosion or blast. The determinant for inanimate movement (*m*) should always accompany this content. Percepts of an explosion "aftermath" such as, "A blast has just occurred and things are lying all over the place," should be coded for other content, or written out in complete form.
Fire	*Fi*	Involving percepts of actual fire, smoke, burning candles, flame given off from a torch, and such. These percepts will ordinarily involve the determinant scoring of *m* to denote the inanimate movement of the "fire" association.
Food	*Fd*	Involving the percept of any edible, such as ice cream, fried shrimp, chicken legs, a piece of steak, etc. The intent or meaning of the association must be clearly associated with "everyday" consumer produce, as in the instance of lettuce, cabbage, carrots, fried foods, etc., or must be presented in such a manner as to suggest that the object

(Continued)

Category	Symbol	Criteria
		perceived is identified as a food substance, that is, "looks like a chicken like we used to have for Sunday dinner."
Geography	*Ge*	Involving percepts of any maps, specified or unspecified, that is, a map of Sicily, or a map of an island, peninsula, and continent. The percepts of *Ge do not* include the actual percept of definite or indefinite land masses which are "real" rather than representations. These type of percepts are scored as *Ls* (Landscape) or written out in rare instances.
Household	*Hh*	Involving percepts of interior household items, that is, chairs, beds, bedposts, plates, silverware, and rugs.
Landscape	*Ls*	Involving percepts of landscapes or seascapes, neither of which would be scored as *Bt* or *Ge*. A tree or a bush might legitimately be scored as *Bt*, whereas "trees," or "a bunch of shrubs" are more ordinarily scored *Ls*. This category includes some underwater scenes where specific animals are not identified, or in some instances as a secondary score as in Card X where a few specific animals may be cited but the bulk of the percept is left vague.
Nature	*Na*	Involving percepts of a wider natural scope than are included in *Bt*, *Ge*, or *Ls*, usually including sky, snow, water, raging sea, a storm, night, ice, rainbow, sun, etc.
Science	*Sc*	Involving percepts that are ordinarily associated with science or science fiction such as bacteria, germs, science fiction monsters, ray guns, rockets, rocket ships, spaceships, etc. In some instances, the symbol *Sc* will be used as the primary content but in other responses, especially those involving science fiction objects, the symbol *(A)* or *(H)* may be assigned as primary and *Sc* as secondary.
Sex	*Sx*	Involving percepts of sex organs or activities related to sex function, that is, intercourse, erect penis, menstruation, vagina, testes, and breasts.

(Continued)

Category	Symbol	Criteria
X-ray	*Xy*	Involving percepts of x-ray, most of which pertain to bone structure, that is, the x-ray of a pelvis, the x-ray of some bones, but may also involve x-rays of organs or organ like structures, that is, an x-ray of the stomach and an x-ray of the intestines. *Shading is always* involved in these percepts.
Vocational (supplementary)	*(Vo)*	Involving percepts which *may* be interpreted as related to the occupation of the subject. This scoring is *never* used as the primary or main content score but may be included as secondary or additional so as to alert the interpreter of a vocational or occupational percept.

From *The Rorschach: A Comprehensive System* (2nd ed.), by J. E. Exner. Copyright 1986. Reproduced by permission of the author.

resources for basic gratification, whereas an extratensive individual is more likely to allow affect to permeate his or her life experience. That is, introversive individuals tend to subdue their feelings when involved in cognitive tasks such as decision making. On the other hand, the cognitive activities of extratensives are more likely to be affected by their feelings and emotions.

The *form-color ratio* (FC:CF+C) denotes the balance or modulation of affect. A higher number on the *color* side of the ratio suggests heightened emotional experiences and possibly impulsiveness. Related to this proportion is the *affective ratio* (Afr), which compares response frequency between the last three inkblots and the first seven blots (recall that the last three cards on the Rorschach contain a variety of colors). The *Afr* indicates an individual's receptivity to emotionally charged stimulation. *Lambda* (L) refers to the judicious use of rational resources and compares the frequency of all pure form (F) responses with all other responses in a record. A very high Lambda points to a pragmatic, somewhat conventional approach to the environment.

Other calculations and derivations in the structural summary include aspirational index, body concern, human interest, depression index, and schizophrenia index. For an in-depth discussion of the structural summary computations see Exner (1986, pp. 170–183, 311–428).

Interpreting Rorschach Responses

Formulating interpretive conclusions from Rorschach data, as in all methods of personality assessment, is an arduous process. Knowledge and extensive experience in personality theory and psychopathology is mandatory, and clinical data from other assessment sources must be considered before worthwhile conclusions can be

Table 11–4		Popular Responses Selected for the Comprehensive System*
Card	**Location**	**Criterion**
I	W	Bat. The response always involves the whole blot.
I	W	Butterfly. The response always involves the whole blot.
II	D1	Animal forms, usually the heads of dogs, bears, elephants, or lambs; however, the frequency of the whole animal to this area is sufficient to warrant the scoring of **P**.
III	D1 or D9	Two human figures, or representations thereof, such as dolls and caricatures. The scoring of **P** is also applicable to the percept of a single human figure to area D9.
IV	W or D7	A human or human-like figure such as giant, monster, science fiction creature, etc.
V	W	Butterfly, the apex of the card upright or inverted. The whole blot *must* be used.
V	W	Bat, the apex of the card upright or inverted, and involving the whole blot.
VI	W or D1	Animal skin, hide, rug, or pelt.
VII	D1 or D9	Human head or face, specifically identified as female, child, Indian, or with gender not identified. If D1 is used, the upper segment (D5) is usually identified as hair, feature, etc. If the response includes the entire D2 area, **P** is coded if the head or face are restricted to the D9 area. If Dd23 is included as part of the human form, the response is *not* coded as **P**.
VIII	D1	Whole animal figure. This is the most frequently perceived common answer, the content varying considerably, such as bear, dog, rodent, fox, wolf, and coyote. All are **P**. The **P** is also coded when the animal figure is reported as part of the **W** percept as in a family crest, seal, and emblem.
IX	D3	Human or human-like figures such as witches, giants, science fiction creatures, monsters, etc.
X	D1	Spider with all appendages restricted to the D1 area.
X	D1	Crab with all appendages restricted to the D1 area. Other variations of multilegged animals are not **P**.

*Based on frequency of occurrence of at least once in every three protocols given by nonpatient adult subjects and nonschizophrenic adult patients.

From *The Rorschach: A Comprehensive System* (2nd ed.), by J. E. Exner. Copyright 1986. Reproduced by permission of the the author.

Structural Summary Blank for the Comprehensive System

Figure 11–2

R =   Zf =   ZSum =   P =   (2) =   Fr + rF =

Location Features	**Determinants** (Blends First)	**Contents**	**Contents** (Idiographic)
W =		H = Bl =	_____ =
D =		(H) = Bt =	_____ =
Dd =		Hd = Cg =	_____ =
S =		(Hd) = Cl =	_____ =
		A = Ex =	_____ =
		(A) = Fi =	_____ =
		Ad = Fd =	_____ =
		(Ad) = Ge =	_____ =
	Single Determinants	Ab = Hh =	
		Al = Ls =	
	M =	An = Na =	
DQ	**M Quality**	FM =	Art = Sc =
		m =	Ay = Sx =
+ =	+ =	C =	Xy =
v/+ =	o =	Cn =	
		CF =	
o =	u =	FC =	**S-CONSTELLATION (Adult)** **Special Scorings**
		C' =	
v =	– =	C'F =	___ FV + VF + V + FD > 2 DV =
	NO FORM =	FC' =	___ Col-Shd Bl > 0 INCOM =
		T =	___ 3r + (2)/R ≤ .30 or ≥ .45 DR =
Form Quality		TF =	___ MOR > 3 FABCOM =
		FT =	___ Zd > ±3.5 ALOG =
FQx	**FQf**	V =	___ es > EA CONTAM =
		VF =	___ CF + C > FC ___ WSUM6 =
+ =	+ =	FV =	___ X + % < .70 AG =
		Y =	___ S > 3 CONFAB =
o =	o =	YF =	___ P < 3 or > 8 CP =
		FY =	___ Pure H < 2 MOR =
u =	u =	rF =	___ R < 17 PER =
		Fr =	_____ TOTAL PSV =
– =	– =	FD =	
NO FORM =		F =	

RATIOS, PERCENTAGES, AND DERIVATIONS

ZSum-Zest =			FC:CF + C =	W:M =
Zd =			Pure C =	W:D =
EB =	EA =		Afr =	Isolate:R =
eb =	es =	} D =	3r + (2)/R =	Ab + Art =
(FM = m = T = C' = V = Y =)			L =	An + Xy =
a:p =	Adj D =		Blends:R =	H + (H):Hd + (Hd) =
Ma:Mp =	Depi =		X + % =	Pure H =
S-Con =	Sczi =		X – % =	(H) + (Hd):(A) + (Ad) =
			F + % =	H + A:Hd + Ad =

From *The Rorschach: A Comprehensive System* (2nd ed.), by John E. Exner. Copyright 1986. Reproduced by permission of the author.

drawn about an individual's personality functioning. Exner (1986) emphasizes that in Rorschach assessment all aspects of the structural summary, accuracy in scoring, verbalizations, and content of response sequence must be evaluated together to form "working hypotheses" and interpretive postulates. Only through a "global" approach can valid data be interpreted to provide a meaningful psychological portrait of a unique person.

In attempting to understand and describe a person's psychological processes, several critical areas of personality functioning are paramount. For example, does a person use cognitive/intellectual resources or emotional reactivity in dealing with the demands of the real world? Moreover, how does a person select an active or passive coping strategy? What defensive styles are used in times of stress? Can the person maintain a rational approach during the process of decision making? Is the person self-focused, task-oriented, conventional, or unique to the point where the consequence is extreme anxiety and interpersonal conflict? Does the person have an inclination toward depressive symptoms, psychopathic acting-out, or schizophrenic ideation?

An intensive and comprehensive appraisal of an individual's Rorschach performance can provide promising clues in attempting to answer the above questions. A synthesis of all Rorschach data should yield a number of preliminary hypotheses, and, when integrated with other clinical information, provide a systematic framework for understanding personality functioning.

Computerized Scoring and Interpretation

Piotrowski's CPR

Zygmunt Piotrowski (1964) developed the first computerized scoring and interpretation system, known as *PAR*, for the Rorschach. Based on clinical observations, Piotrowski provided about 1,000 descriptive personality statements. This pool of interpretive comments and statements focuses on problem-solving strategies, cognitive abilities, and interpersonal effectiveness. Later, Piotrowski's computer-interpretive program was renamed the Computerized Perceptanalytic Rorschach or *CPR*. In applying the procedure, interpretive statements are matched to all Rorschach responses. However, Piotrowski offered no standardization or normative data, or documentation pertaining to the validity of the statements. Because of the idiographic approach favored by Piotrowski, the CPR was criticized for its disregard of pyschometric criteria and has few proponents today.

Miller's and Perline's Programs

Other attempts have been made to exploit the speed and flexibility of computers in Rorschach administration, scoring, and interpretation. For example, Franklin

Miller (1986) developed an online computer-assisted interview program for Rorschach administration that was designed to bring some standardization to the test setting. With more research the interactive computer administration of the Rorschach appears to have a promising future.

A Computer Interpreted Rorschach program, developed by Irvin H. Perline, became commercially available in 1979 from Century Diagnostics. In using this program, which is based on the Klopfer system, the clinician provides Rorschach scores on a tabulation sheet. Percentages and ratios are calculated by the computer and recorded in the Data Summary. The Interpretative Analysis, which is atheoretical, yields interpretive statements based on research with the Rorschach. The Narrative Summary gives information on cognitive, emotional, and interpersonal aspects of personality. Unfortunately, no validity data or reports on the psychometric properties of Perline's program have been published.

The Exner Report

Perhaps the most popular computer-based Rorschach interpretation program is the one developed for Exner's Comprehensive System at the Rorschach Research Foundation in New York. The program follows a logical progression of decision-tree rules yielding a composite of findings that lead to interpretive hypotheses. The Exner Report for the Rorschach Comprehensive System became commercially available from National Computer Systems in 1983.[1] The Report calculates the Structural Summary, scanning all the structural data included in the test, and considers 31 critical clusters derived from 352 scores and derivations of scores. Two categories are represented by the clusters: those related to the examinee's basic personality characteristics (e.g., coping styles, emotional controls, self-esteem, stress tolerance, and perceptual accuracy) and those dealing with psychopathology (e.g., depression proneness, schizophrenia, stress reaction, suicide potential).

A typical computer printout for the Exner Report contains between 18 and 23 interpretive narrative statements. Each statement suggests a hypothesis concerning the personality and behavioral tendencies of the patient. The following two statements are illustrative:

> This person is experiencing considerable mental activity that is being promoted by unmet need states. Such mental activity usually interferes with attention and/or concentration and increases distractibility.

> This person is experiencing considerable emotional irritation because of strong, unmet needs for closeness that are usually manifested as some experience of loneliness. This is made more irritating because some data suggest a preference for dependency on others.

Because scoring, organizing, and interpreting Rorschach data are time consuming activities, a computer program that assists in scanning a large pool of variables and combinations of derived scores can be an asset in terms of speed and reliability of computations. The Exner Report appears promising, but validity and outcome studies are urgently needed to enable clinicians to evaluate the usefulness and credibility of computerized Rorschach interpretation.

Psychometric Issues and Future Prospects

Inadequate validation is a crucial problem with respect to the majority of personality assessment instruments, and the Rorschach is no exception. Satisfactory validity is especially difficult to achieve when the variables are as complex as those comprising the human psyche, including cognitive processes, personality traits, defensive structure, emotional life, and predispositions to behavioral reactivity. To make matters worse, the Rorschach inkblots are not amenable to certain psychometric procedures, for example, determining split-half reliability. Variability in response frequency, unsystematic scoring and administration, and interpreting statements without reference to normative samples are problems that have always plagued the Rorschach. Regardless of such difficulties, it is incumbent upon Rorschach psychodiagnosticians and researchers to verify the psychometric qualities of the test. For many decades, this was difficult to accomplish because of inconsistencies among the five major systems. In fact, reliability and validity studies of the instrument were rare and the findings disappointing.

Because the Rorschach is not a homogeneous test in which different cards or items measure the same variable, internal-consistency coefficients computed across cards are not appropriate and generally quite low. The numbers of responses in different scoring categories (form, color, shading, movement, etc.) are also too small to yield reliable percentages or other stable indices. Furthermore, examinees do not respond independently to different cards; this very interdependence is used by clinicians to assess trends in responses over cards.

Test-Retest Reliability

Whatever earlier studies may have revealed, over the past decade some promising results have been obtained in a series of investigations on temporal stability (test-retest reliability). In a nonpatient adult sample, correlational analyses of 19 Rorschach variables and elements and directional analyses of five ratios indicated that scores based on the Comprehensive System scoring categories are fairly stable over a three-year interval. Four of the five ratios were consistent in direction over the time span, whereas nine of the 19 variables yielded test-retest correlations greater than .80 (Exner, Armbruster & Viglione, 1978). These findings are not particularly surprising because preferred response styles are usually fairly crystallized by the time a normal person reaches adulthood.

Response consistency, however, is not yet apparent in the developing child, and findings concerning the temporal stability of children's Rorschach scores have been equivocal. Exner and Weiner (1982) found low to moderate test-retest coefficients over a 24 to 30 month time period in children's Rorschach scores. A subsequent study of fourth graders retested after a three-week interval obtained test-retest coefficients in the .70 to .80 range for many Rorschach variables and ratios (Thomas, Alinsky & Exner, 1982). However, longitudinal research on the temporal reliability of Rorschach variables points to poor score consistency up to age 14 (Exner, Thomas & Mason, 1985). Perhaps these results are a reflection of inconsistency of response styles, which is expected during the developmental years. Thus, the empirical findings seem to suggest that the Comprehensive System's elements and indices are reliable only for adult samples. In addition to data on normal adults and children, stability data for psychiatric populations are urgently needed; a recent study by Haller and Exner (1985) obtained promising results on an abnormal sample.

Validity

As might be expected, the issue of validity has been a thorny one for the Rorschach. At best, the literature points to inconsistent, ambiguous findings on Rorschach validity. However, several studies have obtained evidence of some empirical validity for response frequency, movement perceptions, use of color, and form level. Rorschach content analysis has been more amenable to validity studies, and the findings of certain investigations in this area are encouraging but not uniformly positive (Goldfried, Stricker & Weiner, 1971; Reznikoff, Aronow & Rauchway, 1982; Zubin, Eron & Schumer, 1965). Although Tamkin (1980) obtained little evidence of a relationship between experience balance and measures of introversion and extroversion derived from personality inventories, Rorschach had originally noted that the two constructs are not necessarily synonymous. And in a longitudinal study of children undergoing residential treatment (Tuber, 1983), Rorschach object relationships and thought organization scores proved to be significant predictors of rehospitalization.

Currently there is much interest in validating Exner's Comprehensive System on psychiatric populations. For example, preliminary research with antisocial personalities, homosexuals, and depressed patients suggests that the Egocentricity Index is related to self-esteem. One study utilized the MMPI Ego Strength Scale as the criterion but found no relationship with the Rorschach Egocentricity Index (Barley, Dorr & Reid, 1985). In addition, scores on the Comprehensive System variables and ratios have been factor analyzed for schizophrenics, depressives, and nonpatient groups. The results reveal distinct personality organizations for the three groups, a finding that supports the discriminatory power of the Comprehensive System variables.

As suggested by the preceding discussion, the issue of the Rorschach's validity is clearly far from resolved. Further research is needed to clarify the psychometric limitations of this instrument, but that task will be facilitated by the availability of the Comprehensive System.

Future Prospects

A resurgence of interest in the Rorschach test occurred during the 1980s, a phenomenon attributable in large measure to the development and application of Exner's Comprehensive System. This methodologically sound framework for administering, scoring, and interpreting the Rorschach has already had positive effects, not only on practitioners of the technique but also on more psychometrically oriented academicians and researchers. In fact, a recent study by Piotrowski, Sherry, and Keller (1985) found that the Exner system is being used by 35% of the practicing clinicians surveyed. Some staunch supporters continue to adhere to one of the original major systems, but even they have been influenced by the work of Exner and his associates.

Alternative approaches to Rorschach administration and scoring, such as content-interview analysis, will undoubtedly continue to be popular. Consensus Rorschach for couples and family therapy (Klopfer, 1984), the Rorschach Prognostic Rating Scale (Garwood, 1977; Shields, 1978) in psychotherapy outcome studies, and other novel approaches (e.g., Blatt & Berman, 1984) are also noteworthy. However, it appears that the Comprehensive System will lead the way in both practice and research.

Despite the fact that the Rorschach has not been a popular assessment instrument in research with adolescents (Leunes, Evans, Karnei & Lowry, 1980), recently there has been a renewal of interest in the Rorschach assessment of children and adolescents (Rabin, 1986, pp. 111–167; Weiner, 1986, pp. 141–171). In part, the resurgence of projective testing is ascribable to the changing roles of psychodiagnostics in general and to the specialty areas of neuropsychological (Chelune, Ferguson & Moehle, 1986) and forensic assessment in particular (see Rogers & Cavanaugh, 1983).

Does the Rorschach really have a promising future? As the foregoing discussion suggests, apparently so. But the future of Rorschach's ten inkblots lies in the continued scrutiny of research data, practical applications, and empirical validity. Questions concerning the ethics of assessment (Brown, 1982) will also play an important role in the future well-being of the Rorschach. If it is to maintain its position against new competitors, continued examination and evaluation of the Rorschach Inkblot Technique should not be feared but welcomed. Hermann Rorschach would undoubtedly have wanted it that way.

Summary

The development of the Rorschach Inkblot Technique has been traced from the publication of Hermann Rorschach's *Psychodiagnostik* in 1921 through its early growth and eventual divergence into five major systems. Over the past several decades the Rorschach has encountered extensive criticism, particularly from academic clinicians, and during the 1960s it declined in popularity. However, John Exner's industrious attempt at a synthesis of empirically sound aspects of each major system and provision of a systematic framework for testing hypotheses concerning personality has resulted in new credibility for the Rorschach technique. Since the mid-1970s Exner's Comprehensive System has been the most popular Rorschach method, not only among clinical practitioners but also among psychometricians and others concerned with research involving projectives.

The Rorschach technique is best conceptualized as a perceptual-cognitive task, a broad-band instrument, and a method for assessing and understanding personality functioning. Despite advances in research and practical applications, the Rorschach must meet the criteria of empirical validation. Research using the Rorschach continues at a brisk, productive pace. In sum, it would appear that the technique has weathered the storms of the past 65 years but has not yet completed its voyage.

Exercises

1. Define each of the following terms in a sentence or two:

achromatic color	introversive
affective ratio	lambda
association phase	location
blend	movement response
chromatic color	organizational activity
Comprehensive System	PAR
content analysis	perseveration
CPR	popular response
determinants	psychodiagnostic method
experience balance	shading
extratensive	special score
form-color ratio	structural summary
form quality	testing the limits
free association phase	texture
inquiry phase	

2. Construct an inkblot picture by putting a large drop of black ink in the middle of an 8 ½ inch by 11 inch sheet of white paper, folding the sheet in half so the ink is inside, creasing the sheet in the middle and pressing it flat, and then opening up the sheet and letting the blot dry. Repeat the process with other sheets until you obtain five fairly detailed, preferably symmetrical inkblots. Then administer your inkblot test to several friends, directing them to tell you what they see in each blot, where on the blot they see it, and what it was about the blot (shape, color, texture, or other quality) that caused them to give that response. Record the one or more responses made by each examinee to each inkblot, and then see if you can tell

anything about the examinee's personality from his or her responses to the five inkblots. Compare the test results with your personal knowledge of the individual and any other test results that are available. Summarize your findings in a report.

3.   What are the major characteristics of the Rorschach scoring and interpretative systems devised by Beck, Klopfer, Hertz, Rapaport-Schafer, and Piotrowski? How do these five major systems differ from Exner's Comprehensive System?

4.   Do you believe that the form of the responses to Rorschach cards is more revealing of unconscious processes than the content of those responses? Why or why not?

5.   Read reviews of the Rorschach Inkblot Technique and Holtzman Inkblot Technique in *The Mental Measurements Yearbook* or *Test Critiques*, and then write a comparative summary of the major characteristics of the two instruments.

6.   Why do you believe that the Rorschach has remained relatively popular among clinical psychologists even though its psychometric characteristics (validity, reliability, norms) leave much to be desired?

Suggested Readings

Atkinson, L. (1986). The comparative validities of the Rorschach and MMPI: A meta-analysis. *Canadian Psychology, 27,* 238–247.

Beck, S. J. (1981). Reality, Rorschach, and perceptual theory. In A. I. Rabin (Ed.), *Assessment with projective techniques: A concise introduction* (pp. 23–46). New York: Springer.

Cundick, B. P. (1985). Review of the Holtzman Inkblot Technique. In J. V. Mitchell, Jr. (Ed.), *The ninth mental measurements yearbook* (Vol. I, pp. 661–665). Lincoln, NE: Buros Institute of Mental Measurements of the University of Nebraska-Lincoln.

Erdberg, P. (1985). The Rorschach. In C. S. Newmark (Ed.), *Major psychological assessment instruments* (Vol. I, pp. 65–88). Boston: Allyn & Bacon.

Erdberg, P., & Exner, J. E. (1984). Rorschach assessment. In G. Goldstein & M. Hersen (Eds.), *Handbook of psychological assessment* (pp. 332–347). New York: Pergamon.

Exner, J. E. (1983). Rorschach assessment. In I. B. Weiner (Ed.), *Clinical methods in psychology* (2nd ed.) (pp. 58–99). New York: Wiley.

Hertz, M. R. (1986). Rorschachbound: A 50-year memoir. *Journal of Personality Assessment, 50,* 396–416.

Holtzman, W. H. (1986). The Holtzman Inkblot Technique with children and adolescents. In A. I. Rabin (Ed.), *Projective techniques for children and adolescents* (pp. 168–194). New York: Springer.

Howes, R. J. (1981). The Rorschach: Does it have a future? *Journal of Personality Assessment, 45,* 339–351.

Weiner, I. B. (1986). Assessing children and adolescents with the Rorschach. In H. Knoff (Ed.), *The assessment of child and adolescent personality* (pp. 141–171). New York: Guilford.

Endnote

[1]A microcomputer (IBM-PC) program based on Exner's Comprehensive System, known as the Rorschach Interpretation Assistance Program (RIAP), is available from The Psychological Corporation.

CHAPTER 12

The TAT and Other Apperception Techniques

Second only to the Rorschach in terms of the number of research citations and clinical usage over the years is the Thematic Apperception Test (TAT). One of the earliest psychometric precursors of the TAT was Binet and Simon's (1905) use of children's verbal responses to pictures as a measure of intellectual development. In a similar manner, Brittain (1907) showed a series of nine pictures to children aged 13 to 20 years, asking them to write stories about the pictures. Qualitative analysis of the responses included degree of imagination and creativity, coherence, length, use of picture details, and use of moral, religious, and social content. Differences were noted between the stories told by boys and girls: boys' stories were concerned more with the consumption of food, whereas girls included more emotional, moral, religious, and social content in their stories. In a related investigation, Libby (1908) examined the relationship between imagination

---

This chapter was prepared by Floyd G. Jackson

and feelings in adolescents, finding a significant difference between the thirteenth and fourteenth year. Predictably, stories told by younger children were more objective and those by older children more subjective.

One of the earliest uses of picture story tests in psychodiagnosis was Schwartz's (1932) Social Situation Test, which consisted of eight pictures and was used in psychiatric interviews of delinquent boys. The technique facilitated the establishment of rapport and assisted in initiating interviews. Another relative of the TAT is the Four Picture Test, which its author, Van Lennep (1951), traced back to 1930.

Christina Morgan and Henry Murray initially published the TAT in 1935. The current version is the second revision. The TAT consists of a set of 31 pictures—30 black-and-white picture cards depicting people in various ambiguous situations (see Figure 12–1) plus one blank card. The 31 cards, which are described in Table 12–1, can be arranged as four overlapping sets of 19 picture cards and the blank card for administration to boys, girls, men, and women. However, a full set of

Figure 12–1 Picture from the Thematic Apperception Test

Reprinted by permission of the publishers from Henry A. Murray, THEMATIC APPERCEPTION TEST, Cambridge, MA: Harvard University Press, Copyright © 1943 by the President and Fellows of Harvard College, 1971 by Henry A. Murray.

Descriptions of TAT Pictures   **Table 12–1**

Picture 1. A young boy is contemplating a violin which rests on a table in front of him.

Picture 2. Country scene: In the foreground is a young woman with books in her hand; in the background a man is working in the fields and an older woman is looking on.

Picture 3BM. On the floor against a couch is the huddled form of a boy with his head bowed on his right arm. Beside him on the floor is a revolver.

Picture 3GF. A young woman is standing with downcast head, her face covered with her right hand. Her left arm is stretched forward against a wooden door.

Picture 4. A woman is clutching the shoulders of a man whose face and body are averted as if he were trying to pull away from her.

Picture 5. A middle-aged woman is standing on the threshold of a half-opened door looking into a room.

Picture 6BM. A short elderly woman stands with her back turned to a tall young man. The latter is looking downward with a perplexed expression.

Picture 6GF. A young woman sitting on the edge of a sofa looks back over her shoulder at an older man with a pipe in his mouth who seems to be addressing her.

Picture 7. A gray-haired man is looking at a younger man who is sullenly staring into space.

Picture 7GF. An older woman is sitting on a sofa close beside a girl, speaking or reading to her. The girl, who holds a doll in her lap, is looking away.

Picture 8BM. An adolescent boy looks straight out of the picture. The barrel of a rifle is visible at one side, and in the background is the dim scene of a surgical operation, like a reverie-image.

Picture 8GF. A woman sits with her chin in her hand looking off into space.

Picture 9BM. Four men in overalls are lying on the grass taking it easy.

Picture 9GF. A young woman with a magazine and a purse in her hand looks from behind a tree at another young woman in a party dress running along a beach.

Picture 10. A young woman's head against a man's shoulder.

Picture 11. A road skirting a deep chasm between high cliffs. On the road in the distance are obscure figures. Protruding from the rocky wall on one side are the long head and neck of a dragon.

Picture 12M. A young man is lying on a couch with his eyes closed. Leaning over him is the gaunt form of an elderly man, his hand stretched out above the face of the reclining figure.

Picture 12F. The portrait of a young woman. A weird old woman with a shawl over her head is grimacing in the background. (see Fig. 12–1)

Picture 12BG. A rowboat is drawn up on the bank of a woodland stream. There are no human figures in the picture.

Picture 13MF. A young man is standing with downcast head buried in his arm. Behind him is the figure of a woman lying in the bed.

Picture 13B. A little boy is sitting on the doorstep of a log cabin.

Picture 13G. A little girl is climbing a winding flight of stairs.

Picture 14. The silhouette of a man (or woman) against a bright window. The rest of the picture is totally black.

(Continued)

Picture 15. A gaunt man with clenched hands is standing among gravestones.

Picture 16. Blank.

Picture 17BM. A naked man is clinging to a rope. He is in the act of climbing up or down.

Picture 17GF. A bridge over water. A female figure leans over the railing. In the background are tall buildings and small figures of men.

Picture 18BM. A man is clutched from behind by three hands. The figures of his antagonists are invisible.

Picture 18GF. A woman has her hands squeezed around the throat of another woman whom she appears to be pushing backward across the banister of a stairway.

Picture 19. A weird picture of cloud formations overhanging a snow-covered cabin in the country.

Picture 20. The dimly illuminated figure of a man (or woman) in the dead of night leaning against a lamppost.

Bellak (1986). Reprinted by permission of the publisher, C.P.S. Inc., Box 83, Larchmont, NY 10538.

20 cards is seldom administered. The following story, given by a young woman in response to the picture in Figure 12–1, is illustrative, but not necessarily typical, of the kinds of stories given to TAT pictures:

> This is a woman who has been quite troubled by memories of a mother she was resentful toward. She has feelings of sorrow for the way she treated her mother; her memories of her mother plague her. These feelings seem to be increasing as she grows older and sees her children treating her the same way she treated her mother. She tries to convey this feeling to her own children, but does not succeed in changing their attitudes. She is living her past in the present, because the feeling of sorrow and guilt is reinforced by the way her children are treating her.

Although still widely employed, the TAT has declined in popularity during recent years, ranking seventh in usage by practicing psychologists during the early 1980s (Lubin, Larsen, Matarazzo & Seever, 1986). The instrument is not only a useful personality assessment device, but also a valuable indicator of verbal achievement and academic socialization (Entwisle, 1972). TAT stories have also been used to measure motives, especially the achievement motive (Veroff, Depner, Kulka & Douvan, 1980).

According to Murray (1943), the TAT reveals underlying tendencies that a person may not be willing to acknowledge or cannot express because the impulses are unconscious. The test also assists the interpreter in determining an individual's dominant needs, emotions, sentiments, complexes, and conflicts, and the perceived external pressures (*press*) impinging on the examinee. It can be especially helpful in understanding the examinee's relations and difficulties with his or her parents and is often included in an assessment in which a variety of other tests such as the Rorschach, the MMPI, the Rotter Incomplete Sentences Blank, the Bender Visual-Motor Gestalt Tests, and the Wechsler Adult Intelligence Scale complement a psychiatric interview.

Administering the TAT

The procedure for administering the TAT varies somewhat depending on whether it is administered to an individual by another person, self-administered, or administered to a group of people simultaneously.

Individual Administration

In administering the TAT individually, it is important to establish good rapport and then situate oneself at a 45 degree angle alongside the examinee so his or her facial expressions can be seen clearly. This position minimizes the examinee's view of the examiner and simultaneously gives the examiner a full view of the former. The examiner can then unobtrusively write down or tape record the stories and related information provided by the examinee.

Two forms of the TAT are available for individual administration (A and B). Form A is suitable for adolescents and adults of average intelligence and sophistication; Form B is for children, adults of below average education and/or intelligence, and psychotics. Murray (1943) recommends the following instructions for administering Form A:

> This is a test of imagination, one form of intelligence. I am going to show you some pictures, one at a time; and your task will be to make up as dramatic a story as you can for each. Tell what has led up to the event shown in the picture, describe what is happening at the moment, what the characters are feeling and thinking; and then give the outcome. Speak your thoughts as they come to your mind. Do you understand? Since you have fifty minutes for ten pictures, you can devote about five minutes to each story. Here is the first picture. (p. 3)

The following instructions are recommended for Form B:

> This is a storytelling test. I have some pictures here that I am going to show you, and for each picture I want you to make up a story. Tell what has happened before and what is happening now. Say what the people are feeling and thinking and how it will come out. You can make up any kind of story you please. Do you understand? Well, then, here's the first picture. You have five minutes to make up a story. See how well you can do. (p. 3)

And the following instructions are recommended for children:

> I have some pictures here that I am going to show you, and for each picture I want you to make up a story. Tell what has happened before and what is happening now. Say what the people are feeling and thinking and how it will come out. You can make up any kind of story you please. Do you understand? Well, then, here is the first picture. You have five minutes to make up a story. See how well you can do. (p. 4)

Bellak (1986) criticizes Murray's opening sentence in the instructions for Form A, claiming that it makes the examinee suspicious and thus impairs his or her performance. Not only is the opening sentence in the instructions for Form A often omitted, but the instructions are frequently adapted to the age, intelligence, personality, and circumstances of the examinee. Karon (1981) maintains that standard instructions are less important than making certain that the examinee tells good stories. He finds the following instructions adequate:

> I'm going to show you a set of ten pictures, one at time. I want you to tell me what is going on, what the characters might be feeling and thinking, what led up to it, and what the outcome might be. In other words tell me a good story.

When the examinee has finished the first story, the examiner says, "O.K., that was pretty good. Now let's see what you can do with this one."

Self-Administration

The following instructions are usually given to people who self-administer the test, that is, write down their stories themselves (Bellak, 1986):

1. Please write a story about each picture in this folder.

2. Do not look at the pictures before you are ready to write.

3. Look at one picture at a time only, in the order given, and write as dramatic a story as you can about each. Tell what has led up to the event shown in the picture, describe what is happening at the moment, what the characters are thinking and feeling; and then give the outcome. Write your thoughts as they come to your mind.

4. It should not be necessary to spend more than about seven minutes per story, although you may spend more time if you wish.

5. Write about 300 words per story, or about one typing page if you write in long hand. If at all possible, please type the long hand story later, without changes, in duplicate, double-spaced, one story per page.

6. Please number the stories as you go along, and then put your name on the front sheet. (p. 47)

This method has the advantage of saving time for the examiner, but there are several disadvantages. For example, the examinee's emotional responses are not observed and recorded by the examiner. The opportunity for the examiner to intervene if the examinee becomes discouraged and the ability of the examiner to control the length of the story are also lost. Finally, the examinee's spontaneity may be affected; shorter, less elaborate stories are usually obtained when examinees write their own responses to the TAT pictures.

Group Administration

Projecting TAT pictures onto a screen by means of an overhead or slide projector makes it possible to administer the test to a large group of examinees simultaneously. In group administration, the instructions given previously for self-administration are presented to the entire group, and everyone is expected to write down his or her own story as each picture is projected. Although efficient, group administration possesses the same disadvantages as those described above for self-administration.

The results of empirical comparisons between individual and group administered TATs indicate that the two procedures are not necessarily equivalent. In a study of 30 university students, Eron and Ritter (1951) found that the stories obtained in oral individual administration were longer, less happy, and less flippant, but essentially equivalent in thematic content to stories obtained in group administration. Fewer differences between individual and group administration were found by Clark (1944) in a study of 50 university students. When the results of administering the TAT to these students as a group were compared with the results of individual administration of a portion of the test to the same students, the differences were negligible. The standard clinical, or individual, procedure proved to be only slightly better than the group procedure. This finding led Clark to conclude that the group administered TAT can serve as an effective screening test when individual administration is not feasible.

Follow-Up Inquiry

Inquiry into the TAT stories of examinees can serve several functions. It can, for instance, ensure that the examinee has followed the instructions and that the stories include the three A's—action, antecedents, and aftermath, along with the characters' thoughts and feelings. Associations or thoughts obtained during the inquiry concerning the proper names of people, places, dates, or any unusual information can be crucial for accurate interpretation of the stories.

Rapaport (1946) suggested that an inquiry be conducted after each story is told. Other clinicians (e.g., Bellak, 1986) suggest conducting an inquiry only after all stories have been told, a procedure that may facilitate the movement of unconscious or preconscious material to consciousness. On the other hand, by conducting an inquiry after each story one can stay with the manifest content and ensure that each story is complete in accordance with Murray's basic instructions.

After the examinee has provided stories for all the pictures presented, and perhaps in subsequent sessions, inquiry can be continued to determine the latent, or less apparent, meaning of the stories. Such an inquiry can also serve as an important tool in psychotherapy.

Shortened TAT Card Sets

Administration of the TAT may not only produce writer's cramp but it can also take a great deal of time. This is especially true when the entire set of 20 cards is administered. Bellak (1986) suggests that an optimal amount of data is obtained from responses to ten TAT pictures, which can be administered in a single hour. He recommends pictures 1, 2, 3BM, 4, 6BM, 7BM, 11, 12M, and 13MF for testing any male and pictures 1, 2, 3BM, 4, 6GF, 7GF, 9GF, 11, and 13MF for testing any female. Bellak includes 3BM in the list of picture stimuli for females because clinically it works well for both males and females and is more effective than its counterpart, 3GF. The specific problem of the examinee is also an important factor in TAT card selection. Cards 12M and 15, for example, are particularly appropriate for patients with reactive depression or acute grief reaction due to the death of loved ones. And cards 9BM, 10, 17BM, and 18BM are considered important in the psychological assessment of individuals with sexual orientation disturbances or fears of being homosexual.

Other recommendations for a shortened TAT card set have been made. From rankings of the ten TAT cards judged most valuable for a basic test set by 170 highly experienced psychologists, Hartman (1970) proposed that cards 1, 2, 3BM, 4, 6BM, 7BM, 13MF, and 8BM be administered for purposes of clinical research and teaching. For assessing adolescent males, Cooper (1981) recommended using cards 4, 6BM, 3BM, 8BM, 10, 18BM, 15, 7BM, 1, 13B. Finally, the Menninger Institute approach to the TAT consists of the following sequence, regardless of sex: 1, 5, 15, 3BM, 15, 10, 7GF, 13MF, 18GF, 12M.

An Illustration: Testing Juvenile Delinquents

In diagnostic workups for a juvenile court system, this author found cards 1, 3BM, 4, 6BM, 7BM, 9BM, 10, 13MF, 13B, 14, 17BM, and 18BM to be most useful. The following response is typical of the stories told by juvenile delinquents to card 1: *The boy is wondering how much money he can get for this violin if he steals it from the school and then sells it on the street.* Another frequent plot is that this boy is just sitting there and thinking about how boring it is to play the violin. Bellak (1986) maintains that card 1 is probably the most useful card with adolescents. It is often descriptive of how examinees deal with impulse control, especially with respect to personal dictates versus environmental demands. It may provide information on parent-child relationships as well as the nature, intensity, and mechanism for the resolution of achievement needs. The most frequently occurring stories given by delinquents to card 1 tend to be characterized by the absence of comments on relationships with parents; such children rarely comment on their relationships with their parent(s), or when made, the comments tend to be negative. This fact can be attributed to the emotional impoverishment suffered by delinquents, whose parents are often absent or provide little emotional warmth. Achievement needs are often present and strong in responses to card 1, but their direction is usually counter to what is considered socially desirable. Narcissism and obsession with elaborate methods of crime are also displayed in stories given to this card.

A typical response to card 3BM is, *This guy just killed himself. No one liked him, and he didn't like himself.* Another frequently occurring plot among delinquents is that this kid has been in a fight. *He got hurt pretty bad, but he was able to hurt a lot of other people.* Bellak (1986) suggests that this highly useful picture elicits themes of guilt, depression, impulse control, and aggression. Guilt is often absent in delinquent protocols, but aggression is strongly expressed. This aggression can be internally directed or, at other times, externally directed. The gun on the floor in the lower left portion of card 3BM is usually significant; it can be used to do harm to oneself or to others. Depression, aggression, suicidal and homicidal ideation, gesturing, and intent may be elicited by this potently useful scene. The themes that seem to be present most often in the protocols of delinquents are those of loneliness, isolation, alienation, depression, aggression, and a lack of sufficient impulse control. If guilt were to arise, it might be a good sign since it can easily be linked to remorse, an indicator of residual strength and health.

Characteristic of delinquents' responses to card 4 can be, *This guy is about to beat up a man who just made a pass at his girlfriend. His girlfriend is trying to stop him, but he breaks away from her and he creams him.* Another frequently occurring plot among delinquents is that *this is Burt Reynolds and his lady. Burt is getting ready to make a drug bust, but his lady friend wants him to stay with her so that they can get high together and have a good time.*

Card 4 also serves as a barometer in appraising the quality of male-female relationships and various feelings, thoughts, attitudes, and beliefs about sex roles. Themes of betrayal and infidelity are common. The man may be depicted as aggressive, distracted, destructive, or fed up. The woman is often depicted as luring, protective, detaining, or controlling. The woman's seductive look and revealing dress elicit sexual commentary. This third party easily suggests a theme of triangular jealousy in which betrayal or infidelity has occurred. Delinquents are often pulled into this theme, expressing dramatic hostility and aggression toward the third party. The picture also stimulates memories of films such as *Gone with the Wind* and the like. Teenagers often idolize Hollywood heroes, identifying with and introjecting many of their characteristics. The woman symbolizes control that is strongly rebelled against and overcome; she ineffectually attempts to control the man; he does as he pleases. The issues of impulse control and autonomy versus dependency, which are manifested in these kinds of stories, are serious problems for delinquents—and to some extent for normal adolescents.

Delinquents tend to respond to card 6BM with stories similar to the following: *This guy is saying goodbye to his aunt before going off to jail.* Another frequently occurring theme is that this guy was called into the principal's office because he missed so many days of school. She tells him that he is not going to graduate from high school. Bellak (1986) suggests that card 6BM is indispensable when testing males because it elicits mother-son relationship problems and similar problems such as those relating to wives and women in general. *Oedipal* themes often emerge. Most juvenile delinquents, however, defend against the recognition of the woman as mother, substituting an aunt, a teacher, or some other woman who is a significant authority figure. She often exerts control, which is usually resisted.

Typical stories told by delinquents to card 7BM are as follows: *This is a guy and his lawyer, and from the look on his face he is not going to be getting out any time soon, or This is a guy and his lawyer. They are talking about his case because they have to go to court.* In response to this card, a child often defends against the father figure, substituting a lawyer. The seriousness of the picture is seldom underestimated, and the outcome is often pessimistic. Bellak (1986) claims that card 7BM is essential in bringing out the father-son relationship and related themes. Attitudes toward authority figures, as seen for example in boss-employee relationships, are evoked and frequently included in the commentary.

One delinquent responded to card 9BM with "These guys have just smoked a whole lot of marijuana and have gotten all high and mellow. These guys don't have anything better to do." According to Bellak (1986), this picture is instrumental in disclosing contemporary man-to-man relationships and insight into social relationships in general. It could be important to determine with whom the examinee identifies. Is he the center of the group, or is he outside the group looking askance at them?

Social prejudices and homosexual issues may also be brought to the surface via card 9BM. Some delinquents tend to relate to the relative inactivity of the men rather than to group cohesiveness and closeness, a fact that may reflect the high degree of idleness of many delinquent children. A large percentage are truant, unemployed, and consequently idle.

A distinction can be made between the responses of socialized and unsocialized delinquents. The child with a socialized conduct disorder tends to associate with the group theme in the picture, whereas the unsocialized child tends to comment on nongroup dimensions. The picture also elicits comments regarding drug abuse, for example, marijuana: as many teenage patients have stated, "These men look wasted." Stories concerned with homosexuality and fears of being homosexual can also be expected in response to card 9BM, but this author's experience is that juvenile delinquents tend to refrain from comments about homosexuality. Exceptions occur more frequently in borderline, and sometimes psychotic, patients, where ego boundaries and defenses are weak and grossly dysfunctional.

Card 10 tends to elicit stories such as, *These people are slow dancing now and later they will be making love, or This man is whispering sweet nothings into his girlfriend's ear, and she falls for it.* This card is designed to bring out feelings, attitudes, and beliefs concerning the relationships between men and women (Bellak, 1986). The arrival versus departure theme may be noteworthy and revealing of dependency, autonomy, and even hostility needs. Bellak suggests that a description of two men embracing or kissing may be indicative of homosexuality or homosexual tendencies.

Dominance and arrogance are typical among juvenile delinquents. Teenage boys are particularly fond of boasting about their own sexual prowess, and sometimes fonder of boasting about the sexual prowess of another male. Consequently, in responding to card 10 they note the overwhelming power that the man has over the woman, partly because he is so "cool" and partly because the woman is so gullible and "easy." In their fantasy and probably in their reality, juvenile delinquents see intimacy as a power struggle where at all costs they need to be in control. Manipulation is a powerful technique in achieving such control.

Here is a response given by a juvenile delinquent to card 13B: "This is Jimmy Carter. When he was a boy he hardly had a house to live in. He hardly had shoes on his feet, or a mother or a father to take care of him. He hardly had food to eat, or kids to play with. When he grew up he became President of the United States, and now we hardly have the United States." Another typical response from a teenage delinquent is that this little boy is lonely. He has no father, and his mother is always busy.

Among juvenile delinquents, card 13B can be a powerful look into earlier childhood experiences. Issues of loneliness, emotional impoverishment, emptiness, pessimism, sadness, and identity confusion (Who am I, and what is life all about?) are drawn out. Emotional impoverishment almost always underlies delinquency, and this card can serve as an effective means of therapeutic communication. In adults, this card similarly evokes childhood experiences that may be dynamically significant for psychotherapy.

A teenage delinquent gave the following response to card 13MF: "This man has just raped and killed this woman, and now he is wiping the sweat from his forehead." Another typical response obtained from delinquents is that this man has just raped his girlfriend because she wouldn't give in to him. Bellak (1986) states that card 13MF helps disclose sexual conflicts in both men and women. Groth-Marnat (1984) maintains that it provides information on a person's attitudes and feelings toward his sexual partner, especially those experienced immediately before and after sexual intercourse. The relationship between the patient's aggressive and sexual feelings is often woven into the story. In a sample of juvenile delinquents tested by the author, the respondents expressed sex and aggression in their plots. In fact, rape is such a common theme in the responses of teenage delinquents that card 13MF has sometimes been referred to as the "rape card." The intertwined display of sex and aggression in the form of rape is indicative of sexual immaturity. The lack of remorse suggests inadequate superego (conscience) development, which is typical among delinquents. The importance of power and lack of impulse control—taking what one desires when one desires it—are also evident in the stories.

A typical delinquent response to card 14 is, *This guy is going to commit suicide. He is about to jump from a high building.* Another common response from juvenile delinquents is that this man is committing a B & E (breaking-in-and-entry) and is getting away with the loot. Still another common response is that the man is looking out on the smoggy city and wondering what's the sense of it all. Bellak (1986) says that it is essential to administer card 14 when one suspects suicidal tendencies, which may be expressed in a story of jumping out of the window. Contemplation, philosophical thought, and wish-fulfillment stories are also expressed in responses to this card. In a sample of delinquents stories range from suicide to B & E to philosophical contemplation.

A delinquent responded to card 17BM, "This guy has climbed up a rope so he can get a free view of the concert." Another common response is that the man is showing off in front of his friends; they dared him to climb to the top and he did it. Bellak (1986) says that this picture is useful in revealing fears, as expressed in stories of flight or escape from fire, another person, or some unknown physical trauma. Oedipal fears (repressed feelings of romantic attraction for the parent of the opposite sex and repressed feelings of threat from the parent of the same sex) or homosexual feelings may also be evoked. Active outgoing people who are achievement oriented often tell stories of a man climbing up a rope (McClelland, 1961; Mira, 1940). Several juvenile delinquents in one sample this author studied expressed an underlying fear of being left out in responding to card 17BM.

A typical delinquent response to card 18BM is, *This man is about to be mugged*. Groth-Marnat (1984) poses some interesting questions regarding the apparent anxiety depicted in this picture. Consider the following: Does the patient see himself as a victim of circumstances in which he is completely helpless? How does he resolve his feelings? Is helplessness a trait or a state? Juvenile delinquents tend to agree that the man in the picture is about to be mugged. The stories usually vary in details such as, *He was walking where he shouldn't have been.* or *Serves him right for being such a whimp.* Delinquents virtually never admit to fantasizing themselves as the victim; they are much more apt to be innocent bystanders or even the aggressor.

Scoring and Interpreting TAT Stories

A variety of scoring and interpreting systems exist for analyzing TAT stories. As with other projectives, it is assumed that examinees project their own needs, desires, and emotional conflicts into the story and its characters, and the stories should be interpreted with this in mind.

Although the usual methods of scoring and interpreting the TAT are highly impressionistic, scores determined by one of the more systematic scoring procedures are fairly reliable and can be interpreted in terms of norms based on standardization studies. Murray (1938) quantified the needs expressed in TAT stories in the context of his theory of personality, which is outlined in Chapter 1. Among the alternatives to Murray's (1938) procedure of scoring stories by rating needs and press on a five-point scale are the systems developed by Wyatt (1947), Eron (1950), Dana (1955), McClelland (1971), and Bellak (1986). A variety of derived scores, such as Wynne and Singer's (1963) communication deviance measure and Karon's (1981) pathogenesis index, have been found useful in the diagnosis of psychopathology.

Clinical Interpretation

A basic ground rule in the clinical interpretation of TAT stories is that the interpersonal scenario described by the examinee cannot be taken at face value as reflecting the examinee's actual current or former relationships. The analysis is an analysis of fantasy, and waking fantasy has about as much correlation with reality as dreams do. To understand, and therefore correctly interpret, the fantasies expressed in TAT stories the clinician must consider them against a background of psychiatric interview findings, the results of a mental status examination, observational and historical data, and other psychological test data. The most important guideline in interpreting a series of TAT stories is to search for recurrent themes and determine how the TAT responses fit into the context of interview and other test findings. In using TAT stories to diagnose psychological disorders, clinicians often look for certain *signs*. For example, slowness or delays in responding may indicate depression. Overcautiousness and preoccupation with details suggest obsessive-compulsive disorders, and stories by male examinees that include negative comments about women or affection for other men may point to homosexuality. However, these interpretations should be viewed as hypotheses, to be confirmed by other data, rather than as final diagnoses.

Interpretation is an activity that is common to all sciences, but a certain artistic ability is required for good psychodiagnostic work. Karon (1981) maintains that a fundamental principle in interpreting the TAT is to consider the stories one at a time, sentence by sentence, while asking oneself: Out of all the possibilities that exist, why would a human being say that? Murray (1943) talks about having a certain flair for the task of interpretation, possessing rigorously trained critical intuition, and having an extensive background of clinical experience. In addition, thorough training in the use of the test instrument, the TAT, is required. Thus, Murray recommends that the interpreter have considerable practice in analyzing stories in contexts where the conclusions can be checked against known facts about thoroughly studied personalities.

Murray's Interpretative System

Murray's (1943) system of analyzing the content of TAT stories incorporates six elements:

- The main character(s) or *hero(es)*.
- The motives, trends, and feelings of the hero(es).
- The environmental forces (*press*) in the hero(es) environment (which may be benign or inimical).

- The *outcomes* (happy or unhappy? results of actions by hero or environmental forces?).
- The *themas*, and the *interests* and *sentiments* expressed

The first step in the analysis is to determine in which character the storyteller is most interested. This hero character is the one who is most integrally involved in the outcome and plays a leading role in the plot. He or she is often the character who most resembles the storyteller in age, goals, sentiments, sex, status, and perhaps other areas. The story is frequently told from the main character's perspective, and his or her feelings and motives are most intimately portrayed. The main character may, of course, be a heroine, or there may be two main characters—a hero and a heroine, or any combination of the sexes.

The second step in interpretation is to examine the personalities of the heroes. What do they feel? What are their motives and unusual or unique characteristics? Most importantly, what are their needs and how are they satisfied? (See Table 12–2.) In quantifying the needs of the hero, Murray (1943) recommends using a five-point scale on which 1 indicates the slightest hint of a need and 5 a potent form of the need or a repeated occurrence of a milder form. In addition to rating the needs, duration, frequency, and relevance or relative importance of the needs in the plot in combination determine the strength of the need.

An assessment of the hero's environment constitutes the third step in interpretation. What are the physical and interpersonal environments, in other words the press, on the hero(es)? (See Table 12–3.) Similar to those of needs, ratings of press

Table 12–2	**Murray's List of Psychogenic Needs**	

Needs concerned with power, prestige, or knowledge

Achievement	Construction	Exposition
Acquisition	Counteraction	Recognition
Aggression	Dominance	Understanding

Needs concerned with love, praise, sympathy, and dependence

| Affiliation | Nurturance | Succorance |
| Deference | Sex | |

Needs concerned with change, excitement, freedom, and play

| Autonomy | Excitance | |
| Adventure, change, travel | Playmirth | |

Other needs

Abasement	Harm avoidance	Retention
Blame avoidance	Passivity	Sentience
Cognizance	Rejection	

Adapted from Murray, 1938, pp. 152–226.

Murray's List of Press		Table 12–3

Press of deprivation

Acquisition	Retention

Press of emptiness and rejection

Lack	Rejection
Loss	Uncongenial environment

Press of force and restraint

Dominance	Imposed duty, task, and training

Press of aggression

Aggression

Press of danger, death, and injury

Affliction	Physical danger
Death of a hero	Physical injury

Press of love, respect, friendliness, and dependence

Affiliation	Sex
Deference	Succorance
Nurturance	

Other press

Birth of offspring	Example
Claustrum	Exposition
Cognizance	Luck

Adapted from Murray, 1938, pp. 291–292.

are made on a 1 to 5 scale with 5 being the most intense press. The criteria for strength of a press are intensity, duration, frequency, and general significance in the plot. The basic difference between needs and press is that needs are forces originating within the person whereas press are forces originating from the environment.

The fourth step in Murray's interpretative system is a comparative strength analysis of hero versus press forces. Do needs dominate press or vice versa? Is the hero's path to achievement difficult or easy? When confronted with obstacles, does the hero get stronger, overcoming his adversary, or succumb? Is the hero active, making things happen, or is he merely reactive, allowing things to happen to him? Is he more dependent or autonomous? Does he succeed when others help him or when he strives alone? After a misdeed, does the hero get rewarded or punished? How much energy does the hero direct against himself? How does the hero react to failure? Under what conditions does he fail? What role do others play in his failure? What is the ratio of failures to successes? And finally, what is the ratio of happy to unhappy endings?

The fifth step in Murray's system is a consideration of simple and complex themas. A *simple thema* is an interaction of the hero's need(s), press, or fusion of press with the outcome (e.g., the success or failure of the hero). *Complex themas* are combinations and networks of simple themas. Common themas focus on issues such as conflict of desires, love, punishment, war, achievement, and the like. Murray notes that the interpreter need not score separate variables in order to make a thematic analysis. Some of the common themas or themes elicited by the 31 TAT pictures are given in Table 12–4.

The sixth and last step in Murray's interpretative scheme is an evaluation of interests and sentiments. What characteristic interests and sentiments does the storyteller attribute to his hero or heroes? What is the nature of these interests and sentiments? How and why does the narrator choose them? In what manner does he deal with these interests and sentiments? What are men and women, young and old, attracted to? How are they related to their "loved object(s)?" How do men relate to men and women to women? What is the mechanism of their relationship formation and maintenance?

Murray (1943) states that the conclusions reached by an analysis of TAT stories must be regarded as good leads or working hypotheses to be verified by other methods, rather than as proved facts. Two tentative, and therefore potentially correctable, underlying assumptions are made regarding interpretation. One assumption is that the attributes of the hero—his needs, motives, emotional states, interests, and sentiments—reflect and represent the storyteller's own personality tendencies. A second assumption is that the press variables symbolize forces and energy systems in the current, previous, and future environments as perceived by the storyteller. Keeping these assumptions in perspective, the skilled TAT interpreter never loses sight of the fact that this instrument is a device for eliciting fantasies. And in order to obtain an accurate appraisal of the examinee and his or her use of defense mechanisms—repression in particular, the interpreter must operationally distinguish between what is fantasy and what is reality.

Psychometric Issues and Research

It should be noted that many other interpretive systems have been developed for the TAT; Bellak (1986) reviews almost two dozen. Polyson, Norris and Ott (1985) report a recent decline in TAT research, but suggest that a renewal of interest will most likely require a synthesis of scoring and interpretation methods. They attribute the decline to the dated quality of the TAT pictures, a lack of standardization in card selection, administration, and scoring procedures (Stein, 1978; Vane, 1981), as well as relatively unimpressive or undetermined reliability and validity (Klopfer & Taulbee, 1976; Schwartz, 1978).

Reliability

As is the case with most open-ended, free-response techniques such as projectives, the reliability of the TAT has been difficult to establish by conventional psy-

| Typical Themes Elicited by TAT Pictures | Table 12–4 |

Picture 1. Relationship toward parental figures; achievement; symbolic sexual responses; aggression, anxiety, body image or self-image; obsessive preoccupations; sexual activity.

Picture 2. Family relationships; autonomy versus compliance; heterosexual and homosexual attitudes; pregnancy; compulsive tendencies; role of the sexes.

Picture 3BM. Latent homosexuality; aggression.

Picture 3GF. Depressive feelings.

Picture 4. Male-female relationships; triangular jealousy.

Picture 5. Mother who may be watching; masturbation; voyeurism; primal scene; fear of attack; rescue fantasies.

Picture 6BM. Mother-son relationships.

Picture 6GF. Relationship of females to father; father-son relationships.

Picture 7GF. Relationship between mother and child in females; attitude toward expectancy of children.

Picture 8BM. Aggression, ambition; Oedipal relationship.

Picture 8GF. Contemporary man-to-man relationships; homosexual drives and fears; social prejudices.

Picture 9GF. Depression and suicidal tendencies; paranoia.

Picture 10. Relationship of men to women; latent homosexuality.

Picture 11. Infantile or primitive fears; fears of attack; oral aggression, anxiety.

Picture 12M. Relationship of a younger man to an older man; passive homosexual fears.

Picture 12F. Conceptions of mother figures.

Picture 12BG. Suicidal tendencies; depression.

Picture 13MF. Sexual conflicts in both men and women; economic deprivation; oral tendencies; obsessive-compulsive trends.

Picture 13B. Stories of childhood.

Picture 13G. Not a very useful picture.

Picture 14. Sexual identification; fears in relation to darkness; suicidal tendencies; esthetic interests.

Picture 15. Death in the immediate family; fears of death; depressive tendencies.

Picture 16. May be extremely valuable with verbally gifted subjects.

Picture 17BM. Oedipal fears; homosexual feelings; body image.

Picture 17GF. Suicidal tendencies in women.

Picture 18BM. Anxiety in males.

Picture 18GF. How aggression is handled by women; mother-daughter conflicts.

Picture 19. Sometimes useful with children, but otherwise not notable.

Picture 20. Fear of dark (females).

Bellak (1986). Reprinted by permission of the publisher, C.P.S., Inc., Box 83, Larchmont, New York 10538.

chometric techniques. Various sources of error contribute to the low reliabilities of these assessments. Not only must one account for differences in the stories told by the same person on different occasions, but also differences in the scoring and interpretation of those stories.

A number of older studies (Tomkins, 1947; Sanford, 1943; Harrison & Rotter, 1945) found most interrater reliability coefficients for the TAT to be modest. With respect to test-retest reliability, Tomkins (1947) determined the test-retest coefficients of TAT protocols, scored according to Murray's needs-press system, as a function of time in three groups of 45 young women. A decrease was noted in reliability from .80 at a two-month interval to .60 at a six-month interval and .50 at a ten-month interval between initial testing and retesting. More recently, however, Winter and Stewart (1977) reported the median test-retest reliability from various studies of the TAT to be approximately .30. The relatively unstructured nature of the test task and the lack of objectivity in scoring are important contributory factors to the low reliability coefficients found in psychometric research on the TAT. Other possible sources of error leading to unreliability are discussed by Kraiger, Hakel, and Cornelius (1984).

In conducting diagnostic workups for court hearings on juvenile delinquents, which requires testing and retesting defendants accused of repeated offenses, the author frequently encountered the problem of relatively low test-retest reliability coefficients of the TAT. Among children and teenagers there is a high degree of personality plasticity that contributes to the low reliabilities of the test. Furthermore, children may remember the stories that they told the first time and want to create something different, leading to low test-retest coefficients (White, 1943; Sanford, 1943). The examinee's emotional state and the conditions under which the test is administered can also affect TAT responses, and hence the reliability of the test. For example, Bellak (1942) found a significant elevation of expressed aggression in the content of TAT stories when examinees' initial stories were sharply criticized.

Validity

In view of the fact that the TAT is an instrument for analyzing fantasy, which may or may not reflect actual behavior, the problem of determining the validity of the TAT is extremely complex. The validity of the instrument has usually been investigated consensually, or by a construct validation approach, by determining its relationships to performance on other projective techniques, case history material, and other fantasy material such as dreams. As is the case with most projective techniques, a wide range of validity coefficients have been obtained with the TAT.

A fundamental point that must be kept in mind in analyzing the validity of the TAT is that the measurement of any variable (e.g., need or press) by this technique, or any other projective technique for that matter, is accompanied by errors of measurement that tend to lower its validity coefficients. Another important point is that the validity of the TAT is limited by its internal consistency, that is, the extent to which different pictures tap the same variables.

With respect to diagnostic validity, the TAT has been found to discriminate among normals, neurotics, and psychotics on measures of story organization, popular references, and superfluous commentary (Dana, 1955, 1959) and on measures of emotional tone, story outcome, and activity level (Eron, 1950; Ritter & Effron, 1952). However, the test has failed to differentiate depressives from normals in terms of story tone (Eron, 1950; Sharkey & Ritzler, 1985). The validity of evaluating ethnic minorities and other groups such as the aged and the disabled by means of the TAT has also been questioned. Furthermore, the TAT has been criticized because of the negative, sad tone of many of the pictures, which too easily induces pessimistic and depressive reactions or at least exerts a negative stimulus pull on the storyteller (Eron, Terry & Callahan, 1950; Goldfried & Zax, 1965). As a result, many modifications and new apperceptive devices have been developed—instruments that present clinicians and researchers with new psychometric problems.

TAT Modifications and Other Apperception Tests

Criticism of the TAT in its original form has stimulated the development of a number of modifications. For example, reported misdiagnoses of black and Hispanic children have encouraged the production of more culturally appropriate apperception techniques (Thompson, 1949; Malgady, Costantino & Rogler, 1984). Other modifications have been made for children, the elderly, and the disabled (Bellak & Bellak, 1973; Wolk & Wolk, 1971). Criticisms regarding the dated quality of the TAT pictures, the limited range of human experience depicted in them (Ritzler, Sharkey & Chudy, 1980), the predominant sadness in most scenes (Eron, Terry & Callahan, 1950; Goldfried & Zax, 1965), the relative lack of specificity in the instructions for administration (McClelland, 1971), the low test-retest reliability (Entwisle, 1972; Winter & Stewart, 1977), and the decline in TAT research (Polyson, Norris & Ott, 1985) have prompted other changes.

Minority Groups

Although there has been an unfortunate history of abuse and misuse of projective techniques among minority children (Anderson & Anderson, 1955), the need to develop reliable and valid tests for the personality assessment of ethnic, racial, and linguistic minority groups cannot be overestimated (Padilla, 1979).

Thompson TAT   On the assumption that blacks identify more readily with pictures of other blacks than with those of whites, 21 of the original TAT pictures were redrawn with black figures and published as the Thompson Modification of the TAT (T-TAT) (Thompson, 1949). The figures on the T-TAT were designed to be similar to those on the standard TAT, but they are not completely comparable in facial expression or situation to those on the latter instrument (Murstein, 1959; Cowan & Goldberg, 1967).

Thompson (1949) believed that identification with the figures in the pictures is greatest when the picture stimuli reflect the culture of the storyteller. He found that blacks told longer stories to the T-TAT than to the standard TAT pictures, a result confirmed by several other researchers (Cowan & Goldberg, 1967; Cowan, 1971; Bailey & Green, 1977). Entwisle (1972) suggested that the number of words used in telling a TAT story is an indicator of verbal achievement and academic socialization, and consequently there should be a positive relationship between achievement motivation and the length of stories told. However, Bailey & Green (1977) reported that black youths do not necessarily obtain higher need achievement scores on the Thompson TAT than on the standard TAT, but that white youths obtain higher need achievement scores on the standard TAT than matched black youths.

TEMAS Special TAT-like tests have also been developed for other groups. One such apperception technique is the TEMAS (Spanish for "themes" and an acronym for "tell me a story"), which consists of 23 chromatic pictures depicting Hispanic characters interacting in urban settings (Costantino, 1978). Malgady, Costantino and Rogler (1984) reported that TEMAS discriminates between Puerto Rican clinical samples and matched samples of school children. These investigators also found the reliability and validity of TEMAS to be respectable, supporting the diagnostic and clinical usefulness of the instrument. In another study, Costantino, Malgady, and Vasquez (1981) found that Hispanic children are more verbally fluent in telling stories about the TEMAS pictures than about the TAT cards.

Picture Tests for Children

Two of the main sources of criticism of the TAT and modifications of it are the lack of representativeness and variety in the stimulus material, lack of psychometric rigor in design, standardization, and validation, and inappropriateness of the test for certain age groups. Illustrative of TAT-like instruments constructed specifically for younger age groups are the Symonds Picture Story Test, the Children's Apperception Test, and the Blacky Pictures. Each of the 22 pictures on the Symonds Picture Story Test by P. M. Symonds (Teachers College Press, 1948) was designed to be more appropriate for adolescents than the TAT pictures. However, the Symonds has not been as popular as the following apperception tests for children.

Children's Apperception Test Bellak and Bellak (1949) constructed the CAT (The Psychological Corporation, 1949, 1974) because the TAT was not considered appropriate for young children. Based on the assumption that young children identify more closely with animals than humans and hence will tell more elaborate stories about them, the CAT consists of ten pictures of animals in various situations (see Table 12–5). The ten CAT cards, selected from an original set of 18, were designed for children from three to ten and depict animal figures involved in human activities portraying common childhood conflicts.

Descriptions of the CAT Pictures	Table 12–5

Picture 1. Chicks seated around a table on which is a large bowl of food. Off to one side is a large chicken, dimly outlined.

Picture 2. One bear pulling a rope on one side while another bear and a baby bear pull on the other side.

Picture 3. A lion with pipe and cane, sitting in a chair; in the lower right corner a little mouse appears in a hole.

Picture 4. A kangaroo with a bonnet on her head, carrying a basket with a milk bottle; in her pouch is a baby kangaroo with a balloon; on a bicycle, a larger kangaroo child.

Picture 5. A darkened room with a large bed in the background; a crib in the foreground in which are two baby bears.

Picture 6. A darkened cave with two dimly outlined bear figures in the background; a baby bear lying in the foreground.

Picture 7. A tiger with bared fangs and claws leaping at a monkey which is also leaping through the air.

Picture 8. Two adult monkeys sitting on a sofa drinking from tea cups. One adult monkey in foreground sitting on a hassock talking to a baby monkey.

Picture 9. A darkened room seen through an open door from a lighted room. In the darkened room there is a child's bed in which a rabbit sits up looking through the door.

Picture 10. A baby dog lying across the knees of an adult dog; both figures with a minimum of expression in their features. The figures are set in the foreground of a bathroom.

Bellak (1986). Reprinted by permission of the publisher, C.P.S., Inc., Box 83, Larchmont, NY 10538.

In a recent review of the CAT, Hatt (1985) concludes that the CAT is a useful clinical tool with children, but the unstandardized administration and scoring of the test permits considerable subjectivity. In addition, the interrater, internal-consistency, and test-retest reliabilities are poor, and the validity of the test is inconclusive. However, the lack of adequate norms for the CAT is not viewed by Bellak (1986) as an overwhelming shortcoming; he feels that norms are not essential for projective techniques because each record is an adequate sample of the examinee's needs and behavior. Bellak also designed an additional series of ten irregularly shaped picture cards, the CAT Supplement (CAT-S), for further exploration of sources of tension in children. An extension of the CAT to older children, the CAT-H, composed of pictures of humans in situations paralleling those of the CAT animal pictures, is also available from The Psychological Corporation.

Considerable training is required to administer, score, and interpret the CAT. Stories given in response to both the CAT and CAT-H cards are interpreted from the viewpoint of psychodynamic theory, specifically in terms of conflicts, anxiety, and guilt. Scores may be determined on reality testing, regulation of drives, object relations, thought processing, ego functioning, defense mechanisms, stimulus sensitivity, autonomy, integrational ability, and mastery-competence. Because of developmental changes in children, analysis of the CAT differs from that of the TAT. Allowance must be made for a child's relative immaturity, a different quality of defensiveness, a greater frequency of primary process (wishful) thinking, in addition to confabulated (confused or mixed) and perseverative (repetitious) responses. A checklist, the Haworth Schedule of Adaptive Mechanisms, is available to assist in interpreting CAT and CAT-H stories.

Blacky Pictures   As with the CAT, development of the Blacky Pictures (Blum, 1950) was based on the premise that children (age five years and over) identify more readily with animals than humans. The Blacky Pictures consist of a set of 11 cartoons depicting the adventures of the dog Blacky and his canine family. The characters are Mama, Papa, Tippy (the sibling), and Blacky. Each cartoon is described in a standard sentence by the examiner, who then asks the child to make up a story about the situation. Afterward, a set of standard questions is asked. For example, the examiner presents Card II (anal sadism) by saying "Here Blacky is relieving himself (herself) . . . "After the child finishes telling his or her story, the examiner presents the following multiple-choice questions:

1. What was Blacky's main reason for defecating there?
     a. He wanted to spite somebody. . . . Who?
     b. He was doing what Mama and Papa told him to.
   *c. He picked the spot by accident.
     d. He wanted to keep his own area neat and clean.
2. Which one of the following is Blacky most concerned with here?
     a. Throwing dirt over what he did so that it will be neatly covered up.
   *b. Relieving himself so that his system feels more comfortable.
     c. Getting rid of his anger.
3. Why is Blacky covering it up?
     a. He wants to make as little mess as possible.
     b. He doesn't want Mama and Papa to find out.
   *c. He's automatically doing what he's been taught.

The starred choices are the correct, or the least conflict oriented, responses.
     Stories given to the Blacky Pictures are scored on 13 dimensions and interpreted from the viewpoint of psychoanalytic theory, specifically in terms of stages of psychosexual development, conflicts, anxiety, and guilt. Sibling rivalry, guilt feelings, ego ideals, love-objects, oral eroticism, oral sadism, anal sadism, Oedipal intensity, and masturbation or penis envy may be noted in the stories. The pronounced psychoanalytic orientation, in addition to the ambiguous theoretical premises regarding maladjustment and development, have been sources of criticism of the test. However, the reliability and validity of the Blacky Pictures are respectable (Blum & Hunt, 1952). Although it was initially standardized on adults, children

find the Blacky Pictures with animal figures portrayed as a family attractive and tend to be quite responsive. In addition, the instrument is an effective therapeutic tool.

Michigan Picture Test-Revised (MPT-R)   The MPT-R by M. L. Hutt (Grune & Stratton, Inc., 1953–1980) was designed for older children (8–14 years) but is considered appropriate for children from first grade through high school. In constructing this test a genuine effort was made to meet the requirements of adequate standardization and reliability. Although it portrays interpersonal relationships more vividly than the TAT, the MPT-R has been criticized for leaving less to the child's imagination. The MPT-R consists of 15 picture cards and one blank card; seven of the 15 pictures are appropriate for both sexes, four being exclusively for girls and four for boys. Responses to the social and emotional situations depicted in the pictures are scored for a Tension Index (needs for love, extrapunitiveness, intropunitiveness, succorance, superiority, submission, and personal adequacy), Direction of Force (whether the central figure acts or is acted on), and Verb Tense (tense of verbs used by examinee). Scores on these three variables may be combined to yield a Maladjustment Index. The interscorer reliability coefficients of the MPT-R are moderately high, and the results of cross-validation studies are encouraging, but evidence for the validity of the test remains unsatisfactory. Norms are provided for grades 3, 5, and 7.

Roberts Apperception Test for Children   An even more recent effort than the Michigan Picture Test to meet the psychometric standards of a good test with a projective technique is the Roberts Apperception Test for Children (RATC) by G. E. Roberts and D. S. McArthur (Western Psychological Services, 1982). Designed for children 6 to 15 years of age, the RATC is also usable with families. The 27 stimulus cards (line drawings of adults and children in modern clothing) on the test emphasize everyday interpersonal situations, including parental disagreement, parental affection, observation of nudity, school and peer interpersonal events, as well as situations of the sort found on the TAT and CAT. The 27 cards are administered in two overlapping sets of 16 cards each, one set for boys and one for girls. Explicit guidelines are provided for scoring the stories on a series of clinical areas, including Conflict, Anxiety, Aggression, Depression, Rejection, Punishment, Dependency, Support, Closure, Resolution, Unresolved Indicator, Maladaptive Outcome, and other measures such as Ego Functioning Index, Aggression Index, and a Levels of Projection scale. Raw scores on each area are converted to standard scores based on norms, by age and sex, obtained on 200 Caucasian children.

   In a review of the RATC, Friedrich (1984) concluded that it is a promising test that generates stories having many different themes and has a well-documented, easy-to-learn scoring system. The 16-card series is rather long for younger children and leads to briefer, more stereotyped stories. Sines (1985) views the RATC as a serious attempt to combine the flexibility of a projective approach and the quantification possible with a more objective scoring system and norms. However, he predicts that users of the RATC may abandon the objective scoring approach and apply a more global and clinical approach to scoring. Both Friedrich (1984) and Sines (1985) end their reviews with a wait-and-see attitude.

Apperception Tests for the Elderly

The 16 pictures on the Senior Apperception Technique (SAT) by L. and S. Bellak (Western Psychological Services, 1973) were designed specifically for older adults and depict elderly people in a wide range of human circumstances. The situations shown in the pictures are designed to reflect themes of helplessness, illness, loneliness, family difficulties, dependence, and lowered self-esteem; happier, more positive situations are also depicted in certain pictures. As on a similar instrument, the Gerontological Apperception Test (GAT) (Wolk & Wolk, 1971), responses to the pictures on the Senior Apperception Technique reflect serious concerns about health, getting along with other people, and being placed in a nursing or retirement home. In interpreting these tests allowances must be made for changes in personality and behavior due to aging. Furthermore, both the SAT and GAT have been criticized for inadequate norms, stereotyping of the elderly, and as possessing no advantage over the TAT in testing the elderly (J. P. Schaie, 1978; K. W. Schaie, 1978). According to Klopfer and Taulbee (1976), these tests portray elderly people in such a way as to discourage active responding and tend to reveal only superficial aspects of personality.

Picture Projective Test

Another alternative apperception test, the Picture Projective Test (PPT), or Southern Mississippi TAT, was designed by Ritzler, Sharkey, and Chudy (1980). Employing a more rigorous methodology and a wider range of picture materials than the TAT, and consequently evoking a broader range of fantasy responses, this test consists of 30 pictures selected from the *Family of Man* photographic collection of the Museum of Modern Art (1955). Interpersonal involvement is stressed throughout the set of pictures, and, unlike the primarily negative themes elicited by the TAT, the PPT pictures incorporate a balance of positive and negative stimulus cues. Approximately half of the pictures show people manifesting positive affect— smiling, embracing, and dancing, whereas people in the remaining pictures display more negative affect. In most of the pictures in the first half of the test the main characters are involved in high energy activities, whereas those in the second half display more subdued energy and activity levels.

Despite a number of noteworthy competitors, the TAT remains the most widely used of all apperception tests, but its limitations with respect to different age, cultural, and disabled groups, in addition to specificity of the clinical problems for which it is an appropriate assessment tool, have led to a search for apperception tests having greater reliability, validity, and utility. Research involving the TAT has been extensive, but quantity does not necessarily imply quality and questions concerning the clinical utility of the TAT and other apperception instruments are mostly unresolved. Among the areas necessitating greater efforts are scoring, interpretation, validity, reliability, standardization, and the construction of better alternative instruments. Unfortunately, there has been a recent decline in TAT research (Lubin,

Larsen & Matarazzo, 1984; Polyson, Norris & Ott, 1985) and some psychologists view it as something of a dead horse that should be spared further floggings.

Summary

The Thematic Apperception Test (TAT), developed originally by Christina Morgan and Henry Murray, consists of 30 picture cards and a blank card. Depending on the examinee's age, sex, and circumstances, an examiner usually selects 10 of the cards for administration. The pictures are designed to elicit stories that reveal the examinee's conflicts, desires, feelings, and life themes. Those that have been found most useful for testing males in clinical contexts are cards, 1, 2, 3BM, 10, 12M, and 8BM, whereas the clinically most useful cards with females are cards 1, 2, 3BM, 4, 6GF, 7GF, 9GF, 11, and 13MF. The cards are presented one at a time, the examinee being instructed to tell a complete story about each card, including what happened before, what is going on now, and how it will turn out. Administration is typically individual, in which case the examiner presents one card at a time to the examinee, but the TAT can also be self-administered or administered to a group. However, the stories obtained from self- or group-administration tend to be less elaborate than those obtained from individual administration of the test.

In testing psychiatric patients or other individuals having serious problems, a set of TAT pictures is selected that are most likely to reveal the dynamics of the particular disorder. Typical stories obtained from a sample of juvenile delinquents to an appropriate selection of TAT pictures (1, 3BM, 4, 6BM, 7BM, 9BM, 10, 13B, 13MF, 14, 17BM, 18BM) are described in this chapter as an illustration of the kinds of responses that are obtained and what they may mean.

Various methods of scoring and interpreting TAT stories, some of them more objective or structured than others, have been suggested. The traditional method of interpretation, as proposed by Henry Murray, is a rather subjective, impressionistic process centering on an analysis of the needs and personality of the main character (the hero), who frequently represents the examinee, and the environmental forces (press) impinging on him or her. The frequency, intensity, and duration of the stories are taken into account in the interpretation. The interpreter also seeks to establish consensual validation by noting overlapping elements and themes in the various stories and their relationships to personality and behavioral data obtained by other methods (interview, other tests, etc.). Although the usual procedure of scoring and interpreting the TAT is highly impressionistic, scores determined by one of the more systematic scoring procedures are moderately reliable and can be interpreted in terms of norms based on standardization studies (Bellak, 1986).

Asking a person to tell stories about pictures would appear to be a more valid approach to personality assessment than asking for responses to inkblots, but TAT stories are affected by the particular environmental context in which the test is taken and do not always differentiate between normal persons and those with psychological disorders (Eron, 1950). Furthermore, many psychologists maintain that less structured stimuli such as inkblots are more effective than picture stories in getting at unconscious conflicts and repressed desires. For these and other reasons the TAT has not proved to be as popular as the Rorschach for psychodiagnostic purposes.

Other apperception techniques have been developed in response to criticisms of the TAT regarding its inappropriateness for groups such as blacks, Hispanics, children, teenagers, and the elderly and its apparent datedness and lack of psychometric rigor. The Thompson Modification of the TAT attempts to appeal to blacks by using black figures in the cards, and it has been successful in eliciting more articulate responses from some blacks. Another ethnically oriented picture-story test is TEMAS, which was designed for Hispanic persons.

The Children's Apperception Test (CAT) and the Blacky Pictures, which consist of pictures of animals in various human-like situations, have been successful in evoking psychologically meaningful stories from children. However, the latter test has been criticized for its strong psychoanalytic orientation. Both the Michigan Picture Test and the Roberts Apperception Test for Children are the products of efforts to combine the flexibility of projectives with the psychometric qualities of a good test (objective scoring, reliability, adequate standardization, etc.), but they are not as popular with clinicians as the CAT. The Senior Apperception Test and the Gerontological Apperception Technique were designed for elderly individuals, but have not proved as successful in eliciting meaningful material from this age group as their designers undoubtedly desired. Finally, the Picture Projective Test (also known as the Southern Mississippi TAT) employs more contemporary pictures from the *Family of Man* photographic collection of the Museum of Modern Art. The pictures on this test have a more uniform balance of positive and negative themes than the TAT, as well as a more contemporary appeal in terms of characters and settings.

Exercises

1. Define each of the following terms in a sentence or two:

complex themas	outcomes
hero(es)	press
follow-up inquiry	sentiments
interests	signs
needs	simple themas
Oedipal	themas

2. For what chronological and ethnic groups is each of the following picture-story tests most appropriate?

Blacky Pictures	GAT
CAT & CAT-H	MPT-R

PPT	TAT
RATC	TEMAS
SAT	Thompson TAT

3.   Show the picture in Figure 12–1 to several people, and ask them to make up a story about it. Tell them to include in their stories what's going on now, what led up to it, and how it will turn out. Following the interpretative suggestions discussed in the chapter, interpret the stories to the best of your ability. Did the stories provide you with any insights into the needs and other personality characteristics of the storytellers? Did this experience lead you to draw any conclusions about the effectiveness of the storytelling technique as a method of assessing personality?

4.   What are the differences in procedure used in individual administration, group administration, and self-administration of the TAT? What relative advantages and disadvantages does each of these three administrative procedures possess?

5.   Another approach to using pictures in personality assessment is that employed by the Szondi Test. This test, which is now out of print in the United States, consists of six sets of photographs, eight pictures per set, of mental patients with different psychiatric diagnoses (hysteria, catatonia, paranoia, depression, mania, etc.). In taking the Szondi Test, the examinee selects, from each set, two pictures that he or she likes most and two pictures he or she dislikes most. The basic assumption underlying the test is that the facial features of the mental patients depicted in the 12 selected and the 12 rejected photographs have special meanings for the examinee, whose needs and personality are presumed to be related to those of the patients depicted in the selected and rejected photographs. What value do you see in this test as a method of personality assessment? Check your evaluation against the several reviews of the Szondi Test appearing in older editions of the *Mental Measurements Yearbook* (3rd, p. 100; 4th, p. 134; 5th, p. 162; 6th, p. 243). Can you think of any other methods of assessing personality that, like the Szondi Test, are based on the identification process?

6.   With respect to Lindzey's (1959) classification of projective techniques into association, construction, completion, arrangement or selection, and expression categories, in which category or categories does the picture-story technique fall? Explain.

7.   Evaluate the TAT in terms of its psychometric characteristics. Check your evaluation against reviews of the TAT in the *Seventh Mental Measurements Yearbook* (1972, Vol. I, pp. 457–462), the *Eighth Mental Measurements Yearbook* (1978, Vol. I, pp. 1127–1130), and *Test Critiques* (1985, Vol. II, pp. 799–814).

Suggested Readings

Bellak, L. (1986). *The TAT, CAT and SAT in clinical use* (4th ed.). New York: Grune & Stratton.

Dana, R. H. (1986). Thematic Apperception Test used with adolescents. In A. Rabin (Ed.), *Projective techniques with children and adolescents* (pp. 14–36). New York: Springer.

Groth-Marnat, G. (1984). Thematic Apperception Test. In G. Groth-Marnat (Ed.), *Handbook of psychological assessment* (pp. 148–199). New York: Van Nostrand Reinhold.

Hall, C. S., & Lindzey, G. (1978). Murray's personology. In C. S. Hall & G. Lindzey (Eds.), *Theories of personality* (pp. 205–240). New York: Wiley.

Haworth, M. R. (1986). Children's Apperception Test. In A. Rabin (Ed.), *Projective techniques with children and adolescents* (pp. 37–72). New York: Springer.

Hutt, M. L. (1986). The Michigan Picture Test-Revised. In A. Rabin (Ed.), *Projective techniques with children and adolescents* (pp. 73–84). New York: Springer.

Pearson, G. S. (1984). The use of storytelling in the psychiatric assessment of children. *Journal of Child and Adolescent Psychotherapy, 1,* 101–106.

Ryan, R. M. (1985). Thematic Apperception Test. In D. J. Keyser & R. C. Sweetland (Eds.), *Test critiques* (Vol. II, pp. 799–814). Kansas City, MO: Test Corporation of America.

Vane, J. R. (1981). The Thematic Apperception Test: A review. *Clinical Psychology Review, 1,* 319–336.

PART V

Other Measures and Issues

CHAPTER 13

Physiological, Perceptual, and Cognitive Measures

As we have seen in previous chapters, behavioral observations, interviews, rating scales, personality inventories, and projective techniques vary in their objectivity, scope, depth, and validity. Nevertheless, all of these methods are used extensively in research and applied settings. Perusal of a typical book or review concerned with personality assessment might leave one with the impression that these methods exhaust the list of possible approaches to measuring personality. However, there remains a variety of interesting techniques that, although not as extensively applied as the above approaches, deserve consideration. Growing dissatisfaction with traditional, self-report and projective techniques of asssessing personality has led to a greater emphasis on less obvious and more structured physiological, perceptual, and cognitive measures or correlates of personality. These indirect, but relatively objective, assessment procedures have great potential because the measurements are not so much under conscious control, cannot be faked as easily, and are not greatly influenced by response sets. Simply because they lack the popularity of rating scales, inventories, and projectives does not necessarily mean that they are less reliable and valid. The major problem is that, at least so far, these procedures do not possess the scope of other assessment techniques and have not been able to reveal as much about human personality.

Physiological and Perceptual Measures

Physiological responses regulated by the sympathetic branch of the autonomic nervous system and prolonged by hormones secreted by the adrenal glands constitute what the physiologist Walter Cannon (1929) referred to as the *emergency pattern*. The components of the emergency pattern, which occurs during excitement, distress, rage, and fear, include changes in the composition of the blood (blood sugar and adrenaline increase, the blood coagulates faster, the acid-alkaline balance changes), redistribution of the blood supply to the surface of the body, increases in blood pressure and heart rate, an increase in the ratio of the volume of oxygen inhaled to the volume of carbon dioxide exhaled, inhibition of gastrointestinal movements, pilomotor response (goose pimples), inhibition of salivary secretion, increased perspiration, enlargement of the pupils of the eyes, and increased muscle tension and tremor. The emergency pattern has the function of permitting short-term expenditure of maximum energy necessary in states of emergency and is consequently very useful in certain situations. But when activated too frequently, it can contribute to disease and other difficulties for human beings. Of particular interest with respect to personality measurement is the level of stress produced by autonomic arousal in the emergency reaction.

Bioelectric Indicators of Emotional and Sexual Arousal

Many types of instruments and procedures have been applied to the measurement of reactions to stressful or arousing situations. Such reactions, which are regulated by the autonomic system, reticular formation, and other parts of the nervous system, are frequently used as indicators of emotional arousal. Among the physiological changes with stress that have been measured and the specialized instruments that measure these responses are

> blood pressure—*sphygmomanometer*
> volume of finger and other body organs—*plethysmograph*
> muscle tension—*electromyograph* (EMG)
> brain waves—*electroencephalograph* (EEG)
> respiration rate—*pneumograph*
> heart rate—*stethoscope* and *electrocardiogram* (EKG)
> electrical resistance of the skin—*galvanic skin response* (GSR) apparatus

temperature—*telethermometer*

vaginal blood volume—*photoplethysmograph*

These instruments may be used individually or in combination, depending on the nature of the research investigation or type of diagnostic information desired. Changes in body chemistry during stress and other emotions can also be determined by chemical analysis.

Although instruments for measuring heart rate, blood pressure, the GSR, and many other physiological indicators have been available for most of this century, advances in medical electronics since the 1960s have resulted in a much greater variety of compact bioelectric instruments. For example, Masters' and Johnson's (1966) finding of a link between sexual arousal and flow of blood into the genitalia has resulted in the development of a variety of instruments to measure sexual arousal by blood flow (Kallman & Feuerstein, 1977). One of these instruments, the pneumatic plethysmograph, uses changes in air pressure to measure variations in the size of a body organ. This instrument has been applied to the study of male sexual responses by monitoring changes in penis size as the person views pictures of other stimuli that produce sexual arousal. A strain gauge that registers changes in the electrical resistance of the skin as the circumference of the penis varies may also be used for this purpose (Barlow, 1977; Zuckermann, 1971). Photoplethysmography, in which changes in vaginal blood volume are measured by means of a photoelectric apparatus inserted into the vagina, has been applied to the study of sexual responses in the female (Geer, 1977).

GSR and Biofeedback

One of the most popular of the psychophysiological instruments used by psychologists who study anxiety and other stressful emotions is a GSR apparatus, which measures the decrease in skin resistance occurring a couple of seconds after exposure to some arousing stimulus. GSR's are produced by perspiration and polarization changes in a palmar or plantar surface of the skin. Also commonly used in biofeedback experiments and treatments are the EMG and EEG. In biofeedback, subjects are fed back information on their level of muscle tension, blood pressure, pattern of brain waves (e.g., alpha waves), or another physiological condition by having them watch a meter needle or attend to some kind of signal. By monitoring his or her particular physiological state at the moment, the individual can learn to control the target condition (blood pressure, muscle tension, etc.). This procedure has proven to be of value in reducing the level of tension and anxiety experienced by certain individuals. For example, by assisting patients in reducing the tension levels of the muscles in the forehead and neck, biofeedback can help decrease the incidence of headaches. Kleinmuntz (1982) suggests that further research involving biofeedback of physiological states will reveal information of value in personality assessment.

However, thus far biofeedback techniques have proven more helpful in therapy than in diagnosis.

Polygraph Tests

When telling a lie most people have an emotional response that is usually not obvious in their overt behavior. However, the emotional response may be detected by an apparatus sensitive to the physiological reactions produced by activity of the sympathetic nervous system. This apparatus, referred to as a lie detector or polygraph, usually measures heart rate, respiration rate, blood pressure, and the galvanic skin response (see Figure 13–1). The usual procedure in a lie detection (or truth verification) test is first to connect electrodes and other attachments to the person. Then a series of relevant questions are asked concerning the person's knowledge of or participation in a crime or other behavior (e.g., Did you take the money?). Relevant (R) questions are interspersed with irrelevant (I) questions (e.g., Are you married?), each question (R or I) to be answered yes or no. If the individual's physiological responses to a given R question are much greater than his or her physiological responses to I questions, then the polygraph operator may conclude

Figure 13–1   Polygraph responses of a person during an actual lie and simulated lies

Respiration

Heart rate

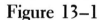
Galvanic skin response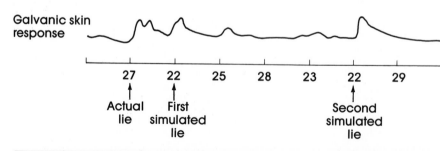

From J. F. Kubis (1962). Cited in B. M. Smith, "The Polygraphy." In R. C. Atkinson (Ed.), *Contemporary Psychology*. W. H. Freeman, San Francisco. Reprinted by permission from the publisher.

that the answer to that particular relevant question was a lie. This relevant/irrelevant (*R/I*) questioning procedure is sometimes made more sophisticated by introducing a third type of question—a control question—referring in a general way to prior misdeeds (e.g., Have you ever taken anything that didn't belong to you?). In addition, city police departments and the FBI, which have used polygraph tests extensively, frequently employ a procedure known as the *guilty knowledge test*: the suspect's responses to questions concerning facts about the crime that could be known only to the guilty person are assessed. Higher accuracy tends to be achieved when using this technique in situations where it is applicable (Yarmey, 1979).

Polygraph tests not only are given to suspects of a crime but also to large numbers of applicants and employees in industry and government to assess their character. They have been used extensively in business and industry to screen out dishonest workers, and by government agencies to detect security risks. A 1983 directive signed by President Reagan requires government employees to take lie detector tests when leaks of classified information are being investigated (Associated Press, 1983). However, a bill passed by the U.S. Congress in 1988 banned most uses of lie detectors in job interviews in government and the private work place.

Despite wide usage of the technique, it has been estimated that lie detector tests are accurate in only about 65% of the cases and that they are more likely to declare innocent people guilty than they are to find guilty people innocent (Lykken, 1983). In a naturalistic study by Kleinmuntz and Szucko (1984), for example, polygraph interpreters incorrectly classified innocent subjects as guilty in 37% of the cases.

The responses registered on a polygraph do not necessarily indicate that the subject was lying; any arousal or emotion—anger, anxiety, and even amusement—may produce a significant reading. Factors other than actual involvement in a crime or other misdeed may cause a person to become aroused by a particular question, including past misdeeds and reactions to the fact that someone even considers that he or she might be guilty. In addition, pathological liars or sociopathic personalities who actually participated in a crime may manifest no physiological changes at all to questions about the crime (Lykken, 1957). And even a normal but guilty subject may, by faking arousal to irrelevant questions, confuse the polygraph examiner.

Although the polygraph is sometimes useful in turning up leads, in provoking confessions, and in obtaining evidence in support of the innocent, state courts consider polygraph data to be insufficiently reliable to be admissible as legal evidence. Furthermore, the Office of Technology Assessment of the United States Congress concluded that "the available research evidence does not establish the scientific validity of the polygraph test for personnel security screening" (U.S. Congress, 1983, p. 4).

Voice Stress Analyzer

More convenient to use than the polygraph, in that it does not require hooking up the subject to electrodes or other connections, is the *voice stress analyzer*. Perhaps because of its simplicity and convenience, there are over 30% more voice stress analysts in the United States than polygraph examiners. A voice stress analysis consists of making a tape recording of a person's voice directly or over the telephone, radio, or television, and playing it through a voice stress analyzer at one-fourth its normal speed. A visual record of the slowed-down voice sounds, or vocal spectrum, is then prepared. As shown in Figure 13–2, the low frequency (8–12 hertz) vocal warble characteristic of a relaxed speaker (left figure) is obliterated when the speaker is under stress (right figure). The device that measures this effect, which is produced by microtremors of the muscles of the vocal apparatus, is called a *psychological stress evaluator* or PSE. Another type of voice stress analyzer measures changes in the frequency spectrum of the voice when the subject is lying. In any event, by employing a procedure similar to that of a polygraph examination, or simply analyzing the voice printout of a speaker who does not know he is being tested, a fairly reliable indication can be obtained as to whether the speaker is under stress. Again, a person who is under stress is not necessarily lying; he or she may be aroused for many different reasons. Even pronouncing different numerals or other word sounds can result in different degrees of measured voice stress. Relatively few studies concerned with the accuracy of the voice stress analyzer have been conducted, and there is no consistent evidence that it accurately measures emotional stress or strain. Clearly further research is needed to determine the validity of this technique and its relationship to other physiological measures of emotion and personality (Lykken, 1981).

Figure 13–2   Voice-stress analyzer printouts for a relaxed speaker (left record) and speaker under stress (right record). Note that the wavelike configuration produced by vocal microtremors oscillating at 8 to 14 hertz in a relaxed speaker (left figure) disappears in the voiceprint of a speaker under stress (right figure).

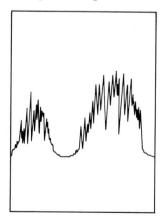 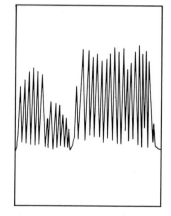

From "Lie Detectors; PSE Gains Audience Despite Critic's Doubt," C. Holden (News and Comment section), Vol. 190, pp. 359–362 (figure on page 360), *Science*, 24 October 1975. Copyright 1975 by the AAAS. Reprinted by permission of publisher.

Fear and Anger

Many researchers have attempted to find evidence of distinctive physiological or biochemical bases for different emotions and personality characteristics, but most of this research has met with little success. The Hippocrates-Galen humoral theory, discussed in Chapter 1, was perhaps the first systematic effort to relate chemistry to personality. However, surely no one today accepts the notion that an excess of yellow bile in the body produces anger, an excess of black bile causes depression, an excess of blood produces aggressiveness, or an excess of phlegm results in laziness!

More recent efforts to relate emotions to physiology stem from the James-Lange theory that the subjective experience of a particular emotion is the awareness of changes in the body organs resulting from an arousing stimulus. Contrary to the common sense notion that "we run because we are afraid," the pioneering psychologist William James (1890, p. 759) maintained that the physiological changes precede the conscious experience of emotion and consequently "we are afraid because we run." Although the physiologist Walter Cannon (1927) rejected the James-Lange theory and proposed instead that both the subjective experience of emotion and the bodily changes accompanying it result from activation of the hypothalamus (the Cannon-Bard theory of emotion), the possibility that distinctive bodily response patterns are associated with different emotions continued to interest researchers. A case in point is the observation made by Wolf and Wolff (1942) of a man whose esophagus had been permanently closed when he drank some piping hot soup. A surgical opening for feeding was made in the man's stomach wall, and the lining of his stomach could be continually observed through the opening. Of interest is the fact that the acidity of the man's stomach varied with his emotional state: anger was accompanied by an increase in stomach acidity and redness of the stomach wall, whereas the acidity level dropped and the stomach wall became paler when he was experiencing fear or sadness.

Ax (1953) also reported some evidence for the physiological differentiation of fear and anger. Using rather ingenious ways to induce fear and anger, he noted a greater decrease in the electrical resistance of the skin, a more rapid respiration rate, and a greater number of peaks in the record of muscular tension during the former emotion. During anger, on the other hand, there were more GSR's, as well as increases in heart rate, diastolic blood pressure, and overall level of muscular tension. These physiological differences between fear and anger appeared to result from different kinds of hormones being secreted by the adrenal medulla during these emotions. The physiological changes observed during fear were associated with the secretion of adrenalin, but those observed during anger were associated with the secretion of both adrenalin and noradrenalin.

Other data bearing on the question of physiological and biochemical differences between fear and anger were obtained by Funkenstein and his colleagues (Funkenstein, 1955; Funkenstein, King & Drolette, 1957). It was found that the amount of adrenalin secreted was relatively greater both in subjects who overtly expressed their anger and in those who were made anxious in an experimental stress situation. In contrast, subjects whose response to the experimental stress was to direct their anger inward toward themselves showed a relatively greater secretion of noradrenalin. Interestingly enough, data on wild animals indicate that timid, fearful creatures such as rabbits secrete more adrenalin, whereas bold, aggressive animals such as lions secrete more noradrenalin.

Despite a few research successes in relating emotions to physiological changes, it is now generally recognized that cognitive factors, such as the individual's appraisal of the specific situation, are as important as physiological arousal in determining the expression of an emotion or temperament trait. The results of research by Stanley Schachter (1971) and other psychologists indicate that the specific emotion expressed results from a complex interaction of physiological arousal, memories of past experiences in similar situations, and the individual's perceptual appraisal of the immediate (social) situation. It should not be concluded, however, that physiological and biochemical measurements do not contribute to the assessment of personality, particularly personality disorders such as schizophrenia and depression, and to the prediction of behavior stemming from those disorders. For example, there is some evidence that physiological or biochemical tests may be useful in the prediction of suicide ("The Suicide Factor," 1982). In addition, the procedure of administering certain drugs and observing their effects on behavior has been employed to identify subtypes of affective disorders (Akiskal, 1979).

Introverts and Extroverts

As noted in Chapter 7, introversion-extroversion is one of the dimensions most consistently referred to in research on personality. Eysenck and Eysenck (1975) describe introverts and extroverts as follows:

> The typical introvert is a quiet, retiring sort of person, introspective, fond of books rather than people; he is reserved and distant except to intimate friends. He tends to plan ahead, "looks before he leaps," and mistrusts the impulse of the moment. He does not like excitement, takes matters of everyday life with proper seriousness, and likes a well-ordered mode of life. He keeps his feelings under close control, seldom behaves in an aggressive manner, and does not lose his temper easily. He is reliable, somewhat pessimistic, and places greater value on ethical standards.
>
> The typical extravert is sociable, likes parties, has many friends, needs to have people to talk to, and does not like reading or studying by himself. He craves excitement, takes chances, often sticks his neck out, acts on the spur of the moment, and is generally an impulsive individual. He is fond of practical jokes, always has a ready answer, and generally likes change; he is carefree, easygoing, optimistic, and "likes to laugh and be merry." He prefers to keep moving and doing things, tends to be aggressive and loses his temper quickly; altogether his feelings are not kept under control, and he is not always a reliable person. (p. 5)

Many different perceptual and physiological factors have been found to be related to the introversion/extroversion dimension. Bakan (1957) and Claridge (1960) reported, for example, that introverts were more vigilant than extroverts in a watchkeeping (vigilance) situation. Harkins and Green (1975) found that introverts do better at signal-detection tasks than extroverts. Other findings are that people with higher introversion scores take fewer involuntary rest pauses in performing a monotonous tapping task (Eysenck, 1967) and are less tolerant of pain but more tolerant of sensory deprivation than extroverts (Petrie, 1967; Lynn & Eysenck, 1961). Extroverts are more readily conditioned than introverts to stimuli associated with sexual arousal (Kantorwitz, 1978). In general, it can be concluded that, compared with extroverts, introverts are more vigilant, more sensitive to pain, more cautious, and more disrupted by overstimulation.

The above findings are consistent with Eysenck's (1967) hypothesis that introversion is associated with a higher level of central nervous system arousal than extroversion. In short, introverts are said to be more awake, less distractible, and more attentive to the task at hand than extroverts. Extroverts, on the other hand, appear to have a greater need for external stimulation and seek out sensations more than introverts. The former are more likely to engage in impulsive acts, such as starting on a trip without appropriate planning, and to say they would like to try parachute jumping (Farley & Farley, 1967). Certain occupations, such as that of fireman or salvage diver, appear to attract extroversive individuals who enjoy thrilling, stimulating experiences.

One researcher (Zuckerman, 1979) designed a Sensation Seeking scale (see Figure 13–3) to measure a person's thrill-seeking behavior—the desire for new experiences or a willingness to take risks. People scoring high on this scale (sensation seekers) were found to have lower blood levels of an enzyme known as monoamine oxidase (MAO) than those who scored low on the scale. The concentration of two neurotransmitters thought to be important in emotion and motivation are regulated by MAO. And because the level of MAO in the blood is affected by heredity (as well as other factors), these findings suggest that risk taking may be due to some extent to biochemical inheritance.

Introversion-extroversion is, of course, only one personality dimension associated with perception and physiology. Other personality variables, such as anxiety, neuroticism, and schizophrenia, have been found to be related to speed of response on several perceptual tasks (e.g., word recognition, identification of incomplete figures, dark adaptation) and to conditionability (e.g., see Chapman & McGhie, 1962; Holzman & Levy, 1977). The majority of these tasks are, however, rather crude measures and show no immediate signs of replacing traditional personality assessment devices. At any rate, as Sarason (1972) suggests, using a combination of physiological measures (EEG, EKG, EMG, GSR, etc.) in a multivariate approach to personality assessment and behavior prediction would seem to be more effective than any single measure.

Figure 13–3

Sensation Seeking Scale.

Directions. For each item, select the response (a or b) that best describes your true feeling. If you do not like either response, mark the one you dislike the least. Do not leave any items blank.

1. a. I have no patience with dull or boring persons.
    b. I find something interesting in almost every person I talk to.
2. a. A good painting should shock or jolt the senses.
    b. A good painting should provide a feeling of peace and security.
3. a. People who ride motorcycles must have some kind of unconscious need to hurt themselves.
    b. I would like to drive or ride a motorcycle.
4. a. I would prefer living in an ideal society in which everyone is safe, secure, and happy.
    b. I would have preferred living in the unsettled days of history.
5. a. I sometimes like to do things that are a little frightening.
    b. A sensible person avoids dangerous activities.
6. a. I would not like to be hypnotized.
    b. I would like to be hypnotized.
7. a. The most important goal of life is to live to the fullest and experience as much as possible.
    b. The most important goal of life is to find peace and happiness.
8. a. I would like to try parachute jumping.
    b. I would never want to try jumping from a plane, with or without a parachute.
9. a. I enter cold water gradually, giving myself time to get used to it.
    b. I like to dive or jump right into the ocean or a cold pool.
10. a. When I go on a vacation, I prefer the comfort of a good room and bed.
    b. When I go on a vacation, I prefer the change of camping out.
11. a. I prefer people who are emotionally expressive even if they are a bit unstable.
    b. I prefer people who are calm and even-tempered.
12. a. I would prefer a job in one location.
    b. I would like a job that requires traveling.
13. a. I can't wait to get indoors on a cold day.
    b. I am invigorated by a brisk, cold day.
14. a. I get bored seeing the same faces.
    b. I like the comfortable familiarity of everyday friends.

Scoring: Count one point for each of the following items that you marked as follows: 1–a, 2–a, 3–b, 4–b, 5–a, 6–b, 7–a, 8–a, 9–b, 10–b, 11–a, 12–b, 13–b, 14–a. Add your total for sensation seeking and compare it with the norms listed below:

0–3: Very low   4–5: Low   6–9: Average   10–11: High   12–14: Very high

Test items courtesy of Marvin Zuckerman.

Field Independence and Dependence

Herman Witkin and his colleagues (Witkin et al., 1962; Witkin & Goodenough, 1977) conducted the most systematic series of investigations of the relationships between personality and perception. Three tests—the Body Adjustment Test, the Rod and Frame Test, and the Embedded Figures Test—were used in these studies to classify individuals according to their degree of field independence or field dependence. On the Body Adjustment Test, the examinee is seated in a tilted chair located in a tilted room and told to adjust the chair to the true vertical position. On the Rod and Frame Test, the examinee is seated before a luminous rod affixed to a luminous square frame in a completely darkened room and instructed to adjust the rod to the true vertical when the rod and frame have been tilted in opposite directions. Several trials are given on both the Body Adjustment Test and the Rod and Frame Test. On the Embedded Figures Test, the rapidity with which the examinee can locate simple figures within each of a series of complex forms is measured (see Figure 13–4). According to Witkin, these three tests, which have substantial positive correlations with each other, measure much the same thing: *field independence* versus *field dependence*, or the ability to differentiate aspects or parts of a complex, confusing whole. Scores on all three tests are combined into a single index; people who score high on this index are referred to as *field independents*, and people who score low as *field dependents*.

Of particular interest is the fact that field independents and field dependents have different personalities. Witkin's description of a highly field independent person is that of a secure, independent, controlled, more psychologically mature, self-accepting individual. Such a person is active in dealing with the environment, tends to use intellectualization (artificially separating emotional content from intellectual content) as a defense mechanism, and is more aware of his or her inner experiences (Witkin et al., 1962). In contrast, a typical field dependent person tends to be tense, less secure, psychologically immature, passive, less attuned to his or her inner experiences, and to possess less self-insight. This person also tends to have greater feelings of inferiority, a low evaluation of the physical self, and to be more likely to use primitive defense mechanisms such as repression and denial.

College major, sex, and sociocultural factors have also been found to be related to field independence-dependence. Field independent individuals tend to do better in engineering, the sciences, and mathematics—fields requiring high analytic ability, whereas field dependent individuals tend to do better in counseling, social sciences, teaching, and other people-oriented professions (Witkin, 1973). With respect to sex and sociocultural differences, boys are usually more field independent than girls, and members of hunting and foraging cultures are more field independent than those in sedentary, agricultural societies (Witkin & Berry, 1975). Field dependent individuals are also more attentive than field independent individuals to facial and other nonverbal social cues (Witkin & Goodenough, 1977).

With respect to intrafamilial factors, significant relationships between the field

Figure 13–4

Sample Embedded Figures Test item. People who have difficulty locating the figures at the left in the complex patterns on the right may be characterized as field dependent.

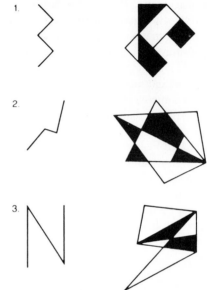

Adapted from Witkin et al. (1977). Field dependent and field independent cognitive styles and their educational implications. *Review of Educational Research, 47,* 1–64. Reprinted with permission from the American Educational Research Association.

independence scores of mothers and sons and fathers and daughters have been reported (Kogan & Kogan, 1970). The parents of field independent children tend to be less restrictive and less authoritarian than those of field dependent children. Compared with typical Anglo-American parents, Mexican-American parents tend to be more authoritarian and family centered in the treatment of their children, discouraging independent and assertive behavior. These differences are believed to contribute to the greater field dependence of Mexican-American children (Witkin et al., 1973; Ramirez & Casteneda, 1974).

Other data indicate that field independence increases progressively up to age 17 in boys and 15 in girls (Witkin, Goodenough, & Karp, 1967). The field independence scores of 10- and 12-year-old children are also positively correlated with scores on the Stanford-Binet Intelligence Scale and Wechsler Intelligence Scale for Children (WISC). This fact, coupled with factor-analytic information and the finding of a positive relationship between field independence and spatial ability (Kogan, 1971), might lead one to consider whether field independence-dependence may be the same variable as nonverbal intelligence.

Identification of the field independence-field dependence style, which may also be referred to more generally as an *analytical* versus *global style*, has led to research on perceptual and conceptual differentiation. A more differentiated conceptual, namely, field independent or analytical, manner of perceiving and interacting with the external world is seen as being associated with greater differentiation or articulation of the self. Analytical individuals tend to view the self as distinct from the environment, whereas global individuals are more likely to view the self and the environment as combined. Furthermore, global individuals come to depend on the external environment, and other people in particular, for definition and direction of the self, whereas analytical individuals are more likely to be self sufficient.

Cognitive Styles

Although field independence and field dependence are perhaps more clearly viewed as perceptual styles, the concepts of global and analytical styles clearly impinge on the cognitive domain. Consequently, a more general term for the collection of strategies or approaches to perceiving, remembering, and thinking that an individual comes to prefer in attempting to understand and cope with the world is *cognitive styles*.

The term *cognition* refers to the processes of intellect (learning, remembering, understanding, thinking), but cognitive style is somewhat broader in that many of the stylistic variables grouped under this term involve motivation and temperament as well as perception and cognition. In general, cognitive styles are strategies or approaches that people employ in their efforts to understand environmental situations so they can cope with them more effectively. Examples of cognitive styles other than field independence-field dependence that have been studied are (Erhardt, n.d.)

- *Broad versus narrow categorizing*—preferring a small number of categories containing a large number of items (broad categorizer) versus a large number of categories with a small number of items (narrow categorizer);
- *Constricted versus flexible*—greater susceptibility to distraction by irrelevant information (constricted) versus resistance to distraction (flexible control);
- *Impulsive versus reflective*—slow and accurate (reflective) in solving a problem versus quick and inaccurate (impulsive) in finding a solution;
- *Internal versus external locus of control*—belief that rewards are the consequences of one's own behavior (internal locus of control) versus belief that one's fate is controlled by forces outside oneself (external locus of control);
- *Leveling versus sharpening*—fitting new stimuli into previously developed memory categories (leveler) versus differentiating new instances from old (sharpener);

- *Risk-taking versus caution*—taking a risk with a low probability of a high payoff (risk-taker) versus preferring a low risk with a high probability of low payoff (caution);

- *Scanning versus focusing strategies*—identifying relevant information in a problem, proceeding in a broad to narrow fashion (scanner) versus proceeding in a trial-and-error fashion (focuser);

- *Tolerance versus intolerance (for incongruous or unrealistic experiences)*—readier adaptation to unusual experiences (tolerance) versus demand for more information before unusual experiences are accepted (intolerance).

Impulsive-Reflective and Locus of Control Styles

Among the cognitive styles that have received the most extensive research attention are the reflective versus impulsive style, measured by the Matching Familiar Figures Test (MFFT) (Kagan et al., 1964), and the internal versus external locus of control of reinforcement style, measured by Rotter's (1966) I-E Scale. The MFFT consists of a set of figures that children must compare for similarities and differences; time and accuracy of response are determined, reflective children responding more slowly and accurately than impulsive children in performing the task. (See Figure 13–5.) The I-E Scale consists of pairs of items, one of which is concerned with the belief that a person can control his or her own life ("internal locus of control"), and the other with the belief that a person's life is controlled by fate or luck. An item of the first type is: "A person gets about as much out of life as he puts into it." An item of the second type is: "Getting ahead is mostly a matter of luck." Both the reflective-impulsive and locus of control styles have been found to be associated with a host of personal and sociocultural variables, but they, like field independence-dependence, are not independent of measures of intellectual abilities.

Other Models of Cognitive Styles

Although the list cited above is fairly complete, it does not exhaust the conceptual dichotomies examined in research on cognitive styles. Other examples are McKenney's two dimensional model of information assimilation and Harvey's conceptual system model.

Two Dimensional Assimilation Model   McKenney and Keen (1974) proposed a two dimensional information assimilation model consisting of the preceptive versus receptive planning modes as one dimension and the systematic versus intuitive modes as a second dimension. Preceptive individuals assimilate information into their own concepts or categories, whereas receptive individuals assimilate information in as raw a form as possible. In other words, preceptives categorize or chunk

Sample of types of items on the Matching Familiar Figures (MFF) Test. On this item the examinee is instructed to select which of the six pictures in the second and third rows is identical to the picture at the top. **Figure 13–5**

From "Reflection-impulsivity: The Generality and Dynamics of Conceptual Tempo," by J. Kagan (1966). *Journal of Abnormal Psychology*, 71, 17–24. Copyright 1966 by the American Psychological Association. Reprinted by permission of the author.

information, but receptives store information as new data rather than as concepts. On the second dimension, systematic people create orderly, sequential plans or strategies, whereas intuitive people prefer ideas rather than plans and skip the part analysis of a problem and move immediately to a whole analysis. Each pole of the two dimensional model is assessed by different tests. An elaboration test is used to assess the preceptive mode, an identical pictures test to assess the receptive mode, a paper folding test to assess the systematic mode, and a scrambled words test to assess the intuitive mode (Haynie, 1985).

Conceptual Systems Model   Another approach to cognitive styles is represented by research on the abstractness-concreteness conceptual systems (Harvey, Hunt & Schroder, 1961; Schroder, Driver & Strufert, 1967). Harvey and his colleagues maintain that people tend to experience the environment at either an abstract level, in which they discriminate among situational requirements and adapt their responses to the situational demands, or at a concrete level, in which they emphasize the similarities among situations and respond in rigid, overgeneralized ways across different situations. Obviously the distinction between abstract and concrete conceptual systems overlaps with several other cognitive styles (e.g., broad vs. narrow categorizing, leveling vs. sharpening, scanning vs. focusing).

There are four systems in the abstract-concrete conceptualization scheme. People who function in system one are conforming to absolute, external standards and were presumably reared in authoritarian homes characterized by intolerance of exploration and deviation from established norms. System two functioning, presumably the result of a laissez-faire or permissive upbringing, consists of rebellion against standards imposed by others. Reflecting overprotective and overindulgent upbringing, people who manipulate others by the use of dependency characterize system three functioning. At the most abstract end of the concrete-abstract continuum is system four functioning. Individuals at this level are characterized by independence of judgment, said to result from a child rearing pattern in which the individual is encouraged to develop standards based on his or her own personal experiences.

Assessing Personality with Cognitive Tests

Research on perceptual and cognitive styles represents only one of many areas of investigation concerned with the relationships of personality to the ways in which people attend to, process, store, and use information from the environment in solving problems. The findings of numerous investigations combining cognitive, affective, and perceptual variables emphasize the fact that these variables are actually inseparable, interwoven processes. They are reciprocally interdependent or interactive, affecting each other in significant ways. Consequently, there is a great deal of overlap among measures of affect, cognition, and perception.

Objective-Analytic (O-A) Test Battery

A definition of personality that includes both affective and cognitive factors has been espoused by certain psychologists for many years. Although measurement specialists have tended to separate the two domains, interest has been growing for a fusion of cognitive and affective instruments. This fact is seen clearly in the Objective-Analytic Test Battery by R. B. Cattell and J. M. Schuerger (IPAT, 1978). These tests were designed to measure ten source traits or factors: Ego Standards (competitiveness), Independence (perceptual accuracy and capacity for intense, self-directed concentration), Evasiveness (self-serving manipulation of social norms), Exuberance (spontaneity and rapidity of thinking), Capacity to Mobilize versus Regression, Anxiety, Realism versus Tensidia (tense, inflexible, dissociation from reality), Asthenia versus Self-Assurance (a kind of inhibited overconformity versus egoistic self-assertion), Exvia versus Invia (extroversion versus introversion), Discouragement versus Sanguinessness (pessimism versus optimism). Each trait on the O-A Test Battery is assessed by seven or eight subtests that can be administered in 21 to 30 minutes. Thus, total testing time for the entire battery is nearly four and a half hours. The tests consist of a variety of perceptual, cognitive, and behavioral tasks that, on the surface, seem more like aptitude than personality measures. Included are tasks of perceptual-motor rigidity, picture perception, endurance of difficulty, criticalness of judgment, humor appreciation, musical preferences, and the like. The test-retest reliability coefficients for trait scores over 3 to 6 weeks range from .58 to .85 (median $r = .69$), and the validities are similar to those obtained with self-report and projective measures of personality.

Intelligence Tests and Personality Variables

Alfred Binet's test has served as a model of intelligence test construction throughout this century. His original aim was to provide a means of identifying children who are not mentally capable of learning adequately in regular school classrooms. Subsequently, the aim of intelligence testing was expanded to that of measuring an entire range of intellectual capabilities in children and adults.

Despite their cognitive focus, it has been clear since Alfred Binet's time that administration of a standardized test of intelligence yields not only an index of intellectual abilities, but also behavioral data on how the examinee approaches problems, how anxious and motivated he or she is, and other indicators of personality. In a sense, an intelligence test is a kind of specialized interview, in which the yield of nontest data can be as useful as whether or not the examinee answers a certain item correctly.

Although Binet was aware of the fact that his Binet-Simon scale elicited affective as well as cognitive data, it was David Wechsler who explicitly included the assessment of noncognitive variables as one of his goals in designing the Wechsler series of intelligence tests. Wechsler's definition of intelligence changed somewhat over the years, and he never seemed entirely clear about what his tests were measuring. In 1958 he defined intelligence as the "aggregate or global capacity of the individual to act purposefully, to think rationally, and to deal effectively with his environment" (Wechsler, 1958, p. 7). By 1975 he had revised the definition of intelligence to the "capacity of an individual to understand the world about him and his resourcefulness to cope with its challenges" (Wechsler, 1975, p. 139). The common core of meaning in these definitions is the ability to cope or deal effectively with the environment. Clearly, however, coping with the environment involves more than cognitive skills; affection (emotional) and conative (striving) factors are also important. Thus Wechsler's definition of intelligence is not restrictively cognitive; it involves other features of personality in a holistic manner. For example, how well one does on an intelligence test, and in solving life's problems in general, depends not only on his or her cognitive abilities but on attentiveness to the task and the dedication with which a solution is pursued. In sum, Wechsler thought of intelligence as multifaceted, multidetermined, and a function of personality as a whole. More intelligent people are capable of dealing more effectively with life's challenges—abstract, practical, or social. Consequently, differentiating between more intelligent and less intelligent individuals requires a multifaceted measure of cognitive, affective, and conative behaviors.

Wechsler Intelligence Scales

Wechsler's first intelligence test was designed for older adolescents and adults, but he subsequently published tests for school-age and preschool children as well. Performance on each of his original tests and their revisions—the Wechsler Adult Intelligence Scale, (WAIS and WAIS-R, ages 16 years and older), the Wechsler Intelligence Scale for Children (WISC and WISC-R, ages 6 to 16 years), and the Wechsler Preschool and Primary Scale of Intelligence (WPPSI, ages four and a half to six and a half years) can be scored on 10 to 12 subtests as well as a Verbal, a Performance, and a Full scale. The Verbal scale, which yields a Verbal IQ, consists of 5 to 6 subtests dealing with verbal tasks; the Performance scale, which yields a Performance IQ, consists of 5 to 6 subtests requiring some nonverbal performance on the part of the examinee. The six verbal subtests on the revised version of the WAIS, the WAIS-R, are listed below:

> *Information:* thirty-three general information questions to be answered in a few words or numbers
>
> *Digit Span:* seven series of digits to be recited forward and seven series to be recited backward
>
> *Vocabulary:* thirty-seven words to be defined in order of ascending difficulty
>
> *Arithmetic:* fifteen arithmetic problems in order of increasing difficulty
>
> *Comprehension:* eighteen questions in order of ascending difficulty and requiring detailed answers
>
> *Similarities:* fourteen items of the type "In what way are 'A' and 'B' alike?"

The five performance subtests on the WAIS-R are as follows:

> *Picture Completion:* twenty-seven pictures on cards, each missing a part
>
> *Picture Arrangement:* ten sets of cards, each card containing a small picture
>
> *Block Design:* ten red and white geometric designs presented on cards, the examinee being instructed to duplicate each design using four or nine blocks
>
> *Object Assembly:* four cardboard picture puzzles presented in a prearranged format to the examinee, who is directed to put the pieces together to make something
>
> *Digit Symbol:* the examinee is directed to fill in each of 93 boxes with the appropriate coded symbol for the number appearing above the box

Similar subtests appear on the revised version of the WISC, the WISC-R.

In administering either the WAIS-R or WISC-R, Verbal and Performance subtests are presented in alternating sequence. The items on each subtest, arranged approximately according to difficulty level, are administered in order until the examinee fails a certain number consecutively. The raw score on each subtest is converted to a standard score scale having a mean of 10 and a standard deviation of 3. The sum of scaled scores on the six verbal subtests is converted to a Verbal IQ, the sum of scaled scores on the five performance subtests to a Performance IQ, and the sum of scaled scores on all 11 subtests to a Full Scale IQ. Each of the IQ scales—Verbal, Performance, and Full—has been standardized to have a mean of 100 and a standard deviation of 15.

Diagnosing Psychopathology from Wechsler Score Differences

Like any other psychologist who has worked in a mental hospital, Wechsler observed that general intelligence is negatively related to psychopathology, in other words that lower-than-average intelligence tends to accompany serious mental disturbance (Gaines & Morris, 1978). Wechsler also reasoned that different kinds of psychiatric disorders have different effects on various cognitive functions and consequently that an analysis of differences between Verbal and Performance IQs as well as differences among subtest scaled scores might be of help in the differential diagnosis of psychiatric disorders. Thus, he expected to find different patterns of subtest scaled scores in schizophrenics, psychoneurotics, and brain-damaged patients, patterns which if sufficiently reliable could be used in the diagnosis of psychological disorders.

Verbal-Performance IQ Differences Despite the failure of research to confirm many of Wechsler's hypotheses concerning the diagnostic significance of score differences on his intelligence tests, large differences between Verbal IQ and Performance IQ have been shown to be of some diagnostic value. Deficiencies in language, education, and other cultural experiences are associated with lower Verbal IQs than Performance IQs. With respect to the diagnosis of organic brain damage, the research findings of Reitan (1966) and his co-workers indicate that a Verbal IQ significantly lower than a corresponding Performance IQ is a diagnostic indicator of left hemisphere damage and that a Performance IQ significantly lower than a Verbal IQ points to right hemisphere damage. Furthermore, if Rapaport and his associates (Rapaport, Gill & Schafer, 1968) are correct in their assertion that Performance test scores are more affected than Verbal test scores by emotional disorders, then one should expect to find Verbal IQs significantly higher than Performance IQs in emotionally disturbed individuals. For example, the Verbal IQs of chronic schizophrenics are usually higher than their Performance IQs. Violent sociopaths, on the other hand, tend to have higher Performance than Verbal IQs (Matarazzo, 1972;

Kunce, Ryan & Eckelman, 1976); the Similarities subtest score is particularly low in these individuals. It must be cautioned, however, that the last finding may be associated with the poorer reading ability of sociopaths, which would tend to lower their scores on several of the Verbal subtests (Henning & Levy, 1967). In any case, it is questionable whether the results can be generalized to other age and ethnic groups than those examined in the Kunce, Ryan and Eckelman (1976) study. A significant difference between WAIS Verbal and Performance IQs has also been found in male homosexuals. Although the American Psychiatric Association now defines homosexuality as a sexual deviation rather than a mental disorder, the finding of higher Verbal than Performance IQs in male homosexuals (Willmott & Brierley, 1984) is of interest.

WISC Score Differences   As in the case of the WAIS, Wechsler hoped that differences among scaled scores on the WISC would be of significance in diagnosing psychopathology and learning disorders. It was believed that specific psychological conditions in children are associated with characteristic profiles of subtest scaled scores and that high scores on certain subtests and low scores on others might be useful psychodiagostic signs. Unfortunately, a survey of studies on the identification of psychological disorders in children concluded that neither Verbal-Performance scale differences nor differences among subtest scaled scores on the WISC-R reliability differentiated among educable mentally retarded, emotionally disturbed, learning disabled, and minimally brain-injured children (Gutkin, 1979).

One reason for the difficulties experienced in attempting to place adults or children in specific diagnostic categories is that these categories themselves are not very reliable or distinctive. Another problem in making such differential diagnoses on the basis of relatively short subtests such as those on the WAIS or WISC is that the scores are not highly reliable and in many instances are substantially correlated with each other. As a consequence, the difference between an examinee's score on two given subtests must be fairly large before it can be viewed as significant or meaningful.

Qualitative Observations on Intelligence Tests

A sensitive psychological examiner does not rely on numerical indexes alone in attempting to understand and diagnose a person's problem. Informal observations of test related and nontest behavior of a person during a testing session can provide clues of an impressionistic sort that suggest certain problems or characteristics. The examiner takes note of the personal style of the individual—how he or she approaches a problem, copes with frustration, interacts in an interpersonal situation, and so on. Mannerisms and other nonverbal behaviors such as squirming, tremors, hesitating, sighing, scowling, avoiding eye contact, and volume and tone of voice often provide more information than numbers about the examinee's personality and problems. Reacting slowly and deprecating one's performance, for example, suggests depression, whereas hesitations and suspiciousness are suggestive of paranoia (Matarazzo, 1972).

Answers to specific WAIS-R or WISC-R items may reflect cultural background, anxiety level, and other characteristics. Overelaborations (including irrelevant details), overinclusiveness (too general), evasiveness (indirect), self-reference (reflecting self-involvement), or bizarreness (idiosyncratic associations) of responses are especially suggestive of psychopathology. Schizophrenia may be indicated by bizarre and overinclusive responses, and a tendency to personalize responses may reflect paranoid thinking. For example, in response to the Similarities subtest item "In what way are a dog and a lion alike?" a mental patient who was subsequently diagnosed as a paranoid schizophrenic gave the following answer: "They use sound to tame them both, and they're using it to try and tame me too!" Finally, flip, self-centered responses, such as answering "I've never been there," when asked how far it is from New York to Paris, are said to be characteristic of sociopathic personalities (psychopaths) (Matarazzo, 1972).

In addition to scrutinizing such qualitatively distinct responses, errors and correct answers can be analyzed for possible insight into the cognitive styles or problem-solving approaches of examinees (Anastasi, 1982). The subtest scaled scores and deviation IQs obtained from administering the WAIS-R or WISC-R, as with subscores or total scores on any other intelligence test, provide a certain kind of information. But administering an individual test in particular should also be viewed as an opportunity to make observations of personal behavior in a controlled situation, an opportunity that can provide a great deal of nontest information and data to confirm or disprove hypotheses concerning the affective and cognitive functioning of the individual.

Summary

This chapter is concerned with physiological, perceptual, and cognitive measures of personality that have been developed in both research and applied contexts. A variety of biolectric indicators or biological transducers, many of compact and even miniature size, are available for measuring general arousal or level of activation, as well as specific responses such as sexual arousal. These measures have been applied in therapeutic contexts as biofeedback devices or to determine when, for whatever reason, the individual is experiencing stress. Prominent among these instruments are measures of blood pressure, respiration rate, heart rate, and the galvanic skin response, which are combined in the polygraph.

The polygraph does not assess lying as such, but rather indicates the increased arousal in various systems stemming from stress of any sort. By comparing the reactions of suspects to questions that are relevant with those that are irrelevant to a crime being investigated, an expert polygraph examiner may be able to judge whether or not the suspect is lying. However, it has been shown that in over one-third of the cases examiners err in the direction of concluding that innocent suspects are lying. This is because people are frequently aroused by questions pertaining to a crime even when they are innocent. Various techniques, such as also asking control questions that refer in a general way to prior misdeeds and applying a guilty knowledge test, may improve the accuracy of the polygraph. Although polygraph findings are typically not admissible as evidence in state courts, the technique continues to be used extensively for employee screening purposes in government and industry. A less intrusive device for determining when individuals are under stress, and perhaps whether or not they have lied, is the voice stress analyzer.

Although several investigators have found evidence for the physiological distinctiveness of fear and anger, in general research has failed to discover characteristic patterns of bodily reactions in different emotions. Specific emotions such as anger, fear, joy, and sorrow are determined by a complex interaction of physiological arousal, memories of past experiences in similar situations, and the individual's appraisal of his or her current situation. Biochemical tests designed to predict certain types of maladaptive behavior or mental disorders are a possibility, but for the time being they remain in the exploratory stage.

Hans Eysenck and his co-workers have accumulated evidence for the differentiation of introversion and extroversion on the basis of specific perceptual and behavioral responses. Herman Witkin and his associates have used data from three perceptual tests—Body Adjustment Test, Rod and Frame Test, Embedded Figures Test, which assess a person's ability to separate or analyze an object from its surroundings—to determine a person's standing on the field-independence/field-dependence perceptual dimension (or analytic vs. global cognitive style). People who score high on field independence are characterized as more secure, independent, controlled, psychologically mature, and self-accepting than those who score low. On the other hand, people who score high on field dependence are said to be more tense, insecure, psychologically immature, and passive, but less attuned to inner experiences and less insightful into oneself than those who score low on this variable. A number of other personality and sociocultural variables have also been found to be related to the field independence-field dependence dimension.

Cognitive styles are strategies or approaches to perceiving, remembering, and thinking that a person comes to prefer in attempting to understand and cope with the world. Among the cognitive styles that have received the greatest research attention are the reflective versus impulsive style of responding, measured by Kagan's Matching Familiar Figures Tests, and the internal versus external locus of control of reinforcement style, measured by Rotter's I-E Locus of Control. Two noteworthy models of cognitive styles are McKenney's two dimensional assimilation model and Harvey's conceptual systems model.

Recommendations for completely objective tests of personality, similar to objective tests of cognition, originated with Charles Spearman (1927), but, because of cost, time, and habit, little progress along these lines has been made. A possible exception is the Objective-Analytic Test Battery, a battery of ten tests consisting of various perceptual, cognitive, and behavioral tasks. The relationship between personality and cognition is also seen in standardized intelligence tests such as the WAIS and WISC. Efforts to diagnose behavioral disorders and other conditions by analyzing Verbal-Performance IQ differences or the pattern of subtest scatter on the WAIS and WISC have not been very successful. However, a great deal of information pertaining to personality and problems can be obtained by careful observation of the examinee's nonverbal behavior while taking an intelligence test and by noting the idiosyncrasies or peculiarities in his or her verbal responses to particular subtest questions.

Exercises

1. Identify each of the following physiological apparatuses or responses:

electrocardiogram	pneumograph
electroencephalograph	polygraph
electromyograph	psychological stress evaluator
galvanic skin response (GSR)	(PSE)
photoplethysmograph	sphygmomonometer
plethysmograph	telethermometer
pneumatic plethysmograph	voice stress analyzer

2. Differentiate between each of the following pairs of cognitive or perceptual styles or strategies:

analytic versus global	internal versus external locus of
broad versus narrow categorizing	control
constricted versus flexible	leveling versus sharpening
field dependence versus field	risk-taking versus caution
independence	scanning versus focusing strategies
impulsive versus reflective	tolerance versus intolerance

3. Numerous articles concerned with the validity and ethicality of polygraph tests have appeared in popular magazines. Consult the *Reader's Guide* or other reference source on popular periodical literature under "polygraph" and "lie detector" for three or four recent articles on the topic. Summarize the evidence and opinions on the usefulness of the procedure in criminal cases and the issues surrounding it.

4. Take and score the Sensation Seeking scale in Figure 13–3. Then administer the scale to several of your friends and score their responses. Compare your score with their's and draw appropriate conclusions. In your opinion, is this scale a valid measure of sensation seeking? Do you think sensation seeking, as a characteristic of personality, is inborn or acquired?

5.   Evaluate the research of Herman Witkin on field independence and dependence and the research of Hans Eysenck on introversion and extroversion. Consult several of the books and articles by Witkin and Eysenck (see references) in making your evaluations.

6.   The following monograph contains Rotter's I-E Scale: Rotter, J. B. (1966). Generalized expectancies for internal versus external control of reinforcement. *Psychological Monographs, 80* (1, Whole No. 609). Make a copy of the I-E Scale, complete and score it. Are the results consistent with your own subjective evaluation of yourself on the internal-external locus of control dimension?

7.   Using a stopwatch or wristwatch with a sweep second hand, determine how many seconds it takes you and each of several of your friends to find the hidden figures in the drawing at the bottom of Figure 13–4. Were there larger individual differences in the times of various people? How are these differences in time to locate embedded figures related to personality?

Suggested Readings

Aiken, L. R. (1987). *Assessment of intellectual functioning* (Chaps. 5 and 6). Newton, MA: Allyn & Bacon.

Biaggio, M. K., & Maiuro, R. D. (1985). Recent advances in anger assessment. In C. D. Spielberger & J. N. Butcher (Eds.), *Advances in personality assessment* (Vol. 5, pp. 71–112). Hillsdale, NJ: Erlbaum.

Blatt, S. J., & Allison, J. (1981). The intelligence test in personality assessment. In A. J. Rabin (Ed.), *Assessment with projective techniques* (pp. 187–231). New York: Springer.

Block, J., Buss, D. M., Block, J. H., & Gjerde, P. F. (1981). The cognitive style of breadth of categorization: Longitudinal consistency of personality correlates. *Journal of Personality and Social Psychology, 40,* 770–779.

Goldstein, K. M., & Blackman, S. (1978). Assessment of cognitive style. In P. McReynolds (Ed.), *Advances in psychological assessment* (Vol. 4, pp. 462–525). San Francisco: Jossey-Bass.

Haynes, S. N., & Wilson, C. C. (1979). *Behavioral assessment* (pp. 342–418). San Francisco: Jossey-Bass.

Haynie, N. A. (1985). Cognitive learning styles. In R. J. Corsini (Ed.), *Encyclopedia of psychology* (Vol. 1, pp. 236–238). New York: Wiley.

Katkin, E. S., & Hastrup, J. L. (1982). Psychophysiological methods in clinical research. In P. C. Kendall & J. N. Butcher (Eds.), *Handbook of research methods in clinical psychology* (pp. 387–425). New York: Wiley.

Kleinmuntz, B., & Szucko, J. J. (1984). Lie detection in ancient and modern times. *American Psychologist, 39,* 766–776.

Lykken, D. T. (1985). Lie detection. In R. J. Corsini (Ed.), *Encyclopedia of psychology* (Vol. 2, pp. 306–307). New York: Wiley.

Wilson, G. (1978). Introversion and extroversion. In H. London & J. E. Exner (Eds.), *Dimensions of personality* (pp. 217–261). New York: Wiley.

CHAPTER 14

Issues and Prospects in
Personality Assessment

It would be comforting to conclude at the end of a textbook on personality assessment that progress in this field has been ever onward and upward during the 70 years since Woodworth devised his Personal Data Sheet. It would also be reassuring to conclude that all the issues and controversies that prevailed during the early years of personality assessment have finally been resolved by compromise among the various disputants. Unfortunately, neither of these conclusions is justified. Progress in personality assessment over the past three-quarters of a century has actually been rather uneven, and at times the field has appeared to go backward rather than forward. Perhaps, however, it merely seems that way to a psychologist who tends to view the halcyon days of yesteryear through rose-colored glasses and does not remember the struggles and uncertainties as clearly as the excitement and successes experienced in a young discipline.

In any case, the issues in personality assessment have not gone away, although some of them have been muted by the passage of time. Thus, personologists no longer debate as energetically about response sets, clinical versus statistical prediction, objective versus projective assessment, hereditary versus environmental influences, holistic versus analytic interpretations, and behavioral versus psychoanalytic versus phenomenological models. On the other hand, the idiographic versus nomothetic, and traits versus situations controversies continue to flourish. Questions concerning the ethics and morality of personality assessment, as well as its applications and validity for particular groups and in specific contexts continue to be of concern. And issues of more recent vintage, such as computer-based assessment, newer tests and methodological procedures, and newer theories or models of personality assessment have become prominent. But, for better or for worse, the 1917 to 1988 time traveler in personality assessment would need to do less catching up than his counterpart in physics or biology. Personality psychologists still have much work to accomplish before their successes are substantially more impressive than those of their predecessors in this discipline. Nevertheless, the prize still seems to be worth the effort—an effort that will require continuing insight and patience on the part of researchers, theoreticians, and practitioners.

Older Issues in Personality Assessment

During their relatively short history, measures of personality have been attacked repeatedly by both psychologists and nonpsychologists. Representative of the most extreme negative reactions to these instruments are the writings of William Whyte (1956) and Martin Gross (1962, 1965) on the applications of personality assessment in business and industry. In commenting on testimony given before a special subcommittee of the U.S. House of Representatives, Gross (1965) severely criticized personality tests on the grounds of invalidity and immorality.

Whyte and Gross were, of course, not the first to castigate personality tests. Indicative of the feelings of some of the lay public toward psychological assessment was the June 1959 burning of certain attitude scales and other questionnaires and tests. The Houston School Board ordered the burning of the answer sheets to six tests and inventories that had been administered to 5,000 ninth graders. The bonfire was a consequence of the strenuous protest by a group of Houston parents who objected to the fact that school children had been required, as part of a psychoeducational research study, to respond to items of the following type (Nettler, 1959):

> I enjoy soaking in the bathtub.
>
> A girl who gets into trouble on a date has no one to blame but herself.
>
> If you don't drink in our gang, they make you feel like a sissy.
>
> Sometimes I tell dirty jokes when I would rather not.
>
> Dad always seems too busy to pal around with me. (p. 682)

It is certainly understandable how a situation of this kind could develop, particularly when one realizes that the public does not always share the "scientific attitude" to which psychologists subscribe nor do they have the same degree of desire to understand human behavior. Furthermore, it has been alleged that many personality test items—especially those concerned with sex, religion, and morals—are not only personally offensive but also potentially destructive to the character of school children.

Strong emotional reactions over the meaning and validity of psychological testing, and social science research in general, also occurred in the debate over Project CAMELOT during the mid-1960s. This project, financed by the U.S. Government, was designed to analyze the causes of counterrevolution and counterinsurgency in Latin America. Public awareness of the project resulted in a rather heated reaction by our neighbors to the south, as well as certain U.S. congressmen. The Project CAMELOT debate, combined with civil suits and attacks on the use of selection tests, led to a congressional investigation of psychological testing in government, industry, and education. One practice examined at length in the congressional inquiry was the administration of personality test items concerning sex and religion to job applicants. Test items of the following types were singled out for special criticism: (1) My sex life is satisfactory; (2) I believe in God; (3) I don't get along very well with my parents. Although the results of hearings concerning personality tests did not lead to an indictment with respect to these tests, the governmental concern manifested by the hearings did prompt psychologists and other assessment specialists to show greater concern for the ethics and values of psychological assessment.

Ethical Issues

Ethical issues such as invasion of privacy, confidentiality of test reports, and privileged communication were dealt with to some extent in Chapter 4, but it will be worthwhile to consider them briefly again here. From a legal standpoint, psychological test data are considered a *privileged communication* to be shared with others only on a need-to-know basis. Examinees should be told at testing time why they are being tested, who will have access to the information, and how the information will be used. Principle 8 of the *Ethical Principles of Psychologists* (American Psychological Association, 1981) indicates that: "in using assessment techniques, psychologists respect the right of the clients to have full explanations of the nature and purpose of the techniques in language the clients understand, unless an explicit exception to this right has been agreed upon in advance." (p. 637) Under such circumstances, examinees or people legally responsible for them are more likely to provide the required informed consent. After being tested, examinees also have a right to know their scores and what interpretations are placed on them. Except under unusual circumstances, as when an examinee is a danger to him- or herself or others, test information is confidential and should not be released without the necessary informed consent. Ideally, psychological assessment findings are treated conscientiously and with an awarenesss of the limitations of the assessment instruments and the needs and rights of examinees. Unfortunately, the ethics of personality assessors have not always been what they should be. Therefore, the adoption by the American Psychological Association and other professional organizations of codes of ethics pertaining to testing and sanctions against their violation was a step forward in personality assessment and the practice of psychology in general (American Psychological Association, 1981; American Educational Research et al., 1985).

Validity of Personality Assessment

In addition to ethical and moral concerns about personality testing, the technical questions of what is measured by such tests, whether those things are worthwhile measuring, and how best to interpret and apply the results have received a great deal of professional and legal attention during the past quarter of a century. It has been stressed in various places throughout this book that the psychometric qualities of personality tests, and projective techniques in particular, often leave much to be desired. Criterion-keyed inventories tend to have higher validities than other assessment procedures, but even their validity coefficients often decrease substantially when they are administered in situations other than those for which they were intended.

Not only is there a need for more reliable and valid personality tests, but improvements in the theoretical bases of these instruments and in the criteria against which they are validated are necessary. For example, the disease model of mental disorders and the associated diagnostic classification system (DSM-III-R) (American Psychiatric Association, 1987), which is basic to the development and scoring of many personality assessment procedures, is in many respects ambiguous and unreliable. Finally, there is the common problem of misinterpreting the results of personality assessments. Such misinterpretations can occur through failure to consider the base rate, or frequency of occurrence, of the event (criterion) being predicted. Misinterpretations of test findings can also result from what is referred to as clinical insight or intuition, but all too often is only a conglomeration of superficial stereotypes, truisms, and other overgeneralizations that may make sense to the personality analyst or diagnostician but are actually misleading.

Despite the shortcomings of these instruments, one cannot help being impressed by the variety of techniques that have been employed in personality assessment. Unfortunately, many of these techniques represent relatively crude attempts to measure characteristics of human behavior and should be viewed primarily as research devices rather than finished psychometric procedures. To be sure, personality inventories and projectives have sometimes contributed to selection decisions. The MMPI, for example, proved valuable in the successful selection program of the Peace Corps during the 1960s. The utility of measures of mental abilities has also been enhanced on occasion by combining them with measures of temperament and motivation. It is generally recognized, however, that none of the available methods of assessing personality is completely satisfactory. The solution to the problem clearly lies in better research and development, but such efforts must be undertaken with a socially responsible attitude and a respect for the rights of individuals.

Test users should also possess a better understanding of statistical and other technical matters pertaining to test design, reliability, validity, and norms. Even when the examiner has adequate knowledge and training and the test is satisfactory for its stated purposes, it is important to keep a record of hits and misses and other indicators of successful and unsuccessful predictions made on the basis of test scores. Over the long run, such information serves as a check on the validity of the test for the stated purposes for which it is used by the examiner.

Sex and Ethnic Bias

Related to both ethical issues and the question of test validity is the matter of whether personality tests are biased against a particular sex, social class, nationality, or racial group. For example, Gynther and Green (1980) maintain that the significant differences between the scores of blacks and whites on the MMPI lead to incorrect diagnoses and treatment. However, Pritchard and Rosenblatt (1980) conclude that such differences are exaggerated and that the MMPI is as valid for blacks as for whites. Other than the work of Gynther and his associates, there has been relatively little systematic research on the matter of ethnic-group, social-class, or nationality-group bias in personality test performance. These are, however, matters that will have to be considered more carefully in the development of new instruments and the revision and restandardization of older instruments.

Because there has been more research and action on the matter of *sex bias* in personality testing, more space will be devoted to this issue. Sex bias can affect the kinds of responses obtained on personality tests and the manner in which those responses are evaluated and interpreted. With respect to test content, the language of many personality and interest inventories has traditionally been somewhat sexist in nature. Sex bias on interest inventories such as the Strong Vocational Interest Blanks and the Kuder Preference Record has long been a topic of concern, with scores on these inventories reflecting sex stereotypes. The fact that the mean scores of females are usually higher on artistic, conventional, and social interest themes, whereas the mean scores of males are higher on enterprising, investigative, and realistic themes (Gottfredson, Holland & Gottfredson, 1975; Prediger & Hanson, 1976) is not necessarily a reflection of sex bias but may simply represent a societal influence. However, it does not follow that women are lower than men in, say, mechanical interest if the majority of items designed to assess this interest deal with apparatus or machines that are more familiar to men.

A traditional response to sex differences in test scores has been to provide separate norms for males and females. More recently, efforts have been made to construct tests in such a way that they are not biased toward either sex. By eliminating sexist language in newer versions of inventories such as the SVIB-SCII and the MMPI, the test authors have succeeded in producing instruments that are fairer to both females and males. Another procedure for reducing sex bias is employed on instruments such as the Vocational Interest Inventory, which is composed of items endorsed equally often by males and females.

Investigations of the effects on personality test responses of the examiner's sex and whether it is the same or different from that of the examinee have yielded inconsistent results. In some studies examiner-examinee sex differences have been associated with differences in the number and nature of the responses given by the examinee to instruments such as the Rorschach (e.g., Harris & Masling, 1970), but in other studies no difference in the number of responses or fewer responses of a certain kind have been found when the examiner and examinee are of different sex (Milner & Moses, 1972).

Sex bias is probably more likely to enter into the picture in the process of test interpretation than in test administration or scoring. This is particularly true when the scales on which the test is scored are, as in the case of the older Strong Vocational Interest Blank, different for males and females. For this reason, on tests such as the SVIB-SCII both same-sex and combined-sex norms are now made available.

Clinical versus Statistical Prediction

One of the most important reasons for obtaining test data is to make behavioral predictions. Unfortunately, personality assessments tend to have rather low predictive validities, a fact which, coupled with their use in personnel screening and clinical diagnosis, has prompted a great deal of research on methods of increasing their validities. As described briefly in Chapter 4, the statistical (or actuarial) approach to data collection and behavior prediction consists of applying a statistical formula, a set of rules, or an actuarial table to assessment data. In contrast, the clinical, or impressionistic, approach involves making intuitive judgments or drawing conclusions on the basis of subjective impressions combined with a theory of personality. Furthermore, the data themselves may be either statistically based information such as test scores or clinically based information such as biographical data and personality ratings.

An early review of research comparing the clinical and statistical approaches to prediction concluded that in 19 out of 20 studies the statistical approach was either superior or equal to the clinical approach in effectiveness (Meehl, 1954). Eleven years later, after summarizing data from some 50 studies comparing the two approaches Meehl (1965) concluded that the statistical approach showed greater predictive efficiency in two-thirds of the studies and was just as efficient as the clinical approach in the remaining studies. A review by Sines (1970) published another five years later concurred with Meehl's conclusion: in all but one of the 50 studies reviewed by Sines the actuarial (statistical) approach was found to be superior to the clinical approach in predicting various kinds of behavior.

Although the data summarized by Meehl and Sines provide impressive support for the conclusion that personality diagnoses and behavior predictions are more accurate when a statistical rather than a clinical approach is employed, Lindzey (1965) demonstrated that an expert clinician can sometimes make highly accurate diagnoses. By using only the information obtained from administering the Thematic Apperception Test, a clinical psychologist proved to be 95% accurate in detecting homosexuality. In this study the statistical approach of employing only certain objective scores obtained from the TAT protocols was not as accurate as the clinical approach.

Continuing the debate, Holt (1970) argued, on various grounds, against the superiority of the statistical or actuarial approach to personality assessment. But despite Holt's objections, it must be concluded that statistical procedures have generally proved superior to clinical or impressionistic approaches, both in terms of time required and accuracy of prediction. Although the debate on this issue has abated during the past 20 years, recognition of the efficiency of actuarial methods led to the construction of so-called cookbooks and to the current emphasis on computer programs for personality diagnosis and behavior prediction.

Heredity and Environment

The extent to which test scores, and personality in general, are influenced by heredity and environment has been a topic of dispute for the better part of this century. The issue is far from settled, but contemporary psychologists recognize that both factors, interactively, influence performance on both affective and cognitive measures. Correlational statistics computed from the scores on personality inventories (CPI, MMPI, etc.) and other measures of personality obtained from individuals with different degrees of kinship have revealed modest but significant contributions of hereditary factors. For example, research on concordance rates (see Report 14–1) for various personality characteristics in identical twins has provided evidence for a significant hereditary influence in introversion-extroversion, activity level, anxiety, dependence, dominance, emotionality, sociability, and certain other personality traits (Eysenck, 1956; Dworkin, Burke, Maher & Gottesman, 1976; Gottesman, 1966; Scarr, 1969; Buss & Plomin, 1975). There is also considerable evidence for a genetic influence in certain mental disorders such as schizophrenia and manic-depressive psychosis (Kallman & Jarvik, 1959; Gottesman & Shields, 1973, 1982). The effects of heredity on personality are, however, far from simple since they vary with age, sex, and other individual differences. Although genetic variables undoubtedly influence personality, they do so by interacting in a complex manner with a person's physical and social environment.

After summarizing evidence for the persistence of various personality characteristics throughout childhood, Thomas and Chess (1977) pointed out that hereditary characteristics both affect and are affected by personal experience. Parents, other people, and the impersonal environment as well react differently to children having different physical and temperament traits. These reactions can, in turn,

Report 14–1   **Measures of Hereditary Influence**

A number of procedures and measures may be used to estimate the proportion or percentage of variance in a characteristic that can be accounted for by hereditary differences in a population. One measure is the *concordance rate*, the percentage of individuals, each of whom is related to a person (an index case) having a particular characteristic, who also have the characteristic. For example, the concordance rate for monozygotic twins suffering from depression has been estimated as 40%, meaning that if one monozygotic twin has the disorder, the probability is .40 that the other twin will also have it (Allen, 1976).

Another useful measure of the influence of heredity is the *heritability index*. This index is roughly defined as the variance in a specified characteristic that is attributable to heredity divided by the variance in the characteristic that is attributable to both heredity and environment. Jensen (1969) estimated the heritability index for intelligence to be approximately .80, which is interpreted as meaning that 80% of the variability among the intelligence test scores of people in an assortatively mating population can be accounted for by differences in heredity and only 20% of the variability by differences in environment.

A more complex statistical method for estimating the relative influences of heredity and environment in determining a psychological characteristic is Cattell's (1965b) *multiple abstract variance analysis* (MAVA). This method involves administering a number of personality tests to the members of a large number of families and then statistically analyzing the results to yield four variance measures: between-family environmental variance, within-family environmental variance, between-family hereditary variance, and within-family hereditary variance. Statistical equations are then employed to estimate the influences of heredity and environment in determining the characteristic. For example, application of the MAVA technique yielded an estimate of 40 to 45 % for the percentage of variance in scores on a test of neuroticism accounted for by heredity. However, considerably smaller percentages of the variance in scores on measures of emotional sensitivity and carefreeness versus cautiousness were accounted for by heredity. From applying the MAVA technique to a wide range of personality variables, Hundleby, Pawlik, and Cattell (1965) concluded that approximately one-third of the overall variance in scores on personality measures is due to heredity and two-thirds to environment.

affect the child's genetically based characteristics, thereby demonstrating the interplay between heredity and environment in shaping personality.

Idiographic and Nomothetic Approaches

Recognizing that, although it is complex and often difficult to understand, human behavior is nevertheless predictable or lawful, many personality theorists and practicing clinicians have opted to search for that lawfulness in individual rather than group behavior. They have argued that the *nomothetic approach* of seeking general laws of behavior and personality, an approach that relies heavily on group norms or averages, is unrealistic and inadequate in attempting to understand individuals. Instead they have advocated an *idiographic approach* in which every person is considered to be a lawful, integrated system to be studied in his or her own right. Thus, the idiographic versus nomothetic battle was joined, usually with more behavioristic and certain trait-factor psychologists taking a nomothetic position and other trait-factor psychologists or personologists, in addition to phenomenologists, taking an idiographic position. Gordon Allport (1937), the psychologist who first described the idiographic-nomothetic distinction in personality assessment, recognized the usefulness of the nomothetic approach but warned of its shortcomings (Allport, 1961):

> Each single life is lawful, for it reveals its own orderly and necessary *process of growth.* . . . Most studies of personality are comparative . . . and these tools are valuable. The danger is that they may lead to a dismemberment of personality in such a way that each fragment is related to corresponding fragments in other people, and not to the personal system within which they are embedded. . . . Psychology is truly itself only when it can deal with individuality. . . . The truth is that psychology is *assigned* the task of being curious about human persons, and persons exist only in concrete and unique patterns. (pp. 572–573)

Rather than personality inventories and other norm-based instruments, Allport advocated the use of personal records (biographies, diaries, etc.), case studies, observations, and other nonstandardized but more individualized assessment procedures.

Many writers in the field of individual differences and personality (e.g., Tyler, 1978) have continually supported the idiographic approach of attempting to understand the complexities of psychological structures and processes within the individual. And even more statistically oriented writers such as Anastasi (1985) recognize that, although many of the idiographic procedures advocated by Allport and others are psychometrically crude, they may "provide a rich harvest of leads for further exploration." (p. xxv) Anastasi sympathizes with the tendency of clinical psychologists to be more receptive than other psychologists to these instruments. Furthermore, she cautions that numerical scores on personality tests and other standardized, carefully designed clinical instruments may create an illusion of objectivity and quantification with no guarantee of being accurately interpreted.

In a new twist on the old idiographic approach, Lamiell (1981) maintains that personality can best be described not by comparing what the individual does with what other people do (normative approach) but rather by comparing what the individual does with what he or she does not do but could do. Consistent with this suggestion, Lamiell proposed an index of a person's standing on a personality attribute as the ratio of the individual's attribute-consistent behaviors to the domain of all possible attribute-relevant behaviors in a specific situation. Comparing such ratios across many individuals results in what Lamiell terms an *idiothetic* psychology of personality and a framework for describing individual personality. According to Lamiell and Trierweiler (1986), such an approach is superior to the use of personality inventories and other psychometric devices that are standardized and validated on groups of people. They argue that, unless the reliability and validity coefficients of assessment devices are perfect, such instruments cannot be interpreted at the individual level. A nomotheticist might counter, however, that although one cannot predict precisely how well an individual will perform on a criterion variable that has less than a perfect correlation with a predictor variable, individual prediction is a matter of probability rather than exactitude and such information may still be useful in counseling and screening even when it is not precise. Furthermore, Lamiell's idiothetic approach to assessment has been criticized on various grounds by Paunonen and Jackson (1986) as well as other measurement specialists.

Continuing Issues: Traits-Situations and Computer-Based Assessment

Although the controversial issues described in the previous section continue, to some extent they have cooled off with time. A possible exception is the heredity-environment issue, which remains a hot topic in intelligence testing. One of the most widely debated issues in personality assessment, which possesses substance as well as fire and has led to some novel research and theorizing, is the traits versus situation controversy. Another issue that has also been associated with many changes in personality assessment is computer-based assessment.

Traits and Situations

The psychology of personality has traditionally assumed that behavior is influenced to a great extent by traits that manifest themselves in a consistent way across different situations. It was recognized that environment (the specific situation) is also a factor in determining behavior, but the emphasis was on personality traits and their measurement. Despite the preoccupation with traits, the fact that the situation is sometimes more important in determining specific behavior was clearly demonstrated by the results of Hartshorne and May's (1928) studies of character in children.

Mischel's Complaint   Four decades after the classic Hartshorne and May studies, in a book that took personality study by storm, Walter Mischel (1968) summarized evidence showing that the behavioral correlates of cognitive abilities are fairly consistent across different situations but that personal-social behavior is highly dependent on the specific situation in which it occurs. Consequently Mischel concluded that inferences regarding personality dynamics or traits are less useful than knowledge of situational variables in predicting behavior. He further argued that assessments of generalized traits of personality are not particularly useful because such traits so often fail to show cross-situational generality (Mischel, 1968).

> Global traits and states are excessively crude, gross units to encompass adequately the extraordinary complexity and subtlety of the discriminations that people constantly make. Traditional trait-state conceptions of man have depicted him as victimized by his infantile history, as possessed by unchanging rigid trait attributes, and as driven inexorably by unconscious irrational forces. This conceptualization of man, besides being philosophically unappetizing, is contradicted by massive experimental data. The traditional trait-state conceptualizations of personality, while often paying lip service to man's complexity and to the uniqueness of each person, in fact lead to a grossly oversimplified view that misses both the richness and the uniqueness of individual lives. A more adequate conceptualization must take full account of man's extraordinary adaptiveness and capacities for discrimination, awareness, and self-regulation; it must also recognize that men can and do reconceptualize themselves and change, and that an understanding of how humans can constructively modify their behavior in systematic ways is the core of a truly dynamic personality psychology. (p. 301)

Rather than analyzing personality into a complex of traits or factors Mischel (1986) proposes a social learning approach, an approach that stresses the fact that people learn to make different responses in different situations and that the accuracy with which a person's behavior in a specific situation can be predicted must take into account his or her learning history in similar situations.

It is widely recognized that social norms, roles, and other group related conditions exert powerful effects on people and often override temperament or style as determiners of action and thoughts. In fact, highly structured situations in which the norms or constraints are quite strong exert an especially powerful effect on individual behavior. On the other hand, more flexible situations in which the norms of behavior are not so clearly delineated provide a greater opportunity for the manifestation of a wide range of personality traits (Monson et al., 1982). Thus, as long as a social situation is fairly constant and the expected behaviors and sanctions are quite apparent, people tend to submerge their idiosyncrasies or individualities and adjust their behavior and thinking to the expectations and reward-punishment schedules provided by others in that situation. It has been amply demonstrated by research in social psychology and by candid television programs that when in Rome all kinds of people do as the Romans do. Acceptance of this truism does not imply, however, that individual personality has no influence on behavior.

Responses to Mischel   Although interpreted by many psychologists as representing merely a one-sided or biased viewpoint, Mischel's criticisms did not go unanswered and actually served to stimulate a great deal of thinking and research on the trait-situation issue and related matters. For example, from the perspective of *attribution theory*, it was noted that people tend to attribute their own behavior to variables in the specific situation but attribute the behaviors of other people to personality traits (Jones & Nisbett, 1972). One possible explanation for this error is that people understand themselves better than they do others and more accurately perceive external circumstances as the primary determinant of their behavior. Also related to the trait-situation debate is Epstein's (1979) demonstration that aggregating (summing) behavioral measures across different times and situations increases both the reliability and validity of those measures. The improvement in validity is, however, greater when behavior is aggregated across time than when it is aggregated across situations.

A number of investigators (e.g., Bem & Allen, 1974; Block, 1977; Underwood & Moore, 1981) have found that the consistency of traits across situations is itself an individual difference variable of which the individual is aware. In an investigation by Bem and Allen (1974) people who believed themselves to be fairly consistent in friendliness and conscientiousness tended to be so, whereas those who perceived themselves as being less consistent tended to be just that.[1]

In another study, Bem and Funder (1978) maintained that a person will behave similarly in two or more situations if he or she perceives the situations as similar. Situations, like people, may be conceptualized as having personalities, and as long as the characteristics of a situation are matched with those of the person, the latter is likely to behave as expected in that situation. Unexpected, or inconsistent, behavior is, according to Bem and Funder, the consequence of a person-situation mismatch. However, the mismatch need not be on all personal characteristics, but only on certain prototypic variables that are important or salient to the individual and the situation. Not all traits are equally relevant for describing a certain person's behavior; some traits characterize some people and other traits characterize other people.

Interaction and Template Matching   As Mischel and other psychologists recognize, a person's behavior in a specific situation is caused by a multitude of factors; among them are personal characteristics and the particular situation in which the behavior occurs. In certain *strong situations*, the features of the situations themselves are more important than personal characteristics in determining how people will react; in other *weak situations*, personal characteristics are more influential than the situation. An example of a strong situation is a religious service or other context in which expected behaviors are more clearly prescribed. Another strong situation is when one is in a different culture or context and doesn't quite know how to behave; usually this dilemma is solved by observing what other people do and copying their behavior. A weak situation is one in which the influence of other people is not so strong, for example when one is at home with only his or her spouse or carousing with two or three close friends.

Rather than personal characteristics or situational variables alone, more generally it is the interaction between personality and situation that determines behavior. Thus, it can be argued that efforts at developing effective measures of personality will be more successful if they begin by providing a conceptual model of how personality dispositions and situational characteristics interact and then develop measures of both sets of variables to make possible a true interactional assessment (McReynolds, 1979). One proposal for understanding the person-situation interaction is Bem and Funder's (1978) *template matching technique*. These investigators conceptualize a situation template as a pattern of behavior characterizing the way in which a person (I) is ideally expected to behave in the situation. Then the extent to which another person (J) behaves in the same way in that situation depends on the match between the personality characteristics of J and those of I.

Computer-Based Assessment

Another issue that promises to persist for some time is that of computer-based assessment. Computers are used for a variety of purposes in psychological assessment, including administering and scoring tests, interviewing, and interpreting assessment results. Computers can also assist in the process of test development by determining norms, derived scores, reliability and validity coefficients, and by conducting item analyses. The uses of computers in interviewing and test interpretation have been discussed in previous chapters of the book, and the details will not be repeated here. The first *computer-based test interpretation (CBTI)* programs were developed in the early 1960s at the Mayo Clinic, the Hartford Institute of Living, and the University of Alabama (Swenson & Pearson, 1964; Rome et al., 1962; Glueck & Reznikoff, 1965). An estimated 200 CBTI programs are now in use, among which are programs that score and interpret personality tests such as the MMPI, the California Psychological Inventory, the 16 Personality Factor Questionnaire, the Millon Clinical Multiaxial Inventory, the Personality Inventory for Children, and the Rorschach Inkblot Test.

Computer-based test interpretations are usually not as individualized as those produced impressionistically by a clinical or counseling psychologist. Many computer programs are designed to take the age, sex, and other demographic information on the examinee into account, but no program considers all of the examinee's personal attributes. Consequently, psychological examiners typically supplement CBTI reports with additional interpretive statements gleaned from their observations and experience. As recommended by the *Guidelines for Computer-Based Tests and Interpretations*, "Computer-generated interpretive reports should be used only in conjunction with professional judgment. The user should judge for each test taker the validity of the computerized test report based on the user's professional knowledge of the total context of testing and the test taker's performance and characteristics." (American Psychological Association, 1986, p. 12) Computer-based test reports are not an adequate substitute for clinical judgment, and a trained clinician should review the report (Butcher, 1978). Some clinicians have resisted using computers, considering them a threat to their control over decision-making (Young, 1982). But, as Madsen (1986) points out, the importance of clinicians, counselors, and other professionals in personality assessment is not diminished when computers are used to administer, score, and interpret tests. Computers can do only what they are programmed to do, and hence are limited in their adaptability, perspicacity, and ability to detect subtle differences in subjective meanings in responses to test materials. When properly applied, computers complement clinicians rather than replace them.

Comments under the guideline quoted in the last paragraph indicate, however, that "a well-designed statistical treatment of test results and ancillary information will yield more valid assessments than will an individual professional using the same information." (American Psychological Association, 1986, p. 13) Consequently, embellishing or altering the computerized interpretation in any way should not be done routinely but only for good and compelling reasons. Be that as it may, a CBTI narrative is not a comprehensive personality analysis or diagnosis, but rather it serves as an indicator of psychological problems or a verification of problems detected by other means (Eyde & Kowal, 1984).

Concerning the reactions of examinees to computer-based test interpretations, the majority of respondents in one study agreed that computer-based MMPI interpretive reports were at least equal in accuracy to those provided by expert clinicians (Johnson, Giannetti & Williams, 1978). In another investigation, computer-based MMPI assessments actually outperformed clinicians in differentiating between neurotic and psychotic patients (Goldberg, 1970) and in predicting suicidal or assaultive behavior (Mirabile, Houck & Glueck, 1970).

Computers, and especially microcomputers, possess many advantages for psychological assessment. In addition to being extremely efficient, computers are adaptable to individual differences in mental and physical characteristics and provide prompt scoring and interpretation of assessment results. Despite their advantages, there are some serious problems with the use of computers in testing. Among these are the cost of the system and the inadequacy of software, as well as the fact that computer-based test interpretations may be inappropriate with certain groups of people (young children, the mentally retarded, people in crisis situations, severe psychotics, etc.). There is also the problem of maintaining confidentiality when computers collect and store important personal information. Examinees have a legal right to control the release of test scores and other personal information, a right that may be too easily violated when such information is stored on a computer. Obviously, CBTI reports should be kept confidential, with the examiner and record keeper acting in accordance with an examinee's right to control his or her own personal information (Herr & Best, 1984; Sampson & Pyle, 1983).

With respect to computer-based test scoring and interpretation services, few of the interpretative programs have been adequately validated and many are based on inadequate norms. Reliability is also a problem with some programs. Consequently, buyers must beware of the proliferation of CBTI programs and demand proof that the service providers adhere to the usual standards of reliability, validity, and representative norms.

There is also a tendency for computer-generated test reports to be endowed with greater status than they deserve—to be viewed as if they were written in stone— even when the validity of such narratives has not been demonstrated. Accepting test interpretations generated by computers as necessarily valid is an illustration not only of the power of the machine but also the *Barnum effect* of believing that personality descriptions phrased in generalities, truisms, and other statements that sound specific to a given person but are actually applicable to almost anyone are accurate. The tendency to use computer-based test interpretations prematurely is more likely to occur in unqualified users who are given access to the interpretations. Turkington (1984) points out:

> The most pressing worry of practitioners is the accuracy of computerized test interpretation. . . . Used by those with little training or awareness of test interpretation validity, computerized testing can do more harm than good. . . . Because test scores and interpretations come from a computer, they give a false impression of infallibility. And because the tests are so easy to use . . . many who are untrained will use them incorrectly for decisions involving employment, educational placement, occupational counseling, mental health diagnosis or brain deficiency assessments. (pp. 7, 26)

According to Skinner and Pakula (1986), Matarazzo's (1983) prediction of a "flood of litigation involving unqualified users of the products of this new technology" (p. 323), which is presumably "just around the corner," will probably name both the test user and test developer as defendents. For this reason, if for no other, developers of CBTI products and organizations that provide CBTI services should make certain that the users of their products are qualified *psychodiagnosticians.* CBTI services should also take care that their products are adequately validated and standardized, follow the *Guidelines for Computer-Based Tests and Interpretations,* and are made available, with all supporting documentation, to qualified reviewers. Reviews of CBTI products are published in professional journals such as *Computers in Human Behavior, Computers in Human Services, Computers in Psychiatry/ Psychology, Computer Use in Social Services,* and the *Journal of Counseling and Development.* After examining these reviews and other documentation on CBTI report products, users would be advised to ask themselves the following questions (Ben-Porath & Butcher, 1986):

> To what extent has the validity of this report been studied?
>
> To what extent does this report rely on empirical findings in generating its interpretation?
>
> To what extent does this report incorporate all of the currently validated descriptive information?

Does the report take demographic variables into account?

Are different versions available for various referral questions?

Is the report internally consistent?

Does the report include practical suggestions?

Is the report periodically revised to reflect newly acquired information? (pp. 173–174)

Finally, it is recommended that students in the human service professions receive adequate computer-based assessment training along the lines outlined by Meier and Geiger (1986). Such training will become increasingly important as new forms of assessment based on administration, scoring, and interpretation by computers are developed. Because the human service professions have traditionally been nontechnologically oriented and have usually attracted people with little computer experience, this requirement is important but likely to prove difficult to meet.

New Methods, Measures, and Theories

The increasing popularity of large-scale testing, combined with criticisms and professional discontent with traditional approaches and instruments, has led to the development and promise of a number of new assessment procedures, instruments, and theories. Among the most significant of these are adaptive testing, the development of measures for assessing environments and for health- and law-related purposes, cognitive theories of personality assessment, and new statistical approaches.

Adaptive Testing

In a traditional test administration procedure the same items are administered to all examinees. Although this approach has not been followed precisely on all tests (for example, on various individually administered tests of intelligence and personality), in general little flexibility has been permitted in deciding what items should be presented. The traditional approach is frequently inefficient, requiring examinees to respond to many items or questions that are inappropriate, unnecessary, or redundant. Adapting the items to be administered to the characteristics (ability level, age, etc.) of the examinee, however, eliminates the need for presenting many items for the examinee's consideration and thereby makes for more efficient assessment. By making the decision concerning which item to administer next contingent on the examinee's response(s) to the previous item(s), *adaptive testing* (also known as branched, sequential, tailored, interactive, or routing testing) makes possible, with no loss of information and equal reliability and validity, the presentation of only a fraction of the number of items required by the traditional testing practice in which examinees are expected to attempt all items.

Item pools for adaptive testing can be assembled by computers employing one of the item response methodologies such as latent-trait theory, item characteristic curve theory, or the Rasch model (see Hulin, Drasgow & Parsons, 1983). It is important, however, that the assumptions of item-response theory (IRT) be met. These assumptions are that all items in a pool measure a single dimension and that the items are independent, that is, the answer to one item does not depend on the answer to any other item. Satisfaction of the first assumption, that of unidimensionality, can be verified by factor-analytic procedures and is more likely to be met by item pools or tests derived by factor analysis.

Although adaptive tests have been used more extensively in achievement and aptitude measurement, applications of adaptive testing methodology to the assessment of personality are also being explored. A particularly useful type of adaptive test for purposes of personality assessment is a stratified adaptive test or *stratadaptive test* (Weiss, 1973, 1985), in which a pool of test items is divided into subsets or strata, based, say, on levels of a personality characteristic or severity of symptoms. Suppose, for example, that the degree of extroversion characterizing a person is to be assessed. An examinee who endorses an item in the direction keyed for extroversion in one stratum goes on to an item pertaining to extroversion at the next higher stratum (next higher level of the characteristic). Various termination and scoring rules are possible. For example, the process of presenting items at successively higher strata might continue until the examinee fails to endorse an extroversion item at a given level; his or her score would then be determined by the highest level reached and the item within that level that was endorsed. Similarly, an examinee who fails to endorse an item in the direction keyed for extroversion in one stratum would be presented an extroversion item at the next lower level, and so forth until he or she endorses an item in the extroversion direction or we run out of strata. In each stratum, items are so arranged that the most discriminating items are presented first (Weiss, 1985).

Sapinkopf's (1977) study with the Dominance (*Do*), Femininity (*Fe*), and Social Conformity (*Sc*) scales of the California Psychological Inventory is illustrative of the use of stratadaptive testing and item-response theory in personality assessment. Compared with the conventional method of administering these scales, stratadaptive testing proved to be more efficient both in terms of the number of items administered and testing time. Of course, efficiency should not have the last word in evaluating a testing procedure; efficiency is meaningless without some knowledge of the reliability and validity of the stratadaptive approach compared with other computer-based and noncomputer-based approaches to assessment.

Environmental Assessment

As the research summarized by Mischel (1968) demonstrates, situational factors play an important role in determining behavior. Consequently, combining *environmental assessments* with measures of ability and personality should improve the prediction of behavior in specific situations. Data obtained on environmental characteristics may also prove useful in comparing different situations. However, the effects of the situation on the person do not constitute a one-way street. People certainly react to environments in different ways and select and structure situations in terms of their own personalities. But there is also a reciprocal interaction, or *transaction* between person and environmental context, with the person both affected by and affecting the environment. Thus far, personality assessment is only on the threshold of devising techniques for analyzing this dynamic, two-way interaction and instruments for assessing it. However, the work of Rudolf Moos and his associates (e.g., Moos, 1976, 1979; Moos & Moos, 1986) on ecological measurement is indicative of how social environments can be conceptualized and evaluated.

Recognizing that the ways in which people perceive environments affect their behaviors in those environments and that the environments are, in turn, influenced by personal perceptions, Moos has directed his efforts toward understanding and assessing human milieus. His assessments of the personalities of environments and their effects on individual functioning may be described in terms of three broad dimensions: (1) the nature and intensity of personal relationships, (2) personal growth and self-enhancement influences, and (3) system maintenance and change. In general, people are more satisfied and comfortable, less irritable and depressed, and experience greater self-esteem in environments that they perceive as highly relationship oriented.

Moos maintains that an analysis of environments in terms of the three dimensions listed above can lead to the formulation of criteria for the ideal environment and optimal methods for instituting environmental changes. To provide a means of assessing these dimensions, a number of Social Climate Scales (available from Consulting Psychologists Press) were constructed. Each scale consists of 90 to 100 items and yields 7 to 10 scores covering the three dimensions referred to above. Based on the assumption that people can distinguish different dimensions of social environments, the items on each scale are answerable in 15 to 20 minutes by individuals who are functioning in or cognizant of the particular social environment.

Moos and his collaborators have devised measures of the following social environments: classroom, community oriented programs, correctional institutions, family, group, military, university residence, ward atmosphere, and work. Different forms of these instruments (Social Climate Scales) measure people's perceptions of the actual social environment (*Form R*), the ideal social environment (*Form I*), and the expectations one has of a particular social environment (*Form E*); short forms (*Form S*) taking 5 to 10 minutes to complete are also available. Illustrative profiles of scores on the ten dimensions of the Family Environment Scale (Moos & Moos, 1986) are given in Figure 14–1. Note in the top graph of Figure 14–1 the differences in perceptions of parents and children of the real or actual family environment, and in the bottom graph the differences in how one child (Beth) perceived her actual family environment (*Form R*) and her preferred family environment (*Form I*).

A number of other measures of the characteristics of particular social environments are available, including McKechnie's Environmental Response Inventory

Profiles for parents and children on Form R (top) and for a particular child (Beth) on Forms R and I (bottom) of the Family Environment Scale **Figure 14–1**

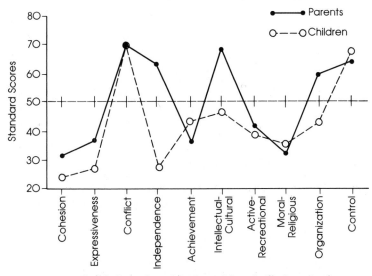

Form R Profiles for Parents and Children

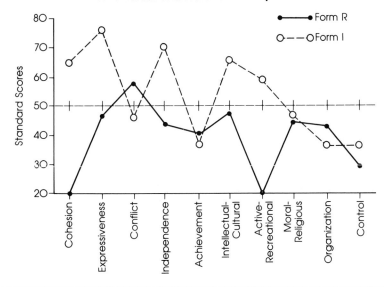

Beth's Actual and Preferred Family Environment

(Consulting Psychologists Press) and Stern's Classroom Environmental Index, College Characteristics Index, Elementary and Secondary School Index, High School Characteristics Index, and Organizational Climate Index (Evaluation Research Associates). Unfortunately, none of these instruments, including the ones devised by Moos and his collaborators, is based on an adequate taxonomy of situations relevant to people (Frederiksen, 1976; Kenrich & Dantchik, 1983).

In a kind of marriage of computers and environmental assessment, it has been proposed that microcomputers can assist psychologists in their efforts to understand how a person's behavior pattern varies as a function of the environmental situation (Tennyson & Tennyson, 1982). By simulating external or environmental variables on a computer, assessments could be made of how situations influence affective (and cognitive) responses. Tennyson and Tennyson (1982) maintain that the nonjudgmental objectivity of a computer should make such a testing procedure more acceptable to examinees and less biased than other methods of assessment.

Assessment in Health Psychology and Legal Psychology

Two contexts in which there has been an increasing demand for psychological services during recent years are health and legal settings. Both areas are attracting some of the best students in psychology, and a number of universities have instituted graduate degree programs focusing on these areas.

Health Psychology   Interest in the role of attitudes, self efficacy, and other psychological factors or personality variables in health is not limited to so-called psychosomatic disorders such as duodenal ulcers and migraine headaches, but includes more life-threatening illnesses such as cardiac disorders and cancer (see Holroyd, 1979). Psychologists are called upon not only to identify psychological factors related to various medical conditions and to help diagnose specific disorders but also to assist in planning intervention or treatment.

Several health-related personality inventories, including the Jenkins Activity Survey for identifying coronary prone Type A personalities, the Eating Disorders Inventory for assessing behavior traits associated with anorexia nervosa and bulimia, and the Millon Behavioral Health Inventory for assisting in formulating a comprehensive treatment plan for adult medical patients were described in Chapter 7. The use of these kinds of instruments is indicative of the growing interest in the field of *health psychology*, which includes specializations such as neuropsychology, pediatric psychology, geropsychology, and health enhancement (Weiner, 1983).

Among the important topics of research in health psychology are the roles of stress, learned helplessness, depression, information processing, and coping ability in illness. For example, a learned feeling or sense of helplessness has been found to be an important factor in the coronary prone personality (Glass & Carver, 1980). And according to Dana (1984), a feeling of personal efficacy or confidence that one's internal and external environments are predictable and can therefore be controlled, is the single most important mediator of psychological health. In addition, personal efficacy, the opposite of helplessness, is important to physical health. A number of theoretical models have been applied in an attempt to understand the development and consequences of feelings of helplessness and personal efficacy. For example, considerable research on the topic has been stimulated by attribution theory (Abramson et al., 1980). Furthermore, such research has led to the development of instruments such as the Attributional Style Questionnaire (Peterson et al., 1982), a potentially useful diagnostic tool.

In forecasting the practice of personality assessment for the next few years, Dana (1984) points to the need for comprehensive measurement of life stress, including identification of the specific stressors, reactions to stress, and an inventory of potential mediators of stress. Inventories such as the Social Readjustment Scale (Holmes & Rahe, 1967) are illustrative of measures that have been used to investigate the relationship between the stress of change, which requires a readjustment on the part of the individual, and an increase in one's susceptibility to disease. On this inventory, 43 events requiring changes in the pattern of daily living are scaled from 0 to 100, depending on the degree of readjustment required (see Table 14–1).

Dana also notes that we need a workable model of psychological health, good functioning, or human wellness. Currently available measures based on various definitions of good functioning derived from self-actualization, ego development, and psychosocial development theories include the Personal Orientation Inventory (Knapp, 1976), the Inventory of Psychosocial Development (Reimanis, 1974), and the Washington University Sentence Completion Test (Loevinger, 1976). These instruments represent a good beginning, but better measures of coping abilities, resistance to stress, and self-efficacy are needed.

Legal Psychology   Many clinical psychologists have, in recent years, become interested in matters pertaining to the legal bases of psychological practice. This interest has been precipitated in large measure by the fact that psychologists are being asked questions and for their opinions concerning matters of litigation and jurisprudence. Some of these matters deal with the issue of competency—competency to stand trial, civil commitment, understanding of Miranda rights, and issues with elderly persons. Other questions asked of psychologists by legal representatives and officials include: Is a particular person insane? What is the likelihood that a person will engage in dangerous or violent behavior? Who should assume custody of a particular child? Why did a person committed homicide? What are the personal characteristics of a particular murderer who has not been apprehended? How can sex offenders be identified from psychological evaluations and can their future behavior be predicted? How can one tell whether a particular client will be defensive or honest in testifying (Lanyon, 1986)?

The assessment tools that the psychologist can bring to bear in attempting to provide answers to questions such as those listed above are not limited to the MMPI and Rorschach. Clinical interview guides and competency screening instruments of

Table 14–1	**Social Readjustment Rating Scale**	
Rank	Life Event	Mean Value
1	Death of spouse	100
2	Divorce	73
3	Marital separation	65
4	Jail term	63
5	Death of close family member	63
6	Personal injury or illness	53
7	Marriage	50
8	Fired at work	47
9	Marital reconciliation	45
10	Retirement	45
11	Change in health of family member	44
12	Pregnancy	40
13	Sex difficulties	39
14	Gain of new family member	39
15	Business readjustment	39
16	Change in financial state	38
17	Death of close friend	37
18	Change to different line of work	36
19	Change in number of arguments with spouse	35
20	Mortgage over $10,000	31
21	Foreclosure of mortgage or loan	30
22	Change in responsibilities at work	29
23	Son or daughter leaving home	29
24	Trouble with in-laws	29
25	Outstanding personal achievement	28
26	Wife begin or stop work	26
27	Begin or end school	26
28	Change in living conditions	25
29	Revision of personal habits	24
30	Trouble with boss	23
31	Change in work hours or conditions	20
32	Change in residence	20
33	Change in schools	20
34	Change in recreation	19
35	Change in church activities	19
36	Change in social activities	18
37	Mortgage or loan less than $10,000	17
38	Change in sleeping habits	16
39	Change in number of family get-togethers	15
40	Change in eating habits	15
41	Vacation	13
42	Christmas	12
43	Minor violations of the law	11

Reprinted with permission from the *Journal of Psychosomatic Research*, 11, T. H. Holmes and R. H. Rahe, "The Social Readjustment Rating Scale," Copyright 1967, Pergamon Press.

various kinds—Competency Screening Test (Lipsett, Lelos & McGarry, 1971), Competency Assessment Instrument (McGarry et al., 1973), Georgia Court Competency Test (Wildman et al., 1980)—are among the devices used in assessing competency. Child custody evaluations may include the Bricklin Perceptual Scales (Bricklin, 1984) in an effort to understand the child's perceptions of his or her parents in four areas (competence, supportiveness, follow-up consistency, possession of admirable personality traits). In addition, measures of the parents' knowledge and attitudes about child rearing practices could contribute to decision making in child custody cases. With respect to sexual offenses, the Clarke Sex History Questionnaire for Males (Langevin, 1983), which reportedly assesses types and strength of sexually anomalous behavior, may be of help to the psychologist. Perhaps the most frequently administered of all psychometric instruments in legal settings, however, is the MMPI. For example, it has been used to predict dangerous or violent behavior, defensiveness (willingness to tell the truth), and many other matters of concern in court trials. The Rorschach is another work horse in legal settings, but neither the MMPI nor the Rorschach permits unqualified answers and opinions concerning legal matters. According to some authorities (e.g., Lanyon, 1986) what is required are more question-specific instruments, for example, an instrument that can assess the effects of a particular brain injury on criminal behavior. Obviously, psychologists who design and use such instruments should be familiar with the law as well as being capable test designers and clinicians.

Cognitive Theories of Personality

For the better part of this century, cognition and personality have been treated as separate areas of study within psychology. To be sure, the division was never complete, and it was generally recognized that thoughts influence emotions and vice versa. An occasional theorist such as R. B. Cattell argued for a holistic conception of personality that included both affect and cognition. Also holistic in nature, but emphasizing more cognitive terms to describe personality was George Kelly's "man as scientist" approach to personality.

More recently, there has been an increased interest in developing *cognitive* (or information-processing) *theories of personality*, theories that employ such concepts as schema, strategies, attributions, expectancies, and cognitive style to explain the processes by which individuals interpret, organize, and categorize their experiences. Rather than emphasizing generalized predictions about people, these theories tend to limit predictions to specific situations or conditions, with the goal of understanding the behavior of the *person in the situation*. Illustrative of these newer approaches to the study of personality is the research and theorizing of Walter Mischel.

Rather than attempting to define personality in terms of measurements on a collection of general traits, Mischel is more interested in how and why people employ trait constructs and what purposes they serve. And rather than simply predicting behavior, he is interested in analyzing it to better understand basic psychological processes and clarify the structure and functioning of human personality (Mischel, 1984). Like George Kelly, Mischel is a cognitive theorist, but one with a strong behavioristic inclination. Like traditional behaviorists he emphasizes the importance of the environment in determining what people do, but his cognitive social learning approach also recognizes the significant role of person variables. These person variables, however, are not adjectival trait names such as friendliness, conscientiousness, aggressiveness, cooperativeness, but rather "construction competencies, encoding strategies, expectancies, goals and values, and self-regulatory systems." (Mischel, 1984).

The five person variables described by Mischel are linked to basic psychological processes that regulate how a person behaves in particular situations. The first person variable, *construction competencies*, is concerned with an individual's cognitive and behavioral competencies, that is, his or her intellectual, social, and physical abilities to generate diverse behaviors under appropriate conditions. The second variable, *encoding strategies*, is concerned with how people perceive, group and construe events or entities (including themselves), and categorize situations. The person variable of *expectancies* refers to the individual's specific expectancies of what will happen under certain conditions; included among expectancies are self-efficacy expectations (How well will I do?). The fourth person variable is concerned with *goals and subjective values*, which lead people with similar expectations to behave differently because the outcome is not equally important to both of them. The fifth person variable described by Mischel consists of *self-regulatory* (self-control) *systems and plans*, which refers to the different rules or standards that people adopt to regulate their behavior (Mischel, 1984).

Mischel (1973, 1986) argues that cognitive social learning person variables such as self-efficacy expectations (or how effective the individual expects to be in coping with a particular situation) are good predictors of such outcomes as the success of treatment, reactions to stress, and performance attainment (see Bandura, 1982). The research conducted by Mischel and his colleagues on how people can learn self-control by focusing their attention on other stimuli is especially noteworthy (e.g., Mischel & Moore, 1973; Mischel & Baker, 1975). This research, which exemplifies the approach of cognitive behaviorism, illustrates how ideation or cognition can function to facilitate both the prediction and control of behavior.

A Final Word

Despite the seeming disarray in the field of personality assessment, there is a great deal of activity on the current scene and a promise of clarification and restructuring of the field. Prompted by the methodological inadequacy of much research on personality (Block, 1977), some of the current activity involves new methodologies such as structural equation modeling (Bentler & Newcomb, 1986) and taxometric methods (Meehl & Golden, 1982). Other investigations are concerned with the administration and interpretation of personality tests, in other words, the problem of reactivity in which the very process of testing, including the examiner's behavior, influences the examinee's responses (Kleinmuntz, 1982), and the effects of examiner biases and heuristics on clinical judgments (Dawes, 1986).

Despite the problems and difficulties that seem to pervade the field of personality and its assessment, one should not despair. Compared with the technical sophistication of ability testing, personality inventories and other affective measuring instruments seem relatively crude. But the potential value of accurate personality assessment is unquestioned, and recent methodological progress in the construction of certain personality and interest inventories suggests that general improvements in affective assessment are forthcoming. Although it is unlikely that oldtimers such as the MMPI or the Rorschach will be replaced by more psychometrically sophisticated instruments in the near future, newer tests will force a continuing reevaluation of these and other time-honored clinical instruments.[2] In a look at the future prospects for psychodiagnosis Weiner (1983) concludes, "Continued careful research on psychodiagnostic methods and the expert application of psychological test findings in clinical consultation should sustain a bright future for psychodiagnosis and its practitioners." (p. 456)

Summary

Despite notable progress in the methodology and technology of psychological measurement, the assessment of personality continues to be a controversial practice characterized by numerous issues. Among the older issues in personality assessment that are still being debated are clinical versus statistical prediction, idiographic versus nomothetic assessment, the ethics and morality of assessment, and the importance of traits versus situations in predicting behavior. Issues and developments of more recent vintage include computer-based test interpretation, newer tests and revisions of older tests, and cognitive models of personality assessment.

Due to some extent to the adoption of codes of ethics pertaining to assessment and other activities of psychologists and other human services professionals, arguments concerning the ethics and morality of personality assessment are perhaps not as heated today as they were two or three decades ago. Furthermore, several court cases and legislative hearings concerning psychological testing have made clinicians, counselors, and others who use tests more aware of their legal and personal responsibilities as professionals.

The validity of personality assessment instruments, and how validity varies from group to group, is and will continue to be a matter of concern. Attempts have been made to eliminate sex bias in interest inventories and other affective measures by rewriting items to make them relevant and fair to males and females and by providing both separate and combined test norms for the two sexes. With respect to the effects of the sex of the examiner, and whether it is the same or different from that of the examinee, research findings indicate that the sex variable does not appear to have a consistent effect on the way in which personality tests are administered, scored, or interpreted.

Although there is no denying the effectiveness of a trained clinician as an assessor and interpreter of personality and behavior, the bulk of research findings indicates that the statistical or actuarial approach to predicting human behavior is usually more accurate than the clinical or impressionistic approach. And with respect to the relative roles of heredity and environment in shaping personality and determining behavior, research evidence continues to underscore the importance of both factors acting interactively.

After many years of emphasizing the nomothetic approach of seeking general laws of behavior and personality, personality assessment and theory now appears to be reverting, at least to some extent, to a more idiographic approach in which every person is viewed as a lawful, integrated system to be studied in his or her own right. Practicing clinical psychologists, in particular, are more idiographic in their efforts to understand the consistencies and inconsistencies of the individual patient or client, without reference to other individuals. A new twist on the old idiographic approach is Lamiell's idiothetic model of personality assessment.

The issue of whether personality traits or situational variables are more significant in understanding and predicting behavior, an issue rekindled by Mischel's discovery of the low level of cross-situational consistency in behavior presumably governed by personality traits, continues to be debated by many personality researchers and theorists. Responses to Mischel's criticisms of trait-factor theories and assessment include research on attribution theory, Bem and Funder's template matching technique, and various counterarguments to situationism presented by Block, Epstein, and others. Although Mischel has not, as he has sometimes been accused of doing, taken the person out of personality, his research and arguments have led to a renewed emphasis on situational factors and interactions between situations and personal characteristics in determining behavior.

One of the most exciting, if controversial, events in personality assessment during the past 25 years has been the development and use of various computer programs for administering, scoring, and, in particular, interpreting inventories, rating scales, and other personality assessment devices. The increased usage of computer-based test interpretation (CBTI) has been accompanied by its own set of concerns pertaining to the ethics and validity of the many programs in use. However, the recently published *Guidelines for Computer-Based Tests and Interpretations* will assist in ensuring that designers, distributors, and users of CBTI products are cognizant of and attentive to the ethical, measurement, and legal responsibilities concerning the use of these programs and the diagnostic narrative reports generated by them.

Among the newer methods and tests that are significant for personality assessment are adaptive testing, environmental assessment, and research and instrument development in the fields of health psychology and legal psychology. Adaptive testing promises to improve the efficiency of test administration, by making subsequent item presentation contingent upon answers to previous items with no loss of reliability or validity. The various social climate scales designed by Rudolf Moos and his associates represent interesting efforts to assess the personalities of perceived environments, both real and ideal, and to analyze how person satisfaction varies with environmental characteristics. Research and instrument development in the growing field of health psychology are providing a better understanding of the relationships of psychological factors to both physical and mental health as well as a variety of new tests and other assessment procedures related to fitness, wellness, and disease.

The broadening professional involvement of psychologists with litigation and other legal matters (competency to stand trial, civil commitment, understanding of Miranda rights, issues with elderly persons, etc.) in recent years has led to greater emphasis on these matters in graduate training programs, in research, and in the design and use of psychological assessment instruments in law-related settings. In addition to older instruments such as the MMPI and Rorschach, a variety of questionnaires, rating scales, checklists, and other devices have been constructed to provide better information for answering questions concerning competency, insanity, child custody, violence and homicide, sex offenses, and defensiveness in legal contexts.

Although theories of personality have traditionally emphasized affective or temperament variables, certain theories have stressed the fact that personality is holistic, including not only affective but also cognitive variables. Recent cognitive theories of personality employ information-processing concepts such as schema, strategies, attributions, expectancies, and cognitive styles to explain how people interpret, organize, and categorize their experiences. These theories view behavior as less general and more situation specific than traditional trait-factor and dynamic theories of personality. An example of a cognitive-social-situational approach to understanding and predicting human behavior is Walter Mischel's conceptualization of five person variables (construction competencies, encoding strategies, expectancies, goals and subjective values, self-regulatory systems and plans).

Exercises

1. Define each of the following terms in a sentence or two:

    Barnum effect
    adaptive testing
    attribution theory
    cognitive theories of personality
    computer-based test interpretation
     (CBTI)
    concordance rate

    construction competencies
    encoding strategies
    environmental assessment
    expectancies
    goals and subjective values
    health psychology
    heritability index

idiographic approach

idiothetic

legal psychology

multiple abstract variance
  analysis (MAVA)

nomothetic approach

privileged communication

self-regulatory systems and plans

sex bias

stradaptive testing

strong situations

template-matching technique

transaction

weak situations

2.   Summarize research findings on the issues of

(a)   clinical versus statistical prediction of behavior,
(b)   heredity versus environment as determiners of personality,
(c)   idiographic approach versus nomothetic approach to personality assessment,
(d)   traits versus situations as determiners of personality.

3.   Write one or two personality test items (true-false format) that are biased toward men, women, blacks, whites, Americans, Asians, more highly educated people.

4.   Write a brief review of legal issues concerned with personality assessment. You should consult some of the sources cited in this chapter as well as other articles and reports in professional journals and the popular media.

5.   What changes do you forecast for personality assessment during the next 20 years or so? What new kinds of assessment instruments and procedures are likely to be developed? What role will continuing developments in technology, such as computers, play in these changes?

6.   Discuss the ethical issues concerning the use of computers in various phases of personality assessment—test development, test scoring, test interpretation, test use. What steps are being taken and what other steps need to be taken to make certain that computer technology is used wisely and ethically in psychological assessment in general and personality assessment in particular?

Suggested Readings

Butcher, J. N., Keller, L. S., & Bacon, S. F. (1985). Current developments and future directions in computerized personality assessment. *Journal of Consulting and Clinical Psychology, 53,* 803–815.

Dana, R. H. (1984). Personality assessment: Practice and teaching for the next decade. *Journal of Personality Assessment, 48,* 46–56.

Endler, N. S., & Edwards, J. M. (1986). Interactionism in personality in the twentieth century. *Psychology and Individual Differences, 7,* 379–387.

Fowler, R. D. (1985). Landmarks in computer-assisted psychological assessment. *Journal of Consulting and Clinical Psychology, 53,* 748–759.

Lanyon, R. I. (1986). Psychological assessment procedures in court-related settings. *Professional Psychology: Research and Practice, 17,* 260–268.

Knoff, H. M. (1986). Conclusions and future needs in personality assessment. In H. M. Knoff (Ed.), *The assessment of child and adolescent personality* (pp. 635–641). New York: Guilford.

Meier, S. T., & Geiger, S. M. (1986). Implications of computer-assisted testing and assessment for professional practice and training. *Measurement and Evaluation in Counseling and Development, 19*(1), 29–34.

Mischel, W. (1984). On the predictability of behavior and the structure of personality. In R. A. Zucker, J. C. Aronoff, & A. I. Rabin (Eds.), *Personality and the prediction of behavior.* New York: Academic.

Pervin, L. A. (1985). Personality: Current controversies, issues, and directions. *Annual Review of Psychology, 36,* 83–114.

Skinner, H. A., & Pakula, A. (1986). Challenge of computers in psychological assessment. *Professional Psychology: Research and Practice, 17*(1), 44–50.

Weiner, I. B. (1983). The future of psychodiagnosis revisited. *Journal of Personality Assessment, 47,* 451–459.

Endnotes

[1]Chaplin and Goldberg (1984) failed to confirm the findings of Bem and Allen (1974); also see Paunonen and Jackson (1985).

[2]Interesting enough, Kaplan and Saccuzzo (1982) predict the demise of the MMPI but the rejuvenation of the Rorschach in the twenty-first century.

APPENDICES

APPENDIX A

Selected Journals Containing Articles on Personality Assessment

American Psychologist

Applied Psychological Measurement

Behavioral Assessment

Clinical Psychologist

Counseling Psychologist

Educational and Psychological Measurement

Journal of Abnormal and Social Psychology

Journal of Psychopathology and Behavioral Assessment

Journal of Clinical Psychology

Journal of Consulting Psychology

Journal of Consulting and Clinical Psychology

Journal of Counseling Psychology

Journal of Personality

Journal of Personality Assessment

Journal of Personality and Social Psychology

Journal of Projective Techniques and Personality Assessment

Journal of Psychiatric Research

Journal of Psychoeducational Assessment

Journal of Research in Personality

Measurement and Evaluation in Counseling and Development

Multivariate Behavioral Research

Personality and Individual Differences

Personality and Social Psychology Bulletin

Personnel Psychology

Professional Psychology

Psychological Bulletin

Psychological Monographs

Rorschachiana

APPENDIX B

Test Publishers and Distributors

ADI Auxiliary Publications Project, Photoduplication Service, Library of Congress, Washington, DC 20540

American Guidance Service, Publishers' Building, P.O. Box 99, Circle Pines, MN 55014–1796

Andres University Press, Berrien Springs, MI 49104

ASIS/NAPS Microfiche Publications, P.O.Box 3513, Grand Central Station, New York, NY 10017

Biometrics Research Dept., New York State Psychiatric Institute, 722 W. 168th St., New York, NY 10032

Bruce, Martin M., Publishers, 50 Larchmont Road, Box 248, Larchmont, NY 10538

Bureau of Educational Measurements, Emporia State University, Box 18, 1200 Commercial, Emporia, KA 66801–5087

Cambridge University Press, 32 E 57 Street, New York, NY 10022

Camelot Behavioral Systems, P.O. Box 3447, Lawrence, KS 66044

Carney, Weedman and Associates, 2223 El Cajon Boulevard, Suite 307, San Diego, CA 92104

Centre de Psychologie Applique, Department Editions, Square Jouvenet, Paris, France 16e, Mir 68–50

Century Diagnostics, 2101 E. Broadway, Suite 22, Tempe, AZ 85282

CTB/McGraw-Hill, Del Monte Research Park, 2500 Garden Road, Monterey, CA 93940–5380

Consulting Psychologists Press, Inc., 577 College Avenue, Palo Alto, CA 94306

Department of Mental Health Sciences, Hahnemann Medical College and Hospital, 230 North Broad Street, Philadelphia, PA 19102

Development Publications, 5605 Lamar Road, Bethesda, MD 20816

Diagnostic Specialists, 1170 North 660 West, Orem, UT 84057

DLM Teaching Resources, One DLM Park, P.O. Box 4000, Allen, TX 75002

EdITS/Educational and Industrial Testing Service, P.O. Box 7234, San Diego, CA 92107

Educational Testing Service, Rosedale Road, Princeton, NJ 08541–0001

Educators'-Employers' Tests & Services Assn., 120 Detzel Place, Cincinnati, OH 45219

Evaluation Research Associates, P.O. Box 6503, Teall Station, Syracuse, NY 13217

William Fullard, Department of Educational Psychology, Temple University, Philadelphia, PA 19122

Molly R. Harrower, 2841 NW 4 Lane, Gainesville, FL 32607

Robin L. Hegvik, 307 North Wayne Avenue, Wayne, PA 19087

Institute for Personality and Ability Testing, Inc., P.O. Box 188, Champaign, IL 61820

Jastak Associates, Inc., P.O. Box 4460, Wilmington, DE 19807

Jung (C. G.), Institute of San Francisco, 2040 Gough Street, San Francisco, CA 94109

Life Themes, Inc., P.O. Box 265, Palos Verdes Estates, CA 90274

London House, Inc., 1550 Northwest Highway, Park Ridge, IL 60068

Mafex Associates, Inc., 90 Cherry Street, Box 519, Johnstown, PA 15907

Manual Moderno, Avenue Sonora 206, Col. Hipodromo, 06100, Mexico D.F., Mexico

Albert Mehrabian, 9305 Beverlycrest Drive, Beverly Hills, CA 90210

Charles E. Merrill Publishing Company, 1300 Alum Creek Drive, Box 508, Columbus, OH 43216

National Computer Systems, P.O. Box 1416, Minneapolis, MN 55440

Pro.ed, 5341 Industrial Oaks Boulevard, Austin, TX 78735–8898

Psychological Assessment and Services, Inc., P.O. Box 1031, Iowa City, Iowa 52244

Psychological Assessment Resources, Inc. (PAR), P.O. Box 998, Odessa, FL 33556–0998

Psychological Corporation (The), 555 Academic Court, San Antonio, TX 78204–0952

Psychological Publications, Inc., 5300 Hollywood Boulevard, Los Angeles, CA 90027

Psychological Services, International, Inc., 311 Main Street, Worcester, MA 10608

Psychological Test Specialists, Box 9229, Missoula, MT 59807

Psychologists and Educators, Inc., 211 West State Street, Jacksonville, IL 52650

Psychometric Affiliates, Box 807, Murfreesboro, TN 37133

Publishers Test Service, 2500 Garden Road, Monterey, CA 93940–5380

Purdue Research Foundation, Attn: William K. LeBold, Educational Research and Information Systems, Engineering and Administration Bldg., Purdue University, West Lafayette, IN 47907

Research Psychologists Press, Inc., 1110 Military St., P.O. Box 984, Port Huron, MI 48061–0984

Riverside Publishing Company (The), 8420 Bryn Mawr Avenue, Chicago, IL 60631

Scholastic Testing Service, Inc., 480 Meyer Road, P.O. Box 1056, Bensenville, IL 60106

Science Research Associates, Inc., P.O. Box 5380, 155 North Wacker Drive, Chicago, IL 60606

Sheridan Psychological Services, Inc., P.O. Box 6101, Orange, CA 92663–6101

Springer Publishing Co., 200 Park Avenue South, New York, NY 10003

Stoelting Company, 1350 South Kostner Avenue, Chicago, IL 60623–1196

Tests in Microfiche, Test College, Educational Testing Service, Princeton, NJ 08541

Western Psychological Services, 12031 Wilshire Boulevard, Los Angeles, CA 90025

APPENDIX C

Companies Specializing in Computer Services, Software, and Hardware for Psychological Testing

ADEPT, Inc., Box 1117 L.U. Station, Beaumont, TX 77710

Behaviordyne, 599 College Avenue, Suite 1, Palo Alto, CA 94306

Caldwell Report, 3122 Santa Monica Boulevard, Santa Monica, CA 90404

Cattell Research Institute, 1188 Bishop Street 1701, Honolulu, HI 96813

Century Diagnostics, Inc., 2101 East Broadway, Suite 22, Tempe, AZ 85282

Consulting Psychologists Press, Inc., 577 College Avenue, Palo Alto, CA 94306

HMS Software, P.O. Box 49186, Austin, TX 78765

Integrated Professional Systems, Inc., 5211 Mahoning Avenue, Suite 135, Youngstown, OH 44515

Institute for Personality and Ability Testing, P.O. Box 188, Champaign, IL 61820

Manumit Psychological Systems, Inc., 2211 East Winston Road, Suite J, Anaheim, CA 92806

MetriTech, Inc., 111 North Market Street, Champaign, IL 61820

National Computer Systems, P.O. Box 1416, Minneapolis, MN 55440

P.C.A. Diagnostic Laboratory, Inc., 714 South Tillotson, Muncie, IN 47304

Pine Grove Institute, 1188 Montgomery Drive, Santa Rosa, CA 95405

Precision People, Inc., 3452 North Ride Circle S., Jacksonville, FL 32217

Psych Lab, 1714 Tenth Street, Wichita Falls, TX 76301

Psychological Software Specialists, 1776 Fowler, Suite 7, Columbia Center North, Richland, WA 99352

Psychologistics, Inc., P.O. Box 3896, Indialantic, FL 32903

Psychsystems, 600 Reisterstown Road, Baltimore, MD 21208

Publishers Test Service, 2500 Garden Road, Monterey, CA 93940

Reason House, 204 East Joppa Road, Penthouse Suite 10, Towson, MD 21204

Queue, Inc., 5 Chapel Hill Drive, Fairfield, CT 06432

Western Psychological Services, 120341 Wilshire Blvd., Los Angeles, CA 90025

APPENDIX D

Interview and Observation Instruments for Mental Status Examinations

Current and Past Psychopathology Scales (CAPPS) by R. L. Spitzer and J. Endicott, New York State Psychiatric Institute, 1966–1968. Psychiatric patients and nonpatients; combination of the *Psychiatric Evaluation Form-Diagnostic Version* (PEF-D) and the *Psychiatric History Schedule* (PHS); rating scale and optional interview guide for diagnosing or describing mental illness; PEF-D section, dealing with patient's functioning over past month, yields 8 summary scale scores (reality testing-social disturbance, depression-anxiety, impulse control, somatic concern-functioning, disorganization, obsessive-guilt-phobic, elation-grandiosity, summary); PHS section, dealing with patient's functioning from age 12 to past months, yields 18 summary scale scores; Research Assessment and Training Unit.

Mental Status Examination Record (MSER) by R. L. Spitzer and J. Endicott; Research Assessment and Training Unit, New York State Psychiatric Institute, 1971. Psychiatric patients and nonpatients; four-page computer form for providing objective record of mental status examination; 16 traditional mental status categories involving 121 checklist items and 156 rating scales; computer analysis yields 20 derived scale scores.

Psychiatric Anamnestic Record (PAR) by R. L. Spitzer and J. Endicott, Research Assessment and Training, New York State Psychiatric Institute, 1973. Psychiatric patients and non-patients; highly structured interview schedule designed to be administered, with training, by people with little clinical experience; four-page booklet of multiple-choice questions and ratings scales on psychiatric case history information; one section on psychopathological signs and symptoms judged twice: from age 12 up to the last month and within the last month; computer-generated narrative output.

Psychiatric Evaluation Form (PEF) by R. L. Spitzer, J. Endicott, A. Mesnikoff, and G. Cohen, Research Assessment and Training Unit, New York State Psychiatric Institute, 1967–1968. Psychiatric patients and nonpatients; interview guide and rating scale for recording scaled judgments of a person's functioning over one-week period in 19 psychopathological dimensions and role impairment in 3 occupational roles and 2 social roles.

Schedule of Affective Disorders and Schizophrenia (SADS) by R. L. Spitzer and J. Endicott, Research Assessment and Training Unit, New York State Psychiatric Institute, 1978. Psychiatric patients and nonpatients; interview procedure designed to collect data for making diagnoses according to DSM-III; consists of a series of questions concerning specific instances of notably abnormal behavior, including branching to other questions depending on interviewee's answers to previous questions.

The Psychiatric Status Schedules: Subject Form, Second Edition (PSS) by R. L. Spitzer, J. Endicott, and G. Cohen, Research Assessment and Training Unit, New York State Psychiatric Institute, 1966–1968. Psychiatric patients and nonpatients; standardized interview schedule for gathering from a subject information needed to fill out a matching inventory designed to evaluate social and role functioning as well as mental status; 18 symptom scores, 5 role functioning scores, and 20 supplemental scores.

APPENDIX E

Representative Personality and Behavioral Checklists

The Adjective Checklist by H. G. Gough and A. B. Heilbrun, Jr., Consulting Psychologists Press & Publishers Test Service, 1965, 1980. High school through adulthood; untimed, 15–20 minutes; 300 adjectives scored on 37 possible scales.

Bristol Social Adjustment Guides by D. H. Stott, 1956–1966. Ages 5–16; Boy Form and Girl Form; untimed, 10–15 minutes; short phrases descriptive of child's behavior, to be underlined by teacher or other adult familiar with child; scored for five core syndromes (unforthcomingness, withdrawal, depression, inconsequence, hostility) and four associated groups (peer-maladaptiveness, nonsyndromic over-reaction, nonsyndromic under-reaction, neurological symptoms).

Camelot Behavioral Checklist by R. W. Foster, Camelot Behavioral Systems, 1974–1977. Mentally retarded; ratings by parents, ward attendants, and teachers; 11 scores (self help, physical development, home duties, vocational behaviors, economic behaviors, independent travel, numerical skills, communication skills, social behaviors, responsibility, total).

Children's Problems Checklist by J. A. Schinka, Psychological Assessment Resources, 1985.

Ages 5–12 years; untimed, 10–20 minutes; 190 items surveying 11 problem areas (emotions, self-concept, peers-play, school, language-thinking, concentration-organization, activity level-motor control, behavior, values, habits, health).

Depression Adjective Check Lists by B. Lubin, EdITS, 1967–1981. High school through adult; untimed, approximately 5 minutes for each form; each of the A, B, C, and D forms consists of 32 adjectives to which the examinee responds by describing how he or she feels; checklists E, F, and G have 34 adjectives each; differentiates between depressed and nondepressed patients.

Interpersonal Check List by R. LaForge, T. Leary, R. Suczek, & M. Freedman, Rolfe LaForge, 1955–1973. Adults; research use only; 4 summary scores (dominance, love, average intensity, acquiescence) or 20 detail scores at 1–2 levels of personality.

Jesness Behavior Check List by C. F. Jesness, Consulting Psychologists Press, 1970–1971. Adolescents; untimed, 10–20 minutes; 80-item scale measuring 14 bipolar behavioral tendencies in adolescents.

Louisville Behavior Checklist by L. C. Miller, Western Psychological Services, 1977–1981. Age 4–6 years (Form E1), 7–12 years (Form E2), 13–17 years (Form E3); untimed; covers entire range of pathological disorders in children and adolescents; Form E1 scored for 20 scales, Form E2 for 19 scales, and Form E3 for 13 scales.

Marital Evaluation Checklist by L. Navran, Psychological Assessment Resources, 1984. Adults; untimed, 10–20 minutes; 140+ items organized into three main sections (reasons for marrying, current problems, motivation for counseling) to survey interpersonal-emotional, material-economic, social, personal, money and work, sex, personal characteristics, and marital relationship areas.

Mental Status Checklist–Adults by J. A. Schinka, Psychological Assessment Resources, 1986. Adults; untimed, 10–20 minutes; 120 items typically included in comprehensive mental status examination of adults (presenting problem, referral data, demographics, mental status, personality function and symptoms, diagnosis, disposition).

Mooney Problem Check Lists, 1950 Revision by R. L. Mooney and L. V. Gordon, The Psychological Corporation, 1950. Grades 7–9, 9–12, 13–16, adults; untimed, 30 minutes; 4 levels; Junior High School Form (grades 7–9) yields 7 scores (health and physical development, school, home and family, money-work-the future, boy and girl relations, relations to people in general, self-centered concerns); High School Form (grades 9–12) and College Form (grades 13–16) yield 11 scores (health and physical development, finances-living conditions-employment, social and recreational activities, social-psychological relations, personal psychological relationships, courtship-sex-marriage, home and family, morals and religion, adjustment to school work, the future—vocational and education, curriculum and teaching procedure); Adult Form yields 9 scores (health, economic security, self-improvement, personality, home and family, courtship, sex, religion, occupation).

Multiple Affect Adjective Check List-Revised by M. Zuckerman and B. Lubin, EdITS, 1960–1981. High School, college and adult; untimed, approximately 5 minutes for either form; measures anxiety, depression, hostility, positive affect, and sensation seeking, plus two summary scores; consists of 132 adjectives and two forms (General Form for affective traits and

Today Form for day-to-day fluctuations). A revised form, the MAACL-R, was published in 1981.

Normative Adaptive Behavior Checklist by G. L. Adams, Charles E. Merrill, 1984. Infancy to 21 years; untimed; 100+ items on self help, home living, independent living, social, sensory-motor, and language concepts-academic skills; checked by teacher, parents, caregiver, or other responsible person familiar with child's behavior; normed on 6,000 individuals from infancy to age 21; also data on 8,000 mentally and/or physically handicapped persons.

Personal Problems Checklist–Adolescent by J. A. Schinka, Psychological Assessment Resources, 1985. Ages 13–17 years; untimed, 10–20 minutes; 240 items surveying common adolescent problems in 13 areas (social, appearance, job, family, home, school, money, religion, emotions, dating, health, attitude, crises).

Personal Problems Checklist–Adult by J. A. Schinka, Psychological Assessment Resources, 1984. Ages 18–60 years; untimed, 10–20 minutes; 211 items representing 13 areas (social, appearance, vocational, family and home, school, finances, religion, emotions, sex, legal, health and habits, attitude, crises).

Psychometric Behavior Check List by B. G. Berenson et al., University of Maryland Counseling Center, 1960. Adults; for recording unusual test taking behavior.

School Behavior Checklist by L. C. Miller, Western Psychological Services, 1977–1981. Ages 4–6 (Form A1), 7–13 (Form A2); untimed 8–10 minutes; 6 scales (need achievement, aggression, anxiety, cognitive or academic deficit, hostile isolation, extroversion) on both forms; also normal irritability, school disturbance, and total disability on Form A1, and total disability on Form A2.

Walker Problem Behavior Identification Checklist, Revised 1983 by H. M. Walker, Western Psychological Services, 1970. Norms for Preschool/Kindergarten (ages 2–6 years), Primary Grades (grades 1–3), and Intermediate Grades (grades 4–6); untimed; teacher checks 50 statements concerning children's behavior that may interfere with academic performance or school adjustment; scored on Total plus five scales (acting out, withdrawal, distractibility, disturbed peer relations, immaturity).

APPENDIX F

Representative Rating Scales for Personality and Behavioral Assessment

Adult Personal Adjustment & Role Skills by R. E. Ellsworth, Consulting Psychologists Press, 1977–1981. Adults; spouse, parent, or person close to patient rates patient's behavior on 31 items measuring eight dimensions (close relations, alienation-depression, anxiety, confusion, alcohol-drug use, house activity, child relations, employment).

Behavior Rating Profile by L. L. Brown & D. D. Hammill, 1978. Ages 6½–18½, grades 1–12; three student rating scales (home, school, peer), teacher rating scale, parent rating scale, sociogram; pro.ed.

Brief Psychiatric Rating Scale by J. E. Overall and L. E. Hollister, 1982. Adults; clinician rates patient on 18 scales (e.g., somatic concern, anxiety, emotional withdrawal, guilt feelings, hostility, suspiciousness, unusual thought-patterns); ratings compared with those of other psychiatric patients (Overall & Hollister, 1982).

Burks Behavior Rating Scales by H. F. Burks, Western Psychological Associates, 1968–1969. Grades 1–9; parent or teacher rates child on 110 descriptive statements of observed behavior; scored on 19 scales defining possible causes of child's problem behavior (excessive self-blame, anxiety, withdrawal, dependency, suffering, sense of persecution, aggressiveness and resistance as well as poor ego strength, physical strength, coordination, intellectuality, academics, attention, impulse control, reality contact, sense of identity, anger control, and social conformity).

Burks Behavior Rating Scales, Preschool and Kindergarten Edition by H. F. Burks, Western Psychological Associates, 1968–1969. Ages 3–6 years; parent or teacher rates child on 105 descriptive statements; scored on same scales as Burks Behavior Rating Scales, except poor academics.

Child & Adolescent Adjustment Profile by R. E. Ellsworth, Consulting Psychologists Press, 1977–1981. Children and adolescents; parent, teacher, or probation officer rates child or adolescent every three months on 20 items measuring adjustment through five factored dimensions (peer relations, dependency, hostility, productivity, withdrawal).

Child Behavior Rating Scale by R. N. Cassel, Western Psychological Associates, 1960–1962. Preschool through third grade; 78 brief statements to be rated by someone familiar with the child; provides profile of child's adjustment in five areas (self, home, social, school, physical) plus total personality adjustment score.

Hahnemann Elementary School Behavior Rating Scale by G. Spivack and M. Swift, Department of Mental Health Science, Hahnemann Medical College and Hospital, 1975. Elementary school students; 14 items scores (originality, independent learning, involvement, productive with peers, intellectual dependency with peers, failure anxiety, unreflectiveness, irrelevant talk, disruptive social involvement, negative feelings, holding back-withdrawn, critical-competitive, blaming, approach to teacher) plus 2 added items—inattention and academic achievement.

Hahnemann High School Behavior Rating Scale by G. Spivack and M. Swift, Dept. of Mental Health Sciences, Hahnemann Medical College & Hospital, 1971–1972; Grades 7–12; ratings by teachers yield 13 scores (reasoning ability, originality, verbal interaction, rapport with teacher, anxious producer, general anxiety, quiet-withdrawn, poor work habits, lack intellectual independence, dogmatic-inflexible, verbal negativism, disturbance-restless, expressed inability).

Personality Rating Scale by S. M. Amatora, Educators'-Employers' Tests & Services Associates, 1944–1962; Grades 4–12; ratings by classmates and teachers or self-ratings on 22 scales (pep, intelligence, sociability, nervousness-calmness, popularity, religiousness, punctuality, courtesy, cooperation, generosity, persistence, honesty, neatness, patience, interests, disposition, good sport, boisterous-quiet, entertaining, thoughtfulness, sense of humor, dependability).

Rating of Behavior Scale by Carney, Weedman & Associates, 1980. Measures children, adolescents, and adults, sex-role adoption and attitudes for present and ideal roles; rated by self or observer; scored on 13 variables pertaining to masculine and feminine sex-role behaviors, variations and inconsistencies among these roles, present and ideal sex-role behaviors.

Social-Emotional Dimension Scale by J. B. Hutton and T. G. Roberts, pro.ed., 1986. Ages 5½–18½ years; norm-referenced rating scale based on characteristics specified by Eli Bowen; scored on six areas (physical/fear reaction, depressive reaction, avoidance of peer interaction, avoidance of teacher interaction, aggressive interaction, inappropriate behaviors).

APPENDIX G

Representative Commercially Available Sentence Completion Tests

Activity Completion Technique by J. Sacks, Psychological Assessment Resources, revised form of Sacks Sentence Completion Test, 1984. Sixty sentence stems covering four areas (family, interpersonal, affect, self-concept); also conceptualized in 15 categories with four stems per category; computer scoring program available.

Bloom Sentence Completion Survey by W. Bloom; Stoelting Co., 1974–1975. One form, two levels (student, adults); 40 items designed to assess attitudes toward important factors in everyday living; eight scores.

Curtis Completion Form by J. W. Curtis; Western Psychological Services, 1950–1968. Grades 11–16 and adults; assesses emotional maturity and adjustment.

Forer Structured Sentence Completion Test by B. R. Forer; Western Psychological Services, 1957–1967. Ages 10–18 and adults; four forms (men, women, adolescent boys, adolescent girls); 100 items; no formal scoring system; responses grouped into four categories (interpersonal attitudes, wishes, causes of one's own feeling or action, reaction to external states).

Geriatric Sentence Completion Form by P. LeBray; Psychological Assessment Resources, 1982. Ages 60 and over; 30 items designed to reveal problems of later life in the physical, psychological, socioenvironmental, and temporal orientation domains.

Incomplete Sentences Task by B. Lanyon and R. I. Lanyon, Stoelting Co., 1979–1980. School Form (grades 7–12) and College Form; 39 highly structured, behaviorally anchored items designed to assess hostility, anxiety, and dependency.

The Rotter Incomplete Sentences Blank by J. B. Rotter and J. E. Rafferty, The Psychological Corporation, 1950. Three forms (high school, college, adult), each consisting of 40 items scored for conflict or unhealthy responses, neutral responses, and positive or healthy responses.

Washington University Sentence Completion Test by J. Loevinger, R. Wessler, and C. Redmore, 1970; also see Holt, 1980, and Loevinger, 1979, 1983. Forms for adult women, adult men, and younger persons of either sex; classifies responses according to seven stage I-level (ego development) scale: presocial and symbiotic, impulsive, self-protective, conformist, conscientious, autonomous, integrated.

Williams Awareness Sentence Completion by R. L. Williams, Robert L. Williams & Associates, 1972–1976. Forty items designed to evaluate Black awareness and consciousness; six scoring categories (Anglo-centric, dissemblance or dissimulation, Afro-centric, socio-centric, anthro-centric, uncommitted).

GLOSSARY

ABC approach.   Behavioral assessment approach, involving the identification of the antecedent events (A) and consequences (C) of the behavior (B). The behavior is modified by controlling for A and changing C.

Ability test.   A test that measures the extent to which a person is capable of performing a certain task or occupation.

Achievement.   Degree of success or accomplishment in a given subject or task.

Achievement test.   Measure of the degree of accomplishment or learning in a subject or task.

Acquiescence response set (*style*).   Tendency of a person to answer affirmatively ("yes" or "true") on personality test items and in other alternative response situations.

Actuarial approach.   Combining quantified clinical information according to empirically established rules, and then making behavioral predictions or diagnoses on the basis of the results.

Adjustment.   Ability to cope in social situations and achieve satisfaction of one's needs.

Adjustment disorder.   Difficulty in adjusting to stress and in meeting one's psychological needs.

Affective assessment.   The measurement of noncognitive (nonintellective) variables or characteristics. Affective variables include temperament, emotion, interests, attitudes, personal style, and other behaviors, traits, or processes typical of an individual.

Affective disorders.   Mental disorders characterized by extreme disturbance of mood and emotion.

Anal stage.   According to Freud, the period of life (second year) during which the major focus of tension and excitation is the anal region of the body; interest and conflict center on the retention and expulsion of feces. Negativism, manifested by defiance of parental orders and frequently associated with toilet training, is most acute during the anal stage.

Analysis of resistance.   Assessment-therapeutic procedure in psychoanalysis that involves analyzing the behavioral signs of resistance (e.g., appearing late for appointments, refusing to talk about certain matters, bringing presents to the analyst) to therapeutic progress.

Analysis of transference. Assessment-therapeutic process in psychoanalysis that involves analyzing the relationship (positive and/or negative) between the analyst and the patient. Transference occurs when the patient behaves toward the analyst as the former has acted toward some significant other person in the patient's life (e.g., acting as if the analyst were a father- or mother-figure).

Anecdotal record. A written record of behavioral observations of a specified individual. Care must be taken to differentiate between observation and interpretation if the record is to be objective.

Antisocial personality. Formerly called *psychopathic personality*, a disorder of personality characterized by inadequate development of moral and ethical restraints.

Anxiety. Vague feeling of uneasiness or apprehension, not necessarily directed toward a specific object or situation.

Anxiety disorders. Chronic feelings of apprehension or uneasiness. This diagnostic label includes generalized anxiety disorder, panic disorder, obsessive-compulsive disorder, post-traumatic stress disorder, and phobic disorder.

Aptitude. Capability of learning to perform a particular task or skill. Traditionally, aptitude was thought to depend more on inborn potential than actual practice.

Aptitude test. A measure of ability to profit from additional training or experience, that is, become proficient in a skill or other ability.

Arithmetic mean. A measure of the average or central tendency of a group of scores. The arithmetic mean is computed by dividing the sum of the scores by the number of scores.

Assessment. Appraising the presence or magnitude of one or more personal characteristics. Assessing human behavior and mental processes includes such procedures as observations, interviews, rating scales, checklists, inventories, projectives, and tests.

Assessment center approach. Technique, used primarily in the selection of executive personnel, for assessing the personality characteristics and behavior of a small group of individuals by having them perform a variety of tasks during a period of a few days.

Astrology. Pseudoscience of interpreting an individual's personality and future circumstances from data on the individual's birth and the relative positions of the moon and planets.

Attitude. Tendency to react positively or negatively to some object, person, or circumstance.

Attitude scale. A paper and pencil instrument, consisting of a series of statements concerning an institution, situation, person, event, etc. The examinee responds to each statement by endorsing it or indicating his or her degree of agreement or disagreement with it.

Aunt Fanny error. Accepting as accurate a trivial, highly generalized personality description that could pertain to almost anyone, even one's Aunt Fanny.

Automated assessment. Use of test-scoring machines, computers, and other electronic or electromechanical devices to administer, score, and interpret psychological assessments.

Average. Measure of central tendency of a group of scores; the most representative score.

Barnum effect. Belief in a personality description phrased in generalities, truisms, and other statements that sound specific to a given person but are actually applicable to almost anyone. Same as *Aunt Fanny error*.

Base rate. Proportion of a specified population of people who possess a characteristic of interest. The base rate should be taken into account when evaluating the effectiveness of a psychometric instrument in identifying and diagnosing people who have that characteristic.

Behavior analysis. Procedures that focus on objectively describing a particular behavior and identifying the antecedents and consequences of that behavior. Behavior analysis may be conducted for research purposes or to obtain information in planning a behavior modification program.

Behavior modification. Psychotherapeutic procedures based on learning theory and research and designed to change inappropriate behavior to more personally and/or socially acceptable behavior. Examples of such procedures are systematic desensitization, counterconditioning, extinction, and implosion.

Bias. Any one of a number of factors that cause scores on psychometric instruments to be consistently higher or lower than they should be if measurement were accurate. Illustrative of factors that result in bias is the *leniency error*—the tendency to rate a person consistently higher than he or she should be rated.

Biographical inventory. Questionnaire composed of items designed to collect information on an individual's background, interests, and other personal data.

Biorhythms. Theory that one's mental or physical effectiveness on a given day is affected by the physical, mental, and emotional cycles fixed in the individual since birth.

Cardinal trait. According to Allport, a disposition or theme so dominant in a person's life that it is expressed in almost all of his or her behavior (e.g., power-striving, self-love).

Case study. Detailed study of an individual, designed to provide a comprehensive, in-depth understanding of personality. Information for a case study is obtained from biographical, interview, observational, and test data.

Central tendency. Average, or central, score in a group of scores; the most representative score (e.g., arithmetic mean, median, mode).

Central tendency error. General tendency to avoid extreme judgments in appraising or assessing a person, and to assign ratings in the middle categories of a continuum or scale.

Central trait. According to Allport, tendency to behave in a particular way in various situations (sociability, affectionateness), but less general or pervasive than a *cardinal trait*.

Cerebrotonia. In Sheldon's temperament typology, the tendency to be introversive and prefer mental to physical or social activities; most closely related to ectomorphic body build.

Checklist. List of words, phrases, or statements descriptive of personal characteristics; respondents endorse (check) those items characteristic of themselves (self-ratings) or other people (other-ratings).

Classification. Assigning individuals to specified groups or categories on the basis of personal data obtained from various sources (observations, interviews, tests, inventories, etc.).

Clinical approach. Approach to behavioral prediction and diagnosis in which psychologists assign their own judgmental weights to the predictor variables and then combine them in a subjective manner to make behavioral forecasts or diagnoses.

Cluster sampling. Sampling procedure in which the target population is divided into sections or clusters, and the number of units selected at random from a given cluster is proportional to the total number of units in the cluster.

Coefficient alpha.   An internal-consistency reliability coefficient, appropriate for tests comprised of dichotomous or multipoint items; the expected correlation of one test with a parallel form containing the same number of items.

Cognitive assessment.   Measurement of intellective processes, such as perception, memory, thinking, judgment, and reasoning.

Cognitive style.   Strategies or approaches to perceiving, remembering, and thinking that a person comes to prefer in attempting to understand and cope with the world (e.g., field independence-dependence, reflectivity-impulsivity, and internal-external locus of control).

Communality.   Proportion of a test's total variance that is accounted for by common-factor variance; communality equals reliability minus specificity.

Concurrent validity.   The extent to which scores obtained by a group of individuals on a particular psychometric instrument are related to their simultaneously determined scores on another measure (criterion) of the same characteristic that the instrument is supposed to measure.

Construct validity.   The extent to which scores on a psychometric instrument designed to measure a certain characteristic are related to measures of behavior in situations in which the characteristic is supposed to be an important determinant of behavior.

Content analysis.   Method of studying and analyzing written (or oral) communications in a systematic, objective, and quantitative manner to assess certain psychological variables.

Content validity.   A psychometric instrument, such as an achievement test, is said to have content validity if a group of experts on the material with which the instrument is concerned agree that the instrument measures what it was designed to measure.

Contrast error.   In interviewing or rating, the tendency to evaluate a person more positively if an immediately preceding individual was assigned a highly negative evaluation, or to evaluate a person more negatively if an immediately preceding individual was given a highly positive evaluation.

Convergent validity.   A situation in which an assessment instrument has high correlations with other measures of (or methods of measuring) the same construct. (See *Discriminant validity*.)

Correlation.   Degree of relationship or association between two variables, such as a test and a criterion measure.

Correlation coefficient.   A numerical index of the degree of relationship between two variables. Correlation coefficients usually range from -1.00 (perfect negative relationship) through $.00$ (total absence of a relationship), to $+1.00$ (perfect positive relationship). Two common types of correlation coefficient are the product-moment coefficient and the point-biserial coefficient.

Criterion.   A standard or variable with which scores on a psychometric instrument are compared or against which they are evaluated. The validity of a test or other psychometric procedure used in selecting or classifying people is determined by its ability to predict a specified criterion of behavior in the situation for which people are being selected or classified.

Criterion-related validity.   The extent to which a test or other assessment instrument measures what it is alleged to measure as indicated by the correlation of test scores with some criterion measure of behavior.

Critical incident.   A measure of performance, used primarily in industrial-organizational contexts, in which an individual's overall criterion score is determined by the extent to which behavior that is thought to be critical for effective performance in a given situation is manifested.

Cross-validation.   Readministering an assessment instrument that has been found to be a valid predictor of a criterion for one group of people to a second group of people to determine whether the instrument is also valid for that group. There is almost always some shrinkage of the validity coefficient on cross-validation since chance factors spuriously inflate the validity coefficient obtained with the first group of examinees.

Deviation hypothesis.   Berg's controversial hypothesis that there is a tendency for people who make deviant responses in one situation to also make deviant responses in other situations.

Diagnostic interview.   An interview designed to obtain information on a person's thoughts, feelings, perceptions, and behavior; used in making a diagnostic decision about the person.

Discriminant validity.   Situation in which a psychometric instrument has low correlations with other measures of (or methods of measuring) different psychological constructs.

Dream analysis.   In psychoanalysis, analyzing the manifest content of a dream to reveal the underlying latent content containing the patient's unconscious wishes and conflicts.

Ectomorph.   In Sheldon's somatotype system, a person with a tall, thin body build; related to the cerebrotonic (thinking, introversive) temperament type.

Ego.   In psychoanalytic theory, that part of the personality ("I" or "me") that obeys the reality principle and attempts to mediate the conflict between the id and superego.

Electroencephalograph (*EEG*).   Electronic apparatus designed to detect and record brain waves from the intact scalp.

Electromyograph (*EMG*).   Electronic apparatus designed to measure muscular activity or tension.

Empirical scoring.   A scoring system in which an examinee's responses are scored according to a key constructed from responses made by people in certain criterion groups, such as schizophrenics or physicians. This scoring procedure is employed with various personality and interest inventories.

Endomorph.   In Sheldon's somatotype system, a person having a rotund body shape (fat); related to the viscerotonic (relaxed, sociable) temperament.

Extrovert.   Jung's term for individuals who are oriented, in their thoughts or social orientation, toward the external environment and other people rather than toward their own thoughts and feelings.

Face validity.   The extent to which the appearance or content of the materials (items, etc.) on a test or other psychometric instrument is such that the instrument appears to be a good measure of what it is supposed to measure.

Factor.   A dimension, trait, or characteristic of personality revealed by factor analyzing the matrix of correlations computed from the scores of a large number of people on several different tests or items.

Factor analysis.   A mathematical procedure for analyzing a matrix of correlations among measurements to determine what factors (constructs) are sufficient to explain the correlations.

Factor loadings.   In factor analysis, the resulting correlations (weights) between tests (or other variables) and the extracted factors.

False negative.   Selection or diagnostic decision error in which an assessment procedure incorrectly predicts a maladaptive outcome (e.g., low achievement, good performance, or psychopathology).

False positive.   Selection or diagnostic decision error in which an assessment procedure incorrectly predicts an adaptive outcome (e.g., high achievement, good performance, or absence of psychopathology).

Fantasy stage.   The earliest stage in the development of interests, in which a child's interest orientations are not based on an accurate perception of reality.

Field dependence.   A perceptual style in which the perceiver depends primarily on cues from the surrounding visual environment, rather than kinesthetic (gravitational) cues, to determine the upright position in Witkin's rod-and-frame test.

Field independence.   A perceptual style in which the perceiver depends primarily on kinesthetic (gravitational) cues rather than visual cues from the surrounding environment to determine the upright position in Witkin's rod-and-frame test.

Forced-choice item.   Item on a personality or interest inventory, arranged as a dyad (two options), triad (three options), or tetrad (four options) of terms or phrases. The respondent is required to select an option viewed as most descriptive of the personality, interests, or behavior of the person being evaluated, and perhaps another option perceived to be least descriptive of the personality, interests, or behavior of the person being evaluated.

Frequency distribution.   A table of score intervals and the number of cases (scores) falling within each interval.

Genital stage.   The last of Freud's five stages of psychosexual development. Beginning with puberty, interest in the opposite sex becomes predominant during this stage, culminating eventually in heterosexual union.

Graphic rating scale.   A rating scale containing a series of items, each consisting of a line on which the rater places a check mark to indicate the degree of a characteristic that the ratee is perceived as possessing. Typically, at the left extremity of the line is a brief verbal description indicating the lowest degree of the characteristic, and at the right end a description of the highest degree of the characteristic. Brief descriptions of intermediate degrees of the characteristic may also be situated at equidistant points along the line.

Graphology.   The analysis of handwriting to ascertain the character or personality of the writer.

Guess-who technique.   Procedure for analyzing group interaction and the social stimulus value of group members, in which children are asked to "guess who" in a classroom or other group situation possesses certain characteristics or does certain things.

Hallucinogens.   Drugs or chemicals that produce hallucinations.

Halo effect.   Rating a person high on one characteristic merely because he or she rates high on other characteristics.

Ideal self.   In Rogers' phenomenological theory, the person whom the individual would like to be (the self he or she would like to possess).

Idiographic approach.   Approach to personality assessment and research in which the individual is viewed as a lawful, integrated system in his or her own right. (See *Nomothetic approach.*)

Incident sampling.   In contrast to *time sampling*, an observational procedure in which certain types of incidents, such as those indicative of aggressive behavior, are selected for observation and recording.

In-basket technique. A supervisor or executive evaluation technique in which the examinee is required to indicate what action should be taken on a series of memos and other materials of the kind typically found in a supervisor's or executive's in-basket.

Individual test. A test administered to one examinee at a time.

Insanity. Legal term for mental disorder in which a person cannot tell the difference between right and wrong (McNaghten Rule) or cannot control his or her actions and manage his or her life.

Intelligence. Many definitions of this term have been suggested, such as "the ability to judge well, understand well, and reason well" (Binet) and "the capacity for abstract thinking" (Terman). In general, what is measured by intelligence tests is the ability to succeed in school-type tasks.

Intelligence quotient (IQ). A derived score, used originally in scoring the Stanford-Binet Intelligence Scale. A ratio IQ is computed by dividing the examinee's mental age (MA), as determined from a score on an intelligence test, by his or her chronological age (CA), and multiplying the result by 100. A deviation IQ is computed by multiplying the z score corresponding to a raw score on an intelligence test by the standard deviation of the deviation IQs and adding 100 to the product.

Intelligence test. A psychological test designed to measure an individual's aptitude for scholastic work or other kinds of activities involving verbal ability and problem solving.

Interest inventory. A test or checklist, such as the Strong-Campbell Interest Inventory and the Kuder General Interest Survey, designed to assess an individual's preferences for certain activities and topics.

Internal consistency. The extent to which the items comprising a test measure the same thing. The reliability of a test computed by the Spearman-Brown, Kuder-Richardson, or Cronbach-alpha formulas is a measure of the test's internal consistency.

Interval scale. A measurement scale on which equality of numerical differences implies equality of differences in the attribute or characteristic being measured. The scale of temperature (Celsius, Fahrenheit) and, presumably, standard scale scales (z, T), are examples of interval scales.

Interview. Systematic procedure for obtaining information by asking questions and, in general, verbally interacting with a person.

Introvert. Jung's term for orientation toward the self; primarily concerned with one's own thoughts and feelings rather than with the external environment or other people; preference for solitary activities.

Inventory. A set of questions or statements to which the individual responds (for example, by indicating agreement or disagreement), designed to provide a measure of personality, interest, attitude, or behavior.

Ipsative measurement. Test item format (e.g., forced-choice) in which the variables being measured are compared with each other, so that a person's score on one variable is affected by his or her scores on other variables measured by the instrument.

Item. One of the units, questions, or tasks of which a psychometric instrument is composed.

Kuder-Richardson formulas. Formulas used to compute a measure of internal-consistency reliability from a single administration of a test having 0–1 scoring.

L-data.   Cattell's term for personality data (recorded or rated) concerned with the individual's behavior in everyday situations.

Leaderless group discussion (*LGD*).   Six or so individuals (e.g., candidates for an executive position) are observed while discussing an assigned problem to determine their effectiveness in working with the group and reaching a solution.

Likert scale.   Attitude scale in which respondents indicate their degree of agreement or disagreement with a particular proposition concerning some object, person, or situation.

Locus of control.   Rotter's term for a cognitive-perceptual style characterized by the typical direction (internal or self vs. external or other) from which individuals perceive themselves as being controlled.

Machiavellianism.   Personality trait in which the individual is concerned with manipulating other people or using them for his or her own purposes.

Man-to-man scale.   Procedure in which ratings on a specific trait (e.g., leadership) are made by comparing each person to be rated with several other people whose standings on the trait have already been determined.

Measurement.   Procedures for determining (or indexing) the amount or quantity of some construct or entity; the assignment of numbers to objects or events.

Median.   Score point in a distribution of scores below and above which 50% of the scores fall.

Mental retardation.   Below average intelligence, usually indicated by an IQ of below 70. The DSM-III-R categories of mental retardation include mild, moderate, severe, profound, and unspecified.

Mesomorph.   Sheldon's term for a person having an athletic physique; correlated with a somatotonic temperament (active, aggressive, energetic).

Moderator variable.   Demographic or personality variable (e.g., age, sex, cognitive style, compulsivity) affecting the correlation between two other variables (e.g., aptitude and achievement).

Multiple abstract variance analysis (*MAVA*).   Statistical procedure, devised by Cattell, for computing the relative effects of heredity and environment in determining a particular personality characteristic.

Multiple personality.   Dissociative disorder in which two or more personalities exist within the same individual.

Multiple-regression analysis.   Statistical method for analyzing the contributions of two or more independent variables in predicting a dependent variable.

Multitrait-multimethod matrix.   Matrix of correlation coefficients resulting from correlating measures of the same trait by the same method, different traits by the same method, the same trait by different methods, and different traits by different methods. The relative magnitudes of the four types of correlations are compared in evaluating the construct validity of a test.

Need achievement.   Motive to excel or attain success in some field or endeavor; measured and studied extensively by McClelland.

Neuropsychological assessment.   Measurement of cognitive, perceptual, and motor performance to determine the locus, extent, and effects of neurological damage.

Neurosis (*psychoneurosis*).   Nonpsychotic mental disorder characterized by anxiety, obsessions, compulsions, phobias and/or bodily complaints or dysfunctions having no demonstrated physical cause.

Nominal scale. The lowest type of measurement, in which numbers are used merely as descriptors or names of things, rather than designating order or amount.

Nomination technique. Method of studying social structure and personality in which students, workers, or other groups of individuals are asked to indicate the individuals with whom they would like to do a certain thing or the person(s) whom they feel possess(es) certain characteristics.

Nomothetic approach. A search for general laws of behavior and personality that apply to all individuals. (See *Idiographic approach.*)

Nonverbal behavior. Any behavior in which the respondent does not make word sounds or signs. Nonverbal behavior serving a communicative function includes movements of large (macrokinesics) and small (microkinesics) body parts, interpersonal distance or territoriality (proxemics), tone and rate of voice sounds (paralinguistics), and communications imparted by culturally prescribed matters relating to time, dress, memberships, and the like (culturics).

Normal distribution. A smooth, bell-shaped frequency distribution of scores, symmetrical about the mean and described by an exact mathematical function. The test scores of a large group of examinees are frequently distributed in an approximately normal manner.

Normalized scores. Scores obtained by transforming raw scores in such a way that the transformed scores are normally distributed with a mean of 0 and a standard deviation of 1 (or some linear function of these numbers).

Norm group. Sample of people on whom a test is standardized.

Norms. A list of scores and the corresponding percentile ranks, standard scores, or other transformed scores of a group of examinees on whom a test has been standardized.

Objective test. A test scored by comparing the examinee's responses to a list of correct answers (a key) prepared beforehand, in contrast to a subjectively scored test. Examples of objective test items are multiple-choice and true-false.

Oblique rotation. In a factor analysis, a rotation in which the factor axes are allowed to form acute or obtuse angles with each other. Consequently, the factors are correlated. (See *Orthogonal rotation.*)

Observation method. Observing behavior in a controlled or uncontrolled situation and making a formal or informal record of the observations.

Oedipus complex. A composite of sexual feelings toward the mother and dislike of the father in three- to six-year-old boys, viewed by Freud as a universal phenomenon. The comparable situation in girls—disliking the mother and loving the father—is referred to as the Electra complex.

Oral stage. The first of Freud's psychosexual developmental stages, occurring from birth to one and one-half years. During the oral stage, pleasure is derived primarily from stimulation of the mouth and lips, as in sucking, biting, and swallowing.

Ordinal scale. Type of measurement scale on which the numbers refer merely to the ranks of objects or events arranged in order of merit (e.g., numbers referring to order of finishing in a context).

Organic mental disorders. Mental disorders resulting from brain damage.

Orthogonal rotation. In a factor analysis, a rotation that maintains the independence of factors, that is, the angles between factors are kept at 90 degrees and hence the factors are uncorrelated. (See *Oblique rotation.*)

Parallel forms. Two tests that are equivalent in the sense that they contain the same kinds of items of equal difficulty and are highly correlated. The scores made by examinees on one form of the test are very close to those made by them on the other form.

Parallel forms reliability.   An index of reliability determined by correlating the scores of individuals on parallel forms of a test.

Paranoid personality.   Personality disorder characterized by projection, suspiciousness, extreme jealousy or envy, and stubbornness.

Participant observation.   A research technique, used mainly by cultural anthropologists, in which the observer attempts to minimize the intrusiveness of his or her person and observational activities by becoming part of the group being observed, for example, by dressing and behaving like the other group members.

Passive-aggressive personality.   Personality disorder in which aggressive feelings are characteristically expressed in a passive manner (by pouting, stubbornness, refusal to cooperate, etc.).

Percentile.   The *p*th percentile is the test score at or below which *p* percent of the examinees' test scores fall.

Percentile band.   A range of percentile ranks within which there is a specified probability that an examinee's true score on a test will fall.

Percentile norms.   A list of raw scores and the corresponding percentages of the test standardization group whose scores fall below the given percentile.

Percentile rank.   The percentage of scores falling below a given score in a frequency distribution or group of scores; the percentage corresponding to this given score.

Personality.   The sum total of all the qualities, traits, and behaviors that characterize a person's individuality and by which, together with his or her physical attributes, the person is recognized as a unique individual.

Personality disorder.   Maladaptive behavioral syndrome originating in childhood but not characterized by psychoneurotic or psychotic symptoms.

Personality inventory.   A self-report inventory or questionnaire consisting of statements concerned with personal characteristics and behaviors. On a true-false inventory, the respondent indicates whether or not each test item or statement is self-descriptive; on a multiple-choice or forced-choice inventory, the respondent selects the statements that are self-descriptive.

Personality profile.   Graph of scores on a battery or set of scales of a personality inventory or rating scale. The elevation and scatter of the profile assists in the assessment of personality and mental disorders.

Personality test.   Any one of several methods of analyzing personality, such as checklists, personality inventories, and projective techniques.

Phallic stage.   The third of Freud's stages of psychosexual development. During this stage (3–6 years), the genital area is of greatest interest, indicated by rubbing, touching, and exhibiting one's genital organs. It is during the phallic stage that the Oedipus complex develops.

Phenomenology.   Study of objects and events as they appear to the experiencing observer; type of psychotherapy (Rogers, Maslow, etc.) which emphasizes the importance of self-perceptions and impressions of others in determining personality and behavior.

Phobic disorder.   Neurotic condition in which the individual is unreasonably afraid of some situation or object that typically poses no actual threat.

Phrenology.   Discredited theory and practice of Gall and Spurzheim relating affective and cognitive characteristics to the configuration (bumps) of the skull.

Physiognomy. A pseudoscience that maintains that the personal characteristics of an individual are revealed by the form or features of the body, especially the face.

Point-biserial coefficient. Correlation coefficient computed between a dichotomous variable and a continuous variable; derived from the product-moment correlation coefficient.

Predictive validity. Extent to which scores on a test are predictive of performance on some criterion measure assessed at a later time; usually expressed as a correlation between the test (predictor variable) and the criterion variable.

Profile (*psychograph*). Graph depicting an individual's scores on several parts of the same test. By examining the profile of scores on a personality inventory such as the MMPI, a psychologist may obtain information useful in personality analysis and the diagnosis of psychopathology.

Projection. A defense mechanism in which an individual attributes his or her own unacceptable desires and impulses to other people.

Projective technique. A relatively unstructured personality test in which the examinee responds to materials such as inkblots, ambiguous pictures, incomplete sentences, and other materials by telling what he or she perceives, making up stories, or constructing and arranging sentences and objects. Theoretically, because the material is fairly unstructured, whatever structure the examinee imposes on it represents a projection of his or her own personality characteristics (needs, conflicts, sources of anxiety, etc.).

Psychohistory. Biography, such as Erikson's *Young Man Luther* or *Gandhi's Truth*, written from a psychoanalytic point of view.

Psychometrics. Theory and research pertaining to the measurement of psychological (cognitive and affective) characteristics.

Psychosexual disorder. Psychologically based dysfunction in the ability to give or receive sexual gratification.

Psychosexual stages. According to psychoanalytic theory, a series of developmental stages—oral, anal, phallic, latency, genital—through which children pass and which influence their character and personality.

Psychotic disorders (*psychoses*). Extreme personality disorders characterized by loss of contact with reality, bizarre behavior, and distortions of personality; usually requiring hospitalization.

Q data. Cattell's term for personality data obtained from questionnaires.

Q technique. A set of procedures used to conduct research on the individual that center on sorting decks of cards called Q sorts and correlating the responses of different individuals to the Q sorts.

Quartile. A score in a frequency distribution below which either 25% (first quartile), 50% (second quartile), 75% (third quartile), or 100% (fourth quartile) of the total number of scores fall.

Questionnaire. A list of questions concerning a particular topic, administered to a group of individuals to obtain information concerning their preferences, beliefs, interests, and behavior.

r. A symbol for the Pearson product-moment correlation coefficient.

Random sample. A sample of observations (e.g., test scores) drawn from a population in such a way that every member of the target population has an equal chance of being selected in the sample.

Range. A crude measure of the spread or variability of a group of scores computed by subtracting the lowest score from the highest score.

Rapport.   A warm, friendly relationship between examiner and examinee.

Rating scale.   A list of words or statements concerning traits or characteristics, sometimes in the form of a continuous line divided into sections corresponding to degrees of the characteristic, on which the rater indicates judgments of either his or her own behavior and traits or the behavior and traits of another person (ratee).

Ratio scale.   A scale of measurement, having a true zero, on which equal numerical ratios imply equal ratios of the attribute being measured. Psychological variables are typically not measured on ratio scales, but height, weight, energy, and many other physical variables are.

Reactive psychosis.   Severe mental disorder that develops suddenly and is precipitated by identifiable stressors; marked by confusion and intense emotional turmoil.

Real self.   In Rogers' phenomenological theory, a person's perception of what he or she really is, as contrasted with what he or she would like to be (*ideal self*).

Realistic stage.   Final stage in the development of vocational interests, usually occurring during late adolescence or early adulthood. The individual has a realistic notion about what particular occupations entail and the vocation he or she would like to pursue.

Regression equation.   A linear equation for forecasting criterion scores from scores on one or more predictor variables; a procedure often used in selection programs or actuarial prediction and diagnosis.

Reliability.   The extent to which a psychological assessment instrument measures anything consistently. A reliable instrument is relatively free from errors of measurement, so the scores examinees obtain on the instrument are close in numerical value to their true scores.

Reliability coefficient.   A numerical index, between .00 and 1.00, of the reliability of an assessment instrument. Methods for determining reliability include test-retest, parallel-forms, and internal consistency.

Repression.   According to psychoanalytic theory, an automatic process by which anxiety producing conflicts or experiences are relegated to the unconscious, below the level of conscious awareness.

Response sets (*styles*).   Tendencies for individuals to respond in relatively fixed or stereotyped ways in situations where there are two or more response choices, such as on personality inventories. Tendencies to guess, to answer true (acquiescence), and to give socially desirable answers are some of the response sets that have been investigated.

Schizoid personality.   Personality disorder characterized by shyness, eccentricity, oversensitivity, and seclusiveness.

Schizophrenic disorders.   Psychoses characterized by withdrawal from reality, disturbances of thinking, emotion, and behavior; a breakdown of integrated personality functioning.

Self-actualization.   In Rogers' phenomenological theory, attaining a state of congruence between one's real and ideal selves; developing one's abilities to the fullest; becoming the kind of person one would ideally like to be.

Self-concept.   An individual's evaluation of her or his self as assessed by various psychometric instruments.

Self-fulfilling prophecy.   Tendency for a person's expectations and attitudes concerning future events or outcomes to affect their occurrence, that is, the tendency for children to behave in ways in which parents or teachers expect them to behave.

Self-monitoring.   The extent to which people are sensitive to, or monitor, their own behavior according to environmental cues. High self-monitors are more sensitive to what is situationally appropriate and act accordingly. Low self-monitors are less sensitive to external cues and act more in response to their own internal attitudes and feelings.

Self-report inventory. A personality or interest inventory comprised of a series of items that the examinee indicates as being characteristic (true) or not characteristic (not true) of himself or herself.

Semantic differential. A rating scale, introduced by Osgood, for evaluating the connotative meanings that selected concepts have for a person. Each concept is rated on a seven-point, bipolar, adjectival scale.

Semi-interquartile range (Q). A measure of the variability of a group of ordinal-scale scores, computed as half the difference between the first and third quartiles.

Sentence completion test. A personality (projective) test consisting of a series of incomplete sentences that the examinee is instructed to complete as quickly as possible.

Situation(al) test. A performance test in which the examinee is placed in a realistic but contrived situation and directed to accomplish a specified goal. Situation tests are sometimes employed to assess personality characteristics such as honesty and frustration tolerance.

Social desirability response set. Response set or style affecting scores on personality inventories. It refers to the tendency on the part of an examinee to respond to the assessment materials in a more socially desirable direction rather than responding in a manner that is truly characteristic or descriptive of his or her personality.

Sociogram. Diagram consisting of circles representing individuals in a group, with lines drawn indicating which people choose (accept) each other and which people do not choose (reject) each other. Terms used in referring to particular elements of a sociogram are *star, clique, isolate,* and *mutual admiration society.*

Sociometric technique. Method of determining and describing the pattern of acceptances and rejections in a group of people.

Somatotonia. Athletic, aggressive temperament type in Sheldon's three-component system of personality; most closely correlated with a mesomorphic (muscular) body build.

Somatotype. Classification of body build (physique) in Sheldon's three-component system (endomorphy, mesomorphy, ectomorphy).

Source traits. Cattell's term for organizing structures or dimensions of personality that underlie and determine surface traits.

Spearman-Brown formula. A formula for estimating what the reliability of a test would be if its length were increased by a specified amount by adding more items of the same general type.

Split-half coefficient. An estimate of reliability determined by applying the Spearman-Brown formula for $m = 2$ to the correlation between two halves of the same test, such as the odd-numbered items and even-numbered items.

Standard deviation. The square root of the variance, used as a measure of dispersion or spread of a group of scores.

Standard error of estimate. The standard deviation of obtained criterion scores around the predicted criterion score; used to estimate a range of actual scores on a criterion variable for an individual whose score on the predictor variable is equal to a specified value.

Standard error of measurement. An estimate of the standard deviation of the normal distribution of test scores that an examinee would theoretically obtain by taking a test an infinite number of times. It can be stated that if an examinee's obtained test score is X, then the chances are two out of three that he or she is one of a group of people whose true scores on the test fall within one standard error of measurement of X.

Standard scores.   A group of scores, such as z scores, T scores, or stanine scores, having a desired mean and standard deviation. Standard scores are computed by transforming raw scores to z scores, multiplying the z scores by the desired standard deviation, and then adding the desired mean to the product.

Standardization.   Administering a carefully constructed test to a large, representative sample of people under standard conditions for the purpose of determining norms.

Standardized test.   A test that has been carefully constructed by professionals and administered with standard directions and under standard conditions to a representative sample of people for the purpose of obtaining norms.

Stanine.   A standard score scale consisting of the scores 1 through 9, having a mean of 5 and a standard deviation of approximately 2.

State anxiety.   A temporary state of anxiety, precipitated by a specific situation.

Statistic.   A number used to describe some characteristic of a sample of test scores, such as the arithmetic mean or standard deviation.

Stratified random sampling.   A sampling procedure in which the population is divided into strata (e.g., men and women; blacks and whites; lower class, middle class, upper class), and samples are selected at random from the strata; sample sizes are proportional to strata sizes.

Stress interview.   Interviewing procedure in which the interviewer applies psychologically stressful techniques (critical and hostile questioning, frequent interruptions, prolonged silences, etc.) to break down the interviewee's defenses and/or determine how the interviewee reacts under pressure.

Structured interview.   Interviewing procedure in which the interviewee is asked a series of preplanned questions.

Superego.   In psychoanalytic theory, the part of personality that acts according to the moral, idealistic principle, incorporating parental (societal) prohibitions and sanctions.

Surface traits.   Publicly manifested characteristics of personality; observable expressions of source traits.

T scores.   Converted, normalized standard scores having a mean of 50 and a standard deviation of 10. Z scores are also standard scores with a mean of 50 and a standard deviation of 10, but in contrast to T scores they are not normalized.

Target behaviors.   Specific, objectively defined behaviors observed and measured in behavioral assessments. Of particular interest are the effects on these behaviors of antecedent and consequent events in the environment.

Target population.   The population of interest in standardizing a test or other assessment instrument; the norm group (sample) must be representative of the target population if valid interpretations of (norm-referenced) scores are to be made.

Template-matching technique.   Bem and Funder's conceptualization of a situation template as a pattern of behavior characterizing the way that a person (person *I*) is ideally expected to behave in that situation. The extent to which another person (person *J*) behaves similarly in the same situation depends on the match between the personality characteristics of persons *I* and *J*.

Test.   Any device used to evaluate the behavior or performance of an individual. Psychological tests are of many kinds—cognitive, affective, and psychomotor.

Test anxiety.   A feeling of fear or uneasiness that one will not do well on a test.

Test-retest reliability.   A method of assessing the reliability of a test by administering it to the same group of examinees on two different occasions and computing the correlations between their scores on the two occasions.

Time sampling.   Observational sampling procedure in which observations lasting only a few minutes are made over a period of a day or so.

Trait.   A cognitive, affective, or psychomotor characteristic possessed in different amounts by different people.

Trait anxiety.   Generalized level of anxiety expressed in a variety of situations.

Transitional stage.   An intermediate stage in the development of interests; falls between the fantasy stage of early childhood and the realistic stage of late adolescence and early adulthood.

True score.   The hypothetical score that is a measure of the examinee's true knowledge of the test material. In test theory, an examinee's true score on a test is the mean of the distribution of scores that would result if the examinee took the test an infinite number of times.

Type A personality.   Personality pattern characterized by a combination of behaviors, including aggressiveness, competitiveness, hostility, quick actions, and constant striving; associated with a high incidence of coronary heart disease.

Type B personality.   Personality pattern characterized by a relaxed, easygoing, patient, noncompetitive lifestyle; associated with a low incidence of coronary heart disease.

Unobtrusive observations.   Observations made without the awareness of the person whose behavior is being observed.

Unstructured interview.   Interviewing procedure in which the questions asked are not preplanned but vary with the progress or flow of the interview.

Validity.   The extent to which an assessment instrument measures what it was designed to measure. Validity can be assessed in several ways: by analysis of the instrument's content (*content validity*); by relating scores on the test to a criterion (*predictive* and *concurrent validity*); and by a more thorough study of the extent to which the test is a measure of a certain psychological construct (*construct validity*).

Variability.   The degree of spread or deviation of a group of scores around their average value.

Variable.   In contrast to *constant*, any quantity that can assume more than one state or numerical value.

Variance.   A measure of variability of test scores, computed as the sum of the squares of the deviations of raw scores from the arithmetic mean, divided by one less than the number of scores; the square of the standard deviation.

Viscerotonia.   Jolly, sociable temperament type in Sheldon's three-component description of personality; most closely correlated with the endomorhic (rotund) body build.

Word association test.   A list of words that is read aloud to an examinee who has been instructed to respond with the first word that comes into mind. Introduced by the Swiss psychiatrist Jung, word association tests are often used in the analysis of personality.

z score.   Any one of a group of derived scores varying from -00 to $+00$, computed from the formula $z = $ (raw score $-$ mean)/standard deviation, for each raw score. In a normal distribution, over 99% of the cases lie between $z = -3.00$ and $1 = +3.00$.

REFERENCES

Abramson, L. Y., Garber, J., & Seligman, M. E. P. (1980). Learned helplessness in humans. In J. Garber & M. E. P. Seligman (Eds.), *Human helplessness* (pp. 3–34). New York: Academic.

Achenbach, T. M. (1981). A junior MMPI? *Journal of Personality Assessment, 45,* 332.

Adair, F. L. (1984). Coopersmith Self-Esteem Inventories. In D. J. Keyser & R. C. Sweetland (Eds.), *Test critiques* (Vol. I, pp. 226–232). Kansas City, MO: Test Corporation of America.

Aiken, L. R. (1985). Three coefficients for analyzing the reliability and validity of ratings. *Educational and Psychological Measurement, 45,* 131–142.

Aiken, L. R. (1987). *Assessment of intellectual functioning.* Boston: Allyn & Bacon.

Aiken, L. R. (1988). *Psychological testing and assessment* (6th ed.). Boston: Allyn & Bacon.

Aiken, L. R., & Romen, L. (1984). *Attitudes and experiences concerning psychological and educational testing.* Paper presented at the Annual Meeting of the Rocky Mountain Psychological Association (*ERIC Reports* ED 247 322).

Aiken, L. R., & Zweigenhaft, R. (1978). Signature size, sex and status: A cross-cultural replication. *Journal of Social Psychology, 106,* 273–274.

Ajzen, I., & Fishbein, M. (1977). Attitude-behavior relations: A theoretical analysis and review of empirical research. *Psychological Bulletin, 84,* 888–918.

Akiskal, H. S. (1979). A biobehavioral approach to depression. In R. A. Depue (Ed.), *The psychobiology of depressive disorders: Implications for the effects of stress.* New York: Academic.

Albert, S., Fox, H. M., & Kahn, M. W. (1980). Faking psychosis on the Rorschach: Can expert judges detect malingering? *Journal of Personality Assessment, 44,* 115–119.

Allen, M. G. (1976). Twin studies of affective illness. *Archives of General Psychiatry, 35,* 1476–1478.

Allen, M. J. (1985). Review of Millon Behavioral Health Inventory. In J. V. Mitchell, Jr.

(Ed.), *The ninth mental measurements yearbook* (Vol. I, pp. 981–983). Lincoln, NE: Buros Institute of Mental Measurements of the University of Nebraska-Lincoln.

Allport, G. W. (1937). *Personality: A psychological interpretation*. New York: Holt.

Allport, G. W. (1961). *Pattern and growth in personality*. New York: Holt, Rinehart & Winston.

Allport, G. W. (Ed.) (1965). *Letters from Jenny*. New York: Harcourt, Brace & World.

Allport, G. W., & Odbert, H. S. (1936). Trait-names, a psycholexical study. *Psychological Monographs*, 47 (Whole No. 211).

American Educational Research Association, American Psychological Association, & National Council on Measurement in Education. (1985). *Standards for educational and psychological testing*. Washington, DC: American Psychological Association.

American Psychiatric Association. (1980). *Diagnostic and statistical manual of mental disorders* (3rd ed.). Washington, DC: Author.

American Psychiatric Association. (1987). *Diagnostic and statistical manual of mental disorders* (3rd ed., rev.). Washington, DC: Author.

American Psychological Association. (1981). Ethical principles of psychologists. *American Psychologist*, 36, 633–638.

American Psychological Association, Committee on Professional Standards and Committee on Psychological Tests and Assessment. (1986). *Guidelines for computer-based tests and interpretations*. Washington, DC: Author.

American Psychological Association. (1987). *General guidelines for providers of psychological services*. Washington, DC: Author.

Anastasi, A. (1982). *Psychological testing* (5th ed.). New York: Macmillan.

Anastasi, A. (1985). Mental measurement: Some emerging trends. In J. V. Mitchell, Jr. (Ed.), *The ninth mental measurements yearbook* (Vol. I, xxiii–xxix). Lincoln, NE: Buros Institute of Mental Measurements of the University of Nebraska-Lincoln.

Anastasi, A. (1988). *Psychological testing* (6th ed.). New York: Macmillan.

Anderson, H., & Anderson, G. (1955). *An introduction to projective techniques*. New York: Prentice-Hall.

Appelbaum, S. A. (1960). The word association test expanded. *Bulletin of the Menninger Clinic*, 24, 258–264.

Arkes, H. R. (1985). Clinical judgment. In R. J. Corsini (Ed.), *Encyclopedia of psychology* (Vol. 1, pp. 223–224). New York: Wiley.

Armstrong, R. B. (1985). Early recollections. In R. J. Corsini (Ed.), *Encyclopedia of psychology* (Vol. 1, pp. 404–405). New York: Wiley.

Aronow, E., & Reznikoff, M. (1983). *A Rorschach introduction: Content and perceptual approaches*. New York: Grune & Stratton.

Arvey, R. D. (1979). Unfair discrimination in the employment interview: Legal and psychological aspects. *Psychological Bulletin*, 86, 736–765.

Associated Press. (1983, March 12). Leaks fought with lie tests. *Holland Sentinel*, p. 1.

Atkinson, R. L., Atkinson, R. C., Smith, E. E., & Hilgard, E. R. (1987). *Introduction to psychology* (9th ed.). San Diego, CA: Harcourt Brace Jovanovich.

Aust, P. H. (1984). Rational-emotive therapy in the school. *Social Work in Education*, 6(2), 106–117.

Ax, A. F. (1953). The physiological differentiation between fear and anger in humans. *Psychosomatic Medicine*, 15, 433–442.

Bailey, B. E., & Green, J. (1977). Black Thematic Apperception Test stimulus material. *Journal of Personality Assessment, 41*, 25–30.

Bakan, P. (1957). Extraversion-introversion and improvement in an auditory vigilance task. *Medical Research Council*, A.P.U. 311/57.

Bandura, A. (1977). *Social learning theory*. Englewood Cliffs, NJ: Prentice-Hall.

Bandura, A. (1982). Self-efficacy mechanism in human agency. *American Psychologist, 37*, 122–147.

Barley, W. D., Dorr, D., & Reid, V. (1985). The Rorschach Comprehensive System egocentricity index in psychiatric inpatients. *Journal of Personality Assessment, 49*, 137–140.

Barlow, D. H. (1977). Assessment of sexual behavior. In A. R. Ciminero, K. S. Calhoun, & H. E. Adams (Eds.), *Handbook of behavioral assessment*. New York: Wiley.

Bass, B. M., & Berg, I. A. (1961). *Conformity and deviation*. New York: Harper & Row.

Bauerfeind, R. H. (1986). COPSystem Interest Inventory. In D. J. Keyser & R. C. Sweetland (Eds.), *Test critiques* (Vol. V, pp. 76–82). Kansas City, MO: Test Corporation of America.

Beck, A. T. (1970). *Depression: Causes and treatment*. Philadelphia: University of Pennsylvania Press.

Beck, S. J. (1944). *Rorschach's test I: Basic processes*. New York: Grune & Stratton.

Bellak, L. (1942). A note about Adam's apple. *Psychoanalytic Review, 29*(3).

Bellak, L. (1986). *The T.A.T., C.A.T. and S.A.T. in clinical use* (4th ed.). New York: Grune & Stratton.

Bellak, L., & Bellak, S. (1949). *Children's Apperception Test*. Larchmont, NY: C.P.S., Inc.

Bellak, L., & Bellak, S. (1973). *Manual: Senior Apperception Test*. Larchmont, NY: C.P.S., Inc.

Bem, D. J., & Allen, A. (1974). On predicting some of the people some of the time: The search for cross-situational consistencies in behavior. *Psychological Review, 81*, 506–520.

Bem, D. J., & Funder, D. C. (1978). Predicting more of the people more of the time: Assessing the personality of situations. *Psychological Review, 85*, 485–501.

Bem, S. L. (1975). Sex-role adaptability: One consequence of psychological androgyny. *Journal of Personality and Social Psychology, 31*, 634–653.

Ben-Porath, Y. B., & Butcher, J. N. (1986). Computers in personality assessment: A brief past, an ebullient present and an expanding future. *Computers in Human Behavior, 2*, 167–182.

Ben-Shakhar, G., Bar-Hillel, M., Bilu, Y., Ben-Abba, E., & Flug, A. (1986). Can graphology predict occupational success? Two empirical studies and some methodological ruminations. *Journal of Applied Psychology, 71*, 645–653.

Bentler, P. M. (1968). Heterosexual behavior assessments: I. Males. *Behavioral Research and Therapy, 6*, 21.

Bentler, P. M., & Newcomb, M. D. (1986). Personality, sexual behavior, and drug use revealed through latent variable methods. *Clinical Psychology Review, 6*(5), 363–386.

Benton, A. L., Windle, C. D., & Erdice, E. (1957). *A review of sentence completion techniques*. Project NR 151–175. Washington, DC: Office of Naval Research.

Bergner, M., & Gilson, B. S. (1981). The Sickness Impact Profile. In L. Eisenberg & A. Kleinman (Eds.), *The relevance of social science to medicine* (pp. 135–150). Dordrecht, The Netherlands: Reidel.

Bernard, H. W., & Huckins, W. C. (1978). *Dynamics of personality adjustment* (3rd ed.). Boston: Holbrook.

Berne, E. (1966). *Principles of group treatment.* New York: Oxford University Press.

Binet, A., & Simon, T. (1905). Methodes pour le diagnostic du niveau intelectuel des anormaux. *L'Annee Psychologique, 11,* 191–244.

Blatt, S. J., & Berman, W. H. (1984). A methodology for use of the Rorschach in clinical research. *Journal of Personality Assessment, 48,* 226–239.

Blessed, G., Tomlinson, B. E., & Roth, M. (1968). The association between quantitative measures of dementia and of senile change in the cerebral grey matter of elderly subjects. *British Journal of Psychiatry, 114,* 797–811.

Block, J. (1961). *The Q-sort method in personality assessment and psychiatric research.* Springfield, IL: Thomas.

Block, J. (1965). *The challenge of response sets.* New York: Appleton-Century-Crofts.

Block, J. (1977). Advancing the psychology of personality: Paradigmatic shift in improving the quality of research. In D. Magnusson and N. S. Endler (Eds.), *Personality at the crossroads: Current issues in interactional psychology.* Hillsdale, NJ: Erlbaum.

Blum, G. (1950). *The Blacky Pictures.* New York: Psychological Corporation.

Blum, G., & Hunt, H. (1952). The validity of the Blacky Pictures. *Psychological Bulletin, 49,* 238–250.

Blumenthal, J. A. (1985). Review of Jenkins Activity Survey. In J. V. Mitchell, Jr. (Ed.), *The ninth mental measurements yearbook* (Vol. I, pp. 743–745). Lincoln, NE: Buros Institute of Mental Measurements of the University of Nebraska-Lincoln.

Bogardus, E. S. (1925). Measuring social distances. *Journal of Applied Sociology, 9,* 299–308.

Bolton, B. (1985). Work Values Inventory. In D. J. Keyser & R. C. Sweetland (Eds.), *Test critiques* (Vol. II, pp. 835–843). Kansas City, MO: Test Corporation of America.

Bordin, E. S. (1943). A theory of interests as dynamic phenomena. *Educational and Psychological Measurement, 3,* 49–66.

Borg, W. R., & Gall, M. D. (1983). *Educational research: An introduction* (4th ed.). New York: Longman.

Bradley, R. H., & Caldwell, B. M. (1977). Home observation for measurement of the environment: A validation study of screening efficiency. *American Journal of Mental Deficiency, 81,* 417–420.

Bricklin, B. (1984). *Bricklin Perceptual Scales.* Furlong, PA: Village.

Brittain, H. L. (1907). A study in imagination. *Pediatric Seminars, 14,* 137–207.

Brown, D. T. (1985). Review of Millon Adolescent Personality Inventory. In J. V. Mitchell, Jr. (Ed.), *The ninth mental measurements yearbook* (Vol. 1, pp. 978–979). Lincoln, NE: Buros Institute of Mental Measurements of the University of Nebraska-Lincoln.

Brown, F. (1982). The ethics of psychodiagnostic assessment. In M. Rosenbaum (Ed.), *Ethics and values in psychotherapy: A guidebook* (pp. 96–106). New York: Free Press.

Bruvold, W. H. (1975). Judgmental bias in the rating of attitude statements. *Educational and Psychological Measurement, 35,* 605–611.

Buck, J. N. (1948). The H-T-P technique: A quantitative and qualitative scoring manual. *Clinical Psychology Monographs, 5,* 1–20.

Burdock, E. I., Hardesty, A. S., Hakerem, G., Zubin, J., & Beck, Y. M. (1968). *Ward Behavior Inventory.* New York: Springer.

Burger, G. K. (1975). A short form of the California Psychological Inventory. *Psychological Reports, 37,* 179–182.

Burisch, M. (1984). Approaches to personality inventory construction. *American Psychologist, 39*, 214–227.

Buss, A. H., & Plomin, R. (1975). *A temperament theory of personality development.* New York: Wiley.

Butcher, J. N. (1978). Automated MMPI interpretative systems. In O. K. Buros (Ed.), *The eighth mental measurements yearbook* (pp. 942–945). Highland Park, NJ: Gryphon.

Butcher, J. N., & Keller, L. S. (1984). Objective personality assessment. In G. Goldstein & M. Hersen (Eds.), *Handbook of psychological assessment* (pp. 307–331). New York: Pergamon.

Butcher, J. N., Keller, L. S., & Bacon, S. F. (1985). Current developments and future directions in computerized personality assessment. *Journal of Consulting and Clinical Psychology, 53*, 803–815.

Campbell, D. T., & Fiske, D. W. (1959). Convergent and discriminant validation by the multitrait-multimethod matrix. *Psychological Bulletin, 56*, 81–105.

Cannon, W. B. (1927). The James-Lange theory of emotions: A critical examination and an alternative theory. *American Journal of Psychology, 39*, 106–124.

Cannon, W. B. (1929). *Bodily changes in pain, hunger, fear, and rage* (2nd ed.). New York: Appleton-Century.

Carter, H. D. (1940). The development of vocational attitudes. *Journal of Consulting Psychology, 4*, 185–191.

Castro, J. G., & Jordan, J. E. (1977). Facet theory attitude research. *Educational Research, 6*, 7–11.

Cattell, R. B. (1957). *Personality and motivation structure and measurement.* New York: Harcourt, Brace & World.

Cattell, R. B. (1965a). *The scientific analysis of personality.* New York: Penguin.

Cattell, R. B. (1965b). Methodological and conceptual advances in the evaluation of hereditary and environmental influences and their interaction. In S. G. Vandenberg (Ed.), *Methods and goals in human behavior genetics* (pp. 95–130). New York: Academic.

Cattell, R. B., Cattell, M. D., & Johns, E. (1984). *High School Personality Questionnaire.* Champaign, IL: Institute for Personality and Ability Testing.

Chaplin, W. F. (1984). State-Trait Anxiety Inventory. In D. J. Keyser & R. C. Sweetland (Eds.), *Test critiques* (Vol. I, pp. 626–632). Kansas City, MO: Test Corporation of America.

Chaplin, W. F., & Goldberg, L. R. (1984). A failure to replicate the Bem and Allen study of individual differences in cross-situational consistency. *Journal of Personality and Social Psychology, 47*, 1074–1092.

Chapman, J., & McGhie, A. (1962). A comparative study of disordered attention in schizophrenia. *Journal of Mental Science, 108*, 487–500.

Chelune, G. J., Ferguson, W., & Moehle, K. (1986). The role of standard cognitive and personality tests in neuropsychological assessment. In T. Incagnoli, G. Goldstein, & C. J. Golden (Eds.), *Clinical applications of neuropsychological test batteries* (pp. 75–119). New York: Plenum.

Ciminero, A. R., Nelson, R. O., & Lipinski, D. P. (1977). Self-monitoring procedures. In A. R. Ciminero, K. S. Calhoun, & H. E. Adams (Eds.), *Handbook of behavioral assessment.* New York: Wiley.

Claridge, G. (1960). The excitation-inhibition balance in neurotics. In H. J. Eysenck (Ed.), *Experiments in personality.* London: Routledge & Kegan Paul.

Clark, R. (1944). A method of administering and evaluating the Thematic Apperception Test in group situations. *Genetic Psychology Monographs, 30,* 1–55.

Cliff, N. (1987). *Analyzing multivariate data.* San Diego: Harcourt Brace Jovanovich.

Coan, R. W. (1972). Measurable components of openness to experience. *Journal of Consulting and Clinical Psychology, 39,* 346.

Colligan, R. C., Osborne, D., & Swenson, W. M. (1982). *The MMPI: A contemporary normative study.* Paper presented at the 17th Annual Symposium on Recent Developments in the Use of the MMPI, Tampa, Florida.

Cooper, A. (1981). A basic TAT set for adolescent males. *Journal of Clinical Psychology, 37,* 411–414.

Cooper, J. E., Kendall, R. E., Gurland, B. J., Sharp, L., Copeland, J. R. M., & Simon, R. (1972). *Psychiatric diagnosis in New York and London: A comparative study of mental hospital admissions.* New York: Oxford University Press.

Coopersmith, S. (1981). *The antecedents of self-esteem.* Palo Alto, CA: Consulting Psychologists.

Copple, G. E. (1956). Effective intelligence as measured by an unstructured sentence-completion technique. *Journal of Consulting Psychology, 20,* 357–360.

Corsini, R. J., & Marsella, A. J. (Eds.). (1983). *Personality theory, research and assessment.* Itasca, IL: F. E. Peacock Publishers.

Cosden, M. (1984). Piers-Harris Children's Self-Concept Scale. In D. J. Keyser & R. C. Sweetland (Eds.). *Test critiques* (Vol. I, pp. 511–521). Kansas City, MO: Test Corporation of America.

Costa, P. T., Jr., & McCrae, R. R. (1986). Personality stability and its implications for clinical psychology. *Clinical Psychology Review, 6,* 407–423.

Costantino, G. (1978, Nov.). *Preliminary report on TEMAS: A new thematic apperception test to assess ego functions in ethnic minority children.* Paper presented at the Second American Conference on Fantasy and the Imaging Process, Chicago.

Costantino, G., Malgady, R., & Vazquez, C. (1981). A comparison of the Murray-TAT and a new thematic apperception test for urban Hispanic children. *Hispanic Journal of Behavioral Sciences, 3,* 291–300.

Couch, A., & Carter, L. F. (1953). A factorial study of the rated behavior of group members. *American Psychologist, 8,* 236–239.

Cowan, G. (1971). Achievement motivation in lower class Negro females as a function of the race and sex of the figures. *Representative Research in Social Psychology, 21,* 42–46.

Cowan, G., & Goldberg, F. J. (1967). Need achievement as a function of the race and sex of figures of selected TAT cards. *Journal of Personality and Social Psychology, 5,* 245–249.

Crandall, E. (1975). A scale for social interest. *Journal of Individual Psycyology, 31,* 187–195.

Crites, J. O. (1960). Ego strength in relation to vocational interest development. *Journal of Counseling Psychology, 7,* 137–143.

Crites, J. O. (1985). Ohio Vocational Interest Survey: Second Edition. In D. J. Keyser & R. C. Sweetland (Eds.), *Test critiques* (Vol. IV, pp. 478–483). Kansas City, MO: Test Corporation of America.

Cronbach, L. J. (1951). Coefficient alpha and the internal structure of tests. *Psychometrika, 16,* 297–334.

Cronbach, L. J., Gleser, G. C., Nanda, H., & Rajaratnam, N. (1972). *The dependability of behavioral measurements: Theory of generalizability for scores and profiles.* New York: Wiley.

Cronbach, L. J., & Meehl, P. E. (1955). Construct validity in psychological tests. *Psychological Bulletin, 52,* 281–302.

Crowne, D. P., & Marlowe, D. (1964). *The approval motive: Studies in evaluative dependence.* New York: Wiley.

Cunningham, R., et al. (1951). *Group behavior of boys and girls.* New York: Columbia University Press.

Dahlstrom, W. G., Welsh, G. S., & Dahlstrom, L. E. (1975). *An MMPI handbook: Research applications* (Vol. II, rev. ed.). Minneapolis: University of Minnesota Press.

Dana, R. H. (1955). Clinical diagnosis and objective TAT scoring. *Journal of Abnormal and Social Psychology, 50,* 19–25.

Dana, R. H. (1959). A proposal for the objective scoring of the T.A.T. *Perceptual & Motor Skills, 9,* 27–43.

Dana, R. H. (1982). *A human science model for personality assessment with projective techniques.* Springfield, IL: Thomas.

Dana, R. H. (1984). Personality assessment: Practice and teaching for the next decade. *Journal of Personality Assessment, 48,* 46–56.

Darley, J. B., & Hagenah, T. (1955). *Vocational interest measurement.* Minneapolis: University of Minnesota Press.

Davidshofer, C. (1985). Review of Jackson Vocational Interest Survey. In J. V. Mitchell, Jr. (Ed.), *The ninth mental measurements yearbook* (Vol. I, pp. 739–740). Lincoln, NE: Buros Institute of Mental Measurement of the University of Nebraska-Lincoln.

Dawes, R. M. (1986). Representative thinking in clinical judgment. *Clinical Psychology Review, 6,* 425–442.

Dean, E. F. (1972). A lengthened Mini-Mult: The Midi-Mult. *Journal of Clinical Psychology, 28,* 68–71.

Diamond, E. E. (1979). Sex equality and measurement practices. *New Directions for Testing and Measurement, 3,* 31–78.

Disbrow, M. A., Doerr, H. O., & Caulfield, C. (1977, March). *Measures to predict child abuse.* Final report of Grant MC-R530351, Maternal and Child Health. Washington, DC: National Institute of Mental Health.

Dittman, A. T. (1962). The relationship between body movements and moods in interviews. *Journal of Consulting Psychology, 26,* 480.

Dolliver, R. H. (1985). Review of Self-Motivated Career Planning. In J. V. Mitchell, Jr. (Ed.), *The ninth mental measurements yearbook* (Vol. II, pp. 1347–1348). Lincoln, NE: Buros Institute of Mental Measurements of the University of Nebraska-Lincoln.

Domino, G. (1985). Review of Ohio Vocational Interest Survey. In J. V. Mitchell, Jr. (Ed.), *The ninth mental measurements yearbook* (Vol. II, pp. 1090–1091). Lincoln, NE: Buros Institute of Mental Measurements of the University of Nebraska-Lincoln.

Drake, L. E. (1946). A social I.E. scale for the MMPI. *Journal of Applied Psychology, 30,* 51–54.

Dreger, R. M. (1982). The classification of children and their emotional problems: An overview-II. *Clinical Psychology Review, 2,* 349–385.

Drummond, R. J. (1984). Edwards Personal Preference Schedule. In D. J. Keyser & R. C. Sweetland (Eds.), *Test critiques* (Vol. I, pp. 252–258). Kansas City, MO: Test Corporation of America.

DuBois, P. H. (1970). *The history of psychological testing.* Boston: Allyn & Bacon.

Duckworth, D., & Entwhistle, N. J. (1974). Attitudes to school subjects: A repertory grid technique. *British Journal of Educational Psychology, 44,* 76–83.

Duckworth, J. C. & Anderson, W. (1986). *Interpretation manual for counselors and clinicians* (3rd ed.). Munsey, IN: Excelerated Development.

Dunn, S., Bliss, J., & Siipola, E. (1958). Effects of impulsivity, introversion, and individual values upon association under free conditions. *Journal of Personality, 26,* 61–76.

Dworkin, R. H., Burke, B. W., Maher, B. A., & Gottesman, I. I. (1976). A longitudinal study of the genetics of personality. *Journal of Personality and Social Psychology, 34,* 510–518.

Dyer, C. O. (1985). Jackson Personality Inventory. In D. J. Keyser & R. C. Sweetland (Eds.), *Test critiques* (Vol. II, pp. 369–375). Kansas City, MO: Test Corporation of America.

Eaton, M. E., Sletten, I. W., Kitchen, A. D., & Smith, R. J. II. (1971). The Missouri Automated Psychiatric History: Symptom frequencies, sex differences, use of weapons, and other findings. *Comprehensive Psychiatry, 12,* 264–276.

Ebbinghaus, H. (1897). Über eine neue Methode zur Prufung geistiger Fahigkeiten un ihre Anwendung bei Schulkindern. *Zeitschrift fur angewandte Psychologie, 13,* 401–459.

Edmonds, J. M. (Ed. and Trans.). (1929). *The characters of Theophrastus.* Cambridge, MA: Harvard University Press.

Edwards, A. L. (1954). *Manual—Edwards Personal Preference Schedule.* New York: The Psychological Corporation.

Edwards, A. L. (1957a). *Techniques of attitude scale construction.* New York: Appleton-Century-Crofts.

Edwards, A. L. (1957b). *The social desirability variable in personality assessment and research.* New York: Dryden.

Edwards, A. L. (1970). *The measurement of personality traits by scales and inventories.* New York: Holt, Rinehart & Winston.

Ekman, P. (1965a). Communication through nonverbal behavior: A source of information about an interpersonal relationship. In S. S. Tomkins and C. E. Izard (Eds.), *Affect, cognition, and personality.* New York: Springer.

Ekman, P. (1965b). Differential communication of affect by head and body cues. *Journal of Personality and Social Psychology, 2,* 725–735.

Ekman, P., & Friesen, W. V. (1984). *Unmasking the face* (Reprint ed.). Palo Alto, CA: Consulting Psychologists Press.

Entwistle, D. R. (1972). To dispel fantasies about fantasy-based measures of achievement motivation. *Psychological Bulletin, 77,* 377–391.

Epstein, S. (1979). The stability of behavior: I. On predicting most of the people much of the time. *Journal of Personality and Social Psychology, 37,* 1097–1126.

Erdman, P., & Friesen, W. V. (1986). *Unmasking the face* (Reprint ed.). Palo Alto, CA: Consulting Psychologists Press.

Erdman, P. E., Klein, M. J., & Greist, H. (1985). Direct patient computer interviewing. *Journal of Consulting and Clinical Psychology, 53,* 760–773.

Erhardt, H. B. (n.d.). *An overview of cognitive style.* Unpublished manuscript, Mountain View College, Dallas, TX.

Erikson, E. H. (1958). *Young man Luther: A study in psychoanalysis and history.* New York: Norton.

Erikson, E. H. (1969). *Gandhi's truth.* New York: Norton.

Eron, L. (1950). A normative study of the TAT. *Psychological Monographs, 64* (Whole No. 315).

Eron, L., & Ritter, A. M. (1951). A comparison of two methods of administration of the Thematic Apperception Test. *Journal of Consulting Psychology, 15,* 55–61.

Eron, L., Terry, D, & Callahan, R. (1950). The use of rating scales for emotional tone of TAT stories. *Journal of Consulting Psychology, 14,* 473–478.

Exner, J. E. (1974). *The Rorschach: A comprehensive system.* New York: Wiley.

Exner, J. E. (1978). *The Rorschach: A comprehensive system,* Vol. 2. *Current research and advanced interpretation.* New York: Wiley.

Exner, J. E. (1986). The Rorschach: A comprehensive system (Vol. 1, 2nd ed.). New York: Wiley.

Exner, J. E., Armbruster, G. L., & Viglione, D. (1978). The temporal stability of some Rorschach features. *Journal of Personality Assessment, 42,* 474–482.

Exner, J. E., & Exner, D. E. (1972). How clinicians use the Rorschach. *Journal of Personality Assessment, 36,* 403–408.

Exner, J. E., Thomas, E. E., & Mason, B. (1985). Children's Rorschachs: Description and prediction. *Journal of Personality Assessment, 49,* 13–20.

Exner, J. E., & Weiner, I. B. (1982). *The Rorschach: A comprehensive system* (Vol. 3). *Assessment of children and adolescents.* New York: Wiley.

Eyde, L., & Kowal, D. (1984, August). Ethical and professional concerns regarding computerized test interpretation services and users. In J. D. Matazarro (Chair), *The use of computer-based test interpretations: Prospects and problems.* Symposium conducted at the Convention of the American Psychological Association, Toronto.

Eysenck, H. J. (1956). The inheritance of extraversion-introversion. *Acta Psychologica, 12,* 95–110.

Eysenck, H. J. (1960). A rational system of diagnosis and therapy in mental illness. In H. G. Eysenck (Ed.), *Progress in clinical psychology* (Vol. 4, pp. 46–64). New York: Grune & Stratton.

Eysenck, H. J. (1965). The effects of psychotherapy. *International Journal of Psychiatry, 1,* 97–178.

Eysenck, H. J. (1967). *The biological basis of personality.* Springfield, IL: Thomas.

Eysenck, H. J. (Ed.). (1981). *A model for personality.* New York: Springer.

Eysenck, H. J., & Eysenck, M. W. (1985). *Personality and individual differences.* New York: Plenum.

Eysenck, H. J., & Eysenck, S. B. G. (1975). *Manual of the Eysenck Personality Questionnaire.* San Diego: Educational and Industrial Testing Service.

Eysenck, H. J., & Rachman, S. (1965). *The causes and cures of neurosis.* San Diego: Knapp.

Farley, F., & Farley, S. V. (1967). Extroversion and stimulus-seeking motivation. *Journal of Consulting Psychology, 31,* 215–216.

Faschingbauer, T. R. (1974). A 166-item written short form of the group MMPI: The FAM. *Journal of Consulting and Clinical Psychology, 42,* 645–655.

Feldman, M. J., & Corah, N. L. (1960). Social desirability and the forced choice method. *Journal of Consulting Psychology, 24,* 480–482.

Finn, S. E. (1982). Base rates, utilities, and DSM-III: Shortcomings of fixed-rule systems of psychodiagnosis. *Journal of Abnormal Psychology, 9,* 294–302.

Fischhoff, B. (1975). Hindsight = foresight: The effect of outcome knowledge on judgment under uncertainty. *Journal of Experimental Psychology: Human Perception and Performance, 1,* 288–299.

Flanagan, J. C. (1954). The critical incident technique. *Psychological Bulletin, 51,* 327–358.

Flanagan, J. C., Tiedeman, D. V., & Willis, M. C. (1973). *The career data book.* Palo Alto, CA: American Institutes for Research.

Folstein, M. F., Folstein, S. E., & McHugh, P. R. (1975). Mini-mental state. A practical method for grading the cognitive state of patients for the clinician. *Journal of Psychiatric Research, 12,* 189–198.

Forer, B. R. (1948). A diagnostic interest blank. *Rorschach Research Exchange and Journal of Projective Techniques, 12,* 1–11.

Forer, B. R. (1949). The fallacy of personal validation: A classroom demonstration of gullibility. *Journal of Abnormal and Social Psychology, 44,* 118–123.

Forer, R. B. (1950). A structured sentence completion test. *Journal of Projective Techniques, 14,* 15–29.

Frank, L. K. (1939). Projective methods for the study of personality. *Journal of Psychology, 8,* 389–413.

Frank, L. K. (1948). *Projective Methods.* Springfield, IL: Thomas.

Frederiksen, N. (1976). Toward a taxonomy of situations. In N. S. Endler & D. Magnusson (Eds.), *Interactional psychology and personality.* Washington, DC: Hemisphere.

French, J. W. (1961). Aptitude and interest score patterns related to satisfaction with college major field. *Educational and Psychological Measurement, 21,* 287–294.

Freud, S. (1905, reprinted 1959). Fragment of an analysis of a case of hysteria. In *Collected papers* (Vol. 3). New York: Basic Books.

Friedberg, L. (1975). Early recollections of homosexuals as indicators of their life styles. *Journal of Individual Psychology, 30,* 196–204.

Friedrich, W. N. (1984). Roberts Apperception Test for Children. In D. J. Keyser & R. C. Sweetland (Eds.), *Test critiques* (Vol. I, pp. 543–548). Kansas City, MO: Test Corporation of America.

Funkenstein, D. H. (1955). The physiology of fear and anger. *Scientific American, 192,* 74–80.

Funkenstein, D. H., King, S. H., & Drolette, M. E. (1957). *Mastery of stress.* Cambridge, MA: Harvard University Press.

Gaines, T., & Morris, R. (1978). Relationships between MMPI measures of psychopathology and WAIS subtest scores and intelligence quotients. *Perceptual & Motor Skills, 47,* 399–402.

Galton, F. (1879). Psychometric experiments. *Brain, 2,* 149–162.

Gardner, P. L. (1975). Attitude measurement: A critique of some recent research. *Educational Research, 17,* 101–109.

Garwood, J. (1977). A guide to research on the Rorschach Prognostic Rating Scale. *Journal of Personality Assessment, 41,* 117–118.

Geer, J. H. (1977). Sexual functioning: Some data and speculations on psychophysiological assessment. In J. D. Cone & R. P. Hawkins (Eds.), *Behavioral assessment.* New York: Brunner/Mazel.

Gendlin, E. T., & Tomlinson, T. M. (1967). The process conception and its measurement. In C. R. Rogers, E. T. Gendlin, D. J. Kiesler, & C. B. Truax (Eds.), *The therapeutic relationship and its impact: A study of psychotherapy with schizophrenics.* Madison: University of Wisconsin Press.

Ginzberg, E., Ginsburg, S. W., Axelrad, S., & Herma, J. L. (1951). *Occupational choice: An approach to a general theory.* New York: Columbia University Press.

Glass, D. C., & Carver, C. S. (1980). Helplessness and the coronary-prone personality. In J. Garber & M. E. P. Seligman (Eds.), *Human helplessness.* New York: Academic.

Glennon, J. R., Albright, L. E., & Owens, W. A. (1966). *A catalog of life history items.* Washington, DC: American Psychological Association, Richardson Foundation for the Scientific Affairs Committee, Division 14.

Glueck, B. C., & Reznikoff, M. (1965). Comparison of computer-derived personality profile and projective psychological test findings. *American Journal of Psychiatry, 121,* 1156–1161.

Goldberg, L. R. (1970). Man versus model of man: A rationale plus some evidence for a method of improving on clinical inferences. *Psychological Bulletin, 73,* 422–432.

Goldberg, L. R. (1972). Parameters of personality inventory construction and utilization: A comparison of prediction strategies and tactics. *Multivariate Behavioral Research Monograph,* No. 72–2.

Goldberg, L. R. (1980, April). *Some ruminations about the structure of individual differences: Developing a common lexicon for the major characteristics of human personality.* Paper presented at the annual meeting of the Western Psychological Association, Honolulu, HI.

Goldberg, P. (1965). A review of sentence completion methods in personality assessment. *Journal of Projective Techniques and Personality Assessment, 29,* 12–45.

Goldfried, M. R., Stricker, G., & Weiner, I. B. (1971). *Rorschach handbook of clinical and research applications.* Englewood Cliffs, NJ: Prentice-Hall.

Goldfried, M. R., & Zax, M. (1965). The stimulus value of the T.A.T. *Journal of Projective Techniques, 29*(1), 46–57.

Goldman, B. A., & Busch, J. C. (Eds.). (1978). *Directory of unpublished mental measures* (Vol. 2). New York: Human Sciences.

Goldman, B. A., & Busch, J. C. (Eds.). (1982). *Directory of unpublished experimental mental measures* (Vol. 3). New York: Human Sciences.

Goldman, B. A., & Osborne, W. L. (Eds.). (1985). *Directory of unpublished experimental mental measures* (Vol. 4). New York: Human Sciences.

Goldman, B. A., & Saunders, J. L. (Eds.). (1974). *Directory of unpublished experimental mental measures* (Vol. 1). New York: Human Sciences.

Goodenough, F. L. (1926). Measurement of intelligence by drawings. Yonkers, NY: World Book.

Gottesman, I. I. (1966). Genetic variance in adaptive personality traits. *Journal of Child Psychology and Psychiatry, 7,* 199–208.

Gottesman, I. I., & Shields, J. (1973). *Schizophrenia and genetics: A twin study vantage point.* New York: Academic.

Gottesman, I. I., & Shields, J. (1982). *Schizophrenia: The epigenetic puzzle.* Cambridge, England: Cambridge University Press.

Gottfredson, G. D., Holland, J. L., & Gottfredson, L. S. (1975). The relation of vocational aspirations and assessments to employment reality. *Journal of Vocational Behavior, 7,* 135–148.

Graham, J. R. (1977). *The MMPI: A practical guide.* New York: Oxford University Press.

Graham, J. R., & Lilly, R. S. (1984). *Psychological testing.* Englewood Cliffs, NJ: Prentice-Hall.

Gross, M. L. (1962). *The brain watchers.* New York: Random House.

Gross, M. L. (1965). Testimony before House Special Committee on Invasion of Privacy of the Committee on Government Operations. *American Psychologist, 20,* 958–960.

Groth-Marnat, G. (1984). *Handbook of psychological assessment.* New York: Van Nostrand Reinhold.

Guide for Occupational Exploration (1979). Washington, DC: U.S. Government Printing Office.

Guilford, J. P. (1940). *An inventory of factors.* Beverly Hills, CA: Sheridan Supply.

Guilford, J. P., & Martin, H. G. (1943). *The Guilford-Martin Inventory of Factors (GAMIN): Manual of directions and norms.* Beverly Hills, CA: Sheridan Supply.

Guilford, J. P., & Zimmerman, W. S. (1956). Fourteen dimensions of temperament. *Psychological Monographs, 70*(10, Whole No. 417).

Gutkin, T. B. (1979). WISC-R scatter indices: Useful information for differential diagnosis? *Journal of School Psychology, 17,* 368–371.

Guttman, L. (1944). A basis for scaling quantitative data. *American Sociological Review, 9,* 139–150.

Gynther, M. D. (1972). White norms and Black MMPIs: A prescription for discrimination? *Psychological Bulletin, 78,* 386–402.

Gynther, M. D., & Green, S. B. (1980). Accuracy may make a difference but does a difference make for accuracy? *Journal of Consulting and Clinical Psychology, 48,* 268–272.

Gynther, M. D., & Gynther, R. A. (1976). Personality inventories. In I. B. Weiner (Ed.), *Clinical methods in psychology.* New York: Wiley.

Hall, E. T. (1969). *The hidden dimension.* Garden City, NY: Doubleday.

Haller, N., & Exner, J. E. (1985). The reliability of Rorschach variables for inpatients presenting symptoms of depression and/or helplessness. *Journal of Personality Assessment, 49,* 516–521.

Hamersma, R. J., Paige, J., & Jordan, J. E. (1973). Construction of a Guttman facet designed cross-cultural attitude-behavior scale toward racial ethnic interaction. *Educational and Psychological Measurement, 33,* 566–576.

Hamilton, J. (1960). A rating scale for depression. *Journal of Neurology, Neurosurgery and Psychiatry, 23,* 56–62.

Hamilton, R. G., & Robertson, M. H. (1966). Examiner influence on the Holtzman Inkblot Technique. *Journal of Projective Techniques and Personality Assessment, 30,* 553–558.

Hanfman, E., & Getzels, J. W. (1953). Studies of the sentence completion test. *Journal of Projective Techniques, 17,* 280–294.

Hansen, J. H. (1985). Review of Vocational Interest Inventory. In J. V. Mitchell, Jr. (Ed.), *The ninth mental measurements yearbook* (Vol. II, pp. 1677–1678). Lincoln, NE: Buros Institute of Mental Measurement of the University of Nebraska-Lincoln.

Hansen, J. C., & Campbell, D. P. (1985). *Manual for the SVIB-SCII.* Palo Alto, CA: Consulting Psychologists Press.

Harkins, S., & Green, R. G. (1975). Discriminability and criterion differences between extraverts and introverts during vigilance. *Journal of Research in Personality, 9,* 335–340.

Harman, H. H. (1976). *Modern factor analysis* (3rd ed.). Chicago: University of Chicago Press.

Harris, S., & Masling, J. (1970). Examiner sex, subject sex, and Rorschach productivity. *Journal of Consulting and Clinical Psychology, 34,* 60–63.

Harrison, R., & Rotter, J. B. (1945). A note on the reliability of the Thematic Apperception Test. *Journal of Abnormal and Social Psychology, 40,* 97–99.

Hartke, A. R. (1979). Development of conceptually independent subscales in the measurement of attitudes. *Educational and Psychological Measurement, 39,* 585–592.

Hartman, A. H. (1970). A basic T.A.T. set. *Journal of Projective Techniques and Personality Assessment, 34,* 391–396.

Hartshorne, H., & May, M. A. (1928). *Studies in the nature of character. Vol. 1: Studies in deceit.* New York: Macmillan.

Harvey, O. J., Hunt, D. E., & Schroder, H. M. (1961). *Conceptual systems and personality organization.* New York: Wiley.

Hathaway, S. R., & McKinley, J. C. (1943). *The Minnesota Multiphasic Personality Inventory.* Minneapolis: University of Minnesota Press.

Hathaway, S. R., & Meehl, P. E. (1951). *An atlas for the clinical use of the MMPI.* Minneapolis: University of Minnesota Press.

Hatt, C. V. (1985). Review of Children's Apperception Test. In J. V. Mitchell, Jr. (Ed.), *The ninth mental measurements yearbook* (Vol. I, pp. 315–316). Lincoln, NE: The Buros Institute of Mental Measurements, The University of Nebraska-Lincoln.

Haynes, S. N. (1984). Computer-assisted assessment. In R. J. Corsini (Ed.), *Encyclopedia of psychology* (pp. 263–264). New York: Wiley.

Haynie, N. A. (1985). Cognitive learning styles. In R. J. Corsini (Ed.), *Encyclopedia of psychology* (Vol. 1, pp. 236–238). New York: Wiley.

Hedlund, J. L., Sletton, I. W., Evenson, R. C., Altman, H., & Cho, D. W. (1977). Automated psychiatric information systems: A critical review of Missouri's Standard System of Psychiatry (SSOP). *Journal of Operational Psychiatry, 8,* 5–26.

Heilbrun, A. B., Jr. (1969). Parental identification and the patterning of vocational interests in college males and females. *Journal of Counseling Psychology, 16,* 342–347.

Henning, J. J., & Levy, R. H. (1967). Verbal-performance IQ differences of white and Negro delinquents on the WISC and WAIS. *Journal of Clinical Psychology, 23,* 164–168.

Herr, E., & Best, P. (1984). Computer technology and counseling: The role of the profession. *Journal of Counseling and Development, 63,* 192–195.

Hess, A. K. (1985). Review of Millon Clinical Multiaxial Inventory. In J. V. Mitchell, Jr. (Ed.), *The ninth mental measurements yearbook* (Vol. 1, pp. 984–986). Lincoln, NE: Buros Institute of Mental Measurements of the University of Nebraska-Lincoln.

Heymans, G., & Wiersma, E. (1906). Beitrage zur Speziellen Psychologie auf Grundeiner Massenunterschung. *Zeitschrift für Psychologie, 43,* 81–127 and 258–301.

Hoch, A., & Amsden, G. S. (1913). A guide to the descriptive study of personality. *Review of Neurology and Psychiatry, 11,* 577–587.

Holden, C. (1975). Lie detectors: PSE gains audience despite critic's doubt. *Science, 190,* 359–362.

Holland, J. L. (1973). *Making vocational choices.* Englewood Cliffs, NJ: Prentice-Hall.

Holland, J. L. (1985). *Making vocational choices: A theory of vocational personalities and work environments* (2nd ed.). Englewood Cliffs, NJ: Prentice-Hall.

Hollingworth, H. L. (1920). *The psychology of functional neuroses.* New York: D. Appleton.

Holmes, T. H., & Rahe, R. H. (1967). The Social Readjustment Scale. *Journal of Psychosomatic Research, 11,* 213–218.

Holroyd, K. A. (1979). Stress, coping, and the treatment of stress-related illness. In J. R. McNamara (Ed.), *Behavioral approaches to medicine: Applications and analysis.* New York: Plenum.

Holsopple, J., & Miale, F. R. (1954). *Sentence completion: A projective method for the study of personality.* Springfield, IL: Thomas.

Holt, A. (1974). *Handwriting in psychological interpretations.* Springfield, IL: Thomas.

Holt, R. R. (1970). Yet another look at clinical and statistical prediction: Or, is clinical psychology worthwhile? *American Psychologist, 25,* 337–349.

Holt, R. R. (1980). Loevinger's measure of ego development: Reliability and national norms for male and female short forms. *Journal of Personality and Social Psychology, 39,* 909–920.

Holtzman, W. H. (1981). Holtzman inkblot technique (HIT). In A. I. Rabin (Ed.), *Assessment with projective techniques* (pp. 47–83). New York: Springer.

Holzman, P., & Levy, D. L. (1977). Smooth pursuit eye movements and functional psychoses: A review. *Schizophrenia Bulletin, 3,* 15–27.

Honigfeld, G., & Klett, C. (1965). The Nurses' Observation Scale for Inpatient Evaluation (NOSIE): A new scale for measuring improvement in schizophrenia. *Journal of Clinical Psychology, 21,* 65–71.

Hulin, C. L., Drasgow, F., & Parsons, C. K. (1983). *Item-response theory.* Homewood, IL: Dow Jones-Irwin.

Hundleby, J. D., Pawlik, K., & Cattell, R. B. (1965). *Personality factors in objective test devices: A critical integration of a quarter of a century's research.* San Diego, CA: Knapp.

Hunt, J. M. (1982). Personality. *Collier's Encyclopedia* (Vol. 18, pp. 594–594c). New York: Macmillan.

Hutt, M. L. (1969). *The Hutt adaptation of the Bender-Gestalt test* (2nd ed.). New York: Grune & Stratton.

Hutt, M. L. (1977). *The Hutt adaptation of the Bender-Gestalt test* (3rd ed.). New York: Grune & Stratton.

Hutt, M. L., & Gibby, R. G. (1970). *An atlas for the Hutt Adaptation of the Bender-Gestalt Test.* New York: Grune & Stratton.

Interview questions that are (legally) acceptable. (1980, Jan. 20). *News-Chronicle* (Thousand Oaks, CA), p. 8.

I was an imaginary playmate. (1965). *American Psychologist, 20,* 990.

Jackson, C. W., & Wohl, J. (1966). A survey of Rorschach teaching in the university. *Journal of Projective Techniques and Personality Assessment, 30,* 115–134.

Jackson, D. N. (1971). The dynamics of structured personality tests. *Psychological Review, 78,* 229–248.

James, W. (1890). *Principles of psychology.* New York: Holt.

Jarnecke, R. W., & Chambers, E. D. (1977). MMPI content scales: Dimensional structure, construct validity, and interpretive norms in a psychiatric population. *Journal of Consulting and Clinical Psychology, 45,* 1126–1131.

Jenkins, C. D., Zyzanski, S. J., & Rosenman, R. H. (1979). *Jenkins Activity Survey: Manual*. New York: Psychological Corporation.

Jensen, A. R. (1969). How much can we boost IQ and scholastic achievement? *Harvard Educational Review, 39*, 1–123.

Johannson, C. B. (1984). *Manual for Career Assessment Inventory* (2nd ed.). Minneapolis, MN: National Computer Systems.

Johnson, J. H., Giannetti, R. A., & Williams, T. A. (1978). A self-contained microcomputer system for psychological testing. *Behavior Research Methods and Instrumentation, 10*, 579–581.

Jones, E. E., & Nisbett, R. E. (1972). The actor and the observer: Divergent perceptions of the cause of behavior. In E. E. Jones, D. E. Karouse, H. H. Kelley, R. E. Nisbett, S. Valins, & B. Weiner (Eds.), *Attribution: Perceiving the causes of behavior.* Morristown, NJ: Learning.

Jordan, J. E. (1971). Construction of a Guttman facet designed cross-cultural attitude-behavior scale toward mental retardation. *American Journal of Mental Deficiency, 76*, 201–219.

Jung, C. G. (1910). The association method. *American Journal of Psychology, 21*, 219–269.

Kagan, J., & Kogan, N. (1970). Individual variation in cognitive processes. In P. Mussen (Ed.), *Carmichael's manual of child psychology* (3rd ed., Vol. 1). New York: Wiley.

Kagan, J., Rosman, B. L., Day, D., Albert, J., & Phillips, W. (1964). Information processing in the child: Significance of analytic and reflective attitudes. *Psychological Monographs, 78* (Whole No. 578).

Kallman, W. M., & Feuerstein, M. (1977). Psychophysiological procedures. In A. R. Ciminero, K. S. Calhoun, & H. E. Adams (Eds.), *Handbook of behavioral assessment.* New York: Interscience-Wiley.

Kallman, F. J., & Jarvik, L. (1959). Individual differences in constitution and genetic background. In J. E. Birren (Ed.), *Handbook of aging and the individual.* Chicago: University of Chicago Press.

Kane, J. S., & Lawler, E. F., III. (1980). In defense of peer assessment: A rebuttal to Brief's critique. *Psychological Bulletin, 88*, 80–81.

Kantorwitz, D. A. (1978). Personality and conditioning of tumescence and detumescence. *Behavioral Research Therapy, 16*, 117–128.

Kaplan, R. M., & Saccuzzo, D. P. (1982). *Psychological testing: Principles, applications, and issues.* Monterey, CA: Brooks/Cole.

Karon, B. P. (1981). The Thematic Apperception Test (TAT). In A. I. Rabin (Ed.), *Assessment with projective techniques* (pp. 85–120). New York: Springer.

Karson, D., & O'Dell, J. W. (1976). *A guide to the clinical use of the 16 PF.* Champaign, IL: Institute for Personality and Ability Testing.

Kelley, C. K., & King, G. D. (1979). Behavioral correlates of the 2-7-8 MMPI profile type in students at a university mental health center. *Journal of Consulting and Clinical Psychology, 47*, 679–685.

Kelly, E. L. (1987). Graphology. In R. J. Corsini (Ed.), *Concise encyclopedia of psychology* (p. 469). New York: Wiley.

Kelly, E. L., & Fiske, D. W. (1951). *The prediction of performance in clinical psychology.* Ann Arbor, MI: University of Michigan Press.

Kelly, G. A. (1955). *The psychology of personal constructs: A theory of personality* (2 vols.). New York: Norton.

Kendall, P. C., & Norton-Ford, J. D. (1982). *Clinical psychology: Scientific and professional dimensions.* New York: Wiley.

Kenrick, D. T., & Dantchik, A. (1983). Interactionism, idiographics, and the social psychological invasion of personality. *Journal of Personality, 51,* 286–307.

Keyser, D. J., & Sweetland, R. C. (Eds.) (1984–1986). *Test critiques* (Vols. I–V). Kansas City, MO: Test Corporation of America.

Kincannon, J. C. (1968). Prediction of the standard MMPI scale scores from 71 items: The Mini-Mult. *Journal of Consulting and Clinical Psychology, 32,* 319–325.

King, A. D. (1978). Minnesota Multiphasic Personality Inventory. In O. K. Buros (Ed.), *The eighth mental measurements yearbook.* Highland Park, NJ: Gryphon.

Kinslinger, H. J. (1966). Application of projective techniques in personnel psychology since 1940. *Psychological Bulletin, 66,* 134–149.

Klein, M. H., Malthieu, P. L., Gendlin, E. T., & Kiesler, D. J. (1969). *The Experiencing Scale: A research and training manual* (Vol. 1). Madison: Wisconsin Psychiatric Institute.

Kleinmuntz, A., & Szucko, J. J. (1984). A field study of the fallibility of polygraphic lie detection. *Nature, 308,* 449–450.

Kleinmuntz, B. (1982). *Personality and psychological assessment.* New York: St. Martin's.

Kleinmuntz, B., & McLean, R. S. (1968). Computers in behavioral science: Diagnostic interviewing by digital computer. *Behavioral Science, 13,* 75–87.

Klopfer, B., & Kelley, D. M. (1942). *The Rorschach technique.* Yonkers-on-Hudson, NY: World Book.

Klopfer, W. G. (1984). Application of the consensus Rorschach to couples. *Journal of Personality Assessment, 48,* 422–440.

Klopfer, W. G., & Taulbee, E. S. (1976). Thematic Apperception Test. *Annual Review of Psychology, 27,* 543–567.

Knapp, R. R. (1976). *Handbook for the Personal Orientation Inventory.* San Diego: EdITS.

Knapp, R. R., & Knapp, L. (1984). *Manual: COPS Interest Inventory.* San Diego, CA: EdITS.

Kogan, N. (1971). Educational implications of cognitive styles. In G. S. Lesser (Ed.), *Psychology and educational practice.* Glenview, IL: Scott Foresman.

Kohlberg, L. (1969). Stage and sequence: The cognitive-developmental approach to socialization. In D. Goslin (Ed.), *Handbook of socialization: Theory and research.* Chicago: Rand McNally.

Kohlberg, L. (1974). The development of moral stages: Uses and abuses. *Proceedings of the 1973 Invitational Conference on Testing Problems* (pp. 1–8). Princeton, NJ: Educational Testing Service.

Koppitz, E. M. (1975). *The Bender-Gestalt test for young children: Research and application, 1963–1973.* New York: Grune & Stratton.

Korchin, S. J., & Schuldberg, D. (1981). The future of clinical assessment. *American Psychologist, 36,* 1147–1158.

Kraepelin, E. (1892). *Über die Beeinflussung einfacher psychischer Vorgaenge.* Jena, East Germany: Fischer.

Kraiger, K., Hakel, M. D., & Cornelius, E. T. (1984). Exploring fantasies of TAT reliability. *Journal of Personality Assessment, 48,* 365–370.

Kretschmer, E. (1925). *Physique and character*. New York: Harcourt, Brace & World.

Kubis, J. F. (1962). Cited in Smith, B. M. The polygraph. In R. C. Atkinson (Ed.), *Contemporary psychology*. San Francisco: Freeman.

Kunce, J. T., Ryan, J. J., & Eckelman, C. C. (1976). Violent behavior and differential WAIS characteristics. *Journal of Consulting and Clinical Psychology, 44*, 42–45.

Lachar, D., & Alexander, R. S. (1978). Veridicality of self report: Replicated correlates of Wiggins MMPI content scales. *Journal of Consulting and Clinical Psychology, 48*, 1349–1356.

Lachar, D., & Gdowski, C. L. (1979). *Actuarial assessment of child and adolescent personality: An interpretive guide for the Personality Inventory for Children profile*. Los Angeles: Western Psychological Services.

Lah, M. I., & Rotter, J. B. (1981). Changing college student norms on the Rotter Incomplete Sentences Blank. *Journal of Consulting and Clinical Psychology, 49*, 985.

Lamiell, J. T. (1981). Toward an idiothetic psychology of personality. *American Psychologist, 36*, 276–289.

Lamiell, J. T., & Trierweiler, S. J. (1986). Personality measurement and intuitive personality judgments from an idiothetic point of view. *Clinical Psychology Review, 6*, 471–491.

Langevin, R. (1983). *Sexual strands: Understanding and treating sexual anomalies in men*. Hillsdale, NJ: Erlbaum.

Lanyon, R. I. (1986). Psychological assessment procedures in court-related settings. *Professional Psychology: Research and Practice, 17*, 260–268.

Lanyon, R. I., & Goodstein, L. D. (1982). *Personality assessment*. New York: Wiley.

Lazarsfeld, P. F. (1957). *Latent structure analysis*. New York: Bureau of Applied Social Research, Columbia University.

Lee, C. C. (1984). Hall Occupational Orientation Inventory. In D. J. Keyser & R. C. Sweetland (Eds.), *Test critiques* (Vol. I, pp. 300–304). Kansas City, MO: Test Corporation of America.

Leunes, A., Evans, M., Karnei, B., & Lowry, N. (1980). Psychological tests used in research with adolescents, 1969–1973. *Adolescence, 15*, 417–421.

Lewinsohn, P. M. (1965). Psychological correlates of overall quality of figure drawings. *Journal of Consulting Psychology, 29*, 504–512.

Libby, W. (1908). The imagination of adolescents. *American Journal of Psychology, 19*, 249–252.

Lichtenstein, S., Fischhoff, B., & Phillips, L. D. (1982). Calibration of probabilities: The state of the art to 1980. In D. Kahneman, P. Slovic, & A. Tversky (Eds.), *Judgment under uncertainty: Heuristics and biases*. New York: Cambridge University Press.

Likert, R. (1932). A technique for the measurement of attitudes. *Archives of Psychology*, No. 140.

Lindgren, H. C. (1967). *Educational psychology in the classroom* (3rd ed., p. 143). New York: Wiley.

Lindzey, G. (1959). On the classification of projective techniques. *Psychological Bulletin, 56*, 158–168.

Lindzey, G. (1965). Seer versus sign. *Journal of Experimental Research on Personality, 1*, 17–26.

Lipsitt, P. D., Lelos, D., & McGarry, A. L. (1971). Competency for trial: A screening instrument. *American Journal of Psychiatry, 128*, 105–109.

Loevinger, J. (1976). *Ego development*. San Francisco: Jossey-Bass.

Loevinger, J. (1979). Construct validity of the sentence completion test of ego development. *Applied Psychological Measurement, 3,* 281–311.

Loevinger, J. (1983). Personality: Stages, traits, and the self. *Annual Review of Psychology, 34,* 195–222.

Loevinger, J., Wessler, R., & Redmore, C. (1970). *Measuring ego development: Vol. 1. Construction and use of a sentence completion test, Vol. 2. Scoring manual for women and girls.* San Francisco: Jossey-Bass.

Lorr, M., Klett, C. J., McNair, D. M., & Lasky, J. J. (1966). *Inpatient Multidimensional Psychiatric Rating Scale* (rev. ed.). Palo Alto, CA: Consulting Psychologists Press.

Lubin, B., Larsen, R. M., & Matarazzo, J. D. (1984). Patterns of psychological test usage in the United States: 1935–1982. *American Psychologist, 39,* 451–454.

Lubin, B., Larsen, R. M., Matarazzo, J. D., & Seever, M. (1985). Psychological test usage patterns in five professional settings. *American Psychologist, 40,* 857–861.

Lubin, B., Larsen, R. M., Matarazzo, J. D., & Seever, M. F. (1986). Selected characteristics of psychologists and psychological assessment in five settings: 1959–1982. *Professional Psychology: Research and Practice, 17,* 155–157.

Lubin, B., Wallis, R. R., & Paine, C. (1971). Patterns of test usage in the United States, 1935–1969. *Professional Psychology, 2,* 70–74.

Lucas, R. W., et al. (1977). Psychiatrists and computers as interrogators of patients with alcohol related illnesses: A comparison. *British Journal of Psychiatry, 131,* 160–167.

Lyerly, S. B. (Ed.) (1978). *Handbook of psychiatric rating scales* (2nd ed.). Rockville, MD: National Institute of Mental Health.

Lykken, D. T. (1957). A study of anxiety in the sociopathic personality. *Journal of Abnormal and Social Psychology, 55,* 6–10.

Lykken, D. T. (1981). *A tremor in the blood: Uses and abuses of the lie detector.* New York: McGraw-Hill.

Lykken, D. T. (1983, April). Polygraph prejudice. *APA Monitor,* p. 4.

Lynn, R., & Eysenck, H. J. (1961). Tolerance for pain, extraversion and neuroticism. *Perceptual and Motor Skills, 12,* 161–162.

Maccoby, E. E., & Maccoby, N. (1954). The interview: A tool of social science. In G. Lindzey (Ed.), *Handbook of social psychology* (pp. 449–487). Cambridge, MA: Addison-Wesley.

Machover, K. (1949). *Personality projection in the drawing of the human figure.* Springfield, IL: Thomas.

Machover, K. (1951). Drawing of the human figure: A method of personality investigation. In H. Anderson & G. Anderson (Eds.), *An introduction to projective techniques.* New York: Prentice-Hall.

Madsen, D. H. (1986). Computer applications for test administration and scoring. *Measurement and Evaluation in Counseling and Development, 19*(1), 6–14.

Mahl, G. F. (1968). Gestures and body movements in interviews. In J. Shlien, H. Hunt, J. D. Matarazzo, & C. Savage (Eds.), *Research in psychotherapy* (Vol. 3). Washington, DC: American Psychological Association.

Mahler, I. (1953). Attitudes toward socialized medicine. *Journal of Social Psychology, 38,* 273–282.

Malgady, R., Costantino, G., & Rogler, L. (1984). Development of a Thematic Apperception Test for urban Hispanic children. *Journal of Consulting and Clinical Psychology, 52,* 986–996.

Maloney, M. P., & Ward, M. P. (1976). *Psychological assessment: A conceptual approach.* New York: Oxford University Press.

Manaster, G. J., & Perryman, T. B. (1974). Early recollections and occupational choice. *Journal of Individual Psychology, 30,* 232–237.

Marks, P. A., Seeman, W., & Haller, D. L. (1974). *The actuarial use of the MMPI with adolescents and adults.* Baltimore: Williams & Wilkins.

Maslow, A. H. (1954). *Motivation and personality.* New York: Harper & Row.

Masters, W. H., & Johnson, V. E. (1966). *Human sexual response.* Boston: Little, Brown.

Matarazzo, J. D. (1972). *Wechsler's measurement and appraisal of adult intelligence* (5th ed.). Baltimore: Williams & Wilkins.

Matarazzo, J. D. (1983). Computerized psychological testing. *Science, 221,* 323.

McAllister, L. W. (1986). *A practical guide to CPI interpretation.* Palo Alto: CA: Consulting Psychologists Press.

McCabe, S. P. (1985). Career Assessment Inventory. In D. J. Keyser & R. C. Sweetland (Eds.), *Test critiques* (Vol. II, pp. 128–137). Kansas City, MO: Test Corporation of America.

McCall, R. B. (1986). *Fundamental statistics for psychology* (4th ed.). San Diego, CA: Harcourt Brace Jovanovich.

McClave, J. T., & Dietrich, F. H. (1985). *Statistics.* San Francisco: Dellen.

McClelland, D. C. (1961). *The achieving society.* Princeton, NJ: Van Nostrand Reinhold.

McClelland, D. C. (1971). *Assessing human motivation.* Morristown, NJ: General Learning Press.

McGarry, A. L., et al. (1973). *Competency to stand trial and mental illness.* Washington, DC: U.S. Government Printing Office.

McKenney, J., & Keen, P. G. W. (1974). How managers' minds work. *Harvard Business Review, 52,* 79–90.

McReynolds, P. (Ed.), (1970–1977). *Advances in psychological assessment* (Vols. 1–4). San Francisco: Jossey-Bass.

McReynolds, P. (1979). The case for interactional assessment. *Behavioral Assessment, 1,* 237–247.

Meehl, P. E. (1951). *Research results for counselees.* St. Paul, MN: Minnesota State Department of Education.

Meehl, P. E. (1954). *Clinical versus statistical prediction.* Minneapolis: University of Minnesota Press.

Meehl, P. E. (1962). Schizotaxia, schizotypy, schizophrenia. *American Psychologist, 17,* 827–838.

Meehl, P. E. (1965). Seer over sign: The first good example. *Journal of Experimental Research in Personality, 11,* 27–32.

Meehl, P. E. (1973). *Psychodiagnosis: Selected papers.* Minneapolis: University of Minnesota Press.

Meehl, P. E., & Golden, R. R. (1982). Taxometric methods. In P. C. Kendall & J. N. Butcher (Eds.), *Handbook of research methods in clinical psychology* (pp. 127–182). New York: Wiley.

Megaree, E. I. (1972). *The California Psychological Inventory handbook.* San Francisco: Jossey-Bass.

Mehrabian, A., & Weiner, M. (1967). Decoding of inconsistent communication. *Journal of Personality and Social Psychology, 6,* 109–114.

Meier, S. T., & Geiger, S. M. (1986). Implications of computer-assisted testing and assessment for professional practice and training. *Measurement and Evaluation in Counseling and Development, 19*(1), 29–34.

Meir, E. I., & Barak, A. (1974). A simple instrument for measuring vocational interests based on Roe's classification of occupations. *Journal of Vocational Behavior, 4,* 33–42.

Merenda, P. F. (1985). Comrey Personality Scales. In D. J. Keyser & R. C. Sweetland (Eds.), *Test critiques* (Vol. IV, pp. 199–212). Kansas City, MO: Test Corporation of America.

Miller, F. E. (1986). The development and evaluation of an online computer-assisted Rorschach Inkblot Test. *Journal of Personality Assessment, 50,* 222–228.

Millon, T. (1969). *Modern psychopathology.* Philadelphia: Saunders.

Millon, T. (1981). *Disorders of personality: DSM-III—Axis II.* New York: Wiley Interscience.

Millon, T. (1982a). *Millon Behavioral Health Inventory manual* (3rd ed.). Minneapolis: Interpretive Scoring Systems.

Millon, T. (1982b). *Millon Adolescent Personality Inventory manual.* Minneapolis: Interpretive Scoring Systems.

Millon, T. (1987). *Manual for the MCMI-II.* Minneapolis: National Computer Systems.

Milner, J. S., & Moses, T. H. (1972). Effects of administrator's gender on sexual content and productivity in the Rorschach. *Journal of Clinical Psychology, 30,* 159–161.

Minton, H. L., & Schneider, F. W. (1980). *Differential psychology.* Monterey, CA: Brooks/Cole.

Mira, E. (1940). Myokinetic psychodiagnosis. *Proceedings of the Royal Society of Medicine.*

Mirabile, C. S., Houck, J., & Glueck, B. C., Jr. (1970). Computer beats clinician in prognosis contest. *Psychiatric News, 5*(18).

Mischel, W. (1968). *Personality and assessment.* New York: Wiley.

Mischel, W. (1973). Toward a cognitive social learning reconceptualization of personality. *Psychological Review, 80,* 252–283.

Mischel, W. (1984). On the predictability of behavior and the structure of personality. In R. A. Zucker, J. C. Aronoff, & A. I. Rabin (Eds.), *Personality and the prediction of behavior.* New York: Academic.

Mischel, W. (1986). *Introduction to personality* (4th ed.). New York: Holt, Rinehart & Winston.

Mischel, W., & Baker, N. (1975). Cognitive transformations of reward objects through instructions. *Journal of Personality and Social Psychology, 31,* 254–261.

Mischel, W., & Moore, B. (1973). Effects of attention to symbolically-presented rewards on self-control. *Journal of Personality and Social Psychology, 28,* 172–179.

Mitchell, J. V., Jr. (Ed.). (1983). *Tests in print III.* Lincoln, NE: Buros Institute of Mental Measurements of the University of Nebraska-Lincoln.

Mitchell, J. V., Jr. (Ed.). (1985). *The ninth mental measurements yearbook.* Lincoln, NE: Buros Institute of Mental Measurements of the University of Nebraska-Lincoln.

Monson, T. C., Hesley, J. W., & Chernick, L. (1982). Specifying when personality traits can and cannot predict behavior: An alternative to abandoning the attempt to predict single-act criteria. *Journal of Personality and Social Psychology, 43,* 385–399.

Moos, R. H. (1976). *The human context.* New York: Wiley.

Moos, R. H. (1979). *Evaluating educational environments.* San Francisco, CA: Jossey-Bass.

Moos, R. H., & Moos, B. S. (1986). *Family Environment Scale: Manual* (2nd ed.). Palo Alto, CA: Consulting Psychologists.

Mosak, H. H. (1969). Early recollections: Evaluation of some recent research. *Journal of Individual Psychology, 25,* 56–63.

Munroe, R. L. (1955). *Schools of psychoanalytic thought.* New York: Holt, Rinehart & Winston.

Murray, H. A. (and collaborators) (1938). *Explorations in personality.* New York: Oxford University Press.

Murray, H. A. (1943). *Thematic Apperception Test.* Cambridge, MA: Harvard University Press.

Murstein, B. I. (1959). A conceptual model of projective techniques applied to stimulus variations with thematic techniques. *Journal of Consulting Psychology, 23,* 3–13.

Murstein, B. I. (1963). The relationship of expectancy of reward to achievement performance on an arithmetic and thematic test. *Journal of Consulting Psychology, 27,* 394–399.

Murstein, B. I. (1965). *Theory and research in projective techniques (emphasizing the TAT).* New York: Wiley.

Museum of Modern Art. (1955). *The family of man.* New York: Maco Magazine.

Myers, I. B., & McCaulley, M. H. (1985). *Manual: A guide to the development and use of the Myers-Briggs Type Indicator.* Palo Alto, CA: Consulting Psychologists.

Nachmann, B. (1960). Childhood experiences and vocational choices in law, dentistry, and social work. *Journal of Counseling Psychology, 7,* 243–250.

Nettler, G. (1959). Test burning in Texas. *American Psychologist, 14,* 682–683.

Newmark, C. S. (Ed.). (1985). *Major psychological assessment instruments.* Vol, I. Boston: Allyn & Bacon.

Noll, V. H.. (1951). Simulation by college students of a prescribed pattern on a personality scale. *Educational and Psychological Measurement, 11,* 478–488.

Norusis, M. (1985). *SPSS-PC plus.* Chicago: SPSS.

Nunnally, J. (1978). *Psychometric theory.* New York: McGraw-Hill.

Osgood, C. E., Suci, G. J., & Tannenbaum, P. H. (1957). *The measurement of meaning.* Urbana, IL: University of Illinois Press.

Osipow, S. H. (1983). *Theories of career development* (3rd ed.). Englewood Cliffs, NJ: Prentice-Hall.

Overall, J. E., & Gomez-Mont, F. (1974). The MMPI-168 for psychiatric screening. *Educational and Psychological Measurement, 34,* 315–319.

Overall, J. E., & Hollister, L. E. (1982). Decision rules for phenomenological classification of psychiatric patients. *Journal of Consulting and Clinical Psychology, 50,* 535–545.

Overall, J. E., & Klett, C. J. (1972). *Applied multivariate analysis.* New York: McGraw-Hill.

Owens, T. A., & Stufflebeam, D. L. (1969, Feb.). *An experimental comparison of item sampling and examinee sampling for estimating norms.* Paper presented at the meeting of the National Council on Measurement in Education, Los Angeles.

Owens, W. A. (1976). Background data. In M. D. Dunnette (Ed.), *Handbook of industrial and organizational psychology.* Chicago: Rand McNally.

Padilla, A. M. (1979). Critical factors in the testing of Hispanic Americans: A review and some suggestions for the future. In R. Tyler & S. White (Eds.), *Testing, teaching and learning: Report of a conference on testing.* Washington, DC: National Institute on Education.

Pagano, R. R. (1986). *Understanding statistics in the behavioral sciences* (2nd ed.). St. Paul, MN: West.

Paul, G. L. (1966). *Insight vs. desensitization in psychotherapy*. Stanford, CA: Stanford University Press.

Paunonen, S. V., & Jackson, D. N. (1985). The validity of formal and informal personality assessments. *Journal of Research in Personality, 19*, 331–342.

Paunonen, S. V., & Jackson, D. N. (1986). Nomothetic and idiothetic measurement in personality. *Journal of Personality, 54*, 447–459.

Payne, A. F. (1928). *Sentence completions*. New York: New York Guidance Clinic.

Payne, F. D. (1985). Review of Bem Sex-Role Inventory. In J. V. Mitchell, Jr. (Ed.), *The ninth mental measurements yearbook* (Vol. I, pp. 137–138). Lincoln, NE: Buros Institute of Mental Measurements of the University of Nebraska-Lincoln.

Payne, R. W. (1985). Review of the SCL-90-R. In J. V. Mitchell, Jr. (Ed.), *The ninth mental measurements yearbook* (Vol. II, pp. 1326–1329). Lincoln, NE: Buros Institute of Mental Measurements of the University of Nebraska-Lincoln.

Pervin, L. A. (1984). *Personality* (4th ed.). New York: Wiley.

Peterson, C. A. (1985). Review of Bloom Sentence Completion Survey. In J. V. Mitchell, Jr. (Ed.), *The ninth mental measurements yearbook* (Vol. 1, pp. 204–205). Lincoln, NE: Buros Institute of Mental Measurements of the University of Nebraska-Lincoln.

Peterson, C., Semmel, A., von Baeyer, C., Abramson, L. Y., Metalsky, G. I., & Seligman, M. E. P. (1982). The Attributional Style Questionnaire. *Cognitive Therapy and Research, 6*, 287–300.

Peterson, R. A., & Headen, S. W. (1984). Profile of Mood States. In D. J. Keyser & R. C. Sweetland (Eds.), *Test critiques* (Vol. I, pp. 522–529). Kansas City, MO: Test Corporation of America.

Peterson, R. C., & Thurstone, L. L. (1933). *Motion pictures and the social attitudes of children*. New York: Macmillan.

Petrie, A. (1967). *Individuality in pain and suffering*. Chicago: University of Chicago Press.

Petrie, B. M. (1969). Statistical analysis of attitude scale scores. *Research Quarterly* (AAHPER), *40*, 434–437.

Petzel, T. P. (1985). Depression Adjective Check Lists. In D. J. Keyser & R. C. Sweetland (Eds.), *Test critiques* (Vol. III, pp. 215–220). Kansas City, MO: Test Corporation of America.

Petzelt, J. T., & Craddick, R. (1978). Present meaning of assessment in psychology. *Professional Psychology: Research and Practice, 9*, 587–591.

Phares, E. J. (1985). Incomplete sentences. In R. J. Corsini (Ed.), *Encyclopedia of psychology* (Vol. 2, p. 193). New York: Wiley.

Piotrowski, C. (1984). The status of projective techniques: Or "Wishing won't make it go away." *Journal of Clinical Psychology, 40*, 1495–1502.

Piotrowski, C. (1985). Clinical assessment: Attitudes of the Society for Personality Assessment membership. *The Southern Psychologist, 2*, 80–83.

Piotrowski, C., & Keller, J. W. (1983, March). *Psychological testing: Trends in master's level counseling training programs*. Paper presented at the annual meeting of the Southeastern Psychological Association, Atlanta.

Piotrowski, C., & Keller, J. W. (1984). Attitudes toward clinical assessment by members of the AABT. *Psychological Reports, 55*, 831–838.

Piotrowski, C., Sherry, D., & Keller, J. W. (1985). Psychodiagnostic test usage: A survey of the Society for Personality Assessment. *Journal of Personality Assessment, 49*, 115–119.

Piotrowski, Z. (1957). *Perceptanalysis.* New York: Macmillan.

Piotrowski, Z. (1964). Digital-computer interpretation of inkblot test data. *Psychiatric Quarterly, 38,* 1–26.

Polyson, J., Norris, D., & Ott, E. (1985). The recent decline in TAT research. *Professional Psychology: Research and Practice, 16,* 26–28.

Polyson, J., Peterson, R., & Marshall, C. (1986). MMPI and Rorschach: Three decades of research. *Professional Psychology: Research and Practice, 17,* 476–478.

Prediger, D. J., & Hanson, G. R. (1976). Holland's theory of careers applied to men and women: Analysis of implicit assumptions. *Journal of Vocational Behavior, 8,* 167–184.

Pressey, S. L., & Pressey, L. W. (1919). Cross-out test, with suggestions as to a group scale of the emotions. *Journal of Applied Psychology, 3,* 138–150.

Pritchard, D. A., & Rosenblatt, A. (1980). Racial bias in the MMPI: A methodological review. *Journal of Consulting and Clinical Psychology, 48,* 263–267.

Pruitt, J. A., Smith, M. C., Thelen, M. H., & Lubin, B. (1985). Attitudes of academic clinical psychologists toward projective techniques: 1968–1983. *Professional Psychology: Research and Practice, 16,* 781–788.

Rabin, A. I. (1981). *Assessment with projective techniques.* New York: Springer.

Rabin, A. I. (Ed.). (1986). *Projective techniques for adolescents and children* (pp. 111–192). New York: Springer.

Rabin, A. I., & Zlotogorski, Z. (1981). Completion methods; Word association, sentence, and story completion. In A. I. Rabin (Ed.), *Assessment with projective techniques: A concise introduction* (pp. 121–149). New York: Springer.

Rabinowitz, W. (1984). Study of Values. In D. J. Keyser & R. C. Sweetland (Eds.), *Test critiques* (Vol. I, pp. 641–647). Kansas City, MO: Test Corporation of America.

Ragland, D. R., & Brand, R. J. (1988). Type A behavior and mortality from coronary heart disease. *The New England Journal of Medicine, 318*(2), 65–69.

Raines, G. N., & Rohrer, J. H. (1960). The operational matrix of psychiatric practice. II. Variability in psychiatric impressions and the projection hypothesis. *American Journal of Psychiatry, 117,* 133–139.

Ramirez, M., III, & Casteneda, A. (1974). *Cultural democracy, biocognitive development, and education.* New York: Academic Press.

Rapaport, D. (1946). *Diagnostic psychological testing.* Chicago: Year Book.

Rapaport, D., Gill, M. M., & Schafer, R. (1946). *Diagnostic psychological testing.* Chicago: Year Book.

Rapaport, D., Gill, M. M., & Schafer, R. (1968). *Diagnostic psychological testing* (Rev. ed.). New York: International Universities Press.

Reilly, R. R., & Chao, G. T. (1982). Validity and fairness of some alternative employee selection procedures. *Personnel Psychology, 35,* 1–62.

Reimanis, G. (1974). Psychosocial development, anomie, and mood. *Journal of Personality and Social Psychology, 29,* 355–357.

Reitan, R. M. (1966). A research program on the psychological effects of brain lesions in human beings. In N. R. Ellis (Ed.), *International Review of Research in Mental Retardation, 1,* 153–218. New York: Academic.

Remmers, H. H. (1960). *Manual for the Purdue Master Attitude Scales.* Lafayette, IN: Purdue Research Foundation.

Reynolds, C. R. (1985). Review of Personality Inventory for Children. In J. V. Mitchell, Jr.

(Ed.), *The ninth mental measurements yearbook* (Vol. 2, pp. 1154–1157). Lincoln, NE: Buros Institute of Mental Measurements of the University of Nebraska-Lincoln.

Reynolds, H. H. (1966). Efficacy of sociometric ratings in predicting leadership success. *Psychological Reports, 19*, 35–40.

Reznikoff, M., Aronow, E., & Rauchway, A. (1982). The reliability of inkblot content scales. In C. D. Spielberger & J. N. Butcher (Eds.), *Advances in personality assessment* (Vol. 1, pp. 83–113). New York: Erlbaum.

Ritter, A., & Effron, L. D. (1952). The use of the Thematic Apperception Test to differentiate normal from abnormal groups. *Journal of Abnormal and Social Psychology, 47*, 147–158.

Ritzler, B. A., & Alter, B. (1986). Rorschach teaching in APA-approved clinical psychology programs: Ten years later. *Journal of Personality Assessment, 50*, 44–49.

Ritzler, B. A., Sharkey, K. J., & Chudy, J. F. (1980). A comprehensive projective alternative to the TAT. *Journal of Personality Assessment, 44*, 358–362.

Roback, H. (1968). Human figure drawings: Their utility in the clinical psychologist's armamentarium for personality assessment. *Psychological Bulletin, 70*, 1–19.

Robinson, J. P., Athanasiou, R., & Head, K. B. (1974). *Measures of occupational attitudes and occupational characteristics.* Ann Arbor, MI: Institute for Social Research, University of Michigan.

Robinson, J. P., Rush, J. G., & Head, K. B. (1973). *Measures of political attitudes.* Ann Arbor, MI: Institute for Social Research, University of Michigan.

Robinson, J. P., & Shaver, P. R. (1973). *Measures of social attitudes* (Rev. ed.). Ann Arbor, MI: Institute for Social Research, University of Michigan.

Rodgers, D. A. (1972). Minnesota Multiphasic Personality Inventory. In O. K. Buros (Ed.), *The seventh mental measurements yearbook* (Vol. I, pp. 243–250). Highland Park, NJ: Gryphon.

Roe, A. (1956). *The psychology of occupations.* New York: Basic Books.

Roe, A., & Klos, D. (1969). Occupational classification. *Counseling Psychologist, 1*, 84–92.

Roe, A., & Siegelman, M. (1964). *The origin of interests.* Washington, DC: American Personnel and Guidance Association.

Rogers, C. R., & Dymond, R. F. (Eds.). (1954). *Psychotherapy and personality change.* Chicago: University of Chicago Press.

Rogers, R., & Cavanaugh, J. L. (1983). Usefulness of the Rorschach: A survey of forensic psychiatrists. *Journal of Psychiatry & Law, 11*, 55–67.

Rohde, A. R. (1947). *Sentence completions test manual.* Beverly Hills, CA: Western Psychological Services.

Rokeach, M. (1973). *The nature of human values.* New York: Free Press.

Rome, H. P., et al. (1962). Symposium on automation techniques in personality assessment. *Proceedings of the Staff Meetings of the Mayo Clinic, 137*, 61–82.

Rorschach, H. (1921). *Psychodiagnostik.* Bern: Bircher.

Rosenbaum, B. L. (1973). Attitude toward invasion of privacy in the personnel selection process and job applicant demographic and personality correlates. *Journal of Applied Psychology, 58*, 333–338.

Rosenhan, D. L. (1973). On being sane in insane places. *Science, 179*(4070), 365–369.

Rosenthal, R. (1966). *Experimenter effects in behavioral research.* New York: Appleton-Century-Crofts.

Rosenthal, R., Hall, M. A., DiMatteo, M. R., Rogers, P. L., & Archer, D. (1979). *Sensitivity to nonverbal communication: The PONS test*. Baltimore: Johns Hopkins University Press.

Rosenzweig, S. (1978). *Aggressive behavior and the Rosenzweig Picture-Frustration Study*. New York: Praeger.

Rothenberg, M. G. (1985). Graphology. *Encyclopedia Americana* (Vol. 13, pp. 190–191). Danbury, CT: Grolier, Inc.

Rothermel, R. D., & Lovell, M. R. (1985). In D. J. Keyser & R. C. Sweetland (Eds.), *Test critiques* (Vol. II, pp. 570–578). Kansas City, MO: Test Corporation of America.

Rotter, J. B. (1946). The Incomplete Sentences Test for studying personality. *American Psychologist, 1*, 286.

Rotter, J. B. (1954). *Social learning and clinical psychology*. Englewood Cliffs, NJ: Prentice-Hall.

Rotter, J. B. (1966). Generalized expectancies for internal versus external control of reinforcement. *Psychological Monographs, 80* (Whole No. 609).

Rotter, J. B., & Rafferty, J. E. (1950). *The Rotter Incomplete Sentences Blank manual: College form*. New York: The Psychological Corporation.

Rounds, J. B. (1985). Review of Vocational Preference Inventory (7th ed.). In J. V. Mitchell, Jr. (Ed.), *The ninth mental measurements yearbook* (Vol. II, pp. 1683–1684). Lincoln, NE: Buros Institute of Mental Measurements of the University of Nebraska-Lincoln.

Sacks, J. M., & Levy, S. (1950). The Sentence Completion Test. In L. E. Abt & L. Bellak (Eds.), *Projective psychology*. New York: Knopf.

Sampson, J. P., Jr., & Pyle, K. R. (1983). Ethical issues involved with the use of computer-assisted counseling, testing, and guidance systems. *Personnel and Guidance Journal, 61*, 283–287.

Sanford, R. N. (1943). Physique, personality and scholarship. *Monographs of the Society for Research in Child Development, 8*, 705.

Sapinkopf, R. C. (1977). *A computer adaptive testing approach to the measurement of personality variables*. Unpublished doctoral dissertation, University of Maryland.

Sarason, I. G. (1972). *Personality: An objective approach*. New York: Wiley.

Sattler, J. M. (1985). Review of the Hutt Adaptation of the Bender-Gestalt Test. In J. V. Mitchell, Jr. (Ed.), *The ninth mental measurements yearbook* (Vol. 1, pp. 184–185). Lincoln, NE: Buros Institute of Mental Measurements of the University of Nebraska-Lincoln.

Scarr, S. (1969). Social introversion-extraversion as a heritable response. *Child Development, 40*, 823–832.

Schachter, S. (1971). *Emotion, obesity, and crime*. New York: Academic.

Schafer, R. (1954). *Psychoanalytic interpretation in Rorschach testing*. New York: Grune & Stratton.

Schaie, J. P. (1978). Review of Gerontological Apperception Test. In O. K. Buros (Ed.), *The eighth mental measurements yearbook* (Vol. I, pp. 829–830). Highland Park, NJ: Gryphon.

Schaie, K. W. (1978). Review of Senior Apperception Techniques. In O. K. Buros (Ed.), *The eighth mental measurements yearbook* (Vol. I, p. 1060). Highland Park, NJ: Gryphon.

Scherer, K. R. (1974). Acoustic concomitants of emotional dimensions: Judging effect from synthesized tone sequences. In S. Wertz (Ed.), *Nonverbal communication*. New York: Oxford University Press.

Schroder, H. M., Driver, M. J., & Strufert, S. (1967). *Human information processing*. New York: Holt, Rinehart & Winston.

Schuldberg, D., & Korchin, S. J. (1985). Clinical assessment. In R. J. Corsini (Ed.), *Encyclopedia of psychology* (Vol. 1, pp. 222–223). New York: Wiley.

Schulte, J. (1985, Dec. 20). Tying personality to heart attacks. *Los Angeles Times*, pp. V–22–23.

Schwab, D. P., & Heneman, H. G. (1969). Relationship between interview structure and interinterviewer reliability in employment situations. *Journal of Applied Psychology*, *53*, 214–217.

Schwab, D. P., Heneman, H. A., III, & De Cotiis, T. A. (1975). In Behaviorally anchored rating scales: A review of the literature. *Personnel Psychology*, *28*, 549–562.

Schwab, D. P., & Packard, G. L. (1973). Response distortion on the Gordon Personal Inventory and the Gordon Personal Profile in the selection context: Some implications for predicting employee behavior. *Journal of Applied Psychology*, *58*, 372–374.

Schwartz, J. D. (1978). Review of the TAT. In O. K. Buros (Ed.), *The eighth mental measurements yearbook* (pp. 1127–1130). Highland Park, NJ: Gryphon.

Schwartz, L. A. (1932). Social-situation pictures in the psychiatric interview. *American Journal of Orthopsychiatry*, *2*, 124–132.

Selltiz, C., Jahoda, M., Deutsch, M., & Cook, S. W. (1959). *Research methods in social problems*. New York: Holt, Rinehart & Winston.

Selltiz, C., Wrightsman, L. S., & Cook, S. W. (1976). *Research methods in social relations* (3rd ed.). New York: Holt, Rinehart & Winston.

Sharkey, K. J., & Ritzler, B. A. (1985). Comparing diagnostic validity of the TAT and a new picture projective test. *Journal of Personality Assessment*, *49*, 406–412.

Shaw, M. W., & Wright, J. M. (1967). *Scales for the measurement of attitudes*. New York: McGraw-Hill.

Sheldon, W. H., Stevens, S. S., & Tucker, W. B. (1940). *The varieties of human physique*. New York: Harper & Row.

Sheldon, W. H., & Stevens, S. S. (1942). *The varieties of temperament*. New York: Harper & Row.

Shields, R. B. (1978). The usefulness of the Rorschach Prognostic Rating Scale—A rebuttal. *Journal of Personality Assessment*, *42*, 579–582.

Siegelman, M., & Peck, R. F. (1960). Personality patterns related to occupational roles. *Genetic Psychology Monographs*, *61*, 291–349.

Siipola, E. M. (1985). House-Tree-Person Test. In R. J. Corsini (Ed.), *Encyclopedia of Psychology* (Vol. 2, p. 143). New York: Wiley.

Siipola, E. M., Walker, W. N., & Kolb, D. (1955). Task attitudes in word association. *Journal of Personality*, *23*, 441–459.

Simon, A., & Boyer, E. C. (1974). *Mirrors for behavior II: An anthology of observation instruments*. Wyncote, PA: Communications Materials Center.

Sines, J. O. (1970). Actuarial versus clinical prediction in psychopathology. *British Journal of Psychiatry*, *116*, 129–144.

Sines, J. O. (1985). Review of Roberts Apperception Test for Children. In J. V. Mitchell, Jr. (Ed.), *The ninth mental measurements yearbook* (Vol. II, pp. 1290–1291). Lincoln, NE: Buros Institute of Mental Measurements of the University of Nebraska-Lincoln.

Singer, J. L. (1984). *The human personality*. San Diego, CA: Harcourt Brace Jovanovich.

Skinner, H. A., & Pakula, A. (1986). Challenge of computers in psychological assessment. *Professional Psychology: Research and Practice, 17*(1), 44–50.

Small, J. R. (1984). Taylor-Johnson Temperament Analysis. In D. J. Keyser & R. C. Sweetland (Eds.), *Test critiques* (Vol. I, pp. 652–659). Kansas City, MO: Test Corporation of America.

Smith, P. C., & Kendall, L. M. (1963). Retranslation of expectations: An approach to the construction of unambiguous anchors for rating scales. *Journal of Applied Psychology, 47,* 149–155.

Smith, R. J. (1984). Polygraph tests: Dubious validity. *Science, 224,* 1217.

Spearman, C. E. (1927). *The abilities of man*. London: Macmillan.

Spence, J. T., & Helmreich, R. (1978). *Masculinity and femininity: Their psychological dimensions, correlates, and antecedents*. Austin, TX: University of Texas Press.

Spielberger, C. D., & Butcher, J. N. (1982–1985). *Advances in personality assessment* (Vols. 1–5). Hillsdale, NJ: Erlbaum.

Spielberger, C. C., Crane, R. S., & Rosenman, R. H. (1982). The role of anger in Type-A behavior and heart disease. In C. D. Spielberger, I. G. Sarason, and P. B. Defares (Eds.), *Stress and anxiety* (Vol. 9, Chap. 16). New York: McGraw-Hill/Hemisphere.

Spitzer, R. L. (1976). More on pseudoscience in science and the case for psychiatric diagnosis: A critique of D. L. Rosenhan's "On Being Sane in Insane Places" and "The Contextual Nature of Psychiatric Diagnosis." *Archives of General Psychiatry, 33,* 459–470.

Spitzer, R. L., Fleiss, J. L., Burdock, E. L., & Hardesty, A. S. (1964). The Mental Status Schedule: Rationale, reliability and validity. *Comprehensive Psychiatry, 5,* 384–395.

Spranger, E. (1928). *Types of men* (P. J. W. Pigors, Trans.). Halle: Niemeyer.

SPSS Inc. (1983). *SPSS-X user's guide*. New York: McGraw-Hill.

Stahmann, R. F. (1978). Review of Taylor-Johnson Temperament Analysis. In O. K. Buros (Ed.), *The eighth mental measurements yearbook* (Vol. I, pp. 1111–1112). Highland Park, NJ: Gryphon.

Stehouwer, R. S. (1985). Beck Depression Inventory. In D. J. Keyser & R. C. Sweetland (Eds.), *Test critiques* (Vol. II, pp. 83–87). Kansas City, MO: Test Corporation of America.

Steimel, R. J., & Suziedelis, A. (1963). Perceived parental influence and inventoried interests. *Journal of Counseling Psychology, 10,* 289–295.

Stein, M. I. (1978). Thematic Apperception Test and related methods. In B. Wolman (Ed.), *Clinical diagnosis of mental disorders* (pp. 179–236). New York: Plenum.

Steiner, R. L., & Barnhart, R. B. (1972). Development of an instrument to assess environmental attitudes utilizing factor analytic techniques. *Science Education, 56,* 427–432.

Stephenson, W. (1953). *The study of behavior: Q-technique and its methodology*. Chicago: University of Chicago Press.

Sternberg, C. (1955). Personality trait patterns of college students majoring in different fields. *Psychological Monographs, 69,* No. 18 (Whole No. 403).

Stewart, L. H. (1959). Mother-son identification and vocational interest. *Genetic Psychology Monographs, 60,* 31–63.

Stone, P. J., Bales, R. F., Namenwirth, J. Z., & Olgivie, D. M. (1962). The General Inquirer: A computer system for content analysis and retrieval based on the sentence as a unit of information. *Behavioral Science, 7,* 1–15.

Wagner, M., & Schubert, H. (1955). *DAP, quality scale for late adolescents and young adults.* Kenmore, NY: Delaware & Letter Shop.

Walker, C. E., & Kaufman, K. (1984). State-Trait Anxiety Inventory for Children. In D. J. Keyser & R. C. Sweetland (Eds.), *Test critiques* (Vol. I, pp. 633–640). Kansas City, MO: Test Corporation of America.

Walsh, J. A. (1984). Tennessee Self Concept Scale. In D. J. Keyser & R. C. Sweetland (Eds.), *Test critiques* (Vol. I, pp. 663–672). Kansas City, MO: Test Corporation of America.

Walsh, W. B., & Betz, N. E. (1985). *Tests & assessment.* Englewood Cliffs, NJ: Prentice-Hall.

Webb, E. (1915). Character and intelligence. *British Journal of Psychology Monograph Supplement,* III.

Wechsler, D. (1958). *The measurement and appraisal of adult intelligence* (4th ed.). Baltimore: Williams & Wilkins.

Wechsler, D. (1975). Intelligence defined and undefined. *American Psychologist, 30,* 135–139.

Weiner, I. B. (1983). The future of psychodiagnosis revisited. *Journal of Personality Assessment, 47,* 451–461.

Weiner, I. B. (1986). Assessing children and adolescents with the Rorschach. In H. Knoff (Ed.), *The assessment of child and adolescent personality* (pp. 141–171). New York: Guilford.

Weiss, D. J. (1973). The stratified adaptive computerized ability test. *Research Report 73–3.* University of Minnesota, Department of Psychology, Psychometric Methods Program.

Weiss, D. J. (1985). Adaptive testing by computer. *Journal of Consulting and Clinical Psychology, 53,* 774–789.

Wells, R. L. (1914). The systematic observation of the personality—In its relation to the hygiene of the mind. *Psychological Review, 21,* 295–333.

Wertheimer, M. (1923). Untersuchungen zur Lehre von der Gestalt: II. *Psychologische Forschung, 4,* 301–350.

Wesman, A. G. (1952). Faking personality test scores in a simulated employment situation. *Journal of Applied Psychology, 36,* 112–113.

Wheeler, K. G. (1985). Review of Temperament and Values Inventory. In J. V. Mitchell, Jr. (Ed.), *The ninth mental measurements yearbook* (Vol. II, pp. 1535–1536). Lincoln, NE: Buros Institute for Mental Measurements of the University of Nebraska-Lincoln.

White, R. W. (1943). The personality of Joseph Kidd. *Character and personality, 11,* 183–208, 318–360.

Wholeben, B. E. (1985). 16 Personality Factor Questionnaire. In D. J. Keyser & R. C. Sweetland (Eds.), *Test critiques* (Vol. IV, pp. 595–605). Kansas City, MO: Test Corporation of America.

Whyte, W. H., Jr. (1956). *The organization man.* Garden City, NY: Doubleday.

Widiger, T. A. (1985a). Review of Millon Adolescent Personality Inventory. In J. V. Mitchell, Jr. (Ed.), *The ninth mental measurements yearbook* (Vol. 1, pp. 979–981). Lincoln, NE: Buros Institute of Mental Measurements of the University of Nebraska-Lincoln.

Widiger, T. A. (1985b). Review of Millon Clinical Multiaxial Inventory. In J. V. Mitchell, Jr. (Ed.), *The ninth mental measurements yearbook* (Vol. 1, pp. 986–988). Lincoln, NE: Buros Institute of Mental Measurements of the University of Nebraska-Lincoln.

Widiger, T. A., Williams, J. B. W., Spitzer, R. L., & Frances, A. (1986). The MCMI as a measure of DSM-III. *Journal of Personality Assessment, 49,* 366–378.

Wiechmann, G. H., & Wiechmann, L. A. (1973). Multiple factor analysis: An approach to attitude validation. *Journal of Experimental Education, 41,* 74–84.

Wiggins, J. S. (1966). Substantive dimensions of self-report in the MMPI item pool. *Psychological Monographs, 80* (Whole No. 630).

Wiggins, J. S. (1973). *Personality and prediction: Principles of personality assessment.* Reading, MA: Addison-Wesley.

Wiggins, J. S., Goldberg, L. R., & Appelbaum, M. (1971). MMPI content scales: Interpretive norms and correlations with other scales. *Journal of Consulting and Clinical Psychology, 37,* 403–410.

Wildman, R., Batchelor, E., Thompson, L., Nelson, F., Moore J., Patterson, M., & DeLaosa, M. (1980). *The Georgia Court Competency Test: An attempt to develop a rapid, quantitative measure of fitness for trial.* Unpublished manuscript, Forensic Services Division, Center State Hospital, Milledgeville, GA.

Willerman, L. (1975). *Individual and group differences.* New York: Harper's College Press.

Willis, C. G. (1984). Myers-Briggs Type Indicator. In D. J. Keyser & R. C. Sweetland (Eds.), *Test critiques* (Vol. I, pp. 482–490). Kansas City, MO: Test Corporation of America.

Willmott, M., & Brierley, H. (1984). Cognitive characteristics and homosexuality. *Archives of Sexual Behavior, 13,* 311–319.

Winter, D. G., & Stewart, A. J. (1977). Power motive reliability as a function of retest instructions. *Journal of Consulting and Clinical Psychology, 45,* 436–440.

Witkin, H. A. (1973). The role of cognitive style in academic performance and in teacher-student relations. *Educational Testing Service Research Bulletin* (No. RB-73-11). Princeton, NJ: Educational Testing Service.

Witkin, H. A., & Berry, J. W. (1975). Psychological differentiation in cross-cultural perspective. *Journal of Cross-Cultural Psychology, 6,* 4–87.

Witkin, H. A., Dyk, R. B., Faterson, H. F., Goodenough, D. R., & Karp, S.A. (1962). *Psychological differentiation.* New York: Wiley.

Witkin, H. A., & Goodenough, D. R. (1977). Field dependence and interpersonal behavior. *Psychological Bulletin, 84,* 661–689.

Witkin, H. A., Goodenough, D. R., & Karp, S. A. (1967). Stability of cognitive style from childhood to young adulthood. *Journal of Personality and Social Psychology, 7,* 291–300.

Witkin, H. A., Price-Williams, D., Bertini, M., Bjorn, C., Oltman, P. K., Ramirez, M., & Van Meel, J. (1973). *Social conformity and psychological differentiation.* Princeton, NJ: Educational Testing Service.

Wittenborn, J. R. (1964). *Wittenborn Psychiatric Rating Scales* (Rev. ed.). New York: Psychological Corporation.

Wolf, S., & Wolff, H. G. (1942). Evidence on the genesis of peptic ulcer in man. *Journal of the American Medical Association, 120,* 670–675.

Wolff, W. T., & Merrens, M. R. (1974). Behavioral assessment: A review of clinical methods. *Journal of Personality Assessment, 38,* 3–16.

Wolk, R., & Wolk, R. (1971). *The Gerontological Apperception Test.* New York: Behavioral Publications.

Woodworth, R. S. (1920). *Personal Data Sheet.* Chicago: Stoelting.

Wursten, H. (1960). Story completions: Madeline Thomas and similar methods. In A. I. Rabin & M. R. Haworth (Eds.), *Projective techniques with children*. New York: Grune & Stratton.

Wyatt, F. (1947). The scoring and analysis of the Thematic Apperception Test. *Journal of Psychology, 24,* 319–330.

Wynne, L., & Singer, M. (1963). Thought disorder and family relations of schizophrenics. II. A classification of forms of thinking. *Archives of General Psychiatry, 9,* 199–206.

Yarmey, A. D. (1979). *The psychology of eyewitness testimony.* New York: Free Press.

Young, D. W. (1982). A survey of decision aids for clinicians. *British Medical Journal, 285,* 1332–1336.

Zarske, J. A. (1985). Review of Adjective Check List. In J. V. Mitchell, Jr. (Ed.), *The ninth mental measurements yearbook* (Vol. I, pp. 52–53). Lincoln, NE: Buros Institute of Mental Measurements of the University of Nebraska-Lincoln.

Zlotogorski, Z., & Wiggs, E. (1986). Story- and sentence-completion techniques. In A. I. Rabin (Ed.), *Projective techniques for adolescents and children* (pp. 195–211). New York: Springer.

Zubin, J., Eron, L. D., & Schumer, F. (1965). *An experimental approach to projective techniques.* New York: Wiley.

Zuckerman, M. (1971). Physiological measures of sexual arousal in the human. *Psychological Bulletin, 75,* 297–329.

Zuckerman, M. (1979). *Sensation seeking: Beyond the optimal level of arousal.* Hillsdale, NJ: Erlbaum.

Zuckerman, M. (1985). Review of Temperament and Values Inventory. In J. V. Mitchell, Jr. (Ed.), *The ninth mental measurements yearbook* (Vol. II, pp. 1536–1537). Lincoln, NE: Buros Institute of Mental Measurements of the University of Nebraska-Lincoln.

Zuckerman, M., & Lubin, B. (1985). *Manual for the Multiple Affect Adjective Check List-Revised.* San Diego, CA: EdITS.

Zytowski, D. G. (1976). Predictive validity of the Kuder Occupational Interest Survey: A 12- to 19-year follow-up. *Journal of Counseling Psychology, 23,* 221–233.

Author Index

Subject Index

Assessment Instruments Index

This page constitutes a continuation of the permission list on the copyright page.